A CITIZENS' INQUIRY

To all the imaginative and courageous people who contributed their ideas to Initiative '92 and the Opsahl Commission

and to Frank Wright, who would have approved.

A CITIZENS' INQUIRY

THE OPSAHL REPORT ON NORTHERN IRELAND

Edited by Andy Pollak

Torkel Opsahl
Padraig O'Malley   Eamonn Gallagher
Marianne Elliott   Lucy Faulkner
Ruth Lister   Eric Gallagher

THE LILLIPUT PRESS
for
INITIATIVE '92

First published in 1993 by
THE LILLIPUT PRESS LTD
4 Rosemount Terrace, Arbour Hill,
Dublin 7, Ireland.

A CIP record for this
title is available from
The British Library.

ISBN 1 874675 08 2 (paperback)
1 874675 09 0 (cloth)

Cover by Dunbar Design
Formatting by STF, Celbridge, Co. Kildare
(10 on 12pt Janson Text)
Printed in Dublin by Colour Books Ltd of Baldoyle

A Blessing

Initiative Ninety-
Two (-three, -four, -five ...)
Offers space, a clearing
In the jungle for me
And you to stay alive
By sharing thought and word.
Are *you* within hearing?
Am *I* being heard?

MICHAEL LONGLEY

Contents

Two Commentaries

Appendices

Illustrations between pages 254 and 255

Map by Timothy O'Neill

Preface

This is a report of what around 3000 people in 554 written and taped submissions said to Initiative '92's citizens' inquiry into ways forward for Northern Ireland, and the reflections on those submissions of seven eminent observers: Professor Torkel Opsahl, Lady Faulkner of Downpatrick, Mr Padraig O'Malley, Professor Ruth Lister, Mr Eamonn Gallagher, Professor Marianne Elliott and the Rev. Dr Eric Gallagher. The whole exercise — launching the work of the initiative, holding public meetings, canvassing for submissions, organizing 'focus groups' and oral hearings, and preparing, publishing and launching the report — was carried out in the 13 months between May 1992 and June 1993 (see The Work of Initiative '92: An Insider's View).

As Professor Opsahl says in his introduction, this is a document for discussion and debate, not a finely finished work of scholarship proposing panaceas for Northern Ireland's many ills. It is meant to provoke and disturb and inspire. As the people behind Initiative '92 made clear when they launched the project, it represents the beginning of a process, not its outcome. Chapters 11 to 14 are a compilation and summary of an estimated two-and-a-half million words in written submissions from people of many different social, political and religious backgrounds, in Northern Ireland and beyond. This is the source material for starting a 'citizens' debate' about the region's future.

The overwhelming bulk of that material — other than the 20 or so submissions which were confidential, and which have been destroyed — has been lodged, on public access, in Northern Ireland's most famous library, the Linen Hall in Belfast. It is there for anyone to check or consult.

One important point must be made clear at the outset. This is a report of two halves. They can be read in tandem or separately. Chapters 2 to 10 have been written collectively by the members of the Opsahl Commission. Nothing that is said in the people's written submissions in Part II necessarily implies support for arguments or the recommendations of the members of the Opsahl Commission in Part I. These are entirely the Commissioners' own, although based on what they read and heard in the written submissions and oral hearings.

This is also not a report written and compiled for the Opsahl Commission and the contributors to Initiative '92 by one person, as is usually the case in reports of commissions of inquiry. This means there may be some unevenness of style, repetition, variable use of footnotes and quotations, arbitrary categorizations, and even the occasional error. The editor takes full responsibility for these, pleading only that readers appreciate that an extraordinary amount of work was done on this project in a remarkably short space of time.

At its height, the project employed three full-time workers, three people on four- to six-month contracts, and one person on a one-month contract. Compare this to the New Ireland Forum a decade earlier: 19 full-time civil servants worked for a year for the Forum, backed by the full panoply of powers and resources of the Republic of Ireland government and state. Yet they received only 347 written submissions; the Forum heard only 40 oral presentations (the Opsahl Commission listened to nearly 200 at its hearings); and in the end no single compilation of material was produced, although many individual booklets were.

The names in the footnotes in this report refer, unless otherwise stated, to the authors of written (or taped) submissions. If a quote is taken from a presentation at an oral hearing, the date of the hearing is added to the name.

A final note. The members of the Commission fall into the same linguistic traps which most people from Northern Ireland fall into, and which Simon Lee bemoans in his submission. They have tried, for example, to avoid using the terms 'Catholic' and 'nationalist', and 'Protestant' and 'unionist' interchangeably when talking about politics, but sometimes have failed to make a distinction between them in their other chapters. A book could be written about such confusions. This is not that book.

This is a report about what happened when a group of energetic, committed people from a wide range of backgrounds came together to create a 'shared space' for discussion and debate — among citizens, not politicians — away from the barriers of a divided and often violent society. We believe that the effort was hugely worthwhile. We trust that the readers of this book will agree with us.

Andy Pollak
Initiative '92 Co-ordinator
May 1993

Acknowledgments

The Initiative '92 project would never have come to fruition without a host of people. Back in the summer of 1991 there was the idea for the project, thought up by Robin Wilson, editor of *Fortnight*, and Simon Lee, professor of jurisprudence at Queen's University, Belfast. However, it would never have seen the light of day without our funders, led by the Joseph Rowntree Charitable Trust and its wonderfully supportive assistant trust secretary, Stephen Pittam. The other trusts without whom this ambitious and experimental project could never have taken place were the Barrow Cadbury Trust, the Northern Ireland Voluntary Trust, the Nuffield Foundation, the Tudor Trust, the Howard Charitable Trust (Republic of Ireland), First Trust Bank (schools' assemblies sponsorship), the Baring Foundation, the Ulster Telethon Trust, the Community Relations Council, the Arthur McDougall Fund, and many personal donors.

If the funders were the first vital element in the successful completion of our task, the staff were a very close second. They worked extraordinarily long and hard hours, and with what one observer called "a commitment at once passionate and rational" to achieve a series of extremely tight deadlines imposed by the shortness of the timescale. My deep gratitude and thanks to Derval Mooney, Siobhán Rainey, Paul Burgess, Kate Kelly, Rob Fairmichael and Helena Schlindwein in Derry. I am particularly grateful to Derval and Siobhán for respectively managing the computer and the accounts so efficiently.

Next comes the management committee, which gave stalwart support in the 'dog days' in the late summer and autumn of 1992 when money was running out and submissions were slow in coming in. My special thanks to Quintin Oliver (chair), Robin Wilson and Simon Lee (again), Ken Logue (also for holding the fort until my arrival and for overseeing finance), Beverley Jones (also for legal advice), Dorothy Day (also for management advice), Róisín McDonough, Les Allamby, Vivienne Anderson, and Terence Donaghy; also to Mary Lyons, Jan Ashdown, June Campion, Alasdair Mac-Laughlin, David Gallagher and Bronagh Hinds.

Martin Cowley deserves a special mention for coming in at extremely short notice to help me with the task of summarizing and condensing the huge amount of material in the written submissions into digestible form for this report. Clem McCartney did an excellent job in setting up six 'focus groups' all over Northern Ireland, again at very short notice.

We were blessed with two 'super-volunteers', James Nelson and Maggie Beirne, whose contribution to the schools' assemblies was absolutely vital to their success. James stayed on to contribute invaluable assistance to the preparation of this report. Other volunteers who helped us at various times were Conleth Bradley — a rare youthful idealist in these cynical times — Sean Courtney, Patrick Corrigan, Francis Levi, Nathalie Caleyron from France, Tiffany Danitz from the USA, and the other people who helped us with postering in Belfast and Derry.

Steve Patterson and Jim McGrath, our sound engineers during the oral hearings, were a pleasure to work with. Thanks too to Leslie Walsh and Keri Logan, who took a note of the hearings.

A number of patrons helped us with donations 'in kind'. Foremost among these was Billy Hastings, who put up the Opsahl Commission free of charge in one of his splendid hotels so that they could finish this report. Barbara Fitzgerald in Dublin organized the largest public meeting of the 29 we held; Frank Bunting was an enthusiastic member of our 'submission-prodding' subcommittee; Lord Blease helped us to get a hearing in the House of Lords; Seán O'Dwyer provided us with a car during the oral hearings; Betty Black and James Hawthorne helped us to get video and sound recording equipment respectively; David Cook threw a splendid party in his home for the members of the Commission; Benny Marley gave us free printing and John Bush cheap stationery; Paul Sweeney advised us on fund-raising; John Robb chaired a particularly sensitive public meeting in west Belfast; Des Smith helped us with advice on premises; Wilfred Mulryne and Fiona Stephen sat on the schools' assemblies planning committee; George Johnston and Margo Harkin chaired our Derry launch; Fiona Stelfox chaired our Derry public meeting, Forster Richardson our Enniskillen meeting, Paddy O'Hanlon our Newry meeting and Tom McBride our Ballymena meeting; Norman Gibson lent us his economic expertise; Paddy Maguinness lent us a beautiful meeting place in Newry; Paddy McLaughlin persuaded the Mayor of Omagh to open our meeting there; Michael Longley wrote us a poem; Ruairí Brugha, Risteard Mac Gabhann and Father Denis Faul did interviews with Raidió na Gaeltachta; Bishop Samuel Poyntz invited us to address the Church of Ireland's Role of the Church Committee; Sam Burch passed the word around the Shankill; Ann McCann was a 'focus group' facilitator; Eamonn Dwyer advised us on computers; Patrick Buckland distributed material for us in England; Howard Noyes donated the famous Wicklow oak doorstops to give to presenters at the oral hearings.

Another special mention is due to our publisher, Antony Farrell of The Lilliput Press, who appeared from nowhere to offer to take on the arduous task of preparing this large volume for publication, and to our two copy-editors, Robert Bell in Belfast and Jonathan Williams in Dublin.

Others we owe thanks to include Barry Cowan, for chairing the schools' assemblies; Norman Richardson and Ray Mullan, who sat on the schools' assemblies planning committee; Leslie Stannage, who designed our leaflets; Ian Knox and Merv Jones, who drew cartoons for them; Jim Manderson of Digital in Scotland, who provided cut-price computers, and Marcus Smith, who lent his computer expertise; Peter Roebuck, for help with setting up the oral hearing at the University of Ulster in Coleraine; the University of Ulster, Magee College, for free postage; a number of particularly supportive community relations officers, notably Norma McKeown in Dungannon, Aidan Bunting in Omagh, Paul Killen in Newtownards, David Clark in Enniskillen (also Jim Ledwith), Kate Bond in Coleraine, Damien Brannigan in Downpatrick, Esther Mulholland in Ballycastle and Brian Devlin in Craigavon; Coopers and Lybrand (Belfast) and Arthur Andersen (Dublin), for more economic advice; the Foyle Arts Centre; Calvert Office Equipment; the Belfast Institute's School of Office and Secretarial Studies; Marigold Johnson, for contacts in Britain; Godfrey Abbott, for chairing our Armagh meeting; Gary Kent, who arranged a meeting for us in the House of Commons; 'focus group' facilitators Sheila Livingstone, Pat Jordan and Edwin Graham; Una McCarthy and the staff of the Old Museum Arts Centre; John Gray, John Killen, Mary Hughes and the rest of the staff at the Linen Hall Library; Paul Bew, Tom Hadden, David McKittrick (although not his news editor), Jill Russell, John Rainey, Michelle Cassidy, Helen Trew, Oonagh Downey, Peter Shirlow, Kathleen Higgins and the staff at all the community centres, arts centres, business centres, leisure centres, town halls, council offices, universities, schools, libraries, hotels and other places where we held hearings and meetings. If I have omitted anyone from this already lengthy list, I hope they will understand, and also accept our thanks.

Finally I have to add a personal 'thank you' to my beloved wife and partner, Doireann Ní Bhriain, and my two beautiful daughters, Sorcha and Gráinne, who were effectively without a husband and father for 13 months because of this project.

Last of all — and it really should be first (it is: in the dedication) — our profound thanks again to the 3000 or so citizens who contributed to this project, and without whom it would never have happened. This report belongs to them.

Abbreviations

ACE	Action for Community Employment
CCPR	UN Covenant on Civil and Political Rights
CSCE	Conference on Security and Co-operation in Europe
DHSS	Department of Health and Social Services
DUP	Democratic Unionist Party
ECHR	European Convention on Human Rights
EPA	Northern Ireland (Emergency Provisions) Act
EMU	Education for Mutual Understanding
GAA	Gaelic Athletic Association
GCSE	General Certificate of Secondary Education
IDB	Industrial Development Board (NI)
INTERREG	EC initiative to fund projects in border areas
IRA	Irish Republic Army
LEDU	Local Enterprise Development Unit
MBW	Making Belfast Work
MEP	Member of the European Parliament
PR	Proportional Representation
PTA	Prevention of Terrorism (Temporary Provisions) Act
Quangos	Quasi-autonomous non-governmental organizations
RIR	Royal Irish Regiment
RUC	Royal Ulster Constabulary
SDLP	Social Democatic and Labour Party
STV	Single Transferable Vote
TSN	Targeting Social Need
UDA	Ulster Defence Association
UFF	Ulster Freedom Fighters
UUP	Ulster Unionist Party
UVF	Ulster Volunteer Force
YTP	Youth Training Programme

A CITIZENS' INQUIRY

Part I

The Commission

CHAPTER 1

Introduction

Torkel Opsahl

This is the report of the Commission set up by the independent citizens' group, Initiative '92, to inquire into possible ways forward for Northern Ireland. Our mandate from the management committee of Initiative '92 was to give the people of Northern Ireland — and those beyond with a legitimate concern for the region — an opportunity to express themselves, to overcome their sense of impotence and helplessness after nearly a quarter a century of political violence and deadlock.

The suspension of the inter-party talks in November 1992 showed that new energy and ideas were called for in the search for peaceful alternatives to the horrors of violence. In the past year, countries in eastern and south-eastern Europe have offered frightening evidence of what may happen when people allow ethnic conflicts to explode into violence beyond the reach of political controls.

The people of Northern Ireland responded to our appeal for ideas. At first the response was hesitant, and some sections of society — notably republican-minded people from west Belfast, border Protestants and Democratic Unionist Party supporters — never overcame their suspicion of this commission of 'outsiders'. However, as the January 1993 closing date for submissions approached, they were arriving in great numbers from elsewhere.

We were impressed and moved by people's readiness to send us their thoughts and speak their minds at our oral hearings. By voicing their views, many have discovered that they are not powerless. Some who had come together for the first time to prepare submissions saw the value of dialogue and realized that their fears were often based on ignorance. Many recognized that there is no 'big solution' in Northern Ireland; others were impatient that the pursuit of such an illusory ideal prevents agreement on the attainable.

An untidy situation needs untidy answers.[1]

A pragmatic approach to conflict is called for. The distinction between conflict and violence is crucial.

Conflict is neither good nor bad, but intrinsic in every social relationship from marriage to international diplomacy.... The real issue is not the existence of conflict, but how it is handled ... rather than solved.[2]

As Professor Clare Palley, who knows Northern Ireland well, put it at a recent UN seminar on minority rights: 'The only people entitled to talk about solutions are chemists.'

A number of submissions to our Commission pointed out that for political progress to be achieved in Northern Ireland, the protagonists must be persuaded that a gain for one side does not necessarily mean a loss for the other. Politics should not be a 'zero sum' game; it should at least offer the possibility that both sides can win something. Sectarianism is a huge obstacle here, which will have to be overcome — both in politics and the community — by a process of 'building blocks towards a situation where some kind of accommodation can be possible between the two communities and some progress made towards a more consensual society'.[3] Both sides' fears and aspirations must be taken into account in making suggestions and tentative recommendations for progress in Northern Ireland. We have attempted to achieve that balance in chapter 10.

You either play on the fears of the past or take risks with the future.[4]

We have also tried to balance the negative and the positive. On the one hand, we were depressed by the enormity of Northern Ireland's problems, by the depth of its divisions and the deprivation and alienation of some of its working-class areas (although this last misfortune, unhappily, is a phenomenon shared by very many countries). On the other hand, we were profoundly heartened by the resilience of spirit and creativity shown by many of the people who appeared at our hearings, notably the women.

There is the positive matter of what is being achieved, against great odds, in some communities through work for reconciliation and community development. Some Northern Ireland Office initiatives — particularly those to do with community development and the voluntary sector — are to be welcomed. A number of presenters stressed the potential for positive experiment in a society of a manageable size like Northern Ireland. The example of a Bill of Rights was frequently mentioned; the point was made that this would contrast with more negative past 'experiments' in the field of human rights, civil liberties and security. More generally, it was suggested that Northern Ireland 'could become a model for regional development in Europe'.[5]

One thing is clear from the Initiative '92 exercise: the people of Northern Ireland do want dialogue, at every level. The process of dialogue is not helped by the region's weak traditions of political consultation and accountability, particularly on the unionist side: politics in Northern Ireland has for too long been largely disconnected from the process of day-to-day government. The absence of democratic accountability was a strong theme at our hearings: there was a demand for more 'talking shops' like Initiative '92, and for a permanent centre in Belfast for debate, dialogue, interchange and reconciliation.

Encouraging community participation was a theme running through a number of otherwise widely differing submissions, whether dealing with working-class alienation or the 'opting out' of the middle classes. We have made a recommendation about bringing Sinn Féin into the political process, partly because we were struck by how many authors of submissions and presenters at hearings mentioned the alienation of whole communities who believe they are excluded because they support Sinn Féin.

The increasing segregation of communities is another huge problem, particularly in Belfast.[6] The 1991 census returns show a degree of segregation which appears to have surprised even those who live in Northern Ireland.

Like the thin white ribbon that the police use to seal an area, we wrap ourselves in our own territories, where we will know we are safe.[7]

Two ways of loosening the ribbon were put to us: integrated education and 'pilot' cross-community housing projects.

One other important theme which emerged in submissions and hearings, and which time constraints prevented us dealing with fully, was the so-called European dimension. A number of thoughtful submissions, summarized in chapter 11, speak for themselves about what is a relatively recent development in Northern Irish thinking. The clear long-term trend is towards the reduction of the importance of national sovereignty, state borders and territorial jurisdiction, and the increased significance of European institutions and political, economic and cultural co-operation.

This offers new ways and a new atmosphere for the handling of old and enduring problems, such as the Irish conflict.[8] This trend towards internationalization and regionalization will have obvious effects on the controversial and elusive concept of nationalism and its primary formation, the nation-state. Our suggestion to grant this concept a measure of legal recognition in Northern Ireland should be seen against this background: it is an expedient to redress an imbalance from the past, not part of a framework for the future. In future, the nation-state will become only one among many levels of authority in the international political, constitutional and legal order. We believe that the Anglo-Irish Agreement should be seen in the same light. The concept of national self-determination, which is the design behind so much death and destruction in the former Yugoslavia at the moment, is not a helpful one, particularly in a divided society like Northern Ireland.

But these are long-term outcomes. The terms of reference of our Commission did not include the requirement to propose outcomes.

Initiative '92 and this Commission has had only one agenda: to assist the democratic debate in Northern Ireland. This report should perhaps be seen as a Swedish-style 'workbook'[9]: a preliminary compilation of information and opinion which can be built on through further consultations with the people of Northern Ireland — through community, youth and schools debates, local conferences, focus groups and follow-up reports. Initiative '92 is planning just such a programme, to begin in the autumn of 1993.

The origins and development of Initiative '92 are detailed in Andy Pollak's commentary at the end of this book. Commission's task was to study the huge amount of material gathered by its workers in the form of 554 written submissions, notes from seventeen days of oral hearings and two schools' assemblies in Belfast and Derry, the transcripts of confidential 'focus group' discussions held in six Northern Irish towns, academic studies and newspaper reports from May 1992 to April 1993. Our conclusions and recommendations, based on this material, appear in chapter 10, and the analysis on which those are based in chapters 2 to 9.

One thing should be made clear: the report does not stand or fall on the basis of our analysis and conclusions. We are only seven individuals. This report — prepared, compiled and written in the ten weeks after the oral hearings ended in February 1993 — was never intended to be a finely honed work of scholarship. It is meant to be a document for discussion and debate. The value of chapters 11 to 15, which reflect the ideas, hopes and fears of thousands of concerned citizens from Northern Ireland, and beyond, stands on its own, independent of our views. One could validly argue that we, the members of the Commission, have put forward 25 recommendations in chapter 10, and the people who made submissions have put forward over 300 recommendations in chapters 11 to 15.

It is also important to stress that this 'citizens' inquiry' may have something to offer a wider constituency outside Northern Ireland. As Professor Trevor Smith, the vice-chancellor of the University of Ulster and one of the United Kingdom's leading political scientists, remarked when welcoming us to his Coleraine campus, Initiative '92 has been trying to do something to fill the much talked about 'democratic deficit' which could have lessons for both Britain and Europe. This project has been an unprecedented, forward-looking experiment in public participation in political debate in a region that is usually characterized as politically rigid, undemocratic and backward.

In an era when regionalism and citizenship have become popular concepts, it has been a pleasure and a privilege to chair a Commission charged with exploring both. It was also a pleasure to work with the co-ordinator of Initiative '92, Andy Pollak — whose journalistic skills and sensitivity to public life in Northern Ireland were of tremendous help — and with his diligent staff.

I hope Initiative '92 and this report will provoke a fruitful debate about new and imaginative ways forward for the lovely corner of our common Europe that is Northern Ireland. If that happens, as the project's introductory leaflet said a year ago, Initiative '92's task will be complete.

Notes

1. Rev. Brian Lennon.
2. Professor John Darby.
3. Dr Ken Logue.
4. Sisters of the Cross and Passion, oral hearing 23.2.1993.
5. Dr George Quigley.
6. David McKittrick, *Independent on Sunday*, 21.3.1993 and *The Independent*, 22.3.1993.
7. A 15-year-old Catholic girl, quoted by Dr Colin Irwin.
8. *Northern Ireland: A Crucial Test for a Europe of Peaceful Regions* (publication from a conference in February 1993), Norwegian Institute of International Affairs. It discusses, among other things, how an integrated Europe might contribute to the playing down of exclusive terms like unionist and nationalist, British and Irish.
9. Nicholas Sanders.

CHAPTER 2

Politics and the Constitution I:
A Changing Paradigm

The question is not so much what the problem is — Northern Ireland is perhaps one of the most over-researched conflicts in the world[1] — the question is whether there is a will and an urgency to arrive at an acceptable resolution of the problem, and, if so, whether that urgency conveys itself to Northern Ireland's politicians and commits them to compromise. In the course of its inquiry, our Commission found that the reasons for this lack of urgency are multifaceted.

The conflict is manageable. This is not to belittle the memories of over 3000 people who have lost their lives in the conflict during the last twenty years, the tens of thousands injured, the grief of countless relatives, and the widespread destruction of businesses, public buildings and homes. Everyone who lives in Northern Ireland is ultimately affected by the conflict. But the daily impact of the violence and the insecurity that it engenders is borne disproportionately by the poor and the powerless. However, the propensity to see Northern Ireland as a conflict of major proportions relative to the size of Northern Ireland is misleading.

Any large city in the United States has a far greater rate of death by violence — three to four times higher than the death rate by violence in Northern Ireland.[2] Nor is it sufficient to argue that the deaths in Northern Ireland are the product of political violence. It is not the purpose of the violence that counts, but the fact of its taking place and people's response to it. Over the worst eight years of the conflict, the average number of fatalities was in the realm of 200 deaths a year: in the last seven years it has fallen to an average of 80 deaths in a year.[3] Moreover, the spatial distribution of fatalities suggests widely different experiences. North Belfast and west Belfast account for 40 per cent of all deaths; Newry and Armagh for 13 per cent; Foyle for 10 per cent and Fermanagh/south Tyrone for 8 per cent. In twelve of the seventeen Westminster constituencies, fatalities were under 5 per cent of the total, while in four (North Down, Strangford, North Antrim, and East Antrim) fatalities were under 1 per cent of the total. As a result, most people in Northern Ireland are not 'at risk' of being killed, and if you do not live in north Belfast and west Belfast, or in a border area, are not a member or a former member of the security forces, the risk level drops dramatically. Submissions attest to this view. Most people live remarkably normal lives.[4]

Northern Ireland has become a bore in an international context. It's hard to stir up international sympathy since other places replace us with more catastrophic ethnic conflicts.[5]

Questions of ethnicity, nationalism, and minority rights are raging everywhere in Europe. This perspective is essential to place the politics of conflict resolution and human rights in Northern Ireland in their comparative place.[6]

In the context of the rest of the world, Northern Ireland is very small. The death rate from muggings in the US is worse by far than the violence in Northern Ireland. We have to keep a sense of perspective.[7] [8]

In the focus groups which we conducted in connection with the Commission's work, we found that when participants were asked to describe the impact the conflict had on their daily lives, most, invariably, said that it had little or no impact except for the inconvenience of security checkpoints.

Looked at another way: of the 16,000 deaths every year in Northern Ireland, only 100 are due directly to the troubles. Twice that number are due to road traffic accidents, fifty times that number (5000) are due to cardiovascular disease, 3000 deaths are cancer-related, and almost 3000 people die in Northern Ireland each year because of cigarette smoking.[9] When a sample of the population was asked, in the lifestyle report conducted in 1992 by the Department of Public Health Medicine on behalf of the Southern Health and Social Services Board, if they were stressed and what were the causes of stress, the 'troubles' and crime were cited by less than one-third of respondents. These two ranked far behind family illness, work pressures and money worries. In short, despite the intractability of the conflict and its devastating effect on civil society, the situation is not bad enough for people to demand that their elected representatives make the compromises necessary for a settlement.

Because it is a manageable conflict, there is little pressure on the politicians to find a settlement. During the oral hearings, presenters were asked time and again what pressures their elected representatives were under to make an accommodation. Every time the answer was the same: none. This goes for pressure from the middle classes too. The 'opting out' of the middle classes, especially the Protestant middle class, was brought to our attention time and again. Apathy and the absence of a demand on either the political parties or the government to deal with the constitutional question with a lot more urgency and determination cut across all barriers.

There are no pressures on politicians. We have a prosperous middle class in both communities.[10]

It's easy for the politicians to walk away from talks. Then you will get your votes. It's more difficult to stick in there.[11]

The reaction to the recent ending of the talks proves that few expected progress. To many, the political process in Northern Ireland is already irrelevant. The opting out of responsibility of the middle class is a definite factor at play. For those whose work, recreation, or social life is untouched by the community of fear, there is a reluctance to get involved.[12]

After twenty years of violence the North itself is coping with war-weariness. This has brought about a greater polarization in working-class communities and in some affluent ones. Catholic and Protestant middle classes have opted out, having become cynical and disillusioned with the political process and wanting little or nothing to do with it. Little affected by violence, they are content to accept the status quo as long as it does not change too much.... There is not much evidence of an obsessive desire to find solutions. Maybe there has to be a greater depth of despair before there is a massive urge for answers.[13] [14]

The desire for some sort of settlement is very strong in the Protestant community. This desire, however, has not translated itself into a demand, and until that happens, politicians can always move away from the table. There's no demand because of a feeling of hopelessness.[15]

The middle class do very well in this society. The economic situation also contributes to the lack of pressure, in that Northern Ireland is heavily subsidized. The middle classes tend to think they are untouched by the situation and, instead, the burden falls on areas such as west Belfast. The middle classes take no steps to integrate, take no responsibilities.[16]

Another aspect of the province's problem is the deep-rooted reluctance politically among the middle classes to accept responsibility for helping to find a solution. The middle classes, Catholic and Protestant, have largely been cocooned from the problem.[17]

Many people know that politicians here cannot really do anything and most people do not respect them. Able people have abdicated a role in the political system. If elected representatives cannot do things, then the middle classes are not going to contact them about anything... The civil service and quangos have all the power and they are not available to the community.[18]

People have distanced themselves from the problem and their responsibility for it:

People tend to talk about the troubles as an 'it' — that is, when will 'it' be worked out, as though it is something over which they have no control. People seem powerless. The loss of political power in one community and the present lack of power in both reinforces this sense of powerlessness. Allied to this feeling of lack of power is lack of responsibility. We tend to think 'they' are responsible, so that we do not have the duty to search for a solution.[19]

Nor are politicians 'punished' in any way by their respective electorates for their failure to reach a settlement. Elections are run along strictly sectarian lines and incumbency effectively means incumbency for life.

People do not even have the expectation that talks will succeed. Again, in our focus groups we asked participants whether they had expected the talks to fail. They, for the most part, said that they had, and there was almost across-the-board agreement that, even if the talks were to start up again, they would be doomed to failure. A survey taken by the *Shankill People* of 202 residents of the Shankill found that 78 per cent wanted the parties to get around the negotiating table; a similar percentage, however, thought talks would not result in a settlement.[20] The desire for change has not yet become a demand for change.

The lack of pressure on the politicians, and people's scepticism about what talks can deliver, reflect a larger underlying reality: people's alienation from the political process itself, a recurring theme in the submissions and oral hearings:

People are not involved in politics. On the unionist side active involvement in politics traditionally has been deemed unnecessary; the solidly built-in majority has always been safe, and decision-making is left to a few at the top. Nationalist apathy results from sheer hopelessness — political activity is seen as a waste of time.[21]

People do not believe in the political process, and women especially feel excluded.[22]

There is a lot of apathy here. Twenty or twenty-five years ago the professional classes abdicated their responsibility in Northern Ireland. Politics became a dirty word.[23]

Non-involvement stands apart as the most virtuous attitude. It's best not to get involved. Non-involvement is the cornerstone of our present problems. The silence of a majority offers dumb allegiance to the way things are. We must regain our sense of outrage. We believe that the absence of a strong civil society in Northern Ireland has meant a preoccupation with a private life and personal happiness and a neglect of concern for the wider community.[24]

Working-class Protestants feel they have been betrayed and abandoned by the middle classes. There are only two forms of expression for the loyalist cause. One is through paramilitary organizations and the other is OUP/DUP. The majority of working-class Protestants do not relate to that and therefore they have no way of expressing themselves.[25]

Working-class people are too busy simply trying to exist to lobby politicians.... If our politicians had consulted grass roots and not simply covered themselves with rhetoric, they would have found that we were prepared to compromise for peace.[26]

On the one hand, civil society in Northern Ireland has been weakened by the opting out of the middle classes. Clearly, this is not universal, as the number of middle-class people who gave evidence to us demonstrated. There appears to be a number of primarily middle-class groups involved in reconciliation work, integrated schools and so on. On the other hand, there appears to be a very vibrant civil society in many working-class areas made up of community groups, women's groups, and so on.

However, whatever the constitutional developments, we must think how to capitalize on the strengths of Northern Irish civil society, as well as strengthen those areas that are weaker. This points to a consideration of *political* as well as constitutional processes. How can a more participatory and inclusive form of politics be developed that encourages and facilitates the exercise of active political citizenship in and across both communities? As one woman from north Belfast said in oral evidence:

We are involved with politics with a little 'p' on the ground, but we get no recognition for it from politicians who are involved in politics with a big 'p'. There needs to be recognition for those engaged in politics with a little 'p'.[27]

The withdrawal of the middle classes from politics further undermines the efficacy of the political process. The poor are not listened to; the extraordinary silence of the centre more than anything else highlights the spe-

cial nature of this conflict and underscores the necessity to bring the professional, business, and middle classes back into the political process. Until
they can be convinced of their *civic* responsibility to play a role and of the
necessity to find a solution, it is unlikely that the accommodations, which a
settlement will require, will be made.

Adding to the malaise are the malign effects of Direct Rule. The people of
Northern Ireland have no say whatsoever in the government that 'rules'
them. They cannot vote for either the Labour Party, the Conservative
Party or the Liberal Democrats. Northern Ireland business is conducted
by orders in council (at Westminster), and legislation prepared by the
Secretary of State cannot be amended. Government is remote, imperial,
and non-accountable to the electorate, which did not elect it in the first
place. Northern Ireland politicians, other than the seventeen MPs, are not
required to be responsive to their constituents since there is no forum in
which they can meet other than the weak district councils, which, for the
most part, were characterized in our submissions and hearings as largely
irrelevant talk-shops with extraordinarily limited powers, while the real
power resides in the Northern Ireland Office (NIO) or the 'quangos'.

Direct Rule has allowed people to keep to traditional positions. Absence of power has kept
them from acting responsibly and compromising.[28]

Our seventeen MPs have more say in the running of the UK than they do in the running of
Northern Ireland. This gap between the electorate and the civil service leaves the civil service
aloof and unaccountable. The implications of policies from the national Treasury are not
always in our interest. There's no structure for business to effect policy.[29]

To many, the political process in Northern Ireland is already irrelevant. Jobs and lives free
from fear are priorities for many. Direct Rule appears to some to be acceptable because they
see no alternative. Talk of local accountability is often a concept of the selected few — not of
the majority who feel little confidence in what has already been attempted.[30]

At the worst, Direct Rule bestows resources without any challenge or responsibility. This will
never provide the basis for a balanced society. At every level the creeping level of indifference
has to be challenged. Leadership is a key factor in bringing about social change and urgently
needs to be nurtured. A relatively small number of civil servants collectively influence social
and economic planning.[31]

Direct Rule makes our rulers arrogant, deters the best brains from going into politics, breeds
servility in the population and absolves voters of responsibility for their actions.[32]

There is a huge democratic deficit in Northern Ireland between the district councils, which
have distinctly limited powers, and the central government which is responsible for carrying
out many of the functions and responsibilities discharged in Britain below the level of central
government.[33]

In the absence of democratic structures, the powers and influence of the civil service have
increased substantially. Many people, who otherwise might join a political party, choose
instead to join a community organization or voluntary one.[34]

Membership of political parties is less per head of population than in the rest of the West. Parties find it difficult to find people to stand for elections, especially at local council levels.[35]

The structures of local government are undemocratic and unresponsive. The present structures do not encourage local politicians to behave in a responsible manner. Northern Ireland has become a totally bureaucratic state. An institutional structure has been created by the tendency within the bureaucracy to establish new agencies in response to specific demands from the community. There are no clear lines of accountability to the community.[36]

In short, whatever yardstick of democracy one wishes to use, Northern Ireland falls short. Back in 1982, James Prior, the then Secretary of State for Northern Ireland, said:

We have to face the fact that we cannot make Direct Rule work indefinitely. It is a remarkable achievement that we have made it work as well as it has. Direct Rule has brought to the province a fair and impartial system of administration. But it is only a second best. It cannot offer anything more than a temporary solution.[37]

Submissions and the oral hearings made the point over and over again: 'the democratic deficit' is a euphemism for undemocratic rule. When one adds the plethora of power the Secretary of State has at his disposal in the Emergency Powers Act (EPA) and the Prevention of Terrorism Act (PTA), one has the makings of government by diktat.

The absence of democracy and its corollary, responsibility to the electorate, means that politicians in Northern Ireland have no forum in which to develop and *practice* political skills. In particular, they do not learn how to compromise and make trade-offs that are the hallmarks of a functioning democracy. Compromising is a learned behaviour; the compromises made in district councils are inconsequential, since the issues at stake are themselves inconsequential. The result is poor leadership and deficient representation.

We are keeping our politicians in kindergarten.[38]

The quality of leadership is the key to the solution. The decline of responsibility in the political sphere makes the task more difficult. In addition, such is the state of disrespect into which politics has fallen in Northern Ireland that those involved in any way in politics are often penalized for such involvement. Their participation on public, community and voluntary bodies and their employment by such bodies is often seen as problematic. Inevitably this has decreased the number, and presumably therefore the quality, of those prepared to enter public life at a political level.... All parties will testify to the difficulty of recruiting qualitative new recruits to political representation, particularly at the local level. In addition, all political parties suffer from a chronic lack of funding, minuscule membership, offices more shabby than many voluntary agencies, and in many cases, a lack of organizational resources and skills.... The best of leadership in Northern Ireland goes into other areas. There is a disrespect for politicians here.[39]

We produce a poor quality of political representation because of the lack of democracy here.[40]

One of the many and complex problems in Northern Ireland is the low calibre of candidates put forward by the traditional political parties. There should be a 'none-of-the-above' option on the ballot.[41]

The politicians of Northern Ireland need to take a fresh look at their role. Some have been with us for over twenty years and seem to have learned very little. What are they doing to rally ordinary women and men to isolate the people of violence? Do they not often ride on the back of violence, using it to press their own political viewpoint? [42]

How can we persuade our politicians that compromise is not a dirty word? We have had few changes in our main politicians and, with one or two exceptions, they remain as conditioned as Pavlov's dogs.[43]

Most of the political actors on the stage are prisoners of their own past. They have merely been given a good behaviour parole by their constituents; even with the best of will possible, their freedom of action is severely constrained.[44]

Politicians need to do unpalatable things. In Northern Ireland they never have to stand up and 'see' the closure of a hospital or the like because they have no responsibility in the long run. They don't have a budget and they don't have to take account of the demands made on a budget. They never have to make a case for anything. They just keep shouting the same old things.[45]

In short, the debilitating impact of Direct Rule is felt in many ways: political parties are poorly organized in terms of political development and policy-making. All political parties, it was pointed out to us, are in dire need of political training, especially at the district council level. Parties have difficulty recruiting candidates for elections; the middle class, Catholics and Protestants, but especially Protestants, have opted out of politics; the business sector no longer seeks to play a role, and the overall effect is a diminution in the calibre of candidates standing for office, with some of the best people quitting because of frustration, and the lack of real authority. Thus, Direct Rule has lead to a crisis of *leadership*, and without leadership, in the view of many presenters at our hearings, it would be extremely difficult to chart a path to Northern Ireland's future.

While there are many ways in which the democratic deficit can be ameliorated, two ways received frequent mention: (1) give back to Northern Ireland district councils the powers they exercise in the other parts of the United Kingdom (although these powers are being reduced in the UK, Northern Ireland should be a warning to the rest of the UK); (2) give back to Northern Irish councils some measure of this power, with the understanding that a full devolution of residual functions would follow power-sharing arrangements in the councils.

Submissions reflected a range of views:

Local authorities could be offered power on a rolling basis, provided they meet certain criteria for cross-community co-operation.[46]

Further efforts should be made to revive responsible local government. The geography of Northern Ireland appears to be dominated by the two cities of Belfast and Derry. They, with their adjoining town and rural areas, could form the two city-regions for local government and administration. In order to attract a good quality of elected members, the city regions would have to have effective powers and duties.[47]

[A return of power to the local level] would have the great advantage of giving members of both communities more experience of the actual business of government. Local councillors at present have so little real power that they tend to waste time on striking political attitudes. It would also mean that, in areas with a clear majority from one community, there would be a growing sense of responsibility for their own affairs; and in areas without that clear majority, a challenge to find local ways for the communities to work together.[48]

At local level there should be county councils, bigger than the present councils, with a very big say in services, tourism, education, health, social services, the infrastructure necessary for industrial development, police forces, fire brigades and environmental services. Councils should rotate the chair every six months.[49] [50]

Two Paramount Realities

Many submissions listed what they perceived to be the realities of the situation — a practice going back to the days of the New Ireland Forum Report.[51] When realities were talked about, two appeared paramount to the Commission:

(1) Protestants do not want to become part of an all-Ireland state, and the question of forcing them into such an arrangement is not an issue. Leading nationalists and republicans both have come around to this point of view.[52] 'As leaders of our respective parties', said Sinn Féin president Gerry Adams and SDLP leader John Hume, in a joint statement in April 1993,

we have told each other that we see the task of reaching agreement on a peaceful and democratic accord for all on this island as our primary challenge. We both recognize that such a new agreement is achievable and viable only if it can earn and enjoy the allegiance of the different traditions on this island, by accommodating diversity and providing for national reconciliation.[53]

Northern Ireland, therefore, is likely to remain a part of the United Kingdom for a long time, a point made in a number of submissions.

Nationalists will have to accept that Britain is going to remain in Northern Ireland for a very long time. There is no evidence that they are prepared for this.[54]

There are a large number of nationalists for whom the aspiration to a united Ireland is pushed so far into the future as to be almost meaningless, or who would actively resist incorporation into a united Ireland like the present Republic. I am convinced that fair play and treatment within Northern Ireland is the essential demand of many, if not most, Catholics who live here, and that they are far less concerned with changing Northern Ireland's position within the UK. [55] [56]

(2) The Republic of Ireland cannot at present or for the foreseeable future absorb Northern Ireland and continue to subsidize it at current levels of UK expenditures. Moreover, polls indicate that there is a great deal of ambivalence in the Republic on unification: the aspiration is there, but for the most part people do not see unification happening during their lifetimes. The aspiration is strong, the commitment is weak.[57]

In the light of these realities, two submissions succinctly stated the essence of the nationalists' dilemma:

There is no historical imperative that Ireland should ever be united; the case for unity must be judged on its merits alone. Northern Ireland is an 'unagreed' entity, rather than a non-legitimate one.[58]

The Republic should accept that the most important objective to be achieved is to assist nationalists and unionists to work together politically in Northern Ireland. The Republic needs to accept the reality of the situation, that is, that there is unlikely to be consent for a united Ireland for a very long time and that many unionists resent the South having anything to do with the North. Northern nationalists will have to decide which is more important in the near future: a united Ireland or justice and reconciliation in Northern Ireland.[59]

Which is more important? Justice and equity and the ability to participate on an equal basis in *all* spheres of life in Northern Ireland today, or the possibility of a united Ireland in some distant tomorrow? The former is a prerequisite for the latter.

Britain's attempt to portray herself as 'neutral' adds to the problem. Says one commentator:

It is not productive for Britain to claim that she is neutral. Britain is part of the problem. No one is neutral in this game.[60]

According to the Northern Ireland Office: 'The government has consistently explained that it has no blueprint for new political structures.' This adds to the instability and the distrust that appears on both sides of the political divide as Britain seeks to appease two communities that have diametrically opposing aspirations. On the one hand, the British government seeks to convey the impression that Northern Ireland is an integral part of the UK; on the other, that it will not stand in the way of Irish unity, if that is the wish of the majority. Having no long-term objectives, or at least not publicly stated ones, Britain appears to be attempting to achieve short-term objectives. The result is confusion and contradiction, with both communities scrutinizing every government statement for nuances that might make it appear that the government is leaning to its side. The British government's insistence that it is an honest broker, and that the ingredients of a settlement must be worked out by the two communities, adds to the recipe for conflict.

Moreover, claims of neutrality lead the SDLP to argue that the task of nationalists is to persuade Britain to become one of the persuaders; that is, to convince unionists to become part of some form of an all-Ireland state. One could argue, with equal logic, that the task of the unionists is also to persuade Britain to become one of the persuaders, that is, to convince nationalists that their future lies in some form of a Northern Ireland state which is part of the United Kingdom.

Britain may or may not want Northern Ireland to remain in the UK —

many of our submissions and oral hearings were of the view that she did not. It is inconceivable, however, that the UK, given the practices of international law, would unilaterally 'rid' itself of Northern Ireland, without the consent of a majority of the people of the region, more especially so in the post-Cold War world, where ethnic conflicts and disputes over national territory are resulting in violent upheavals across Europe.

Many authors of submissions and oral hearing presenters believed that Britain's undertaking under Article 1 of the Anglo-Irish Agreement — that the status of Northern Ireland would not change without the consent of a majority of the people of Northern Ireland — is unworkable.

Do unionists have the right to say no to an all-Ireland solution? Our answer is no. But whatever their right, in reality unionists can veto a united Ireland, unless we impose it on them militarily.[61]

If you leave the consent formula in place, you have a zero-sum game. One side wins, one side loses. We need a settlement where we are not threatened by each other.[62]

Even if 60 per cent of voters opted for a united Ireland in a referendum, a vast number of Protestants would leave, others would acquiesce, some would fight. I believe in more like two-thirds' consent — 50 per cent plus one is a formula for violence.[63]

Any solution put forward must meet with the approval of two communities voting separately. Any subsequent change in constitutional status must attain majority approval from each of the two communities. Changes in the constitutional status of Northern Ireland following a new political structure should be very difficult. Majorities of over 75 per cent in Northern Ireland, both in parliament and referendum, should be required before either British or Irish withdrawal could be effected.[64]

On the question of the consent of a majority for unification, a majority approval will not solve the problem. We need a consensual approach. It's true that in a divided society you need some kind of decision-making process but decisions cannot be made on the basis of fifty per cent plus one. The consent formula is a recipe for disaster if taken literally.[65] [66]

You can't force Protestants into a united Ireland. Any constitutional change must be by consent of the Protestant people.[67]

Even if Catholics were to emerge as the majority of the electorate at some future stage, the consent formula would be inoperable without the consent of a sufficiently large number of Protestants to forestall a Protestant backlash against forced incorporation into an all-Ireland state, in which they would have had no say in how that state was shaped. Moreover, Protestants are more determinedly against a united Ireland than Catholics are for it. There is little support among Protestants for *any* form of a united Ireland.[68] Most Protestants are not even prepared to see it as a future option. On the other hand, there is far less complete support than imagined among Catholics for a united Ireland. As a long-term objective, it receives widespread acceptance. However, in only one of the vast number of surveys carried out in Northern Ireland did Catholics opt for a united Ireland of some form as their preferred option. Usually a united Ireland is a less favoured option than power-sharing with a devolved government and an Irish dimension.[69]

My nationalist friends are not interested in unity with the South as it is presently constituted. They want their 'Irishness' recognized here [in Northern Ireland] and a united Ireland can be left to the future.[70]

The concept of majority consent is an illusion in the context of Northern Ireland's constitutional status. It is not useful as a tool on which to build policy.

Simple majority consent cannot deliver what it promises. It is regressive since it increases uncertainty about the future of Northern Ireland.

All — the two governments, the opposition parties in Britain and the Republic, and the constitutional parties in Northern Ireland — pay lip service to Irish unity with the consent of a majority. But equally, all must know that even if 50 per cent plus one gave their consent to a united Ireland, a recalcitrant 49 per cent, say 750,000 Protestants, would be just as much an obstacle to unity as would one million. This begs the question: *How large a majority is necessary to give expression to the consent of a majority?* One must clearly distinguish between the consent of *the* majority (the unionist community) and the consent of *a* majority (51 per cent of the community). In our view, given the deep religious, political, and ethnic cleavages that exist in Northern Ireland, it only makes sense to require the consent of a majority of *the* majority (the unionist community) as being a necessary precondition for giving significant expression of the consent of *a* majority of the community as a whole.

A British government may be either unable or unwilling to deliver on its obligations under Article 1 of the Anglo-Irish Agreement, its commitment to introduce and support in parliament 'legislation to secure a united Ireland if in the future a majority of the people of Northern Ireland were clearly to wish for and formally consent to the establishment of a united Ireland'. The historical parallel is obvious: the Home Rule Bill of 1912 passed both houses of Parliament. However, the threat of loyalist resistance was sufficient to ensure its demise. And today, as in 1912, an unwillingness to coerce loyalists is at the core of the British 'problem'.

Eleven years ago, Mr Nicholas Scott, former Minister of State for Northern Ireland, said:

Simple unification seems to me to be absolutely pie-in-the-sky, and I have to emphasize that, even with a majority of people deciding to bring it about, the practical problems of the governments of the UK and the Republic of Ireland would be such that they would actually have to sit down and work out something much more complex than just reunifying Ireland.[71]

There was a wide range of views expressed regarding the role of the Republic in Northern Ireland. To summarize: an acknowledgment that, in the absence of new political structures in Northern Ireland, the Anglo-Irish Agreement and conference must continue as a minimum expression not just of nationalists' aspirations towards Irish unity, but of their desire to have Dublin involved in the running of the affairs of the North as the second guarantor of their position.[72] There was a belief that the Republic's government, political parties, people and Churches could be more aware of and sensitive to Northern fears and sensibilities; that the Republic is so intertwined with nationalist politics in the North that unionist-minded people have justifications for their suspicions; that while this was understandable in the past, nationalist grievances have been, and continue to be, redressed, and it is time the Republic took an interest in *all* the people and traditions in the North; that it should attend to the perceptions of unionists (and many nationalists) that it is a confessional state; that the Republic needs to 'to redefine its position vis-à-vis the North and address the ambiguity there towards the North which still exists'.[73]

Notes

1. See John Whyte, *Interpreting Northern Ireland* (Oxford: Oxford University Press, 1990).
2. In Washington, D.C., a city of 638,432 inhabitants, it was recently reported that 3300 people have been killed in the last eleven years — 453 in 1992 alone.
3. Michael McKeown, *Two Seven Six Three* (Dublin: Murlough Press, 1989).
4. Councillor Raymond Ferguson at oral hearing 4.2.1993.
5. Mr Paul Sweeney at oral hearing 25.1.1993.
6. Mr Robin Wilson and Professor Richard Kearney.
7. Archbishop Robin Eames at oral hearing 17.2.1993.
8. Other submissions used for this section: Dr Mari Fitzduff (oral hearing 25.1.1993); Professor Bernard Cullen; Mr Mark Russell.
9. Faculty of Public Health Medicine, Royal Victoria Hospital.
10. Professor Desmond Rea at oral hearing 17.2.1993.
11. Mrs Marlene Jefferson at oral hearing 25.1.1993.
12. Archbishop Robin Eames.
13. Rev. Sydney Callaghan.
14. Other submissions used for this section: Northern Consensus Group (oral hearing 2.2.1993); Interfriendship; Mr Barry Cowan; Dr Clifford Smyth (oral hearing 3.2.1993).
15. Mr Jackie Redpath at meeting with Commission.
16. Dr Duncan Morrow of Corrymeela Community, at oral hearing 28.1.1993 (and submission).
17. Mr Sam Butler.
18. Mr Alan Sheeran.
19. Mr Joseph Peake.
20. Mr Jackie Redpath.
21. Ms Olive Scott.
22. Mrs Kathleen Feenan and Mrs Mary Leonard.
23. Mrs Marlene Jefferson at oral hearing 25.1.1993.
24. Mr James Nelson and Ms Claire Johnston.
25. Mr Jackie Hewitt.
26. Group of former loyalist prisoners at private hearing.
27. North Belfast women at oral hearing 3.2.1993.
28. Mr Hugh Logue at oral hearing 2.2.1993.
29. Northern Ireland Chamber of Commerce and Industry at oral hearing 3.2.1993.

30. Mr Roy McClenaghan, Ekklesia Christian Fellowship.
31. Northern Ireland Voluntary Trust.
32. Mr Kenneth James.
33. Sir Kenneth Bloomfield.
34. Dr Gabriel Scally.
35. Mr Will Glendinning.
36. Mr Sam Butler.
37. Quoted in Padraig O'Malley, *The Uncivil Wars: Ireland Today* (Belfast: Blackstaff Press, 1983).
38. Mr Kenneth James at oral hearing 22.2.1993.
39. Dr Mari Fitzduff.
40. Dr Clifford Smyth.
41. Councillor T. Carlin .
42. Churches' Central Committee for Community Work.
43. Mrs Sheila Chillingworth.
44. Mr John O'Riordan.
45. Mr Alan Sheeran.
46. Mr Iain Sharpe.
47. Lord Hylton.
48. Sir Charles Carter.
49. Rev. Denis Faul.
50. Other submissions used for this section: Mr Paul Sweeney; Dr Jean and Caroline Whyte.
51. New Ireland Forum Report (Dublin: Stationery Office, 1984).
52. See also Mr Michael Farrell.
53. *The Irish Times*, 26.4.1993.
54. Corrymeela Community.
55. Professor Bernard Cullen.
56. Inter-Church Group on Faith and Politics submission, also used for this section.
57. Dr T.K. Whitaker.
58. Mr Jim Hanna.
59. Pax Christi Ireland.
60. Professor Kevin Boyle at oral hearing 17.2.1993.
61. Bloody Sunday Initiative at oral hearing 26.1.1993.
62. Mr Charles Murphy at oral hearing 26.1.1993.
63. Mr Glen Barr at oral hearing 27.1.1993.
64. Corrymeela Community.
65. Professor Kevin Boyle at oral hearing 17.2.1993.
66. Other submissions used for this section: Mr Eoin Ó Cofaigh; Mr Charles Murphy; Mr James Wilson (New Ireland Group) at oral hearing 27.1.1993.
67. Mr Michael Farrell at oral hearing 19.2.1993.
68. John Whyte op. cit.
69. ibid.
70. Mr Charles Murphy at oral hearing 26.1.1993.
71. Interview with Padraig O'Malley quoted in *The Uncivil Wars: Ireland Today*.
72. Mr Michael Farrell.
73. Inter-Church Group on Faith and Politics.

CHAPTER 3

A Modest Constitutional Proposal

There was a plethora of constitutional models in the written submissions: ranging from resuscitation of some version of majority rule (although there were very few of these), to various power-sharing recipes — with or without an Irish dimension, to forms of an all-Ireland federation or confederation (some ingeniously designed), to models that would place Northern Ireland in the context of Europe, calls for independence — or at least autonomy, models of consociation, joint authority, and cantonization. A number of submissions made arguments for joint authority in the absence of agreement among the political parties on a way forward.[1] There was a suggestion that both contentious legislation in a new regional assembly and change in Northern Ireland's constitutional status should require majorities of 75 per cent;[2] or that the latter should require a majority in both Northern Ireland's communities.[3]

Forty-nine submissions called for a devolved government for Northern Ireland, usually with some form of Irish dimension; forty-four called for some form of all-Ireland state; thirty-three called for joint authority; nine called for constitutional models that would put Northern Ireland in the framework of Europe, and eight called for independence.

In these submissions, a number of points were repeatedly made:

- An almost universal acceptance in the unionist community that power will have to be shared with nationalists.
- An acknowledgment that an Irish dimension exists which must be accommodated, but an absolute refusal on the part of unionists to agree to any new arrangement that would give the Republic an executive role in the government of Northern Ireland. The Commission remarked that, in submissions from a number of constitutional nationalists, all-Ireland political structures for the future of Northern Ireland are put forward as if a unionist community does not exist.
- Widespread disagreement on the form the North-South relationship should take, varying from the 'good neighbours' formulation and variations on 'co-operation on matters of mutual concern' to a relationship that would give the Republic an executive role in the government of Northern Ireland.
- Explicit recognition of the fact that the future of the economies of the two parts of Ireland are inextricably linked to a single-market Europe.

- Widespread agreement that Northern Ireland should be as self-governing as possible.
- A Bill of Rights was almost universally endorsed as being desirable; indeed, many submissions said that it was an indispensable part of any settlement.
- Some kind of proportionate, or equal, power-sharing to give literal expression to the equality of the two traditions.
- Special majorities required to secure the passage of legislation
- Various mechanisms to give veto rights to the minority with regard to matters of particular concern to it.

Whatever the differing allegiances and preferences of the people who wrote to and appeared before the Opsahl Commission, one common thread is clear: there was an almost unanimous desire to have a government and administration that were more accountable to the people of the region, however they perceived it. There is a widely shared opposition to government by non-representative civil service departments or appointed bodies like 'quangos'.

At the same time, the evidence submitted strongly suggests that no internal government can be agreed to that fails fully to respond to the fact that Northern Ireland is essentially composed of two communities: one unionist, one nationalist. However much they have in common, including significant degrees of poverty and deprivation, they differ radically not only on how and by whom they should be governed, but also on what their fundamental political allegiance should be — to Britain, to Ireland, to Northern Ireland. In these circumstances, it is evident that a parliamentary system of government based on the Westminster model is not and — experience has shown — was not a suitable model for the governing of a fundamentally divided society.

In Northern Ireland, as currently constituted, notions which may be discarded are that:

- Northern Ireland is like any other part of the United Kingdom.
- The communities in Northern Ireland will agree to independence.
- The United Kingdom will withdraw from Northern Ireland under pressure of violence.
- The Republic of Ireland will renounce the aim of Irish unity.
- Irish unity is a realistic prospect in the foreseeable future.

It also appeared from what we heard and read that:

- Majority rule in Northern Ireland, whether simple or proportionate, is not currently a viable proposition. The nationalist community has no obligation to agree to it and has the critical mass to prevent its imposition.
- The unionist community will not accept an administration for Northern

Ireland that gives an executive role to anyone outside the United Kingdom.

The Commission further noted that the representative political voices of the nationalist tradition, North and South, without exception, recognize that any agreement is achievable and viable only if it has the consent of both traditions in Ireland. Thus the Tánaiste and Minister for Foreign Affairs, Mr Dick Spring, said in March 1993:

We are working towards an accommodation between the two traditions in Ireland, based on the principle that both must have satisfactory, secure and durable political, administrative and symbolic expression and protection.... We could agree certain fundamental principles to govern all future relationships and entrench them beyond the reach of all changes in regard to sovereignty.[4]

The following month the Taoiseach, Mr Albert Reynolds, said that the Fianna Fáil party was committed to the eventual establishment of a united Ireland, 'but recognizes that realistically it can only come about through agreement and consent, and as a result of a lengthy process of dialogue, co-operation and reconciliation'.[5]

In his speech to his party's 1991 annual conference, SDLP leader Mr John Hume, said:

Difference should be respected and institutions should be created, North and South, which clearly respect our diversity and our difference, but which also allow us to work the substantial common ground between all of us. This approach presents a major challenge to everyone in Northern Ireland, unionist and nationalist. It presents a particular challenge to the Provisional IRA. Do they accept that the basic reasons that they give for their methods no longer exist? The answer that they keep giving is that our approach, because we insist on agreement, gives a veto to the unionists. Could they tell us how a group of people could unite about anything without agreement? Could they tell us how Serbs and Croats, or Greek and Turkish Cypriots could unite without agreement?[6]

In so far as these and similar statements by nationalist leaders both in Northern Ireland and the Republic can be correctly interpreted to mean what they say — and we have been given no reason to doubt this — the task of creating a government for Northern Ireland within the limits described above should not be beyond the realm of the possible and the practicable. (We note that in a Market Research Bureau of Ireland survey carried out in the Republic on 15-16 April 1991, 82 per cent of a representative sample of 1000 voters were prepared to postpone Irish unity in order to achieve an internal settlement in Northern Ireland.)

In essence, we consider that — provided that Irish nationalism is legally recognized in Northern Ireland (*see recommendation 1.3*) — a regional government for Northern Ireland should be put in place, *based on the principle that each community should have an equal voice in making and executing the laws or a veto on their execution, and should equally share administrative authority.* This government should be free to discuss and negotiate its relationships, institutional and other, with the government of the Republic of Ireland.

In these circumstances, immediate changes in the constitutional status of Northern Ireland or in Articles 2 and 3 of the Irish Constitution are unnecessary: in the future, any change in the constitutional status of Northern Ireland would require the consent of the Northern Ireland government, constituted on the basis of the principles proposed, and the consent of the people of Northern Ireland.

Against this, it may be argued that no compromise is conceivable between the traditional unionist position — that only a structure which preserves Northern Ireland as a unionist-governed entity within the United Kingdom is acceptable — and the traditional nationalist position, that only an all-Ireland structure is acceptable.

Our response is that it is possible to sustain Northern Ireland and provide it with a government, on condition that it clearly becomes the equally owned property of both communities; thus, leaving aside the issue of Irish unity unless and until both communities consent to it. What we propose derives from the concept of 'concurrent government' elaborated by the nineteenth-century American Statesman and political philosopher, John Caldwell Calhoun, the son of Northern Irish Calvinist parents. Calhoun argued that the underlying principle of concurrent government must be compromise, whereas, in a divided society, government by numerical majority necessarily will be based on force.[7]

The significance of this proposal is twofold. First, it is premised on the necessity for any solution to the Northern Ireland problem to be based on building trust and confidence between the two communities, so that each comes to see the other as a community without which a workable political future cannot be constructed.

Secondly, it assumes a recognition that, however protected its rights and liberties might be in Northern Ireland (for example, by a Bill of Rights), the nationalist community is bound to feel its minority status, derived from partition, as a continuing source of insecurity. It is for this reason that only equal authority in government can remove their 'second-class' status. The corollary, of course, is that the unionist community will be able to feel more secure in the face of the growth of the Catholic population in Northern Ireland and in the knowledge that there can be no moves towards a united Ireland without its consent (i.e. all such moves can be prevented by using its power of veto).

In order to provide reasonable flexibility, if there is a deadlock at executive/administrative level under this system, the regional parliamentary assembly could be asked to resolve the issue by weighted majority vote. Dr T.K. Whitaker, Mr Jim Hanna, the Corrymeela Community and others have suggested weighting formulas.

The virtue of this new proposal can best be understood perhaps by comparing it with the only other novel proposal of recent years: joint author-ity. Our prime concern, like those proposing joint authority, is to ensure equality within Northern Ireland for the two communities, as well as a sense of security about what the future holds. The difference is that, where joint authority might further the suspicion and polarization generated by 'remote-control' administration, our proposal envisages the breaking down of mistrust through a common project of government. While joint author-ity risks the death of politics within Northern Ireland, our proposal would remedy its 'democratic deficit' and move towards resolving the sterile debate on Northern Ireland's constitutional status without prejudice to long-term consensual change.

One implication of this would be a refocusing of the Anglo-Irish Agreement on the 'east-west' relationship, as the confidence of such a new administration in Northern Ireland grew. As the representatives of both Northern Irish communities felt able to start taking on powers currently under the aegis of the Anglo-Irish Agreement, the involvement of that accord in Northern Ireland correspondingly would diminish. If such agreement to take on equally shared powers and responsibilities was not forthcoming, or if constitutional deadlock resulted, those powers could be retained by or restored to the domain of the two governments.

This necessary provision diminishes the apparent rigidity of the pro-posed formula. The incentive towards self-government, on the unionist side, would be the threat of a return to the full inter-governmental struc-tures of the Anglo-Irish Agreement. On the nationalist side, it would be the formal embodiment in political institutions of the concepts of equality of treatment and parity of esteem.

In discussions and negotiations between such a new government in Northern Ireland and the government of the Republic of Ireland, *both* union-ist *and* nationalist concerns could be accommodated simultaneously. For unionists, no relationship would be established which did not have their con-sent. For nationalists, such relationships as were established would be between Irish men and women, without any involvement by the UK govern-ment. In these non-threatening circumstances, there would be a real possibil-ity that the role of the Irish government could come, in time, to be perceived as one of protecting the interests of both communities in Northern Ireland.

The implications of this recommendation are far-reaching: taking them into account is a matter for the political parties in both parts of Ireland and their respective governments.

Notes

1. For example, Corrymeela Community; Mr Paul Nolan; Mr Michael Farrell; Dr Brendan O'Leary and Dr John McGarry; Mr Jonathan Stephenson.
2. Mr Jim Hanna; Corrymeela Community.

3. Professor Frederick Boal.
4. *The Irish Times*, 6.3.1993.
5. Address in New York, *Financial Times*, 23.4.1993.
6. *The Irish Times*, 25.11.1991.
7. John C. Calhoun was vice-president of the United States (1825–32) and a US senator (1832–44 and 1845–50). See 'A Disquisition on Government' in *The Essential Calhoun* (New Brunswick, New Jersey and London: Transaction Publishers, 1993).

CHAPTER 4:

The Constitutional Parties:
A Widening Gulf?

With regard to the 1992 talks among the constitutional parties, the Commission puts forward, at least for public debate, its understanding of where Northern Ireland's constitutional parties saw themselves as standing when the inter-party talks were suspended in November 1992.

The Alliance Party: The public view of the SDLP is that it wants power-sharing. But now the SDLP does not see power-sharing along the lines of the 1973/74 Sunningdale model as being acceptable. The SDLP is taking a more extreme position than it did 20 years ago. The SDLP is doing exactly what unionists did for a generation: driving the opposition into a corner. When unionists went to Dublin, they found none of the generosity they had been led to expect.

The Democratic Unionist Party (DUP): The SDLP brought to the table a set of proposals which were so outrageous that even its own friends were surprised and puzzled. Everyone thought the proposals were an opening gambit. But it became clear that the SDLP was not prepared to negotiate these proposals. On one occasion concessions were made on all sides. An agreement was reached. But the next morning the SDLP took it off the table. The party's proposals today are in the same shape and form as they were on the first day of the talks. The Irish Government made a number of comments before the talks process, indicating that unionists would be surprised at its generosity, but Dublin was implacable on the question of Articles 2 and 3. They were on the table, but only to be debated. There seemed to be no willingness to reform the Irish Constitution and it was quite clear that there was no business that could be done with them.

The Ulster Unionist Party (UUP): The visit to Dublin became an exercise in semantics. Dublin literally got stuck on whether there could or would be a referendum on Articles 2 and 3, if certain things happened. This issue occupied the better part of two days. The paper that the Ulster Unionist Party put forward on North-South relations was one they thought was a fair, and generous paper, and a good basis on which to have an agreement. But it was not even considered by the Irish side or by the SDLP.

The Social Democratic and Labour Party (SDLP): The SDLP had strong reservations about the government of Northern Ireland being controlled by an assembly. The likelihood would be that it would behave the way local councils behave — in fact, that the assembly would turn out to be a larger version of the Belfast City Council and that what you were against would matter, not what you were for. That would be a disaster. Hence the SDLP proposals for a type of administration formed partly on the European model and partly on the American model. The SDLP was dismissive of the UUP's North-South proposals for three reasons: (1) they were tabled on the eve of the ending of the talks, an ending forced by the unionists; (2) they fell far short of what had been discussed bilaterally between the parties; (3) the UUP appeared divided on them.

One problem, of course, that compounded the difficulties the political parties faced was their opposing perceptions as to the purpose of the negotiating process. The unionist parties wished to negotiate an agreement to replace the Anglo-Irish Agreement; that is, an agreement that would give the Republic of Ireland little or no consultative role in Northern Ireland, whereas the SDLP wanted to negotiate an agreement that would 'transcend in importance any agreement ever made'; that is, an agreement that would give them at least, if not more than, what they had already secured in the Anglo-Irish Agreement. In response to a question in this regard, Mr Mark Durkan, the SDLP chairman, told the Commission:

That's a fair interpretation. We thought everything would be on the table. Other parties arrived, having been given assurances that certain possibilities were not on the table. There was a misunderstanding.[1]

Thus, while the constitutional status of Northern Ireland was on the table for the SDLP, for the unionists it clearly was not. How such a fundamental misunderstanding could occur, given the months of talks about talks, the innumerable bilateral talks between the constitutional political parties and the Secretary of State for Northern Ireland, is difficult to comprehend. It seems to us to be related to the different modes of thinking and articulation the two traditions use; we explore these at more length in chapter 5.

Presenters at the oral hearings expressed a wide variety of opinions about the talks, some blaming the SDLP for their collapse, others blaming the unionists, and some blaming the rationale of the 'nothing will be agreed until everything is agreed' formula.

The indications we are getting are that unionists would be interested in a Sunningdale type of agreement if such an arrangement would bring finality. But unionists are afraid that every attempt at a settlement is a stepping stone to a united Ireland. Unionists in 1985 suffered a great defeat in their own eyes. It's difficult to negotiate when you don't think you are playing on a level playing field. The unionist position represents a considerable advance.[2]

The SDLP should have sought accommodation in Strand One — it's what a lot of people want. I found the SDLP document surprising. They said it was only there for debate. But as I understand it, it was still on the table at the end of the meeting. They proposed joint authority, including Europe and the South.[3]

Unionists are more accommodating today. Unionists say they have now gone as far as they can without getting something in return. The concept of majority rule has been dropped. Now unionists accept power-sharing.[4]

We also question whether the policy that 'nothing is agreed until everything is agreed' should continue. While this may have been an appropriate negotiating tactic at the beginning, it has resulted in six months of talks with nothing to show for it. Surely it would have been better to have some agreement, at least in principle.[5]

There is a fundamental flaw in the approach to the recent talks, that 'nothing is agreed until everything is agreed'. I am inclined to the view that everything never will be agreed, that the situation in Northern Ireland is just not bad enough yet. And perhaps it will never be. In Northern Ireland the treatment required of all interested parties to enable there to be a lasting settlement would demand painful concessions all around. We are not prepared to do so.[6]

Politicians, especially those elected on party tickets, are wedded to a complex package of manifesto commitments which are often so tightly interwoven that compromise on one aspect, however desirable, would so jeopardize the totality that movement becomes impossible. [Moreover,] the regularity with which they have to submit themselves to the verdict of the ballot box means that their hands will be tied for eternity.[7] [8]

Despite such difficulties, there is a widespread wish among the people that politicians should resume open-ended talks as soon as possible and come to agreement on those issues upon which they can agree. Those politicians who showed a willingness to talk won admiration for doing so, and the Ulster Unionists won admiration for their courage in going to Dublin. Our overall impression is that there is tremendous unrequited thirst for dialogue among the people of Northern Ireland and a recognition that there is no 'big solution'. Archbishop Eames pleaded for an end to the 'dramatic gesture'[9] and a slow build-up of trust instead. In the words of another presenter, 'an untidy situation needs untidy answers'.[10]

Another Democratic Deficit

We also heard arguments as to why the mainland political parties should organize in Northern Ireland. Northern Ireland may be a special case, but not so special that the ordinary, taken-for-granted tenets of democracy should not apply. One of those tenets specifically requires that the citizens of a country have the right to vote for a party that will govern them; that no citizen should be denied the right to have a say in who will govern them.

[We] argue that the exclusion of the province from full participation in the party system of the state of which it is a part is an intellectual denial of basic democratic rights, and, secondly, that sectarianism and extremism can be challenged if the citizens of Northern Ireland have the opportunity to participate in those British political parties which have no stake in perpetuating sectarian voting blocks.[11]

In our view, as long as Northern Ireland remains in the UK, its citizens should have the same voting rights as citizens in the rest of the state. In particular, the people of Northern Ireland should be able to vote for or against the parties that actually govern them. They should not be restricted to regional parties, which mostly represent communal or sectarian interests. Citizens of the Republic of Ireland or any country can join the Labour Party. Opinion polls indicate that the demand that the parties of government open their ranks to local people is more popular amongst Catholics and Protestants than any other political initiative.[12] [13]

In its essence, the call for the British parties to organize in Northern Ireland is simple: exclusion from the party system means that politics in Northern Ireland is exclusively communal. Parties in Northern Ireland are not political parties in the real sense because they are not concerned with the business of governing the UK. They represent only Catholic and Protestant interests.

An Ulster Marketing Surveys poll in February 1989 showed that 53 per cent of people (57 per cent of Protestants, 45 per cent of Catholics) said they would be prepared to vote for the main British political parties if they stood in elections in Northern Ireland.

The essentially sectarian nature of politics in Northern Ireland was brought to our attention by a member of the SDLP. 'My party', he said, 'should not rest comfortably. One question it should ask itself: Why, after twenty years of existence, is it still a Catholic party that draws only Catholic support? Why has our party such a sectarian image?'[14]

Whatever the arguments for or against British parties organizing in Northern Ireland, the Commission is convinced that the current democratic deficit requires greater choice to be available to the Northern Ireland electorate.

Articles 2 and 3

Articles 2 and 3 of the Irish Constitution figured prominently in a number of submissions, the case being made for their retention, amendment, or outright deletion. The two Articles read as follows:

Article 2: The national territory consists of the whole island of Ireland, its islands and territorial seas.

Article 3: Pending the reintegration of the national territory, and without prejudice to the right of the Parliament and Government established by this Constitution to exercise jurisdiction over the whole of that territory, the laws enacted by that Parliament shall have the like area and extent of application as the laws of Saorstát Eireann and the like extra-territorial effect.

A sample of the range of opinions on Articles 2 and 3 includes:

Now people are keyed up emotionally over Articles 2 and 3. If a referendum were held today, I don't know if it would pass. And if the results were negative, the situation would be much worse than it was before.[15]

Articles 2 and 3 are unworkable and are kept there only to annoy unionists.[16]

Articles 2 and 3 *must* go.[17]

Articles 2 and 3 should be amended to make unity conditional on the will of the majority in the North. However, it should be done only in the context of a final settlement.[18]

There is now, at least on paper, a majority in the Dáil for reform or removal of these Articles. There are, nonetheless, very powerful reasons why the Irish government might not wish to reform Articles 2 and 3. Firstly, it would be seen as a betrayal and abandonment of the Northern nationalist community. Second, it would be seen by nationalists in the South as a recognition of the legitimacy, as opposed to the fact, of partition, and there would probably be strong opposition to such a proposal. Thirdly, the question of the entitlement of Northerners to Irish citizenship would have to be resolved to ensure that people from the North could carry Irish passports.[19]

Should the British government or the unionists give a sufficient executive role in the government of Northern Ireland to nationalists, it is difficult to see how nationalists could avoid meeting unionists' demands for changing Articles 2 and 3 and for proper formal recognition of Northern Ireland and its structures of government. Without a decision to give a sufficient executive role, it probably will be impossible for nationalists to change Articles 2 and 3. Nationalists would probably better their case by saying explicitly that they are committed to recognizing Northern Ireland when and if such decisions are made.[20]

I would support an amendment to Articles 2 and 3 which would express the deeply held desire of most citizens of the Republic of Ireland: that the people of this island should be united in their wish to live together in peace, recognizing in our laws and political structures the diverse traditions which we cherish equally.[21]

The question of whether the Irish government is prepared to recommend repeal for Articles 2 and 3 appears to have become a major obstacle to agreement at the inter-party talks. Such a reaction is quite disproportionate to the importance of these Articles. To have a constitutional imperative which it has neither the power nor the desire to enforce must be a source of embarrassment for the Irish government. Perhaps the bigger disadvantage of Articles 2 and 3 is that they provide an excuse for some unionist politicians to obstruct the progress of inter-party talks. However, if Articles 2 and 3 were repealed, it is likely that these politicians would find another excuse to impede progress. We urge all politicians to ignore Articles 2 and 3 and to concentrate on the real issues.[22]

To be honest, if the Free State did away with Articles 2 and 3, it would put the politicians here in the position of having to do something. Maybe they are using Articles 2 and 3 as an excuse for not doing something. If the South removed the Articles, then maybe there would be a chance of progressing towards peace. But the South would have to do that first.[23]

To propose to amend or remove these Articles, other than in the context of an overall settlement, would be disastrous for the following reasons: in a situation where the future is being negotiated, fears and anxieties will be increased only by proposals for unilateral concessions in advance; any such referendum would be very divisive in both Northern Ireland and the Republic, creating an atmosphere which would not be conducive to constructive dialogue; any change in the Constitution arguably would undermine constitutional nationalism and would allow the gunmen to claim that they were the only ones concerned with the rights of the nationalist community in Northern Ireland; the grossly over-simplistic and unhelpful view that the Republic is 'a foreign country' and that Northern Ireland is just a normal part of the United Kingdom would be strengthened; finally and crucially, there is absolutely no guarantee that any referendum in the Republic would be successful — the risk involved in an unsuccessful referendum and the damage it would do, having raised expectations, far out-weighs any dubious benefits of a successful referendum.[24]

Articles 2 and 3 represent the assertion of sovereignty by the Irish nation over the national territory, a sovereignty not fully accomplished as yet. As such, Articles 2 and 3 are a normal statement of national sovereignty, such as can be found in other national constitutions, but tailored, of necessity, to the abnormal situation created by the British presence in Ireland. Without these Articles, the British claim stands unopposed.[25]

A consensus of a kind emerges: Articles 2 and 3 should be amended as part of a final settlement. In our view, the most pertinent argument against a unilateral referendum in the Republic on Articles 2 and 3 is the one in which the electorate would reject the proposed alternative in the absence of any proposals being on the table regarding the future government of Northern Ireland — a situation that would only exacerbate the problem in the North. This points to the need for consensus among the political parties in the South on the question of what to do about Articles 2 and 3. Our commission of inquiry did not speak to these parties. However, if opinion hardens along traditional party fault lines, this consensus will not emerge. Hence the need for the political parties in the South to be in broad agreement regarding what structures they would like to see in place in Northern Ireland and what institutional arrangements between the North and the South would supply a sufficiently legitimate expression of the Irish Dimension.

In this regard, we believe that such a consensus should acknowledge the following:

• That a majority in Northern Ireland does not want to become part of a united Ireland.
• That, in the absence of a broad-based consensus for unity, a majority will support structures that will allow the people of Northern Ireland to govern themselves, provided that Irish nationalism is legally recognized in Northern Ireland and the government of Northern Ireland is based on the principle that each community has an equal voice in making and executing the laws, or a veto on their execution, and equally shares administrative authority (as outlined in the previous chapter).
• That part of that expression will be reflected in North/South institutional arrangements.
• That in accepting that there is no consent for unity, Irish governments in future will put forward only proposals which reflect that reality.
• That there is a clear acknowledgment that the people of Ireland cannot now, nor in the foreseeable future, pay for the costs that unification would bring with it.
• That if the need arises and in line with the principles of 'concurrent government' elaborated in chapter 3, Articles 2 and 3 eventually could be amended to say that unity of Ireland will come about only with the

freely given consent of a majority of both communities in Northern Ireland, or by means of a special weighted majority with which both communities agree.

A final reflection: one matter brought to our attention on a number of occasions was the asymmetrical structure of the Anglo-Irish Agreement. If the South speaks for Northern nationalists and the British government is neutral, who represents the interests of the unionists? The Commission recognizes the strength of the argument that this does not make for 'a level playing field'.

Notes

1. Mr Mark Durkan, SDLP chairman, at oral hearing 25.1.1993.
2. Mr Terence Donaghy at oral hearing 2.2.1993.
3. Professor Desmond Rea at oral hearing 17.2.1993.
4. Mr Roy Montgomery at oral hearing 18.2.1993.
5. Northern Consensus Group.
6. Professor Bernard Cullen.
7. Mr Barry Cowan.
8. Other submissions used for this section: Professor Tom Hadden; Mr Frank Curran; Mr Paul Sweeny; Dr Leo Smyth.
9. Archbishop Eames at oral hearing 17.2.1993.
10. Rev. Brian Lennon at oral hearing 19.1.1993.
11. Campaign for Equal Citizenship.
12. North Down Labour Representation Group.
13. Other submissions used for this section: Mr Mark Langhammer; Democracy Now; Councillor James O'Fee.
14. Mr Declan O'Loan.
15. Very Rev. Victor Griffin at oral hearing 27.1.1993.
16. Mr Roy Montgomery at oral hearing 18.2.1993.
17. Senator Gordon Wilson.
18. Lord Holme.
19. Mr Iain Sharpe.
20. Rev. Brian Lennon.
21. Mr Peter Barry TD.
22. Northern Consensus Group.
23. Mr Joseph Beattie.
24. A Belfast Catholic lawyer from a nationalist background.
25. Irish National Congress.
26. Other submissions used for this section: Mr John Robb; Professor Tom Hadden; Mr Michael McKeown; Committee for National Democracy and Peace; Lord Hylton.

CHAPTER 5

The Two Communities:
A Widening Gulf?

Part of the problem the Commission came face to face with is the problem of language itself:[1] what Protestants perceive to be Catholic indirectness versus Protestant directness, and hence the Protestant propensity always to think in terms of the hidden agenda.

'Presbyterians', Dr John Dunlop, moderator of the Presbyterian Church, told us, 'have little time for ambiguity. We were told with the Anglo-Irish Agreement that we should read between the lines. We don't want to read between the lines.'[2]

In other contexts, the following remarks were made to a member of the Commission.[3] 'The Protestant work ethic, the Protestant use of language, is very straight up and down', said Dr Godfrey Brown, a former moderator of the Presbyterian Church. 'There is a literalism, sometimes an over-literalism, about Protestantism and Protestant reaction to things political.' 'Northern Protestants', Rev. Sydney Callaghan, past president of the Methodist Church in Ireland noted, 'believe that Catholics do not say what they mean, that they are profligate with words, past masters of the art of the fine point, the innuendo and the half-truth.' And, said Dean Victor Griffin,

Protestants are really puzzled by what they feel is the ambiguous attitude of Catholics and their failure to define ordinary concepts in a clean, straightforward way. There is much more of what I would call sophistry, casuistry, in the Roman Catholic approach to honesty. Protestants generally find that Catholic concepts of right and wrong and truth and honesty are more complicated. Honesty and truth and right and wrong have a rather simplistic, straightforward, uncomplicated meaning for Protestants, and Protestants sometimes find it very difficult to understand the sophistry, the playing with words which we (sometimes) get from Catholics.

Another submission reinforces these attitudinal perceptions. 'The major conflicts in the world,' the author says, 'including ours, all have some kind of religious component.'

The religious component is usually that the thinking process in the culture has been determined to some degree by the theology that operates in each of the cultures. In our situation, we inherit two very different theologies — the main difference between them is the pre-Reformation theology of Aquinas which was deductive in form, and the post-Reformation theology of Calvin and Luther which was inductive. We have seen how that happens in political life. The SDLP puts down a deductive principle — a general framework — then never budge from it and there is no movement; the unionists put down a number of similar propositions —

the two just bypass each other and no wonder they do not agree. In my opinion, this has happened in every negotiation.[4]

These differing elements of thinking and uses of language are of fundamental importance if the two communities are to learn how to accommodate their differences. Numerous submissions made the point that you had to establish a basis of trust between the two communities; that as communities become more segregated, this becomes more difficult, that there was a need for some interactive process that would enable each community to 'learn' the language and mode of thinking of the other. This is especially true in relation to the Protestant community, which is highly distrustful of the Catholics' 'hidden' agenda: to somehow deceive them into becoming part of a united Ireland. (See also chapter 9 on culture, religion and identity.)

Distrust is, of course, related to uncertainty, especially uncertainty over the constitutional status of Northern Ireland, and therefore there is a need for some mechanism to make that status a non-issue. If political consensus is to emerge, then mutual trust and respect, tolerance of others, and a willingness to compromise *must* exist at *all* levels of society within Northern Ireland.

In this regard, when there is a transparent absence of trust on each side of the divide, due in part to ingrained cultural differences with regard to language and conceptualization, a negotiating process and practices on the basis that 'nothing is agreed until everything is agreed' sets up a situation more like a poker table than a negotiating table. According to people who work in the field of conflict resolution, the formula 'nothing is agreed until everything is agreed' discourages openness and risk-taking, and encourages both sides to play their cards close to their chests, making it difficult to create the ambience in which accommodation emerges. They say that, at each level, negotiation should involve the inherent risk of compromise. Each compromise is a building block, and as the parties grow to trust each other, they move from one compromise to the next, with concessions, though difficult, being made on all sides. Each party becomes invested in the process, each develops a stake in seeing the other succeed, and a sum of mutual investment develops which provides the cushion when it comes to the crunch issues.

The Importance of Demography

In this regard three aspects are important: the rate of growth of the respective populations, the spatial distribution of the populations, and the increasing segregation taking place across Northern Ireland, but especially in Belfast and Derry.

The 1991 census shows that the Catholic population came to 41.4 per cent and is probably rising, while the Protestant population is at 54.1 per cent and most likely falling. 'What is all the more disconcerting', Mark Brennock wrote in *The Irish Times*, 'is the relative speed of the changes. Twenty years ago Catholics stood at 34.7 per cent. This population has increased by 7 per cent in the last two decades.'[5] Moreover, recent studies point to a higher number of Protestants than Catholics leaving Northern Ireland. Almost 40 per cent of Northern Ireland university students go to colleges in Britain. More than two-thirds of them are Protestants. At present more than half the students at Queen's University, Belfast, are Catholics. This is probably due to the level of Protestant emigration. However, it is also due to the children of the previous generation of Catholics, with their higher birth rates, reaching the age at which they can attend college. The school population in Belfast is now believed to have an equal balance between Catholics and Protestants. West of the Bann, Catholics have a majority of up to three to one in the schools.[6]

The political effects of the change can be seen most starkly in the North's twenty-six local government areas. Seven had Catholic majorities in 1971, eleven had Catholic majorities in 1991, with a further two having a Catholic proportion of over 40 per cent and rising. Most dramatically, the Catholic proportion of the Belfast population rose from 31.2 per cent in 1971 to 42.5 per cent in 1991.[7] What all this underscores is that the concepts of majority and minority are changing in Northern Ireland.

The religious divide is also striking in geographical terms. Almost every local authority west of the river Bann has a Catholic majority, as has that area taken as a whole. Currently three counties — Derry, Fermanagh and Tyrone — have Catholic majorities, so that there are in fact two minorities in Northern Ireland, one east of the Bann and one west of the Bann. Moreover, since 1978 the number of Catholics born each year has exceeded the number of Protestants, while seven out of ten deaths are of Protestants. This suggests a younger, growing Catholic population and an older, more slowly growing, Protestant population.[8]

As a result of the geographical dispersion of the population, Mr Frank Curran, the Derry journalist, who has tracked demographic changes in Northern Ireland for many years, informed us that politicians would have to take into account the anatomy of Northern Ireland before developing political structures for the whole unit. He believes that, in a restructured Northern Ireland, special arrangements would have to be made, especially for policing on the west side of the Bann. 'It is impossible,' he concluded, 'to police west of the Bann with the RUC.'[9]

Concern over demographic changes was raised several times in our focus groups, especially with Protestants, given their history of fear of absorption and their reaction to population shifts. We found that the situation in

Derry illustrates the psychological intensity that gives the conflict its special character, and hence the special difficulties that lie in the way of resolution. Over the last twenty years the Protestant population has moved across the river Foyle to Waterside so that there are, in effect, two Derrys: Catholic Derry on the West Bank, Protestant Londonderry on the Waterside. Protestants, having lost control of their Londonderry — the gerrymandered city that had existed before 1972 — have chosen, in a sense, to marginalize themselves.

Community leaders in the Waterside articulate a strong sense of exclusion and separateness.

I was a co-founder of Boston-Derry Ventures. Two years ago I resigned because the Waterside was not being given a fair deal. People on this side of the river saw no development, only on the city-side. In the early days of the troubles, Protestants would shop in Limavady and lunch in Coleraine. Caravans left on the weekend. We needed a heart in Waterside to stop this drift. The central government believes resources must be invested in the SDLP to stop Sinn Féin. Britain throws all the money at Catholic areas. That's why the city-side has enjoyed so much more development. The power-sharing rotation of the mayoralty means nothing to Protestants. We are still in a position of no influence. Protestants see money from both governments and outside agencies going exclusively to Catholics.... [If nationalists want to help overcome Protestant alienation] they should encourage greater development in Protestant areas, particularly in community work. Until Protestants get a better and fairer deal in Derry, they won't cross the bridge. Not because they feel unsafe. They just don't want to be part of that city.[10]

In the Waterside there is a feeling that the other side has won. Protestants have excluded themselves by choice.[11]

Protestants have fled to the Waterside. In a situation of a Catholic majority, Protestants move away. Protestants are happier and safer when they feel they are in the majority.[12]

Protestants won't cross the river to shop in the West Bank. It's like crossing the border — crossing that river is like crossing to the South. They think it's not their Derry anyway. Many Protestants won't cross the bridge.[13]

And thus the paradigm of how Protestants might see themselves in an all-Ireland state:

Unionists can't see themselves in any state that would diminish their population. Their existence is at stake in their minds. A united Ireland is equivalent to extinction.[14]

The Catholic community, on the other hand, feels perplexed and even a little aggrieved at Protestant attitudes. Although they control the city council, they share power with the Protestant parties and believe that their treatment of Protestants in Derry is a paradigm for the way Protestants should be treated in an all-Ireland state. It is, however, a community on the march, confident of itself and the contribution it is making. It has transformed the city-side with shopping malls, museums, craft and heritage centres; it has won Derry an international reputation for cultural events and community development initiatives.[15] The Catholics of Derry see themselves as having had to fight to get where they are, they believe they are sharper than Protestants, that they get things done, that Protestants are short of leaders. They see the question of Waterside Protestants saying that they have not held power for the last twenty years, as being a question of perception, not reality. The Derry City Council, they believe, is fair.[16]

One senior local unionist who spoke to us privately in Derry paints a dramatically different picture:

The Protestant perception is that the Catholic agenda is such that they will use whatever means, they will change whatever tactics have to be changed, in order to reach that agenda. The agenda never changes. The agenda is to drive the Protestants out. We are excluded from the West Bank. We are being made to feel that the system, the framework for any social life, business life, for anything that the community would involve itself in, will happen on the west bank of the river, and that Protestants are not heard, that they are just the exception. They are outside the pale. We would like in, but we are different, and that gives an ostracizing effect.

The SDLP says that, although it controls the city council, it is careful not to exercise simple majority rule.

There's a vibrancy to our work here and a strong sense of place. In Derry, through gesture and practice, the majority Catholic community has tried to be fair to the whole city. This justice is reflected in the central office rotation. We have a DUP mayor, even though that party has only four councillors.

Alienation is a question for the unionist community to address. How can they include themselves? In the tricentenary of the Siege, where we even had a Siege Symphony, unionists boycotted it, even though it celebrated their own history. It hurt us deeply last year when there was a campaign to have boundaries redrawn in an attempt to partition Derry. Even in Derry, where we've been so generous, they wanted partition to control their own area.[17]

Another senior SDLP official was privately dismissive of Protestant grievances:

The Waterside has not been excluded. There is a form of attitude, putting it mildly, and it's a very tough thing to say and I've never said it publicly, but there are people in this society who, when Catholics moved onto their streets, started moving out. That's nothing to do with being excluded. Just as in the United States when black people move into an area, whites move out. There is a unionist mentality which says we are being excluded, but there is also a unionist community that works very closely with us.

Such are the paradoxes and anomalies of Northern Ireland: the deeply held different perceptions; the bitterness, anger, sense of loss and grievance on the part of one community, and a sense of vibrancy and self-perceived generosity on the part of the other. Derry appears to be symptomatic of what is happening all over the region. A detailed analysis of population trends based on the 1991 census and disclosed by the *Independent on Sunday*, shows that the degree of physical separation between Catholics and Protestants is increasing year by year, with the number of segregated areas more than doubling in the last two decades. Among the findings:

- About one-half of the province's 1.5 million people live in areas more than 90 per cent Protestant and 95 per cent Catholic.
- Fewer than 110,000 people live in areas with roughly equal numbers of Catholics and Protestants. Analysis of the data often reveals that an apparently mixed ward contains two separate communities, sometimes physically parted by a twenty-foot high reinforced wall, known as a 'peace line'.
- In the last two years, of the 566 district council wards, the number of predominately Catholic wards has increased from 43 to 120. Areas almost exclusively Protestant rose from 56 to 115.
- Of Belfast's 51 wards, 35 are at least 90 per cent of one religion or the other. In Belfast, substantial religious integration exists in only two middle-class populations, the north and south.[18]

Thus, even if the level of violence has fallen in the last fourteen years, the level of polarization and segregation, amounting in many areas to *de facto* apartheid, has not been conducive to enabling a climate that will bring to fruition the seeds of trust, tolerance and mutual understanding which will provide the necessary underpinnings of a settlement.

Some presenters recognized this:

Most Catholics and Protestants don't meet each other. We Catholics project the worst of ourselves on to Protestants and vice-versa.[19]

The level of contact between Catholics and Protestants has been falling over the last twenty years. This promotes ignorance and suspicion and distrust which are the basis of prejudice.[20]

There has been a tendency over the years for houses once owned by non-Catholics to be occupied by Catholics.[21]

'Nationalists are winning' — that is the perception of the Protestant working classes; that, and the belief that, if nationalists hold to their demands, refuse compromise, they eventually will prevail when Britain finds a way out of Ireland and abandons Northern Protestants to their own devices. These themes recurred frequently in Belfast, where there was a marked difference between the attitudes in both working-class communities on the Falls Road, the Shankill Road and north Belfast. On the Catholic side, there was a preoccupation with the behaviour of the security forces, the constant harassment of young people, the intimidation, the unacceptability of the RUC, the maladministration of justice, the marginalization of their political representatives, and unemployment and deprivation.[22]

But while unemployment and deprivation were also one among many concerns in Protestant working-class areas, Protestants were obsessed with a deeply felt sense that they are losing, even though they often find it difficult to articulate exactly what it is they are losing. They believe that they are somehow being pushed out, that the concerns of the Protestant working class are being ignored, that the Protestant working class is being mistreated, that they are being made the scapegoat for the actions of the Protestant ruling classes in the past.

Protestants feel they have been giving everything for the last 20 years; Catholics feel they have not caught up. There is scarcely any recognition among Protestants that Catholics were discriminated against and had a lot of catching up to do. The Commission was told that Protestants in working-class areas do not accept the claim that Catholics are still more than twice as likely to be unemployed, and they see the Fair Employment Commission as a way of 'doing Protestants down'.[23]

Central to the sense of anger in Belfast is the feeling working-class Protestants have of being squeezed out. They equate this with the belief that Catholics are winning, and that loss of territory is evidence of an advancing Catholic community; that their current experiences in Northern Ireland are a precursor of what fate awaits them in some future all-Ireland state.

The Rise in Loyalist Violence

'There has been a hardening of attitudes among Protestants,' the North Belfast women told us.

They feel under siege and see all Catholics as legitimate targets. It comes down to territory. Ardoyne is bulging, but you can't move the peace wall and therefore the territorial boundary. With peace walls, young people don't meet and are taught to fear and hate the other side. Young loyalist paramilitaries are not motivated by politics, but by sheer sectarianism. Protestants believe their numbers are in the balance. Their areas are emptying, becoming derelict. Nationalists perceive themselves as the future, and loyalists feel their backs are up against the wall. There are two perceptions: an ascending Catholic community, growing in confidence and power, and a beleaguered, isolated, diminishing Protestant one. No one represents Protestants. Protestants would like to replicate the community structures you have in Catholic areas. But there's a low spirit among Protestants — maybe since the Anglo-Irish Agreement. They feel almost apologetic about being Protestant.[24]

'The recent rise in loyalist violence is the result of frustration,' says the Church of Ireland Bishop of Connor, Dr Samuel Poyntz. 'And a feeling that violence works.'

Loyalists claim that when empty ground is found, it's always on their side of the peace wall. They are seeing their land disappear — for example, in Suffolk. And there are huge numbers of people leaving the Shankill. On the Shankill only 4 per cent passed the Eleven plus in 1987. Only ten children passed in 1988. The number of schools on the Shankill has declined. There's only one secondary school for the whole area, while in the Falls there are plenty. The Shankill is not getting educated, but the Catholics have a good set-up.[25]

Part of the problem, he told us, is the ambivalent relationship working-class Protestants had in the past with their social superiors:

In the past, Protestants had trouble admitting they had a problem. It seemed disloyal. Now there is an increasing awareness of injustice and alienation. Catholics are more cohesive.

Protestants offer no cohesive voice to the government. The loyalist perception is that 'they don't listen to us'. The perception is that the government will only listen to Twinbrook.[26]

The Rev. Walter Lewis amplifies:

Protestants don't have any expectations. The Shankill has become demoralized. They feel at sea. They feel a lack of dignity. They place no emphasis on education. For Catholics, education is the way forward. But the Shankill has lost hope.[27]

Twenty years ago the population of the Shankill was 76,000; today it is 27,000. The Protestant population of north Belfast has fallen from 112,000 in 1982 to 56,000 today.[28]

'Deprivation has different effects in each community', Mr Jackie Redpath told us.

Protestant deprivation reinforces a sense of siege, of retreat, almost of defeat. Even middle-class Protestant communities have retreated into their own middle-class ghettos mentally and physically, largely outside of Belfast. The Protestant working-class culture is rubbished in the media. No one defends it. What we have here is a Catholic community in the ascendant. Protestants, on the other hand, are in retreat mentally, physically, in every aspect of life. This is not understood. Protestants have less confidence in themselves, with their siege mentality. In sectarian communities, you can't find space to look at yourself or your own society.[29]

Protestants, we were told, are going through a process of grief. Up to 1969, working-class Protestants thought they were being looked after by their government. The early civil rights marches focused on slums in Derry and the Falls — which awakened the Shankill when people said, 'Those houses are just like ours.'[30]

This sense of loss, real or not, is part of a process of grieving. First anger, then denial—acting as if nothing had happened — from denial to apathy, and then from apathy to depression. A recent survey taken in the Shankill indicates that 80 per cent of young people feel depressed.[31] 'The political cultures of Catholics and Protestants are now different', says Mr Mark Langhammer.

The Catholic political culture is vibrant, active, with a dynamic civil society — they have, for example, a profusion of community groups. The Protestant community, by comparison, is apolitical. Outside the public life of its Churches, civil society barely exists.[32]

There is, moreover, a perception among Protestants that Catholic grievances have been dealt with. The Church of Ireland Primate, Dr Eames, told us that 'for far too long, Catholics have been obsessed with grievance. Psychologically that sense of grievance remains. But at what point does reality not square with grievance?'[33] That sense of grievance is now matched and, in many ways, overtaken by the Protestant sense of grievance as the disadvantaged in both communities wrestle for scarce resources.

A Class War

Archbishop Eames told the Commission: 'They are not fighting each other on the Malone Road. It took me years to understand the implications of that remark. There are two communities here, and one is involved in violence, suffering, unemployment, and injustice. The demarcation is class.'[34]

There are in fact two wars in Northern Ireland. The class war, reflected in the data for fatalities for north and west Belfast especially, and the border war, conducted in rural areas along more traditional nationalist/unionist lines. Over 40 per cent of all deaths in the 'troubles' have occurred in west or north Belfast. Areas of greatest deprivation are also the areas of greatest violence. Forty-five per cent of Northern Ireland's unemployment and 65 per cent of the violence are in these areas.[35] 'There are two divisions,' Mr Joseph Peake from Enniskillen informed us, 'a vertical one and a horizontal one. The vertical one is between Catholics and Protestants; the horizontal one between haves and have nots. In Northern Ireland, it's when the two intersect that the conflict is the worst.'[36]

This is the context in which the upsurge in loyalist political violence must be considered. Between 1969 and 1989, loyalist paramilitary organizations were responsible for 691 deaths, or 25 per cent of the total. Usually loyalist violence has come in cycles and ebbs and flows with variations in political circumstance, in recurring patterns of tit-for-tat killings. In the last three years there has been an upsurge in loyalist paramilitary violence which has given cause for concern. In 1991 loyalist paramilitary organizations were responsible for 42 dead or nearly 45 per cent of fatalities; in 1992 for 35 dead (also nearly 45 per cent of fatalities), and in the first four months of 1993 for 15 dead (or over 53 per cent of fatalities). These totals are greater than for killings by republican paramilitary organizations in the same period.

What makes this cycle of loyalist violence more ominous is the manner in which it differs from the violence of loyalist paramilitaries in the 1970s. It is more ruthless, more efficient, and less open to infiltration.[37] It is also generationally different. Members of the UDA or UVF in the 1970s were there to protect the status quo; in many respects that they were convinced they had the implicit encouragement of the unionist parties and were, in some instances, their armed surrogates. Members were part of the 'old Northern Ireland', grew up under successive unionist regimes, believed that Northern Ireland was a Protestant state for a Protestant people, and even if they did not share in Protestant privilege and power, they felt they were members of the superior group and wanted to preserve their position. The Protestant working classes were marginally better off than their Catholic counterparts if only in the sense that they 'belonged' to the ruling sectarian community. Even for those Protestants who were close to the bottom of the economic heap, it was comforting to know that Catholics, as a class, were worse off. It fed the myth of superiority, of exclusivity.

All that has changed. It is sometimes forgotten now that Northern Ireland has been under Direct Rule for twenty-two years, for almost one-third of the life of the Northern Ireland state. Today's loyalist paramilitaries are different. Many were born after the conflict erupted in 1969; they have no reference point for Protestant privilege and power, never knew Stormont rule. Given the increasing alienation that has taken hold in working-class Protestant areas, they see themselves as constantly losing, see nationalists as winning, and see their relative position continue to decline.

During the oral hearings, we asked a number of presenters to evaluate the nature and content of current loyalist paramilitary capacity. A certain consistency occurs in their responses:

My main concern is that the Protestant paramilitaries are now becoming proficient and efficient and are becoming more appealing to the younger elements in the Protestant community. There is hero-worship at the moment, and the UVF/UFF are now able to hit [identifiable targets]. Protestants are saying that maybe this was not an innocent Catholic, it could have been a Provo or Provo supporter. Therefore they are entitled to be hit as well as we are. Young people believe no one listens to talk and the only answer is to imitate the IRA. We face a holocaust in three or four years unless the politicians solve the constitutional process.[38]

Eight years on from the Anglo-Irish Agreement and we are back in the '70s. The Anglo-Irish Agreement has not worked. Loyalist violence must be partly the result of the perception that violence has paid for the IRA. Young people's resentment is of authority. We don't have institutions to respect here. They are not accountable. That realization helps to explain the upsurge in loyalist violence. There's a conviction that violence pays.[39]

The recent upsurge in loyalist violence stems from the feeling of having been on the losing side and now hitting back in kind at the element that caused them to lose. I think it's something new in terms of the people organizing it and running it. The leadership of the UDA is new. There is a theory behind it, and the theory, I believe, without being absolutely certain, is that they have set an agenda to bring this situation to a climax by ensuring that the Provos understand that every act of violence they perpetrate will be responded to in kind and more — on a discriminate or indiscriminate basis, that response will be inflicted on the Catholic community. It is based on a belief that violence has paid for others.[40]

The violence as we now know it today is coming from a different generation of people. It's coming from a generation of young people who have grown up knowing nothing but violence — British troops on the streets, IRA bombings. On the one side you have the UVF. They have actually started to say, 'We don't hit people in the Catholic community unless they are actively involved in supporting the Irish Republican movement, or in some way contribute to the armed struggle.' On the other side you have the UDA, a group of people who are young, in their twenties. They are in control of the organization, have lots of power. They are probably people who never would have power in any other way and they feel they have to react against the British Government, to show that they do not accept the Anglo-Irish Agreement. There is also an element that really feels they need to react. Loyalist paramilitaries in working-class areas have support or they would not be able to function. People have to turn a blind eye to things that are going on. A lot of the support is lip service rather than being proactive. But I would say you have a good percentage of support in terms of lip service.[41]

Loyalist violence is up because violence seems to pay. From this side of the fence, it looks as though they [the republicans] have bombed their way through twenty years and got everything they wanted. Young Protestants, nineteen or twenty years old, are taking over the violence in north and west Belfast. The older fellows are afraid of them. The young say: We have been told that Northern Ireland would always be in the UK and that Dublin would never be a part of our future. But now Protestants have no one to turn to and so they turn to their own methods to achieve what they want.[42]

This is the extreme loyalist reaction to the general perception in working-class Protestant areas of powerlessness, hopelessness in the face of growing and unfamiliar unemployment, absence of political and community leadership, abandonment by Britain, and the conviction that they are 'losing' and the other side is 'winning'. Loyalist paramilitaries have empowered themselves in the way their experiences teach them to: in their eyes, the gun works.

Notes

1. For an exposition on the language of the debate in Northern Ireland, see Professor Simon Lee.
2. Dr John Dunlop at oral hearing 19.1.1993.
3. Interviews with Padraig O'Malley conducted during 1987–89 in *Biting at the Grave: The Irish Hunger Strikes and the Politics of Despair* (Belfast: Blackstaff Press, 1990).
4. Mr Peter McLachlan.
5. *The Irish Times*, 14.11.1992.
6. ibid.
7. ibid.
8. Mr Frank Curran at oral hearing 25.1.1993.
9. ibid.
10. Mr Glen Barr at oral hearing 27.1.1993.
11. Mrs Marlene Jefferson at oral hearing 25.1.1993.
12. Mr Frank Curran at oral hearing 25.1.1993.
13. ibid.
14. ibid.
15. Mr Kevin McCaul; Holywell Trust.
16. Mr Paddy Doherty at oral hearing 25.1.1993.
17. Mr Mark Durkan, SDLP chairman, at oral hearing 25.1.1993.
18. David McKittrick, *Independent on Sunday*, 21.3.1993.
19. Mr Paddy Doherty at oral hearing 25.1.1993.
20. The Churches' Central Committee for Community Work.
21. Mr D. Gordon Kelly.
22. Mrs Elizabeth Groves; Mrs Sally McErlean.
23. Mr Roy Montgomery at oral hearing 18.2.1993.
24. North Belfast women at oral hearing 3.2.1993.
25. Dr Samuel Poyntz at oral hearing 16.2.1993.
26. ibid.
27. Rev. Walter Lewis at oral hearing 16.2.1993.
28. Mr Jackie Redpath.
29. ibid.
30. Mr Jackie Redpath at oral hearing 18.2.1993.
31. Mr Roy Montgomery at oral hearing 18.2.1993.

32. Mr Mark Langhammer at oral hearing 18.2.1993.
33. Archbishop Robin Eames at oral hearing 17.2.1993.
34. ibid.
35. Figures from Mr Jackie Redpath.
36. Mr Joseph Peake.
37. Group of former loyalist prisoners at private hearing.
38. Mr Glen Barr.
39. Mr Ray Smallwoods at oral hearing 3.2.1993.
40. A community worker from Belfast in a private hearing.
41. Group of former loyalist prisoners at a private hearing.
42. Pastor Jack McKee at oral hearing 18.2.1993.

CHAPTER 6

Sinn Féin and the Paramilitaries: Coming in from the Cold?

On the question of Sinn Féin involvement in the negotiating process, there was almost across-the-divide agreement among presenters at the oral hearings that a settlement that excluded Sinn Féin would be neither lasting nor stable and that some way had to be found to bring Sinn Féin into the process. Most submissions reflected this view only in general terms, without spelling out what forms such involvement might take in practice. No contributor specified what kinds of exchanges of signals, informal contacts, concrete steps leading to a reduction in violence or a ceasefire, formal negotiations or even talks leading to a constitutional settlement would be necessary or desirable.

Even among Protestants, while there was no enthusiasm for any such moves, there was a grudging acknowledgment that at some point Sinn Féin, or the political wing of the IRA, would have to be included. There was strong support for the claim that Sinn Féin spoke for the working-class voters of west Belfast, who resented their exclusion from any political talks and saw it as a form of disenfranchisement.[1] Moreover, many were indignant that support for Sinn Féin was automatically taken to mean support for violence. We are republicans, but we do not support violence, the Commission was told at the West Belfast oral hearings; we vote Sinn Féin because they are a young party, they have a high profile on the ground and we relate to them in a community context; yet the more they move towards the ballot box, the more they seem excluded; if you want to talk to us, talk to the people we elect.[2] Ironically, there was also respect for Sinn Féin's community work among some Protestant community workers.

However, the overwhelming opinion of those submissions which spoke of Sinn Féin was that its claim to be a political party should be tested by accepted democratic norms, and that, if it did aspire to function as a constitutional party, it should be given a helping hand over the hurdle of violence. At present, it is said, Sinn Féin has little incentive to seek a cessation of such violence.[3] Marginalizing it by the media ban, exclusion from council chambers and the 'political vetting' of community groups in republican areas were thought to be playing into the hands of those who preferred violence.[4]

However, almost all presenters we heard from felt that, before Sinn Féin could earn a seat at the negotiating table, it would have to renounce the use

of violence. The Sinn Féin presentation to the Commission was uncompro-
mising: all actions would follow from an explicit expression of a desire on
the British government's part to end partition, including a declaration of
intent to withdraw from Northern Ireland. Sinn Féin talks about this
process taking place 'in the shortest time possible, consistent with obtaining
maximum consent for the process and minimizing costs of every kind.'[5]
'Democracy and practicality', it notes, 'demand that this be done in consultation and co-operation with the representatives of the Irish minority, the
Northern unionists, as well as with the representatives of the Northern
nationalists.'[6] 'A non-reunited Ireland is short-sighted', Mr Mitchel
McLaughlin told us. 'It only delays a problem that inevitably will come up
again. After all, demographically, the six counties will soon have a majority
nationalist population.'[7] The presenters recognize that Protestant fears of a
united Ireland are real, but republicans 'should not be expected to bend
over backwards to accommodate unionists'.[8] One senior Sinn Féin official
told the Commission:

If the British government changes its policy on partition, there's something to discuss. At present unionists can sit on their fears. It's the British government that must break the log-jam
and deploy international forces with experience in conflict resolution. Sinn Féin is committed
to peaceful campaigning as a practical strategy. The connection between Sinn Féin and the
IRA has been greatly exaggerated by unionists and by the media. It's used as an excuse not to
talk with us.

Sinn Féin points out that there is a distinction between a party's advocating the right to use violence in certain situations, and a party's direct or
even indirect use of violence. Sinn Féin claims the former right and rejects
allegations of its involvement in the latter.

Would Sinn Féin join in asking the IRA to lay down its arms? 'We all
have views on many conflicts. Whatever those views, that doesn't mean we
are not working peacefully. The work we do defines what we do. There is
no substitute for removing conditions that create violence.'[9]

The following is a cross-section of opinion from authors and presenters
regarding the role of Sinn Féin in the political process:

An approach must be made to Sinn Féin.... But Sinn Féin must renounce the use of violence.[10]

There can be no lasting stable resolution that did not include Sinn Féin. Ultimately, the talks
have to include everybody. The question is when Sinn Féin is likely to be included — only
after the constitutional parties have made some progress.[11]

Sinn Féin should call a halt to the violence. Then I hope for a period where their sincerity is
tested before allowing them to participate in talks.[12]

It's unrealistic for the British not to talk with Sinn Féin until they renounce violence. The
reverse order is more likely. Republicans must be convinced that politics will work before they
put away the gun.[13]

The peace process must be inclusive. We are critical of a process that excludes Sinn Féin and
the republican community. This exclusion is not based on a consistent principle. Sinn Féin is a

political party whether or not you like the politics.[14]

You can't leave the paramilitaries out. They are both protectors and oppressors. We all support an end to violence. We want the paramilitaries out — but we must negotiate what we need to survive.[15]

Many of the paramilitaries, especially on the republican side, see we are in a cul-de-sac. These people may be in a minority, but they must be encouraged. We need to talk, although the government line is: Don't talk to paramilitaries.[16]

As regards the involvement of Sinn Féin in the talks, the general view is that they couldn't countenance the question. They [Protestants] don't want to think about it or face up to it. It is probably too hard for the Protestant community to contemplate at the moment.[17]

It would be best if Sinn Féin joined the talks, but it's not possible. The unionists would boycott. Whatever you think of the policy theoretically, the reality is that you cannot include them.[18]

The present talks are doomed to fail because they exclude political parties and groupings who are part and parcel of the problem.[19]

We are opposed to preconditions of all kinds.[20]

Only one initiative is likely to lead to a significant reduction in the level of anti-security force violence in Northern Ireland. This is the holding of talks between representatives of Sinn Féin and of the British government. Unpalatable as it is, it may be that such talks will just have to occur.[21]

We believe there will be no peace until Sinn Féin is allowed into the process. We accept that will require Sinn Féin to renounce the use of violence.[22]

We believe that any attempt to find a solution which does not bring into the political arena those engaged in paramilitary activity is doomed to fail.[23]

I see the cessation of violence as the vital key to a peaceful solution. Without it, I cannot see how any proposed constitutional solution will work. The IRA must be convinced to abandon the armed struggle and have a place at the negotiating table.[24]

It is clearly not possible in a democratic framework to negotiate with a group who, if they don't get what they want, will go back to shooting. On the other hand, unless some of the concerns of the marginalized nationalist communities are dealt with, their alienation is likely to continue. Sinn Féin will have to make a declaration to end its violence before it can be involved in talks. The only way Sinn Féin could be persuaded to give up violence would be when it is politically clear to them that the only way forward was to be at the negotiating table.[25] [26]

In private hearings with a senior member of Sinn Féin, we found a more conciliatory tone, an acknowledgment that if there was to be a lasting and stable peace, there would have to be a *rapprochement* with the Protestant community in the North, and more importantly, an acknowledgment that 'we [republicans] cannot and should not even try to coerce the Protestant people into a united Ireland. We must convince them of the rightness of our cause and of the benefits accruing to them from advocacy of our cause.' We were given to understand that discussion was taking place within Sinn Féin to express a shift in policy emphasis on this.

As we understand it, the proposed new emphasis envisages a declaration of intent by Britain to withdraw from Northern Ireland within a specified time period (there are differences over the length of that time period, some wanting it to be as soon as five years and others prepared to wait thirty or more years). The IRA would call a ceasefire. Plans for British withdrawal would be drawn up and, as the ceasefire held, troops would be withdrawn. All parties would come to the negotiating table. Sinn Féin would accept that the consent of unionists would have to be won to any form new constitutional arrangements might take, and that if unionists could not be persuaded of the benefits of joining a united Ireland, then other constitutional arrangements would have to be considered.

We should emphasize that these opinions are not part of present Sinn Féin policy. However, another senior Sinn Féin official agreed that his colleague's scenario was under serious consideration, but that the time limit envisaged for a declaration of intent from Britain to withdraw from Northern Ireland was a matter of debate. Moreover, the first Sinn Féin official who spoke to us did indicate that the movement had authorized him to canvass branches of Sinn Féin throughout the country regarding their reactions to the scenario he had outlined for us.

Whether or not this scenario becomes a part of Sinn Féin's official policy, we should point out two other events which we feel are significant. One is the speech given at Coleraine in December 1992 by Sir Patrick Mayhew, Secretary of State for Northern Ireland. 'It is not sensible to suppose that any British government will yield to an agenda for Ireland that is pursued by means of violence', he said. 'There have been welcome signs that the truth is getting through to some republicans. There are leading Sinn Féin officials who voice their wish for a peaceful solution and their desire to follow a constitutional path. Provided it is advocated constitutionally, there can be no proper reason *for excluding any political objective from discussion.*[Our emphasis.] Certainly not the objectives of an Ireland united through broad agreement fairly and freely achieved.'[27] Sir Patrick called on Sinn Féin to renounce the use of violence and to demonstrate over a sufficient period that its renunciation is for real.

In the event of a genuine and established cessation of violence, the Secretary of State said, 'the whole range of responses that we have had to make to end violence could, and would, inevitably be looked at afresh'.

Thus, when terrorism is seen to have genuinely ended, there will indeed be profound consequences for the maintenance of law and order, and for the administration of justice. Freed from the threat of death at every corner, the Royal Ulster Constabulary would be free to give fresh priority to the quality and accessibility of its service. The preventive measures that have been such a necessary part of everyday life in the province could be relaxed dramatically. The routine support of the armed forces would no longer be required: the army could return to its garrison role, as in the rest of the United Kingdom.

To quote my predecessor's Whitbread speech again: 'The United Kingdom has of course no vested interest in maintaining these high force levels a day longer than is necessary. This kind of high military profile was made necessary by violence, will be maintained as long as there is violence, but will certainly be reduced when violence comes to an end.' Similarly, the emergency legislation on which many of these responses are founded would have served its purpose. Normality could return.[28]

The other event of significance took place in February 1993 at the Sinn Féin Ard Fheis in Dundalk. There, Sinn Féin president, Gerry Adams, called on the British government to undertake an initiative in Northern Ireland. 'As part of such an initiative,' he said, 'the British government should be invited by Dublin to explore in discussions with all interested parties the steps that would be made to get *Northern majority consent* [our emphasis] to Irish reunification, and the guarantees and assurances that would be needed to safeguard Protestant rights and interests in such a situation.' Talks, he said, between the British government and Sinn Féin were 'inevitable and long overdue'. The government had already conceded the principle and is currently setting down its conditions.[29]

This statement, it seems to us, is an explicit acknowledgment that Sinn Féin officially accepts that, at the very least, the consent of a majority of Northern Ireland is a prerequisite for unification. Furthermore, it seems to us that Sinn Féin is therefore in a position to renounce support of violence, since republican violence reinforces Protestant opposition to a united Ireland. Moreover, British withdrawal is predicated on the consent of a majority for Irish unification. Should that consent emerge, Britain is obliged to withdraw according to her current legal obligation. (Article 1 of the Anglo-Irish Agreement states that 'if in the future a majority of the people of Northern Ireland clearly wish for and formally consent to the establishment of a united Ireland, they [the British and Irish governments] would introduce and support in the respective Parliaments legislation to give effect to that wish.')

If Sinn Féin really wants to address itself to the question of obtaining the consent of a majority for its new Ireland, a renunciation of violence is a necessary first step. Indeed, a declaration of intent to withdraw on the part of the government would, in the short run at least, further reinforce Protestant opposition to Irish unification. The obstacle to Irish unity is not the British presence in Northern Ireland, but the absence of consent from a majority for a united Ireland. Sinn Féin strategy should aim at getting that consent. If it gets that consent, British withdrawal will follow. However, if it insists on British withdrawal before consent is forthcoming, it is only reinforcing opposition to what it wants to achieve.

We should point out that Sinn Féin refers to unionists as the Irish minority. 'It's hard to think of yourself as being Irish', one prominent Protestant representative told us, 'when your community is being killed in the name of Ireland.'[30]

Reducing the Violence

The Commission had a private meeting with a group which had contacts with both the IRA and the security forces, and which, on occasion, acts as an intermediary between the two. We were told that in the area they work in, for example, violence had dropped dramatically:

The IRA responds to provocative behaviour from the police, for which the community demands they retaliate. But the level of police harassment depends on the level of IRA activity. It's a vicious circle and the only way to beat it is by unilateral de-escalation. This can be accomplished by gestures. Either the security forces or the IRA must make a commitment to this de-escalation.

Yet, too often, in their experience, signals are sent but are unreceived. 'For gestures to be taken on board, we must first build up mutual trust.' As a result of these meetings with the army, police, and Sinn Féin, they have come to the following conclusions:

- The IRA does not believe it can defeat the British militarily, but it has no shortage of volunteers. They believe as long as they have four or five volunteers and enjoy support in their community, they will persevere.
- Paramilitaries are not stupid people. The one thing they fear is the people in their own area. 'If they bomb a city shopping centre or downtown, they would be finished.'
- The IRA has a responsibility to its own people and its own personnel; it would have to get something out of a ceasefire.
- The British cannot appear to be giving in to violence. The IRA would have to declare a ceasefire in advance of British moves.
- When the former Secretary of State Mr Peter Brooke made his 'no strategic interest' speech in November 1990, the IRA decided to hold off and give British policies a chance.[31] Over two years have gone by without any substantial British initiative. If there is no British initiative, the hawks in the IRA will reassert themselves.
- The British army admits to there being a stand-off with the IRA. When the IRA reduces operations, security operations are commensurately reduced.
- Only now are republicans taking loyalist violence seriously. In the past they had been perceived as puppet creations, part of the British structures in Northern Ireland. That attitude has changed. Loyalists have been more successful, copying the IRA cell structures, and their operations are now more successful. Republicans now realize that they are a force to be reckoned with in their own right.
- The perception that there is a split in the IRA between hawks and doves is off-target. There is a flexibility in the leadership, a willingness to explore whether, in a safer political situation, a relaxation of violence is

advantageous. If it proves disadvantageous, the organization goes back on the offensive.

- When a senior member of Sinn Féin spoke to members of their group, the group unanimously agreed afterwards that he was trying to send a message to the British government: 'We want to get out of violence, but you have to help us.'
- The British army claims to have a lengthy list of possible de-escalation measures.
- Even in the event of a ceasefire it will be extremely difficult to win over unionists to talk with Sinn Féin.

Both the security forces and the IRA have told them in discussions that there are peace-building moves they would like to make, but that they don't trust the other side.

Their fear is that, long before this could happen, they would lose support in their own community. They believe they might have trouble getting quality recruits. On the other hand, they believe that if they were to reduce the level of violence, Northern Ireland would fall to an even lower place on Britain's agenda. They would be giving away their strongest card for future negotiation; there would be no guarantee of a sufficient response; the morale of volunteers would plummet. They fear that the security establishment would take advantage of any ceasefire to weaken them.

There is a way to make peacekeeping moves without suffering the repercussions. The IRA could make a unilateral move—such as the elimination of 'coffee-jar bombs', or a larger one such as the ending of the bombing of commercial buildings. The move might be designed to reduce direct pressure on the security forces or to reduce the threat to lives. The move could be publicly announced or conveyed to the security establishment through intermediaries. In any event, they would be making clear that they expected a response. It is of the utmost importance that such a message be signalled, whether privately or publicly. There have been periods of inactivity which the IRA hoped the British government would read as signals of intent, but the message was not understood. There must be a clear message.

The security forces, too, admit they can't win the war. For them to increase their offensive activity would mean an unacceptable price in the Catholic community without any certainty of military gain. Army officers say they have prepared a long list of 'de-escalating measures' which [they] would be willing to make step by step to answer IRA moves. In fact, they have implemented some, but each side so distrusts the other and finds it difficult to interpret the intention behind the action. One must give clear signals of what one intends.

Each side needs some help from the other. The IRA needs some help in the form of political recognition from the government to reduce its own violence; the security establishment needs help from the IRA if it is to take its presence off the Catholic side of the community.

In short, the only way forward is for each side to take a series of unilateral steps, which can be halted or even reversed if the other side takes advantage of them. Gradually trust will build. . . . Since the early moves each side makes will be made in the dark, they should be tested out at the local level. Once the security establishment and the IRA were clearly responding to each other, violence would begin to drop, taking the excuse away for any loyalist campaign. The signalling of intentions to one another would come close to negotiations.

We recommend, accordingly, that informal channels of communication should be opened with Sinn Féin with a view to persuading the IRA first to move towards a de-escalation in the level of violence and eventually to a ceasefire that would lead to a drastic reduction in the number of security forces deployed in Northern Ireland, and/or their return to barracks. Though we respect the refusal of the current political parties to have Sinn Féin officially at talks on the future of Northern Ireland until it shows signs that it is willing to work within an agreed constitutional structure, the party nevertheless should be given help and encouragement to join the constitutional process, if that is what it desires. As Mr Gary McMichael of the Ulster Democratic Party, which reflects the thinking of the UDA, told the Commission:

I look forward to the day when they [Sinn Féin] could become involved, but when that happens they would not be Sinn Féin in its present form because then they would have become an active constitutional party.[32]

Notes

1. For example, Mrs Elizabeth Groves.
2. ibid.
3. Focus Groups, December 1992.
4. Mr Michael Farrell.
5. Sinn Féin.
6. ibid.
7. Mr Mitchel McLaughlin at oral hearing 20.1.1993.
8. Mr Pat McGeown at oral hearing 20.1.1993.
9. Ms Mairead Keane at oral hearing 20.1.1993.
10. Very Rev. Victor Griffin at oral hearing 27.1.1993.
11. Professor Kevin Boyle at oral hearing 17.2.1993.
12. Archbishop Robin Eames at oral hearing 17.2.1993.
13. Mr Michael Farrell at oral hearing 19.2.1993.
14. Bloody Sunday Initiative at oral hearing 26.1.1993.
15. North Belfast women at oral hearing 3.2.1993.
16. Bishop Samuel Poyntz at oral hearing 16.2.1993.
17. Mr Jackie Redpath at oral hearing 18.2.1993.
18. Sir Kenneth Bloomfield.
19. Mr Patrick Devlin.
20. Mr Mark Durkan, SDLP chairman, at oral hearing 25.1.1993.
21. Professor Brice Dickson.
22. Drumcree Faith and Justice Group.
23. Pax Christi Ireland.
24. Senator Gordon Wilson.
25. Dr Duncan Morrow at oral hearing 28.1.1993.
26. Other submissions used for this section: Dr Mari Fitzduff; Mr Paddy Doherty; Mr Paul Sweeney; Mr Roy Montgomery; Mr Jim Creighton; Mr Eugene O'Shea; Mothers for Peace; Mrs Sheila Chillingworth; Mr Fergal Henchy; Mrs Sally McErlean; Mrs Eilish McCashin.
27. Speech by Sir Patrick Mayhew, at the Centre for the Study of Conflict, University of Ulster at Coleraine, 16.12.1992.

28. ibid.
29. Reported in *The Irish Times*, 22.2.1993.
30. Presbyterian moderator, Dr John Dunlop, at oral hearing 19.1.1993.
31. Speech by Mr Peter Brooke, during which he said: 'The British government has no selfish, strategic or economic interest in Northern Ireland.' 9.11.1990.

CHAPTER 7

Law, Justice and Security I:
Beyond the Dividing Labels

The words 'justice' and 'security' as they relate to 'law and order' are particularly controversial in a divided society scarred by political violence. Given this background, the Commission readily endorses a suggestion that key organizations in Northern Irish society — such as Churches, public service bodies, trade unions, businesses and others — should be challenged to 'each create an internal working group to look at how their particular organization could contribute to an improvement of law and order with a view to ensuring justice'.[1] The author of this submission believes that 'without such a lead, it is hardly surprising if 'security' and 'justice' remain easy catchwords for 'gesture' politics, or the marginalized concern of a few committed activists.... It is not sufficient that an unresponsive and largely unaccountable security and political apparatus on the one side, and small activist groups like the Committee on the Administration of Justice on the other, have the field to themselves.'

Unlike the frozen constitutional and political situation since the introduction of Direct Rule in 1972, there have been a number of developments in law, justice and security; for example, a shift from a 'military security' approach to a 'police prosecution' approach in confronting terrorism.[2]

Before the outset of the 'troubles', complaints about injustice in Northern Ireland centred on social and political discrimination against the minority community. The civil rights campaign of the 1960s led to changes in several fields, both for better and for worse. On the one hand, the position of Catholics has improved as a result of legislation and other means which have produced 'significant progress'[3] (although we recognize that there continues to be evidence of discrimination).[4] However, in return, the violence of the 'troubles' and security measures which deeply affect everyday life are often seen by the same community as threats to human rights. 'Significant violations have not produced peace, far from it'.[5] It is evident that many sore points persist.

This Commission, however, was never intended to serve as a tribunal to make findings on such grievances. Nor has any material been submitted which would enable it to form opinions — for instance, on whether the emergency measures were in the circumstances justifiable departures from normal obligations, or whether incidents in a particular street or prison violated certain rights. It would be wrong for this Commission to judge such matters, and its recommendations must be understood accordingly.

Violence and the paramilitaries

The argument that security problems would not exist were it not for terrorism was accepted by most people. That said, the politicians on all sides were almost alone in their steadfast refusal to include the paramilitaries in a search for solutions. Even among many Protestants and loyalists, the Commission found a pragmatic acceptance of the need to include the paramilitaries in the search for a settlement and a recognition that no political solution would be workable against a background of continuing violence.[6] Discussion centred rather on how and at what stage they should be involved,[7] almost all who touched on the topic recommending involvement in the talks process only after a period of ceasefire.[8] Most Protestants thought that loyalist paramilitary action was reactive and felt it would stop in the event of an IRA ceasefire. Catholics, and some Protestants, recognized that levels of loyalist paramilitary violence were also related to perceived moves to weaken the link with Britain and towards Irish unity. However, most discussion centred on the IRA. There was a sense among some nationalists that, while they recognized the reasons for the emergence of the IRA campaign, after nearly a quarter of a century it had achieved little and the IRA 'could make a more positive contribution to its cause by announcing an indefinite ceasefire'.[9] There was considerable anger and resentment at perceptions that all nationalists somehow support the IRA.

That said, it is clear that violence is in-built into the Northern Ireland situation at many different levels, including the use of force by the state, and that ambivalence is rife.

While the numbers directly involved in paramilitary organizations are relatively small,' cautioned one thoughtful submission, 'it is fallacious to dismiss paramilitarism as a phenomenon of a few fanatics or organized crime gangs. Many people in Northern Ireland are ambivalent towards political violence, many are highly selective in their condemnations of violence.... . The first stage in seeking a resolution to the conflict in Northern Ireland is to confront the reality that those involved in paramilitary organizations are very much an integral part of our community.[10]

This home truth ought to trigger some reconsideration of the oft-used reason for not talking to the paramilitaries — that violence should not be seen to pay.

We have already dealt with the question of the paramilitaries and attitudes to them in more detail in chapter 6.

The police and the army

We agree with those submissions which, like that from Rev. Brian Lennon, emphasized that, as with political structures, the key questions about policing in Northern Ireland have to do with accountability and responsibility. Policing is currently controlled by the Secretary of State, the RUC Chief Constable, the army and the Police Authority. However, because the Police Authority has such limited powers, control effectively lies with the first two of these. Unless genuine representatives of both the unionist and nationalist communities are given an executive and administrative role in relation to policing, they cannot take responsibility for it.[11]

Our impression was that policing was much less an issue among working-class Protestants than working-class Catholics. Among the latter there was still a sense of the police as a purely Protestant force, and there were memories of the B-Specials in border areas and among some older Catholics. One Catholic priest from Armagh made the point that it was unreasonable and unworkable for young Protestant RUC officers from north Down and north Antrim to police strong nationalist areas like south Armagh, east Tyrone and west Belfast. He suggests that a study should be made of the possibility of regional divisions, or perhaps a second-line force that would separate the armed RUC from an unarmed civilian police force.[12]

However, we also found some willingness to give credit for the reforms that have taken place, and some recognition that more nationalists would have to be encouraged to join the RUC, although this was accompanied by a feeling that both the state and the police authorities would have to be more proactive in bringing this about. There was agreement on all sides that there was frequent and gratuitous harassment of young nationalists, and that this played a major role in recruitment into the republican paramilitaries. In general, the British army came in for more criticism than the RUC. Protestants felt this too. 'The troops cause annoyance in nationalist areas and the RUC has to sort it out', said someone in the Shankill Road focus group. The army was felt to be largely unaccountable for its actions.

We noted that Catholic reluctance to enlist in the police was due less to fear of reprisal from the IRA and more because of the nationalist perception of the RUC as the instrument of a state which is still seen as British and unionist, and therefore as not 'belonging' to their community. We believe that Catholic support for and significant recruitment to the RUC will take place only in the context of new political structures for the region, in which power and authority go hand in hand with responsibility.

Currently nationalists still consider the RUC to be an inherently anti-nationalist force; as one community worker in west Belfast said, it is not very 'user-friendly' for nationalists.[13] Harassment is more likely if one has a Catholic-sounding name. Senior police officers told the Commission that the police training programme specifically includes warnings that such harassment is a breach of discipline. However, given the very large number of references to such harassment in submissions from all over the region, and given the equally wide recognition that such practices increase recruitment into the paramilitaries, more priority should be given to eliminating it.

'Why does Northern Ireland have a "royal" police force, a recognizable instrument of the state', it was asked at an oral hearing, 'when the rest of the UK has regional police forces?' Whatever the reforms, this failure of a 'Crown' police force to shake off the symbols of the unionist state, appeared time and time again as an explanation for Catholic reluctance to join the RUC. For many nationalists, a change in the name of the force would be a step in the right direction. The same point was made about the symbols of justice in the province, all seen as continued tokens of a state deemed to be anti-Catholic. 'The constant emphasis on the unionism and pro-Britishness of the state of Northern Ireland is almost triumphalist, and it is an attempt to proclaim its Britishness at the expense of a very large section of its citizens, who do not feel that way.'[14]

Even so, the silence of the SDLP on the subject of non-enlistment in the police — and of its failure to take up seats on the Police Authority and various liaison committees — was criticized by Protestants and some Catholics.[15] 'The failure of the Catholic community, through its political and Church leaders, to address seriously the issue of policing undermines their criticism of the police. If Catholic criticism of the police is to be helpful, there is a need for positive proposals, which in a different context would enable nationalists to play a prominent role in future policing structures.'[16]

Senior RUC officers expressed a desire for proper research into why young Catholics do not join the force. Despite saying that 'the last thing a nationalist in difficulty in Armagh City wants to do, is to seek the help of the RUC', Father Raymond Murray suggested meetings of Catholics to which senior members of the RUC would be invited. Given such a clear desire expressed by all sides, the RUC and Catholic Church ought to consult each other on pursuing such a suggestion. The anomaly of a predominantly Protestant force policing predominantly Catholic areas, and the potential of this for exacerbating sectarian tension, was recognized by all. In the short term, 'separate community police forces for nationalist and unionist areas' to deal with non-paramilitary crime were suggested. The Commission sees many dangers inherent in introducing possible polarization within the RUC itself.

A powerful case was put to us that, if the RUC did act more forcefully against ordinary crime, it would elicit considerable community support, even in areas such as west Belfast, where the police's abdication from such a role has allowed the IRA to pose as community 'crime-busters'. The problems created by the RUC's conflicting security/policing roles is felt by police and public alike. But the claim by one submission 'that there *is* a level of faith in the police authorities to handle ... non-paramilitary crime' in nationalist enclaves,[17] and a willingness, particularly on the part of community workers, to facilitate normal policing, found endorsement in many others. A study should be made of the feasibility of decentralized and different levels of policing (such as exist in almost every other country outside Ireland and the UK).

There is a desire (expressed forcefully in north and west Belfast and the Lower Ormeau area) for the kind of community participation in policing which is encouraged in the UK generally, and signs that sensitive appointments of local commanders, willing to listen and respond to the local community, were welcomed and produced results. Women seemed particularly willing to work with the police, especially in cases of ordinary crime, in defusing tension and generally to improve police-community relations, if such co-operation could be facilitated. The structure of the Police Liaison Committees should be improved. At present people feel that they have little access to them; they do not know whom to contact. It was suggested that one officer in each station should be the local contact and should be much more accessible to the community. The powers of liaison committees were considered to be too limited; they had no power to discuss the kind of security issues which immediately affected the community (notably harassment by security forces and paramilitaries, and problems presented by security/peace walls). There was also fear that such complaints might lead to further harassment.

The general absence of community policing[18] because of the security situation was a cause of regret. Such policing remains the long-term ideal. But, in its absence, it was felt that some mechanism should be established whereby problems could be discussed locally and informally. In the earlier years of the 'troubles', there was direct communication to the security forces through 'incident centres'. Today such issues are taken to community advice centres, but they do not have such direct lines of communication to the security forces.

We were particularly impressed by the submission of Mr Douglas Hegney, as an example of how sensitive leadership and 'community policing' can improve relations between police and public in a deprived 'borderline' area of Belfast — in this case the nationalist Lower Ormeau. Here the arrival of a new subdivisional commander who regularly meets residents and community leaders to discuss mutual difficulties and to explain the circumstances of arrests, strikingly changed the atmosphere. Harrassment and mutual hostility were replaced by consultation and a diminution of tension and unrest. The Commission was also told of a recently formed informal complaints system in Derry, organized by a local peace group, which was being used by people who have grievances against the security forces.

A wide range of submissions pointed to the RUC and the army's lack of accountability and the impression created that the security forces considered themselves to be above the law. The Commission was also made aware of feelings within the RUC that such a totally independent body would be welcomed by them. The underlying message in many submissions was 'if the police treat the people with respect, they will get it in return'.[19] Where there is consultation, it is appreciated.

All in all, we found confusion and frustration in the Catholic community about policing matters: some recognition of the difficult and dangerous situation in which the RUC operates; some sense of wanting to trust and participate in normal policing if shown the way, but also that such a 'way' still faces huge obstacles: 'Who is there to turn to, to alleviate the situation?'[20] was how one of the best portrayals of this dilemma summarized things. 'Those sent to protect us have at times been in collusion with those who attack us, and the perception is that justice is not carried out with due process.... There is much confusion as to whom to turn to for support or for a solution to the problem. There is a level of faith in the police authorities to handle what might be described as non-paramilitary crime, but any collaboration with the police outside of this is fraught with mistrust.'[21] Such an analysis leaves the RUC in a no-win situation. In their attempts at policing, their lives are put at risk. With less than 8 per cent Catholics in their ranks, they are seen to support a British rule of authority, therefore a unionist rule, therefore a Protestant rule. That being the perception, they have the almost impossible task of having to enforce the law impartially and of being seen to be doing so.[22]

As with the role of the RUC, so with that of the British army: there was widespread recognition that normal conditions could not prevail in the current climate of violence, and few submissions called for a withdrawal of the army, most of them from people living in England and the Republic. However, there was even less affinity for the army than for the RUC. The high profile of the army on the streets was said to increase fear and tension; the constant circling of helicopters and frequent pointing of loaded weapons at civilians were considered to be intimidating, and the army was singled out for the 'crude frisking of young men, coupled with abusive comments and snide remarks'.[23] Some submissions thought that, given the problem of allegiances in the province, the British army was perhaps not the best security agent for the area.[24] Few could suggest any realistic alternative, although several suggested EC or UN forces, without going into how feasible or likely such an intervention would be.

Criticism of Security Legislation:
EPA and PTA

The Commission has noted a number of human rights concerns in security legislation and the way it is practised.[25] It also is aware of the argument that certain measures in the past, such as internment, have increased, rather than reduced, the level of violence and insecurity.

At present the main relevant measures are based on the Northern Ireland (Emergency Provisions) Act of 1991 (EPA) and the Prevention of Terrorism (Temporary Provisions) Act of 1989 (PTA). The former follows the lines of similar Acts since 1973, which again (after the introduction of internment in 1971 and the later report of the Diplock Commission) had replaced the Special Powers Act of the 1920s. The PTA applies to the whole of the United Kingdom, and is the fourth 'generation' of this piece of nationwide emergency legislation since it was first introduced as a 'panic Act'[26] after IRA bombs killed 21 people in Birmingham in 1974.

The Commission has not carried out any specific inquiry into this legislation. However, on the basis of some of the submissions, various points can be highlighted. More detailed studies and professional criticisms are available elsewhere.

The emphasis and strength of the criticisms submitted vary considerably. There are calls for the early repeal or abolition[27] of the relevant Acts, because they are in part seen as unnecessary; arguments in favour of a policy of dismantling them as a measure of reducing the conflict;[28] and the possibility of permitting some elements to lapse in return for concessions on the part of the 'men of violence', as conveyed by the Secretary of State in December 1992.[29]

The features of these laws cannot be discussed in detail here. Compared to the ordinary law of the land they grant the police and army wider powers to arrest and detain persons suspected of involvement in terrorism, with special rules on photographing, fingerprinting, bail and preliminary enquiry; trials take place before a single judge sitting without a jury; confessions are admissible evidence without corroboration, and there are certain special rules regarding burden of proof. The lack of jury trial has been replaced by allowing an extended right of appeal against conviction to the Court of Appeal. There are, however, no special laws dealing with the use of force by security forces or with the status of prisoners in Northern Ireland. The Acts are the subject of annual reporting and renewal.[30]

The Commission is aware of detailed expert criticisms and proposals for amendment to this legislation. On the PTA, it has been argued, on the one hand, that it includes 'core controls' which should not be temporary (annual report by Lord Colville), but that, on balance, its present form of renewal is a danger to necessary review. The need for and usefulness of its powers of proscription of organizations and exclusion of persons have been questioned, also in official reports. On exclusion, 'a formidable list of objections can be marshalled': unfairness, preferable alternatives, declining importance'.[31] While action against paramilitary funds may be appropriate, the special police powers of arrest and other police powers come in for detailed criticism. It is convincingly shown that official reviews have caused trends toward an expansion of powers but also towards better safeguards. By contrast, Parliament and the European Convention have had little impact.[32] Even the judgment in the *Brogan* case (see p. 69), where the power, of arrest were not sufficiently 'promptly' checked by court, as required by the European Convention, resulted in derogation not amendment in the short run.

On the EPA, a detailed set of possible amendments — apparently without result — was presented by the Standing Advisory Commission for Human Rights before the present Act was adopted.[33] The argument was that, while some emergency powers are needed in Northern Ireland, much more attention should be paid to *safeguards*, for two main reasons: the legal risk of being held in breach of human rights and the pragmatic view that reasonable laws are more likely to be acceptable to the public.

The Commission observes generally that, for all the reasons suggested, well-informed criticism of this legislation certainly deserves attention. If recent bomb attacks in England result in amending the PTA or other legislation — for instance, adding further to police powers, as suggested in certain newspapers (April 1993) — the Commission is of the opinion that, during such a review, the latest atrocities should not overshadow the points made or echoed in various submissions. Many of them seem valid. Accordingly, the Commission has also made some more specific recommendations in chapter 10.

Discrimination

The issue of discrimination still looms large among grievances, although, perhaps surprisingly, it did not occur frequently in submissions to us. However, there seems to be a general view that much past injustice has been rectified by resources and laws to benefit disadvantaged groups and the minority community. Some such points (social, economic, religious, sexual) are dealt with in other chapters.

Suggestions that 'protection against discriminatory laws and practices are essential' for human rights and freedoms,[34] and that a Bill of Rights 'should have an equality clause' to tackle the continuing deficit,[35] ought to command widespread support. In this context, the proposal to extend the principles of the 1989 Fair Employment Act to goods and services[36] should also be noted.

Human Rights: The International Dimension

Most countries have a written constitution or other legislation which explicitly recognizes human rights as a category to be defined and protected. In the United Kingdom, including Northern Ireland, this is not the case; instead, there is a strong domestic common law tradition in this field. Many submissions seemed to agree that there is a need for a reform (see Bill of Rights section below).

To discuss human rights for Northern Ireland, therefore, easily leads to ambiguity. They are no longer essentially a matter of the domestic jurisdiction of the sovereign government and parliament. Both the United Kingdom and the Republic of Ireland are bound by very important and comprehensive conventions in this respect: notably the European Convention on Human Rights (ECHR, 1950), with accompanying instruments and institutions, such as the European Commission and European Court, competent to deal with complaints; and the United Nations International Covenants on Human Rights (CCPR, 1966). Both these instruments make necessary a process of adjustment between national and international norms.

This international dimension of human rights fundamentally affects Northern Ireland. However, this does not necessarily mean higher standards than before, a fact which may run counter to widely held views about law and policy. For instance, trial by jury, or a suspect's right to silence, are not internationally recognized to be human rights. Departures from these traditional principles of common law are controversial on the domestic level. Assuming that the national principles represent a higher level of protection, the conventions themselves state that this level cannot be lowered on the pretext that the conventions do not afford the same protection.[37]

Self-determination and Minority Protection

Under the auspices of the United Nations, the right of all peoples to self-determination has become a point of departure for the human rights of individuals, whether civil and political or economic, social and cultural (common Article 1 of the two 1966 International Covenants on Human Rights).

In a broad perspective, the links between self-determination, democracy and human rights are obvious. The same can be said about present concerns regarding the protection of minorities, but in this respect international standards have not been given a similar form, general and legally binding.

Both concepts can be seen as highly relevant to the situation in Northern Ireland and the aspirations of the two communities. They belong to the political and constitutional context as well. However, we doubt their usefulness as guidelines for a solution or settlement. Scepticism is called for when one sees how hate, cruelty and intransigence thrive among those who rely on arguments about self-determination and the protection of minorities. Even the promotion and protection of 'collective rights of minorities' can have unintended side-effects, such as social polarization and segregation, leading to the perpetuation of sectarianism.

The European System

The Commission has noted, in the submissions and elsewhere, a considerable body of favourable opinion on the role of the European Convention and its organs in Northern Irish affairs. Recently it was even argued[38] that there would have been no need for the civil rights movement of the late 1960s to take to the streets, and for the unending crisis which that step precipitated, if discrimination had been contested in Strasbourg, and even less if the Convention had been incorporated into domestic law at an early stage (as it still is not — see below).

Given the limitations of the Convention system, the Commission cannot fully share these views. The Convention does not cover grievances about employment and housing, irrespective of whether there was a derogation or not. If such grievances were the original causes of the 'troubles', the ECHR could not have changed the chain of events.

It should be noted, however, that, for Northern Ireland as elsewhere, human rights were at the time no longer essentially matters of domestic jurisdiction for the sovereign power. These rights had their international dimension since before the start of the present 'troubles'. This new dimension has fundamentally affected the domestic legal order both in the United Kingdom and in Ireland, through the available recourse to European and other international institutions. In particular, if domestic remedies should prove ineffective, the available international remedies already provide a kind of — very limited — 'direct rule' from Europe, by means of the European Commission and Court in Strasbourg.

There were and are important matters on which the European Commission and Court could pass opinion and judgment, especially concerning the duty of the state to protect the rights to life, integrity and liberty. These rights were alleged to have been affected by the application of the Special Powers Act and other actions by the security forces. A main issue was internment without trial, its possible justification, and allegations of discrimination in the internment of republican, as opposed to loyalist, paramilitary suspects from 1971 onwards. An enormous litigation, lasting for years, between the two governments of the Republic of Ireland and the United Kingdom ended with a judgment by the European Court of Human Rights in 1976. It should be recalled that the Court (like the European Commission) found that internment of persons suspected of paramilitary activity had been justified by the political violence, and not to have been applied with discrimination during the relevant periods.

Complaints about deaths caused by security forces usually did not lead very far, including those in Derry on Bloody Sunday in January 1972, which were declared inadmissible (because domestic remedies had not been exhausted). But ill-treatment contrary to the Convention was found in a series of cases. Apart from instances of simple brutality, there was the use of special techniques of investigation on some detainees after the introduction of internment in August 1971. Besides the important inter-state case, great numbers of individual applications were considered.[39] As regards the 'troubles', the most important of these cases may be *Brogan and others*, which the Court decided in November 1988; it found that detention of certain suspects under the Prevention of Terrorism Act had violated the guarantee of 'prompt' judicial review, a provision from which derogation had not been made at the time. Derogation was later introduced, thus effectively removing the basis for similar complaints in the future.

The efforts invested in the Strasbourg proceedings in these cases did not seem to have much real effect on the conflict, either on the actions of the authorities or on the occurrence of political violence. Moreover, new allegations of rights violations by the security forces have continued to be made. Apparently such matters as instructions to the RUC and the army have been reviewed, and control of their practices perhaps tightened, but this Commission is not able to tell how far this is due to international supervision or has other causes.

Both the United Kingdom and the Republic of Ireland are still among the few states which have not incorporated these international norms on human rights into their own constitutional and legal order. Thus their domestic application as part of the law has not yet been secured. On the other hand, certain standards of domestic law (for example, trial by jury and the right to silence) are traditionally seen as individual guarantees, but are not reflected in the international conventions. If special security legislation affects them, recourse to the convention organs may be of no avail.

A Bill of Rights

A new deal in the shape of a Bill of Rights for Northern Ireland seems to have much to commend it. It seems easier to agree on this than on self-determination, although many in the past may have felt that 'civil rights was a stick to beat the unionists with'. However, a Bill of Rights of some kind is favoured in many submissions across the whole political spectrum, unionist and nationalist.

The idea is advocated either in a general form, as part of a proposed constitutional framework for the future, or independently. It seems also to have been endorsed on behalf of all the main political parties. Some more specific points are taken up by, among others, two expert bodies, the governmental body, the Standing Advisory Commission on Human Rights and the independent Committee on the Administration of Justice, neither of which takes any position on political or constitutional issues.

Such a reform of the law does not require constitutional change, and even less does it assume any change in constitutional status. It may be brought about as an act of Direct Rule. Although this might not be entirely satisfactory for those who emphasize self-determination, it is one of the steps which might create a better climate of understanding. But what should be the content of the Bill of Rights?

In all parts of the world, countries in rapid transition are rather quick to adopt Bills of Rights as part of their new constitutions, and in recent years many of these are modelled on, or incorporate, the chief international instruments of human rights. In view of this, it is not surprising that the European Convention seems to be the obvious and only candidate for such a role for Northern Ireland, rather than elaborating a 'national' or domestic version. Such incorporation has taken place in one form or another in most Council of Europe countries. Apart from Ireland and the United Kingdom, the exceptions are Sweden, Norway and Iceland, and these three are now taking steps to follow the others, as Denmark did in 1992.

Thus, one might ask, why hesitate any longer? It is tempting to suggest that a Bill be introduced as soon as possible, by a simple legislative enactment, making the European Convention the law of Northern Ireland. Optimistically, one might consider action within weeks or months. It does not seem to require any complex text or many deliberations.

However, such legislation may be delayed by what some may see as details, but which are not. A simple Bill to incorporate the European Convention and make it the law of the land, took the Danish experts a couple of years to prepare, because its implications had to be studied, and the Norwegian experts, who had a wider mandate and had to consider also other conventions, have needed three-and-a-half years to report.

The European Convention is far from complete; it is silent about important matters governed by other human rights conventions, and was drafted at a time when values and opinions differed a good deal from those of today. The idea of a more modern Bill of Rights, and perhaps one more tailor-made for Northern Ireland, is likely to come up. One submission sees the 'process of fashioning' it as a way in which 'the leaders of the two divided communities can come together in an institutional dynamic, for the first time in living memory, and act in common cause'.[40] It is possible that they would find the task of drafting such a composite document and elaborating means of enforcing it domestically more difficult than they expected.

There are alternative formulations. A distant parallel may be the Hong Kong Bill of Rights, enacted by an ordinance of 5 June 1991, clearly as a measure to prepare for the transfer of sovereignty to China in 1997. It incorporates into the law of Hong Kong the (United Nations) International Covenant on Civil and Political Rights of 1966. A lively process of Hong Kong case law has since been developing.

Given this background, several alternative approaches to submissions proposing a new Bill of Rights suggest themselves, even if they are limited to the special needs of Northern Ireland. The idea of a home-made document, based on the traditional principles of the rule of law and civil and political liberties as developed in these islands over a long time, might attract some; but the international dimension is more forward-looking and may be more trusted in a divided society. Most of the proposals favour the early incorporation of the European Convention on Human Rights of 1950 with later amendments and additions. The Commission is of the opinion that a reform in this field is overdue and should be undertaken as soon as possible, bearing in mind the widely felt urgency, and the apparently uncontroversial nature of the general idea.

It should be stressed, however, that the incorporation of the European Convention into a Bill of Rights for Northern Ireland, while relatively simple, would be a minimum solution. Although practised as a living and dynamic instrument, it is far from complete, being silent, for example, on non-discrimination and minority protection. In the present situation, however, the legal and symbolic value of such an enactment, making the Convention the law of the land, and accompanied by a review of the available domestic remedies, is strongly recommended. This should not be made a bargaining-point under the principle that nothing is agreed until everything is agreed.

Notes

1. Ms Maggie Beirne.
2. Kevin Boyle in *Lessons from Northern Ireland* (Belfast: SLS, Queen's University, 1990), p. 111.
3. The Standing Advisory Commission on Human Rights (SACHR).
4. Professor Brice Dickson; Dr Gerard Quinn.
5. The Committee for the Administration of Justice (CAJ).
6. South Tyrone Focus Group; Shankill Road Focus Group; Mrs Marlene Jefferson.
7. Peace and Reconciliation Group, Derry.
8. The vote at the schools' assembly for immediate involvement of Sinn Féin in political talks was unusual.
9. Senior Prefects' Committee, Omagh Christian Boys' School (also oral hearing 5.2.1993).
10. Mr Paul Sweeney (Senior Prefects' Committee Omagh CBS; New Ireland Group; Mr Michael McKeown all make the same point.)
11. Rev. Brian Lennon.
12. Rev. Raymond Murray.
13. Mrs Elizabeth Groves.
14. Dr Brian Gaffney at oral hearing 16.2.1993.
15. Mr Alan Houston; Mr Declan O'Loan.
16. Northern Ireland Religious for Justice and Peace.
17. ibid.
18. Which does exist in some predominantly Protestant areas.
19. Northern Ireland Religions for Justice and Peace.
20. Northern Ireland Religious for Justice and Peace.
21. ibid.
22. ibid.
23. Little Sisters of the Assumption.
24. Mr Stephen Plowden; Mr Patrick Dunne; Ms Olive Scott; Mr Douglas Hegney.
25. For example, Committee on the Administration of Justice; Youth for Peace; Pax Christi Ireland.
26. Clive Walker in *Lessons from Northern Ireland* (Belfast: SLS, Queen's University, 1990) p. 163.
27. Committee on the Administration of Justice; Pax Christi Ireland; Youth for Peace.
28. Mr Michael Farrell.
29. Brice Dickson, *The Legal System of Northern Ireland*, 2nd ed.(SLS, Belfast 1989).
30. This summary is based on Dickson, op. cit, p. 123-5.
31. Walker, op. cit, p. 146-7.
32. Walker, op cit, p. 162.
33. Standing Advisory Commission on Human Rights (SACHR) 16th Report 1990-91 Annex C pp 86-109.
34. Standing Advisory Committee on Human Rights.
35. The Committee on the Administration of Justice.
36. Professor Brice Dickson.
37. Articles 60 of the ECHR and 5 of the CCPR.
38. Kevin Boyle in *Ireland and Northern Ireland in a European Context* (Oslo: Norwegian Institute of International Affairs, 1993), forthcoming.
39. See for a survey, for example, Brice Dickson, 'The European Convention on Human Rights and Northern Ireland', in *Mélanges offerts à Jacques Vélu* (Bruxelles: Bruylant, 1992, pp. 1409-29.
40. Committee for a New Ireland (Boston)..

CHAPTER 8

The Economy and Society I: Some Hidden Agendas

The Economy

Northern Ireland is one of the least prosperous regions in the European Community — 126th out of 171. Since the early 1970s, the region's manufacturing sector has been in decline: between 1973 and 1990 manufacturing output fell in absolute terms by 25 per cent, and dropped from 31 per cent to 17 per cent in terms of its share of total regional output. Less than 20 per cent of the Northern Irish workforce is now employed in manufacturing.

During this period, the region's traditional industries — shipbuilding, tobacco, textiles and aircraft manufacture — fell into particularly steep decline. At the same time the multinationals, which had flooded into Northern Ireland in the 1960s — causing the region to lead the UK in annual increases in manufacturing output — began to pull out. There was a 40 per cent fall in the number of externally owned factories in Northern Ireland between 1973 — when they accounted for over half of its manufacturing jobs — and 1990. In the same period the numbers employed in indigenous small manufacturing firms also fell sharply. 'All in all, the past 20 years have seen a huge contraction in the province's industrial base.'[1] Against that background, the public sector has come to dominate the local economy, with 44 per cent of the workforce employed directly in it and many more jobs dependent on public spending. Public expenditure outstrips locally raised taxes by nearly £2.5 billion. The UK subvention which makes up the shortfall, excluding spending on security, amounts to about £1300 per annum for each Northern Ireland resident. Thus, even with its economic problems, 'Northern Ireland enjoys a standard of living not warranted by the performance of the underlying economy.'[2]

However, large numbers of its people do not enjoy that artificially high standard of living. Unemployment in Northern Ireland traditionally has been the highest in the United Kingdom. In April 1993 it was officially 14.2 per cent. In some official 'travel to work' areas, male unemployment rises to well over 25 per cent, and in some local communities it is as high as 70 or 80 per cent. These areas and communities tend to be where Catholics are in a majority.

The majority of submissions on the Northern Ireland economy stressed that if the region's economic prospects were to be improved and unemployment significantly reduced, a political settlement was crucial. Professor Desmond Rea of the University of Ulster, Jordanstown says there will no serious inward investment to Northern Ireland as long as the violence continues, and therefore a political settlement is needed as a prior step to bringing that violence to an end. Such a settlement, he believes, should involve devolution: 'with the latter, we can argue more successfully with the British government and seek more direct lines to Brussels, and, incidentally, not be hidebound by ideological Tory principles'.

The Northern Ireland Chamber of Commerce and Industry believes that, irrespective of whether or not the politicians are able to agree on a political way forward, business people must involve them in planning for a future regional economic strategy. In an oral hearing, Mr Noel Stewart, the Chamber's president, argued convincingly that the lack of self-esteem and resources of the region's small business sector — its inability to 'think big' — meant that there was a need to switch the policy emphasis from trying to attract inward investment in the face of fierce international competition, towards expanding markets for indigenous firms. He urged local political leaders to join with the main business bodies and the government in the regional economic think-tank already set up by the Chamber. He pointed to the dramatic results when politicians and business people did work together, as in the Derry-Boston Venture, the Tyrone Economic Development Initiative, Down-Chicago Links and other similar projects.

Both the Northern Ireland Chamber and the Northern Ireland Committee of the Irish Congress of Trade Unions were also concerned about the weakness of the region's representation in Brussels, believing that the government treated Northern Ireland like any other part of the UK, rather than as a special case, when it came to distributing EC funds, with the result that the Republic of Ireland received proportionately much more. A number of submissions urged that the Northern Ireland Centre in Brussels — which is currently purely a private sector initiative — should be strengthened by government involvement.

A wide range of authors — many of them business people with no political agenda — supported closer cross-border economic relationships within the EC as an important step forward. Foremost among these was the chairman of the Ulster Bank and former Secretary of the Department of Economic Development, Dr George Quigley. He urges an 'island economy', which would have to be 'an exercise in synergy, not a 'zero-sum' game, where a wholly insufficient quantity of existing island wealth is simply redistributed'. Equally important is the perception that both parts of Ireland would see such a movement as beneficial. Dr Quigley suggests specifically that the European Community should allow the island 'a block of resources for allocation between the two governments on a basis agreed with the EC'.

In tandem with this, Dr Quigley repeats his suggestion, first made in 1992, for the creation of a Belfast-Dublin 'economic corridor'. The context for this is the 'remarkable upsurge in business enthusiasm for North-South economic integration in the last few years'.[3] This stems from a shared sense of peripherality and the fear that heightened competititon in the single market will lead to further marginalization, with economic activity and wealth becoming increasingly concentrated in the EC's core economic regions. There is a growing realization that the two parts of Ireland have broadly similar problems — low international competitiveness, comparatively low economies of scale, low incomes, high unemployment, and a heavy reliance on agriculture and multinational branch plants with limited domestic linkages — and that 'if the two parts of Ireland do not swim together, they may sink separately'.[4]

In their submissions, both the Confederation of British Industry (CBI) and the Northern Ireland Committee of the Irish Congress of Trade Unions (ICTU) agreed on the importance of stronger cross-border economic links, with the former emphasizing the importance of developing the island's transport and energy infrastructure. One economist stresses that there is no question of greater North-South economic co-operation involving any weakening of Northern Ireland as part of the United Kingdom economic union, or losing its large fiscal transfers from London. 'Rather, the project is about forging more intimate and symbiotic relationships between companies, institutions and social partners on both sides of the border so that a new commercial environment may be established'.[5]

A number of significant messages come from these and from other economic submissions:

(1) A sense of loss: the region has moved from being one of the industrial centres of Europe to a peripheral region dependent on the public sector, a transformation which has hit Belfast's Protestant workforce particularly hard.

(2) A sense of isolation: as seen from continental Europe, the Republic of Ireland is hidden behind the United Kingdom; Northern Ireland is hidden behind both.

(3) There is agreement from the CBI to local community groups that job creation is the number one priority. We found an overwhelming plea, particularly from community groups, for 'real' jobs rather than temporary schemes. Official figures show that between 1 April 1992 and 31 January 1993, 70 per cent of those leaving an ACE (Action for Community Employment) scheme moved into unemployment, 20 per cent into employment and 2 per cent into further education or training.[6] The case was made for a strategic regional plan, embracing the

social as well as the economic, and providing a continuum from industrial development down to community development. The point was
also made that, because of the widespread agreement that jobs are the
priority, this could be a potential means of cross-community co-operation through some kind of job creation agency. In this respect, more
use might be made of the powers given to local councils by the
Miscellaneous Provisions Order 1992 to strike a rate to raise money
for local economic development. This might provide a vehicle for
more community involvement in economic development and for
involving the middle classes.

(4) Given the importance of ensuring that job creation does not mean
simply transferring people from the poverty of the dole to the poverty
of low pay, we can readily appreciate the CBI's version of a high wage,
high productivity economy, based on achieving high performance.

(5) There is no ignoring the fact that common membership of the
European Community has altered economic relations between the
United Kingdom and the Republic of Ireland. As a number of submissions point out, economic and commercial factors shape politics even
more than the other way round.[7] The new economic and political synergy between the Republic and the UK as a whole inevitably spills over
into North/South relations.

We therefore readily endorse the numerous pleas for greater cross-
border economic co-operation. This surely must make sense whatever
happens constitutionally, particularly in the European context. As the Irish
Minister for Foreign Affairs, Mr Dick Spring, said in March 1993, there is
a 'demonstrable need' for a body which can take as its brief 'the collective
needs and the economic logic of the island as a whole'.[8]

Social Policy and Community

Putting social policy on the agenda

The consequences of the domination of the Northern Ireland political
agenda by the 'troubles' — however unsurprising — have nevertheless
been very damaging for the fabric of Northern Irish society. Major dimensions of inequality and discrimination, other than those directly associated
with the Protestant/Catholic divide, have remained largely undisturbed.
The fundamental challenge of poverty and disadvantage has been insuffi-
ciently met. Important facets of social policy, affecting the everyday lives
of the people of the region, occupy a low position on the political agenda.
Yet it is clear from the evidence that the Commission received from a

number of quarters that these issues are of burning importance for many of the citizens of Northern Ireland.

Two dimensions of inequality and disadvantage which must be resolved, if all who live in Northern Ireland are to be full citizens in the political, civil and social spheres, are poverty and gender divisions. We look at these issues separately below.

There are, in addition, a number of minority groups in the region which cannot be said to enjoy full rights of citizenship. The understandable pre-occupation with discrimination on grounds of religion has meant that, until recently, the question of racial discrimination has not been seen as an issue. The government is currently consulting individuals and organiza-tions on this matter and there is clearly strong support in some quarters for the extension of British race relation legislation to Northern Ireland.[9] This would provide protection for the growing Chinese and Muslim com-munities.

If such legislation is to provide protection for the group singled out by many as the most disadvantaged and vulnerable, it must explicitly cover travelling people as a minority ethnic group. Although the Commission received no evidence directly from representatives of travelling people, it was clear from the evidence that we did receive from others that the travel-ling people is the ethnic group most lacking in basic amenities and oppor-tunities. Concern was expressed about the discrimination which travellers can face: their health, housing and educational status, and policies which operate against their nomadic culture and lifestyle.[10]

The absence of anti-discrimination legislation on the grounds of disabil-ity or sexual orientation was also mentioned by some groups. In these instances, Northern Ireland is in the same position as Britain. However, the point was made that, in the same way that the region has been singled out in the past for the restriction of human rights, it could now provide a model for their extension.[11]

The position of disabled people is particularly important. There are more disabled people than unemployed people in Northern Ireland, as one local MP noted in a recent Commons debate on disability. He cited a dis-ability rate of nearly one in five, which is higher than in Britain. Research has revealed that disabled people are a group whose needs have been over-looked in Northern Ireland.[12] It was suggested to the Commission that attitudes towards disability, combined with the more general lack of atten-tion paid to 'secondary' areas of discrimination in the region, have meant that there is not yet a disability movement fighting for anti-discrimination legislation, as in Britain. However, it was also suggested that this is begin-ning to change.[13]

The lack of attention paid to the needs of the large minority of disabled people is symptomatic of the generally low priority given to social policy issues in Northern Ireland, despite the important work being done by a number of people in this field. While this partly reflects the domination of the political and constitutional agenda, it also is a product of the 'democratic deficit', which leaves voluntary organizations feeling powerless to influence social policy decisions taken at Westminster. In turn, the virtual absence of social policy issues from the political agenda was cited as one of the reasons why women's participation in formal politics is particularly low in the region.

The author of one submission to us argued that 'this poverty of social policy debate and understanding substantially debilitates Northern Irish society in grappling with the many substantial problems that affect people in addition to the problems of violence', and that it will handicap the development of potential democratic government structures.[14] The Eastern Health Board's director of public health, Dr. Gabriel Scally, in a personal submission, put forward a proposal for raising the level of social policy debate which echoes the call in another submission for a better collaborative framework for the development of social policy.

The proposal is for the establishment of a series of policy fora covering the major social policy questions: 'the objective of an individual forum should be to explore and develop policy questions through the analysis of problems, the generation of public debate and the proposing of measures designed to achieve progress or solve problems. The forum would have the ability to commission research or reports, invite submissions and publish and publicize its proceedings and conclusions.' It is suggested that, as a minimum, the government and its officials should be required to consider any conclusions and recommendations and respond to them.

As well as raising the level of social policy debate, such fora should widen the level of participation in public affairs and draw on the talents and knowledge of a broad range of people. Such an approach, based on maximum public participation, would be very much in the spirit of Initiative '92 and should be explored as one of the possible steps forward, following the Commission's report. Another proposal was for something in the nature of an Economic and Social Affairs Committee, made up of representatives of the political parties, the social partners, and independent people, which would comment on matters referred to it by the government and act as a forum to work out an agenda for government. In this way, it was argued that the emphasis of the political parties might shift from the path to power to the uses of power.[15]

It is clear from many of the submissions received that there are a large number of 'bread and butter' issues which could be examined by such policy fora or by a more formal committee. Proposals on one of these, health, was detailed in a submission from the Healthy Cities Project which, it was suggested, might provide a model for other policy matters. Other examples, beside the overriding issues of jobs and poverty, include housing and homelessness, local community facilities, the position of older people, the hidden costs of education — such as school uniforms, support for ex-prisoners and the wives of prisoners, and the needs of rural areas.

A focus on such issues would be important in its own right in dealing with the everyday concerns of many people, especially those in poorer areas. It could also be important as part of the peace and reconciliation process in building trust, confidence and a sense of security about concerns that potentially unite the two communities. As one presenter stated, 'it is difficult to envisage stability when so many have so little stake in society'.[16]

Poverty and exclusion

Underlying many of these specific 'bread and butter' concerns is the fundamental challenge posed by poverty levels that, in the words of one eminent Church of Ireland witness, can only be described as 'obscene'.[17] Presenter after presenter at the oral hearings — Protestant as well as Catholic — spoke of the poverty and deprivation which is entrenched in their communities; of how poverty dominates the lives of many families and effectively excludes them socially, politically and culturally from the mainstream.

Poverty sweeps through working-class Catholic communities in swathes; it is concentrated in working-class Protestant communities in pockets, often obscured by ward statistics which combine areas of relative affluence and intense poverty. It has been suggested that the Protestant community has found it harder to acknowledge the label of poverty, reflecting their deep-seated attitudes towards self-reliance and also a desire not to appear disloyal.[18] However, it was felt that, since unemployment and deprivation are taking an increasingly heavy toll on Protestant communities, attitudes are beginning to change.

Unemployment and the lack of real jobs were cited as the cause of much of Northern Ireland's poverty. Joblessness means high levels of reliance on social security benefits. Official statistics show that 17 per cent of Northern Ireland's population are reliant on income support, compared with just under 14 per cent in Britain. A recent Child Poverty Action Group report shows that the proportion of primary school children receiving free school meals (and therefore being members of families on income support) is 27 per cent in Northern Ireland, nearly double the 14 per cent in England. Similarly, the regional proportion of average gross weekly household income accounted for by social security benefits is nearly double that in England, 19.4 per cent, compared with 10 per cent.

Social security levels, therefore, are central in determining the living standards of many people in Northern Ireland. A number of submissions maintained that these living standards had fallen in recent years. The replacement of single payment lump sum grants by the cash-limited, discretionary social fund, which mainly provides loans, was seen as a major factor in the deterioration of living standards.

Unemployment is not the only factor associated with poverty. The incidence of recorded sickness and disability is also higher in Northern Ireland than in the rest of the United Kingdom, and the proportion of families headed by a lone parent is similar. Significantly higher proportions of both men and women in Northern Ireland than in Britain are earning low wages . At the same time, living costs for poorer people tend to be higher because of the relatively high cost of food, transport and, in particular, fuel, a point that has been underlined more than once by the Social Security Advisory Committee.

Over and over again, witnesses testified to alarming levels of marginalization and alienation and an overwhelming sense of powerlessness among many living in poor working-class communities, Catholic and Protestant. The point was made that such phenomena are not unique to Northern Ireland, but it was felt that the combination of the nature of government in the region and the impact of sectarian conflict did create a situation different from that in other deprived areas of the UK.

The evidence from those who live daily with the effects of this deprivation often provided powerful statements of the relationship between social and economic exclusion on the one hand and political exclusion on the other. A situation in which many people, especially young unemployed people, feel that they have no stake in society provides fertile ground for the paramilitaries.

While no one would argue that deprivation is the cause of the violence in Northern Ireland, many did see a clear relationship between the two and felt that the roots of much of the violence lay in deep deprivation and frustration. It was suggested that there was a geographical correlation between areas of intense deprivation and high levels of violence. There appeared to be a wide consensus that part of any 'solution' had to lie in tackling the poverty and deprivation which fester at the heart of the problem. In the words of two west Belfast women who gave evidence to the Commission: 'until the basic standard of living has been improved and people have confidence in their ability to participate, the divisions in our community will never be overcome'. At a very minimum level, the sheer energy required to survive on a poverty income can leave little over for trying to overcome the community divide. As a member of the audience at one of our oral hearings put it, 'everyone is so wound up in their own poverty, neither side has any inclination to mix with the other'.

Clearly, the relationship between Northern Ireland's socio-economic problems and any political and constitutional settlement is a complex one. No one suggests that successfully tackling the former (which in any case is a major challenge in its own right) will lead to the latter. Nevertheless, many people felt that it could help to do so.

Tackling poverty and empowering those living in poor communities would be part of the confidence-building process, seen by many as crucial to making people more open to political and constitutional change. Some went further and argued that true peace has to be rooted in social justice.[19] Others suggested that unless the conditions underlying the widespread social alienation were improved, any constitutional settlement would be at risk.[20]

The message is overwhelming: if Northern Ireland is to move forward on the political and constitutional front, it cannot afford to allow significant numbers of its citizens to continue to face levels of poverty and deprivation which are excluding them from the social and political mainstream and thereby providing the breeding ground for violence.

It is encouraging that there are signs to suggest that it is a message that is being heard by those responsible for the government of Northern Ireland. Nevertheless, the government's response is still far from adequate, in the face of the scale and depth of the deprivation endured by so many.

Through the Targeting Social Need (TSN) programme, which has been adopted as a third public expenditure priority alongside law and order and the strengthening of the economy, the government has publicly accepted that 'there is a need to eradicate the significant inequalities which persist in the social and economic conditions experienced by both Protestants and Catholics' and that 'greater equality can be achieved by improving the social and economic conditions of the most disadvantaged areas and people in Northern Ireland'.[21] In December 1992, the Northern Ireland Secretary, Sir Patrick Mayhew, declared that 'the government is wholly committed to a fair, equitable society where the sharp edges that constitute injustice may at least be taken off its dividing lines'.

Such declarations are welcome, provided they are translated into effective action. One leading member of the voluntary sector suggested to the Commission that the TSN programme does indeed have the potential to make a real impact on poverty and inequality in Northern Ireland.[22] However, whether or not this potential will be realized depends on a number of factors.

There is a widespread feeling that insufficient attention has been paid to the views of those living in poor communities (see below). It has been suggested that, with the exception of the Department of Health and Social Services (DHSS), government departments have not yet really taken Targeting Social Need into account in shaping their programmes. Clear goals need to be set: the Central Community Relations Unit (CCRU), which has been given responsibility for monitoring TSN, needs to be strengthened in order to perform this role effectively. More generally and fundamentally, TSN needs to be allocated new resources, rather than simply be the recipient of the redistribution of existing resources, and the programme must be pursued with greater vigour and a greater sense of urgency.

Targeting Social Need has an important role to play in job creation and training, within the constraints of the wider economic situation. What TSN cannot do is tackle the poverty that results from low levels of social security benefits. Benefit levels are set for the UK as a whole. There is a growing body of evidence throughout the UK that these levels are insufficient to enable recipients to participate fully in society. There is also a growing body of evidence, including from government-commissioned research, that the social fund is failing in its aim of targeting help for those in greatest need. This is certainly what the people of Northern Ireland have said to us.

These are important issues that need to be tackled by the British government, but it is worth emphazising again their particular significance for Northern Ireland, where social security levels determine the living standards of a relatively high proportion of the population. It is significant that the Northern Ireland Social Attitudes Survey shows that social security is a high priority for increased public spending, particularly among the Catholic population. The higher living costs (which for those on social security are not offset by the lower housing costs in Northern Ireland) have caused some to argue for a higher level of benefit in the region. This demand has not been supported by the Social Security Advisory Committee, but it has argued that restraint in raising fuel costs is vital to those living on social security in Northern Ireland. In this context, it is essential that social security recipients are compensated in full for the proposed imposition of VAT on domestic fuel.

Women: the other divide

In Northern Ireland, as elsewhere, poverty often wears a female face. Women are more vulnerable to poverty than men, and it is mainly women who bear the burden of managing poverty, which can be both stressful and time-consuming. Their alienation from the political system is more acute than men's. Yet it is women who are often the mainstay of community groups and the kind of informal politics that they can represent.

The evidence we received from various quarters has been important in putting a spotlight on a source of inequality which is, in some ways, as deep as that between the Protestant and Catholic communities. The position of women in Northern Ireland has been described by two social policy commentators as 'a problem postponed'.[23] The evidence we have received supports their conclusion that 'gender inequality cannot be separated from other forms of inequality in Northern Ireland — and it is a problem that should no longer be postponed'. Indeed, the Equal Opportunities Commission (NI) argued at an oral hearing that improving the status of women in Northern Ireland should facilitate the alleviation of problems which undermine social, economic and political progress generally.

As the EOC emphasized, the inequality and marginalization suffered by women in the economic, political and social spheres undermine their status as full citizens. In order to deal effectively with the discrimination still faced by women, the importance of consolidating the various pieces of legislation covering different aspects of sex discrimination and equal pay in Northern Ireland was emphasized.

In the employment field, attention was drawn to the ways in which the labour market continues to be segregated, with women concentrated in low paid and increasingly peripheral and casualized jobs. Concern was expressed about the likely impact of the abolition of wages' councils on women. It was felt that employers could do much more to put gender equality on the agenda.[24]

Women's access to relevant education and training is widely seen as a priority. Women are underrepresented in many training programmes and tend to be concentrated on courses in traditional 'female' areas. Women's particular education and training requirements need to be identified and attended to, taking account of the specific needs that may arise where women face access problems, be it as a result of disability or lack of transport in rural areas. A number of witnesses suggested that many women prefer and feel safer in community-based training schemes and that these need to be better resourced.[25]

If women with children are to be able to take full advantage of any employment or training opportunities open to them, their child care needs must be adequately met. The issue of child care — for both pre-school and school-age children — was a number one priority for many who represented women's interests to the Commission. The UK as a whole has a very poor record on the provision of child care, compared with other members of the EC; within the UK, Northern Ireland has the lowest level of provision. A recent study carried out in the Shankill area of Belfast demonstrated how women's lives are dominated by child care and revealed the great need for more and better provisions, both pre-school and out-of-school.[26] The region-wide Women's Working Lives survey confirmed the ad hoc and complex nature of many women's child care arrangements.[27] There needs to be a comprehensive child care strategy for Northern Ireland. As a first step, at the very least the government's new out-of-school child care programme should be extended to the region.

Child care is an example of an issue affecting women which it has been difficult to get taken seriously on the political agenda. A number of women expressed a feeling that their concerns are not really being articulated or tackled through the political system and that their voices are not heard.

This is both a contributory cause and a consequence of women's under-representation in the formal political system. There are no women MPs or MEPs in Northern Ireland; only just over one in ten local councillors are female, and women are scarce on public bodies. Women are thus effectively excluded from an important sphere of public life, even though research has shown that women can be very active politically, both as local councillors and in political parties at grass-roots level. This activity is too often invisible.[28] The barriers which exclude women (and which handicap those who nevertheless overcome them) are by no means unique to Northern Ireland, but they are that much higher than in the rest of the UK and the nature of formal politics in the region is even more alienating of women than elsewhere. The lack of a clear route from local to national politics affects women in particular.

It is not only women who lose as a result of this, but the society as a whole; it is clear from all the evidence received about women's participation in civil society that they have an enormous amount to offer to the political system and to the search for a peaceful settlement. Typical of evidence we received were the comments of two women that 'in our experience, Catholic and Protestant women find it easy to co-operate when the deliberations and activities are directed towards the issues which matter in their lives'.[29] We heard of many instances where Protestant and Catholic women's groups were working together for the mutual good of both their communities. The following quotations illustrate the significance of the work being done by women, generally unrecognized by the formal political system: 'Women in north Belfast have played a pivotal role in drawing attention to the problems of social and economic deprivation in the area. In addition, women have often been the key players in attempting to resolve the overt sectarian conflict within the area.'[30]

'The development of women's groups in Northern Ireland, the Women's Aid Federation writes in its submission, 'whether community or service-based, has provided one of the most positive areas of growth within the wider political arena in the region during the last two decades, often unacknowledged by the more established and traditional political mechanisms,' The Northern Ireland Voluntary Trust (NIVT) goes further, drawing the Opsahl Commission's attention to 'the phenomenal contribution of local women's groups keeping hope alive within and between the divided communities of Northern Ireland'.

There was wide agreement that this contribution must be recognized and that the work of such groups should receive adequate and secure funding. Other ideas for ways in which women's contribution could be better recognized were a Commission on the Status of Women — along the lines of the equivalent body in the Republic [31] — and a special women's forum or think-tank, in which women from all walks of life would be encouraged to participate.[32]

Whatever the mechanism, women's existing contribution to public life in the sphere of civil society should be recognized and supported, and the formal political system must be more responsive and open to their needs and demands. At the same time, the barriers which keep women out of the formal political system should be dismantled. While there is no simple relationship between women's political participation and the resolution of conflict, the experience of women's involvement in local community groups suggests that they could have an important contribution to make in the search for a political and constitutional settlement.

Children and young people

A number of important points were made to us regarding the position of children and young people; their interests were clearly a priority for a number of people.

Two general points should be made. Northern Ireland prides itself on being a child-centred society, and yet the general view seemed to be that the provisions made for children are totally inadequate. The case for a co-ordinated policy to attend to children's needs was made in one submission.[33]

One cannot overstress the importance of adequate support for children and young people. As one submission put it, there can be 'no greater priority in a community undergoing economic dislocation and political turmoil than to invest in the human development of its future generation'.[34] A big improvement in nursery education, child care facilities for pre-school children, and out-of-school facilities for school-age children were widely seen as priorities.[35]

A number of submissions also stressed the importance of play provision, both to meet the needs of children and as a potential force for integration, especially in mixed communities where travel would not be a problem. Research has pointed to a lack of safe play areas and suitable/affordable recreation facilities for older children. It was suggested that the youth service could be more supportive of parents' groups working with children and young people.

There was strong criticism of the selective education system. One presenter at an oral hearing summed up the position of young people in poor working-class areas who leave school at an early age, 'degraded by the process and with little faith in themselves and no faith in the future'.[36] One teachers union argued that the labelling of children at such an early age represented an infringement of children's rights.[37] (See also chapter 10.)

Training was another issue that a wide range of people stressed, from the Confederation of British Industry (CBI) to local community groups, although their perceptions of current training schemes were rather different. A number of groups from local communities were critical of the quality of training schemes. They pointed out that poor quality schemes could lead to disillusionment and frustration.

A major concern among community groups was that Youth Training Programme (YTP) schemes increasingly place too much emphasis on vocational skills at the expense of pre-vocational work — building up confidence and self-esteem, and developing personal skills. Some young people need counselling support as well. The CBI, while emphasizing the importance of the vocational element, did accept that there should also be a personal skills element in training and pointed to inter-personal skills, problem-solving and numeracy.

It was also argued that there is an urgent need for integrated youth schemes, to counteract the impact of a segregated educational system (see chapter 10). Most youth provision is denominational, either because of its location or because it is organized by a particular Church. There are parallel Catholic and mainly Protestant scouts and guides movements. One presenter at an oral hearing pointed to the positive impact of an integrated youth training scheme which had led to cross-community friendships.[38] However, it was argued that changes in the rules governing training schemes have militated against an integrated approach. If this is the case, it should be looked at; every encouragement should be given to integrated schemes. However, it has to be recognized that many young people appear to be frightened to move outside their own area for training.

A general, very worrying point, made by a number of witnesses, concerned the growing alienation, acute sense of powerlessness and lack of hope among young working-class people. This goes back to the effects of the education system and the lack of jobs. In this context, the paramilitaries are seen to provide the only achievement structure. A recent trend is the growing recruitment of Protestant young men to the paramilitaries. In this context, it is absolutely vital that the work of local community groups which are trying to involve young people in the community in more positive ways, and to develop their skills, should receive recognition.

This all adds up to the necessity for us to make the needs of children and young people in Northern Ireland a major priority. They are the citizens of the future and, yet, the education system is preparing many young people in their separate communities for a form of second-class partial citizenship which the community divide largely obscures from the domain of public policy.

Community development and the voluntary sector

Many of the women's groups which submitted evidence to the Commission did not talk about women's issues as such but about the general needs of their communities and, in particular, those of young people (see earlier section of this chapter). The energy and creativity of these groups, working often in adverse circumstances, is truly remarkable. Much is being achieved in education and training, job creation, support for young people, and cultural and environmental activities. Although there is a longer tradition of community development in working-class Catholic communities, it is also beginning to take root in some Protestant communities.[39]

This community development work is important not only for its tangible achievements, but also for the less tangible impact it has on deprived communities. Working together in this way has improved morale and increased confidence. This is exemplified in the definition of community development offered to us by one group of presenters: 'a process which gives people an opportunity to develop their own skills and the ability to improve the quality of their own lives so that they have control over the decisions that affect them'.[40]

The importance of confidence-building as part of any process of reconciliation and reconstruction was emphasized by a range of oral hearing presenters. Thus, to quote one submission, community development is a 'vital element in the regeneration processes that need to take place throughout Northern Ireland'.[41] Another argued that 'community development challenges prejudice, sectarianism and the unequal distribution of resources'.[42]

Community development takes place both within and between the two communities in Northern Ireland. On the one hand, the importance of cross-community work was underlined, and a group of women from north Belfast argued that the kind of community work being done had helped to ensure that the area was relatively free of conflict.[43] On the other hand, some suggested that people needed to build up their confidence and self-esteem within their own communities before they would be willing and able to cross the community divide. One group of women — Catholic and Protestant, representing a number of community projects in west Belfast — explained that their idea of cross-community work was to build up confidence within communities first and then encourage rather than impose co-operation between communities.[44] In their case, they operated within a network through which they collaborated with each other on issues of mutual benefit to the two sides of the community.

There can be no 'correct' answer about the proper relationship between intra- and inter-community development work, and it is important that government funding policies are sensitive to both approaches. It was suggested that there is a danger that an overemphasis on cross-community work in government-funding criteria is jeopardizing some valuable projects that do not have an explicit cross-community remit and is distorting the work of others.[45]

This was one of a number of criticisms of government policies towards community groups. Broadly, these criticisms fell under three inter related headings: lack of accountability; a failure to recognize the knowledge and skills of local people; funding policies.

There was a very strong feeling that, although the government talks the language of 'bottom up', its policies and procedures are, in fact, still very much 'top down'.[46] Expectations about consultation had been raised but, with a few exceptions (in particular, the work of the Belfast Action Teams), appear not to have been realized. As one group put it, 'in practice local people feel that often their involvement is of peripheral interest to those who control these consultations'.[47] Without access to the kind of information and resources available to those in control of the consultation process, such consultation as does take place can lead to a sense of frustration.

Underlying the criticisms was a feeling, voiced by many, that those with authority do not recognize and value the knowledge, ideas, experience and skills of those actively involved in deprived communities. 'No one recognizes us as people', one woman told us.[48] There was a call for positive recognition by government that local projects managed by local people have the capacity to respond to the needs of their communities. This then feeds through into funding policies. There was a sense that these were informed by the agendas of those in power, rather than of those in the neighbourhood who know what is needed in their communities.[49] A number of groups, working with statutory agencies, complained about the lack of core funding for their work. Energies were being diverted from the purposes of the projects in order to raise money. Another complaint was that it was difficult to get funding for innovative projects.

There was a strong sense of not being trusted with public funds. This was exacerbated by resentment at 'political vetting' of community groups applying for funds. It was disturbing that some community groups in west Belfast expressed anxiety about submitting evidence to the Commission for fear that, if they stepped out of line in what they said, they might lose their funding. Such a climate of anxiety and self-censorship is not conducive to good community development work. We recommend that the political vetting of community groups be replaced by strict accounting procedures so as to ensure that funding is used only for community work.

There was also a feeling among some groups that the government is not really committed to community development; that it has been replaced as a priority by community relations work and economic development.[50] It is thus encouraging that in February 1993 Sir Patrick Mayhew made, on behalf of the government, 'a clear statement of the importance which we attach to the work of community groups, and to the process of community development that can make so significant a difference to life within the province'. The statement is made in a new government document entitled

'Strategy for the Support of the Voluntary Sector and for Community Development in Northern Ireland'. This explicitly recognizes the value of community development methods in building 'capacity for social change' and that 'the experience of local community groups in identifying local needs, skills and strengths, and responding in imaginative and effective ways can be a significant factor in the formulation of social and economic policies'.

Clearly there is a significant gap between the rhetoric of this document and the reality experienced by the community groups. The hope must be that the publication of this strategy document signals a serious intention on the part of government to work towards bridging this gap, both in terms of genuine community participation and also adequate funding for community development. The point was made to the Commission that the government has a tendency to produce policy statements without the resources necessary to implement the policies properly.

A number of ideas were put to us as to how community development and participation could be better facilitated. A common theme was the importance of information, education and training within local communities. While some stressed the importance of local leadership, there was also a recognition that leaders can easily become either burnt out or divorced from their own communities. If more people are trained to take responsibility, there is less of a danger of reliance on a small number of leaders. Community development requires audits, which measure both what a community needs and what it has to offer (examples of such initiatives were given to us).

One group suggested a number of ways in which the work of community groups could be better understood and valued.[51] These included seconding civil servants to work in voluntary organizations so that they can gain a better understanding of inner city communities; evaluation of community development, to be carried out by those with experience of community work, employed alongside civil servants, and with a greater emphasis on qualitative process as well as quantitative outcomes; users of services being represented on decision-making bodies; the creation of city centre neutral venues to enhance cross-community collaboration.

Model demonstration projects were suggested by a group of religious sisters as a useful way forward.[52] One submission on the Healthy Cities Project suggested that it could serve as a model of inter-sectoral collaboration and community participation, which would allow issues to be tackled in a non-confrontational way. Other suggestions included model co-operatives for young people and the establishment of cottage industries, supported by community workers with business back-up.

One submission made a specific proposal for the establishment of locally based community development trusts.[53] The authors defined such a trust as 'an independent, not for profit organization which takes action to renew an area physically, socially and in spirit. It brings together the public, private and voluntary sectors, and obtains financial and other resources from a wide range of organizations and individuals. It encourages substantial involvement by local people and aims to sustain their operations at least in part by generating revenue.'

In bringing together the statutory, private and voluntary sectors, and combining social and economic development, such trusts are in line with the government's own thinking. The idea has considerable potential as a means of building on existing work in local communities and putting it on a firmer and more secure financial footing. The proponents of the idea argued that the establishment of community development trusts would help erase feelings of powerlessness and frustration and would give those involved a sense of being in charge of their own development. It would also be a recognition of the time, energy and commitment that people are already investing in their communities — for no reward. A small number of demonstration projects would represent a positive step and could be funded on a tripartite basis by the statutory, private and charitable sectors.

Community development is one aspect of the work of the voluntary sector which plays a very significant role in the civil society of Northern Ireland. We have noted elsewhere the view that, because of the nature of Northern Irish politics and the democratic deficit in which they are played out, some of the brightest talents have chosen to put their energies into the voluntary sector rather than into formal politics. This further underlines the importance of the voluntary sector and its potential contribution to the search for a settlement and the process of reconstruction that would need to follow it. A number of submissions pointed to the widening of the concept of social partnership at EC level[54] to encompass the voluntary sector and recommended that the same should happen in Northern Ireland as part of the process of filling the political vacuum.

In this context, the recent government strategy document referred to above, which talks of a real partnership between government and the voluntary sector, is to be welcomed. In the press release announcing the report and the establishment of a new Voluntary Activity Unit within the DHSS, the Secretary of State declared that 'for the first time, government has a clearly defined strategy which acknowledges the contribution of the voluntary sector to many aspects of life in the province'.

There is, though, a potential danger in this partnership and it was drawn to the Commission's attention. It is part of the government's wider policy for the provision of welfare services — based on the 'purchaser-provider' split and the 'contract culture'— to draw voluntary organizations, including church-based organizations, increasingly into the role of providers of services. Whatever the merits or otherwise of such a policy in general, it carries the risk in the context of Northern Ireland of leading to parallel welfare systems operating within the two communities. This would exacerbate an existing tendency: we were astonished to hear, for example, that Catholic and Protestant children with hearing impediments are taught different sign languages. If this tendency were to continue, it would mean welfare policies cutting directly across the government's community relations policy. This serious danger needs to be recognized and averted.[55]

The role and significance of the voluntary sector look set to increase. The sector contains a diverse range of groups, and some are more prepared than others to respond to the challenge that current developments create. One voluntary sector representative argued that 'the task for the next ten years and into the next century is to achieve a more mature vision about the kind of society people stand for through a programme of work within voluntary organization structures and networks which will help articulate that vision'. His own vision reflected the principles of social citizenship, which he argued have 'had remarkably little effect on the conflict in Northern Ireland', despite evidence of implicit support for them.[56]

In order to take forward such a programme of work, a university-based Centre for Voluntary Sector Study has been proposed. Among other things, such a centre would explore the relationship between the aims of the voluntary sector and the political structures within which it operates. We understand that discussions are already taking place about the creation of such a centre and we hope that they will be fruitful. Such developments contribute to the strengthening of civil society in Northern Ireland and to the role that it can play in the process of conflict resolution and reconstruction.[57]

Finally, a point should be made about submissions on cross-community housing projects. A number of people argued for pilot schemes, suggesting that people could be encouraged to live in new 'mixed' estates by lower rents (although this would not help those on income support, so long as they remain on benefit).

This was seen as a way of counteracting the growing segregation taking place, especially in Belfast. This segregation, exacerbated by the erection of 'peace walls' was described to us by women from north Belfast.[58] They argued that the peace walls were erected by the security forces at least once without any consultation with local communities, in an area where the two communities were living together peacefully (others, however, did see the need for such dividing lines to prevent sectarian attacks). They suggested that the walls were more for the security management of the population than for tackling underlying problems. A comment from an unnamed government source in the *Independent on Sunday*[59] appears to give some support to this view: 'On the one hand, general government social policy would theoretically favour a mix. But then security policy would probably favour a separation because it keeps things distinct and under control.'

It was felt that the Housing Executive could do more to support those who express a wish to live in a mixed community. And it was suggested that either the Executive or the Community Relations Council could provide a forum for discussing how spatial segregation could be reduced.

Notes

1. Mr Paul Teague.
2. ibid.
3. Mr James Anderson.
4. ibid.
5. Mr Paul Teague.
6. Hansard, 23.2.1993, col. 533.
7. For example, Councillor Raymond Ferguson.
8. Speech to the Irish Association, 5.3.1993.
9. For example, Pax Christi Ireland; Peace People; Committee on the Administration of Justice (CAJ).
10. For example, Royal Victoria Hospital Faculty of Public Health Medicine; CAJ; Council for the Homeless; Mrs Kit McClarey.
11. For example, CAJ; Northern Ireland Committee Irish Congress of Trade Unions.
12. D. Birrell, E. Evason, R. Woods, 'A Qualitative Study of Life in the Disadvantaged Areas of Belfast', Northern Ireland Voluntary Trust (NIVT), 1992.
13. Mr Nick Acheson at oral hearing, 22.2.93.
14. Dr Gabriel Scally.
15. Dr George Quigley.
16. ibid.
17. Bishop Samuel Poyntz.
18. ibid.
19. Peace People; Quaker's Peace and Service, Northern Ireland Committee.
20. New Ireland Group.
21. Mr Jeremy Hanley, Minister of State, DHSS, 27.2.1991.
22. Mr Paul Sweeney at a private meeting.
23. C. Davies and E. McLaughlin, 'Women's Employment and Social Policy in N. Ireland: A Problem Postponed', Policy Research Unit, University of Ulster, 1991.
24. Northern Ireland Committee, Irish Congress of Trade Unions; Equal Opportunities Commission; Amalgamated Transport and General Workers' Union, Region 2 Women's Committee.
25. For example, Ballybeen Women's Centre.
26. R. Taillon, J. McKiernan, C. Davies, 'Who Cares? Child Care and Women's Lives in the Shankill Today', University of Ulster, 1992.
27. J. Kramer and P. Montgomery, 'Women's Working Lives', Equal Opportunities Commission (Northern Ireland), 1993.
28. E. Rooney and M. Woods, 'Women, Community and Politics in Northern Ireland', University of Ulster, 1992.
29. Mrs Kathleen Feenan and Mrs Mary Leonard.
30. North Belfast women.
31. Amalgamated Transport and General Workers' Union (ATGWU), Region 2 Women's Committee.
32. Ms Grace Bennett.
33. Playboard.

34. Mr Paul Sweeney.
35. Playboard; Ormeau Woodcraft Folk.
36. Mrs Sally McErlean at oral hearing, 19.1.1993.
37. Irish National Teachers' Organization (INTO).
38. Mr Glen Barr.
39. Report of a seminar entitled 'Community Development in Protestant Areas', CDPA Steering Group, 1991.
40. The Springfield Group.
41. Northern Ireland Voluntary Trust (NIVT).
42. Dr Ken Logue.
43. North Belfast women.
44. The Springfield Group.
45. Mr Paul Burgess.
46. Rural Community Network.
47. The Springfield Group.
48. Mrs Sally McErlean.
49. The Bridge Centre.
50. For example, Ballybeen Women's Group.
51. The Bridge Centre.
52. Sisters of the Cross and Passion, Larne.
53. The Springfield Group. The term 'community development trust' here refers to small local agencies rather than the kind of major trust — for example, Inner City Trust — established in Derry. We support both as models of community development.
54. Mr Robin Wilson and Professor Richard Kearney; Ms Róisín McDonough.
55. Mr Nick Acheson.
56. ibid.
57. ibid.
58. North Belfast women
59. *Independent on Sunday*, 21.3.1993.

CHAPTER 9

Culture, Religion, Identity and Education I: The Articulation of Confusion

Culture and Identity

Few would question the idea that, central to our problems in Northern Ireland is a conflict, even a confusion, of identity. The 'troubles' and attendant political developments have shattered old certainties. Nationalism and unionism are no longer the monoliths they once were. The IRA's brand of republicanism has alienated many from the nationalist cause, and the Commission found little confirmation among ordinary nationalists — whatever about their political leaders — of the Protestant perception of nationalists as 'winning'. Nor was there much foundation for some nationalists' belief that unionists seek only to continue their ascendancy. Although we are still forced to use the language of stereotypes for analysis, the stereotypes no longer apply. This is the reason for the withdrawal into private life and apparent apathy of so many Northern Irish people — the fragmentation of the old identities, the abuses to which this has given rise, but the inability to arrive at anything new which carries the same clarity.

It is difficult to articulate confusion. Yet if there was one common denominator in most of the submissions to the Opsahl Commission, it was the attempt to do just this. One presentation by a group of evangelical clergy, while outlining their traditional fears of 'political catholicism', recognized their past neglect of biblical teachings on justice. 'The troubles have been a humbling experience ... the old certainties have gone, there's a sense we don't know what we want.'[1] There is still much suspicion, but also a new will to understand, if people can be given some help to do so.

There can be little doubt that religious practice in Northern Ireland has sectarian and politicized undertones, however subconscious — a definition of oneself against the idea of 'the other'. There still is a frequent resort to stereotypes and 'a demonization of one side by the other' to justify one's own stance;[2] the ideal of religion removed from the 'political' sphere to the realms of private conscience and practical Christian concern for the com-

mon good is still a long way off. There is, however, a recognition, particularly among the young, that such politicized religion is part of the problem
and there was criticism of clerics participating in party politics.

For many Protestants, religion is a far more important element in defining their identity than their 'unionism' or 'Britishness'. Their attitudes to
the Republic of Ireland are explained almost entirely in religious terms:
Catholicism is seen not just as a religion, but as a threatening political system with international dimensions. Catholicism and Irish nationalism are
seen as two parts of the same system, with Articles 2 and 3 of the Irish
Constitution symbolic of its threat. Catholicism is still perceived as an
authoritarian religion, wielding considerable power over its flock, and the
stance of the Catholic clergy on integrated education was cited repeatedly
as an example of this. There is still a belief among some Protestants that
the Catholic Church teaches hatred of Protestantism. Protestant fears and
mistrust of the Catholic Church are so deeply and sincerely felt that both
the Catholic Church itself, and leaders of society in the Republic of
Ireland, must move to allay them. In the opinion of the Commission it is
time for an in-depth examination of the role of the Church in the Republic, paying particular attention to its perceived influence in the ethos of
such state-funded and controlled sectors as health and education. It is
specifically concerned about the continuing threat to the existence and
ethos of the Republic's only Protestant-run general teaching hospital, the
Adelaide, and points to the effect such a threat has in reinforcing the poor
image of the Republic among Northern Protestants. The Commission also
supports those submissions which asked the Catholic Church to be more
sensitive to the needs of couples in mixed marriages and of Catholic parents who wish to have their children educated in integrated schools.[3]

There is also a sense that Protestants' culture is 'rubbished', 'vilified
nationally and internationally'.[4] 'We are treated like white South Africans',
commented one person from the Shankill Road. There is a defensiveness
about Protestant culture, which is not helped by a certain inarticulateness[5]
and inability to explain, let alone share it.

Catholics do not have the same problem with Protestantism as a religion
and are more tolerant of Protestants as individuals. They do not understand Protestant fears of their Church. They are baffled and offended by
Protestant 'anti-popery'; at the offensive treatment of Catholicism in some
evangelical writings; and the political consequences of this — one submission pointed to advertisements for such literature in UDA newsletters.[6]
Because of a lack of understanding of the religious reasons for such attitudes (and the past failure of Protestants to explain them), the belief per-
sists among many Catholics that Protestants cling to the connection with
Britain simply to retain their 'ascendancy'. The Catholic complaint is still
with the politicians and the state; they still have a sense of being victimized

and 'pigeon-holed' politically because of their religion. There is resentment among west Belfast Catholics, in particular, that they are perceived
as being highly politicized and treated accordingly.[7]

Much of the defensiveness of Protestants comes from ignorance of their
own history and of Irish history generally, a sense that history will be used
as a weapon against them, and a tendency in consequence to dwell on
those events in which they too were victims, and to ignore the rest. In this
sense, all sides in Northern Ireland are prisoners of a victim theology
which sees the other side as the aggressor.[8]

But do Protestants really need to be so defensive and apologetic about
their culture? We think not. There was less sign than in the past of the
nationalist tendency to view Protestants as somehow un-Irish; only a few
submissions used the old planter/native stereotypes, and these came almost
exclusively from people from the South or older border nationalists. Very
many Protestants can boast as sound a Gaelic lineage as Catholics (if they
only studied their own history). In this respect, the new trend of
Protestants tracing links with pre-historic Ulster is a beginning,[9] though
the tendency to claim exclusive 'ownership' is the reverse image of the
IRA's version of Irish history. No one group has a monopoly of Irishness
or indeed Ulsterness.

The Commission was made aware of a strong desire among many
Protestants to be 'made to feel at ease with their Irishness'.[10] The belief is
still there that nationalists generally have appropriated the Irish language
and Irish history as political weapons.[11] The truth of this was recognized
by many nationalists. But few Protestants acknowledged that they too had
contributed by their own rejection of both. There is a clear desire among
nationalists to move away from such exclusiveness. This, unfortunately,
has taken the form of omitting Irish history from some Catholic schools
because it is potentially divisive. Yet there was a desire among both
Catholic and Protestant sixth-formers at the schools' assemblies that both
Irish history and the Irish language be made available in all schools.
Perhaps, too, if more were known about the history of Ulster, more common ground might be established.

For their part, Protestants should look at the anti-Catholic nature of
some of their culture. The emphasis by the Orange Order on marches
seems singularly unimaginative. Its continued insistence that these should
take traditional routes, even when the areas through which they pass have
become predominantly Catholic, is indefensible, and transmits the negative signals about their culture which many Protestants wish to deflect.
The Commission points out that such marches do not accord well with the
qualifications laid down for Orangemen by their own organization: 'He
should cultivate truth and justice, brotherly kindness and charity, concord
and unity and obedience to the laws; his deportment should be gentle and

compassionate, kind and courteous.'[12] One submission suggests that a summer festival would give people a way of celebrating Protestant and Orange culture without emphasizing religious antagonisms.[13]

Protestants privately acknowledge injustices which existed under the Stormont regime, but few will say as much, and they resent being reminded of them. Yet Catholics desire this simple recognition, and it would win considerable respect if made.

Time and time again we heard Protestants talk of Catholics' greater proficiency at organizing themselves; what once would have been dismissed as a herd-like tendency, now wins admiration and an acceptance that in the voluntary and community sector Protestants have much to learn (see chapter 8). Certainly there are signs of a weak political culture generally among Northern Ireland Protestants and a recognition that the public voice of Protestantism sounds bigoted.

The Churches were considered not to have done enough either to represent the fears of their communities or to take a lead in assuaging them. It is all very well for the religious leaders to act in unison, the Commission was told, but the 'trickle-down effect' is perceived as very limited. However, submissions reflected considerable debate and movement amongst a wide range of clergy and a recognition that they can do more.[14] The Churches should encourage more explanation of their theologies and their cultural and political implications. In the Belfast schools' assembly there was a demand for more religion to be taught, not less. A purely secular atmosphere in schools is not what most young people want. Rather, they asked for 'mixed' religious education classes, where they could actually hear other young people talking about their religion. The discussion groups preceding the assemblies were a model of what could happen: frank discussions about beliefs and identities. Could existing integrated schools and those state schools that are mixed — as well as schools linked through the Education for Mutual Understanding (EMU) programme — run pilot projects along these lines and involve the respective Churches?

The Catholic Church bears a particular responsibility for this (given the depth of Protestant suspicion outlined above). The submission from the Inter-Church Group on Faith and Politics pointed to a number of ways in which the Catholic Church could help defuse 'the deep-seated distrust among Protestants, of Catholic ecclesiastical power', among them 'offering communion to inter-church couples when requested, or not putting obstacles in the way of those who wish to give experiments in integrated education a fair trial, or altering some of the rules for mixed marriages'.

Protestants in the South should be encouraged to talk to their co-religionists in the North, and explain that they do not feel threatened. Northern Protestant clergy, for their part, should be sensitive to elements conducive to sectarianism in their own statements and practices. A more thoughtful and concerned religious leadership could not be imagined than those representing the Presbyterian Church and Government Committee, who appeared at the first week's oral hearing in Belfast. And yet they had difficulty explaining the implications of one of Presbyterianism's central doctrinal documents: the Westminster Confession of Faith, with its description of the Pope as the 'anti-Christ'. Many Catholics were also critical of their Church's stance on integrated education, pointing to the obstacles placed in the way of some Catholic parents wishing to send their children to integrated schools.[15]

While Catholics were comfortable with their Irish identity, the difficulties for Protestants in this sphere was a recurring theme. Many felt no difficulty in being British and 'Irish only in the geographical sense'.[16] However, others echoed the outgoing Presbyterian moderator, Dr John Dunlop, in asking 'How can Protestants claim to be Irish when their neighbours are being killed in the name of Ireland?' Many Protestants addressing the Commission admitted to being less inclined to call themselves Irish because of the 'troubles'.

If the schools' assemblies were taken as a guide, many young Protestants west of the Bann appeared to see themselves as British rather than Irish, while those in the east were more open to seeing themselves as Irish first. Young Catholics west of the Bann were less inclined to recognize a common local identity than those in the east, where an identity with the geographic region of Northern Ireland was stronger, regardless of religion.[17] But there is more duality and confusion than is generally recognized. Where older Protestants spoke of the monarch, the British constitution and the Protestant succession, young Protestants had difficulty defining their Britishness and tended to point to things like sport. Family traditions seemed paramount: where the family was highly politicized, the young felt strongly British (although, even here, there was a sense of being second-class British citizens). Where Irish history was offered at school, Protestant pupils felt more comfortable in accepting an Irish identity, when coupled with British citizenship.[18] Given such attitudes, there appears to be a case for offering people in Northern Ireland some way of recognizing such mixed identity, other than the simple option of holding British or Irish passports.

The young Catholics at the schools' assemblies defined their Irishness almost entirely in terms of culture; there was a desperate eagerness that it should be shared and little sign that they wanted it used as a political weapon. 'As a Protestant who has never had a problem with embracing my Irishness', writes Sam McAughtry in his submission, 'I have been aware for many years that this single gesture brings with it more warmth and goodwill from Catholics than any other Protestant response within the context of our divisions.'[19]

In fact, nationalists have come a long way since the 1960s. They have reconsidered their history in a way that unionists have not. Unionism could benefit from a similar reconsideration — 'we need to take the history of our antagonism seriously'.[20] 'Britishness' needs to be redefined in the context of Northern Ireland. Political Britishness, defined simply in terms of the political connection, no longer gives Protestants the confidence in their identity that they once had. Religion is clearly the most fundamental element in defining Protestant identity and, if that is generally explained and recognized, they could have, and be given, more confidence in the future. Equally, Irishness needs to be redefined as something more pluralist than at present; it was, after all, happily used by Protestant and Catholic alike until the foundation of Northern Ireland.

A number of other specific suggestions were made to the Commission, such as the organization of local festivals, including Orange festivals. One innovative scheme was for a Northern version of the schools-based heritage collection project, based on the one mounted in the Republic in the 1950s, 'which not only established a valuable cultural archive, but also created a shared sense of cultural, communal history and identity among the pupils who collected the material'.[21] Another was for a community-based Centre for the Media, Arts and Communication, to be established on the Belfast 'peace line' to increase awareness of the culture and traditions of both sides.[22]

Catholics concerned about the Irish language and culture should condemn their use for divisive political ends and generally should help Protestants to feel more at ease by recognizing Protestant culture as part of an Irish identity. There should be a progressive depoliticizing of cultural beliefs, with attempts to find new Northern Irish symbols and emblems with which both traditions can identify. A monolithic national identity is inappropriate to the experiences of the people of Northern Ireland: 'In practice its citizens pick 'n mix from a range of cultural choice ... . Thus acknowledgement of *de facto* affiliation to two islands must inform any new institutional framework.'[23] There are many signs that the British government and the Northern Ireland Office have recognized this need; there are fewer from the Republic.

Religion

Church apologists have consistently argued that the Northern Ireland problem is not religious. Land, power and nationhood are identified as the issues. But when the good land and power have for centuries been in the hands of a group on one side of the traditional religious divide, and when the lack of both land and power has been experienced by a group on the

other side, a religious content in the struggle is inevitable. When Protestants claim to be British and when Catholics assert their Irishness and
want to be rid of any British connection, the mixture of religion and
national identity makes for a volatile brew.

While both sides may in some ways deny that they are engaged in a religious war, their art forms and mores tell a different story. Loyalist murals
depict warriors ready for action under the words 'For God and Ulster'
emblazoned on gable walls. Republicans, on the other hand, have for generations thought, spoken and written in terms of blood-sacrifice. They
have their hagiography of the men and women who have died 'for the
cause'. The suffering of those who died on hunger strike is still compared
with the sufferings and sacrifice of Christ on the cross. Every one of the
more than 3000 people who have been killed in the present 'troubles', irrespective of whether or not they were paramilitary activists, has been given
a Christian burial

Religion may or may not be the prime cause of the conflict: it is certainly a potent component of it — probably more so for Protestants than for
Catholics. It was evident in more than one submission that the real 'hate
figures' for Protestants are likely to be the priest and the Pope — the
human personification of Roman clericalism — while for Catholics it is
almost certainly the loyalist politician, the RUC and the UDR (now the
RIR), rather than the Protestant clergyman or minister.[24]

It simply comes to this: the Northern Ireland conflict is in part economic and social, in part political and constitutional, and also in part religious,
and damagingly so. Accepting the religious factor in the equation, are the
Churches obliged to respond? Have they any obligation to do anything?

In so far as the Churches succeed in relieving suffering; in persuading
activists to lay down their arms; in persuading others not to take them up;
in providing ideas or suggestions that may lead to a settlement, or indeed
in reaching out and mediating, they may be considered as part of the solution. In so far as they fail to do any or all of these things, they are part of
the problem. Responsibilities and obligations consequently rest on all the
Churches. They cannot assert that they are not affected or involved in a
struggle which is tearing apart Northern Ireland society, causing deaths
and destruction on a scale even the greatest pessimist would have considered impossible twenty-five years ago.

What then has been the contribution of the Churches, good or bad, to
the Northern Ireland problem over the last quarter of a century ? Let it be
said at once that in the early 1900s and as late as 1912, when the Home
Rule crisis came to a head, the Churches had no hesitation in taking sides.
There was no doubt about the stance of any of them. The newspaper
reports and public rallies of the period are witness to adamant Protestant
Church opposition to Home Rule and to Catholic Church approval of it.

Not so in the years of the current unrest. The mainstream Churches at least have organized no public religious-political rallies and engaged in no public agitation, whatever may be the inner wishes and aspirations of their members.

The Commission received over fifty written submissions from official church bodies and individual clergy and lay people. These included important voices from the three main Protestant Churches, in the form of key Presbyterian and Methodist committees and three Church of Ireland bishops. Regrettably, the Northern Catholic bishops did not contribute, although members of religious orders and individual priests did.

In both the written submissions and oral hearings, the Commission had clear evidence of a wealth of Christian compassion in Northern Ireland over the years.[25] The relatives of the murdered have been comforted, counselled and helped; refugee and rest centres have been provided when needed; housing has been made available through Church-based housing associations; Christian organizations and communities like Corrymeela have been at work supporting the victims of violence; holidays for children from ghettos have been arranged on a cross-community basis year after year by Church-related organizations and by associations whose aims and members are avowedly Christian. There is much worth in what has been done.

Nonetheless, the Churches would be ready to admit that all this is only a fraction of what needs to be done. At best they can hope only to provide a back-up and to complement what the state can and ought to provide. In any case, only the Churches can say what more they could have done. The submission of the Irish Council of Churches referred to the many thousands of pounds contributed through the Churches Emergency Fund to organizations and groups engaged in cross-community and ameliorating projects. However, all the money distributed has come from Germany, the United States and Britain. None of the Irish Churches seem to have contributed to the Fund.

The late Cardinal Conway once reflected that perhaps the Catholic Church should have been more concerned about unemployment and other social issues.[26] The other Churches could well have said the same. The gospel the Churches profess to believe, preach and practice has much to say, in addition to its insistence on the grace of God, about the search for justice, concern for the poor and equal rights, and love for self, neighbour and enemy. Those are the criteria and principles that the Churches must apply to what they say to politicians and to what the politicians wish to propose.

How then have the Churches measured up to that obligation? The Commission was reminded that the Presbyterian Church had published studies on Irish republicanism and loyalism;[27] that the Methodist Church's

Council on Social Welfare had done work on poverty and deprivation in Northern Ireland and on the Anglo-Irish Agreement.[28] It was aware of books by Cardinal Daly and Archbishop Eames, calling for the application of Christian principles to any solution offered for Northern Ireland's agony.[29]

The Commission took note of the reference in the Irish Council of Churches' submission to the recommendations of the 1976 report from the Working Party on Violence in Ireland, appointed by the Catholic Hierarchy and the Protestant Churches of the Council. The report recommended that the Churches should actively support peace and reconcilation movements; they should support the principle of a Bill of Rights to protect minorities; there should be action by the Churches to ensure that they are not compromised by paramilitary organizations at funerals and commemorations; there should be urgent experiments in the youth service to make it both non-denominational and appealing to those young people hitherto not attracted to it; a joint committee should be established to consider closer contact and co-operation between Catholic and other schools; the Churches should set an example to society in the place they give to women; a sustained programme of education within the Churches should be initiated to make their members more aware of the political and social implications of Christianity for Irish society, and of democratic methods for promoting justice and peace; and a Christian Centre of Social Investigation should be set up, to conduct research into the problems underlying the conflict and to monitor progress in removing discrimination and other injustices related to the occurrence of violence. The Commission regrets that there is much unfinished business as far as many of these recommendations are concerned, notes that they are as relevant now as they were then, and calls for renewed action on them.

How have the Churches in Northern Ireland discharged the ministry of reconciliation? The late Bishop Philbin of Down and Connor once wrote that the world could with justification keep aloof from the Churches as long as the Churches kept aloof from one another. What then has been happening in Northern Ireland?

The Commission learned from both written submissions and oral hearings that there has been a marked development in ecumenical services and in the growth of cross-community prayer and Bible study groups. However, it was claimed that the majority of Catholic clergy attending those services come from the religious orders (rather than from priests in parishes), and the majority of Protestants also appear to be from non-congregational or non-parish sectors. Furthermore, it was claimed that the lay attendances are for the most part Catholic.[30] This seems to bear out a comment made by the late Professor John Whyte in his posthumously published book *Interpreting Northern Ireland* that more than 50 per cent of both Presbyterians and Methodists are opposed to such ecumenical services. The intensity of that opposition may be gauged from some sentences in a written submission made to the Commission by a former moderator of the Presbyterian Church.

Many unionists see ecumenism as but another means of undermining their Protestant heritage by blurring the fundamental differences between the Reformed and Unreformed faiths. It is clear that in all the Protestant Churches, whatever the clergy may pretend or even wish, the people are determined that their Protestant faith and heritage are not for sale.[31]

So much for reaching out in ecumenical services. What of actual attempts to make peace? Probably the full story of such initiatives will never be completely known. The Commission is aware that meetings between churchmen — whether or not officially accredited — and republican and loyalist activists have taken place which have never been publicized. Some of those encounters have not been without positive effects. However, it should be noted that the much publicized 1974 Feakle encounter between leading Protestant churchmen and the IRA had far from unanimous support inside the Protestant Churches, and one of the party was publicly disavowed by his superiors. The Peace People, the unnumbered peace groups and organizations, the Sadie Pattersons, Ruth Agnews and others whose names are history, the Gordon Wilsons of today, are witnesses to the fact that somewhere along the line the Churches have succeeded in producing persons who are prepared to work and struggle as well as to pray for peace. Tragically, more is needed to end the conflict.

There is one other factor to be considered. To a remarkable extent, the Churches have succeeded in maintaining 'quality of life' inside their own communions and particularly within individual parishes and congregations. Members of those congregations have been able to attain a degree of caring for each other and norms of acceptable behaviour that might not have been expected. At a minimum, thousands of adults and young men and women have been encouraged and persuaded to refrain from activity that would foment or increase unrest. It is, of course, undeniable that large numbers, who at one time were under the tutelage of the Churches, have resorted to violence.

At a time when the credibility of the Churches is increasingly being called into question, their maintainance of a regular pattern of worship and practice, often in the face of intimidation and danger, has been no mean achievement .

The summaries of the written submissions in Part II give some indication of the record — good and bad, successful and failed, encouraging and depressing — of the Churches in Northern Ireland over the last quarter century of strife. There has been concern; there has been action of different kinds, but there is still an alarming amount to be accomplished.

Education

The role of education in Northern Ireland was a central issue: around seventy submissions referred to it in some way. Northern Ireland has much to be proud of in its education system, which compares well with the rest of the United Kingdom and is arguably superior to the Republic's. During the oral hearings, the Commission was impressed again and again by the highly articulate and well-informed contributors, the vast majority of them products of the region's educational system — whether state, voluntary or Catholic schools — who appeared before it. The school students at the two schools' assemblies were likewise impressive.[32] A similar compliment can be paid to the remarkably high standard of logical argument evidenced in the written submissions. Clearly the grammar school system has put an emphasis on excellence that has served many people from both communities very well indeed.

However, there were also contributions from people highly critical of a system that determines the type of education deemed suitable for children at the early age of eleven. The trade union which organizes mainly Catholic teachers, the Irish National Teachers' Organization (INTO), said:

One of the greatest social evils persisting in Northern Ireland is the continuation of a selective system of education at secondary level. The Northern Ireland second level of education is provided with a dual level of selective grammar schools (30 per cent of pupils) and non-selective secondary schools (70 per cent of pupils) which do not enjoy parity of esteem. The selective process has had an adverse impact on the primary school curriculum and ensures that at least two-thirds of our young people are categorized as 'failures' at the age of eleven years. The success of pupils in obtaining higher percentages of A-level passes than England and Wales is achieved at a disproportionate cost to the rest of the education system, with the result that more children leave secondary education without any form of qualification than anywhere else in the United Kingdom'.[33]

The same point was made by the principal of a Catholic secondary school for girls in Fermanagh: 'the secondary school is less esteemed, less well-resourced, and among its pupils are the least able academically, the socially deprived and the educationally alienated'.[34] It was confirmed by the Department of Education's publication of its first 'league table' of school exam results on the eve of the oral hearings. That table amply justified the claims made for the merits of the grammar schools, but equally demonstrated the consistent level of underachievement in the secondary sector. Most alarming were the statistics from schools in deprived or under-privileged housing areas, where there was a clear correlation between underachievement and absenteeism on the one hand and unemployment and deprivation on the other. A higher proportion of young people leave school without qualifications in Northern Ireland than in other parts of the UK: 13 per cent, compared with 7 per cent in England and Wales, for example.[35]

It was put to us that an alarming number leave school unable even to read or write. In effect, a significant proportion of the children of Northern Ireland are condemned as failures at the age of eleven. It then becomes very difficult to motivate these children and young people. The Commission will not soon forget the comment made by one west Belfast mother at an oral hearing. She told how one of her children had been absenting himself from school for three years: 'I did not know it and the school did not know it either.'[36] The Commission is convinced that the system of selection at eleven needs to be radically overhauled, and greater provision must be made for pupils who reject or fail to adapt to the normal educational system.

The requirements of the new national curriculum have also placed heavy demands on all schools, and particularly on secondary schools because of their lesser funding and the requirements of the science and technology curriculum. The result is that the parity of esteem between the grammar and secondary sectors, for which many educationalists have argued, seems more and more difficult to attain. More serious still is the correlation between deprivation and underachievement. Elsewhere in this report attention is drawn to the high level of alienation from society and authority to be found in deprived and segregated areas. The fact that parents and their parents before them have had little or no experience of paid employment is certainly no encouragement to children in these areas. It must be difficult, if not impossible, for conscientious teachers not to lose heart in an atmosphere where deeply alienated young people can easily find an attractive alternative in violence.[37]

A new factor in the 1980s and 1990s is the emphasis on cost effectiveness and the management culture. In education, as in the health service, this has led to rationalization and, more often than not, to the closure of small and/or contracting schools. Too often the consequence is significant damage to the fabric of local small communities, both urban and rural.[38] Concern about these matters was evident in submissions on the new school curriculum. For the most part, there was approval for the new courses on Education for Mutual Understanding (EMU) and Cultural Heritage, the joint Irish Commission for Justice and Peace/Irish Council of Churches peace programme and similar projects (although some cynicism was expressed about them in the schools' assemblies).[39] But the fear was expressed that the pressure to control budgets is leading to underfunding of such vital subjects in the Northern Irish context. Contributors were aware that courses like these could not in themselves remove the evils of sectarianism. The Commission nevertheless recognizes that they can play a valuable role in the ameliorating process, and urges the government to ensure that they are adequately resourced.

Of the 36 submissions which favoured integrated schooling, nine came

from joint groups or cross-community organizations, twelve from perceived Protestant sources, six from Roman Catholics, and two from people
whose religion was not identifiable. Recent legislation has provided for 100
per cent capital grants for integrated schools. The result is that in 1993
there are fourteen integrated schools — compared to only two ten years
ago — out of a total of 1336 primary and secondary schools in the region
(that is, around 1 per cent).

The Commission noted the argument from the All Children Together
(ACT) group that integrated education represented 'a very radical form of
reconciliation' in the Northern Irish context. The group believe that this
reconciliation does not merely touch pupils, but has 'a cascade of positive
influence' which touches parents, grandparents, brothers and sisters, relations, friends, and staff working in the schools.[40] The Commission also
noted the argument of Dr Colin Irwin, a social anthropologist from
Queen's University, Belfast: because of opposition of local community
leaders, Churches and school boards, 'the Northern Ireland Office and the
Department of Education have failed to provide every child in the
province with a real option of attending an integrated school'.[41] The consequences of significant demographic change in recent years — with the
1991 census figures revealing that at least half the population now lives in
areas which are more than 90 per cent either Protestant or Catholic — has
significant implications for the spread of integrated education.[42] The creation of a large, region-wide integrated school system along the lines
envisaged by Dr Irwin is going to be difficult, even if there was a marked
determination to work towards it. In these circumstances, it is difficult to
see any significant increase in the number of such schools in the near
future, although in principle the Commission welcomes educational integration at all levels thoughout the school system.

Equally significant are the attitudes of local community leaders and the
opposition of the Catholic Church. While it is true that the Protestant
Churches have given guarded approval to integrated schooling, the same
cannot be said of Protestant community leaders.[43]

The position of the Catholic Church, as set out by the Second Vatican
Council, states that the Catholic Church has the right to expect from the
state sufficient finance to enable it to establish and maintain schools at
every level, and asserts unequivocally that Catholic parents have a duty 'to
entrust their children to Catholic schools, when and where this is possible'.

Since the promulgation of that declaration in 1965, the Irish Hierarchy
has regularly reaffirmed that position. However, the Commission recognizes that, while the Hierarchy's position is accepted by most Irish
Catholics, there are those who wish to see a less rigorous stance being
adopted. There seems to be an identifiable, though slowly growing,
demand inside Northern Catholicism for integrated schools. It should also

be noted that there are significant numbers of Catholic children enrolled in the Protestant voluntary grammar schools. The Commission, while understanding the strength of the case for the Catholic school, asks if it might not be possible to establish safeguards and conditions which would make integrated schools acceptable to the Hierarchy. It is aware that in England and Wales, the Catholic Hierarchy has responded to a request from its national pastoral conference to consider setting up shared Christian schools, by promising to 'investigate the possibility of further shared schools, not on a merely pragmatic basis, but in order to discuss the potential for ecumenism and other reasons'.[44] The Commissioners would welcome a similar investigation taking place in Ireland.

The Commission agrees with the many people who appeared before it that integrated education is no panacea for Northern Ireland's many problems of violence and division, but at least it can contribute to their resolution. It would represent a small brick in the wall of peace-building, and could percolate through the society beyond the school walls. We heard from one group in Londonderry how the process of setting up an integrated school had helped to build trust — 'an experience of hope and renewal'.[45]

In the meantime, the almost complete segregation of young people of school age from differing traditions will continue unless some ameliorating provision can be made. Suggestions made by contributors to the Opsahl Commission included: more teacher exchanges between Catholic and other schools, and between schools in the Republic and schools in the North, as already organized for some years by Co-operation North;[46] the 'twinning' of schools from different traditions;[47] a history curriculum common to all schools in Northern Ireland and the Republic;[48] a nursery school on the Belfast 'peace line' available to children (and their mothers) from each side;[49] more sixth-form conferences along the lines of the Initiative '92 schools' assembly; joint visits to other countries and enrolment for service at home and abroad in a Northern Irish 'peace corps'.[50]

The Commission draws attention again to the educational recommendations of the 1976 *Violence in Ireland* report of the Churches, widely acclaimed although not satisfactorily followed up after they were first made public. The report recommended, *inter alia*, that the Churches should encourage and — where they were in a position to — produce pilot schemes to exchange teachers between Catholic and other schools, particularly on sensitive subjects such as history, civics, Irish language and culture, and the history of the Churches; shared sixth-form colleges; common nursery schools in suitable areas; shared school debates, cultural and folk-cultural activities, sports and games, with an emphasis on the diversification of the last of these to increase their potential for sharing. The Commissioners regret that, for the most part, these recommendations have not been acted upon, and urges the Churches to give them urgent attention.

The topic of religious education figured prominently in a number of submissions. There were those who objected to the recent Common Core Syllabus of Religious Education, published by a committee officially representative of the Church of Ireland, the Methodist Church, the Presbyterian Church and the Catholic Church.[51] The Commission is aware of the common Christian basis of the syllabus and points out that it claims only to be a core to which schools can, at their discretion, add educational material relevant to other world religions. Again the Commission echoes the statement of the *Violence in Ireland* report:

The stereotypes which each community may have inherited regarding the religious beliefs and positions of the other must be finally rejected and replaced by exact and sympathetic understanding. It will often be desirable to invite representatives of the other tradition to come to the schools to talk about their own traditions.

The Commissioners acknowledge how exposure in both the oral hearings and the schools' assemblies to proponents of various points of view helped to remove stereotypes and preconceived ideas. They believe that exposure of school students to similar open fora on a regular basis could well have similar results.

One final, novel proposal was for the establishment of a 'Friendship University' on the border between Northern Ireland and the Republic. Such an initiative, it was suggested, would serve two purposes: the practical one of providing places for the rapidly expanding number of potential third-level students in the Republic and for at least some of the students from Northern Ireland who currently go to Britain: and the visionary one of promoting a centre of excellence and enlightenment, a place where a new generation of young people can begin 'to share an all-Ireland perspective in the non-threatening, indeed liberating, atmosphere of a centre of learning, debate and research'.[52] The Commission endorses the conclusion of this submission that, on the eve of the twenty-first century, it is time for a new intellectual vision in Ireland. Perhaps education in Northern Ireland can begin to provide it.

Notes

1. The Witness-bearing Committee of the Reformed Presbyterian Church at oral hearing, 18.2.1993 (also submission).
2. Sisters of the Cross and Passion; Dr Ken Logue.
3. Mrs Ursula Birthistle and Mr Niall Birthistle.
4. Mr Jackie Redpath at oral hearing 18.2.1993.
5. Professor Edna Longley brings this out well.
6. Rev. Patrick McCafferty.
7. Mrs Elizabeth Groves at oral hearing 19.2.1993.
8. Sisters of the Cross and Passion at oral hearing 23.2.1993.
9. Ulster Motherland Movement.
10. Mr Jackie Redpath at oral hearing 18.2.1993; Mr William O'Neill.

11. For example, Sam McAughtry.
12. M. W. Dewar *Why Orangeism?*, (Grand Orange Lodge of Ireland, 1959).
13. Mr and Mrs Morgan.
14. For example, Sydenham Methodist Church; Presbyterian Church in Ireland, Church and Government Committee; Sisters of the Cross and Passion, Larne; Northern Ireland Religious for Justice and Peace; and some particularly impressive submissions from Catholic religious orders.
15. Mrs Ursula Birthistle and Mr Niall Birthistle.
16. Rev. Robert Dickinson.
17. Schools' assemblies working groups on identity and belief.
18. ibid.
19. Mr Sam McAughtry.
20. Inter-Church Group on Faith and Politics.
21. Dr Bob Curran.
22. Mr Paddy Fleming and Sister Genevieve.
23. Professor Edna Longley.
24. Presbyterian Church in Ireland, Church, and Government Committee.
25. Strongly implied in submissions from Irish Council of Churches; Quaker Peace and Service; and various religious orders.
26. *Christians in Ulster: 1968-1980*, Stanley Worrall and Eric Gallagher (Oxford: Oxford University Press, 1982).
27. Presbyterian Church in Ireland, Church and Government Committee at oral hearing 19.1.1993.
28. Methodist Church Council on Social Welfare.
29. Cahal Daly, *Violence in Ireland and Christian Conscience* (Dublin: Veritas, 1973); Cahal Daly, *The Price of Peace* (Belfast: Blackstaff Press, 1991); Robin Eames, *Chains to be Broken* (Belfast: Blackstaff Press, 1992).
30. Corrymeela Community at oral hearing 28.1.1993.
31. Rev. Robert Dickinson.
32. Also see submissions from Senior Prefects' Committee, Christian Brothers School, Omagh; three Methodist College sixth-formers.
33. Irish National Teachers' Organization (INTO); Northern Ireland Voluntary Trust.
34. Sister McQuade.
35. House of Commons, Hansard, 18.3.93, col. 393.
36. Mrs Sally McErlean.
37. INTO; Mrs Sally McErlean; Mrs Kathleen Feenan and Mrs Mary Leonard.
38. INTO.
39. Mr Trevor Halliday; Churches' Central Committee for Community work; INTO.
40. All Children Together (ACT).
41. Dr Colin Irwin.
42. *Independent on Sunday*, 21.3.1993; *Belfast Telegraph*, 19.4.1993.
43. 'Christians in Ulster' op. cit.
44. ibid.
45. Foyle Trust for Integrated Education; Oakgrove Integrated Primary School at oral hearing 27.1.1993.
46. Mrs Evelyn Berman and Mrs Catherine Lyle.
47. Mr Tony Gasson.
48. Irish National Teachers' Organization; Methodist Women's Association.
49. Mr Paddy Fleming and Sister Genevieve.
50. F. John Herriott.
51. Baha'i Community Religious Education Committee, Newtownabbey; Mr Arthur Green.
52. Mr Andy Pollak.

CHAPTER 10

Conclusions and Recommendations

These conclusions and recommendations should be read in the context of the analysis by the Commission of politics and the constitution, law and justice, economic and social concerns, and religious, cultural and other issues, contained in chapters 2 to 9 The analysis is based on a reading of the written submissions summarized in chapters eleven to fourteen, and the evidence of the schools' assemblies and the oral hearings (chapter 15 and commentary), as well as six focus groups, a number of private meetings and other sources.

Politics and the Constitution

1.1 On the process towards future government

The Commission recommends that if the current or resumed round of political talks should fail, and in view of the strong desire we found in a great many submissions for a system of government in Northern Ireland that is accountable to its people, the British Government should, in consultation with the Irish Government, set up a Commission[1] to study the situation and put forward views and recommendations. This Commission should consider, *inter alia*, the proposals contained in *recommendation 1.2*. Its views and recommendations should be the basis for a further consultation with the political parties and, if necessary, for direct consultation with the people of Northern Ireland. In this regard, the Commission also should consider how best the people of Northern Ireland may be consulted directly, given that simple majorities do not work in a divided society.

1.2 On future government

It is evident from the views submitted to the Commission that a parliamentary system of government based on the Westminster model, with its emphasis on majority rule, is not a suitable model for the governing of this fundamentally divided society.

In Northern Ireland, as currently constituted, notions which may be discarded are that:

- Northern Ireland is like any other part of the United Kingdom.

- The communities in Northern Ireland will agree to independence.
- The United Kingdom will withdraw from Northern Ireland under pressure of violence.
- The Republic of Ireland will renounce the aim of Irish unity.
- Irish unity is a realistic prospect in the foreseeable future.
  It also appeared from what we heard and read that:
- Majority rule in Northern Ireland, whether simple or proportionate, is not currently a viable proposition. The nationalist community has no obligation to agree to it and has the critical mass to prevent its imposition.
- The unionist community will not accept an administration for Northern Ireland that gives an executive role to anyone outside the United Kingdom.

The Commission further noted that the representative political voices of the nationalist tradition, North and South, without exception recognize that any agreement is achievable and viable only if it has the consent of both traditions in Ireland.

The task of creating a government for Northern Ireland within the limits described above should not be beyond the realm of the possible and the practicable. In essence, we consider that — provided that Irish nationalism is legally recognized in Northern Ireland (see *recommendation 1.3*) — a government of Northern Ireland should be put in place, based on the principle that each community has *an equal voice in making and executing the laws or a veto on their execution, and equally shares administrative authority*.[2] This government should be free to discuss and negotiate its relationships, institutional and other, with the government of the Republic of Ireland.

In these circumstances, immediate changes in the constitutional status of Northern Ireland or in Articles 2 and 3 of the Irish Constitution are unnecessary: in the future, any change in the constitutional status of Northern Ireland would require the consent of the Northern Ireland government, constituted on the basis of the principles proposed, and the consent of the people of Northern Ireland.

1.3 On the legal recognition of nationalism

We were impressed by one submission which stressed that an interim step should be 'recognition of the nationalist community in a legal sense'.[3] This, it is argued, could start a process which would change thinking in both communities.[4]

So far, the law and authorities in Northern Ireland and the British government, while accepting expressions of Irish identity and the right to work by peaceful means for Irish unity, have only tolerated such expressions of and aspirations towards nationalism. Their exercise has never been granted any form of recognition in domestic law.

'Parity of esteem' between the two communities should not only be an ideal. It ought to be given legal approval, promoted and protected, in various ways which should be considered. Such recognition could be made operational at the highest level by an Act of Parliament. We recommend that the government moves to examine the feasibility of drafting such legislation explicitly to recognize Irish nationalism in Northern Ireland in relevant ways.

Practical aspects of this matter are already part of Irish law, such as the right for people from Northern Ireland to choose dual citizenship, vote in the Republic, use Irish passports, and so on.

We hope that, as understood in this manner, self-determination for Irish nationalists would become more acceptable. In this regard, the importance of the border is already diminishing as a result of the integration process of the European Community.

This would be a future-oriented concession, recognizing the role of a constructive nationalism within Northern Ireland. It would be a kind of constitutional change without altering the status of the territory — only of that of its population in constitutional and international law.

It should be stressed that if this parity of esteem is to be achieved, the legal recognition of Irish nationalism should not mean the diminution of 'Britishness' for unionists.

1.4 On the training of politicians

We endorse the proposal put to us for an expanded programme of education and training for political leadership.[5] It was pointed out that countries like the USA, Germany and Sweden have privately and publicly funded training programmes for politicians. Such training should be cross-community in nature and be tailored both to present and prospective politicians; being trained in this way should be part of the commitment undertaken by those entering politics, and they should be financially compensated for it. It should include information about other democratic systems, and particularly those representing pluralism at its best; briefings on economics, the environment and other issues from relevant boards and government departments; community relations training — for example, how to counteract sectarianism; effective political discussion skills, the eradication of prejudice and conflict management.

1.5 On the position of Sinn Féin

There was widespread agreement that any settlement that which had entirely excluded Sinn Féin from the negotiating process would be neither lasting nor stable, and that some way had to be found to involve the party in future talks. However, in most cases this view was stated only in general terms, without making specific either the form in which Sinn Féin might be involved, or at which level or stage this should be (see also *recommendation 2.2*).

Many submissions urged that Sinn Féin's claim to be as representative as any other political party should be tested by accepted democratic norms, and that if it did genuinely aspire to function as a constitutional party, it should be given a helping hand over the hurdle of violence.[6] Even among some Protestants, there was a grudging acknowledgment that Sinn Féin would have to be involved eventually.[7] However, almost all the authors of submissions and presenters at hearings felt that, before Sinn Féin could earn a seat at the negotiating table, it would have to renounce its justification of the use of violence.

We believe that marginalizing Sinn Féin in Northern Ireland by means of the broadcasting ban, excluding it from local council committees and other activities, and removing funding from community groups in the areas where it is strongest, only plays into the hands of those who prefer the use of violence,[8] and is a policy that should be reconsidered. We therefore recommend that the government open informal channels of communication with Sinn Féin with a view to testing the party's commitment to the constitutional process, without resort to or justification of violence.

We also believe that the broadcasting ban in the Republic should be reconsidered.

Law, Justice and Security

2.1 On the need for public debate about reform

The words 'justice' and 'security' as they relate to 'law and order' are particularly controversial in a society divided by political violence. Given this background, we readily endorse a suggestion that key organizations in Northern Irish society — such as Churches, public service bodies, trade unions and businesses — should be challenged to 'each create a working group to look at how their particular organization could contribute to an improvement of law and order with a view to ensuring justice'.[9]

2.2 On reducing the violence

Clearly the single most important and most difficult task for law enforcement in Northern Ireland is the reduction and eventual elimination of political violence. None of the submissions we read and heard believed that a 'military solution' could achieve that. Many believed, often with great reluctance, that the way forward lay in the eventual involvement of the paramilitary organizations in any peace-seeking process.[10]

It is difficult to see how talks with the paramilitaries could be brought about, given the universally felt sense of revulsion at their atrocities. In the majority of submissions touching on this issue, an extended cessation of violence was the *sine qua non* for any such talks with either the IRA or its loyalist counterparts.[11]

In practice, any involvement of paramilitary organizations in a ceasefire and talks might best be handled by non-governmental agencies,[12] and a clear distinction would have to be made between talks on the constitutional future, which should involve constitutional political parties, and peace talks to bring the conflict to an end, which might involve the paramilitaries.

A number of contributors suggested that there was a need for confidence-building measures to reduce the violence by the security forces and paramilitaries alike. In this regard we endorse the proposal from a mediation group we met during the oral hearings that the security forces and the IRA each should make exploratory unilateral moves towards reducing the violence. Moves from the IRA could be announced publicly or conveyed to the security establishment through intermediaries, in the expectation that a response would be forthcoming. It is vital that such moves should be signalled distinctly and that clear, albeit informal, channels of communication be opened. This group said that the British army claims to have a lengthy list of possible de-escalatory measures, which could become relevant in such a circumstance. As they were explained to us, a series of such steps could provide a means of reducing republican violence, thus taking much of the excuse away for loyalist violence. The signalling of intentions by each side could come close to negotiations.[13]

In the light of the above, we recommend that the British Government — either directly or through intermediaries — open informal discussions with Sinn Féin, in the first instance, with a view to persuading the IRA first to move towards a de-escalation in the level of violence and eventually to a ceasefire that would lead to a drastic reduction in the number of security forces deployed in Northern Ireland and/or their return to barracks.

2.3 On policing

As with political structures, the key question about policing is how to ensure its acceptance by the nationalist community, given that community's traditional suspicion of the RUC as the arm of a unionist state. Unless genuine representatives of the nationalist community are given an executive and administrative role in relation to policing, they cannot take responsibility for it.[14] It is unreasonable to expect a police force made up largely of members of one community to be acceptable to the other community in a divided society like Northern Ireland.[15]

We believe that nationalist support for and significant recruitment to the RUC will take place only in the context of new political structures for the region, in which power and authority go hand in hand with responsibility.

In the interim — while being conscious of the extremely difficult and dangerous work the RUC is currently forced to undertake — we suggest that a study should be initiated into alternative decentralized and multi-level models of policing, as exist in most other European countries outside the UK and Ireland.

We welcome the recent appointment of an Independent Commissioner for Holding Centres. Other suggested reforms which we endorse are:

(a) The Ombudsman's office should take over the functions of the Independent Commission for Police Complaints, which does not enjoy public confidence. Senior RUC officers told us that they would welcome a totally independent complaints body. Such functions eventually could be extended to deal with the army and even undercover forces.[16]

(b) The immediate introduction of at least visual recording of police interviews to protect the right of both the suspect under questioning and the police officer doing the questioning; also the extension of the scheme under which 'lay visitors' inspect cells in police stations to the three holding centres where terrorist suspects are detained.[17]

(c) Improved mechanisms for communicating and mediating between the security forces, particularly the RUC, and local people and community leaders, about grievances and ideas on more locally accountable policing.[18] We particularly commend for further study the work of an informal complaints system in Derry, and an example of how sensitive leadership and 'community policing' can improve relations between police and the public in a deprived, nationalist area of Belfast.[19]

(d) The RUC should be relieved of the responsibility for making decisions on the routing of Orange and other controversial marches, which reinforces nationalist perception of the police as an anti-nationalist force.[20]

Given the widespread references in submissions and hearings to harassment, particularly of young nationalist men, by the security forces, and the equally wide recognition that such practices serve to increase recruitment to the paramilitaries,[21] we also recommend to the RUC Chief Constable and the General Officer Commanding the army that immediate steps should be taken to resolve this problem.

2.4 On strengthening the protection of human rights

A Bill of Rights for Northern Ireland is strongly favoured in many submissions across the political spectrum.[22]

Most of the proposals favour the early incorporation of the European Convention on Human Rights of 1950, with later amendments and additions. The Commission notes that, for Northern Ireland, as elsewhere, human rights are no longer essentially matters of domestic jurisdiction for the sovereign power. However, both the United Kingdom and the

Republic of Ireland are still among the few states which have not incorporated international human rights norms into their own constitutional and legal order. Given this background, several alternative approaches to the proposals for a new Bill of Rights suggest themselves, even if they are limited, as most of them are, to the special needs of Northern Ireland.

The Commission is of the opinion that a reform in the field of human rights is overdue and should be undertaken as soon as possible, bearing in mind the widely felt urgency for special action for Northern Ireland, and the apparently uncontroversial nature of the general idea.

To enact a Bill of Rights for Northern Ireland in the form of incorporating the European Convention, making it the law of the land, and accompanied by a review of the available domestic remedies, is relatively simple. This is strongly recommended, and it need not be made a bargaining-point under the principle that 'nothing is agreed until everything is agreed'.

2.5 On discrimination

On the subject of political and religious discrimination, we recognize that, in the words of one leading academic lawyer's submission, the 1989 Fair Employment Act is one of the few pieces of legislation with 'the potential to heal wounds in Northern Ireland'.[23] We endorse the recommendation of the Standing Advisory Commission on Human Rights, that this law's provisions should be extended to protect not just people's employment rights, but also their rights in the provision of goods and services.

2.6 On criminal justice

We also endorse a number of the proposals, put forward by the Committee on the Administration of Justice and others, for improving the fairness and accountability of the criminal justice system in Northern Ireland. In doing this, we are concerned that abuses and distortions in the justice system have been a factor in alienating people, particularly in deprived areas, from the institutions of the state in Northern Ireland and making the arguments in favour of the use of violence more attractive. However, we also recognize that, during an extended period of terrorist violence, any state has the right to take legal measures to safeguard the security of its citizens. We therefore endorse the following proposals:

(a) That the single judge in the juryless Diplock courts, who currently decides all issues of law and fact, should be joined by one or two judicial or lay assessors, as is the practice in other jurisdictions where jury trials are not the legal norm.
(b) That the inquest process in Northern Ireland requires reform because of the long delays in bringing cases (particularly those involving killings in disputed circumstances) to court, and other inadequacies.

(c) The introduction of a charge of manslaughter in cases involving the intentional use of lethal force. Because of the absence of such a charge in these cases, it has proved impossible to secure convictions where the use of some force was permissible, but the use of lethal force was excessive in the circumstances.

(d) The suggestion for an independent appeals tribunal within the criminal justice system in Northern Ireland. This could take the form of an independent appeal commissioner, who would investigate cases of people claiming to have been unfairly convicted, and request new evidence or question the original evidence. In appropriate cases, the commissioner should have the power to refer matter back to the courts.[24]

(e) The ending of indeterminate sentences for prisoners under eighteen convicted of terrorist offences, and a re-examination of the life sentence review system to make it more open and even-handed.

Economic and Social Issues

3.1 On economic co-operation with the Republic

We endorse the numerous submissions in favour of greater cross-border co-operation in all kinds of economic activity,[25] and we propose that the creation of an appropriate cross-border economic institution should be an immmediate priority of the Irish Government and the new Northern Ireland Government, set up in accordance with *recommendation 1.2* in the political and constitutional section. In the meantime, in view of the urgent demand for economic improvement both North and South, we recommend that all possibilities of economic co-operation for mutual advantage should be officially encouraged.

3.2 On a strategic regional plan

We consider that the proposal put forward by groups, ranging from the Northern Ireland Chamber of Commerce and Industry to the Northern Ireland Voluntary Trust, for a strategic regional plan, embracing both social and economic goals, should be pursued vigorously and without delay.

3.3 On tackling deprivation

We believe that the government's 'Targeting Social Need' programme has the potential to make a major contribution to tackling deprivation in Northern Ireland. However, it needs to be given higher priority in the allocation of new resources; clearer goals should be set; the responsibility for monitoring its progress must be strengthened, and the whole programme should be pursued with greater vigour and urgency.[26]

3.4 On community development

We welcome the government's recent statement of support for community development in Northern Ireland. This should be backed up with adequate resources and funding policies which reflect the priorities of the communities themselves.[27] We also recommend that the 'political vetting' of community groups[28] should be replaced by procedures which ensure strict accountability in the use of funds. What is important is that public funding should be used for the benefit of the communities involved, and not for political purposes.

We were impressed by the arguments put forward for the empowerment of people through the establishment of locally based community development trusts.[29] These were defined as independent, non-profit-making organizations, bringing together the public, private and voluntary sectors with the people of a local area in order to renew it 'physically, socially and in spirit'. We endorse and urge support for both community development trust models outlined during our hearings: the small local agencies proposed by a group of women in west Belfast, and the larger trusts already successfully in operation for a number of years in Derry.[30]

3.5 On women in politics

The Commission believes that women have an important contribution to make to the political life of Northern Ireland and to the search for a settlement. On the one hand, this will require action to remove the barriers which exclude so many women from formal politics:[31]

- The political parties should set targets for the number of women MPs and local councillors representing them. The effectiveness of such a strategy is illustrated by the experience of Norway and other Scandinavian countries.
- The Northern Ireland Office should set targets for the number of women on public bodies.
- The political parties should give higher priority to the social issues that are of particular concern to many women.

On the other hand, support and recognition should be given to the work that women already do in civil society in Northern Ireland. We endorse the demand for adequate and secure funding for the important work of women's groups, much of it done on a cross-community basis.[32] A key issue for women with children is the provision of child care, which is at a low level in Northern Ireland compared to other European countries. We support calls for a comprehensive childcare strategy covering both preschool and school-age children.[33]

3.6 On poverty and social security

The Commission wishes to draw attention to the evidence it received of
the failure of social security benefits and the social fund to prevent poverty
among a significant proportion of the population in Northern Ireland.[34]
Given the relatively high cost of fuel in the region, it also adds its voice to
those calling for full compensation to social security recipients for the proposed imposition (after the 1994 budget) of VAT on domestic fuel.

3.7 On integrated housing

In response to a number of strongly argued submissions, we suggest that
the Housing Executive should examine the feasibility of setting up a number of 'pilot' integrated housing schemes,[35] with subsidized rentals and
other support mechanisms, in order to encourage those who wish to be
involved in the necessary process of reversing the drastic segregation of
housing in Northern Ireland to do so.

Religious, Cultural and Other Issues

4.1 On the Catholic Church in Ireland

In the light of the widespread and deep fear and mistrust we encountered
among Northern Protestants about the Catholic nature of Southern society and the intentions of Southern people with regard to Northern
Ireland,[36] we believe that the government of the Republic of Ireland must
move — and be seen to move — to make good the claim in the 1916
Declaration that it cherishes all the children of the Irish nation equally.

Recalling the Irish Hierarchy's declaration to the New Ireland Forum
that it did not wish to have the moral teaching of the Catholic Church
become the criterion of constitutional law or to have its principles embodied in civil law, and its reference to the need for a balanced examination of
the role of the Church in a changing Ireland, we urge that this examination — and a public debate on it — should take place now. To this end we
suggest the setting up, by a university or other reputable independent
body, of a wide-ranging public inquiry into the role of the Catholic
Church in Ireland.

More specifically, the Commission urges the Irish government to move
quickly to remove the perceived threat to the existence of the Republic's
only Protestant-run general teaching hospital, the Adelaide, and points to
the effect such a threat has in reinforcing the poor image of the Republic
among Northern Protestants.[37]

4.2 On Churches and confidence-building

In the light of the same fears, we echo the request by the Inter-Church Group on Faith and Politics to the Catholic Hierarchy, to consider such confidence-building steps as: offering communion to 'inter-church' couples when requested; altering the rules for mixed marriages; and not putting obstacles in the way of those parents who wish to send their children to integrated schools. We also add our support to the proposal first made in the *Violence in Ireland* report, that the Churches should set up a Christian Centre for Social Investigation to research, sponsor debate and publish material on the religious divides in Irish society.[38]

4.3 On the Protestant Churches in Northern Ireland

We believe that the Protestant Churches should re-examine — and revise, where they can in conscience — any of their formulations that give offence to Catholics.[39] We draw their attention to the criticisms of Protestant schoolchildren about the involvement of ministers of religion in party politics.[40] We recommend that they look again at the recommendations of the *Violence in Ireland* report, with special reference to their role in encouraging contacts between mainly Protestant and Catholic schools, noting the view expressed strongly at the Initiative '92 schools' assemblies that pupils wanted mixed religious education classes, where questions of belief, culture and identity could be discussed frankly and openly as they were in the assemblies' working groups.

   We also urge those Church members involved in the Orange Order and other similar bodies to use their influence to persuade those organizations to consider imaginative alternatives — such as summer festivals — to marches along 'traditional' routes through areas which are now predominantly Catholic.

4.4 On Churches and community understanding

We believe that Protestant Church leaders, clergy and community leaders should acknowledge, on behalf of their community, that the Catholic community suffered discrimination in Northern Ireland for many years.[41] They should encourage Protestants to see themselves as Irish people with British citizenship[42] and take pride in the Christianity and culture they share with their Catholic neighbours. Equally, we believe that Catholic Church leaders, clergy and community leaders should give credit, on behalf of their community, to the Protestant community for those changes in attitude that have taken place: it is not adequate, for example, for nationalists to say to unionists, when they agree to some form of power-sharing, that 'the bus has moved on since 1974'.[43] Catholic leaders should encourage their community to view the emblems of 'Britishness' which they dislike, as part of the culture of their fellow Irish men and women, and respect them as such.

4.5 On integrated education

While not pretending that integrated education by itself can solve the problems of a divided society, we are convinced, from the wide representation of submissions in favour of it, that integrated schooling at all levels — from nursery to sixth-form — is a valuable aid to the kind of reconciliation that necessarily will have to accompany any political and other accommodations.[44] We suggest to the Catholic Hierarchy that it should follow the example of the English Catholic bishops and investigate the possibility of setting up 'shared schools' as part of the process of ecumenism.

We also urge the government to ensure at this time of spending cuts that the vital work of the Education for Mutual Understanding (EMU) programme is properly funded and further developed; also that the weakening of traditionally mixed rural communities through the closure of their primary schools is minimized.

4.6 On school projects for understanding

Having been impressed by the high level of debate at the schools' assemblies, the Commission urges a range of projects to be initiated to stimulate further such contact and debate. We note with approval the submissions suggesting a schools-based heritage collection project on the model of the one carried out in the Republic in the 1950s, to bring children together in a search for their shared and different local traditions;[45] the proposals for various innovative educational institutions, from shared nursery schools and a cultural centre on the Belfast 'peace line'[46] to shared sixth-form colleges;[47] and the proposal for a new all-Ireland 'Friendship University', a joint venture between the public and private sectors, to be situated close to the border.

4.7 On a common Irish history and culture

Once again, using the arguments and wishes expressed at the schools' assemblies, we recommend that a common Irish history course be introduced at all schools in Northern Ireland and, eventually, in the whole of Ireland. The Commission was made aware of a real desire by many Northern Protestants to regain their sense of Irishness, and to reacquaint themselves with Irish history, culture and the language,[48] which they believe have been expropriated by nationalists as political weapons. We believe that Irish culture has a great potential for uniting people in Northern Ireland, and urge all its proponents to ensure that it is made unthreatening and attractive to Northern Protestants.

Notes

1. The idea of a commission came from Sir Kenneth Bloomfield. Our proposed body would be set up in consultation with the Irish Government and have a much broader brief.
2. This proposal did not come directly from any single submission. However, its inspiration was the strong emphasis on the need for absolute parity of esteem between the two communities in Northern Ireland in a number of submissions;for example, the Corrymeela Community; Mr Charles Murphy; Dr Brian Gaffney; Professor Bernard Cullen; Mr Jim Hanna.
3. Confidential submission from a prominent Catholic nationalist lawyer.
4. It also appears to be in sympathy with the ideas of the SDLP leader, Mr John Hume, in his defence of the SDLP's proposals at the inter-party talks, which he said were aimed at giving 'minimal' recognition to the nationalist identity in Northern Ireland, together with strong recognition to the unionist identity (address at St Thomas's Church of Ireland, Belfast, reported in *The Irish Times*, 10.5.93).
5. Dr Mari Fitzduff, Dungannon Community Relations Workshop.
6. Mr Michael Farrell.
7. For example, Very Rev. Victor Griffin; Mrs Sheila Chillingworth; Archbishop Robin Eames; Mr Roy Montgomery; Professor Brice Dickson; Senator Gordon Wilson; Dr Duncan Morrow.
8. Mr Michael Farrell.
9. Ms Maggie Beirne.
10. For example, North Belfast women; Bloody Sunday Initiative; Dr Samuel Poyntz; Pax Christi Ireland; Senator Gordon Wilson; Mr Michael Farrell.
11. For example, Archbishop Robin Eames.
12. Mr Eugene O'Shea.
13. See chapter 6 for further details.
14. Rev. Brian Lennon; Northern Ireland Religious for Justice and Peace; Corrymeela Community.
15. Rev. Raymond Murray; Mr Frank Curran.
16. Professor Brice Dickson.
17. Mr Ian Paisley Jnr.
18. North Belfast women.
19. Mr Douglas Hegney.
20. A senior RUC officer in a private meeting.
21. For example, Little Sisters of the Assumption.
22. For example, Standing Advisory Commission for Human Rights; Committee on the Administration of Justice; Committee for a New Ireland; Community of the Peace People; and many individual submissions.
23. Professor Brice Dickson.
24. Mr Ian Paisley Jnr.
25. For example, Dr George Quigley; Northern Ireland Chamber of Commerce and Industry; Confederation of British Industry (NI); Co-operation North; and many individual submissions.
26. Mr Paul Sweeney.
27. Northern Ireland Voluntary Trust; Dr Ken Logue.
28. Mrs Elizabeth Groves.
29. The Springfield Group (Ms May Blood, Ms Kate Kelly, Mrs Geraldine O'Regan).
30. For example, Inner City Trust; Holywell Trust (see submissions by Mr Kevin McCaul).
31. E. Rooney and M. Woods, *Women, Community and Politics in N. Ireland* (University of Ulster, 1992).
32. Equal Opportunities Commission for N.Ireland; Northern Ireland Voluntary Trust;

Northern Ireland Women's Aid Federation; and many women's groups and individual women.

33. Playboard.

34. For example, North Belfast women; Ballybeen Women's Centre.

35. For example, Sisters of the Cross and Passion; Mr D. Gordon Kelly.

36. For example, Rev. Robert Dickinson; Presbyterian Church, Church and Government Committee; Rev. R.S.Ross; Mr Wilfred Grundle; Inter-Church Group on Faith and Politics; Mr David Bleakley.

37. Mr Desmond Smith; Very Rev. Victor Griffin.

38. Also Mr Brian Lambkin.

39. Rev. Patrick McCafferty.

40. For example, Cookstown High School, lower-sixth form group.

41. Inter-Church Group on Faith and Politics.

42. Mr Sam McAughtry.

43. Phrase used by a Northern Ireland Office official when discussing the inter-party talks.

44. All Children Together; Foyle Trust for Integrated Education; Windmill Integrated Primary School; and many individual submissions.

45. Dr Bob Curran.

46. Sister Genevieve and Mr Paddy Fleming.

47. Irish Council of Churches (from *Violence in Ireland* report).

48. For example, Dr Bob Curran; Cookstown High School, lower sixth-form group; Mr Sam McAughtry; Mr Jackie Redpath.

Part II:
The Citizens

CHAPTER 11

Submissions' Summary:
Politics and the Constitution II

A total of 554 submissions were made to Initiative '92's citizens enquiry, representing the collective work of approximately 3000 people in Northern Ireland and beyond. In line with the publicity material put out by Initiative '92, this summary of those submissions will be in four major chapters: one on politics and the constitution; one on law and justice; one covering social and economic concerns; and the last on culture, identity, religion and other issues. In rounded percentage figures, 54 per cent were on politics and the constitution, 10 per cent on law and justice, and 18 per cent on social and economic concerns and religious, cultural and other issues respectively (religion accounting for just over 3 per cent). However, large numbers of submissions covered more than one of these questions, as indicated in the subject index and the cross-references.

Devolution

The political structure that attracted the greatest number of proposals (49) was some form of devolved government on the basis of power-sharing, proportionality or weighted majorities, usually with an institutional Irish dimension. However, this tended to be favoured more by unionists than by nationalists.

SIR KENNETH BLOOMFIELD, the former head of the Northern Ireland Civil Service, says he has no doubt that 'the optimal solution would be to restore in Northern Ireland a devolved local legislature with some form of executive to it, running the 'old' Northern Ireland Departments'. Such an institution would have to command 'widespread acceptance across the community'.

In the face of repeated declarations from the two unionist parties that 'institutionalized power-sharing' would be unacceptable to them, he suggests that the 1974 arrangements 'do not represent the only available model for broadly based government and administration in the province'. However, he stresses his opinion that the SDLP is 'highly unlikely, in any foreseeable circumstances, to accept the recreation of any 'top table' of government at which only the representatives of the majority would sit, whatever safeguards for minority interests might otherwise be built in'.

On the question of what kind of powers such a devolved institution would have, Sir Kenneth quoted from the 1972 British government Green Paper that 'law and order powers' were 'fundamental to the operation of anything which can be characterized as a government', and that 'the more real and pressing problems are, the more important it is to force representatives of the community concerned to face up to them'.

In the event of the constitutional parties not being able to agree on such a devolved institution, Sir Kenneth suggests that a Royal Commission-type body should make urgent recommendations for the restoration of 'an elected and democratic tier of administration below the level of central government, and with broadly comparable powers to those exercised by local government in Great Britain'.

However, he does not agree with the argument in the 1970 Macrory Report in favour of a single elected local government-type body for the whole of Northern Ireland. 'If it should prove too difficult to share power, then the answer may well be to diffuse power and to build in the strongest possible safeguards against any abuse of power by elected majorities in any part of the province.'

DR T.K. WHITAKER, the former Secretary of the Republic's Department of Finance, is also concerned about the need to qualify majority rule. 'It is pretty widely accepted amongst unionists that simple majority rule, as in the old Stormont, cannot obtain in any future assembly or parliament in Northern Ireland', he says.

He believes that the normal government/opposition system is healthier than power-sharing, which at best can be only transitory because 'it confines opposition to the privacy of the cabinet room rather than ensuring that issues are debated in parliament in the hearing of press and public'. He suggests 'a qualification to simple majority rule which combines two safeguards for the minority: (a) the need for a weighted — say 70 per cent — majority for a narrow range of major matters, and (b) an advisory committee for each Department, chaired by the Minister, on which the political parties would be represented according to their parliamentary strength.'

Dr Whitaker emphasizes the long-term potential of proportional representation, which he calls 'a great political asset of Northern Ireland, not so far shared by Great Britain'. 'In a less tense political situation it could produce a more realistic (and therefore fragmented) representation of the community, opening up the possibility of various parliamentary groups coming together, even across the political divide, to form an alternative government.' He is one of the scores of contributors who recommended that, given the difficult community and security pressures in Northern Ireland, the rights of the individual should have the special protection of a Bill of Rights.

Dr Whitaker says that the Anglo-Irish Agreement should be no more than a transient arrangement on the way to an acceptable system of devolution: 'It would be neither just nor practicable to exclude unionists for ever from having a direct and proper say in managing the affairs of Northern Ireland.'

He also points out that by signing the Anglo-Irish Agreement, registered with the United Nations as an international instrument, the Republic of Ireland has bound itself to the principle of Irish unity becoming possible only with the consent of a majority in Northern Ireland.

Logically, one consequence should be a readiness to at least rewrite in aspirational terms Articles 2 and 3 of our 1937 Constitution. This would require a referendum and no one could be quite sure of the outcome of a campaign confused by emotional irredentist rhetoric. It is safer, and should suffice, to recognize that these Articles have been significantly qualified by acceptance of the majority-consent principle.

Dr Whitaker, calling himself 'a peaceful and patient Irishman' who wants to leave the door open to an eventual coming together of Irish people in a new constitutional framework, stresses that the spiral of violence should impel Northern Ireland's politicians to arrive at a political arrangement that would enable the two communities to live together peacefully and co-operatively. This should take place while

leaving open the possibility of a significant number of either community being persuaded at some time in the future to change their mind on the constitutional issue. It is important that any new political arrangement should have this built-in potential for evolution, as well as for additional transfer of powers. It would be wrong to interpret acceptance of the majority-consent principle as implying abandonment forever of the ideal of Irish unity in some form. The politics of urging moves towards unity should be as legitimate as the politics of consolidating UK membership. On the other hand, evolution should be just that — it should not be allowed to boil over disruptively. The question of preferred constitutional status need be tested by referendum only every 20 years or so, and all members of a devolved assembly should swear allegiance to the existing constitution [of Northern Ireland] until it is validly changed.

Immediate pursuit of a widely accepted political arrangement for Northern Ireland should not be impeded by arguments implying that this is a 'failed' concept, or that the wider London-Belfast-Dublin relationship must first be satisfactorily settled. What brings peace to Northern Ireland should be the overriding consideration for all concerned. The aims of any particular political party should not be pressed to the point of precluding the accommodation essential to a workable compromise. The two sovereign governments, for their part, should be disposed in principle towards accepting whatever political arrangement may be arrived at by the Northern Ireland constitutional parties. They should see their role as that of overseeing from the sideline the effective and equitable working of any devolved system. With such a system in place, the Maryfield secretariat, whose symbolism was always provocative, could be closed down. It might make for political stability, as well as denying any shred of justification to guerrillas, if the consent of the two governments was confirmed by plebiscite in Ireland, North and South; such a referendum might provide a promising opportunity in the Republic to amend Articles 2 and 3.

The PRESBYTERIAN CHURCH'S CHURCH AND GOVERNMENT COMMITTEE, which includes 1993's outgoing moderator, Dr John Dunlop, stresses the importance of confidence-building measures within Northern Ireland, between North and South, and between the Republic and Britain, warning that 'political strategies which are not accompanied by or even preceded by these measures may not succeed'. (The need for such confidence-building measures, particularly between the two Northern communities, is a regular theme in submissions.)

In welcoming continuing assurances that Northern Ireland would remain part of the UK until a majority wishes otherwise, the Committee also warns that 'the political, financial and security implications of a British government withdrawal would be calamitous for the whole of Ireland'.

The Committee sees the challenge in Ireland as being essentially 'one of finding some way in which we can move from an "I win — you lose" scenarios to ones marked by co-operation, mutual affirmation, honour and respect, in which we are all winners'. At present nationalists (in both parts of Ireland) are not seen and heard to be concerned about the well-being of unionists, and the same is true of unionists' lack of concern for the well-being of nationalists. The Committee regrets the one-sided concern expressed in Article 4(c) of the Anglo-Irish Agreement, which declares that: 'The Conference shall be the framework within which the Irish government may put forward views and proposals on the modalities of bringing about devolution in Northern Ireland, in so far as they relate to the interests of the minority community.'

The Committee points out that the system of church government in the Presbyterian Church (by far the largest Protestant church in Northern Ireland) is so concerned about the protection of minorities that a majority decision in the ruling General Assembly is not enough to change the Church's constitution; it also has to be approved by a majority of the second, local level of the Church — the presbyteries.

In recommending a devolved government involving the representatives of both communities in 'the politics of co-operation', the Committee also suggests that a second chamber, composed of 'experienced people nominated by a wide range of bodies within Northern Ireland' with initiating, scrutiny and delaying powers, might be helpful. 'It could be that the second chamber might be the place into which some input could be invited from people from the Republic of Ireland. A similar input might be invited from Northern Ireland people into the deliberations of the Senate in the Republic of Ireland.'

The Committee also urges that, in the event of Direct Rule and the Anglo-Irish Agreement continuing, and 'if the Irish government represents the interests of the nationalist community at the Inter-Governmental Conference and the British government is impartial, some means must be found to represent the interests of the unionist community'. (See also Culture, Religion, Identity and Education: Identity.)

THE METHODIST CHURCH'S COUNCIL ON SOCIAL WELFARE also favours 'some form of devolution which will command the support and approval of a majority of both the majority and the minority. A corollary of that support must be a willingness to share in the responsibilities and risks of playing a full part in the running and security of the whole community.' The Council believes that such a system of government, in which both traditions are involved and with which they can both identify, is an urgent necessity. 'The way forward may be to seek means whereby the two traditions could achieve a common allegiance not only within Northern Ireland but also within a wider context.' It says that it has set up a working party on pluralism to consider what policies should be adopted in both Irish jurisdictions so that all people on the island should have the same rights, privileges, responsibilities and opportunities.

The NORTHERN CONSENSUS GROUP (NCG), a group of professional people from both main traditions in Northern Ireland, believes that 'perhaps the greatest impediment to political progress in Northern Ireland is lack of political confidence'. This was evident among influential people on both sides of the community divide, with certain nationalist politicians advocating an executive role for the Republic in the government of Northern Ireland, and some unionists advocating the integration of the region into the UK. 'The only way forward for Northern Ireland is for both traditions to have enough self-confidence to participate in a devolved government in which responsibility is shared by the two traditions. It is notable that there appear to be substantial numbers of members of all the parties to the recent talks who share this view', the Group continues.

The group urges the British government and the other parties involved in the latest talks to end the secrecy surrounding them, and to publish an account of the proceedings, including the papers submitted, so that 'an informed public debate can take place'.

We also question whether the policy that 'nothing is agreed until everything is agreed' should continue. While this may have been an appropriate negotiating tactic at the beginning of the talks, it has resulted in six months of talking with nothing to show for it. Surely it would have been better to have some agreements at least in principle (if this was possible) that could be built upon in future talks.

The Group also wonders why the Anglo-Irish Inter-governmental Conference was required to convene while the talks were in progress.

If the aim of the Anglo-Irish Agreement is to produce an agreed, presumably devolved government for Northern Ireland, the provisions of the Agreement should not be used to impede progress towards this aim. Since British and Irish Ministers were meeting weekly during the talks process, it is difficult to see why a formal meeting of the Conference had to take place, except for symbolic reasons, which should have no place in matters of such importance.

The Group believes that the unionist opposition to Articles 2 and 3 of the Irish Constitution, which seemed to be a major obstacle to agreement at the talks, was 'disproportionate to the importance of these Articles'.

To have a constitutional imperative which it has neither the desire nor the power to enforce must be a source of embarrassment for the Irish government. It may also be a source of frustration to some Northern nationalists. It is difficult to see why it should cause any practical problems for unionists. Why should the constitution of what they regard as another country be of concern to unionists? It is sometimes suggested that Articles 2 and 3 give legitimacy to republican terrorism. It is surely naive to suppose that repeal of these Articles would influence terrorism in any way. Perhaps the biggest disadvantage of Articles 2 and 3 is that they provide an excuse for some unionist politicians to obstruct the progress of inter-party talks. However, if Articles 2 and 3 were repealed, it is likely that these politicians would find another excuse to impede progress.

We urge all politicians to ignore Articles 2 and 3 and concentrate on the real issues. Clearly the Articles will have to be repealed or amended at some time, but in the meantime they should not be an obstacle to attempts to reach agreement.

The Northern Consensus Group is critical of the SDLP's proposal at the talks that an Irish government representative (and an EC representative) should have an executive role in the administration of Northern Ireland. They surmise that Northern nationalists would prefer to participate in the government of the region through their own elected representatives, rather than through Irish government (and EC) representatives, who would have received no electoral mandate from the people of Northern Ireland and would not be answerable to their elected representatives in any parliament.

We also question the motives of the SDLP leadership in going into the talks with a proposal which they knew would be unacceptable to the other parties, and apparently refusing to move from this position during the talks. We also question whether the SDLP still adheres to the Anglo-Irish Agreement, which clearly envisages a devolved government consisting of elected representatives from Northern Ireland, with a reduction in the influence of the Anglo-Irish Conference when such a government comes into operation.

DR CHRISTOPHER McGIMPSEY and MR MICHAEL McGIMPSEY, the former an honorary secretary of the Ulster Unionist Party and both members of that party's team at the 1992 inter-party talks, state that 'mutual ignorance and suspicion between nationalists and unionists is the tragedy of Northern Ireland. Identification of common interest and a mutual understanding of each other's position is a necessary prerequisite to political progress and co-operation.'

They believe that the real problem for nationalists 'is their inability to accept the legitimacy of the Irish unionist identity', which means in Northern Ireland the deep desire to be and stay British. In this, unionists are 'entitled to the same esteem as Irish nationalists in either jurisdiction'. In failing to recognize that unionists will never consent to a united Ireland, or to any 'process or settlement which would precipitate movement towards a united Ireland', Irish nationalists are making 'a fundamental and enduring mistake'.

For unionists, the union with Britain is 'inviolate'. 'To countenance an independent 32-county Irish Republic is for unionists, by definition, impossible. If that can be accepted, then all matters pertaining to a working arrangement are open for discussion and we will consider any reasonable and workable suggestions.'

The McGimpseys say that the recent history of failed settlements, from Sunningdale in 1973/74 to Hillsborough in 1985, 'demonstrates clearly that unionist involvement is an obvious prerequisite for the achievement of peace, stability and reconciliation'.

They believe that the historic breakdown in relations between unionists and nationalists

can best be overcome through the establishment of (a) a benevolent, liberal and pluralistic democracy in Northern Ireland in which both communities share; which disadvantages neither and which fully protects all individuals and groups; (b) a North-South mechanism to facilitate business between Belfast and Dublin administrations, in which the two could co-operate, as equals, to achieve social and economic benefits for the Irish people as a whole.

Out of the diametrically opposed dominant strands of political philosophy in Northern Ireland had come division and terrorism. 'It is the task of our political parties to break down this division and thus end the resulting violence.' It is the parties' responsibility 'to reach an accommodation to which most of the people of the province can subscribe. In other words, to find a way forward, a way of sharing the province, that can unite the people, and thus isolate the men of violence. And thereby make terrorism redundant.'

Three thousand people have died in the present 'troubles', they point out, and over 30,000 have been injured. In the United Kingdom this would be the equivalent of 100,000 dead and over one million injured.

The costs in economic terms have been a permanent recession, with 15 per cent permanently unemployed and an artificial economy where 60 per cent of those people in work are employed either directly or indirectly by the government. In addition, a substantial proportion of those at work are involved directly or indirectly with the security sector.

It is no exaggeration to say that, without the support of the British Exchequer, the economic consequences of terrorism would have been very grim indeed. And it is further no exaggeration to say that without the support of the British army in the province, the violence would be very much worse. In fact, we would be dealing with a Yugoslavia situation and a general break-down in law and order.

The McGimpseys stress the very great benefits, not only to Northern Ireland, but to the rest of Ireland and the rest of the UK as well, of an 'honourable accommodation' among the constitutional politicians. They emphasize their belief that such an accommodation can lead to a resolution of the conflict, political stability leading to economic stability and 'thereby a real increase in prosperity for all the people of this island'. The advantages of North-South co-operation are obvious, with both jurisdictions sharing common economic and social problems, notably unemployment and a peripheral location in the EC, which could benefit from a common approach. However, they warn that such co-operation cannot take place fully while the Republic retains, through Articles 2 and 3 of its Constitution, a 'harsh and irredentist claim over the people and territory of Northern Ireland'.

MR ALAN HOUSTON from east Belfast identifies an internal power-sharing assembly and executive as the second in a three-legged scheme which also has nationalist and, unusually, unionist integrationist elements. The former would see the Irish government changing Articles 2 and 3 to a long-term aspiration, in return for a guaranteed, proportional place for Northern nationalist representatives on that executive, together with a cross-border council. The latter would see a Northern Ireland Select Committee at Westminster, and all three main British parties organizing in Northern Ireland. This could be interpreted by unionists as a *quid pro quo* for more nationalist involvement in the internal government of the region.

DR FREDERICK BOAL, professor of human geography at Queen's University, Belfast, incorporates power-sharing into his 'mutuality solution', first outlined in a book in the early 1980s. He sees Northern Ireland as an overlap of the 'British' and 'Irish' realms in the archipelago, and believes that attempts to pull Northern Ireland into one of these two realms is unacceptable and unworkable. 'Northern Ireland must be developed in such a way as to give the two basic identities ('Irish' and 'British') full and equal recognition.'

He proposes the development of an autonomous Northern Ireland, with the British and Irish governments acting as guarantors of the two communities and the region governed on a power-sharing basis. However, he emphasizes that 'any solution put forward must meet with approval from *each* of the two communities, *voting separately*. Any subsequent change in constitutional arrangements for Northern Ireland must obtain majority approval from *each* of the two communities.'

Currently there is a 'British' majority in Northern Ireland. However, despite this, constitutional arrangements must be designed that give equal standing to the 'Irish' minority. Equally, if at some future date an 'Irish' majority should emerge, that majority should not be permitted unilaterally to overturn a constitutional arrangement that gave 'British'-'Irish' equality. If equality of institutions are a requirement now, when there is a 'British' majority, this same condition must apply in any circumstance where an 'Irish' majority were to emerge. The Irish nationalist position cannot eat its cake and have it at the same time.

The ULSTER DEMOCRATIC PARTY (UDP) — which is generally considered to reflect the political views of the Ulster Defence Association and whose submission is largely based on the 'Common Sense' document of the late UDA leader John McMichael — says that whatever may be the relationships between Northern Ireland and the Republic, and the Republic and Britain, 'the fundamental reality' is that 'it is the people of Northern Ireland who must work out a way of living together'. To this end, it proposes the scrapping of the Anglo-Irish Agreement; a devolved legislature and government 'based on shared power and responsibility, with proportional representation for all elections'; a written Constitution for Northern Ireland, a Bill of Rights, and a Supreme Court charged with upholding both.

We believe that the vast majority of the people of Northern Ireland support a Bill of Rights and even that political parties should be represented in government in proportion to their electoral strength. In short, it could be said that they support power-sharing in its fullest sense. It can also be inferred from the occasional policy documents produced by tendencies within the UUP and DUP that many within these parties could live with power-/responsibility-sharing.

The group claims that the leaders of both these parties, Mr James Molyneaux and Rev. Ian Paisley, now accept both a Bill of Rights and proportional representation, and, at least, a form of committee government. This puts them somewhat ahead of other UK parties, which are committed to the adversarial Westminster model.

In an oral submission, A GROUP OF FORMER LOYALIST PRISONERS say they believe that the majority of Protestants in Northern Ireland would not want a return to pre-1972 Stormont-style majority rule.

'With regard to the Protestant population, I think the days of the mass protest are over', says one. 'I don't think they will really fall for that again. It's been done in the past and nothing has changed, and they have seen that. I think they would have to be really desperate before they could mobilize them again. It would have to be that a united Ireland was in sight. People would not want a united Ireland for a whole lot of reasons, economically as well as Church-State.'

In the present day people are more worried about jobs and their incomes — bread and butter issues — and that is not being talked about.... Everyone is worried about themselves and how to survive, and there's nobody fighting for that in parliament. I think the majority of

Protestant people would agree with power-sharing. I don't think it's the bogey man that the politicians have made it. It might have been in 1973/74, but it is not any more. People accept it. Power-sharing is probably a necessity if we are going to get anywhere. I suppose the bugbear there is Sinn Féin — whether they would accept if power-sharing would be enough.

The group also believes that many Protestants would be prepared to accept the Irish government having some input into Northern Ireland's social and economic affairs, but would be opposed to any involvement in constitutional or security matters. Some kind of tripartite British-Irish-Northern Irish arrangement was suggested.

Other pro-devolutionist viewpoints — often from Church-based groups — echo Dr T.K. Whitaker's stress on weighted majorities on sensitive issues, as a brake on pure majority rule, rather than the proportionality in cabinet and committees emphasized by unionist groups.

REV. BRIAN LENNON, a Portadown-based Jesuit priest, goes further. He points out that the basic weakness of the Anglo-Irish Agreement is that Northern nationalists have no executive role in it. The Agreement's strengths are that it has given Northern nationalists a degree of confidence; it has reduced conflict and increased communication between the British and Irish governments; and it has 'started a process which will lead inevitably to a further narrowing of the gap between the two countries and governments within the context of the EC'.

However, its negative aspects are that it has increased the dependency of Northern nationalists on the Republic, and they now turn to Dublin to argue on their behalf with the British government. Because neither the Northern nationalists nor the Irish government has executive power in Northern Ireland, this inevitably leads to frustration. 'The Irish claim credit for any positive changes, the British are blamed for any refusals; the lack of an executive role reinforces dependency.'

Until Northern nationalists have such an executive role, they will not have to take responsibility for any difficult decisions — over policing, for example. 'It is important to recognize that unless nationalists are offered and accept an executive role in Northern Ireland, there will be no substantial progress, because without such a role they can never own Northern Ireland.'

Father Lennon points out that, normally, minorities are catered for by passing laws protecting them culturally, or perhaps economically. Yet this makes them dependent on the majority for the implementation of these laws, leaving them in the position of 'owning nothing and having responsibility for nothing'.

Many argue that giving an executive role to nationalists is giving them too much. What such arguments overlook is that, with an executive role, nationalists take on responsibility. They then have to face difficult decisions; for example, in relation to policing. They have to commit themselves to Northern Ireland as it then would be, with all the inevitable compromises in nationalist ideology that would be required. An executive role also involves working together with unionists and British people, with whom nationalists often disagree profoundly. It means working within the context of real economic limitations and implementing the decisions necessary in the light of such realities.

Father Lennon suggests that it may be considerations like these which explain the decline in nationalist enthusiasm for power-sharing between 1974 and the present.

He believes 'the best level for nationalists to play an executive role is within Northern Ireland, provided the Dublin government continues to have an advisory role'.

Giving both nationalists and unionists an executive role within Northern Ireland can happen either by having a Northern Ireland Executive Assembly with the minority having a disproportionate number of seats; or else by giving each community — where they are deeply segregated — its own form of local government.

He claims in response to those who would say that the latter course reinforces sectarianism, that it is 'arguably better to have two separated peoples involved to some degree in government than to have neither involved in government. There are many areas in Northern Ireland where optimism about the two communities working together is simply 'pie-in-the-sky'. Either we accept the fact that such areas must remain politically powerless, or we allow some separate political structures (unless we are open to majority rule, which in such areas is politically undesirable).' (See also Law, Justice and Security: Policing.)

MR RUAIRÍ BRUGHA, from Dublin, a former Fianna Fáil Northern Ireland spokesman, suggests that a referendum should be held 'seeking the approval of the electorate for the formation of an elected administration, each of those elected having undertaken in advance, if selected, to participate in an administration to run Northern Ireland. If the proposal is approved by the electorate, a general election should be held using the proportional representation (PR) system.

Following the election, the parties would be brought together to select a cabinet based on a pro rata allocation of positions, but subject to the portfolio of justice/security being jointly shared by a unionist and nationalist representative. In the event of a party or person selected for office failing to participate in an administration, the vacancy or vacancies should be filled from among those willing to do so until such time as those entitled to act agree to do so

Whereas Father Lennon and Mr Brugha approach power-sharing from a broadly nationalist perspective, SIR EDWARD ARCHDALE, an Ards borough councillor, looks at it from a unionist standpoint. He proposes a 'model for consensus government', based on a 68-strong assembly elected by single transferable vote PR. The executive would consist of a chief minister, who would be the leader of the party with the most votes, and six senior ministers, drawn from parties which had received at least ten per cent of the votes cast in the assembly election. They would be appointed in departmental ranking sequence (with justice and home affairs, the latter controlling the police, being the most senior ministries) using the D'Hondt highest average voting system, or by negotiation between the parties.

The ULSTER UNIONIST CHARTER GROUP (UUCG) proposes a Constitutional Community Coalition 'reflecting the will of the majority' which would 'invite and include the minority as partners in the executive' of a new Northern Ireland devolved assembly.

Using the analogy of a large business company, Northern Ireland plc, which would have majority and minority shareholders (the electorate), the Group explains:

The devolved government would consist of the board of directors, which will have an executive management accountable to the shareholders through the elected forum. The executive management would be formed by the leader of the party holding the most seats at the elected forum, or the agreed leader of a coalition of parties able to count together the most seats. It would be binding upon such a leader to obtain from the Prime Minister approval for the measures he or she would seek to implement over a fixed term. It would be binding upon such a leader to then offer to the leaders of the other parties posts in the devolved administration. It would not be binding upon any other leaders to accept such posts. But it would be expected that any party accepting the offer to participate in government would do so with honourable intentions, and would work for the common interest of the shareholders [electorate].

The Group, while stressing its belief in the importance of an internal Northern Ireland settlement which is not aimed at placating the long-term aspirations of nationalists, says that a bilateral liaison body between the administrations in Belfast and Dublin should then be set up to deal with matters of common concern which do not conflict with east-west British-Irish relations.

Twenty-one-year-old GLYN ROBERTS, from east Belfast, has worked out a more detailed system of devolved government. He rejects the nationalist analysis that it is impossible to have democratic structures in Northern Ireland because the region is not a natural political entity. He accepts that in the past the region has been unfairly governed and that discrimination and one-party rule have convinced a significant nationalist constituency that the Northern state is unreformable.

He believes that, given a say in the fully accountable government of the region and partnership with the Republic, Northern nationalists will be able to express their Irish, political, as well as cultural, traditions within Northern Ireland.

The structures he proposes to achieve this are a 12-member executive elected directly by the people of Northern Ireland by PR, with the region as one constituency. The chief executive would be the candidate who receives the highest number of first preference votes, with the next 11 filling the rest of the places on the executive. The chief executive's post would be rotated — perhaps on a yearly basis — among the parties whose leading members make up the executive.

To take office, this executive would need to win a weighted vote — Mr Roberts suggests it should be 80 per cent — in a separately elected 102-member regional assembly. The assembly would be required to pass most legislation by means of differently weighted majorities, ranging from 80 per cent for sensitive matters like security, 65 per cent for education and housing, to normal 50 plus one majorities for non-controversial matters.

He also proposes a 52-member Senate, made up of members appointed by the Secretary of State, the new executive, the Irish government (five members), the main churches, the business and trade union organizations, the universities and Belfast and Derry city councils. The Senate would scrutinize all legislation and be able to propose amendments.

Like so many contributors, Mr Roberts proposes a Bill of Rights, but he also suggests a Northern Ireland Civil Rights Commission, both to monitor that Bill of Rights and to be the region's highest appeal court. He further suggests that the commission's four judges should be appointed respectively by the British and Irish governments, the European Commission and the new executive.

To deal with cross-border issues, he proposes an executive conference, bringing together on a monthly basis Ministers of the Irish government and the new Northern Ireland executive to discuss and make decisions on matters of mutual concern. Any decision reached by this conference would have to be ratified in Northern Ireland by the new assembly.

MR MARK RUSSELL, a law student at Queen's University, Belfast, proposes a more modest form of 'semi-devolution' as the most realistic chance of more accountable government for the region. Rather than have 'faceless bureaucrats' running Northern Ireland's government departments, he proposes that small teams of local politicians, drawn from an elected provincial council, should be appointed by the Secretary of State for Northern Ireland to do the job under his Whitehall-appointed deputy, the Minister of State. The constitutional parties would be allocated junior ministerial posts in those teams according to their strength on the council. All ministers, including the Secretary of State, would be accountable to the provincial council.

There would also be a consultative structure involving the Irish government. A junior minister from each departmental team would join the

Secretary of State and Ministers of State in a twice-yearly Council of Ministers, to discuss matters of mutual concern with their Dublin opposite numbers.

MR GORDON JACKSON from Banbridge sees a devolved Northern Ireland 'council' as the upper tier, with blocking powers, in a system at whose heart would be four elected regional councils, covering matters comparable with the health and education boards, and representing approximately 375,000 people each. The regional council representatives would be nominated to a number of cross-border committees with their Southern counterparts, covering everything from security to economic development, agriculture and tourism. He also suggests that the Anglo-Irish secretariat at Maryfield should be replaced by an Irish Ambassador in Belfast, who would have a consultative role on the upper tier council.

VERY REV. VICTOR GRIFFIN, the former dean of St Patrick's Cathedral in Dublin, now living in Limavady, suggests that the restoration of the office of Governor of Northern Ireland might help to alleviate unionist fears of a sell-out. The Governor would have to be satisfied before signing any legislation passed by a new assembly that it is fair to both principal communities.

Similarly, to allay nationalist fears, he suggests a resident Minister from the Republic's government to keep a watching brief in Belfast and promote North-South co-operation. A new Northern Ireland administration might have a similar Minister in Dublin.

The former Alliance Lord Mayor of Belfast, MR DAVID COOK, is of the opinion that there are only two ways Northern Ireland might be governed other than by direct rule from London: one a form of government he calls 'the Irish Confederation', the other 'some means of creeping joint authority' between the British and Irish governments. If Direct Rule were to last indefinitely, the latter, involving, for example, the joint appointment of some Ministers and civil servants, might become a possibility in the absence of agreement on any other system. He is opposed to joint authority, believing that 'it would condemn the people of Northern Ireland to a perpetual political childishness which they do not deserve and for which they will not be grateful'.

His confederation scheme envisages a regional parliamentary institution, consisting of an assembly elected by single transferable vote PR; the election of a partnership executive from the assembly on the basis of proportionality; minority blocking mechanisms; a political right of appeal; the same procedures to be applied to a reduced number of amalgamated local government authorities; and a Bill of Rights. He accepts that this first piece may be the most difficult part of his jigsaw to complete.

If it can be completed, he sees a confederal North-South institution arising from 'an agreement between the Republic of Ireland and Northern Ireland acting as two equals', small at first but with further functions being assigned to it as agreement takes place. At first, aspects of energy and industrial policy, the environment, transport and agriculture could be assigned to it. It would have executive, not legislative, powers, and initially its business would be conducted by Ministers from the Irish government and the Northern Ireland executive. Irish people, North and South, while retaining their British or Irish passports, could, if they so wished, also describe themselves as citizens of this 'Irish Confederation', and it could have a symbolic flag.

PAX CHRISTI IRELAND (PCI) does not propose any specific constitutional structures, but makes a more general observation.

Agreed structures of government for Northern Ireland will not in themselves bring an end to the conflict but they may be a contributory factor. Where there is a lack of political consensus, hatred and enmity, violence and sectarianism, distrust and disunity will all continue to prevail — and the paramilitaries on both sides will seek to fill that vacuum in their own destructive ways.

We believe that political consensus, based on mutual trust and respect, tolerance and honorable compromise, must exist on a variety of levels: at local government level, at Northern Ireland inter-party level, at North-South level and at British-Irish level.

(See also Law, Justice and Security: Reducing the Violence.)

The ALLIANCE PARTY presented the papers it put forward at the 1992 inter-party talks. In these, it envisages an 85-member devolved assembly for Northern Ireland, elected by the single transferable vote PR system. Such an assembly would have executive and legislative powers initially for all main domestic matters except security, which might be transferred to it at a later date.

Following inter-party talks, the Secretary of State would appoint a small responsibility-sharing executive, drawn from and answerable to this assembly. He or she should be satisfied that this executive was widely representative of the community, reflecting as far as practicable the balance of constitutional parties in the assembly. For it to take office, it would have to be voted in by 70 per cent of the assembly's members. Thereafter, its continued acceptability could be tested by a resolution supported by at least 15 per cent of the assembly members not more than once every parliamentary year.

Alliance believes that the most likely problems in this process would be due either to a lack of consensus for the executive's original appointment, or changing political circumstances which would make the executive unacceptable to the assembly. In either circumstance, the Secretary of State should have the power to hold a fresh election so as to give the population an opportunity to break the log-jam.

The party's proposals would also include a Bill of Rights and a political right of appeal for aggrieved minorities to the Westminster Parliament, which would require 30 per cent support within the assembly.

Given that very significant powers, including security, would remain in London, Alliance further proposes a tripartite structure involving the British government, the Irish government, and the new Northern Ireland administration, to ensure consultation and co-operation on matters of common concern. This could be accompanied by a tripartite inter-parliamentary body. Within that framework, consultative North-South institutions could be set up in economic development, tourism, agriculture, and environmental and cultural affairs. Where practical, common cross-border programmes and strategies could be developed.

Party leader Dr John Alderdice stresses that it is not the physical partition of the country which is the problem in Ireland, but, in the words of Professor J.C. Beckett, the partition 'in the minds of men'. 'The sense of identity which is Irishness is not particularly a matter of statehood', he goes on, pointing out that President Robinson said in her 'inspiring' inaugural speech that 'the state is not the only model of community with which Irish people can and do identify'. Dr Alderdice continues: 'Her expression of freedom, which for me broke the link between mere state allegiance and a sense of Irishness, meant that her election could be a matter of joy in east Belfast as well as in Ballina.'

LORD HOLME, the Liberal Democrats' spokesman on Northern Ireland, believes that discussing the problem of Northern Ireland in terms of 'sovereignty' is unhelpful. 'For both the UK and the Republic of Ireland, whatever the residual shreds of national pride which still flutter over their respective positions, Northern Ireland, far from being a valuable disputed property, has become a costly and apparently insoluble embarrassment which they would rather not have to deal with but are saddled with by history.' He believes the classic British constitutional definition of sovereignty, exercised 'top down' by the 'Crown in Parliament', is similarly unhelpful.

For Liberal Democrats, the starting-point is that

the people of Northern Ireland have the right to govern themselves; and not only the right, but the responsibility. It is difficult to believe that the paternalism of the Northern Ireland Office, and direct rule from Westminster, whatever problems it solves in the short term, does not sap the civic virtues of the people of Northern Ireland and encourage feelings of cynical impotence. A change of culture and context both demand that people in Northern Ireland come to terms with their responsibility, as well as their right to govern themselves.

Lord Holme argues that 'because of the sharply defined communitarian divisions, such self-government must be by power-sharing' and that it should be government limited by the codified rights of the citizen' in a Bill of Rights. On the question of sovereignty, he stresses that once it is accepted — as it is by him — that 'ultimate sovereignty is vested in the people of Northern Ireland themselves', then the only answer to whether the region should be part of the UK or the Republic of Ireland is whatever the people themselves decide. 'Interestingly, Article 1 of the Anglo-Irish Agreement, in itself an extraordinary constitutional precedent, makes that very commitment to the wishes of the majority of the people of Northern Ireland.' He believes there should be a regular referendum, say every ten years initially, to measure changing attitudes towards the region's constitutional status.

Lord Holme quotes the late Professor John Whyte, one of Ireland's most distinguished political scientists, in support of power-sharing: 'I know of *no* case where a divided society has been stable without power-sharing ... in all of them there is some set of arrangements whereby the different segments of the population share power roughly in proportion to their numerical strength.' Lord Holme suggests a 100-member assembly elected by PR; this body would elect a ten-member executive committee by PR which would contain members of every party which had secured between five and ten per cent of assembly seats. As long as sectarian politics continued to dominate, the chief minister at the head of this executive would be a unionist. However, it is possible that the later preferences of nationalist and other assembly members could influence which unionist is elected, and would encourage the selection of someone who enjoys cross-community support. He also urges a Bill of Rights to be enshrined in any new constitutional settlement. 'The present political climate in the UK is perhaps especially conducive to constitutional reform, given the breakdown of confidence in the political elite.' Lord Holme rejects the argument that a Bill of Rights in only one UK region would create a constitutional anomaly, arguing that Northern Ireland throws up special problems requiring special constitutional structures. Liberal Democrats would be 'happy if such a Bill increased pressure for the protection of rights in the UK as a whole'.

Finally he proposes the creation of a constitutional court, which 'would rule on the constitutionality of measures and structures proposed by government, as well as protecting the rights of the citizen'. He suggests that its membership might consist of six judges: one from Northern Ireland, two from Britain, two from the Republic of Ireland, and one from Europe, either from the EC Court of Justice or the European Court of Human Rights: 'This sort of composition would be one way of giving tangible shape to the role of the UK and the Republic of Ireland as guarantors of the new constitution, and to the legitimate interests of a European Community of which all these territories are part.'

DEMOCRATIC LEFT (DL) begins its submission by pointing out why and how unionists hate the 1985 Anglo-Irish Agreement, although the party accepts that in the short term it is here to stay. However, to unionists it is an agreement entered into without consultation with them to give the Republic a say in Northern Ireland's internal affairs; it appears to unionists that, both in its conception and operation, the Irish government speaks for and consults closely with the SDLP, while the British government sees itself as neutral between unionists and nationalists. 'Is it any wonder that unionists feel alienated?' the party asks.

Democratic Left says it is not opposed to institutional links between the Republic and Northern Ireland, but believes that 'to be successful, they must have the support of both unionists and nationalists'. It calls for Articles 2 and 3 of the Republic's Constitution to be replaced with 'a formula of words which would acknowledge an aspiration towards unity, while explicitly accepting the present legitimacy of Northern Ireland's position within the United Kingdom'.

The party urges the British and Irish governments to put new pressure on the main Northern Irish political parties to reach agreement about power-sharing devolved government.

Devolved government for Northern Ireland represents a compromise between total absorption into the Irish Republic or total integration with Britain. Providing it is established on a basis acceptable to the community at large, it can lay a foundation for political stability and aid economic regeneration.

The party also concurs with unionist demands for an all-party grand committee of the Westminster Parliament to monitor Northern Ireland's affairs, agreeing that the present system 'by which Northern Ireland matters are passed by order in council with minimal debate is undemocratic and damaging to the political process'.

THE WORKERS' PARTY proposes a devolved assembly of between 85 and 102 members elected by the single transferable vote system. The members of the assembly would then, by the same method, elect eleven committees, covering all matters, including security. Those committees would each elect chairpersons who collectively would form an executive, which would then elect its own chairperson. At first the committees would only scrutinize their relevant government department, but the party envisages the committees moving towards assuming responsibility for as much of their work as possible. Before decision-making powers could be given to a committee, 60 per cent of the assembly's members would have to agree. The security committee would have no operational functions, but would act as a link between the security forces and public representatives. Decisions of the executive would require the approval of 60 per cent of the assembly. The assembly's first act should be to set up a drafting committee for a Bill of Rights, to receive the widest possible representations from all sections of Northern Ireland society.

THE NORTHERN IRELAND OFFICE contributed a paper entitled 'H.M. Government's approach to political development in Northern Ireland'. It begins with a paragraph on the constitutional position:

What follows should be read in the light of the government's commitment that Northern Ireland will not cease to be part of the United Kingdom without the consent of a majority of the people who live here. Such majority desire for a change in status, as demonstrated in successive elections in Northern Ireland, clearly does not exist at present and seems unlikely in the foreseeable future. However, if in the future a majority of the people of Northern Ireland clearly wish for and formally consent to the establishment of a united Ireland, the government is committed to introduce and support in Parliament legislation to give effect to that wish. A corollary of that commitment is that the government will continue to defend the democratically expressed wishes of the people of Northern Ireland, as of any other part of the United Kingdom, against those, from whatever quarter, who try to promote political objectives, including a change in the status of Northern Ireland, by violence or the threat of violence.

It then summarizes government policy under the headings of security policy, economic and social policy, and political development. The government's approach to the last of these is 'to seek to transfer substantial political power, authority and responsibility to locally elected representatives in Northern Ireland on a basis which would be stable, durable and widely acceptable across the community'. The submission continues: 'The prime motive for seeking such a political settlement is that it represents the best chance of bringing about a workable and lasting political accommodation both between the two main parts of the community in Northern Ireland and between the two main traditions in the island of Ireland as a whole.' Such an accommodation would

give genuine parity of esteem to both major traditions, and allow a situation to emerge in which the whole community would be better able to identify with, and give allegiance to, whatever new institutions were agreed upon. That, in turn, could be expected to generate a greater political consensus and wider public support for, and confidence in, the security forces and the administration of justice, enabling law and order in Northern Ireland to be maintained more effectively. Such an accommodation would also mean that decisions about local matters, distinctive to Northern Ireland, would be taken by locally accountable politicians with special knowledge of all the relevant issues. It could also be expected to maximise the opportunity for achieving the benefits of contact and co-operation between the two parts of Ireland.

The submission goes on to underline the government's belief that the way forward lies through the talks process, involving the British government, the four main Northern Irish constitutional parties, and the Irish government discussing 'an eventual settlement across the three relevant sets of relationships' (within Northern Ireland, within Ireland and between the two governments). The government emphasizes that it has no 'hidden agenda' nor blueprint for what form any new institutions should take.

As well as providing greater responsibility, on a fair and equitable basis, for locally accountable representatives in Northern Ireland, the government envisages that a political accommodation would also encompass a commitment to a new relationship between any new institutions in Northern Ireland and the government and people of the Republic of Ireland. What form this commitment will take is for the main constitutional parties and the Irish government to decide in direct discussion and negotiation within the talks. But there are several subjects that could lend themselves to a common approach.

The remainder of the submission consists of a statement on security policy and a number of relevant speeches by the present Secretary of State, Sir Patrick Mayhew, and his predecessor, Mr Peter Brooke.

MR W.A. LEONARD, from Co. Armagh, outlines a power-sharing scheme based on Arend Lijphart's ideas on 'consociation'. He proposes a power-sharing central assembly, together with seven county councils, to replace the present 'unwieldy' 26 district councils. Relations with the Republic should be handled by a separate directly elected council. All parties inside and outside Northern Ireland agree on the need for a North-South relationship: the Irish government wants to be imaginative and is conscious of Articles 2 and 3 of its Constitution; Northern nationalists want such a relationship to proceed towards unity; the British government has long accepted the reality of such a relationship; while unionists, although trenchantly opposed to Articles 2 and 3, realize the need to be good neighbours. 'The difficulty is how to frame this relationship without loss of identity, aspiration and constitutional security.' Mr Leonard foresees changes in the 'nation-state concept', brought about largely by the EC, which could facilitate this.

Dealing with matters of common concern for the island should be through machinery closely allied to the EC, to avoid, as far as possible, threats to loyalties and identities. Similarly, he stresses the importance of ensuring that the internal affairs of Northern Ireland are dealt with by the central assembly and county councils, and that the 'non-territorial council responsible for relations with the Republic' is separate, although there may be some overlap in its elected membership. He hopes that, with minimal work, Dublin, London and Brussels could reallocate significant EC funds to such a council — which he suggests should be called the 'European Council for Ireland' — to make it work. He proposes that MEPs from both parts of the island should sit on it, together with the directly elected members from North and South. It could deal with economic co-operation — he cites Ulster Bank chairman Dr George Quigley's ideas on the 'island economy' as an example — with harmonization of social policy within Europe, security co-operation, cultural relations, common European citizenship, agriculture, education, tourism, transport and energy.

Mr Leonard suggests that decisions of the European Council for Ireland should first be referred to the Belfast assembly and to the London and

Dublin parliaments for comment; their observations should be referred back to it, and the proposed measure should then be channelled through the EC legislative machinery. This might look cumbersome, he concedes, but it would have the advantages of adopting a consensual approach, which would minimize fears and, without sidestepping the nation-states, it would be 'availing of a less threatening arbiter, which ultimately could be more acceptable to all sides, that is, the European Community'.

Other submissions that dealt, among other things, with the need for devolved, partnership government, were: members of the Belfast Rotary Club (one of several different proposals), Mr Terence Donaghy, Mr Trevor Halliday, Mr Jackie Hewitt, Labour '87, Mr Allan Leonard (with Bill of Rights), Liberal Democrats (Northern Ireland), Mr Thomas Lyttle, Rev G.B.G. McConnell, Ms Jeanette McCormack, Mrs Helen and Mr Thomas McCormick, Mr Alistair MacLurg, Mr Charles Murphy, New Consensus (Britain), New Consensus International, Northern Ireland Community Study Group, Rev. Cecil Orr (Church of Ireland Dean of Derry), Scrabo Presbyterian Church, members of Stormont Presbyterian Church (one of several different proposals), members of Sydenham Methodist Church and the Ulster Political Research Group. (See also Local government)

United Ireland

The second most popular political structure among contributors to Initiative '92 (38 submissions) was some form of united Ireland, usually brought about by the withdrawal of the British presence from Northern Ireland. If the proposals for a federal Ireland were added, the number in this category rose to 44. In addition, a significant number of submissions proposing joint authority or joint sovereignty (see next section) saw that as a staging post on the way to a united Ireland. There was a tendency among many of these nationalist submissions to stress the desirability and inevitability of a united Ireland, rather than to examine how it might come about, and how unionist opposition to it might be accommodated or overcome.

One broadly republican submission which did not do this came from the BLOODY SUNDAY INITIATIVE (BSI) in Derry, which concentrates on the problems of peacemaking. Its members believe that 'the most significant step' towards creating the conditions for peace should be 'a declaration by the British government that it wishes to begin the process of withdrawal from Ireland and to facilitate the process by which all shades of political opinion in Ireland can come together to agree on new constitutional arrangements for Ireland as a whole'.

All the major nationalist and republican political parties have said that the political representatives of the unionist community will have a major role to play in shaping any new constitution. They would also have a major role in determining the kind of relationships which might well exist within the British Isles, especially since the break-up of the United Kingdom is increasingly a distinct possibility. Political representatives of the unionist community, on whatever basis they are elected, will be able to play a full role in an Irish parliament. Indeed they may well provide members of a future all-Ireland government.

The group compares this with 'the charade that passes for democracy at the moment in Northern Ireland', with the unionist community's ability to influence political events following the Anglo-Irish Agreement 'virtually nil'.

The Bloody Sunday Initiative is very critical of the kind of 'peace process' that would exclude Sinn Féin and the marginalized, impoverished and angry community it represents. It accepts that the issue of political violence must be dealt with, but calls for a recognition that 'to some degree everybody in this community, as well as in Britain, has supported violence, has suffered intensely from it and has gained by it materially and politically. Scapegoating one section of the community, or one or two of the combatants to the conflict, cannot and should not be the basis for any genuine peace movement.'

The group accepts that a powerful case can be made against political violence, particularly that perpetrated by the IRA. It is often rightly characterized as sectarian, and its most negative legacy is the 'culture of militarism' which inhibits the development of genuine radical politics in working-class areas. However, the group also points out that an equally powerful case can be made for the effectiveness of political violence as a catalyst for change: whether in bringing down Stormont and the power-sharing executive, or bringing in the Anglo-Irish Agreement.

Whatever the pros and cons about violence, its use by the IRA or the loyalist paramilitaries 'is not going to be argued or reasoned away'. 'How then to bring to an end the various military campaigns, including that of the IRA, remains a central issue which no peace movement or proposed peace process to date has adequately addressed.'

The group is also critical of republicans for their 'failure adequately to acknowledge the deep-rooted hostility to violence held by many people, and the degree to which the IRA campaign has turned off many former supporters of the nationalist cause, especially in Southern Ireland'; their too ready acceptance of the 'inexcusably high number of civilian casualties and the sectarian bias in too many IRA operations'; and their attempts to ignore or to justify 'the violations of human rights which armed struggle inevitably involves'.

Republicans have also failed to acknowledge or deal adequately with the aspirations of the unionist community and to articulate how national self-determination could include those who, rightly or wrongly, see themselves as British or as Ulster people. For many, this remains the most serious political criticism of republican approaches to peacemaking.

The Bloody Sunday Initiative goes on to suggest the setting up of a new kind of peace movement, provisionally known as Peace 2000, around the following agenda:

(1) That peace negotiations should begin to resolve the conflict between Britain and Ireland and within Ireland, and that all parties to that dispute should be able to attend, including Sinn Féin;

(2) That the British government publicly announces that repealing the government of Ireland Act 1921 (and subsequent amendments) would be on the table and that the British government and parliament would support and facilitate an all-Ireland solution;

(3) That the IRA agrees that a permanent end to armed struggle would be a central agenda issue;

(4) That any constitutional settlement would recognise religious and political liberty, diversity and the principle of non-domination.

Peace 2000 would declare that its goal would be to attempt to establish peace (that is, an end to armed conflict in Ireland) by the year 2000 at the latest, and that its objective was to seek support for a historic compromise in which all sides of the conflict commit themselves to a negotiated peace, without preconditions and excluding nobody, but with a willingness to show real generosity and reciprocity. The Bloody Sunday Initiative believes that there is an increasing desire for a genuine discussion to begin about how armed conflict in Ireland can be ended once and for all and a genuine and lasting peace secured.

MR JOHN GRAY from Belfast, an author and librarian, also believes that the creation of a united Ireland is the only way the Northern Ireland constitutional question can be resolved.

While this solution does not at present command broad cross-community acceptance, there is little doubt that, if achieved, and with whatever difficulty, it would constitute an irreversible step. That is a valid argument in the context of the historical continuum of Britain's declining commitment to the Protestant community in Ireland, and of the declining confidence of that community itself. If, indeed, a united Ireland can offer a permanent settlement in a way that no other option can, it at least deserves far more serious consideration than it has been given, even by liberal academics from the Protestant tradition.

He accepts that the form and practice of the Southern Irish state in the past has reinforced the fears of Northern unionists that their cultural Britishness would be threatened by 'the increasingly ultramontane and exclusive Catholicism of Irish nationalism'. However, he believes that this has now changed.

There is little doubt that a process of political and cultural modernization in the Irish Republic is now rapidly under way. This has been most markedly evidenced by the election of Mary Robinson as President, and the recent general election which has produced the most significant change of any general election North or South since 1922. There is now a real prospect of the transformation of the Republic from a clerically dominated state into a pluralist one, and this without the assistance of Northern Protestants.

The time is now surely overdue for Northern Protestants to respond to and encourage these developments, that is if they have any interest in living in a pluralist state. If they do not, that, of course, has the most gloomy implications for the possibilities of an internal settlement in

Northern Ireland itself. They should also be aware that any assumption that an Ulster Protestant culture is a British one is now alien to multicultural Britain itself, especially when associated with concepts of dominance. Viewed from Britain, we are 'all Paddys now'. Meanwhile, the notion that Irish culture in the Irish Republic is exclusively Irish (and Catholic), which was never entirely true, is now less so than ever before, in a society where aspects of a British cultural heritage and a native Irish one readily coexist.

The economic argument of 70 years ago that the interests of Northern industry, with its imperial and international markets, were at variance with the protectionist needs of the small-scale and stagnant Southern economy has also been overtaken, says Mr Gray.

Northern Ireland has ceased to have an industrial economy of any great significance — we are all public servants now if we have work at all. In so far as Northern Ireland has a surviving industrial sector, its interests in the international marketplace are very similar to those of the far more rapidly developing industrial sector in the Republic of Ireland. Within the EC and the single market there is now virtually no scope for the adoption of significantly divergent trade policies as between North and South. Access to the levers of power within the EC is increasingly important, and here the North, as a large part of Ireland as a whole, could enjoy far better access to influence through Irish membership, as opposed to insignificant importance in the context of British membership.

While the Republic still has acute problems, reflected in levels of unemployment even higher than the North and in great social inequality, real growth there in recent decades has been far faster and on a more secure basis.

The gap that remains between the two areas is an entirely artificial one, arising from the huge funding transfers from Britain to Northern Ireland. To assume that these would simply become a net loss on the creation of a united Ireland is myopic in the extreme. It first of all assumes that Britain is willing to maintain this level of subvention in perpetuity in support of a war-torn Northern Ireland, which is by no means necessarily the case. It secondly assumes that Britain would immediately withdraw all support if a united Ireland were agreed. This is unlikely, on the presumption that Britain approved the settlement. A more likely scenario would be a tapering-off of support.

In fact, Mr Gray believes that such beneficial new factors as reductions in the cost of security, increased inward investment and tourism, and a higher rate of growth would rapidly eliminate the consequences of any loss of British transfers.

However, he accepts that because of the opposition, even bitter opposition, of the vast majority of Northern Protestants, progress towards a united Ireland will have to be slow and undramatic: 'any immediate moves to unity almost certainly would produce a backlash', with a major threat from many thousands of well-armed and hostile unionists, an extreme reluctance by either the British or Irish armed forces to take them on, and a mass exodus of Northern Protestants from Ireland. He points out, in the light of all this, that the simplistic republican solution of holding an all-Ireland referendum, which would almost certainly produce a vote in favour of a united

Ireland, just would not work; it 'would not make its creation one jot easier than in the scenario described above'.

However, he also believes that, just as such an all-Ireland mandate would be unable to dictate a settlement, so the constitutional guarantee to the unionists, allowing them to veto any settlement other than a British one, should not provide an 'absolute and overriding right to impede any particular settlement'.

Mr Gray believes that such interim solutions as repartition or devolution within a British framework will not work, as they have not worked in the past, because they fail to resolve the problem of constitutional insecurity.

His proposed interim solution involves a new treaty, under which the Irish government would 'entrust' the British government with jurisdiction over Northern Ireland until such time as both governments should agree otherwise (or either government should wish to derogate from the treaty). This would give 'immediate recognition to the reality of British jurisdiction in Northern Ireland, but makes clear the conditional basis for this'. There would have to be appropriate amendments to Articles 2 and 3 of the Irish Constitution and the 1973 Northern Ireland Constitution Act — the latter replacing the veto previously given to 'the majority of the people of Northern Ireland' by the concept of constitutional change by agreement between the two governments.

At the same time, provision would be made for a Northern Ireland regional parliament, to be elected by PR, and the formation of a 'majority rule' — that is, in the first instance, almost certainly unionist — government from that parliament with responsibility for all matters other than security and defence.

However, the treaty should also provide for a separate Northern Ireland commission — made up of equal representation from the British and Irish governments, and a third party, possibly the EC — which would have the power to recommend to the British government the vetoing of unfair legislation passed by the Northern Ireland parliament. It could also recommend to the British government the suspension of the regional parliament and government, or any local council, if they 'sought persistently to prevent good and fair government, or refused to operate at all'. The commission would also have a responsibility to monitor the British authorities' operation of their security and defence powers in Northern Ireland.

Mr Gray concludes by stressing that his commission proposal could be applied to changing circumstances. While initially the commission might be seen as a safeguard against unionist majority abuse, if population or political change were to alter the balance of power, it might come to serve as the guarantor of the rights of unionist or Protestant minorities. 'Indeed if, at some point in the future, steps to a united Ireland were taken, this might well be on a federal basis, with a Northern Ireland Commission still in place.'

SINN FÉIN argues that 'partition, which created the six-county statelet on the basis of a sectarian headcount, was imposed undemocratically by Britain on the Irish people and is maintained by force. That is the fundamental problem. The search for a sustainable solution can only begin by understanding the need to reverse this partition of Ireland. For over 70 years the national rights of all the Irish people have been negated by partition. Consequently, the Irish people have been prevented from creating the necessary all-Ireland constitutional forum which would resolve the complexities of Irish nationhood in an open and pluralist manner.'

Sinn Féin says that Northern Ireland, since its inception, 'has been maintained by force of arms and has survived on a diet of repression, discrimination and institutionalized brutality, which falls, almost exclusively, on the shoulders of the nationalist population'. It 'feeds conceptions of superiority amongst its supporters', and despite verbal commitments to reform by Britain, 'the official statistics and the actions of the state and its servants proclaim the second-class citizenship status of nationalists'.

'Britain must leave Ireland', the party concludes.

All proposals which maintain partition are merely 'quick fix' solutions. The past 23 years of conflict demonstrate the validity of this observation.

It is essential to recognize that the basic problem is not just one of community relations within the six counties. Such a definition allows the British government to pose as the 'honest broker' seeking a settlement between two opposing factions, or as a 'peacemaker' whose armed forces are 'keeping the warring sides apart'.

Sinn Féin says that this misleading view, so important to British government strategy, 'masks Britain's historical and contemporary colonial role in Ireland'.

None of this is to deny the deep divisions which exist within the six counties or to minimize the huge challenge this poses to all who are concerned with seeking a way forward out of the present political impasse. The gulf between the unionist and nationalist communities is deep and will not easily be overcome. But sectarian divisions do not have their basis in differences of religion or race. They arise directly from the political situation and specifically from the injustice inflicted on one section of the population — nationalists — by the state, to the advantage of another section of the population — unionists.

Sinn Féin believes that the unionist veto on moves to end partition is central to the Northern Ireland conflict — 'the cornerstone of the British government's public rationale for its continuing exercise of sovereignty over the six counties'. Northern Ireland was created as 'the maximum area which could accommodate a unionist majority, thus perpetually guaranteeing that undemocratic veto over the constitutional future of Ireland. Thus to seek an end to the unionist veto is not to deny the rights of the unionist people. It is to assert that, as in any other society, those rights must be exercised with respect to the rights of others; in this case, the majority of their fellow citizens.'

If there is to be movement towards conditions in which the debate about national reconciliation can take place, the British government-bestowed unionist veto needs to be removed. We believe it is necessary to break out of the present conception of politics prevalent in Ireland, where one person's gain is conceived automatically as another person's loss.

Outlining its 'conditions for peace and democracy', Sinn Féin stresses that, 'without the explicit expression of a desire on the British government's part to end partition, unionists are unlikely to be convinced of the need for change and will remain intransigent, in the confidence that the British government will continue to underwrite their contrived majority with force and finance'.

Therefore the primary responsibility for allowing a peace process to develop rests with the British government. The elements which are needed to bring about conditions for peace are:

(1) A British government which makes the ending of partition its policy.
(2) A Dublin government which has the same policy end.
(3) Co-operation between the British and Dublin governments to bring about their joint purpose in the shortest time possible consistent with obtaining maximum consent to the process and minimising costs of every kind.
(4) Democracy and practicality demand that this be done in consultation and co-operation with the representatives of the Irish minority, the Northern unionists, as well as with the representatives of Northern nationalists. This, in effect, would be a process of national reconciliation.

In their submission, the REPUBLICAN PRISONERS AT THE MAZE put forward many of the same arguments as their colleagues in Sinn Féin, but with some different emphases, particularly when they recognize unionist fears of a united Ireland. Emphasizing the primary responsibility of Britain for the legacy of conflict in Ireland, they quote the Anglican Bishop of Salisbury, Dr John Austin Baker, during the 1980 prison hunger strike: 'Our injustice created the situation [in Northern Ireland]; and by constantly repeating that we will maintain it so long as the majority (in the North) wish it, we actively inhibit Protestant and Catholic from working out a new future together. This is the root of the violence, and why the protestors think of themselves as political offenders.'

They conclude by saying:

The British government must be persuaded to accept its responsibility to become involved in a serious search for peace. Any political transformation must be away from structures of dominance and sectarianism. We do not believe that peace and justice are possible within the six-county state. Unionism, when backed by the British presence, is an ideology of supremacy. That said, we fully recognize that unionists have genuine fears of being dominated within a 32-county state and we believe it will be a vitally important task to overcome those fears as fully as possible.

The task of creating a shared future, free from oppression, will be difficult, but that nettle must be grasped if a genuine and lasting peace is to endure. If the central issue of British involvement is not tackled, the conflict will be bequeathed to future generations.

(See also Law, Justice and Security: Prisons.)

A leading businessman from a unionist background writes that he prefers 'an old-fashioned solution — a united Ireland within the Commonwealth', an outcome which he believes 'may be a little more realistic than it was even two years ago'. He says that he has long believed that (1) the average Ulster Protestant is more Irish than he would like to admit; (2) within the European context, we would be better off economically as part of Ireland than of the UK; (3) the UK government is becoming tired of and exasperated by the Northern Ireland problem; (4) we need to find a way to ensure that elections are along standard economic lines, rather than for or against the Union; (5) we need to face up to the united Ireland position once and for all — a power-sharing solution is far from ideal and will do little more than paper over the cracks.

Recent changes have provoked a number of other thoughts. He believes that 'the Republic's standing in the eyes of Northern Ireland Protestants and the world at large is much improved by Mary Robinson and to a lesser extent Albert Reynolds'. He notes that 'the Commonwealth is now such a tenuous arrangement that it cannot be seen as threatening — Commonwealth countries have their own Presidents, national anthems and identities. The role within Europe would be more important than the role within the Commonwealth.'

Would such an approach encourage party politics on the basis of economic and social beliefs, rather than on history and bigotry? There would be a need for a division of government between Dublin and Belfast. All sorts of interesting possibilities come to mind. Police forces could be combined with obvious benefits, but the military solution is much more difficult, in view of Ireland's neutral stance. The Church and state would require to be totally separated, and this made clear in any constitution. Symbolism in anthems, flags and emblems would have to be neutral. It is possible to be Irish *and* British without a sense of betrayal. Look at the examples on the sports field.

This businessman puts these proposals in the context of the multiple problems facing Northern Ireland. He writes about unemployment blackspots like west Belfast and Strabane, where the work ethic disappears and societies break down, with the result that the temptation to join paramilitary groups becomes hard to resist. 'There is a desperate need to create self-pride, self-confidence and the will to succeed. Jobs are crucial.'

He also writes about the level of apathy brought about by more than 20 years of 'troubles', with people of all social backgrounds too easily learning to 'adapt to the 'It's part of life here' approach, and 'there will never be a change', so why worry.' He is concerned about the poor calibre of leadership:

There are many people in the province with leadership qualities and initiative in all walks of life, but they would not enter politics. Until we have more able politicians who look to the future rather than live in the past, we will have little chance to progress. Which comes first — a new breed of politicians or a new environment?

He accepts that tribalism still exists. 'How can we create a framework which allows individuals to hold on to beliefs and cultures but devote their energies to solving common problems? There is much more that unites than divides people, wherever they live and to whatever economic strata they belong — that message needs to be hammered out by leaders of every kind.' He insists that Northern Ireland has 'much more happening within communities and across communities now', as well as 'many superb community leaders who with training and guidance can widen horizons and develop esteem'. He stresses that the paramilitaries 'must not be portrayed as idealists; they are thugs and gangsters and must be seen as such by the people they 'protect'.' He asks the media to focus more on 'initiatives and work for good rather than the totally black'.

Although people feel 'distant and possibly sceptical' about the talks process, it must be used to isolate the extremists and 'to focus on what people have in common rather than what divides them', the businessman goes on. 'People must understand — the participants in the talks and the public — that life is about negotiation and fair solutions, not winners, and losers.' If people talk about winners, they should think of the international successes in the sports and entertainment arenas which break down barriers — the Olympic medallists, the Eurovision Song Contest winners, the successful rugby and soccer teams.

A PROMINENT CATHOLIC NATIONALIST LAWYER argues that

a planned, stage by stage progression to joint British-Irish authority in Northern Ireland, followed by a federal format which would allow of final British withdrawal, is the only means by which even-handed justice can be done to all traditions in Ireland and permanent peace brought to pass. The timescale envisaged is 10-15 years, to be so proclaimed from the beginning, but this period could be shortened or extended as circumstances dictate.

He sees the problem of Northern Ireland as one of allegiance. On the unionist side he identifies three broad groups: those who take pride in their sense of being part of Britain, just as nationalists do about Ireland; those who are motivated by fear and hatred of Catholicism, seeing Britain as their protection against Rome; and those who see themselves as British and Irish, and take pride in both traditions. This latter group, 'if satisfied that their British citizenship and identity would be safeguarded, would be most likely to negotiate reasonably for a permanent settlement. They could be joined in this by elements in the first group, but never the second.' If this analysis is valid, then 'one is not faced, in seeking a solution, with unionism as a unified and monolithic structure'.

Since the inception of Northern Ireland, 'the British allegiance has enjoyed full and free expression in the matters of national, religious and cultural identity'. The unionists displayed — some might say flaunted — all the outward signs of their British rule and identity, without a single generous or compensatory gesture to Catholic neighbours who had lost their Irish identity through partition.

It is this gross imbalance, this palpable injustice, which is at the heart of the problem, and at the same time offers the key to its resolution.

Both justice and democracy demand that the nationalist community be placed on equal terms with the unionist community in matters of identity, culture, and above all, allegiance. To do so requires no less than the dismantling, over a planned period of years, of the constitutional structures erected by the government of Ireland Act 1920, while at the same time putting in place a new, and fairer, political design, which for the first time since partition places the two Northern Ireland communities on a completely equal footing. It is essential that at each and every stage of this process, the agreement, or at least the acceptance, of as many as possible from both communities be sought and obtained.

The lawyer urges the British government to follow the logic of the statement by Peter Brooke that Britain has no interest in remaining in Ireland by going on to say that

it is the intention of the government to begin working for the creation of conditions under which Britain could leave, without fear of leaving behind a state of civil conflict. This statement, of course, will make it very clear that no precipitate withdrawal is contemplated, and that the process will be by managed stages, and over a period of years. It would be probably better if a final date was proposed. It would be a vital and absolutely necessary component of such a declaration that the Protestant and unionist people were given positive guarantees that their right to British citizenship and their Protestant heritage would be protected by all possible means, including such statutory provisions and international treaties as seemed necessary.

He then deals with the situation of great danger and violence that will be created by such a 'momentous development'. First, there would be every reason to hope that the IRA would cease its violence, meaning that the security forces would have to fight on one front only, in the event of loyalist violence. He does not personally believe that

our Protestant neighbours will in large numbers fall on us and murder us wholesale. For one thing, it is not in their nature. For another, one does not imagine that a bald statement at a Stormont press conference will be the first intimation of British intentions, but that the ground will have been most carefully prepared for many months in advance of any formal statement. By this means it will be made known that nobody seeks victory over the unionist people, but only to begin a slow and careful process towards permanent peace in Ireland; that at every step the unionist people will be consulted; and that the British heritage and citizenship of the unionist people will be permanently protected. Unionist confidence will grow as the rewards of the new departure become clear to them, and loyalist gunmen, of whom it is accepted there will at the beginning be many, will find themselves, with little public support, face to face, on impossible terms, with the RUC and the British army. One is entitled to question whether there would be anything remotely like the 3000 deaths already caused by the British failure to meet the problem adequately, not to mention those which will continue to occur if present policies, or lack of them, are maintained.

He then goes on to outline a series of legal, political and constitutional steps to be taken. These include the legal recognition of the right to Irish citizenship; the election of a power-sharing regional assembly and executive; the establishment of a commission by the British and Irish governments to examine the equalization of the laws, North and South; the setting up of a second unarmed police service, separate from the RUC, with an emphasis on community policing and dealing with ordinary crime, with its religious composition mirroring those of the areas in which it operates.

The submission of THE NATIONAL PLATFORM (Dublin), written by its convenor, Dr Anthony Coughlan, asks whether this is not the appropriate time for 'Dublin and the SDLP to use the Anglo-Irish process to invite the British government (a) to join in a process of exploration of the steps that might be needed over time to secure majority consent in Northern Ireland to a dissolution of the Union, and (b) to take the first steps in that direction?'

Could Britain reasonably refuse such an invitation? If it did, would it not be indicating that, contrary to Peter Brooke's statement (that the British government has 'no selfish strategic or economic interest in Northern Ireland'), it does have an interest in staying in Ireland after all?

If Britain could be induced to join in such a process, aimed at obtaining Northern majority consent, it would mean that for the first time since 1920 the British government was throwing the weight of its influence on the side of coming-together rather than the division of the two communities in Ireland. That surely would open the way, as nothing else could, to a qualitatively new era of friendship and co-operation between the peoples of the two islands.

As for Northern unionists, could they reasonably deny Britain's right to embark on a process of exploration of the terms for getting majority consent to dissolving the Union — a process in which they should, of course, be given every encouragement to join — as long as it was made clear that there was no question of their being pushed into a united Ireland, either hurriedly or against their will? They could appeal in opposition only to the non-existent principle of a unilateral 'right to union'. But, being hard-headed people, most would surely see the absurdity of that. For how, concretely, can one party assert an illusory right to union if the other party is bent on divorce? No one can reasonably deny that the British government and people have the right to seek to separate from the unionists if they want to, so long as all legitimate unionist rights — those attaching to a large minority within Ireland — are guaranteed in the final settlement at the end of the process of securing northern majority consent to reunification.

If both governments took such a course, indicating that they intended to base their policy henceforth on working together to secure the consent of a majority in the North, over however long a necessary timespan, it would open the way to bringing violence on the nationalist side to an end. For republicans too have a pragmatic interest in obtaining majority consent; while the Northern nationalist community would at last have a clear prospect of vindicating their democratic rights, denied for 70 years, as part of the political majority in the whole of Ireland. For unionists it would mean that both governments were embarked on a policy of encouraging them to a final reconciliation with the majority of their fellow-countrymen, with whom they could build together a genuinely better Ireland.

THE SENIOR PREFECTS COMMITTEE AT OMAGH CBS (CHRISTIAN BROTHERS' SCHOOL) favours a federal solution. It recommends that

talks, attended by all important groups in Northern Ireland, including those currently excluded from the process, and by representatives of the British and Irish governments and the EC,
and possibly chaired by a US peace envoy, should take place. The IRA could help to initiate
such a process by announcing an indefinite ceasefire. The talks should have a broad agenda,
and should *not* confine themselves to discussing solutions within the context of Northern
Ireland as part of the United Kingdom and the Republic of Ireland as a foreign country.

The Committee unanimously agrees that the best solution which could
emerge from such talks would be a federal Ireland, with a central government in Dublin, but with substantial powers being delegated to provincial
executive bodies, which would control a considerable degree of social and
economic affairs, including policing and education. In this way, we believe,
the desire of the overwhelming majority of people on the island of Ireland
for an independent, united country can be fulfilled, while delegation of
powers to locally elected bodies would safeguard the interests of the Ulster
Protestants.

The group criticizes the current talks process for not addressing the
issue of partition. Partition, which 'has never been put before any part of
the Irish electorate, North or South, in a referendum', should be 'nego-
tiable, not taken as the framework within which a settlement must be
agreed'. The committee quotes the 1973 British government White Paper
as defining the central problem as 'disagreement not just about how
Northern Ireland should be governed but as to whether it should exist at
all'.

The group wants Sinn Féin and the paramilitaries on both sides to be
involved in this process: only in that way, it believes, 'can there be real
agreement on a settlement'.

If paramilitaries laid down their arms in return for talks with the British government, the government should accept this offer. The government should then issue invitations to all interested parties to talk with the broadest agenda possible; if these invitations are not accepted by any
particular political group, it must be made clear to that group that its viewpoint will not be
represented at such a crucial conference.

MR DECLAN O'LOAN, a teacher and SDLP member from Ballymena,
says that the essential problem in Northern Ireland is very simple: 'it is
constitutional uncertainty'. He goes on to warn that a bare majority for
any solution would not be adequate.

Suppose the day were to come when 51 per cent of those who voted in a Northern Ireland referendum favoured a stated form of united Ireland, and 49 per cent were against. Suppose further that those 49 per cent were deeply and implacably opposed to the idea. Would we really
go ahead on that basis? We in the Catholic community have surely learned little from our
experience over the years if we would be prepared to ride roughshod over the deeply held
views of half the population. Surely for the pragmatic reason that we want a constitutional settlement to work, we should seek the 'whole-hearted consent' of the people of Northern
Ireland, or at least a widespread level of consent combined with acquiescence from the majority of those who are not actively in favour.

However, Mr O'Loan then goes on to dismiss three of his four 'simple solutions' to the Northern Ireland problem — integration into the UK, devolved government within the UK, and independence — and plumps for the only possible constitutional framework which he believes will produce a permanent solution to that problem: a united Ireland. He stresses that he does not mean merely adding the present six counties of Northern Ireland to the existing Republic of Ireland, but a modern, updated, confident, European state, which would be brought about by 'changes as great in the South as in the North'.

He accepts that many unionists look forward to a united Ireland 'with all the enthusiasm they would display towards the return of the Plague. But I suspect that a large number of unionists are convinced that a united Ireland is going to come about. For that reason they have feelings of loss, resentment and betrayal.' He counters unionist fears about a threat to their Protestant heritage, culture and way of life by pointing to the decline of Catholic control over political matters in the Republic. 'Society in the South of Ireland has become much more pluralist, secular and irreligious; indeed, that might be a greater concern for sincere Protestants.'

Mr O'Loan then spells out a number of steps which he thinks will help the process towards what he sees as the inevitability of a united Ireland, although he also sees them as being of value in themselves. He urges the British government to begin to promote the idea — and thus getting the unionists accustomed to it — that 'it sees the ultimate solution to the Northern Ireland problem as being in some form of united Ireland'. He also suggests that the British government should initiate talks with Sinn Féin without preconditions, and he suggests a phased amnesty for paramilitary prisoners, with the government announcing that if a paramilitary group announces a permanent ceasefire, 'then all its prisoners will be released, starting with a large group after six months, and continuing with other groups at fixed intervals, so long as the violence is not resumed. In this way, it would be clearly seen that the only people keeping the prisoners in jail would be the paramilitary leaders themselves.'

Mr O'Loan warns unionists that their 'Ulster says no' attitude is not working, and they have few political allies left in London, where it matters to them. He urges them to 'go through a process of exploring and assessing what their own interests are' and to be prepared for a process of real negotiation.

They may not get everything they want out of that, but if they do not take part, ultimately others will make the decisions and they will have to take what is offered. Everyone will be the losers in that situation. Ireland as a whole stands to gain much from the remarkable qualities of the unionist population if they do not continue to turn in on themselves.

MR PADDY DOHERTY, the director of the Inner City Trust (ICT) in Derry (in a personal, oral submission), begins by saying it is 'a major tragedy that the unionists did not really accept the native Irish as equals. What has happened in the North of Ireland over the last 20 years has been a flowering of the native population and it has frightened them out of their wits.' He is concerned that if the two communities do not come to 'some kind of arrangement about living together on this island, then there will be a major confrontation when the [population] figures for native Irish Catholics are greater in electoral terms than Protestants. With their present mind-set the unionists will attempt to assert themselves by force of arms, [and that would be] disastrous for them, as well as ourselves, because that will initiate the involvement of the whole Irish race, and that would be a major tragedy.' He believes that, in such an event, the unionists would attempt a repartition, but they are misreading the situation if they think Britain would back them in this.

Britain will have to join the persuaders. I would like to see a commitment by the British government to put a lot of money into bringing a unity of purpose to both Catholics and Protestants and to indicate that it is no longer possible for Britain to maintain its responsibility to the people of Northern Ireland indefinitely.... If Britain fails in persuading both communities in Northern Ireland to appreciate their differences and work together, the loyalists are going to find themselves out on a limb — angry, aggressive and without friends.

Mr Doherty has no objection to Britain

playing a supportive role as long as it is understood that the elected representatives, all of them, of the Irish people, would have to hammer out the structures of government. It could well be that all of Ireland may decide that a federation of Britain and Ireland could be the most suitable arrangement as both countries battle for economic survival. I honestly believe that a united Ireland would be a non-starter initially and could happen only when sufficient trust had been built between the Northern unionists and the rest of Ireland. However, there are a variety of constitutional variations which could apply, and I will accept any of these as long as they are negotiated by the elected representatives and agreed by the Irish people. However, an independent Northern Ireland with the unionists back in charge would test my tolerance to the limit.... My own preference would be a state wherein the principle of subsidiarity was the keystone: that is, the interference of central government to be confined to the macro-decisions and locally to be confined to those areas where the local structures are unable to cope.

He believes the sticking-point for many unionists is to accept that majority rule is only one aspect of real democracy, and that the real mark of a democratic society is how it treats its minorities. (See also Religious, Cultural and Other Issues: Identity.)

MR P.A. McNAMEE, a County Antrim man now living in Dorset, begins his submission with an amusing if sharply drawn account of growing up as a Catholic in a Protestant area in the 1920s and 1930s. He believes that Northern Ireland, once 'the loyal hub of the Empire', is now seen by Whitehall as being 'surplus to requirements'.

Ulster, from being a grossly flattered, cosseted favourite, has become a bore and a nuisance. Yet the Ulster-Scots — self-respecting, dynamic and courageous — still snuffle abjectly at

England's heels. This is totally out of character, so why do they do it?

He cites as a principal reason that they 'seem honestly to believe the most childish of all myths, that Home Rule is Rome Rule'; their leaders have encouraged this state of mind.

The real victims of partition are the rank and file loyalists. They have been betrayed, misused, misled, blinded to their best interests and even cajoled out of their identity. They may still regard us Catholics as white niggers, but feeling superior to an *untermenschen* is about the only privilege they can boast.

On the Catholic side, Mr McNamee tells of visiting relatives in Derry recently. He asked them if they were aware that demographic change meant that Derry and Armagh had now joined Tyrone and Fermanagh in having Catholic majorities. 'Their response was emphatic. They knew well, and they looked forward to freedom (their word) as a coming certainty.' He thinks the mid-2020s is the probable date for the coming of a united Ireland. He believes that one effect of this population change is that 'unless the situation changes radically, the nationalists will have no interest in settling for anything less than what is already on the table — a federal Ireland.'

Mr McNamee recommends that the British government should propose a federal Ireland to the unionists, and give them an ultimatum to accept it or face a British withdrawal. Those who wish to be 'repatriated' to Scotland or elsewhere should be helped to do so. He doubts if five per cent would actually leave.

The important thing is for Britain to mean what she says. Once the loyalists realize that the old cow is really going to kick over the bucket and hightail for the horizon, they will accept the new situation and flint out the best possible deal with the bog Paddies down south. Some people talk about a bloodbath if England goes. They take no account of the sea-change it [a withdrawal] would produce in the loyalist outlook. Their whole playpen way of life grew out of their long dependence on England. With the playpen gone, the unused dynamism of this very positive people would assert itself constructively. If a bloodbath would bring England back, it just might be worth a try. But nothing on earth would bring England back once she had escaped from the Ulster imbroglio, and what other possible purpose would a bloodbath serve?

MR GAVIN WRIGHT from north Down, stressing that he is not an IRA sympathizer, argues that a British withdrawal from Northern Ireland 'need not be a traumatic experience for Protestants. We could look, for example, at a staged withdrawal taking place over a 20-50-year timescale. The British army would not need to disappear overnight for the Provos to consider a long-term ceasefire. Dual citizenship could also be offered for an indefinite period after withdrawal had begun, and business and economic links could also be maintained, particularly now that trade barriers throughout Europe are being brought down.'

Other submissions which dealt, among other things, with the united Ireland or federal Ireland solutions, were from: Mr William Burns, Mr Peter Cadogan of the Gandhi Foundation, Mr R.J. Clements, Committee for National Democracy and Peace, Mr Michael Cunningham, Mr Steve Dawe, Mr Patrick Devlin, Mr Alan Evans (a socialist Ireland), Mr Sean Gallagher, Mrs Elizabeth Groves, Mr Joseph Healy Jnr, Mr Barry Hurley, Irish in Britain Representation Group, Irish National Congress, Irish Studies Workshop (Soar Valley College), Captain James Kelly, Mr Brian McKeown, Mrs Anne McQuillan, Mothers for Peace (Ilkley), Ms Clara NíGhiolla, Mr Dermot O'Brien (an all-Ireland responsibility sharing body with increasing powers), Mr Gabriel O'Keefe, Dr Seán Ó Mearthaile (a socialist Ireland), Dr Máire O'Rourke, Mr Philip Perry, Mrs Ursula Perry, Ms Eva-Maria Reidinger, Republican Sinn Féin, Mr Hubert Rooney, Mr A.E. Gordon Rudlin, Mr E. Ruttledge and Stormont Presbyterian Church (one of several different proposals).

Joint Authority/Sovereignty

Various and widely differing forms of administering Northern Ireland with an input from both the British and Irish governments provided the third most popular category of suggested political structures for Northern Ireland (33 submissions). These tended to be divided into two kinds: those written from a broadly nationalist viewpoint, which saw joint authority structures as a stepping-stone to a federal or otherwise more unified Ireland; and those which stressed that, in order to gain some unionist support for them, joint authority, or something less than joint authority, would have to be seen as an end in itself. Frequently the submissions under this heading overlapped into proposals for a united Ireland, a federal Ireland or an autonomous Northern Ireland (see separate sections). Interestingly, only one submission in this section came from an organization or institution.

MR DOMINIC LOUGHRAN from Newry writes:

Like many northern nationalists, I would be quite happy to see the link between Northern Ireland and Britain maintained, if it is in a context in which there is also a substantial political link between North and South in Ireland. I am sure many nationalists here have no wish to dispossess unionists of their link with Britain — they simply want political institutions which reflect the attachments of the nationalist community to the rest of Ireland, alongside those of the unionist community to Britain.

I believe the involvement of both Britain and the Republic is crucial to the stability of Northern Ireland. Any proposal for British withdrawal would undoubtedly cause civil conflict, but equally one has only to look back to the political landscape before 1985, when the defining question was how the alienation of the nationalist community could be addressed — a question no longer asked — to realize that there must be a role for the Irish government in any political settlement here. Just as the unionists do not see Britain as an occupying power, so nationalists do not see the rest of Ireland as a foreign country, and any discourse predicated on either of those bases is, by definition, exclusive of one community here.

The question is whether nationalists can accept the maintenance of the link with Britain if there is also a significant linkage between North and South, and whether unionists can accept such a linkage in a context in which the place of Northern Ireland within the UK is subscribed to by all sides, including the Irish government. I believe that such acceptances are more possible now than they were at any time in our history.

The current affairs group of the CORRYMEELA COMMUNITY begins its submission by emphasizing that 'attempts to develop or impose political structures on Northern Ireland which deny the reality that one part of the population is hostile to the British state while another is hostile to an all-Ireland state will always founder on the rock of sociological and empirical fact.' The current affairs group warns that, since elements in both groups have resorted to force, and political violence has deepened polarization between and within communities, there has been an acceleration of 'the marked and near-universal disillusion with the democratic political process'.

Continuing to believe that the competing national and cultural groups in this one geographical area will one day 'disappear' while there is ongoing political violence is cloud-cuckoo land. Simplistic attempts at 'integration' into either Britain or Ireland without the majority assent of both communities will always rely on the military suppression of one part of the community.

We in Northern Ireland are faced with a difficult choice: either we begin to develop political structures which seek to accommodate this dual or bi-national reality or each group will continue to seek militarily to suppress the other. For as long as Britain is prepared to maintain present policy, this may be by the relatively humane instrument of the British army. The British army remains sensitive to international outrage and the democratic norms of British society. Alternatively, it may be the result of uncontrolled ethnic pogroms. Without wishing to be unduly alarmist, the example of ethnic cleansing in Bosnia, unpredicted in the West, should alert us to what the suppression of one group by the other in ethnically divided societies can actually mean.

The group says the two key aspects of the Anglo-Irish Agreement which should be retained in any future agreements are: '(1) the recognition at international level of the dual or bi-national reality of Northern Ireland, and (2) the obligation on both the United Kingdom and the Republic of Ireland to work together.'

Irish involvement in Northern Irish affairs must be both real enough to reassure nationalists and limited enough to reassure unionists. The unionist community needs to be reassured that the addition of Irish national involvement in Northern Ireland is not the same as the subtraction of British involvement. In other words, the Anglo-Irish Agreement is part of a 'both British and Irish' conception which rectifies nationalist fears but is not part of a slippery slope, the end of which is the coerced reunification of Ireland and the substitution of unionist fears for nationalist ones. In this regard, the Irish Republic legitimately could be asked to re-examine the language of Articles 2 and 3 of the Irish Constitution, to ensure that they cannot be interpreted as support for republican terrorism.

They should 'clearly state that any unity will be by consent of the Northern population'.

Equally the nationalist community 'needs to be reassured that the Anglo-Irish Agreement is not a temporary measure, except where that Agreement is replaced by a new agreement arrived at by general consent. The right to Irish citizenship should be guaranteed. The British government should be asked, in the light of appropriate changes in Articles 2 and 3, to formally recognize the involvement of the Irish Republic in Northern affairs.'

No agreements can be made which are not guaranteed by both Britain and Ireland. No purely internal arrangements for Northern Ireland, based on particular interpretations of democracy or even of internal courts, can survive the internal pressures and suspicions. Everybody must be clear that there is *no* possibility that any group in Northern Ireland can coerce the other by force. This applies to both unionists and nationalists. Only the certainty of a unified and consistent monitoring by both Britain and Ireland can give this assurance. Changes in the constitutional status of Northern Ireland following a new political structure should be extremely difficult. Majorities of over 75 per cent in Northern Ireland, both in [a Northern Ireland] parliament and in popular referendum in Northern Ireland should be required before either British or Irish withdrawal could be effected. This should be ratified by both the UK and the Republic of Ireland in an international treaty. In this way both communities can be assured of their own ties without threatening the other.

The group then suggests a devolved Northern Irish parliament elected by proportional representation, with a regional government ruling 'according to the broad principles of power-sharing', 70 per cent majorities required for new legislation and a Bill of Rights along the lines proposed by the Committee on the Administration of Justice. (See Law, Justice and Security: Changing the Law).

The group goes on: 'Settlement in Northern Ireland will require real institutional changes in the relationship of the Irish Republic and the UK. Both will have to accept the involvement of the other in each other's affairs for the foreseeable future.' This ultimately would include joint decision-making structures, at least in Northern Ireland. There will have to be unique international agreements recognizing that Northern Ireland is 'a special problem between them'.

This will involve Irish nationalists in an acceptance of Britain remaining in Ireland, for which there is little evidence that they are really prepared. Furthermore, it will involve the acceptance by Britain that its international boundaries in relation to Ireland are open. British-Irish relations are so involved, that complete separation is no longer possible without enormous costs. Official recognition, ultimately through joint institutions, of a common heritage and future will have to transcend historical antagonism between Ireland and Britain, if Northern Ireland is to find a way forward.

New political arrangements between the two countries would involve special financial arrangements. 'It must be recognized that the present imbalance of financial ability to pay represents a serious difficulty to joint sovereignty.' North-South relations should be promoted at all levels. To prevent unionists seeing this as dealing with the entire problem only in an Irish context, rather than one that also involves Irish nationalists' equally difficult relations with Britain, 'the triangular structure, Britain-Ireland-Northern Ireland, will have to be maintained in all things, including cultural exchange'.

The group sees involvement by the Republic of Ireland in Northern Ireland's legal and security structures as the single most difficult political obstacle. It makes a number of minimum suggestions: a Bill of Rights; appeal cases to be heard by courts with judges drawn from British, Irish and Northern Irish jurisdictions; police complaints to be handled by a body independent of the Police Authority structures, with all investigations involving representatives from both Britain and the Republic.

Only when there is an internal structure for the government of Northern Ireland which can command the loyalty of nationalists will it be possible to recruit nationalists to the police in numbers commensurate with the nationalist share of the population. Without direct Irish involvement in security, it is difficult to see nationalist distrust for the police changing. Policing in Northern Ireland should be subject to annual review by the British and Irish governments. All appointments at high levels in the RUC should be subject to both British and Irish approval. Candidates for such posts may be selected from police services in Britain, Northern Ireland or the Republic. Political representation on the Police Authority should include representatives from across the political spectrum in Northern Ireland and from Great Britain and the Republic of Ireland.

The Corrymeela submission stresses that whatever Northern Ireland's formal structures — and many groups will see new agreed arrangements as a betrayal of their causes — there will be a continued need for models of trust at all levels of society. These will range from the Anglo-Irish Conference at the top, through the work of the Community Relations Council, bodies working for fair employment and fair policing, Education for Mutual Understanding and integrated education, to inter-church and cross-community groups at the grass roots.

Governments in Britain and the Irish Republic must be unequivocal in their own support for such developments. The two governments inevitably will have to develop their own cross-national co-operation to such an extent that there is no possibility for local political interests to portray Britain and Ireland as enemies, each working to impose their own, conflicting agendas for Northern Ireland. Only if the politics of division and separation are shown to be pointless and hopeless can a new agenda of trust and inter-community relationships appear to be more rational to the majority of people in Northern Ireland. Unless the commitment to inclusive forms is actually made in both Dublin and London, the politics of pessimism and fear, based on very real experiences of violence in Northern Ireland, will always appear more 'realistic'.

(See Culture, Religion, Identity and Education: Religion.)

MR RAYMOND FERGUSON, a Fermanagh unionist councillor, says that, 'whereas the unionists in 1973 were able to persuade not only the British government but the government of the Irish Republic and the SDLP to set up and take part in an administration with significant powers devolved from Westminster alone, it is now difficult to conceive of any form of devolved government that will not be supervised by both London and Dublin'.

Mr Ferguson stresses that what sustains and fortifies the IRA is 'the state of political limbo that Northern Ireland has purposely been allowed to exist in since 1972'. He points out that all the major British political parties are 'determined that Northern Ireland shall remain apart and distinguished from the rest of the kingdom'. Their 'constant wishful thinking has been that (a) Protestants and Catholics, unionists and nationalists shall in some way see the futility of their quarrel and agree to co-operate in a new and separate government on terms acceptable to both sides, and (b) that whenever this arrangement is in place, the province will adopt a sensible and friendly *modus vivendi* with the Republic of Ireland.'

Since the 1985 Anglo-Irish Agreement, British policy has been 'to try to weary unionists, in particular, into a state of mind where they eventually accept what Whitehall policy-makers conceive to be the inevitable — that their political future lies on this island and not on the British mainland, and that they really have to make the best of it'.

The unionist leadership has been unable or unwilling to confront its followers with this reality. Devolved government is still held out as a major policy aim, and furthermore devolved government without power-sharing. The leadership is well aware that the chances of achieving this demand are so unlikely as to make it irrelevant, almost ridiculous. In fact, although lip service is still paid to the desirability of a Stormont-like administration with both legislative and administrative powers, the unionist leadership has long since abandoned any real hope of achieving such. What is now envisaged is a type of county council with administrative power only. If there is a discernible policy, it is to have Northern Ireland's legislative matters dealt with by a Special or Grand Committee at Westminster and, of course, to have the Anglo-Irish Agreement abolished.

Mr Ferguson believes that 'a large proportion of the unionist electorate does not readily identify with Westminster as its democratic outlet. If a sort of creeping integration is to be the outcome of the present policies, then it is tolerated only because there appears to be little alternative. The result is a debilitating and dangerous demoralization that in the short term can only succour the terrorist and in the long term will see a continuation of the emigration of the best young people.'

He worries too about the dependency that has resulted from the huge amounts of money poured into Northern Ireland by the British Treasury in order to give the 'appearance of normality and even prosperity', which he says does little for the self-respect of the ordinary Northern Irish citizen.

No one enjoys being beholden to anyone else for their existence; Northern Ireland people have long prided themselves on their self-reliance. They find that their inability to influence their political destination, combined with such a considerable financial dependency, is a double blow to their pride.

Mr Ferguson concludes by looking at the inevitable consequences of Northern Irish business expanding into the all-Ireland market of five million people as part of the removal of EC trade barriers: 'to the vast majority of Northern Ireland businessmen, this market is much more readily accessible and understood than the markets of Britain and the rest of Europe'.

It is to this new commercial situation that unionist politicians must now address their minds. To date, the attitude of unionists to Europe and the Common Market has been negative, even begrudging. It is time for a radical change. A positive attitude to the removal of trade barriers is needed. Northern Ireland business should be encouraged to take advantage of this new market on their doorstep. There should likewise be a new attitude to the improvement of North/South infrastructure — better roads and communications. For the period from the middle of the 19th century to the 1950s, Northern Ireland business, largely due to its linen and shipbuilding interests, was faced towards the Great Britain market. For the past 70 years, because of the protectionist policies of successive Southern governments, it has been forced to disregard its Southern market.

Because of the greater facility with which business can be transacted on the same land mass rather than over sea journeys of 30-300 miles and longer, it is entirely foreseeable that regardless of what attitude is adopted by politicians North or South, commerce will develop and grow between the North and South of Ireland. This will inevitably give rise to the need for political direction and structures to deal with the demands and problems created. It is difficult to see how the Unionist Party could sensibly ignore these developments. Of necessity, political representatives of the North will become involved in dealing with representatives of the government of the Republic. To date unionists have fought shy of acknowledging any entitlement of the Republic's government to input into Northern Ireland affairs. This may have been the inevitable result of having had the Anglo-Irish Agreement foisted on them, but as time passes it will become clear that this position is no longer tenable.

MR JONATHAN STEPHENSON, a vice-chairman of the SDLP but writing in a personal capacity, says that 'the logic of history is that, regardless of current constitutional arrangements, the six counties of Antrim, Armagh, Derry, Down, Fermanagh and Tyrone are populated by men and women who owe their allegiance not to a single nation–state, as has been the norm in Western Europe (whatever the fluctuating boundaries of states might have been from time to time), but to two'. He believes the important thing is that the political arrangements for governing Northern Ireland should recognize the reality of this divided allegiance.

In the immediate short term, that might just mean working the existing Anglo-Irish Agreement more vigorously to give some teeth to its provisions and to allow 'nationalists' in Northern Ireland to feel that the Irish Republic did indeed have a genuine right to protect the interests of those people in the North whose cultural and political identity are regarded by them as Irish. Moving the Agreement further down the road towards the concept of joint responsibility (while leaving the symbols of United Kingdom *sovereignty* untouched) would be, it seems to me, an appropriate short-term response to the failure of all-party negotiations to reach agreement.

My preferred option would be for joint responsibility for Northern Ireland exercised by the two governments and the elected representatives of the people of Northern Ireland, with formal sovereignty remaining with the UK, unless or until a majority of the Northern Irish people decide otherwise.

Mr Stephenson notes that others have sought to add a European element to this process, and agrees that, if achievable, this would be desirable. However, he believes that a 'Europe of the regions' will have to evolve into the next century and cannot successfully be imposed ahead of its time. What is important is that the region's people should take back a stake in their own government, while at the same time being able to express to the full 'their different but equal senses of nationhood'.

His suggested model for how this might work would be along the following lines. It would involve a three-person directly elected commission governing Northern Ireland, with a likely membership of two unionists and one nationalist, but requiring consensus to exercise power, including the initiation of legislation. Alongside this executive would be a proportionately elected Assembly, perhaps operating a proportionate committee system, with initial consultative and review functions, broadening into weighted majority legislation and veto powers over the proposals of the commissioners as confidence in the institutions is established. The commissioners would appoint departmental Ministers from the assembly and they would be answerable to the assembly.

The three commissioners and their junior Ministers would sit in a Council of Ministers, with Ministers from Dublin, to reach decisions on 'a whole range of strategic island-wide social and economic issues, including financial questions and, crucially, including all-island security policing, which I would like to see separated out from 'community' policing, which would remain accountable to the assembly. Northern, Southern and British Ministers would meet regularly in an inter-governmental conference with powers of review. Formal sovereignty over Northern Ireland would remain at Westminster. Any deal would need to be ratified by referenda in both parts of Ireland, and a referendum in the South might provide an excellent opportunity to tone down the symbols of territorial nationalism seen by some to be contained within Articles 2 and 3.'

Mr Stephenson believes that neither the history of the last 23 years, nor the present record of Belfast City Council, can give anyone confidence that an unfettered assembly, even one with ingenious but highly artificial power-sharing arrangements, is likely by itself to gain the support of the wide range of people that any new political institutions in Northern Ireland would require. On the other hand, he says that many nationalists have 'for some time accepted that the old ideal of a politically united unitary state of Ireland with one flag, one Dáil Eireann and one President is impossible and that Northern Ireland must be shared'. What is required now is for many unionists to come to the same conclusion 'vis-à-vis their ambition for Northern Ireland to be exclusively part of the United Kingdom. The parrot cries of 'Brits Out' and 'No Say for Dublin' are but two sides of the same base and outdated constitutional coinage, and it is more than time that that coinage was removed from respectable circulation.'

In their submission (which is a chapter of a book published in January 1993), DR BRENDAN O'LEARY of the London School of Economics and DR JOHN McGARRY of the University of Western Ontario in Canada quote the late Professor John Whyte, in support of their case. Joint authority, he wrote in 1990,

responds to the analysis of the Northern Ireland problem as one of a clash of identities... it is the logical goal towards which the Anglo-Irish Agreement of 1985 seems to be pointing, whether or not the signatories intended that fact ... it is the point towards which various forces in the conflict appear to be converging — unionists' adamant refusal to be ruled by Dublin; nationalists' insistence on symbolic as well as practical equality in Northern Ireland; the declining interest of opinion in the South in outright unification; and possibly a British readiness for detachment from the problem without taking the risk of abandoning all say in how it should be handled.

Dr O'Leary and Dr McGarry believe that 'British and Irish arbitration through joint authority would be more disinterested and productive in outcome than simply British or Irish arbitration'. Majority rule inevitably would provoke conflict unless it dealt only with non-contentious issues or took place within a joint authority framework. Joint authority would allow for experiments in Swiss-style cantonization in which powers could be devolved to new and very small local political units. 'Under joint authority, both the British and Irish governments could continue to promote consociational (i.e. power-sharing) solutions, with no worse prospects of success than under present circumstances, and with some medium-term prospects of creating more widely legitimate structures of government.'

The joint authority option, say the two political scientists, involves

the appealing idea of splitting the difference: both sides would gain because their national identity is respected by membership of their preferred nation-state, and by being governed by their preferred state; and both sides would lose because their national aspiration is accomplished at the expense of sharing the regional territory with another nation-state and another national community. However, given that the status quo is one of British sovereignty over Northern Ireland, tempered by the Anglo-Irish Agreement, it must be acknowledged honestly that Ulster unionists would experience an actual loss from joint authority, whereas nationalists face a speculative opportunity-cost from the creation of joint authority: the prospect of immediate or medium-term national reunification.

Dr O'Leary and Dr McGarry recall that the first appearance of joint authority as a serious policy option came in the 1984 New Ireland Forum Report, when it emerged as the third preference of the convened nationalist parties, after a unitary state and a federal Ireland. The sketchy version outlined in that report 'implied a permanent system of dual direct rule in Northern Ireland, with British and Irish ministers governing the region. Joint direct rule, through legal, policing and military organizations responsible to the appointees of both states, would be tantamount to joint sovereignty'.

They then refer to the different form of joint authority suggested by the majority of the members of an independent group of UK-based academics, journalists and politicians in the Kilbrandon Report (also in 1984). Under their scheme of 'co-operative devolution, a five-person executive, consisting of one representative of the UK and Irish governments, and three (elected) representatives from Northern Ireland, would govern the region and resolve any disputes by majority rule'. This would make the system of government non-colonial, and create incentives for unionist and nationalist representatives to participate in the executive. The Kilbrandon Report made clear that, in its preferred model, the British government would be the dominant partner.

Dr O'Leary and Dr McGarry concede that opinion polls have shown that this 'comparatively novel idea' has little public support in Northern Ireland. In a July 1991 poll, 19 per cent of people interviewed in the Republic of Ireland, 10 per cent in Britain and 7 per cent in Northern Ireland gave first-preference support to 'a devolved government jointly guaranteed by and responsible to the British and Irish governments' (26 per cent in Britain, 25 per cent in the Republic, and 11 per cent in Northern Ireland gave it second-preference support). The same poll showed that 49 per cent of those asked in Britain were very willing to give the Irish government a major role in any new settlement (25 per cent a minor role), while 28 per cent in the Republic envisaged a major role for the British government and 40 per cent a minor role. However, the poll showed that joint authority enjoyed much greater support among Catholics than among Protestants in Northern Ireland.

Given unionists' dislike of the Anglo-Irish Agreement, it is not surprising that they reject joint authority. Moreover, the few critics who have examined its merits have usually observed that most condominium precedents have been colonial (for example, Boyle and Hadden in 1985). They have also maintained that joint authority would be undemocratic because it would have to be imposed against the wishes of a majority of Northern Ireland's citizens.

When answering the undemocratic charge, proponents of joint authority reply pragmatically that any micro-constitutional solution, apart from returning Northern Ireland to unionist majority control, has to be imposed against the first preferences of a majority in the region, including British direct rule; and they observe that the British and Irish governments have already imposed the Anglo-Irish Agreement against the wishes of a majority of the region's electorate. In a principled rather than a pragmatic way, proponents of joint authority can argue that Northern Ireland cannot be a successful democracy if it is to be purely British or purely Irish. Furthermore, they can maintain that, since both communities in Northern Ireland regularly express their wish democratically to be governed by the British or the Irish states, there is no good reason why they should not be (partly) governed by both those states. Finally, since the governments and electorates of both Britain and the Republic of Ireland have direct stakes in Northern Ireland, there is no argument in democratic theory that can show why they should not create a form of shared political responsibility in which the British, Irish and Northern Irish governments and peoples participate.

MR MICHAEL FARRELL, the former People's Democracy leader, now a solicitor, writer and civil liberties activist in Dublin, argues strongly that 'an end to emergency laws would help to secure a cessation of republican violence, which in turn would create a more fertile climate for discussions about the future of Northern Ireland.' (See also Law, Justice and Security: Reducing the Violence.)

However, he also argues that 'future structures must at the least represent the bi-communal nature of Northern Ireland and the all-Ireland allegiance of a substantial section of the population. I also suspect that growing disenchantment with its role in Northern Ireland will lead to progressive disengagement by Britain'. Mr Farrell believes that the 'simplest and most logical arrangement' would be an all-Ireland state with strong safeguards for unionist and Protestant interests, whether through a federal structure, dual citizenship, or internationally guaranteed human rights protection.

However, he recognizes that unionist agreement to such an all-Ireland state does not seem likely in the near future, so in the short term he opts for a maintenance and strengthening of the Anglo-Irish Agreement and in the medium term for a form of joint authority. Mr Farrell believes the Anglo-Irish Agreement and Conference must continue as 'a minimum expression not just of nationalists' aspirations towards Irish unity, but of their desire to have Dublin involved in the running of the affairs of the North as the second guarantor of their position'.

He then digresses to defend Articles 2 and 3 of the Irish Constitution in the same terms. Although previously nothing much was expected of them by many Northern nationalists — who saw them as a clever piece of verbal republicanism concocted by de Valera — they were nevertheless regarded 'as a minimum response to Britain's actual exercise of jurisdiction over the North'.

In today's circumstances, when the question of Dublin involvement has become a much more immediate issue to many nationalists, to delete those Articles, otherwise than as part of a wider settlement which continued to express the aspiration to unity and gave it a more concrete form, would be seen by many nationalists as an act of betrayal or abandonment by the Republic. It would engender great bitterness and a feeling that they were isolated. It would give a considerable boost to those who argue that the political road cannot bring redress for nationalist grievances.

Joint authority would mean a structure involving the British and Irish governments 'sharing authority and responsibility for the government of Northern Ireland'.

If military forces were still required, it would mean they would be drawn from the armies of both states, possibly with the addition of troops from other member states of the EC as well. The police force should be disarmed, civilianized and restructured to reflect the two communities which it would be serving, there should be no locally recruited armed militia, and the administration should function subject to an entrenched Bill of Rights or to the enactment of the European Convention of Human Rights into the domestic legislation of Northern Ireland.

A local assembly and executive, whenever agreed, could administer the area under the supervision of the joint authorities, while a powerful independent Human Rights Committee, with personnel drawn from the UK, the Republic and the EC or the US, could be given a mandate to vet all proposed legislative or administrative measures and to monitor the activities of the security forces and the administration.

The potential for friction between the two governments would be considerably lessened by the fact that both are members of the EC, which would have a substantial interest in avoiding conflict between member states and could act as an arbiter in disputes, while more and more areas of policy effectively would be determined at EC level anyway.

If Britain moves towards disengagement from Northern Ireland,

that would of course mean a lessening of Britain's financial contribution to the economy of the area. Under a joint authority arrangement, however, Britain would still have a substantial commitment for as long as this lasts, while a cessation of violence should mean a considerable 'peace dividend' to the UK authorities.

Eventually Mr Farrell feels that 'a period of good and fair administration under joint auspices would lessen unionist fears about Dublin, and that, combined with a British desire to disengage from Ireland, would lead to agreement on a transition to an all-Ireland administration, with whatever safeguards unionist representatives required. They would also have the reassurance that if anything went wrong, they could always seek redress from the EC authorities, with whom the Irish government would be very reluctant to clash.'

MR TED O'SULLIVAN from Dublin sees the basis of a solution in 'shared sovereignty' between the UK and the Republic; this would not necessarily be joint sovereignty, since the powers held by each government would not have to be symmetrical. Pointing out that Catholics are now in a majority in over half the land area of Northern Ireland, he suggests that 'within this framework possibly there could be a type of repartition creating two cantons, made up of the areas where each community is in a majority. Each community would have its own bailiwick. Each one could develop a special character suitable to the majority within it, but respecting the minority. The fact that each held a captive minority would act as a check on the other.' After a time, the Southern state could take on more responsibility for the nationalist canton.

Elsewhere in his submission, Mr O'Sullivan points out that the people of the Republic of Ireland aspire to a united Ireland, but the key word is 'aspire'. 'Nobody lies awake in bed at night worrying about it. There is great willingness for compromise. The fear of the South that unionists have is partly caused by politicians playing on their insecurities, and partly due to a misunderstanding of the 'aspirational' culture of the South.'

MR STEPHEN PLOWDEN from London outlines a 'first sketch' of a joint authority constitution. Citizens of an autonomous Northern Ireland would enjoy dual citizenship. They are currently able to vote for a Northern Ireland assembly (when in existence) and the House of Commons; they should also be able to vote for the Irish parliament, the Oireachtas. To avoid the anomaly of Northern deputies voting on issues which do not affect their constituents (for example, taxation), there could be different categories of legislation on which they could and could not vote. Alternatively, Northern Ireland could be represented in the Seanad but not in the Dáil.

In civil law cases, parties to a contract in Northern Ireland could state whether it should be governed by British or Irish law, which in any case are very similar. Legal proceedings would start in the same lower courts in Northern Ireland, but appeals would go to London or Dublin. Judges in criminal cases need not all come from Northern Ireland, nor even from Britain and Ireland, but from any common-law country. A final court of appeal could be set up in Northern Ireland, staffed by judges from common-law countries other than Britain or Ireland.

Mr Plowden proposes a new (or renewed) office of Governor or Chief Magistrate, elected either by direct popular vote or by a regional assembly, who would appoint the Chief Constable of the RUC, perhaps renamed. Policemen from other countries should be eligible for this post. If it was necessary for the military to act in support of the police, the soldiers should come from the EC. 'For the time being, the Chief Magistrate would have to address any request for help direct to individual heads of state, but there is an increasingly strong case, quite apart from Northern Ireland, for the Community to develop its own peacekeeping force.' (Now see Law, Justice and Security: Reducing the Violence.)

REV. JOHN BRADY S.J., of the National College of Industrial Relations (NCIR) in Dublin, says 'the political structure which appears to reflect most accurately the pluralist nature of Northern Ireland would be that of a semi-autonomous region of the EC, over which the governments of Great Britain and Ireland exercise joint sovereignty, while encouraging the development of regional political structures which allow for the participation of elected representatives of both traditions in government'.

He outlines one possible model, which incorporates a British Secretary of State working with a Minister of State nominated by the Irish government. There would be a 13-person executive appointed by the Secretary of State with an independent chairman, representatives of all the constitutional parties — who could be members of an elected assembly, but need not be — and from both governments. The objective would be an executive reflecting both traditions, but in which neither unionists nor nationalists have a majority. The US-style provision for non-elected people in cabinet could help to break the political impasse by allowing talented people from outside politics to be brought into government. 'The political parties would experience a new political reality, namely that they may participate or not as they choose, but they cannot block progress being made in devolved structures of government.'

Father Brady proposes that such a new structure should be given a two-year trial period so that people can see it working in practice before it is put before the electorate, North and South, for popular endorsement by referendum.

The aim should be to devise a structure which has a reasonable chance of attracting a majority of about 60 per cent from both unionist and nationalist voters.... There would also be a high level of support in the Republic of Ireland for them. Hence there would be a possibility of around a 70 per cent majority support in the whole island in a referendum held on the same day in both parts of Ireland. This would be a strong message to the IRA to end its campaign of violence.'

A BELFAST NATIONALIST LAWYER also supports moves towards joint authority, which he suggests is the current direction of both the Anglo-Irish Agreement and British government policy. However, apart from the enormous practical problems, he sees the main political obstacle highlighted by the strength of unionist opposition to the Anglo-Irish Agreement. 'Up to now, given the 'winner takes all' nature of the conflict, unionists understandably have seen any progress towards significant change as the 'thin end of the wedge' leading to a united Ireland. This genuine fear would need to be assuaged. All parties would need to agree the new arrangements as a historic compromise and not a stop-gap.' He emphasizes the importance of building in 'the greatest possible degree of local democracy with the necessary safeguards to protect the interests of both communities'.

If such a structure can be developed and can cater to the sensitivities, hopes and fears of both communities, then the conflict can be brought to an end. If both communities can identify with the institutions and arrangements in any new set-up (and a stable economy and adequate standard of living are guaranteed), any remaining gunmen on either side will be deprived of that well of alienation, fear and anger which allows them to continue to operate with a high level of public support, or at least ambivalence, as at present.

MR PAUL NOLAN says that sometimes the reconciliation of unionist and nationalist ambitions seems like 'a hopeless quest to square the circle'; at other times that 'we are moving — although with glacial slowness — towards the building of a new consensus'. He identifies two elements in a political framework that might encourage the latter possibility. First, with signs that in the 'new Europe' the importance of the nation-state is breaking down, 'a new emphasis on regional and on cross-national arrangements could facilitate a repositioning of Northern Ireland in ways that will extend beyond traditional loyalties'.

Secondly,

both the British and Irish governments are moving towards a position which might best be described as a 'whatever-the-two-sides-can-agree' position. This preparedness to pass over sovereignty is healthy and co-operative, provided it is accompanied by a further commitment to jointly sharing responsibility until new arrangements are in place — in other words the next step must be an acceleration of the Anglo-Irish Agreement to something approaching dual sovereignty. Inside Northern Ireland the people must be entrusted with some form of executive powers if they are not to be kept in a state of political infancy. It is this tier of government which is, frankly, the most difficult to envisage. Is it to be appointed or elected? How can it be trusted not to misuse its powers? The danger of a Belfast City Council with real power is enough to frighten even the most stout-hearted. On the other hand, it has to be recognized that, in some ways, it has been the lack of power at local level that has allowed the political stage to be occupied by the crude sectarians now in post. As the recent Rowntree-funded research into district councils has argued, the return of power to the councils may attract back more able and creative individuals. It would be prudent, however, to accept, as the Rowntree Report accepts, that the return of powers could be staged only as a rolling process of devolution, as a response to proven exercises of consensually based power-sharing.

(See also Culture, Religion, Identity and Education: Identity.)

A former independent senator in the Republic, MR BRENDAN RYAN, says that the future government of Northern Ireland must be based on institutions that incorporate both a continuing permanent link with the UK — to be broken only with the consent of its people — and a 'clear and identifiable link with the rest of Ireland'. The key must be the institutionalization of both links on the basis of equality. In return for accepting the continuing link with Britain, the Irish government should be granted a 'status equivalent to co-supervisor of institutions in Northern Ireland'.

Unionists would be asked, in return, for the 'copper-fastening of the future of Northern Ireland's link with Britain', to sacrifice some of its 'external symbols'; for example, the introduction of an oath to uphold and respect the law and the constitution of Northern Ireland, rather than an oath of allegiance to the monarch, or a separate flag and anthem for Northern Ireland. The equivalent sacrifice for the nationalists would be that they would be asked 'to accept the reality of the continuing link with Britain, in return for which they will get institutional guarantees about their equality within the state of Northern Ireland and their links with the Republic'.

SIR ROBIN DAY suggests, as a new mechanism for working towards a solution, a treaty between the British and Irish governments to create a UK-

Irish 'Community', based on the idea of partnership between sovereign nations institutionalized in the European Community. The treaty would specify those matters with which the Community and its institutions would be concerned on both sides of the border: for example, security, law enforcement, religious discrimination, civil rights, education, economic development and constitutional reform (including Articles 2 and 3 of the Irish Constitution).

The new Community institutions would be broadly similar to those of the EC: a council of ministers, a commission, a court and an assembly. 'If this sounds cumbersome and complicated, that in itself might have the positive merit of harnessing and diverting the energies of conflict into new channels of constructive discussion.' Sir Robin foresees that in such a UK-Irish Community the border issue would come to matter less and less. 'The influence of the Community institutions would evolve, *by mutual consent of the two sovereign treaty partners*, through a step-by-step process at a speed varying with the problems in each area of the Community's concern.'

The apex of the Community would be the council of ministers, which would include Ulster ministers, if some form of devolved government had been created. The 'engine or powerhouse' of the community would be the commission, made up of administrators, senior police and security officers, economists, diplomats and churchmen, who would serve the community's common interest, whatever their own national or religious backgrounds. 'The commission would examine problems within the limits of the Treaty, and propose action to the council of ministers.' There would also be a court of justice to rule in disputes arising out of the treaty, and an assembly, made up of MPs from both national parliaments, with the right to question and criticize the commission and council. The new community would have to be endorsed by referendum in both the UK and the Republic.

The new UK-Irish Community would 'express the overwhelming need for two sovereign neighbours to exist in peace, yet *with no surrender of long-held loyalties and aspirations on either side*'. Nothing in the treaty would imply the abolition of the border, or weaken allegiance to the Crown, or derogate from the Republic's independence. Nothing in it would be a bar to a united Ireland if, in the future, that were to be the wish of a majority of Northern Irish people. The fact that the treaty would be between the UK and the Republic would be welcome to unionists, since Northern Ireland's involvement in the new Community would be as part of the UK. 'A new atmosphere might gradually be created in which violent extremism would be less able to flourish. And cross-border operations against terrorists could be intensified.'

MR STEPHEN SHELLARD of Dumfries in Scotland proposes a 'supra-national assembly' elected by all the people of Ireland. When a consensus of its members existed, it would have powers to pass legislation which would be binding on both sides of the border. This assembly would not govern 'in the sense of making day-to-day decisions regarding the management of the country; this responsibility would remain firmly with, on the one hand, the Dáil, and on the other a Stormont parliament in relationship to Westminster'. The assembly would require a consensus — for example, a two-thirds majority — to take decisions, with the result that most important legislation would continue to be passed by the Dublin and Belfast parliaments. However, in such a forum, the unrestricted discussion of matters affecting all Irish people would in itself be a useful function, and make it of particular symbolic importance to nationalists. Unionists could make its setting-up conditional on the removal of Articles 2 and 3 of the Irish Constitution. They also would know that the Republic of Ireland's right, through the assembly, to have a say in Northern Ireland's affairs, would be balanced by their right to intervene in the Republic.

EOIN Ó COFAIGH from Dublin offers a radical new strategy for devising governmental structures acceptable to all the people of Northern Ireland. This 'might start from the premise, not of sovereignty by either one of two governments over the territory of Northern Ireland and all its people as a result, but rather, from that of permitting the Northern people individually to give their allegiance either to the government in London or that in Dublin'. Thus Northern nationalists could elect representatives to the Oireachtas, choose to be answerable to Irish law and to be tried by the Republic's courts, and pay their taxes to the Irish government. Unionists would be *encouraged* by the Irish people to continue doing the same vis-à-vis Britain.

He accepts that such a structure would involve great constitutional and legal change, immense practical problems and enormous consequences for structures of taxation, security, administration of justice, health and welfare, and so on. He accepts that the proposal appears to offer more to nationalists, with a greater change in the status quo, than unionists. 'However, the unionist people gain two things: peace with their neighbours (this only has a chance if everyone agrees), and the knowledge that neither their neighbours nor the Irish people as a whole will ever seek to have them leave the protection of the British Crown.'

Some form of joint authority is implicit in the submission from MR CHARLES MURPHY of Maghera, Co. Derry. He argues that any future political settlement must satisfy the following requirements:

(1) It must recognize and give expression to the sense of Britishness of the unionist people and

their allegiance to the British Crown. (2) It must provide the unionist people with realistic protection from the possibility of incorporation into a united Ireland against their will. (3) It must
recognize and give expression to the sense of Irishness of the nationalist community and its
allegiance to the Irish nation. (4) It must provide the nationalist community with realistic protection from the possibility of rule by a unionist majority within Northern Ireland. (5) To be
stable and lasting, any such settlement would have to be seen as a settlement for the foreseeable future which would hold even if unionists were to become a minority within Northern
Ireland.

All these requirements are essential: the omission of any one of them will leave the roots of
the conflict unchanged. If unionists are left secure in their Britishness and protected from a
united Ireland, their sense of threat will be diminished and the motivation to discriminate
against nationalists will be removed. If a constitutional settlement within Northern Ireland
gives recognition to the Irishness of the nationalist people, it will earn their allegiance; it will
remove their sense of not belonging and will remove the traditional argument for a united
Ireland which so threatens the unionists.

Mr Murphy points out that the current constitutional position 'gives
complete recognition to the British/unionist identity and no recognition to
the Irish/nationalist identity. The flag is the Union Jack; the head of state
is the British monarch; our MPs sit in the British parliament at
Westminster; our police are the Royal Ulster Constabulary; the army is
the British army. Any settlement representing a middle way must involve a
move towards the nationalist position.' However, Mr Murphy believes that
only if people can learn to live together in peace within Northern Ireland
will there be the possibility of a united Ireland sometime in the future. A
move to such a new middle-way constitutional settlement would require
'an immense act of faith and goodwill from both communities. However, if
reasonable people cannot resolve their differences, they cannot be surprised if less reasonable people push such differences to the point of violence, bloodshed and sectarian murder.'

He therefore proposes a new pluralist constitution which 'formally recognizes that there are two major communities, one British and one Irish.
Any government of the state must clearly represent both these communities. The constitution should be guaranteed by the United Kingdom, the
Republic of Ireland and the EC. The continued existence of the state
should not be dependent on one of the communities forming a simple
majority.'

DR DONAL O'TIERNEY of Newry, Co. Down, argues similarly that the
demographic reality in Northern Ireland is such that a one-culture state
can never be politically stable. To force the 19 per cent unionist minority
into a 'one-culture united Ireland' could not produce a peaceful island, and
it is even less feasible to subsume a 40 per cent nationalist minority into a
'one-culture loyalist Ulster'. He believes that 'only a two-culture Northern
Ireland administration, where there is equality of esteem for both traditions and the symbols and institutions reflect that equality can bring stabil-

ity'. He suggests that the Westminster Parliament should bring in a new two-culture Northern Ireland constitution to which nationalist Ministers would take an oath of loyalty, rather than to the Crown. The Irish Constitution could then be amended to give parallel recognition to this new Northern constitution. In the new two-culture Northern Ireland administration,

the authorities would have to be at pains to ensure that the quality of esteem is reflected in the symbols of state and that the official phraseology will defer to both unionist and nationalist sensitivities. We have the example of how a sustained policy of removing sexist terminology in our language can bring about a change of attitude in the treatment of women in our society.

PROFESSOR BRICE DICKSON, of the Department of Public Administration and Legal Studies at the University of Ulster, says that 'an obvious way in which to accommodate the extreme nationalism of the republican and loyalist paramilitaries, and to counter claims that being British is more desirable than being Irish, or vice-versa, is to highlight the benefits attached to having both nationalities. In practice, people living in Northern Ireland already enjoy these benefits, but they are not fully enough articulated by the respective governments. A study could usefully be undertaken of how joint territorial sovereignty has operated in other parts of the world, and a blueprint for its introduction should be produced. This would have to be promoted not as a staging-post to the reunification of Ireland, but as a desirable constitutional status in itself.' (See also Law, Justice and Security: Changing the Law/Reducing the Violence)

MR JOHN CHRISTOFFERSEN from New York believes joint authority is attainable because it involves reaching agreement between the two governments, rather than between the more unreconcilable unionist and nationalist leaders. It is economically sound because it would leave intact Britain's large financial subvention to Northern Ireland. It would remove the sovereignty dispute, thus making co-operation between unionists and nationalists easier. However, it would have to be presented as a permanent solution, rather than a halfway house to a united Ireland. 'If legal mechanisms could be put in place to guarantee the permanency of joint authority, this could go a long way towards overcoming loyalist fears.'

The former Alliance Party politician, MR WILL GLENDINNING, warns that unless joint sovereignty is

seen as the final settlement, then unionists will have moved, but the nationalist aspiration for a united Ireland will remain and joint sovereignty will just be another step in what unionists fear, that is, the loss of their identity. For joint sovereignty to be worth moving to from a unionist point of view, nationalists would have to be prepared to accept that their ultimate goal of a united Ireland would have to be dropped. Only in that situation is joint sovereignty a true compromise, with both sides giving up their first options of a permanent place in the UK and a united Ireland. Even if that position is reached, there are other problems and difficulties to look at. For example, joint sovereignty or authority presumably means joint responsibility for finance and resolving disputes which arise. Are both the UK and Irish governments prepared to pay equal amounts for the running of what is now Northern Ireland? Are they prepared regularly to be put in the position of being asked to arbitrate on behalf of one community because of the actions of the representatives of the other? Will the existence of permanent outside referees assist in the development of politics based on some form of judgment apart from the tribal one that currently rules, or will it perpetuate the present position?

PROFESSOR EDNA LONGLEY's submission is essentially a cultural perspective, and is detailed in that section of this report. However, one paragraph is worth quoting here: 'As a border zone, a Bosnia, an Alsace-Lorraine, Northern Ireland does not lend itself to domination by any single 'national' ethos. In practice, its citizens pick 'n mix from a range of cultural choices every day of their lives. Thus acknowledgment of *de facto* affiliation to two islands must inform any new institutional framework. A spirit of condominium would serve to undermine *both* absolute claims.'

Other submissions that dealt, among other things, with some form of joint authority or sovereignty were from Mr Barrie Brooks, Rev. Gregory Dunstan, East Belfast Protestant and Catholic Encounter, Rev. Denis Faul, Mr B. Gordon, the Inter-Church Group on Faith and Politics, Ms Marie-Therese McGivern, Mr M.B. McGovern, Mr Austen Morgan, Mr William Potter and the SDLP.

Autonomy/Independence/Repartition

For ease of presentation, these three rather different — although often related — options are being placed in the same section. There were twelve submissions which dealt, among other things, with repartition (nine of them from outside Northern Ireland); eleven that dealt with some form of autonomy for Northern Ireland within the UK; and eight dealing with independence.

Autonomy

The most detailed submission in this section, proposing an autonomous Northern Ireland within the United Kingdom with control over security and an institutionalized Irish dimension, was by MR JIM HANNA from Belfast. This summary can give only a superficial flavour of it. He stresses that 'a key to redefining the problem in a manner which does not involve compromise of principle would be for each side to separate the 'essentials' of their respective positions from the 'non-essentials'. The essentials, and therefore the key to an accommodation between unionists and nationalists, are the equal validity of the two traditions in Northern Ireland, and the equal protection of their essential interests and aspirations.'

Acknowledgment by unionists of the equal validity of the nationalist philosophy means that unionists would accept that if the nationalist case were to become accepted by an agreed weighted majority of the electorate — he suggests 75 per cent — then Northern Ireland should become united legitimately with the Republic. On the other hand, nationalists must acknowledge that 'there is no historical imperative that Ireland should ever be united — the case for unity must be judged on its merits alone'. Northern Ireland is an 'unagreed' entity, rather than a non-legitimate one. Nationalists must accept that unionism is entitled to the same respect as nationalism as a legitimate political philosophy, and that unionists are entitled to persuade the people of Ireland — and especially nationalists in Northern Ireland — of the merits of the unionist case.

It is essential, Mr Hanna goes on, that 'nationalists are free to actively safeguard and promote their political, cultural, religious and other interests and goals — and that there is a mechanism whereby they may achieve the eventual realization of their nationalist aspiration'. Equally, it is essential that unionists should have their interests safeguarded against being absorbed unwillingly into a united Ireland. To this end, they would seek nationalists' agreement to the criterion of 'widespread community consensus' (75 per cent of the electorate) as the condition for ending partition.

Mr Hanna suggests a new structure, based on pragmatism and compromise, by which he believes every side would gain (and lose) something. This would involve Northern Ireland becoming a self-governing unit within the UK, with a devolved assembly in which contentious legislation would be passed only by this 'widespread community consensus', and a 20-year border referendum would be subject to the same requirement. As a result of this 'parity of privilege', unionists would consent to substantial recognition of an institutionalized Irish dimension, involving inter-governmental and inter-parliamentary roles for the Republic. The British army would withdraw — subject to a cessation of paramilitary violence — to be replaced by a military Ulster Guard, not part of the army but responsible to a new independent security authority (itself partially answerable to the new assembly), and an Ulster Police Service.

Mr Hanna suggests that by this arrangement unionists could secure nationalist recognition of and commitment to a devolved Northern Ireland, and would be made more secure by the 75 per cent border poll provision. Nationalists would gain the safeguard of the 75 per cent weighted vote in the assembly and unionist acceptance of a substantial Irish dimension. Republicans, by accepting this limited version of British 'withdrawal', would be able to return to the mainstream of Irish political and cultural life and might also secure an amnesty for all the prisoners of the 'troubles'. 'The ultimate political destiny of Northern Ireland — whether with Britain or the Irish Republic — would be determined by peaceful political rivalry under clearly defined neutral rules.'

YOUTH FOR PEACE, the youth wing of the Peace People, believes that Northern Ireland should move towards being 'a largely autonomous region, still within the UK, with a maximum devolution of legislative powers.' Youth for Peace does not believe an elected regional assembly should be based on a Westminster-style 'majority rule' model, but should contain 'structures that safeguard the rights and aspirations of all minorities'. The organization also wants a reform of local government, with increased powers and responsibility given to local councils 'on the basis of reward for cross-council co-operation and power-sharing'.

An all-Ireland consultative body should be set up to play an important role in

institutionalizing relations and effective communications between North and South. It should investigate and discuss mutually important issues and pass its findings and recommendations on to the relevant authority (a Northern Ireland assembly, Westminster, Dublin or Brussels). The membership of this forum should draw from all areas of life (on the island for example, politicians (Northern Irish, Southern Irish and British), institutions such as the Confederation of British Industry (CBI), the Confederation of Irish Industry, and the Irish Congress of Trade Unions (ICTU), farmers' organizations, educational organizations, and so on. There should also be specifically elected local representatives. This would allow a broad range of matters to be covered, particularly matters of economic concern, such as regional development, inward investment, infrastructure and tourism.

Youth for Peace believes that 'as Northern Ireland demonstrates its political maturity, it should operate within the EC with a degree of autonomy rather than being fettered by Westminster or the Dáil', thus becoming a functioning part of 'Europe of the regions'. It also recommends a Bill of Rights and an independent commission, perhaps modelled on the European Court of Human Rights, to which individuals who feel their civil rights have been infringed can appeal. (See also Law, Justice and Security: Changing the Law.)

MR B. GORDON of east Belfast urges a solution based on a common identification with Northern Ireland, which would not be seen by the two communities as shedding their Britishness or Irishness. He proposes a self-governing political entity that would have close relationships with both Britain and the Republic of Ireland. He sees Puerto Rico — 'described as a self-governing commonwealth attached to the United States' — and the Isle of Man as possible models. Initially he suggests two voting registers electing representatives to two separate, but equal, regional parliaments, with a liaison body between them. Eventually he would like to see one such body but with absolute equality of representation in it between the two communities. Only in this way could a sense of loyalty to the new entity and its structures be built up.

Other submissions which deal, among other things, with a measure of autonomy for Northern Ireland, either as part of the UK, or with links to both the UK and the Republic of Ireland, are those from: Ursula and Niall Birthistle, Mr Garret Brophy, Dr Michael Carr, Mr H.W. Gallagher, Mr A. Kaluarachichi and Mr Nevin Taggart.

Independence

REV. HUGH ROSS, the president of the Ulster Independence Committee, writes:

The UK government, with or without the help of the Eire government, has been unable to defeat terrorism and achieve political stability within Northern Ireland. The crux of our Ulster problem — a divided society with divided loyalties — has to be addressed. The only solution that does not involve defeat or humiliation for one section or other of our people is for us to put a united Ulster first, before a united Ireland and before a United Kingdom. Our divided allegiances to England and to Eire must be replaced by a common allegiance to Ulster. The Anglo-Irish Agreement has failed and a replacement agreement will continue to divide and rule the Ulster people as before. The only 'art of the possible' way forward is to become *one* community, governed in accordance with the articles of an agreed constitution and Bill of Rights in an independent Ulster. Constitutionally negotiated independence is the only way forward, so that the people may unite and be loyal to a state founded on the principles of equality for all and special privilege for none.

MR GLEN BARR, the former UDA leader and former Northern Ireland Assembly member who is now a prominent community leader in the Waterside area of Londonderry, maintains in an oral submission that his 1979 document, *Beyond the Religious Divide*, with its argument for negotiated independence, still holds the key to the way forward. He says his major concern at present is that the loyalist paramilitaries are becoming 'more proficient and efficient' and therefore more attractive to the younger elements in the Protestant communities as a way of hitting back at the IRA. 'There is hero-worship at the moment, with the UFF and UVF able to hit [identifiable targets] and Protestants now saying maybe that person was not just an innocent Catholic — he could have been a Provo or a Provo supporter and therefore is as entitled to be hit as we are.' He worries that the paramilitaries will become 'more ruthless, harder to talk to and harder to change'.

Mr Barr believes that the two communities in Northern Ireland must learn that they will win some things and lose others. 'If you have a constitutional settlement which involves Dublin, it will not be accepted by the Protestants, and if you have a constitutional settlement which involves

long-term rule by London, this will not be accepted by Catholics.' Therefore both outside protagonists will have to be removed from the scene: the
Protestants will have to give up their *de facto* and *de jure* British guarantor
in return for asking the Catholics to give up their dream of a united
Ireland. 'We would be giving up more than we are asking the Catholics to
give up.'

He recalls that in *Beyond the Religious Divide* he suggested that the Northern Ireland Supreme Court, the final guarantor of people's constitutional
rights under his independence constitution, should contain a judge from a
friendly country, like the United States, who would ensure the fair over-
sight of the system. He also suggests a US-style direct election for the post
of Prime Minister, a powerful Speaker to run the legislature (who would
have to be elected by two-thirds of its members, or at least by a percentage
that would require the agreement of some minority parties) and US-style
separation of executive, legislative and judicial powers throughout the system. He believes that it is particularly crucial that a Prime Minister should
be able to start horse-trading with minority parties to put a majority executive together.

If we can create the right climate in Northern Ireland where the state offers everyone a fair
deal through political involvement at all levels and there is a constitution and a Bill of Rights
which protects every individual within the state, and everyone has equal rights, then I believe it
would be in the interests of everyone to support law and order.

The writer BRIAN INGLIS, who died in early 1993, was a long-standing
advocate of independence. In his submission he wrote:

All Irishmen, north and south of the border, are thought of as Irish, think of ourselves as Irish,
and make no discrimination between North and South if, say, supporting an Irish team or
player in some event. Historical circumstances have made it impossible, for the foreseeable
future, for a political union between North and South.

Northern Protestants are unionists only for protection from the South's political domination. They are 'loyalist' only to the extent that they have relied on Britain to provide that protection; when that has been in doubt, as in 1912-14 (and more recently), they have had no hesitation in being disloyal. Their fear of the Republic — understandable in the past — is now
unnecessary. The great majority of the Republic's electorate now accepts the political division
and has no desire to overturn it.

The overwhelming majority of the British electorate would be relieved to see Northern
Ireland leave the United Kingdom, if a way could be found to grant a form of independence
that would satisfy the Catholic minority as well as the Protestants. The only real strength of
the IRA and Sinn Féin lies in the British 'occupation' of Northern Ireland. If independence
were achieved, they would wither away.

The main arguments against the setting up of an independent state, with a constitution guaranteed by Britain and the Republic, are unconvincing. Northern Ireland's size no more means
that it would not be viable, than the size of Luxembourg means that it is not viable. Financial
backing would certainly be required, but with the reduction of violence it could soon be reduced.
Those unionists who want to remain citizens of the UK, with all the attendant benefits, could
maintain their citizenship — just as Southerners born before 1921 have been able to do.

Other submissions which deal, among other things, with independence, include those from: Mr Wilfred Grundle, Mr M.J. Kelly, Mr William Ruskin (Ulster Motherland Movement), Mr M.G. Thompson and Mr Gerald Tottin (dominion status).

Repartition

MR WILLIAM BROWNE of Wexford, who lived in Northern Ireland for sixteen years from the 1950s to the 1970s, proposes the 'readjustment' of the border 'in accordance with the wishes of the inhabitants, in so far as this is compatible with geographic and economic considerations'. These would be gauged by means of a referendum, which unlike the 1973 Border Poll, would have to contain a question like: 'Do you want the area in which you live (a) to remain part of the UK? (b) to be joined with the Republic of Ireland? Perhaps (b) might be divided into (1) within the Commonwealth (2) outside it.' The areas referred to would have to be of realistic size; for example, electoral divisions or wards. No such adjustment could avoid the problem of the large number of Catholics in Belfast and pockets elsewhere whose wishes expressed in such a referendum could not be met. Grants might be offered to those of them who wished to move.

MRS MÁIRE MACSWINEY BRUGHA of Dublin says that for the past 25 years she has 'watched many efforts to redress the injustices and lack of civil rights of the nationalists — with many successes. However a funda-mental injustice still remains, viz. that an Irish person, living in the North, cannot claim Ireland as his native country. He is, as it were, living in exile in Ireland.' Although stressing that the activities of the IRA are unaccep-table, she suggests that 'the IRA is not the cause of the 'troubles' but the inescapable consequence. The same phenomenon would arise in any other part of the world in the same circumstances.'
    She believes that

by refusing to address oneself to the fundamental cause, no fundamental solution can be found. We are told that a majority of the population of Northern Ireland want to remain British and democracy demands that the wish of the majority must prevail. I would point to the results of the last British general election which applied to the whole 32 counties in 1918. The result was over 70 per cent in favour of setting up a parliament in Dublin. Even taking the six north-east-ern counties separately (which is not a way to judge election results democratically), Fermanagh and Tyrone returned a substantial majority for a Dublin government, as well as south Armagh, south Down and parts of Derry. Very little notice was taken of the democratic wishes of the people at that time, nor when creating the six counties.
    However, the question now is how, in spite of centuries of injustice and conflict, do we find a way for the people of this island to live together in harmony with neither ethnic group in domination over the other. I can see no other solution today than to allow the areas where the nationalists live in a majority to rejoin the present Irish state if they so wish. The areas where the British live should be given autonomy — possibly within the framework of a federal Ireland. Switzerland and Germany find this form of government very successful.

I realize that at this suggestion many people throw up their hands in horror. Repartition? One objection I have heard is that we would be abandoning the nationalist areas of Belfast. I have even been told the people there would be slaughtered. Perhaps Belfast could be made a self-governing 'free city' on the model of Danzig and Trieste, possibly as a protectorate of the EC.

MR FRANK CURRAN, a former editor of the *Derry Journal*, argues that the British justification for Northern Ireland has been based on a myth, created by Lloyd George in 1920, that the area has 'a fairly solid population, a homogeneous population, alien in race, alien in sympathy, alien in religion, alien in tradition, alien in outlook from the rest of the population of Ireland'.

Mr Curran uses the 1911 census figures to show that at the time of partition, of Northern Ireland's total population of 1,250,000, slightly more than half, 700,000, lived in Belfast, County Antrim and the northern part of Down, with a Protestant majority of 552,000 to 149,000. 'That area, it could reasonably be claimed, met Lloyd George's parameter of 'homogeneity'.' In the other four-and-a-half counties there were 281,000 Catholics and 268,000 Protestants. 'That area, containing about two-thirds of the total land mass of the six counties, therefore, held a nationalist majority. Today the nationalist-Catholic majority in that area exceeds 60,000.'

Mr Curran goes on:

Where would you find a more homogeneous area than Derry, Fermanagh and Tyrone? They have common borders, they have borders with the Republic, there are nationalist majorities in all three counties. The three counties measure 2714 square miles, more than half the six counties' total area. Add Armagh, with common borders with Tyrone and Monaghan, and a growing Catholic proportion of the population, and you see that not only is Antrim-Down the area where 70 per cent of the unionist population lives, but that Antrim and Down are the only two counties without a land border with the Republic.

I am not advocating a simple repartition after 70 years. It is obvious that no Dublin government could rule Antrim-Down in peace and stability, as it is that no unionist government can ever hope to get real allegiance from west of the Bann. I am saying that if politicians continue to try to reach agreement based on the homogeneity or the right of the six counties to be regarded as a natural political unit, and fail to allow for the fact that there is a nationalist majority in the greater part of the land mass, they will be drawing a spurious blueprint, not for peace but for unending further disaster. The last 70 years has proved not that 'Ulster is British', but that Derry, Tyrone and Fermanagh are as Irish as Kerry, Dublin or Tipperary. No hyperbole can remove that fact.

The plain truth is that in a restructured Northern Ireland, even inside the United Kingdom, special arrangements must be made about contentious factors like the police and new laws about their control and accountability in the nationalist counties. British Ulster expects recognition, Irish Ulster must have no less.

Other submissions dealing with repartition, among other things, are those from: Mr James Brogan, Mr Fergal Henchy, Mr R.B. Leahy, Mr Brian

Minchin, Ms Máire Mullarney, the Newry Plan Group, Mr Andrew Patterson and Mr Michael Singh.

Integration/Other Unionist Proposals

There are 11 broadly integrationist submissions in this section — both from Labour and Conservative viewpoints — together with another 12 which could be described as unionist without being specifically in favour of either integration with Britain or devolution for Northern Ireland. It is noteworthy, perhaps, that there were no submissions specifically proposing a return to Stormont-style 'majority rule' devolved government.

Integration

DR CLIFFORD SMYTH, the author and former unionist politician, argues that Ireland lacks a balance of power, a lack made more acute by the ideology of the Irish nationalist majority which views the eventual unification of the island as not merely a matter of faith, but something that is inevitable.

Those, a minority in Ireland, who support the Union, are deeply factionalized and atomistic. The political leadership of all the major factions of unionism is inept, inarticulate and lacking in both creativity and imagination, which explains why the working-class loyalists, who have borne the brunt of the war with the Provisional IRA, will state candidly that Ulster's British and Protestant people are 'lions led by donkeys', a phrase redolent of the heroic role of Ulstermen in another campaign of attrition, the Somme in July 1916.

It can be seen, therefore, that the Irish nationalists are able to maximise their position beyond that of being the natural majority on the island — while the unionists are perceived to be, indeed perceive themselves to be, weaker than they are in reality. The unionists have a defensible homeland and have shown unflagging determination, resolution and conviction in their prescriptive (God-given) right to be both British and Protestant in the north-east corner of the island, in that region known as Ulster.

The whole drift of British policy through the present prolonged period of unrest has been to tilt the internal balance in Ireland in favour of the Irish nationalist position. As a consequence the Ulster unionists have rejected numerous proffered 'solutions' favoured by successive British governments out of an intuitive sense of self-preservation.

Dr Smyth voices a common unionist belief that neither the British nor Irish governments 'will support any political initiative which either shores up the status quo, that is, Northern Ireland's continuance within the United Kingdom, or even worse, from the point of view of the Dublin-London axis, actually strengthens the Union'. As an example of this, he cites the campaign for British parties to contest elections in Northern Ireland, the response to which had shown that the British political elite had 'no enthusiasm for this most democratic way to peace'.

'The unwillingness to defend the Union is seen most explicitly in "security" where the British policy has been one of containment. Provisional

IRA violence is not to be permitted to get out of hand or to be seen to be so excessive as to alert public opinion on the mainland.' He says the fact that this 'scandal' does not intrude upon public opinion 'can be accounted for by the profound bias in the media against the British and Protestant population in Ulster and by the bipartisan approach to the region adopted by the main parties at Westminster'. Dr Smyth believes that because the British government and army cannot defeat the IRA militarily, it follows that 'it will be necessary to defeat the unionists politically, in order to end "the violence"'.

Throughout this prolonged period of civil disturbance and constitutional uncertainty, a clear pattern is discernible in which events have been alternately dominated by surges of republican physical force violence and political aggression against the unionists by self-styled 'constitutional' nationalists. The combined effect of these two flanking movements on the part of irredentist Irish nationalism has been to weaken the Union over time. The whole weight of upholding the continued unity and integrity of the United Kingdom of Great Britain and Northern Ireland therefore rests upon the will, determination and resolve of the pro-British portion of the population within the peripheral region of Ulster.

Dr Smyth warns that the concept of the unionist 'siege mentality' is a double-edged one: 'those whose attitudes are shaped by a 'siege mentality' may be expected to prove immoveable and intransigent, but also present will be qualities of patience, tenacity and determination'.

Dr Smyth believes that it is through the flexible adaptation of the Westminster Parliament that an innovative resolution of Northern Ireland's major political problems can be found. He suggests that a fortnight after a British general election, a second vote should be held in Northern Ireland in order to elect a regional executive committee from among the 17 Northern Irish MPs. The election would be by PR, with Northern Ireland being treated as one constituency. The Secretary of State would then appoint the various executive committee members to run the Northern Ireland government Departments, and the Northern Ireland Office would be disbanded. He suggests that seven Minister of State-style offices should be created for the MPs who have gained the first seven places in that second ballot. The committee, chaired by the Secretary of State, would be bipartisan in its make-up.

The holding of a second ballot for offices in such a Northern Ireland executive committee 'would encourage parties in Northern Ireland to enter into negotiations with each other to secure a place for their candidate. In time, such a political process could help to rebuild the centre ground in Ulster politics and promote the emergence of an elite consensus. An elite consensus is absent at present and represents a serious obstacle to political progress in any direction.'

Two of the departments to be administered in this way would be new (or renewed) ones: Home Affairs and Community Relations. The former would have some limited responsibility for policing, a role that would expand 'as the security situation improves and general police matters cease to be politically contentious'. The executive member with responsibility for the latter would be the link between the new executive committee and the Anglo-Irish talks. 'Since these talks have been a source of suspicion to the unionists in the province, there might well be a political gain to be made from giving this post initially to a unionist in order to allay fears in the province.' This department would also fund academic research into aspects of the 'Irish Question' and support community relations work among young people in Northern Ireland. The work of the executive committee could be scrutinized by a Northern Ireland Grand Committee at Westminster, although both it and the Secretary of State would be answerable to Parliament.

Dr Smyth believes that the participation of Northern Ireland's Catholic MPs in this bipartisan executive committee would open up the possibility of a growing percentage of their electorate supporting such a solution. 'Finally, the abandonment of a parochial solution for Northern Ireland would open up the region to new political horizons and the prospect of the emergence of a different style of political leadership.'

MR MARK LANGHAMMER, a member of the East Antrim Labour Representation Group and an unsuccessful candidate in the 1989 European elections, says (in an individual submission) that 'the central political abnormality of Northern Ireland is that politics is disconnected from government. Those who govern Northern Ireland are not electorally accountable to the people of Northern Ireland. Government is entirely without mandate.'

The British Labour Party 'operates a boycott of Northern Ireland by refusing to organize constituency parties, by refusing to stand candidates and by refusing to accept members in Northern Ireland'. He says that since the party started an overseas membership scheme, Northern Ireland is the only place in the world where one cannot join the Labour Party. The Liberal Democrats have a similar policy. The Conservatives, following a grass roots revolt at the 1990 party conference, do allow Northern Irish people to join the party, but there has been little support for local Tories from Conservative Central Office.

This 'arm's length' principle underlying British policy in Northern Ireland has resulted in Britain keeping a 'reluctant sovereignty' over the region for 70 years. This has three aspects: the party boycott; the refusal of British governments to refer the Republic of Ireland's territorial claim in Articles 2 and 3 of its Constitution to the International Court at the Hague; and insistence on some form of devolution in Northern Ireland 'whether it is demanded or not, effectively reducing Northern Ireland to 'homeland' or 'bantustan' status. Where devolution has not been possible

— that is, 1974 to the present — a separate 'Government of Northern Ireland' has been kept in waiting with a distinct body of law (even where the law is a very close replica, if not word for word) and a distinct administration with separate government departments. In this way, devolution is used by the British political establishment as a replacement for the proper politics of government and as a means of avoiding responsibility for the region.'

Mr Langhammer believes that the border question — on which all constitutional parties and the two governments are committed to the principle of no change without consent — should be resolved by consent, i.e. by periodic referenda, as laid down in 1973 legislation. 'Pending consent for change, the border question is no excuse for keeping Northern Ireland out of, and at 'arm's length' from, the political life of the rest of the United Kingdom.'

Northern Ireland's exclusion from the British party system means that 'politics in Northern Ireland is exclusively communal. This is not the fault of the local political parties. Given the history of Northern Ireland, it is inevitable that parties exclusive to Northern Ireland will be either Protestant or Catholic. They are not political parties in any proper sense, since they are not concerned with the business of governing the United Kingdom. They are concerned only with representing Catholic or Protestant interests.' He goes on to stress the importance of the party system in ensuring the success of Britain as a multinational state, in that the British parties 'contest every seat and every inch of ground and actively seek to draw into their ranks numbers of every religious or ethnic group'. That process has helped Britain to absorb substantial numbers of immigrants from India, Pakistan and the West Indies without major social disruption.

Mr Langhammer says that at successive opinion polls since 1986 'a consistent figure of over 60 per cent of both Catholics and Protestants are shown to be in favour of the development of the party system in Northern Ireland. Within the trade union movement, a growing body of opinion is in favour of normal party politics.' He points out that in the only union to ballot its members on the issue — the Union of Communication Workers — over 70 per cent were in favour of the Labour Party organizing in Northern Ireland (since then the members of the Amalgamated Engineering and Electricians Union have also supported such a change).

'There is little chance of local, communal parties agreeing on anything substantial. This has been borne out yet again by the failure of the substantial and protracted 'talks' process. This is not meant as a criticism but as a statement of fact,' says Mr Langhammer.

Elections in Northern Ireland are reduced to highly inaccurate border polls (countless opinion polls have consistently shown that a significant proportion of SDLP voters and even some

Sinn Féin voters are not very interested in a united Ireland in the short term). If Westminster wants a border poll, it should be organized properly and not be called an election. If Westminster wants Northern Ireland to have proper votes at general elections, it should end Northern Ireland's exclusion from the party system.

THE CONSERVATIVE INTEGRATION GROUP (CIG) says that 'the policy of separate political development for Northern Ireland has failed and so a policy of closer involvement between Great Britain and Northern Ireland is both necessary and morally right'. The Group claims that the 'vast majority' of people of all religions wish to continue to live in the UK, and because Britain is a multidenominational, multicultural society, Northern Ireland fits easier with it than with a country that aspires to be mono-denominational and mono-cultural'. The group quotes a range of opinion polls between 1987 and 1991, showing that integration was the single most popular option with those interviewed, with between 28 per cent and 39 per cent of those polled choosing it as their preferred form of government for Northern Ireland.

The Group then outlines its integrationist proposals for Northern Ireland. It says district councils should have the power to decide on planning applications, like their counterparts in Britain. The powers of the Audit Commission should be extended to Northern Ireland, to compel district councils to give the public the same details of spending as their British counterparts. It suggests that a Northern Ireland regional council, with similar powers to an English county or a Scottish regional council, should be responsible for education, libraries, health and welfare, roads and transport, housing, the fire service, and, for the time being, have an advisory role in the running of the police force. 'In view of Northern Ireland's troubled past', it thinks that the chairmanship of this regional council's committees should reflect the composition of the council as a whole and that this should become a statutory requirement. On the potentially controversial area of housing — which was removed from local government in the early 1970s — the Group says a regular review by the Local government Boundary Commission could reduce the danger of gerrymandering and it proposes legislation to outlaw religious and racial discrimination in housing allocation. On policing, it urges a single UK-wide police force, not least because 'terrorists operate throughout the UK'.

The Group believes that legislative powers should continue to be held by the Westminster Parliament. However, it is opposed to the present unamendable order in council system, with each House of Parliament voting whether to accept or reject an order in its entirety after a debate lasting no more than three hours.

Most of the legislation mirrors legislation for Great Britain or England and Wales which has been passed by Act of Parliament after a full debate and generally after a number of amendments have been made. There is no reason why such legislation should not be extended to include Northern Ireland. Where there is a need for separate legislation, it should be considered by a Northern Ireland Grand Committee or Standing Committee, just as Scottish legislation is dealt with by the Scottish Grand and Standing Committee. A Northern Ireland Select Committee should be set up to scrutinize the work of government departments in Northern Ireland.

MR JAMES O'FEE, a Conservative councillor in north Down and an individual member of the Conservative Integration Group, notes that the people of Northern Ireland, of whatever background, are from an ethnic minority within the UK as a whole, since it is 'a multinational state in which each nation has certain rights, including, ultimately, the right to secede if that becomes the settled opinion in any of the four constituent nations'.

Mr O'Fee says that integration 'does not imply the rejection or suppression of anyone's religious or cultural heritage; however diverse, these are perfectly consistent with loyalty to a tolerant multinational kingdom where diversity is accepted'. He believes that the UK is 'a more tolerant and pluralist society than any of those states created by the one nation/one state dogma of strident nationalism — including the Irish Republic'. He points out that the British Conservative Party has always opposed the creation of devolved parliaments in Scotland, Wales and England, and calls for the same consistency to be applied to Northern Ireland. 'Conservatives have traditionally had a feeling for the British Isles as a community — economically, socially, culturally and politically', he says, quoting, to support his argument, the Irishman Edmund Burke, 'the founder of Conservative thought', and Sir Edward Carson — who saw clearly that 'a Northern Ireland Parliament and government would have a sectarian character'.

Mr O'Fee quotes a 1992 pre-general election opinion poll which showed that 46 per cent of Northern Irish people interviewed were in favour of a campaign to put pressure on the main British political parties to stand for election in the region (32 per cent of Catholics, 52 per cent of Protestants and 61 per cent of other people).

THE CAMPAIGN FOR EQUAL CITIZENSHIP (CEC) is 'committed to supporting a diverse civil society and is hostile to the proposition that the condition of political and social life in Northern Ireland is eternally limited to two — and only two — traditions. The political task of the 1990s should be to extirpate sectarianism and not to legitimize it; to depoliticize communalism and not to legislate for it. For the CEC believes that the choice today, not just in Ireland but throughout Europe, is between an open society based on liberal principles and a closed one based on ethnic belonging.'

The Campaign strongly criticizes British government policy for being founded on what it sees as the fundamentally flawed thesis that there are two permanent and opposed communities in Northern Ireland, and the basis of a historic compromise depends on the Protestant unionist and Catholic nationalist political leaders 'delivering' their respective cohesive voting blocs in favour of it. The Campaign's position is that this 'perpetuates the sectarian animosities it is designed to dispel. It only institutionalizes sectarianism in a most unstable political form (and contradicts positive civic action by government in other fields, such as the promotion of integrated education)'.

We argue that the political consequences of the two-community thesis are regressive for the following reasons. Firstly, from the moment we are born to the moment when we die, we are assumed to be members of two entirely separate communities. Our communal identity is our fate and we cannot escape it. All of us in Northern Ireland are confined by circumstance and history to be part of one or the other identity. Choice and reflection do not enter into it.

The CEC concludes that 'this is a formula which insults just about every liberal value in Western civilization'.

Secondly, the two-community thesis proposes that we have no other choice but to act according to the communal principles of our respective political identities. There is no real interest and no real purpose in doing otherwise. Indeed, if we follow the logic of the two-community thesis to its conclusion, there seems to be no need at all for democratic elections or political debate. We have simply been assigned perceived communal/religious identities. Why not simply get the communal parties to establish electoral lists and, on the basis of a statistical sectarian computation, allocate seats proportionately in some new assembly? Such a system is profoundly traditional, because freedom is only understood in terms of fidelity to the community — in sum, it is reactionary.

By making the idea of the two communities into a form of political absolute, government policy has encouraged the consequent denigration of individual rights and liberties. It has meant the attempt to promote and to sustain an organic relationship between individual, community, political party, regional assembly (of some sort) and central state authority. It has meant the attempt to inculcate an unshakable political correspondence between personal need, communal cohesion, political allegiance and constitutional 'aspiration'. It is an organic vision for all parts of the polity become functional to the rest in the service of a preordained end. That preordained end is assumed to be peace, stability and reconciliation (as stated in the Anglo-Irish Agreement, the two-community theory's greatest political success to date). What has really been promoted has been the perpetuation of sectarian antagonism which has affected and implicated everyone in Northern Ireland. It has frustrated the possibilities for proper governance rather than advanced them.

The Campaign for Equal Citizenship wants to 'explode the two-traditions stranglehold in order to provide Northern Ireland's civil diversity with an alternative political voice'. The CEC's 'liberating project' is a movement to 'reform Direct Rule from Westminster and make it more accountable. Devolution of regional functions, a relationship with the Republic of Ireland and relationships within the EC should take place in that reformed context. Protestants and Catholics have their different grievances but the vast majority recognize the important stability Direct Rule has provided — all other constitutional options considered. Poll evidence suggests that they now want a say in and an influence over the policies of state which affect their everyday lives. They also want the opportunity to join and vote for the major parties of that state. The Campaign says that Direct Rule has also changed the relationship between many Northern Ireland Catholics and the British state.

For many Catholics, and in particular the Catholic middle class of professionals and business people, important new opportunities have opened up. They can participate more fully in public life simply because they no longer need to feel complicity with institutions of Protestant supremacy. The working class, Catholic and Protestant, continue to acknowledge the comparative material advantages of membership of the British state.

MR JEFFREY DUDGEON, a long-time campaigner for integration and for the British Labour Party to organize in Northern Ireland, believes that the experience in the former Yugoslavia of the 'dismantling of a multinational state and its replacement by sovereign ethnic national states' provides 'an exemplary insight into what could so easily happen here'. He believes that 'the length and extremity of the war here is a direct and simple result of Northern Ireland being politically excluded from the multinational aspects of the United Kingdom state, and being forced to search in vain for an internal solution'.

Mr Dudgeon believes, therefore, that 'disputes centred on opposite national aspirations are insoluble; that reconciliation between such parties is only practical and possible in some greater entity, especially if the relative size of the minority has reached a critically high level'. There is no need for any British government to adopt a policy of integration, he goes on, but 'rather to abandon its absolute insistence on a policy of devolution and, pending any other magic solution, to: (a) consider upgrading local government functions, especially to curb the supremacy of the Department of the Environment; (b) write Northern Ireland into all new legislation and end (*pro tem* if so desired) the continuing adherence to maintaining a rigidly separate body of Northern Ireland law, thus enabling us to feel the benefit of reform immediately (and to pay the price if that is necessary); (c) permit local Conservatives the normal access to decision creation and decision-making that they would not only be permitted but would insist on in England, Scotland and Wales.'

Mr Dudgeon says that it is 'a denial of human and civil rights' for the Labour Party to ban Northern Irish people from membership. He believes that the aspiration to Irish unity or nationhood would not be diminished by equal citizenship within the UK, 'since some similar structure existed in Ireland throughout the 19th century and it did not stop Home Rule becoming the dominant political aspiration of Southern Catholics.' He does not believe Northern Catholics want a devolved parliament and government, citing opinion poll evidence that the overwhelming majority of both communities (96.6 per cent of Protestants and 92.2 per cent of Catholics, according to the 1978 Northern Ireland Attitude Survey) want the same laws as Britain. At the same time, such a move towards integration would be a significant blow to the IRA which 'has had only political victories and concessions for 20 years, which has led inexorably to a ridiculously long and bloody war'.

Other broadly integrationist views (although some of them objected to the description) were expressed by: Democracy Now, the Foyle Labour Group (urging the British Labour Party to organize in Northern Ireland, while hoping that one day there will be a cross-community consensus for a united Ireland), Mr Stanley Jamison, the South Belfast Constituency Labour Party (while not ruling out a socially progressive unification of Ireland achieved by consent), and the North Down Labour Representation Group.

Other unionist proposals

The most concise expression of the more traditional unionist case came from MR JIM SIMPSON, an Ulster Unionist councillor from Ballymoney, Co. Antrim. Since the compromise formula of the 1920 government of Ireland Act divided Ireland into a majority-unionist Northern Ireland and a majority-nationalist Irish Free State, 'unionists have continually declared through the ballot box their determination to remain part of the United Kingdom', he writes.

Yet this democratically expressed wish is continually ignored or diluted by those who wish to see the Union broken. If unionists are to have the political security to which they are entitled as the result of that clear expression of their democratic wishes, then it should be clearly stated and understood by all that Northern Ireland is part of the United Kingdom *without qualification*. To avoid any confusion in the eyes of the world, a referendum could be held on whether or not the people of Northern Ireland wish to be part of the UK and the result of this — which will certainly be 'yes' — would be final. After all, if Northern Ireland were to vote itself out of the UK no doubt that result would be regarded as final.

He cites the Anglo-Irish Agreement as an example of nationalist misconceptions about how in time unionists can be persuaded to go along with movement towards a united Ireland, whereas, in fact, unionists are as opposed to that Agreement now as when it was signed.

It is the continual attempts by various means to subvert the democratic wishes of the majority of people in Northern Ireland that make it so difficult to achieve a system of accountable government in Northern Ireland. Unionists' desire to be part of the United Kingdom and their opposition to being incorporated into an independent Irish Republic remain totally undiluted. The clear recognition of this reality will represent the beginning of wisdom in achieving a democratic and accountable system of government in Northern Ireland.

REV. ROBERT DICKINSON, a former Presbyterian moderator, contributes a strong traditional Protestant unionist perspective:

Unionists, of whatever political shade or religious adherence, see their destiny, and that of the province, as being linked indissolubly with the British Crown and Constitution. Whatever the reasons or historical antecedents, unionists, with rare exceptions, regard themselves as 'Irish' only in the geographical sense, and have little or no affinity with the 'Irish' in the cultural sense. This is what, to the vast majority, makes repugnant the persistent attempts to deny to unionists their deeply ingrained claim to Britishness, and to foist on them a new identity or brand of 'Irishness'.

Thus when unionists repudiate the right of the government of the Republic to have any part in determining the affairs of the province, they are not just being politically obstructive. They are, in fact, reasserting not merely the constitutional integrity of Northern Ireland as a part of the United Kingdom, and their abhorrence of republicanism, but also the far more fundamental reality of their cultural, ethical, educational, moral and religious estrangement from all that they see the Republic of Ireland to represent — a Gaelic culture, a foreign nationality and an unreformed and dominant religion.

Unionists owe allegiance not to a particular shade of political government but to the monarch as head of the state. Moreover, they see the monarch under the British Constitution not only as the supreme ruler by whose decree and under whose authority all others govern, but also as being charged with the preservation of the Protestant succession to the throne. This is why they reject the assertion that opposition or resistance to the decisions of the so-called sovereign government, which they believe to be wrong or unjust, is in any way in conflict with their ardent profession of 'loyalty'.

Dr Dickinson worries that the 1991–92 inter-party talks were less a search for a just and democratic political solution than 'a cleverly contrived process being carried on (so far as possible) behind closed doors, so as to prevent the unionist people from knowing what is going on in the hope that the sell-out of their British heritage can be accomplished without the possibility of their resistance or refusal to accept'. He then details five ways in which the unionist representatives at the talks were put at a disadvantage, ranging from British government proposals, which 'amounted to little short of joint rule by Westminster and Dublin', to the refusal to ban Sinn Féin (while banning the UDA) 'in order to facilitate the participation of representatives of terrorists at some point in the 'talks' process'.

He concludes by outlining the way forward for Northern Ireland, as he sees it, in the form of six points:

(1) Northern Ireland must remain an integral part of the United Kingdom. (2) Either Northern Ireland must be totally integrated into the United Kingdom and governed in exactly the same way as every other part of that Kingdom, or *democratic institutions of government must be established which are just and fair to all but must not endanger the constitutional integrity of the province.* (3) The right of the government of the Republic to have any say in the affairs of Northern Ireland must be abrogated. (4) Articles 2 and 3 of the Constitution of the Republic of Ireland must be removed if normal and friendly relations between North and South are to become possible. (5) Normal relations must be established between the governments at Westminster and Stormont and the Dublin government based solely on mutual respect and co-operation for the good of all concerned. (6) *The minority in Northern Ireland must be prepared to identify with and take a full part in the institutions of the state, as Roman Catholics do in the rest of the United Kingdom.*

Several unionist submissions emphasized the IRA's campaign of violence as Northern Ireland's overriding problem. MR J. EAGAR of Belfast said 'the reality of the Northern Ireland situation is that it is the terrorists who are the problem and until the British and Eire governments take the necessary resolute action to remove them from society, then the problem will continue'. Mr Eagar voices a common unionist protest that 'over the past 20 years the IRA terrorists have been allowed to set the whole agenda' and gives the example of the Anglo-Irish Agreement, which 'would never have come into being had the IRA not been in existence'.

MR KENNETH JAMES, secretary of the Stranmillis branch of the South Belfast Ulster Unionist Association (writing in a personal capacity), strongly criticizes Direct Rule, which he says 'makes our rulers arrogant, deters our best brains from entering politics, breeds servility in the population, promotes clientelism in local politicians, prevents elected representatives from learning how to govern, and absolves voters from accepting responsibility for their actions. Direct Rule is a recipe for political stagnation in which the terrorist thrives.' Mr James also complains about the difficulty of attracting young, able people into politics, with people turned off by Direct Rule and worried about violence, and the middle classes — business people or academics — seeing political involvement as a hindrance to their careers.

Other broadly unionist submissions came from Mr Jim Creighton, who argued for a Labour wing within unionism; Mr Arthur Green, Mrs Elizabeth McCullough, Rev. R.S. Ross,and Mr R.L. Walshe, who quoted Cardinal (then Bishop) Cahal Daly's warning in January 1986 that the unionists had been 'humiliated before the world through being presented as a community of bigots. Indeed, many of them must feel ashamed at being misrepresented by bigots who claim to speak in their name. Unionists have seen their cherished institutions dismantled, their control over Northern Ireland affairs decapitated, their sense of security suddenly undermined. They feel they have been forced against their will and without consultation into a future of insecurity and powerlessness.'

Local government reform

A significant number of submissions in other categories suggest, in passing, that more powers and responsibilities should be returned to local councils which practice power-sharing. This section adds a few more and includes one cautionary submission.

MR SAM BUTLER, a former editor of the *News Letter*, believes the best approach to Northern Ireland's problems is 'a gradual evolutionary one' because one of the most fundamental of those problems is 'the deep sense of insecurity felt by the Protestant/unionist community'. The Anglo-Irish Agreement has exacerbated this. 'This community finds itself caught in a vice between a government in London which has indicated a desire to withdraw from Northern Ireland and the transparently sectarian campaign of the IRA/Sinn Féin, which is regarded as being a form of genocide, particularly by the Protestant community in the south and west of the province.'

The unionist siege mentality has been

brought to the surface by pressure on unionism from all sides — the IRA; a perception that the government lacks the will to tackle the IRA effectively; the actions of nationalist politicians; the Irish language campaign; the Irish-American lobby; agencies such as the Fair Employment Commission and initiatives such as Education for Mutual Understanding. The whole thrust appears to unionists to be aimed at elevating the Irish identity at the expense of Protestant/unionist culture. This has produced an alienation within the majority community. Thus the burden of grievance has been transferred from the shoulders of nationalists to those of unionists. There can be no hope of progress while any significant section of the community feels a sense of grievance and injustice.

Mr Butler believes that this problem of unionist insecurity needs to be tackled 'by building on the political structure which already exists, and which the Protestant/unionist section regards as a fundamental element in its Britishness'. He suggests that the order in council system for passing Northern Ireland's laws through the Westminster Parliament, which implies that the government is only interested in the marginalizing of Northern Ireland compared to other UK regions, should be made more accountable by the introduction of a grand committee to scrutinize the province's legislation.

He recommends that more powers in non-controversial matters, such as economic development, should be devolved to local councils. 'The greatest progress is likely to be made at local level where regular contacts are easier and co-operation and trust between various sections of each community already exists.' He believes that the frustration of both local politicians and community-based groups is being exacerbated by existing undemocratic local government structures. The lack of effective local powers also deters key sections of the community — business people, for instance — from becoming involved.

Mr Butler points out that the present councils were the result of proposals from a commission in the early 1970s headed by Sir Patrick Macrory, which also recommended an upper tier of local government to inject authority and responsibility into the structure. This tier has never been put in place; successive governments have instead 'concentrated on what has proved to be a futile search for a more ambitious assembly-type institution'. Mr Butler believes that 'a central body, not necessarily a Stormont-type parliament or assembly, is needed to prevent fragmentation'. He sees clear signs that border regions around Derry, Newry and Enniskillen now have stronger relationships with neighbouring areas in the Republic than with Belfast. 'The trust which will make power-sharing possible has to be nurtured at local level. This approach could, perhaps, be extended to an upper tier of local government to deal, in the first instance, with non-controversial matters.'

He worries too that since 1972 Northern Ireland has become a totally bureaucratic state. 'An institutional culture has been created by the tendency within the bureaucracy to establish new agencies in response to specific demands from the community. Thus a series of Chinese walls has been created to separate the administration from the people. There are no clear lines of accountability to the community.' He finds it remarkable that Northern Ireland, 'a region about the size of Yorkshire, should require five education and four area health boards, in addition to Departments of Health and Education'.

Mr Butler urges the government to look to build on existing local structures — for example, the 30 Chambers of Commerce in Northern Ireland. At present, the Chamber of Commerce movement is forced to survive on limited finances because most of the services its equivalent bodies in continental Europe supply to local business are here supplied free by government agencies like the Local Enterprise Development Unit (LEDU) and the Industrial Development Board (IDB). Because of this, there is little incentive for business people to become involved. He suggests that the Local Enterprise Agencies — now financed throughout Northern Ireland by the International Fund for Ireland — 'should become a focus for co-operation between local politicians and business bodies such as Chambers'.

Similarly, Mr Butler suggests that local councils should be encouraged to take on more responsibility for matters like employment, education and health. He welcomes the government's move in 1992 to provide a role for local councils in economic development by giving them the power to levy a charge on the rates for economic development schemes.

Trust is the key needed to unlock the door to progress. The best way to build trust is by promoting contact and dialogue on practical non-controversial matters. It is not my intention to suggest that the main political issues should be ignored or avoided. I would contend that there has been an over-concentration by government and other bodies on addressing areas of conflict. The balance needs to be shifted to foster co-operation in other areas which have a more immediate impact on ordinary people.

He cites the work done by initiatives such as Derry-Boston Ventures, the Fermanagh Initiative, the Tyrone Economic Development Initiative, the Phoenix West Belfast Trust and the Greater Shankill Development Agency, and successful power-sharing in councils like Dungannon, Down, Newry and Mourne and Derry. 'Belfast City Council remains the most serious and enduring problem.'

Mr Butler is also concerned that after 20 years of violence and political upheaval, 'conflict defines Northern Ireland in the minds of people in the province and elsewhere. There is a need to tackle this conditioning and negative attitude, an attitude also heavily influenced, indeed reinforced, by a media which is driven by violence and political confrontation.' (See also Culture, Religion, Identity and Education: Culture.) He believes that 'a state of paralysis exists because the absence of a 'solution' has become the justification for a lack of action, an inability and/or unwillingness to look to the future. People have become narrow, selective and introverted. They are obsessed with today, but the context of their existence is the past. People at all levels are tired of the violence and political turmoil, war-weary, but there is no mechanism for mobilizing these emotions and channelling them into positive action.' He repeats that one way out of this 'stasis' would be a government strategy of involving business and other middle-class people in initiatives to regenerate local areas, and of involving business leaders more in Northern Ireland's future development. 'The way to break the inertia, particularly among the middle class, is to provide opportunities for more people to contribute in such matters as the economy, health and education. A 'can do' mentality has to be fostered.'

SIR CHARLES CARTER, the former chairman of the Northern Ireland Economic Council and currently chairman of a large independent inquiry into UK local government problems, suggests that devolving more powers to local level might be more advisable than putting so much emphasis on obtaining a constitutional settlement at regional or national level.

This would have the great advantage of giving members of both communities more experience of the actual business of government. Local councillors at present have so little real power that they tend to waste time on striking political attitudes. It would also mean that, in areas with a clear majority from one community, there would be a growing sense of responsibility for their own affairs; and in areas without that clear majority, a challenge to find local ways for the communities to work together (as indeed has occurred in some places).

The objections usually raised to the return of functions to local authorities are twofold. First, that Northern Ireland authorities are mostly too small. But this is not true by European standards: in many countries, wide functions (including education and health) are exercised by communes which are smaller than the Northern Ireland authorities. The second objection is that local authorities cannot be trusted to avoid sectarian bias. But that is a problem at national as well as local level: it has to be dealt with by appropriate safeguards, not by the non-democratic expedient of permanent colonial rule.

My proposal is, therefore, that there should be a rolling return of functions to local government, beginning with local planning, libraries, more local environmental measures, and the maintenance and lighting of local roads — but not excluding possible future functions in housing, primary education, the social services and local health services, if the initial experiment works well. The return should be subject to two conditions: first, that it should be by way of a licence, to be withdrawn if, in the opinion of an impartial watchdog body, the local authority shows substantial evidence of sectarian bias in its activities; second, that the licence should be conditional on a degree of power-sharing in the internal management of the local authority, reflected for instance in the membership of committees and the distribution of chairmanships. Such a system would offer incentives for good behaviour, and its operation over a period of years might lead to a firmer settlement at the national level.

MS MAGGIE BEIRNE, from London but presently based in Belfast, uses research material gathered for a recent thesis on power-sharing in local government to make a number of points. She finds that the rotation of the chair, deputy chair, and (to a lesser extent) the sharing of committee posts on a proportional basis between unionists and nationalists is happening in 11 out of Northern Ireland's 26 councils: six of them nationalist-controlled, and five unionist-controlled. In fact, all six nationalist-controlled councils in the region are engaged in power-sharing, the single common factor being that they are all controlled either by the SDLP or by a combination of nationalist parties within which the SDLP has a relatively strong voice.

On the unionist side, the three factors distinguishing the five power-sharing councils from the other 15 unionist-controlled councils are: (a) in all cases except one (Banbridge), there is a close nationalist-unionist electoral balance, with demographic and electoral trends suggesting an increasing nationalist percentage of the vote; (b) in all cases the Ulster Unionist Party is the dominant party within the unionist bloc; (c) there is little or no representation of what might be called non-aligned parties. None of the unionist-controlled councils, with the exception of Dungannon, yet rotate the chairperson's position, and all have engaged in office-sharing for the first time in this current term of office. Ms Beirne speculates that several factors played a role in this: the confrontational and sterile period before 1989; the consolidation by both the SDLP and the Ulster Unionists of control over their respective sectarian blocs, allowing more freedom to manoeuvre; and the positive example presented by Dungannon District Council after 1988:

Overall, one is led to the conclusion that power-sharing occurs when *either* the SDLP is able to determine the outcome, and rigorously applies its centrally agreed policies (in the past this does not seem to have been done consistently), *or* when the unionist parties choose not to rigorously apply their negative stance on power-sharing and leave it to be determined in the light of pragmatic electoral needs at the local level. In the latter case, local unionists (so far, the Ulster Unionist Party only) study the threat posed *both* by the nationalist parties, and the balance of power within the unionist bloc.

In addition, a case study of Dungannon District Council had shown that many councillors there felt the need to lead the way in bringing an end to 'sterile adversarial politics, in a common commitment to the financial and general well-being of the Dungannon area; they found in a common opposition to political violence that they had more in common than previously recognized.' Ms Beirne says 'there seems to have been no obvious public pressure for such an initiative in advance, but those most directly concerned with the move to power-sharing all increased their vote in the elections that followed soon after their innovation. There seems to be a generally positive assessment of the move, with claims that the area has materially benefited from this public expression of communal co-operation.'

She concludes that power-sharing in local government can work. 'Most importantly, it is possible for the political leadership at this level to see common external threats (political violence and economic disinvestment) and share district-wide loyalties.' Rev. Denis Faul also strongly emphasized this point in the context of Dungannon and Tyrone. However, Ms Beirne points out that

since these same prerequisites cannot be met at the province-wide level, the positive experiences of power-sharing at local government level do not necessarily presage wider changes. Indeed it is not even possible to say that power-sharing at local government level is necessarily going to flourish in all district council areas; if my assessment that pragmatic electoral considerations are crucial is correct, many district councils will never 'need' to engage in power-sharing. Nor is it possible to urge that more powers be devolved to power-sharing councils by way of an incentive to them and others. Many would argue that the current positive trends in bridge-building are occurring at local government level precisely because the power at issue is limited. Increase the stakes and the whole process may collapse. The enormous diversity of experiences on the ground seems to give further weight to John Whyte's plea that 'perhaps the search for a solution in future should envisage the possibility that different arrangements will be required in different areas'.

(See also Law, Justice and Security: Introduction.)

THE INTER-CHURCH GROUP ON FAITH AND POLITICS writes:

In parts of Northern Ireland the two communities are for the most part geographically separated (for example, west Belfast, Derry/Londonderry, Portadown). In other parts this is not true. In some areas both communities could work together, in others this will not be possible. Within the wider Northern Ireland structure it might then be worth examining the possibility of a local government structure based on quite small areas, some nationalist, some unionist, each with a certain amount of autonomy. Basic community needs and services would have to remain under the control of a Northern Ireland-wide administration. It would obviously be preferable if relations between the two communities developed in such a way that autonomous areas were not necessary.

(See also Role of the Republic; and Culture, Religion, Identity and Education: Religion.)

MR KEVIN McCAUL, a retired senior official with Derry City Council, explains in an oral submission how the independent trust movement — also referred to by Paddy Doherty — has fuelled the regeneration of Derry. When the new Conservative government came to power in 1979, following large cutbacks in public funding to Derry, its emphasis on the private sector and the 'enterprise culture' was seized on by a group of community development workers in the city to set up a number of private community-based independent trusts. Out of this came the Inner City Trust, involved in major inner city regeneration; the Holywell Trust, publications and conferences; the Northland Centre, work with alcohol and substance abuse; the Guildhall Press, local history publications; the Acorn Project, environmental work; the Creggan Initiative; the various Maydown/Ebrington centres run by Glen Barr in the Waterside, and so on. 'These are unique to Derry. For example, in the year 2000 the Inner City Trust will have £10 million capital infrastructure in the city and one million pounds per year in rent.'

The city council has also become involved in partnerships with these trusts, and Mr McCaul believes that this partnership will be the city's 'theme for the next 20 years'. An example of this was the Siege of Derry museum, which was built by the Inner City Trust, largely by using government job creation schemes, and presented to Derry City Council. He says there was a feeling in the 1970s that Derry would no longer be the 'second city' of Northern Ireland, but would be a city with a unique identity, making a contribution of its own. Out of that feeling had come, for example, last year's Impact '92 (an acronym for International Meeting Place for the Appreciation of Culture and Tradition) celebration. 'This was Derry's celebration of the new European single market opening up and of Derry's contribution to Europe's regions: Northern Ireland is obviously one of those regions, but we decided that the region here is Derry and Donegal.'

Mr McCaul concedes that most of the work over the past 20 years has been on the overwhelmingly Catholic west bank of the Foyle. The principal future task is 'to release the energy and creativity on the (mainly Protestant) east bank'. He emphasizes that, unlike Belfast and other places, the old community work structures, built on geographical boundaries, have given way to major projects with a single focus or activity.

People are stepping out from their own particular communities to develop a single focus and achieving excellence within that, which lets them develop relations and contacts throughout the world. That is the major difference between Derry and Belfast. The work that people have been involved in has had a wider national and international dimension, and the huge release of energy through people's participation in these single focus activities has meant that their concentration was on the issue rather than on a piece of ground. I think that the particular methodology used in Derry was unique to the city. I do not think you would find such a high level of co-operative development, comprehensive community development or social animation anywhere.

He gives as an example of Derry's new international dimension the 1992 Beyond Hate conference, run by the Centre for Creative Communications, which brought in prominent speakers from areas of conflict all over the world, to address meetings and hold discussions in local community centres, schools, and even police stations and prisons.

Mr McCaul compares Derry with Belfast, where the City Council's Community Services Department employs around 130 people. In contrast, Derry City Council identifies a particular trust-run project but, instead of employing city community workers on it, its own leaders are paid and employed — 'so you have two workers from Derry City Council and the community employs up to 50 people. This strategy is the best way to approach community development.... The major players in the city now are the independent trusts. They are bigger than both the private or the public sector because they have the enterprise of the private sector but the social contacts of the public sector.' At the same time he sees people in Derry — Catholic and Protestant — identifying with a particular issue because it concerns their city: he gives the example of the successful public campaign to prevent the Du Pont chemical company opening a toxic incinerator in 1991. 'The Du Pont issue brought together a conglomeration of people both from inside and outside Derry, including Greenpeace, and this international dimension reinforces people's self-worth and self-image and it develops the city as a centre of learning.'

MR ANDREW FREW of Belfast notes that in Northern Ireland

in the absence of control by local popular vote, the local administration reflects the interests of a generalized middle-class constituency. Without the imperative to accommodate local groups through the political process, a policy of manipulating them, of excluding them from power, has been implemented. The power of quasi-governmental organizations has been developed to present an illusion of consensus and 'normality'. For a large section of the salaried middle class, the maintenance of this illusion is financed by the UK exchequer. This has a hugely distorting effect on economic development, and effectively underwrites unrealistic political positions while stifling new developments.

All this means that 'responsiveness to local interests is largely in the hands of civil servants'; there is no funding for local parties or pay for local politicians; there is 'little payback for lobbying locally'; and, as a result, 'a young person trying to develop a political career is likely to suffer low pay and a lack of related career opportunities'. Mr Frew makes a number of proposals, including six full-time paid councils in Northern Ireland; eventual funding for local political parties; modifying taxation and benefit arrangements for local needs; and international experience programmes for local representatives.

MR C. HUDSON, of Irvinestown, Co. Fermanagh, tells of his small town of 3000 people — about 60 per cent Catholic and 40 per cent Protestant — which he says has had good community relationships over many years

in good part due to the inter-community organizations which are active in it. These bodies — the Fairs and Markets Trustees, the Women's Institute and the Chamber of Commerce — are all concerned with the well-being of the community as a whole and are not sectarian or biased in any way. It is my opinion that if the cultivation of mutual trust, as encouraged in the three organizations mentioned, could be infused into the whole Northern Ireland community, it would go a long way towards improving the situation.

He stresses that the great problem is how to encourage trust. He makes six suggestions: (1) the ordinary people must be made to feel that they matter and have a say in the running of Northern Ireland; (2) people must feel that they are all treated justly and all get a fair hearing; (3) integrated education would be a step forward, but if this is not possible, there should be more interrelationship between schools; (4) there should be more co-operation at local level on community problems between Churches; (5)

where possible, housing estates should not be sectarian; (6) there should be urgent action on job provision, with as much attention paid to indigenous industry as to inward investment.

Other submissions which dealt, among other things, with local government were from Councillor T. Carlin, Archbishop Robin Eames, Mr Robert Hayes, Mr Gordon Jackson, Mr Michael McKeown, Mr Robert Mooney (equal representation for women in local government by the introduction of salaries for local representatives, and equal gender representation for each area), Ms Margot Smith, Pax Christi (London) and Youth for Peace.

The European dimension

There were nine submissions which dealt with the place of Northern Ireland as a region of the EC, although several of them were detailed and significant contributions. Several other contributors suggested, in passing, an EC peace-keeping force to take over security duties from the British army.

MR BERNARD CONLON, a Brussels-based writer and journalist, sees the EC's process of international integration as one of a number of positive outside influences that can help break down 'the insularity and intellectual introversion' that is endemic in Northern Ireland. He warns that if such influences are to provide successful and viable alternatives to the 'culture of paramilitarism', they must not exclusively come through government channels. 'Yet a bottom-up movement of community and local interest groups might be the source of imaginative initiatives capable of taking advantage of some of the resources and opportunities afforded by the EC.'

He also warns that the process of integration into the EC is 'very much a double-edged sword'. Despite the perception in both parts of Ireland that the EC is a panacea for all ills and a source of unlimited finance with no strings attached (itself a product of the country's neo-colonial dependency culture), the single European market 'will inevitably produce a brain drain, sucking in more and more of the young, skilled and educated section of the population, North and South, to the economic core of the Community. No amount of Structural Funds money will compensate for the negative consequences of this.'

However, Mr Conlon believes that the EC can make a positive contribution to resolving Northern Ireland's problems. This would require the British government to stop regarding the region solely as an internal matter, and to concede that if the Anglo-Irish Agreement could recognize the Republic's 'legitimate interest' in Northern Ireland, it could concede that the EC has a similar interest ('regardless of the abstraction of subsidiarity').

This could pave the way for the creation of an entirely new EC concept such as an area or region of Special European Interest. Small beginnings in this direction have already been made. For example, the Community has enacted a special budget line to contribute to the International Fund for Ireland. Also, Northern Ireland was granted Objective One status under the EC's Structural Funds as a politically motivated concession. Such a special status should entail EC observation and monitoring of a whole range of policy matters, including security and judicial measures.

He concludes his submission with a promise and a warning:

During this decade, with the changes in Europe, both parts of this island will have a one-off opportunity for self-examination. There will be a choice between casting off long inculcated hang-ups, while rediscovering the vast wealth of a varied heritage and culture which, if tapped, will give people North and South, the self-confidence to be proactive participants in the new millennium.... However, if we remain trapped in our respective trenches and narrow mind-sets, we face, in the North, the prospect of becoming a violent sideshow on the edge of Europe — of which Yugoslavia should be the nightmare reminder. While the South could descend into a golfing and fishing theme park for affluent continentals, with Dublin as a centralized, cosmopolitan Euro-Pale.

DR RICHARD KEARNEY and MR ROBIN WILSON argue that 'a repositioning of Northern Ireland in a set of European contexts, guaranteeing democratic participation and minority rights, economic development and cultural diversity, offers a way out of the current impasse — not one in which conflict ends, but one in which it is rendered non-violent, indeed becomes a healthy feature of a pluralist and democratic society'. Their vision is of 'a federal 'Europe of the regions' in which European integration and enlargement is marked by a progressive transfer of power down to regions from nation-states, as much as by a transfer of power upwards through economic and monetary, and political union'. This new European 'architecture' would be buttressed by a 'new concept of European citizenship underpinned by human rights guarantees, overseen by pan-European institutions'.

They compare the conflict here with parallel clashes of competing nationalist groups and 'double minority' problems in the former Yugoslavia and Nagorno-Karabakh. 'It would be easier by far if in each of these situations, one side was clearly 'right', the other 'wrong'. But just as it was 'reasonable' for the Armenian majority in Nagorno-Karabakh to resist domination by the much larger Azerbaijan, so also it was 'reasonable' for the Azeri minority in Nagorno-Karabakh to fear a handover to Armenian sovereignty. Similarly, it was, and remains, entirely 'reasonable' for Northern Ireland Catholics to feel fearful of their fate under a unionist regime. And unionists, conscious of their minority position on the island, can 'reasonably' fear that accommodation of Irish nationalism, given its ultimate goal, will be to their constitutional disadvantage.'

The new Europe raises fundamental questions about the nature of sovereignty, the meaning of words like nationalism and unionism and their 'winner take all' premises, say Dr Kearney and Mr Wilson. 'These conventional notions of 'national sovereignty' in Ireland have historically entailed either colonial dependence or nationalist independence. The idea of European interdependence, combined with the principle of subsidiarity, can, however, for Northern Ireland transcend both.' A map of Europe divided into regions to which government has been devolved shows 'the sheer geographical size' and 'centralized power' of the Republic and England in comparison. 'However 'artificial' its foundation, Northern Ireland, by contrast, is approximately the size of the Italian autonomous regions, or Wallonia and Flanders in Belgium, or the smaller German *länder* and French regions.'

Dr Kearney and Mr Wilson cite the beneficial effect of the European integration process on such regional problems as Spain's internal conflicts with the Basques and Catalans and Italy's German-speaking South Tyrol. They point to the example of the Istrian peninsula (mainly in Croatia), which has been 'so far insulated from the ex-Yugoslav maelstrom, despite its combination of Croats, Slovenes and Italians'. 'What matters is that no community tries to claim ownership of the territory', they quote one observer as saying; 'an Istrian is simply someone who lives and works there.'

They also quote the Conference on Security and Co-operation in Europe (CSCE) on the rights of national minorities: their rights 'to freely express, preserve and develop their own ethnic, cultural, linguistic and religious identity and to maintain and develop their own culture in all its aspects, protected from all attempts of assimilation against their will'. The CSCE also underlines its right to maintain contacts with citizens of other states with whom they have a common national origin, and the importance of their representatives being included democratically in decision-making or consultative bodies. At its 1992 Helsinki meeting, the CSCE agreed, in the face of objections from Britain, the US and Turkey, to set up a High Commissioner for Minorities, who would gather information on and monitor emerging conflicts in Europe.

Recalling the CSCE's recognition that its processes should involve citizens as well as states, Dr Kearney and Mr Wilson then cite Cyprus as an example where incorrect 'top down' methods have only perpetuated conflict. In Cyprus — and 'the Northern Ireland resonances are clear' — over two decades of UN peacekeeping forces have, by separating communities, made achieving peace, if anything, harder. The island's destructive processes have not been directly confronted because the UN's strategy was 'concerned with mediation efforts involving the leaders of the various communities'. They quote one observer who advocates, instead, attempts both to change the negative attitudes that the parties to the conflict have of each other and to tackle socio-economic problems which 'feed destructive behaviour'. This observer identifies economic development, confidence-building measures, education for mutual understanding and the overcoming of prejudice as key 'peace-building' tasks.

In Northern Ireland the 'pragmatic' sense of regional identity seen in the example of Istria has been reflected in co-operation between the normally adversarial local parties on European issues, like the establishment of a Northern Ireland Centre in Brussels. And as the Scottish political scientist Elizabeth Meehan has pointed out, there is already in Northern Ireland 'extensive participation by public agencies, professional bodies and voluntary associations in trans-European networks that deal with culture, poverty, employment, training, urban and rural regeneration and sex equality'. This involvement with inter-regional networks will grow through economic necessity in the context of the EC single market, Dr Kearney and Mr Wilson point out.

Northern Ireland, however, also lacks an appropriate European institutional *culture* in discussion of regional development. In part, this is because unionists to date have refused to accept the pluralistic, coalition type of administration widely practised elsewhere in Europe — an administration which could marshal *all* the resources and talents of civil society to a dynamic, developmental project.

It is also because British Conservative governments have been 'out of synch' with more successful European administrations which have involved 'social partners' in planning and regulating economic development.

'The idea of a 'Europe of the regions' holds out the prospect of a new, more modern Northern Ireland, in which pluralist, democratic and participatory institutions could acquire legitimacy, traditionally withheld by nationalists because of its association with the 'unionist aspiration', through pragmatic acceptance of its status as the Northern Irish region of the evolving Europe.' Similarly, the European integration process has the potential to make the 'nationalist aspiration' less unpalatable to unionists. 'It becomes possible, in this context, to present closer relations between North and South as pragmatically desirable in a single-market Europe without frontiers, where people, goods and capital move freely across former barriers. Such a focus could help modernize nationalist politics on the island in the process, away from the traditional emphasis on border change and territorial unity towards a stress on the unity of peoples.' They quote the then presidential candidate, Mary Robinson, in a 1990 speech in Belfast, saying that closer co-operation across the border was simply common sense and required 'no ideological strings' to be attached.

For Dr Kearney and Mr Wilson, the Committee of the Regions envisaged in the Maastricht treaty is one aspect of the way forward for Northern Ireland. They point out that the four countries most in favour of this committee were Spain, Germany, Belgium and Italy — all of which already have effective regional government — and the two least eager were the UK and the Republic of Ireland, the EC's most centralized states, with two of the Community's worst economic and human rights records.

They conclude with a number of recommendations aimed at constituting Northern Ireland as a region exercising maximum 'subsidiarity' within the UK and therefore able both to develop to the full its 'special relationship' with the Republic and play its part in the new Europe. These include an elected regional assembly with a high degree of autonomy, comparable to those sought for Scotland by the Scottish Constitutional Convention, with powers to intervene in the economy and to represent Northern Ireland in the EC; the closest possible relationship with the Republic, particularly in economic affairs; guarantees of pluralism in regional government, with an executive sustained by weighted majority support and the right of appeal to the European Parliament; a Bill of Rights; the implementation of an innovative policy of embracing cultural diversity within the region; and a constitutional requirement to extend democratic participation through multi-partner partnerships with business and trade union bodies, the community and voluntary sectors, with EC assistance.

A NORTHERN IRISH RESIDENT OF BRUSSELS, in an unattributable submission, warns against excessive optimism about the death of the nation-state and 'a brave new future of harmonious regions within a supra-national European structure'. He says it is now apparent that 'a strong and at times aggressive sense of nationalism threatens the liberal veneer of many Western European countries, and such aggression has found in the process of greater European integration one of its most favoured targets'. He warns of continuing serious difficulties in Corsica, Catalonia and the Basque country, with a move towards a form of federal autonomy reflecting serious strains within Belgium. 'From a political point of view, the process of European integration has proved most effective in reconciling member states — notably France and Germany — to each other, and scarcely at all in reconciling member states with their regions or minorities.'

He believes that 'European integration functions at a level which is not likely to influence strongly the evolution of regional conflicts. This is consistent with the division of competences within the Community and with the kind of areas which are the object of Community intervention. To pose a European Community solution to the problems of Northern Ireland would be to stand subsidiarity on its head, and there is in the present situation little likelihood of this.' He believes that 'ultimate progress [in Northern Ireland] can emanate only from within ourselves'.

He also warns that sooner or later the cushioning effect of being part of the UK market will not prevent Northern Ireland's trading climate from becoming substantially altered by membership of the EC single market.

Northern Ireland must take seriously a number of things: better, broader and more training and education, preferably involving placement in other European regions; language training; better management skills; promotion of intra-Ireland trade and economic co-operation; strategic collaboration and partnership with companies, regions and educational institutes in other parts of Europe; improved and more co-ordinated industrial relations models, based on the kind of understanding of social partnership prevalent throughout the most successful economies in the EC — Belgium, Germany and France. Above all, we must face the fact that continued political and community division is stifling economic growth and development. Since 1970, when for obvious reasons we turned in on ourselves and our perception of ourselves became dominated by our internal divisions, much has happened in the world, including a technological and economic revolution, little part of which we seem to have mastered or participated in. Generous public expenditure is not likely to shield us for ever from the effects of this omission. Failed politics has its price to pay.

He believes that the 'process of inclusion' which has accompanied the distribution of EC aid to Northern Ireland has been a 'positive experience'. For example, the requirement for the regional authorities to consult with local bodies to ascertain their needs has involved 'an unprecedented level of consultation and involvement within Northern Ireland concerning the region's developmental priorities in a European context'. He thinks this has tended to 'open local economic planning to alternative and on occasion more integrated strategies'. He points out that the EC's work in the region often remains unknown to local people — 'an unfortunate consequence of the lack of prominence often afforded to EC-funded projects in the UK'.

Thus the EC's INTERREG initiative has facilitated economic regeneration in cross-border areas long neglected by both governments. However, here there is another problem, one which requires 'urgent reflection and attention', he says. 'Northern Ireland does not generally have that dense tissue of dynamic local economic actors which remains the hallmark of the more successful economies'. When it comes to absorbing INTERREG monies, the complaint that centrally based organizations and civil servants 'muscle in' is not entirely untrue. He points out that this need to 'lead from the centre' is because local communities have become used to a lack of involvement. 'But the effectiveness of certain EC programmes is dependent on local involvement and empowerment and on a more acute sense of local responsibility. Excellent models of this kind of collaboration are to be found in Belgium, Germany and in many border areas of the Benelux countries. We could learn much from them.'

Despite his warnings about the limited impact of movement towards political union as mapped out at Maastricht, the EC civil servant says the new concept of a common European citizenship 'may in time erode the common Anglo-Saxon principle of exclusive and sovereign citizenship. In the longer term, such a model may provide an attraction for partisans of more asymmetrical forms of citizenship within Northern Ireland itself and may provide, at long last, some political space within the region for expression of national or cultural traditions and identities which cannot be packaged, even in a climate of liberal tolerance, to accord with the uniform and unique symbols of exclusive statehood'.

However, the Brussels resident also notes that until now the European experience has had little impact on most people's attitudes. 'Little of that sense of Euro-euphoria, however naive it may seem, which has characterized intellectuals and political parties, churches and citizens in the South, has been manifested in the North. Unlike the South, Northern Ireland continues to function in relative isolation from what a European standard just might be, instead, contenting itself to be, ideally, the best in the UK.'

He concludes that the best thing Northern Ireland might learn from the EC is that 'it is not alone as a divided society in Europe, and that limits to our capacity to tolerate each other are characteristic of most, if not all, European peoples'. He says that Northern Irish people might come to appreciate that although 'ours is a fundamental quarrel ... we need not portray ourselves or be portrayed by others as a permanent enigma defying all "civilized" thought'. He compares the restraint and tolerance often found in Northern Ireland with the 'xenophobic reactions' of many richer Belgians, French or Germans to the small and poor minorities brought into their countries as cheap labour. 'We need not, on every occasion, think of Europe from a position of moral inferiority. For we are not always the worst.'

The EC affords many examples of societies as culturally and historically complex as that of Northern Ireland. The track record of resolution remains somewhat more impressive than our own. In this sense, it may be that the European experience may yet help heal our own experience of ourselves. But the condition for this is that Northern Ireland gets to know other regional role models.

He ends by warning that a European experience can help to ease Northern Ireland's 'straight-jacketed cultural identities' only if the symbols of state there can begin the process of reflecting and publicly expressing the loyalties of both communities. He believes that its citizens will not be able to work through their 'crisis of truncated identity with the help of the tenuous space that some sense of European belonging might give', unless its public institutions recognize this.

LABOUR '87, the group established by members of a number of small Northern Ireland-based Labour parties, has a strong European dimension in its plan for devolved government for the region. 'Our vision is one of Northern Ireland as a unique regional unit within a modern Europe based on power-sharing, extended democracy, social justice, equality and the protection of individuals through a Bill of Rights.'

The group believes in a Northern Ireland under democratic regional control as part of a British, Irish and European federal system as the eventual way of overcoming the continuing 'intense disagreement' about its constitutional arrangements. Unless regional democracy is established, future international developments will increasingly marginalize Northern Ireland — as well as other peripheral regions in Britain and Ireland made politically weak compared to more affluent regions within unitary state structures. 'Ultimately, we envisage organs of independent regional government in Britain and Ireland with a tier of independent local government below and independent national and European government above.' Labour '87 points out that 'in Scotland, Wales and the North of England groups based in different political movements are arguing for regional government as a basis for economic recovery and the extension of democracy'.

Labour '87 is one of the few groups to propose ways of financing future political arrangements.

We do not advocate a self-financing Northern Ireland. Centuries of exploitation have deprived the region of a resource base on which this could be established. We envisage a significant element of redistribution at national and European levels. This would be done by redistributing a fixed proportion of taxes raised by the UK government on the basis of how weak or strong the existing tax base (incomes, wealth and property) of Northern Ireland is, compared with other UK regions. Ideally we would like to see this formula applied to all the UK regions and ultimately extended to all the regions of the European Community. A fixed proportion of taxes raised by national government would be for regional functions and distributed to each region to supplement the taxes that can be raised from the region's own taxation base. Thus poorer regions would receive large contributions, while more affluent regions would receive little, if any, contributions.... Thus the wealthier regions will be providing tax revenue which will be redistributed to the poorer regions until all regions have a broadly similar resource base (incomes, wealth and property values per head). Together with a regional tax, this will provide for spending on those functions under the control of regional authorities, which we argue should be elected assemblies.

The group says that 'the experiences of Germany and Japan show that economic planning and industrial development can be administered on a regional basis extremely successfully, especially when backed up by a regional bank'.

It also seeks a two-chamber devolved government for Northern Ireland within the UK. The major legislative chamber would be directly elected by PR single transferable vote in multi-member constituencies, and 'power would be shared in cabinet and government committees in proportion to party representation in that assembly'. But it also recommends a second chamber to involve representatives from other key sectors of society. 'One quarter of its membership would represent the employers' side of industry, including nationalized undertakings; one quarter would represent trade unions; one quarter the district councils and one quarter a diverse grouping, including consumer and voluntary organizations, professional and educational organizations and farmers.' Labour '87's submission also includes a detailed outline for a Bill of Rights.

PROFESSORS KEVIN BOYLE and TOM HADDEN conclude their submission (see also the next category, Improving the Anglo-Irish Agreement) with three ideas for developing a European dimension to a new British-Irish Agreement.

(1) They believe that some form of direct EC recognition of or involvement in Northern Ireland as 'a distinctive inter-state region' would be formally possible in a protocol to the Rome or Maastricht treaties. Such a proposal probably would meet considerable resistance from other member states. 'The better approach may be to promote the recognition of Northern Ireland as a distinctive region within established EC programmes and to develop structures for the representation of Northern Ireland within established EC institutions.'

(2) 'It may be easier to develop specific provisions for the protection of individual and communal rights in Northern Ireland within the context of the Council of Europe' (rather than the EC). 'It may be possible in this way not only to develop some form of European guarantee for any new settlement but also to make provision for a European involvement in any procedures for adjudication and enforcement on relevant matters.'

(3) 'The Conference on Security and Co-operation in Europe has already developed a wide range of internationally agreed standards on matters of special interest in Northern Ireland, such as the treatment of minorities, the operation of emergency powers and the general protection of individual human rights. The CSCE has also developed a number of procedures through which other states may raise issues of concern and arrange for missions of investigation.' The most important of these are the agreed mechanism for monitoring human rights and the newly constituted High Commissioner for Minorities. 'Though the UK government has entered reservations to the relevant CSCE documents which appear to reduce their potential application in Northern Ireland, it should be possible within a new British-Irish Agreement to ensure that these provisions for international monitoring on issues of security, minority protection and human rights are accepted as a useful safeguard against potential or actual abuses.'

MR HUGH LOGUE, formerly an SDLP Assembly and Convention member and now a senior EC civil servant, puts forward a European model of government institutions for Northern Ireland which he calls the 'trialogue'. He points out that 'the essential strengths of the effort made by Robert Schuman and Jean Monnet in 1950 in setting out to overcome the aftermath of World War II, were to:

(1) build on what is here and now; (2) refuse to look back or enter into recrimination; (3) think positively, based on a desire for reconciliation; (4) create institutions robust enough to establish a positive momentum, yet flexible enough to accommodate the differing positive points of view. By 1957 the Common Market was established with six member states; today it is a vibrant single market, with a Community of 325 million citizens in 12 member states.

Mr Logue proposes that the EC's Council of Ministers, Commission and Parliament should be a model for new Northern Irish institutions. No direct participation by EC institutions is envisaged. A commission for Northern Ireland would act as an executive, introducing policy initiatives and implementing them. The commission's president would be appointed by the council, which would be made up of three members each from the British and Irish governments and the three Northern Irish MEPs (alternatively the local members could be directly elected by PR with the region as one constituency, as the MEPs are at present). The Northern Ireland parliamentary assembly would correspond broadly to the present British-Irish inter-parliamentary body, and would be composed of all Northern Ireland members of the House of Commons and equal representation of members from the Commons and the Dáil. The assembly's role would be to advise, consult, monitor and hold accountable the other two institutions for their decisions and actions, as does the European Parliament in the EC (for example, no budget could be adopted without the assembly's approval).

The commission president would be appointed by the Council from nominations received from those Northern Ireland parties which receive, for example, 10-15 per cent of the vote in the single constituency election. In consultation with the council, he or she would then appoint a Commission of not more than ten additional people from among the other nominations. All members of the commission would come from within Northern Ireland. Although nominated by the main parties, they need not be elected politicians, but could include people from local government, industry, the unions and the universities, thus 'intertwining the political process with the technocratic executive approach of many modern, successful democracies'. The commissioners, upon appointment, would be required to renounce all political affiliation, all offices of profit and take an oath to serve without favour the people of Northern Ireland. As with the European commission, where successive presidents are not from the same country, so successive Northern Ireland commission presidents would not be from the same party.

DR ELIZABETH MEEHAN, professor of politics at Queen's University, Belfast, urges the unionists to consider more carefully the way in which they speak with two voices about the EC — 'hostile at home, because of the possible implications for the idea of the Union, and co-operatively with the SDLP away from here in order to maximise benefits for Northern Ireland'. She suggests that a way must be found of making people aware that unionists co-operate at the EC level, as they do on some councils. (See also The Economy and Society: Women's Issues.)

Other submissions with some European angle came from The Inter-Church Group on Faith and Politics, Mr L. McArdle (a 'European school' for Northern Ireland), Professor Paul McNulty and Mr Tom Magner.

Improving the Anglo-Irish Agreement

There were a small number of significant submissions urging that, rather than take dramatic new initiatives which would be doomed to fail, the British and Irish governments should work to build on what already exists, notably the Anglo-Irish Agreement.

MR PAUL SWEENEY, director of the Northern Ireland Voluntary Trust (NIVT), in a personal submission, says that there is much in the Anglo-Irish Agreement to which he can relate. 'Second only to the Sunningdale accord, it provides a process that could enable Catholics and Protestants to readjust themselves into political arrangements hitherto not contemplated.' Living in a violent and divided area of Belfast, he is conscious of both unionist and republican opposition to the Agreement, but he believes it has been 'a major catalyst to development in these islands' and echoes the regrets of one of its architects, the former Irish diplomat Michael Lillis, that neither the British nor Irish governments has maximized its potential. 'An indecisive, half-hearted, wait and see, hope and pray approach to any Anglo-Irish Accord is in itself a very irresponsible and dangerous arrangement.'

He says that since the Agreement was signed, the British government has 'made very genuine attempts to give greater recognition to the legitimacy of the 'nationalist tradition' in Northern Ireland'. One of the major changes he has seen since 1985 has been the 'gingering role' throughout all government departments of the Central Community Relations Unit at Stormont. Similarly, he believes there has been considerable achievement in the fields of fair employment, equal opportunities, race relations and cultural traditions. Mr Sweeney urges the Opsahl Commission to encourage debate on a Bill of Rights, which has considerable cross-party support and which could be an important requisite for the 'realignment process' he seeks to encourage. He also suggests that the appointment of a Minister for Equality for Northern Ireland — modelled on the new portfolio in the Republic's recently formed coalition government — 'could significantly capture the public imagination and galvanize the eradication of discrimination and the pursuit of equity throughout all facets of life in Northern Ireland'.

Mr Sweeney believes that, in the context of a more dynamic working of the Anglo-Irish Agreement, 'the emergence of a credible devolved regional political chamber in Northern Ireland will remain an unachievable objective in the short to medium term'. He hopes that in time the political talks will resume, but believes that 'the need to build on the Anglo-Irish Agreement should not be superseded to create space for the talks to take place'. In the absence of a devolved regional authority, local government should be encouraged more.

As part of a deliberate piece of social engineering, I believe that resources should be awarded to those councils which put forward policies and programmes which command cross-party support and which will be implemented with a power-sharing approach.... To many purists, this will appear undemocratic. However, what passes for democracy in some councils is far from being in the interests of the public good. Northern Ireland has for too long been too tolerant of inappropriate models of democracy. We should have the leadership and confidence to redress this where necessary. Government special initiatives (for example, Making Belfast Work, the Londonderry Initiative), the International Fund for Ireland, Departmental funding — all should strive to reward good practice in local government.'

Mr Sweeney believes that it is only a matter of time before the political structures on the island of Ireland give greater expression to its 'economic and social coherence'. 'I am convinced that terms such as 'united Ireland' are redundant and delay any sophisticated discussion of pan-Ireland issues.' In this regard, he was impressed by the British government's document, 'Overcoming lack of adequate channels of communication between North and South', which was submitted to strand two of the 1992 talks.

This document contains a challenging agenda for those seriously committed to regenerating the social and economic fortunes of Ireland. While Britain might put some imagination into how they present this, the maximisation of cross-border co-operation in the island of Ireland and between the island of Ireland and Britain should be a central plank of British government policy.

Parallel with this, 'every effort should be made in the Republic of Ireland to constantly convince a besieged unionist community in Northern Ireland that their welfare can be advanced by the forging of closer relationships with the South'. He hopes that, despite the lack of statesmanship and imagination of successive Irish governments in their approach to the North, 'a new political realism is evolving in the Republic'. He would like to see Articles 2 and 3 of the Irish Constitution rephrased in an aspirational tone more fully reflective of public opinion in the Republic, but recognizes that progress on a wide range of issues to do with the North would be a prerequisite for a successful referendum to change them.

Mr Sweeney emphasizes the direct correlation between deprivation and political violence in both Northern Irish communities (see also Talking to Sinn Féin and the paramilitaries): to remain indifferent to these levels of deprivation is to remain indifferent to peace. The need for a targeted programme of social and economic regeneration has been recognized in the government's 'Targeting Social Need' programme, but 'much more resources, commitment, imagination, urgency and resolve will be required if we are to make any substantive difference to the quality of life in the most disadvantaged areas'. Such a major programme of recovery would have to alleviate poverty in both Catholic and Protestant areas and would have to involve their people in its design and implementation. Above all, it would have to be aimed at young people growing up with little hope of employment, and, as a result, lacking in self-esteem and alienated from the mainstream of society. 'Our young people whose lives have been blighted by the sins of their fathers need major compensatory programmes and life opportunities if they are to become the leaders, parents and citizens of tomorrow.'

In conclusion, Mr Sweeney argues for 'a dynamic Anglo-Irish Agreement with strong cross-border linkages, which reflect the political and cultural diversity of Northern Ireland. This may appear as government by imposition rather than consent; however, in the viciousness and despair of Northern Ireland, enlightened manipulation is preferable to democratic stagnation. For too long both communities have exercised their vetoes and proven their ability to cancel progress. The management of diversity requires a different approach for the greater good of all. Let history judge its merits.'

PROFESSORS KEVIN BOYLE and TOM HADDEN open their submission by saying that its purpose is 'to reaffirm the vision of the 1980s, as incorporated in the Anglo-Irish Agreement of 1985, and to restate and refine its major provisions in a form suitable for adoption in a new British-Irish agreement for the 1990s'.

They concede that the immediate hopes for the 1985 Agreement have not been fulfilled, primarily because of the 'total rejection of the agreement by unionists, due in part to their effective exclusion from its preparation and to the related failure to deal convincingly with the disputed claim by the Republic over Northern Ireland in Articles 2 and 3 of the Irish Constitution'.

They suggest a number of ways in which the principles of that agreement need to be developed and refined. First, in the wake of events in the former Yugoslavia, the extent of intermingling between the two communities in Northern Ireland 'makes it essential in any new agreement to stand firm against the pressures for ever-increasing communal separation and to emphasize the need in the interests of peace and stability for the development of structures which will accommodate both traditions rather than those which will facilitate or encourage further separation'. They suggest one way of doing this might be to develop the 'legal recognition and protection of the rights not only of those who wish to assert their communal identity, but also of those who wish to assert their belief in pluralism and integration in appropriate matters'.

Professors Boyle and Hadden also stress 'the need to create democratic space at all levels'. Although the principle of regional democracy was built into the 1985 Agreement, it had not been pursued with any initial urgency. However, a good deal of effort had been put into remedying this in the 1991/92 talks process. A commitment to structures which 'will permit and encourage accountable democracy at appropriate levels of decision-making, in accordance with the so-called principle of subsidiarity, should be re-emphasized in any new agreement'.

They then suggest a number of broad matters for action. The first of these deals with Northern Ireland's 'internal dimension', where the basic objective should be 'to create space for regional and local democracy within a framework which recognizes and respects the essential interests, identities and aspirations of the two major communities without imposing or encouraging any form of communal separation'. Within this framework there would be a need for 'workable legal controls on any abuse of majority power' and lists three such mechanisms:

(a) A Bill of Rights for Northern Ireland, based on the European Convention of Human Rights, but incorporating additional protections.

For example, there might be an enforceable duty on all government bodies to respect the identity and interests of both major communities, and some special provision to protect against the illegitimate or one-sided introduction or implementation of emergency powers of any kind. There may be scope for the provisions of such a Bill of Rights to be interpreted and enforced by a court in which members of the European Commission or Court of Human Rights might play a part.

(b) The development of internal government structures which

allow space for flexible internal coalitions, rather than fixed or proportional communal representation in government. The dangers of the abuse of majority power might then be controlled either by specific provisions for weighted voting on specified matters or through an expanded 'judicial review' procedure, under which any alleged abuse of a constitutional duty for all public bodies to respect and esteem both major traditions would be subject to review by a judicial or quasi-judicial body. There might be a role for both British and Irish as well as European representatives on such a supervisory body. This kind of supervisory jurisdiction would be preferable to any form of direct British, Irish or European involvement in the administration of those matters within the jurisdiction of a Northern Ireland government.

(c) Some form of constitutional entrenchment to prevent the imposition of different structures by future British and Irish governments without reference to the people of Northern Ireland.

This could be done by involving the European Community or the Council of Europe as a party to any new British-Irish agreement, through a protocol to the treaties of Rome or Maastricht, or an appropriate Council of Europe convention.

The second subject for action suggested by the two law professors is the North-South dimension. Here they see the most useful way of developing a working relationship between Northern Ireland and the Republic of Ireland — in order to develop cross-border consultative and executive bodies on questions like the economy and the pursuit of EC funding — as 'full mutual recognition as a basis for agreement on reciprocal co-operation on specific functions'.

This would best be achieved by agreement on identical wording on the status of Northern Ireland in both UK and Irish law. Any such statement might include both the right of a majority within Northern Ireland to opt for adhesion to either the UK or the Irish Republic, and an appropriate statement of aspiration for members of both communities.

This too could be the subject of a protocol in the treaties of Rome or Maastricht. (See also The European dimension.)

MR IAIN SHARPE of Watford, Hertfordshire, argues that, given the entrenched positions of all parties to the conflict, an agreed settlement is not possible in the foreseeable future. He urges an end to the pretence that any such agreement is possible. This gives the impression that 'an agreement is there for the taking, but that the Northern Irish people are too narrow-minded to accept it. It promotes apathy and ignorance about the conflict in Britain and in the Republic where people are content to let the Northern Irish bicker among themselves. It also gives rise to false hopes which are then inevitably dashed. Therefore the emphasis should be not on an agreed settlement, but on the smaller steps towards progress which can be made by the various parties involved.'

He then lists a series of 'positive steps' which can be taken by all parties 'once the red herring of a final settlement is out of the way'. These, he hopes, would result in a reduction in the intensity of the conflict, and would mean 'slow but steady progress towards *eventually* ending the conflict'.

(1) There appears to be room for 'give' on both sides on the issue of reforming Articles 2 and 3 of the Irish Constitution in return for some unionist acceptance of an Irish government role in Northern Ireland as exists at the moment under the Anglo-Irish Agreement. 'In the meantime the Anglo-Irish Agreement must continue to operate, not because of its own intrinsic merits, but because. if it was abandoned, the triumphalism of the unionists would be unbearable and would mark a big step backwards, and because there might be a falling away of SDLP support back to Sinn Féin.'

(2) Continued political talks are a good thing, but they should be low-key and exploratory. 'If the pressure to find a solution is off, then there is greater scope for flexibility.'

(3) 'The UK and Irish governments should continue to develop and improve cross-border security co-operation. The Irish government, if it

aspires to Irish unity in the long term, must give equal value to the lives of all its citizens and potential citizens and must be unequivocal both in condemning and in combating terrorist killing on both sides of the sectarian divide.' In turn, the British government must accept that 'counter-terrorist activity which is of questionable (to say the least) morality and legality, for example the Gibraltar shootings, are unacceptable by any standards and do more harm than good.'

(4) Emphasis should continue to be placed by the UK government on equal opportunities and an end to sectarian discrimination, particularly in employment — not as a sop to the Catholic population, but because it is right in itself.

(5) The UK government would be on weak ground in introducing a Bill of Rights in Northern Ireland when Britain lacks one. However, with all the local parties agreeing on the need for one, 'it is vital that individual citizens in Northern Ireland know where they stand in relation to the state and are able to assert their rights as citizens'.

(6) Given that there is little prospect of devolved rule, 'local authorities could be offered increased powers on a rolling basis, provided they meet certain criteria for cross-community co-operation within the council and for fair employment practices. This would give a real incentive for councils to eliminate sectarian discrimination.'

(7) Northern Ireland parties should make a point of developing links with all parties on the mainland to help to dispel some of the widespread ignorance, even among politically aware people, about politics in Northern Ireland. Greater understanding would result from more representation of Northern Irish parties at British party conferences, and from links and exchanges between councillors and party activists on both sides of the water. There should also be more contact with parties in the Republic.

(8) 'The same applies to the voluntary sector in Northern Ireland, particularly the peace and reconciliation groups. In my view there is a problem of isolation of Northern Ireland from the rest of the UK and from the Republic. There is a need to break this down. Perhaps the situation in former Yugoslavia will help to demonstrate to those of us who face no threat to our national identity, that those who do face such a threat are not bigots, but victims of history and circumstance. The aim must be to change the image of Northern Ireland as a backwater. Peace and reconciliation groups can help to achieve this by raising their profile on the 'mainland', in addition to carrying out their vital work in the province. The recent bombings in London appear to many people to be more an 'Act of God' than a product of a political dispute with which their country is involved. It is vital to break down this attitude. From my point of view, the Northern Irish groups with the highest profile on the 'mainland' are Troops Out and the Irish Freedom Movement. A wider cross-section of opinion needs to

have a high profile to ensure that all views are heard and understood.'

(9) Detecting some new thinking among republicans about the 'armed struggle' (for example, the Bloody Sunday Initiative), Mr Sharpe asks them to explore questions like whether or not it would be possible in a future united Ireland for Britain to have an officially recognized role in defending the interests of the Northern Protestants, similar to that afforded the Republic with regard to Northern Catholics under the Anglo-Irish Agreement. 'If not, can they ever expect Protestants who identify as British to accept a united Ireland which has no intrinsic links with Britain?' On the other hand, he asks unionists to ponder 'how respect for Irish identity, as opposed to mere fair treatment of Catholics in employment, education, and housing, can operate successfully without a united Ireland'.

LORD BLEASE, formerly the Northern Ireland officer of the Irish Congress of Trade Unions, believes that a number of major hurdles have to be crossed before political talks on Northern Ireland's future can resume: Articles 2 and 3 have to be tackled; there must be a commitment from all the Northern Ireland constitutional parties that they will participate fully in any agreed settlement; an Inter-Irish Relations Committee, made up of members of the British and Irish parliaments and a proposed new Northern Ireland assembly, should be set up; and a Bill of Rights should be enacted.

He maintains that power-sharing devolution is an attractive concept but not a realistic one. 'Nationalists will not agree to power-sharing unless the settlement includes a strong Irish dimension and because they aspire to a united Ireland. Unionists will not share power under a strong Irish dimension. These divisions are fundamental and have lain at the root of the Northern Ireland political crisis since 1921.' Given this, there is no 'solution' that can gain 'the enthusiastic support of a majority of both communities'. Lord Blease believes the future of the region would be served best by a continuation and reform of Direct Rule and the Anglo-Irish Agreement, and proposes a list of reforms to this end. These include a Northern Ireland Standing Committee at Westminster, the extension of the powers of the 26 local councils, a new regional council (based on a large English county council) and a three-year strategic programme for good government, covering security, economic development, social need and a Bill of Rights.

MR W.J. BRITTON of Donaghadee, Co. Down, makes numerous proposals, of which improving the Anglo-Irish Agreement is one. He begins: 'I sense a disillusionment among the ordinary people of Northern Ireland with their political leaders and believe that they are more prepared now than ever before to modify some of their entrenched views in return for lasting peace, stability and prosperity. Government *must* now have the courage to test their goodwill.' He proposes that the British government, in conjunction with the Irish government where appropriate, should prepare a series of proposals for constitutional and political change. Among these he suggests the following. There should be a mandatory poll on the continuing existence of the border not less than every ten years, rather than the present open-ended arrangement. As a means of reassuring unionists, each new British government should be required by statute to publish a proclamation recommitting itself for the life of that parliament to the principle of no change in the sovereignty of Northern Ireland as part of the UK for as long as the majority wishes it. He believes the Anglo-Irish Agreement serves to reinforce this principle at international level and provides a forum for much closer North-South co-operation. However, 'there is no discernible framework of co-operation at present. I suggest that permanent committees are established from relevant departments North and South with remits to harmonize working relationships, regulations and practices wherever possible. Annual reports on achievements should be published.' Mr Britton wants Articles 2 and 3 to be revoked or amended to incorporate the above consent principle; this would allow the Republic to replace the Maryfield secretariat with a conventional consulate to conduct Anglo-Irish business. He also proposes that the Secretary of State should appoint three Ministers of State, drawn from the elected MPs of the three largest Northern Ireland parties, to run Northern Ireland Departments of State. He suggests that the oath of allegiance to the Crown be made optional or be reworded to satisfy nationalist MPs.

Talking to Sinn Féin and the paramilitaries

Eighteen submissions mentioned, among other things, the need to involve Sinn Féin, in some way, in discussions about the future of Northern Ireland; to open lines of communication to the IRA and other paramilitary organizations; and/or to end the broadcasting ban on such parties and groups.

The most powerful argument for this came from MR PAUL SWEENEY. He believes that 'a negotiated renouncement of violence can be achieved only by an inclusive dialogue which actively involves those, directly or indirectly, engaged in political violence'. He says it is 'fallacious to discuss paramilitarism as a phenomenon of a few fanatics or organized crime gangs. Many people in Northern Ireland are ambivalent towards political violence, many are highly selective in their condemnations of violence, many can be quite sanctimonious about the existence of violence. The first stage in seeking a resolution of the conflict in Northern Ireland is to confront the reality that those involved in paramilitary organizations are very much an integral part of our community.'

In Northern Ireland, Sinn Féin — whose elected representatives should be recognized in the same way as any other party's elected representatives — represent 'an extremely important section of our community, who desperately need to be convinced that they can benefit from the political process'. He says in this regard that Sir Patrick Mayhew, in his 'Culture and Identity' address in December 1992, went further than any other British government spokesperson. Mr Sweeney believes that Britain should now open channels to Sinn Féin: 'Britain stands to gain by either convincing Sinn Féin that political violence does not advance its cause and that compromises can be achieved, or by challenging Sinn Féin to prove that violence has not itself become a principle and a manifestation of that movement's own brutalization. That constituency from which Sinn Féin musters its support is a mature and sophisticated people. If Britain can prove its sincerity in being neutral on the future of political arrangements in these islands (which I believe is the case), then demonstrate this openly by engaging with Sinn Féin. Ultimately, it will be the marginalized people in republican areas who will decide if the IRA is to be denied its authority to prosecute a campaign of violence on their behalf.'

Mr Sweeney does not believe that the British government should insist on an IRA ceasefire as a precondition to such talks. 'A resolution of conflict and cessation of violence should be the outcome of and not the precondition to political dialogue.' In the meantime, the broadcasting ban on Sinn Féin and the UDA should be repealed: 'If violence is to be effectively flushed from the political process in Northern Ireland, dialogue, debate and critical exchanges will require an inclusive and dynamic media.'

MRS ELIZABETH GROVES from Andersonstown, Belfast, making an individual oral submission (not in her role as chairperson of the Falls Community Council), says that people in west Belfast vote Sinn Féin for a whole range of different reasons. They vote for them for the same reason that their grandparents voted for them in 1918, for an all-Ireland aspiration that has still to be realized. On the other hand, 'Sinn Féin is a very young and very progressive party within its own community in that they are the ones who are out in the street helping with housing problems and social problems and giving advice on a wide range of welfare rights. People do not always vote Sinn Féin to support violence, which is the common perception, but certainly people relate to them in a community context because they are the people who are seen on the street working for the people.'

She points out that people had attempted, as they had been told to for years, to 'try the legal way forward, to put away the gun and try the ballot box' — ordinary people who had never used the gun in the first place went out and voted Sinn Féin, and still they were excluded from talks, even when loyalist parties who in the past had supported violent organizations were there at the conference table. 'And that is a very, very strong point that the nationalist people in west Belfast want to get across. If you want to hear our views, if you want to talk to us, then talk to the people we are electing, because that is not happening at the minute.'

(See also Law, Justice and Security: Policing; and The Economy and Society: Social Policy and Community.)

THE CENTRE FOR RESEARCH AND DOCUMENTATION (CRD), a west Belfast-based 'think tank' staffed by former workers in developing countries, argues that in many parts of the world governments have said they would never talk to 'terrorists' and all ended up doing so. It says that in talks with the warring factions in the former Yugoslavia, international mediators like David Owen and Cyrus Vance do not see the use of violence as a block to talking when the aim is a cessation of violence from all sides so that there can be a political solution to a political problem. The Centre quotes an Irish Jesuit, Oliver Rafferty, observing: 'It seems that there is, if not a hierarchy of political truths, then at least a pecking order of 'terrorist' organizations with which the [British] government will talk: those involved in distant conflicts may be nodded to more readily than those who are active on these islands.' The CRD continues:

Sinn Féin and the IRA have their roots in the most marginalized and oppressed section of the nationalist community, and the former represents a significant section of it. If there is to be a solution to the conflict in Ireland, all parties must be included. Excluding them perpetuates the problem. Ways must be found of involving Sinn Féin, the IRA, UDA and UVF in the negotiations, along with all the other political parties and governments. If there are preconditions, those preconditions should exist for everyone. No one in this conflict is neutral. The British government is not neutral; they need to stop pretending they are. International pressure should be aimed at broadening the base of negotiations and at finding genuinely interested but neutral arbiters to facilitate a resolution.

From a different perspective, but reaching a (reluctantly) similar conclusion comes MRS SHEILA CHILLINGWORTH, a retired educational psychologist who has worked in disadvantaged areas of north and west Belfast for over 20 years.

We have had few changes in our main politicians, and with one or two honourable exceptions (Ken Maginnis, for example), they have remained as conditioned as Pavlov's dogs. I should, however, continue with the Anglo-Irish talks. Constant dialogue with people who think differently from oneself can sometimes lead to a meeting of minds. More realistically, as long as our politicians are occupied in talks and sworn to silence, we can get on with our lives without being deluged by floods of predictable rhetoric every week.

On the other hand, I have an uneasy feeling that any decision they might make could prove irrelevant. It seems clear that eventually discussions will have to take place with Sinn Féin after a cessation of violence. They may be a small part of our community, but I am forced to admit that they are too big to be ignored. This is bound to introduce a completely new set of variables into the dialogue. I confess I cannot (indeed dare not) speculate about the outcome.

Other submissions mentioning the need to talk to Sinn Féin (and loyalist paramilitaries) and/or to end the broadcasting ban on them came from Mr G.T. Burton, the school student group of the Derry Peace and Reconciliation Group, Ms Joan Jackson, a group of former loyalist prisoners, Mothers for Peace (Ilkley), Scrabo Presbyterian Church (after renouncing violence and a allowing period of time to elapse to ensure that the renunciation is genuine), and Sisters of the Cross and Passion (Larne).

The role of the Republic

It will have become apparent that Articles 2 and 3 of the Republic's Constitution are a frequent secondary theme of submissions dealing with the constitutional issue. Below are several more which deal specifically with Articles 2 and 3, and others that concentrate on the role of the Republic in any resolution of Northern Ireland's problems.

MR PETER BARRY TD, the Republic's former Minister for Foreign Affairs, writes: 'I would support an amendment of the Articles which would express what is the deeply felt desire of most citizens of the Republic: that the people of this island should be united in their wish to live together in peace, recognizing in our laws and political structures the diverse traditions which we cherish equally. We cannot undo 70 years of our history but must recognize the realities they have produced and look to our future rather than our past.' Mr Barry, while conceding that unionists continue to view the Anglo-Irish Agreement as a 'hateful instrument which must be replaced', asks them to recognize two significant developments which have coincided with its operation:

Firstly the eclipse of Sinn Féin as the focus of non-unionist support, and the quadrupling of SDLP representation at Westminster, which could have come about only if the nationalist community saw that their wrongs would be redressed through political action. Secondly, the unlocking of the political log-jam in Northern Ireland which has led to the first talks this century involving all the key political players in these islands.

A BELFAST NATIONALIST LAWYER warns of the Articles' enormous symbolic importance for Northern nationalists. 'Political parties in the Republic are prepared to change these Articles in what they see as a conciliatory gesture (which can also be seen as their being entirely fed up with the situation and willing to do anything which seems superficially helpful). Not one nationalist political or community figure in Northern Ireland has spoken in favour of the unilateral abolition or amendment of these Articles.'

He believes that to remove or amend these Articles, other than in the context of an overall political settlement, would be disastrous for a number of reasons: 'In a situation where the future is being negotiated, fears and anxieties will be increased only by proposals for unilateral concessions in advance; any referendum on Articles 2 and 3 would be very divisive in both Northern Ireland and the Republic, creating an atmosphere that would not be conducive to constructive dialogue; any change to the Constitution arguably would undermine constitutional nationalism and allow the gunmen to claim that they were the only ones concerned with the rights of the nationalist community in Northern Ireland; the grossly oversimplified and unhelpful unionist view that the Republic is a 'foreign country' and that Northern Ireland is just a normal part of the UK would be strengthened; finally, and crucially, there is absolutely no guarantee that a referendum in the Republic would be successful — the risk involved in an unsuccessful referendum and the damage it would cause, having raised expectations, far outweigh any dubious benefits of a successful referendum.'

MR MICHAEL NUGENT of New Consensus in Dublin suggests that first the territorial claim contained in Articles 2 and 3 should be replaced by 'an aspiration to self-determination for all the people on the island'; secondly, 'we should enshrine in our Constitution the right of anyone born on the island to Irish citizenship'; and thirdly, 'we should allow Irish citizens living in Northern Ireland to be represented either in the Dáil or (perhaps more practically) in the Seanad, and to vote in Irish presidential elections'. This third suggestion would work by creating an extra-territorial Dáil 'constituency' (or Seanad panel) to represent Irish citizens living in Northern Ireland, who could register to vote on production of an Irish passport. In this way, Mr Nugent says, 'we would have removed our territorial claim while, in real terms, advancing the actual political unity of the Irish nation'.

At the same time he suggests that the 1920 government of Ireland Act should be amended to grant self-determination to the people of Northern Ireland — 'to make clear that Northern Ireland is part of the United Kingdom, not because the Westminster parliament says so, but because a majority of the people of Northern Ireland say so. Such a change should also make it legally binding that the Westminster parliament cannot veto any future decision by a majority of the people of Northern Ireland to leave the United Kingdom and enter into a new constitutional relationship with the people of the Republic of Ireland.' Mr Nugent suggests that the most appropriate way to combine these changes would be to incorporate them into a new Northern Ireland Constitution Act, jointly underwritten by the two governments and by the EC.

DR BRIAN EGGINS, a chemistry lecturer at the University of Ulster and an Alliance Party activist, argues that the existence of Articles 2 and 3 does not in itself pose a threat to unionists, whatever the McGimpsey judgment might imply.

If they were removed or modified, it would not change the reality of the situation one iota. The fact is that many (most?) people in the Republic of Ireland are not pressing for an immediate united Ireland. If they were offered it, they would be embarrassed; they would not know what to do about it. They would not, could not, want to enforce it unless the majority in the North agreed.... But if Articles 2 and 3 were abolished or amended, it would make no difference to the feelings of those Irish people North and South who see unity as logically desirable, in that Ireland is one island with a common cultural identity. They would still have their 'aspirations' for a united Ireland.

However, abolition or amendment 'would allay the fears of the unionists and reduce the perceived threat which partially triggers loyalist paramilitary violence. It might also affect IRA violence. As long as Articles 2 and 3 remain in their present form as a 'constitutional imperative', the IRA feels that it has a quasi-legal justification for violence.' (He admits that elsewhere in his submission he also believes that the opposite might happen: that the IRA might use the excuse of the Articles being diminished to redouble its violence — 'but then the IRA is no respecter of logic!')

MR SAMUEL BOYD, a Belfast man now living in South Wales, says that the challenge facing anyone contemplating a new initiative is to devise some means of containing the nationalist desire for Irish unity within a governmental structure that would allow Northern Ireland's politicians to grapple with the region's serious economic and social problems.

He suggests a referendum every ten years to take place throughout Ireland — perhaps to coincide with elections to the European Parliament — on specific constitutional proposals drawn up by the Irish government for a future unified state. The proposals would have to be carried by *more* than a simple majority in each jurisdiction before any moves towards implementing them could take place.

This would give the Republic's government and people the opportunity to present a set of proposals which might in time be sufficiently attractive to interest the people of Northern Ireland, while allowing the final decision on their constitutional status to rest with the people of the North. 'Contained within this machinery is the essential ingredient of time — time for the healing of grievous wounds and for co-operation on mutual economic problems.' In the meantime, an elected assembly in Northern Ireland would be freer to concentrate on social and economic matters.

MR TERENCE DONAGHY, a Belfast solicitor and founder member of the Northern Consensus Group, says that two things, above all, have inhibited the search for a new arrangement to replace the flawed 1921 settlement.

(1) The conviction of the unionist population that the nationalists will never be satisfied until they have achieved a united Ireland. Many sincere unionists will point to the fact that all the original demands of the Civil Rights Movement from the 1960s have been met in full: yet we are as far away from peace as ever. John Hume's statement in the heat of battle ('It's a united Ireland or nothing') has never been forgotten, despite everything he has said since.
(2) The fact that republican violence seems long since to have become endemic. The brutal nature of the republican murder campaign, especially in the border areas, has created a sense of intense anger, coupled with a despairing sense of helplessness among too many unionists.

To meet these two great inhibiting factors, John Hume has made what must be one of the most sensible proposals put forward by any politician from any camp, that is, that a political settlement, hammered out by elected politicians, should be put to the test of joint referenda, North and South of the border, simultaneously. Common sense would strongly indicate that the outcome of such referenda would be a resounding endorsement of the proposed settlement, but most particularly if Sinn Féin could be brought into the settlement negotiations.

This would be the 'clinching factor' in reaching a permanent settlement, although Mr Donaghy accepts the immense problems it poses. However, he is convinced that the outlines of such a settlement are 'already clear to the political leaders on both sides of the divide'.

REV. SYDNEY CALLAGHAN, a Methodist minister who was born in the Republic but has long lived in Belfast, says people in the South 'could not care less about what is happening 'up North' so long as it does not affect them — as it may in border areas or in the tourist industry. Behind a polite conversational gambit, they simply do not want to know.' He says there are political posturings — mainly for overseas consumption — and the necessity to make nationalist noises, but in general elections Northern Ireland and Irish unity are not big issues. 'If the ex-pats, particularly in America where they are living on and with the romantic myths of all their yesterdays, can be encouraged to believe the quest for Irish unity is still alive and well back home, then all is well — but the possibility that it might happen would scare the living daylights out of any Irish government.... The concept of a pluralist society — as it would have to be — is something to be talked about but not worked out. So far as a solution to the current malaise is concerned, there is no real will to find one.'

After 20 years of violence, the North itself is 'coping with a certain war weariness. This has brought about a greater polarization in working-class communities, while the affluent middle class, of both Catholic and Protestant traditions, are largely 'opting out', having become cynical and disillusioned with the political processes and wanting little or nothing to do with it.' Little affected by the violence, they are content to accept the status quo as long as it does not change too much.

In the meantime the poor and deprived are becoming poorer and poorer as government policies begin to affect more and more people in the Protestant and Catholic ghettos and areas of high unemployment. Despite all this, and some excellent inter- and cross-community projects, and vastly improved housing stocks, there does not seem to be any real wish to find a solution. In the South no real will. In the North no real wish. The significant word is *real*.

Rev. Callaghan suggests that perhaps the time has come 'when there has to be a forthright spelling out of what Britain's short-term and long-term plans are for Northern Ireland. If goals were clearly defined and possible arrangements spelled out without any blurring of the edges, it might help to concentrate the minds of both people and politicians all over Ireland. For example, how much longer can the British economy maintain its financial involvement in Northern Ireland? It could be that financial factors and not political ones will be the deciding factor. If this is so, why not say so?'

The lack of cross-border communication is a theme that occurs in a number of submissions. CATHAL and CATHERINE BRUGHA of Dublin believe that 'one of the reasons for the failure to resolve the problems in Northern Ireland has been the expectation that politics can provide solutions to a situation that has major cultural and religious aspects'. They argue that, if there is a first step to be taken, it should be to deal with unionist fears. 'Very few people in the Republic have any wish to take over Northern Ireland. Similarly, very few Roman Catholics would wish to impose their religious beliefs on Christians of other denominations. Indeed there is very little understanding in the South of the depth of unionist/loyalist fears. A particular starting point for breaking the impasse would be to focus on unionist/loyalist fears of being threatened politically, culturally and religiously by the Republic.'

In this context they believe that people in Dublin are not as 'trapped' as the unionists and the nationalists in the North.

Much of the memory of hundreds of years of abuse of the Irish by the English is fading in Dublin. This memory remains strongest in country areas. Most rural townlands will have an elderly person who has talked with a grandparent who lived during the Famine when English rule amounted to a policy of genocide. It is not well understood by unionists and in Britain that it was government policy in much of the last century to destroy the Irish politically, culturally and religiously. To an extent the Irish were saved by emigration. The flood of impoverished Irish into English cities, and the threat of growing Irish influence in America, apparently had the effect of mitigating the starvation policy to the point of emigration. The nationalist/Roman Catholic culture in Ireland certainly has a sensitivity to ethnic genocide which, when they overcome the hurt of it, could make them highly responsive to unionist/loyalist fears. Of all parts of the Republic, Dublin is very much more open to change and to forgetting and forgiving past grievances. In many ways a Dubliner has more in common with someone from Belfast. There has for long been a tendency for Belfast people from both sides of the divide to come to Dublin whether to visit, to study or to live. Dublin people, generally, have not reciprocated in this regard, apart from some shopping excursions.

A cross-border communication between the two premier cities would help to deflate irrational fears and create a sensitivity to justifiable fears. This would be particularly valuable if it took place on an individual or family basis, where the communication could be real. Also it would have more effect if the people were not from the upper class, who by their wealth are removed from the problems and consequently are more apathetic about their solution. Ideally those from the South should come from a nationalist tradition; otherwise, they would not be seen to be credible when talking on behalf of the Southern view. Likewise those from the North should come from the Presbyterian or strictly loyalist tradition, in which the fears more certainly are centred. Those from the Church of Ireland tend not to have the same feeling of abandonment by England. Because they have so much more in common with the English, they have more of an option to emigrate to England, and so are not as emotionally involved in looking for a solution.

Once together and in dialogue a lot could be done to resolve the log-jam of inter-community blockages. There are many issues on which to focus: Articles 2 and 3 of the Republic's Constitution; our common Christian faith and Bible studies. Many Irish towns are twinned with others in Europe and further afield. A twinning between Dublin and Belfast could give a lead to others; for example, Cork and Derry, Ennis and Enniskillen. An unusual possibility of tripletting would be the three Dundrums in Counties Down, Dublin and Tipperary. Such direct contact would be beneficial in reducing tension within Northern Ireland, but it would also be good for the people of Dublin and in the South generally.

CO-OPERATION NORTH, which has done much of this cross-border work since the late 1970s, believes that 'community links are essential to any lasting political solution'. Given the lack of current political consensus, the organization stresses the importance of strengthening existing North-South relationships and building new ones in the fields of business, tourism, social and community activities, sport and culture. 'It is important to build and manage a process of continual dialogue between the differing communities. This process mirrors the process by which the European Community was gradually built up from the ruins of world war, but is more intimate because of the more intimate nature of our conflict.' It urges that proper financial resources should be invested in building individual and community linkages across the border — 'currently the cost of one day's violence far exceeds the cost of one year's peace building'.

THE INTER-CHURCH GROUP ON FAITH AND POLITICS believes that 'there is still a lot of ambiguity among people in the Republic about the question of a united Ireland and this ambiguity has a serious effect on people within Northern Ireland. People in the Republic need to establish realistic relationships with the United Kingdom as a whole and with both communities in Northern Ireland in order to clarify further what sort of political structures they hope to achieve ultimately and what responsible measures they are using to achieve them. The extent to which many people both in the Republic and Britain — even at the highest political level — remain unaware of many of the realities of Northern Ireland is a cause for serious concern.' (See also Local government Reform; and Culture, Religion, Identity and Education: Religion.)

MR CHRIS HUDSON, Dublin trade unionist and chairperson of the Southern committee of the Peace Train Organization, writes about the indifference and 'Northern Ireland fatigue' of Southern society, including the media. He suggests, as a Southern Protestant, that his religious/cultural community has failed to use its good offices 'in order to tease out issues which perhaps could help heal the divide'. He suggests that a delegation of Southern Protestants could visit Northern Ireland, listen carefully to both sides and report back to each side the feelings, fears and hurt of the other, as well as to the Irish government. He believes that 'Protestants from the South talking to Northern Protestants about their hopes, fears and wishes for Southern society' could be a positive and interesting development.

(See also Professor Edna Longley, Religious, Cultural and Other Issues: Culture and language.)

Other political submissions

There were some 40 submissions on broadly constitutional and political themes which could not easily be fitted into any of the above categories. They ranged from criticisms of British government policy for being too pro-nationalist, through innovative schemes for preferenda, cantonization and 'minimum percentage' electoral systems, to pleas for renewed political leadership and a realization that the world was soon going to pass Northern Ireland by.

MR MICHAEL McKEOWN, a writer and lecturer originally from Belfast but now living in Dublin, identifies a number of trends that he believes could lead to attitudinal changes over the next decade which 'might generate a political climate more congenial to positive initiatives'. These include: (a) a radical change in the demographic profile of Northern Ireland; (b) the emergence of a significant Roman Catholic meritocracy; (c) constitutional changes in the United Kingdom; (d) a growing demand for enhanced local powers; (e) attitudinal changes within the population of the Republic; (f) reactions to the impact of the EC on social and community life in Northern Ireland.

The first two of these factors are interdependent, linked to the rise in the Catholic proportion of the population over the past 20 years, the probable continuance of this trend because of the greater numbers of Catholic children and young people, and the larger numbers of Catholic recruits to management jobs in the public service. 'A consequence of this is that, as the Catholic population grows numerically and in political influence, it might no longer be as homogeneous politically as it has been in the past. While nationalist spokesmen in the period between the 1930s and 1960s sought the support of the Catholic population as the tribunes of the dispossessed, there is now emerging a Catholic middle-class sector which has access to power and position. This has been a consequence of academic achievement and the operation of fair employment procedures.' Mr McKeown does not believe that this new meritocracy will be drawn either to militant republicanism or to unionism, and will 'furnish a leadership which will be more disposed to evolutionary rather than revolutionary changes'.

The reactions of the Protestant majority to these developments are likely to be ambivalent. The perceived threat to the guarantee of an assured majority must give rise to apprehensions in some circles and fuel the fervour and animus of extremist groups. On the other hand, the increased identification of the new meritocracy with the institutions of the state might serve as a reassurance to more moderate Protestant opinion. Such a response would be likely to accelerate the search for an accommodation with the expanding minority community. That search might be made easier by the constitutional and social changes which Britain is likely to have to confront in the immediate years ahead. Many of the British institutions and symbols which have commanded the loyalty and commitment of Northern Protestants are likely to lose their sacramental potency. The diminution of sovereignty consequent upon the Maastricht treaty, the need to find some devolutionary solution to the Scottish demand for more autonomy and a changed role for the British monarchy will reduce the gravitational pull towards London and will offer the Protestant community alternative models of government to the Westminster model. The Crown in Parliament which has been the validating and consecrating mechanism for unionist legitimacy will be less significant and less alluring than before.

Mr McKeown believes that the implication of all this is that within a relatively short period of time 'a cross-community constituency' could merge which would be disposed to change and would look for structures 'reflective of the changed social and political circumstances'. He believes one matter where this might manifest itself could be in a demand for greater local authority powers. 'There are sufficient examples over recent years of cross-community co-operation in local councils to suggest that bipartisan strategies will emerge in response to the new opportunities.'

Mr McKeown sees unionists' 'not an inch' stance as based on a number of fears. These include absorption in a 32-county Irish Republic; loss of their British citizenship and rights; Irish government intervention in the government of Northern Ireland; concern about key aspects of devolved administration falling under nationalist control, either at local or regional government level. He believes that nationalists must consider how far they can accommodate these concerns 'without totally compromising the integrity of their own aspirations'. He suggests, for example, that an amending clause should be added to Articles 2 and 3 of the Irish Constitution to 'incorporate the concept of consent as a precondition to the reintegration of the national territory'. He points out that the British assurance to unionists about Northern Ireland's continuance as an integral part of the UK is less than rock solid, because it derives from a pledge of the Westminster Parliament (underwritten by the Anglo-Irish Agreement), and no parliament can bind a future parliament. 'If the government of the Republic was to bind itself constitutionally and under international law to become the first guarantor of unionist aspirations, it should afford unionists more confidence in the outcome of future talks.'

Mr McKeown believes that 'a more confident unionist community could be expected to be more co-operative in other fields as well; one such might be local government'. At present local government is very enfeebled, offering little scope for significant co-operative decision-making. He warns that the 'shared authority situation in the Hillsborough consultative model' or an executive version do little to promote the sense of restraint needed to prevent majority communities from abusing power. 'In many ways emphasizing the paternalistic role of the sovereign authorities might only encourage the elected representatives at all levels to be even more irresponsible than they have been.' Noting that, despite the behaviour of some (such as Belfast unionist councillors), there has been welcome evidence recently of this restraint at local council level, he urges that 'it is time the mantle of paternalism was discarded and power and responsibility returned to local politicians'.

Such 'managed changes' are designed to 'reinforce the strength of the moderate wing of unionism and encourage it in its attempts to secure an assured role for the unionist community in a changed world', says Mr McKeown. He emphasizes that the two communities' first options are well known. 'It will require a sensitive instrument to establish what their second options are, but these are the only ones likely of fulfilment and with the passage of time they could well become first options.' (See also Law, Justice and Security: Reducing the Violence.)

THE CADOGAN GROUP, a group of six academics and former civil servants, said that their submission was born out of 'a concern that official policy on Northern Ireland, and most serious comment on it, was moving further and further from reality' (the quotes are from an article summarizing the group's arguments by one of its members, Dr Dennis Kennedy).

The group believes that current British government policy is not working, despite the very wide consensus for it, because the analysis on which it is based is wrong. 'Since that analysis is essentially a nationalist one, and the policy based upon it has been primarily concentrated upon satisfying — some might say appeasing — nationalists, then our conclusions are indeed critical of that side of the divide. This does not mean that the group is motivated by unionist convictions.'

The Group says that a remarkable consensus has emerged over the past decade, based on seeing the central issue as the need to satisfy the desire of Northern nationalists to have the right to political expression of their Irish identity. The Anglo-Irish Agreement results from policy based on that analysis. Mr Kennedy says that it is 'rather a fancy way of stating an old-fashioned nationalist claim. It is, in a way, what Serbs in Bosnia are saying when they demand a state within a state.'

Logically the only way to give nationalists the 'right to political expression of their Irish identity' is to modify, in some way, the constitutional status of Northern Ireland. No nationalist spokesperson, North or South, has given any indication that such an expression of Irish identity can be achieved within a wholly United Kingdom context. As another element in current policy, regularly affirmed by British Ministers and assented to by all others, is that there can be no change in the constitutional position without majority consent, we have a rather glaring departure from realism.

The Group's submission (also published as a booklet entitled 'Northern Limits') 'challenges the view that sees the history of Northern Ireland as a simple tale of unionist guilt and nationalist suffering; this is historically inaccurate and has led to a facile assumption that nationalism is 'right'. We point out that civil rights demands were satisfied 20 years ago and that minority grievances today stem from a situation created by terrorist violence and the security response to it — a situation which has existed for two decades, during which unionists have had no political power in Northern Ireland.'

Yet much comment on the position today still tends to present an unreal picture of Catholics as an oppressed minority. The pamphlet does not seek to exonerate unionists from all charges of past misrule, or to deny that Catholics can still be socially and economically disadvantaged, but it does contend that both historical and cultural reality are more complex than the simplistic nationalist picture often portrayed.

We argue that, in these circumstances, to present Irish unity as a distinct possibility, as the Anglo-Irish Agreement does in Article 1c and as British Ministers frequently do, or to insist that the minority nationalist aspiration to dismantle Northern Ireland is of equal validity to the majority desire to maintain it, is unrealistic and destabilizing. Ireland was partitioned in the 1920s for the same reason Yugoslavia was partitioned in the 90s — there was no basis for unity. So the idea that partition was somehow wrong or undemocratic has to be discarded, along with Articles 2 and 3 of the Republic's Constitution, which are no more than a crude territorial claim.

The submission also criticizes 'lack of reality on possible European Community roles in achieving an agreed Ireland'. It points out that no real costing of constitutional change has been done by supporters of it, and that even joint authority would place an unacceptable burden on Southern finances. It says that while income levels North and South are similar (although Northerners pay less tax), standards of living are about 40 per cent higher in the North; consumer spending is one-third higher; and government spending per head on public services (not including defence, business subsidies and debt interest) is two-thirds higher. This difference is maintained by British taxpayers, who make a substantial contribution to the running costs of government in Northern Ireland through the tax and fiscal system, on the principle that to maintain parity of services throughout the UK, public funding has to be channelled from the richer to the poorer areas. 'The combination of well-funded public services with lower tax revenues than in the rest of the UK means that Northern Ireland almost certainly has a larger net inflow of public funds than any part of

Great Britain.' In recent years this has been running at close to £2000 million annually, and rose to £2500 million in 1991-92.'

The group argues in the light of these figures that there is no prospect that the burden of supporting living standards in Northern Ireland could be taken over by the Republic.

For this reason alone, a political unification of the island without continued UK financial support is not a realistic option. Nor is it conceivable that the EC or any other outside agency would fill the financial gap. At present the EC makes a net contribution of only around £100 million (or 4 per cent of the contribution made by UK taxpayers). The financial impossibility of unification is well recognized within government in the Republic, and is a significant part of the ambiguity, not to say hypocrisy, of the territorial claim.

Similarly, shared sovereignty over Northern Ireland, unless the Republic was to pay an impossible proportion of the costs involved, would

abrogate the almost universal principle that political authority should be exercised by the representatives of those who pay for government.... Some nationalists argue that under shared sovereignty, financial contributions to Northern Ireland might be made by Britain and the Republic in proportion to the sizes of their respective populations. This would, however, leave the Republic with perhaps 17 per cent of the influence, under the SDLP scheme, while contributing only 5 per cent of the finance necessary to maintain living standards.... If such an eventuality were to come about, however, we must realize that it would involve politicians elected in the *Republic* having a major say in spending the money of taxpayers in *Britain* on behalf of people in *Northern Ireland*. Any contribution from the Republic would involve Southern taxpayers in subsidizing living standards in Northern Ireland higher than their own. Arrangements of this nature would surely attract major protest in all three jurisdictions and are hardly likely to survive in the long term.

Any future agreement must be a real settlement, not a staging post on the way to something else, and not a formula for providing temporary accommodation of two incompatible but supposedly equally valid political traditions. The nationalist project of pushing for an increasingly enhanced 'Irish' dimension will ensure that mutually acceptable institutions for the good governance of Northern Ireland remain unattainable.

On the other hand, the Group advocates 'the greatest possible Irish dimension in a practical sense, with maximum and institutionalized cross-border co-operation. Inside Northern Ireland within the United Kingdom everyone should be able to live in dignity and security in a pluralistic society accommodating various nationalities, cultures and identities, with exceptional remedial measures to assist the economically and socially disadvantaged, and with the fullest guarantees of civil and other rights.

The best hope of achieving this lies within a European Community where national citizenship is of decreasing importance, where the concept of a common European citizenship alongside freedom of movement and mutual recognition of rights makes citizenship an incidental of residence — not a badge of nationality or cultural identity. This could leave the residents of Northern Ireland in the happy position of deeming themselves to be Irish or British or both as they wish, while remaining constitutionally citizens of the UK, and of the EC.

PROFESSOR JOHN DARBY of the Centre for the Study of Conflict at the University of Ulster argues for a more pragmatic approach to Northern Ireland's divisions than has been evident in past or present policies. He says that during the early 1970s many observers believed that the upsurge of violence could lead to one of two outcomes: 'the belligerents would either be shocked into an internal accommodation, or propelled into genocidal massacre'. Neither has occurred, he points out, and the violence, though remarkably persistent, has not intensified. On the contrary, the evidence is that it has diminished: from a peak of 468 deaths in 1972 to under 100 in every year since 1981. The proportion of civilian deaths has also diminished, and in 1990 it was difficult to find 'any examples of the direct sectarian confrontations which had been the main form of violence in 1969 and 1970'.

Why is this? Professor Darby asks. He argues that the conflict operates under a number of controls: the presence of the army, whatever other problems it causes, is a barrier against collapse into genocidal conflict; the paramilitary organizations are limited by both military and communal factors; but most important are 'the social mechanisms which people have evolved within local communities to regulate and manage their differences'. Examples of these are the kinds of co-operation based on mutual self-interest; for example, farmers joining to bring in the harvest, or, in a city, the two communities co-operating to ensure that a government training centre comes to their area. Such mechanisms act as restraints on the conduct of the two conflicting communities, reducing and managing the effects of sectarian differences. 'In effect, they are obstacles to absolute group cohesion for both communities, and therefore to a more genocidal form of violence.' He believes that not enough attention has been paid to the identification and support of these control mechanisms, and they would need to be considered as an element in any future settlement.

Professor Darby notes that the current outbreaks of ethnic violence throughout the world provide a measure for the conflict in Northern Ireland. 'They assure us that we are not singled out by some genetic birthmark, pariahs doomed forever to slaughter each other. There is no curse of Cuchulainn or Carson. The issues being contested here — human rights, ethnic violence, aggression, reconciliation, cultural pluralism — are not peculiarly Irish. They are universal themes.' He believes that there is much to be learned from the comparative study of other ethnic conflicts: 'from Malaysia, about how to manage ethnic tensions through electoral reform; from Holland, its approach to educational diversity; from Belgium, its treatment of minority languages; from equal opportunity approaches in Canada and the South Tyrol'. More selectively, 'we may aspire to Switzerland's decentralization without embracing its treatment of women and immigrants; we might consider the Lebanon's power-sharing experiments, but perhaps should stop short of imitating some other aspects of the Lebanese experience'.

He points out that this is not a one-way traffic: the surgical techniques and emergency procedures developed at Belfast's Royal Victoria Hospital have become a model for hospitals in Israel and other societies experiencing street violence; the educational research carried out at the University of Ulster on integrated education and education for mutual understanding is regarded as a model for educational researchers and policy-makers in other countries.

Professor Darby says that the Centre for the Study of Conflict has recently launched the Ethnic Studies Network, with the aim of encouraging international co-operation between researchers working in societies experiencing ethnic conflict. It is also in negotiation with the United Nations University to establish a research and training centre at the University of Ulster to serve as an international focus for such ethnic studies.

He urges that the Northern Ireland issue should stop being regarded as a problem, 'with its implication that a solution lies around the corner for anyone ingenious enough to find it'. Rather, it is a tangle of interrelated problems: the central constitutional problem; a continuing problem of social and economic inequality, especially in employment; a problem of cultural identity; a security problem, with people being killed because of it; a problem of religious difference; and a problem of the day-to-day relationships between the people who live in Northern Ireland. He points out that at certain times there is a chance of movement on some of these, while on others progress is impossible. It makes sense, then, to adopt a pragmatic approach, with initiatives determined by opportunity and circumstance. He says that during the last few years there have been changes in the educational and fair employment fields which would have been 'unthinkable' five years ago.

He urges an integrated approach to change.

Educational reforms will be frustrated if they are not accompanied by the removal of fundamental inequalities in the distribution of jobs. It is foolish to seek a political settlement which does not acknowledge that each tradition has cultural expressions which are non-negotiable to them but anathema to many of their opponents. It is ridiculous to devise security policies — peace lines, undercover operations — without trying to anticipate their effect on community relationships. There is evident and immediate need for a structure which integrates more effectively the different arms of government policy in the broad field of community relations, and especially which integrates security policies into the mainstream of policy-making. It is obvious that security policy has peculiar needs, but the security blanket is used much too frequently at present to frustrate policies in other fields of government activity.

Professor Darby concludes by repeating that conflict is something to be handled rather than solved.

Government policy since the 1970s has been directed towards seeking to expand the middle ground and marginalizing more extreme elements. This has clearly not been successful. It is now obvious that any significant improvement will require the acceptance of elements from the other culture which seem to be confrontational. For Catholics it means regarding Orange processions, which seem so triumphalist to many of them, as a legitimate expression of cultural distinction. For Protestants it means acknowledging the position of the Irish language, which seems so threatening to many of them. An even more unpalatable pill for both communities to swallow is the inevitable problem of how, when the violence ends, to reintroduce to the community those who have been engaged in using it. Respect for diversity will not come naturally, and it cannot depend on vague good wishes. Initially at least, it will need the force of the law to back it up.

Support for the middle ground is, of course, important. Moderate opinion, expressed through reconciliation groups, the Churches and political action, has played its part in keeping this society together during 20 years of violence. It will have a major role in conflict management in the future. But now it must move over for unsavoury bedfellows. Altruism is an unreliable basis for conflict resolution. Better to rely on hard negotiation, firmly based on self-interest.

ARCHBISHOP ROBIN EAMES, the Church of Ireland Primate, in a personal submission, writes that the 'real problem for Northern Ireland is the accommodation of difference' and the 'real problem for Ireland as a whole is the accommodation and respect for minorities'. He continues: 'The Protestant majority in Northern Ireland is much more aware of its minority role in Ireland as a whole than it is of its majority position in Northern Ireland. That is the major change which has occurred in the thinking and attitudes of Protestants here during the past 25 years.... This leads to many of the uncertainties and fears which are expressed about their relationship to the United Kingdom and their attitude towards the Republic.' That fear and uncertainty, he believes, is the root of the problem on the Protestant side, just as sectarianism on both sides 'remains the root cause as well as the dominant consequence of attitudes and relationships in Northern Ireland'.

He also believes that, beside Northern Ireland's traditional 'two communities', two other communities are emerging: one is composed of both Protestants and Catholics and is one of growing trust and confidence, although it is still 'a tender plant'; the other is the 'community of fear' which reaches out into the first through violence, intimidation and threat. 'As long as these two communities exist in a juxtaposition, the uncertainty and fear to which I refer will continue. No political reform or social development will improve the situation as long as this basic fear and uncertainty prevail.... An imposed solution or any solution which fails to listen to the message produced by those two communities will fail.'

Archbishop Eames then poses a number of questions and essays answers to them:

(1) 'Is there sufficient evidence today of a desire by most ordinary people to see a new way forward?' At times he detects 'a general willingness to accept political progress, but the reaction to the ending of 'the talks' proves that few expected progress. There is a need to restore public confidence in the political process.... A speedy renewal of the process is essen-

tial. But it is equally important to find ways of preparing society for the fact that progress will mean compromise.

(2) 'How far has society become immune to the need to progress because of the trauma and effects of years of violence and division?' He believes the point has been reached where this danger exists. 'An acceptable level of violence is one thing — but an acceptable level of *acceptance* of violence is of greater importance. It holds many and varied psychological implications. I fear it is present today in many parts of our community...it would be fatal to any solution to ignore the fact that as time passes more and more people come to accept a situation as inevitable.

(3) 'Is it possible that people in large numbers have come to accept the status quo not because they welcome or accept it, but because they have lost the will to see a different path?' He believes people will generally accept social or political change if (a) they see it is to their advantage; (b) they do not feel threatened by it; (c) they have a trust in those motivating it; (d) it is something which *can* work.

(4) 'At what point does a community become so accepting of a situation that the amelioration of its problems becomes irrelevant?' Dr Eames warns that 'to some, the political process in Northern Ireland is already irrelevant — jobs and lives free from fear are priorities for many. Direct Rule appears to some as acceptable because they see no alternative. Talk of local accountability is often a concept of the selected few — others feel little confidence in what has already been accepted.'

(5) 'Is there today any real credibility for the political process, given two factors: the apparent failure of political parties to reach accommodation on the future government of Northern Ireland and the clear opting-out of so many from public involvement?' Dr Eames says: 'the opting out of responsibility by the middle class is a definite factor today. For those whose work, recreation or social life is untouched by the 'community of fear', there is a reluctance to get involved.'

'I have become convinced that we must no longer think in terms of grandiose or short-term political objectives', Archbishop Eames concludes.

The temptation to engage in dramatic initiatives or gestures must be avoided. Slow, steady progress in building up inter-community confidence and trust must be allowed to overcome the divisions of generations. There are many ways in which this process is already taking place. Emphasis should be laid on co-operation between religious and political groupings where this is possible. Efforts to bring new investment, provision of social amenities, health care and education on a basis which can easily be identified by all community groupings as essential for their well-being as a whole can be positive and lasting. Unemployment is not the prerogative of any one section of this community.

He ends with a number of specific suggestions: (1) more power should be returned to local councils involved in responsibility-sharing; (2) political parties should be encouraged to unite on issues such as unemployment to show what can be achieved by co-operation; fair employment policies should be continued and developed; (3) there should be a community-wide effort to gain new investment, with groups adopting the joint approach of the four Church leaders in their 1993 visit to the USA; (4) 'support for terrorism will continue so long as there is no alternative; that alternative will only appear once the efforts to build confidence in a political process of change become relevant and obvious.'

THE GREEN PARTY says that 'any solution to the problems of Northern Ireland must involve a degree of compromise. As an absolute minimum, therefore, we need a decision-making process by which compromise decisions are at least possible'. The party proposes 'multi-option consensus voting', or the best-known version of this, the so-called 'preferendum'. Such a process would, for example, help to avoid the clash between those who want a 32-county state and those who want a six-county state, both believing that those are the only options.

The process is the following. By awarding points to all (or most) of the policy options on a ballot paper according to preference, each voter would recognize the validity of their neighbours' legal aspirations (on the constitutional issue, for example, the options might run right across the spectrum from full integration with Britain to a unitary Irish state). Secondly, by adding all the points cast for each option and choosing that which achieves the highest score, the system would ensure that (almost) everyone participates in the democratic process, and not just 50 per cent and a bit. 'No longer should it be a question of British or Irish, as if these were the only two options. No longer should it be poll tax: yes or no? Or abortion: never or on demand? There should be both a rational discussion on all valid viewpoints, and a rational decision-making process; that is, one which is also multi-optional.' (See also Law, Justice and Security: Policy; and Culture, Religion, Identity and Education: The Environment.)

Other submissions recommending the use of the preferendum came from Mr Annett Agnew, Mr Peter Emerson, Mr Dave Little and the Northern Ireland Community Study Group.

The Witness-Bearing Committee of the REFORMED PRESBYTERIAN CHURCH says that 'our conflict in Northern Ireland is not, as some people care to portray, a holy war. It is the weary reaction of men and women who over many years have been brutalized and stripped of their dignity. It is the galvanic reaction of men and women who are too frightened to trust those who stand beside another flag and wrap themselves in another culture. The gospel of Christ tells us that they are frightened, vulnerable sinners just like us. It also tells us that we do not find our everlasting security or our highest dignity in earthly political structures. Rather, we find in Christ one who is able to reconcile us to God, to straighten out our twisted natures, and by taking away fear and hate gradually removes our sense of alienation from our fellow men.'

In Northern Ireland the minority community, feared by the majority community as subversive aliens, was marginalized to areas where their influence could cause no damage to the state. Excluded and brutalized, this community has given rise to a new generation of brutalizers. The majority community, although in a position to govern the province for 50 years, have fared little better. They are told by an aggressive majority on the island as a whole that they are not really a viable community and have no real rights of self-determination. Their only real right is to help influence what sort of united Ireland they will live in. A generation of inter-communal violence has added tears to fears, and the atmosphere of a blood feud to feelings of political alienation.

The Committee urges that 'a consensus around a new set of values must be sought before there can be real constitutional renewal. Whatever form it might take, our politicians and community leaders (including Church leaders) must lead us to and through a process whereby our sacred principles are aired and discussed and our fundamentals are thrashed out in the form of a constitutional covenant. That will include a statement of rights and responsibilities that we can all accept and agree with. We may care to call it a 'Bill of Rights', but it must be a formulation that will command the respect of all.... A structure that is produced outside Northern Ireland and imposed from without is counter-productive, because the process of producing a political covenant is as important as the final product. When we produce this ourselves (or at least feel that our voice has contributed to its formation) we will feel a sense of ownership of our constitution and a corresponding loyalty to its institutions.' This covenant will seek 'to express the ethos of our political culture by declaring what is sacred and accepted and this will act as a focus for unity'. The Committee recognizes that it cannot change hearts — it believes that only salvation through Jesus Christ can do that — 'but it can engender attitudes and promote behaviour which recognize the rights and dignity of others'. It will be a legal document, but more than that it will also be 'a moral declaration, providing the moral framework for government'. The Committee contends that it is also the place to make a declaration that any proposed government of Northern Ireland must be subject to the authority of Jesus Christ, making it a focus for loyalty 'in a society with a strong sense of the sacred' and able to command the respect of all denominations.

The submission of MR ROY JOHNSTON, the Dublin-based scientist, long-standing political activist and member of the Irish Green Party, is visionary in a very different way. He begins by describing three potential European scenarios: the first malign — a powerful, centralized EC with a dominating central core attracting labour from a declining fringe; the second benign — minimal central authority with all power devolved to regional governments or cantons; the third malign again, with Europe breaking up into fighting fringe tribes and a defensive imperial heartland.

He then outlines some steps towards a possible benign scenario in Ireland, based on decentralization and cantonization. Cantons would need to be new political entities with their own devolved governments, formed as an EC project with the blessing of London and Dublin 'as steps in the direction of resolving the old and costly dispute'. They should be viable enough to support at least one third-level education institution each. Mr Johnston suggests three networks of towns which could be the cores of such cantons: (1) Derry, Strabane, Omagh, Donegal, Letterkenny; (2) Enniskillen, Ballyshannon, Sligo, Boyle, Carrick-on-Shannon; (3) Dundalk, Newry, Armagh, Dungannon, Monaghan, Cavan. The first of these would involve the regeneration of the Derry hinterland based on the old Donegal light railway. Pointing out that the regional technical colleges in Derry and Letterkenny are already linked by EC programmes, he suggests that 'it should be possible to develop a pilot political dimension, via the existing local government bodies, in the joint supervision of a network of college-related enterprise centres and local business-funded college-based projects, in such a way as to give the initiative a positive image from the start.' A 'development council' should be set up, with an input from existing local authorities, which would deal directly with Brussels, and should go on to work out the future role of cantonal government, being helped by the EC to study regional and cantonal systems of government elsewhere in Europe.

Mr Johnston envisages one or two more cantons in the north of Ireland: the first around greater Belfast, with a possible second centred on the Ballymena-Coleraine axis. 'Thus, instead of a six-county entity, we would have a five-canton entity involving twelve counties, of which six would be from the Republic.' He emphasizes that the cantons would have to be demilitarized zones, with a possible nominal UN presence, and that all sides would have to feel that they had gained from the process: the British because it would be the end of 'an ongoing nightmare'; the IRA because the British army would leave; the Catholics because a situation would have ended which effectively excluded them from politics; and the Protestants because it would mean the end of any threat of rule from Dublin.

On a more immediate note, the director of the Community Relations Council (CRC), DR MARI FITZDUFF, in a personal submission, says that 'in situations of conflict, whether these be of a constitutional, territorial, cultural or political nature, the quality of leadership available to the opposing parties is likely to be the most crucial factor in determining a successful outcome'. It is particularly important that those committed to the political process alone — without any dependence, either explicit or hidden, on violence to achieve their aims — are able to demonstrate its adequacy for dealing with even the most difficult situations. She emphasizes how difficult the task of politics is in Northern Ireland, and the strain politicians there are under-balancing the personal pressures from their constituents against the local, regional, national, and (increasingly) European require-ments of their profession, all against a background of sectarian division.

In addition, such is the state of disrespect into which politics has fallen in Northern Ireland that those involved in any public way in politics are often penalized for such involvement. Their participation on public, community and voluntary bodies and their employment by such bodies is often seen as problematic. Inevitably this has decreased the number (and presumably therefore the quality) of those prepared to enter public life at a political level.... All parties will testify to the difficulty of recruiting qualitative new recruits to political representation, particu-larly at the local level. In addition, all political parties suffer from a chronic lack of funding, minuscule membership, offices more shabby than many voluntary agencies, and in many cases, a lack of organizational resources and skills.

All this testifies to a situation where the political process suffers from 'a pari-ahship' which has diminished its capacity to deliver an acceptable and sustain-able political solution for the region — 'and such a demand upon it will con-ceivably continue, unless our pretensions to democracy are to be abandoned'.

She then proposes that the present minimal training and education for political leadership should be greatly expanded, pointing out that countries like the USA, Germany and Sweden have privately and publicly funded training programmes for politicians. Such training should be cross-com-munity in nature and be tailored to both present and prospective politi-cians; being trained in this way should be part of the commitment under-taken by those entering politics, and they should be financially compen-sated for it. It should include information about other democratic systems, and particularly those representing pluralism at its best; briefings on eco-nomics, the environment, planning issues and so on from relevant boards and government departments; community relations training — for exam-ple, how to counteract sectarianism; effective political discussion skills; overcoming prejudice; conflict management; cultural traditions work.

Dr Fitzduff also suggests that more public, community and voluntary bodies should consider engaging politicians in their work, on a cross-party basis if they can. She believes the work of the Northern Consensus Group (see Devolution) should be studied and allocated financial resources. She argues for increased powers for councils that have been sharing power. And she proposes the setting up of a working group, drawn from the polit-ical parties, the government and charitable trusts, to study how the prob-lem of inadequate party funding can be overcome.

Finally she urges all British and Irish government spokespersons to extend the range of individuals and groups to whom they talk. In particu-lar, Irish government spokespersons 'should be encouraged to take all opportunities possible to hear from and talk with all sections of political interest in Northern Ireland, thereby increasing their capacity to appreci-ate the complexities which inform the conflict'.

MR DES SMITH from Dublin, a former member of Fianna Fáil's national executive and of the Progressive Democrats' Northern Ireland Committee, begins by quoting the 19th-century Protestant nationalist patriot, Thomas Davis, urging Irishmen of different faiths to unite 'in the other's weal'. Mr Smith says that, after having stood over too many graves and talked to too many distraught and bewildered people, he has 'no stomach left' for piece-meal reforms. He urges an acknowledgment that 'the problem is the age-old one between Britain and Ireland which we have shunted northwards'. While rejecting the Northern Ireland state, he admits that the Republic offers 'no credible alternative'. 'To the vast bulk of Ulster Protestants, the Republic offers no attractions as a permanent and safe home where their heritage, ethos and traditions would be protected, secure and welcome. The aspiration to such security is their birthright, and until nationalist Ireland can muster the sensitivity and confidence to guarantee it, through all the suffering and grief 'Ulster' will cling to what it has.'

Mr Smith cites four examples of 'national shortcomings and failures' in the Republic: the ban on anyone attached to the Northern Ireland security forces being a member of the Gaelic Athletic Association, which he calls 'nakedly sectarian' in that it applies almost entirely to Protestants; the 'crass insensitivity' of laws which do not allow Protestants in the Republic to make up their own minds on matters of conscience and personal moral-ity, laws which have greatly damaged the state's pluralist credentials; the 'cloud of uncertainty' that hangs over the future of the Republic's only Protestant teaching hospital, the Adelaide in Dublin, which 'does not encourage the North to look South with any degree of confidence'; and the Catholic Church's *ne temere* decree, which demanded of the Catholic partner in a mixed marriage a written undertaking to bring up its children as Catholics, now to all intents and purposes a thing of the past.

Mr Smith concludes with a radical proposal: that in return for unity, the present Republic should dissolve itself. 'I believe strongly that only an offer of such proportions will capture the interest of the Northern unionist community.... If accepted in principle, the two great traditions in Ireland could sit down in co-operation and mutual respect finally to design and construct a house in which they could comfortably live together.'

THE NEW IRELAND GROUP (NIG) wants the British and Irish govern-ments to declare jointly that in due course they will withdraw all claims to sovereignty over the people of Northern Ireland, and in the meantime will jointly sponsor a process to seek a solution consistent with the principle of self-determination based on consensus (in the event of such a solution being found, they will also jointly guarantee its outcome). The aim of such a joint declaration would be the removal of loyalist fears of absorption into an extension of the present Irish Republic and the reassurance of republicans that British sovereignty over Northern Ireland would not last forever. As part of this process, Articles 2 and 3 should be amended; the Anglo-Irish Conference should be replaced in the interim by the Anglo-Irish Inter-Governmental Council, set up by Margaret Thatcher and Charles Haughey in the early 1980s; and the media prohibition should be lifted on Sinn Féin and other banned elected representatives.

Once the external powers had set the scene in this way, the Group would urge an earnest attempt to negotiate a permanent ceasefire with an amnesty, and the establishment of an Initiative '92-style public forum to bring the people into the search for self-determination based on consensus. After this, a Northern Ireland constitutional convention should be set up to consider the final report of the public forum, to initiate a debate on the various possible constitutional options, and finally to vote by means of a preferendum (see Green Party) or similar method to find the option which has the greatest degree of consensus. This would then be put to the Northern Irish electorate, with the requirement that it would have to win at least two-thirds of the votes cast. In the event of failure, the convention would reconvene, to amend or alter the proposal in order to seek the people's ratification again. Ultimate failure would result in a reactivation of the Anglo-Irish Conference, or consideration of European protectorate status for Northern Ireland as an interim measure.

The New Ireland Group itself would be urging some of the following elements to be included in any blueprint: an appropriate degree of autonomy for Northern Ireland; association with the Commonwealth; a Bill of Rights; a 'community charter', to give citizens the means of participating effectively at local level; explicit separation of Church and state; the dissolution of the Republic of Ireland as presently constituted; an all-Ireland conference (if the delegates at the Northern constitutional convention agreed) to test whether Southern representatives were able to meet Northern conditions for a new Ireland; and a new Ireland constitution to be put to the Northern and Southern electorates, requiring a weighted (perhaps two-thirds) majority in each jurisdiction.

MR JAMES CANNING, an independent Dungannon councillor, repeats the common theme that, before any progress can be made in solving the Irish constitutional problem, 'we must find a way of removing fear and lack of trust within our community from the bottom up'.

We are often told that the people of Northern Ireland — Protestant and Catholic, nationalist and unionist, loyalist and republican — have more things in common than we have dividing us, and I believe this to be true. What we need is a forum where people, representing all opinions, can meet and discuss and explore the common ground which will be of mutual benefit to all.

He suggests that a PR election should be held to elect an 85-member general council for Northern Ireland which would be given the job of agreeing policy in the following matters covered by the following government departments: Environment, Agriculture, Health, Education, and Economic Development. The council would be banned from debating security and constitutional issues 'because from experience, if allowed to do so, they would talk about nothing else'. Mr Canning believes that members of such a body would find they had a great deal in common on these 'bread and butter' issues, and that it would attract people from business and community groups who normally do not involve themselves in party politics. 'It would also allow groups like Sinn Féin, if elected, to be part of a six-county forum, involved in drawing up policies which affect the well-being of us all.' He hopes this would lead to greater respect of and tolerance for the opinions of others and might eventually allow moves towards discussing agreed solutions to the constitutional problem.

MR BARRY COWAN, the broadcaster and film-maker, believes that the idea that only elected politicians can arrive at a successful formula for the future government of Northern Ireland is a flawed one. All previous political initiatives have foundered on the problem of elected politicians feeling that their hands were tied by voters whom fear and mistrust have made deeply suspicious of any inventiveness, initiative or compromise. He also thinks the 'benign dictatorship' of Direct Rule has become for many 'the least undesirable of the political options...the 'referees' who have occupied Stormont Castle for the last 20 years have, through dogged persistence and the application of common sense, cleared the way for slow and sensible reconciliation without much of the historical excess baggage which continues to burden the older generation.'

He believes the best hope for the future lies with two groups, which must be persuaded to return to the political process, whatever the cost: the middle classes, who have 'largely turned their backs on what they see as a discredited machine', and the young, who 'see old men bickering over issues which have no relevance to them'. These are the people who want to see jobs for themselves and their neighbours, who have preserved a semblance of normality over the past 25 years, who 'do not see solutions in terms of victory or defeat'.

Mr Cowan believes there is 'a relatively non-sectarian backbone' in Northern Ireland — people already sitting on area boards, on non-governmental agencies, on the Arts Council and Sports Council — which is prepared to listen and contribute. 'Why not offer realistic financial rewards to such people to take on the full-time job of assisting in, or even leading, the search for political solutions and agreed institutions? Because they would not be hostages to the lowest common electoral denominator, they might have the courage and foresight to think the unthinkable.'

He proposes the setting up of a 60-80 member 'council of state' with members appointed by a special committee of the Anglo-Irish parliamentary tier. Members should be well-paid and represent the widest possible social and religious spectrum. They should accept that 'initial progress must be made within the political status quo — Northern Ireland within the United Kingdom', although other aspirations must not be precluded. The council should not be considered a 'government in waiting'.

However successful they may be in discovering new models or adapting old ones, there can be no question of the council having any of the levers of power handed to them. Those must remain with the two governments under the terms of the Anglo-Irish Agreement until such time as the people give their verdict at the ballot box. If that verdict is 'yes', then the workings of the new model must be handed over to the elected politicians, while the council remains as a second chamber, like the Lords at Westminster or the Senate in Dublin. If the verdict is 'no', then the council must return to the drawing-board until such time as a new model can be agreed or the council decides itself that no further progress in possible and is dissolved.

LORD HYLTON, president of the Northern Ireland Association for the Care and Resettlement of Offenders (NIACRO), in a personal submission, lists a number of suggested reforms that could be brought in before or during new political arrangements. These include:

(1) Bright young graduates of Northern Irish universities should be attached on short-term contracts to the private offices of government Ministers and to organizations like the Belfast Action Teams and the Fair Employment Commission, the object being 'to create a pool of intelligent and well-informed young people with some practical experience, who would be capable of providing future political leadership'.

(2) There could be direct elections for seats on the Housing Executive and other statutory boards, starting with a minority of seats but with the ultimate aim that they should become 100 per cent elected bodies.

(3) There should be wider responsibilities for local councils that practice office-sharing. Local government could be further revived by forming Belfast and Derry, together with their adjoining towns and rural areas, into 'city-regions' for administrative purposes. 'In order to attract a good quality of elected member, the city-regions would have to have effective powers and duties. If the present statutory boards continued as providers of services, the city-regions would need to be accountable for the policies and practices of the boards within each region.'

(4) There should be a thorough examination of ways in which nationalists can be helped to accept state institutions in Northern Ireland and work with them, with studies made of the best practices in pluralist countries like Canada. He suggests a thorough review of all symbols used by government bodies. Similarly, he wonders whether the administration of the law could be made more acceptable by recruiting jurists from other common-law jurisdictions to act as magistrates and judges in Northern Ireland.

(5) Northern Ireland could become a Special EC Region, or an auton-

omous region under EC supervision, in the way Gibraltar is being talked about at the moment, and may well become necessary in the Balkans.

RT. HON. DAVID BLEAKLEY, the former general secretary of the Irish Council of Churches, says that what is needed is a new concept of 'interdependence' between the peoples of England, Wales, Scotland and the two Irelands. Such an Islands of the North Atlantic (IONA) federation of equals would be particularly difficult, yet also liberating, for England, allowing it to get away from centralized parliamentary domination and so explore to the full its post-colonial status. Such a system would mean the development of new forms of more expansive and flexible citizenship, not dependent on residence of a particular side of the Irish Sea. There would also be room for greater common welfare, educational, taxation, social services and pension benefits. More specifically, Mr Bleakley asks how far are Britain and the Republic willing to realize that real peace in Northern Ireland depends on a partnership between Protestants and Catholics working together for a common destiny. Increasingly the question from the North to the Republic, in particular, must be: 'How far are you willing to let our people go? What, for instance, if Northerners, Protestant and Catholic together, can make a lasting peace *outside* the context of a united Irish republic? Would, in those circumstances, the Republic be willing to pay the price for peace in the North and bring its public political stance into line with the new circumstances?'

DR DAVID CHAPMAN, of the Democracy Design Forum in Suffolk, puts forward two different electoral systems as 'alternative means of obtaining a Northern Ireland government which is responsive to both Catholics and Protestants'. (This summary can provide only the briefest overview of a complex and meticulously detailed set of proposals.) The first system operates by giving a party seats according to its 'minimum percentage' (or MPC), that is, its percentage of votes in those areas where it receives its *lowest* percentage of votes. The idea of this is to reward a party for getting votes in every area of the region — among Protestants and Catholics, unionists and nationalists — and to penalize a party which gets few or no votes in any areas. Thus, for example, if a hard-line unionist party gets few votes in a Catholic area, it will get a low MPC and will be penalized by losing seats. 'Thus, in so far as the two communities are geographically segregated, the system gives each party the incentive to get votes from both Catholics and Protestants.'

The system elects the party whose MPC is highest as the single-party government, and gives it a fixed 55 per cent majority of seats, thus enabling it to govern. The other parties share the remaining 45 per cent of seats, partly according to their ordinary votes, and partly according to their MPCs.

Another feature of the system is the division of Northern Ireland into small 'tracts', many of them mono-sectarian, groups of which would make up constituencies. This would facilitate the calculation of each party's 'overall percentage' and 'minimum percentage'. According to Dr Chapman's hypothetical calculations, the main beneficiaries of this system might be the Alliance Party and the Ulster Unionist Party. Whatever the outcome of such a system, he emphasizes that it would exert powerful incentives upon each party towards 'pan-sectarianism'.

Dr Chapman's second system is a modified version of single transferable vote PR, already used in Northern Ireland for elections to a regional assembly and local councils. The votes would be counted so that, in effect, candidates are divided into 'sets' of those similar in political tendency and sectarian allegiance. One candidate is then elected from each set by a balanced electorate, so that the candidates in a set have to compete for the votes of both Catholics and Protestants.

The former Alliance politician, MR WILL GLENDINNING, who now works for the Community Relations Council, stresses that of equal importance to the contents of any initiative or agreement is how it will be sold to each community. The political leaders must learn not to sell any 'deal' as beneficial to — or even a victory for — their own community at the expense of the other community. He warns that if any agreement is produced, it is the same local politicians who are regularly blamed for the current impasse who will have to implement it. Politics in Northern Ireland is often seen as a 'dirty game', and membership of political parties is proportionally less than in most western democracies. Outside the handful 'at the top', being an elected representative is likely to be a hindrance to the development of a career. Each time a political initiative fails, another batch of people drops out of the political process, never to return. A recent survey showed 'a much lower level of qualifications and status within the community' for local councillors in Northern Ireland than for their counterparts in Britain.

Politicians need to be understood and not dumped on for all our wrongs. They have, after all, stood for election and people have voted for them. They must be the people who negotiate any deal or settlement since they are the ones who will have to sell it to the people and who have to operate and defend it. They are most likely to do this if they see it as their deal. They are least likely if they feel that it is imposed on them and there is nothing of them in it. There is nothing strange in this: it is what is used in many systems of conflict dispute such as marriage guidance.

Pointing out that public pressure had played an important part in keeping the politicians at the talks table last year, Mr Glendinning stresses that those of us outside political parties but still part of the political process need to make things as easy as possible for the negotiators. They must feel that there is a majority for some form of compromise. It may take a long time for this to develop or it may develop quickly as a result of external changes. We need to develop policies in as many spheres of life as possible which increase contact between the two communities. These should not be artificial but natural — through the social, sporting, working, cultural and other activities which people undertake together. We should look at policies for housing and education to see if these are increasing or decreasing contact. Both communities are well aware that they are capable of destroying an initiative or bringing down a system of government in Northern Ireland. Only if we reach the position that sufficient people from both communities are prepared to support and defend a form of government can we hope for stability. (See also Joint Authority/Sovereignty.)

REV. DENIS FAUL, the Dungannon priest, stresses that the solution to the problem of government for Northern Ireland must be based on 'the real day-to-day problems of the area'. These include security, with each community living in fear of violent extremists from the other; people who wish to work for peace being prevented from doing so by Paisleyites and republican 'fanatics'; continuing discrimination; the well-founded impression in the Catholic community that the security forces and the courts are biased against them; and opposition to Catholic education and Irish culture.

He believes Northern Ireland's problem is primarily a spiritual one.

Forces such as generosity, kindness and friendship across the community divides are essential. Laws are of little effective use if they are not built on sincerely held values. These values of generosity and kindness are best built by co-operation. This is being encouraged by the funds (international, US and European) which are coming into the country in a cross-community and cross-border fashion. Granted that a degree of friendship, generosity and kindness has been achieved, the governmental structures should be built as follows:

(1) At local level there should be county councils (bigger than the present councils), with a very big say in services, tourism, education, health, social services, the infrastructure necessary for industrial development, police forces, fire brigades and environmental services. Councils should rotate the chair every six months.

(2) At provincial level there should be a Senate with nominated members from the local councils. This should have only consultative powers, not executive.

(3) Executive power should reside in London/Dublin in varying degrees; in London at first, with an increase in power to Dublin as time goes on. A condominium is the ideal, with 50 per cent of power in either direction.

(4) The courts of justice should have a Northern Catholic, Northern Protestant, British and Southern membership, with additional judges from Europe and the USA. These courts should have effective power to stop any act of the administrations detailed at (1), (2) or (3), and to compensate victims of injustice. They should have particular vigilance over the administration of the local councils.

MR EUGENE O'SHEA of Killarney believes that the 'first requirement of any peace initiative in Northern Ireland should be the brokerage of a ceasefire'. He believes that any political talks taking place against a background of violence stand very little chance of success. (See also Law,

Justice and Security: Reducing the Violence.) Following such a ceasefire, he envisages a preliminary but lengthy bilateral talks stage, involving all the parties, including Sinn Féin and perhaps the political wing of the UDA. He proposes that unionist fears could be assuaged by a declaration that 'specifically rules out a united Ireland as an option, since any such entity would carry within it exactly the same democratic deficit as Northern Ireland does as presently constituted'. If these bilateral talks were to break down, the Secretary of State should determine by referendum whether the electorate nevertheless wanted them to move to the multilateral stage: a weighted majority would be required for them to proceed in this way. Those who had caused the breakdown at the bilateral talks would be invited back in to the multilateral stage.

'The purpose of the multilateral stage would be to arrive at an agreed new constitutional status founded in a true consensus of the people(s) involved.' This would take at least two years, perhaps longer. The multilateral stage would have two parts: the first would be an open Initiative '92-style forum, with a wide range of parties, groups and individuals involved, to 'set the parameters' for the final plenary stage. The latter would consist of round-table talks with representatives of the major parties — or directly elected representatives of the people — and of the two governments, discussing 'a range of constitutional options consistent with the parameters as set out in the open forum report'. If at any stage this process were to break down, the Secretary of State should again invite the electorate, through a referendum, to decide whether it should continue or be dissolved. If the electorate decided for continuation, and those who had caused the breakdown still chose to stay out of the process, the people of Northern Ireland again should be asked to decide — this time by means of a multi-choice referendum or 'preferendum' (see Green Party) — on a list of options drawn up by the open forum's secretariat. This would give the electorate 'the opportunity to express its opinion across a range of carefully chosen options which lie between two mutually exclusive alternatives, thereby rendering consensus possible in a way that a border poll never could.'

Mr O'Shea suggests that the constitutional options to be discussed at the round-table talks could include the following: (1) an independent EC region with institutional links with Britain and the Republic; (2) an autonomous region within a new British Isles-wide ('Anglo-Celtic') confederation; (3) part of a two-part federal Ireland linked institutionally to Britain and within the Commonwealth; (4) repartition, so as to leave a 90 per cent consensus on each side of the new border.

Seventeen-year-old JOSEPH O'HANLON from Bangor, Co. Down, says he believes passionately that a major factor in the Northern Ireland problem is that 'neither side ever gets to hear the other side's position first-hand'.

For example, he would very much enjoy 'being part of a young nationalist group meeting with young unionists in order to explain our respective positions and to alleviate any mutual anxieties'. He proposes the establishment of some kind of institutionalized forum — he suggests it might be set up by Initiative '92 — to allow each side to engage in this kind of explanation and exchange.

MR CORMAC McALEER of Carrickmore, Co. Tyrone, says that it would be a joke, if it were not so deadly serious, for the dominant power in the Irish situation, Britain, 'to suggest that somehow it is an honest broker trying to barter a peace between two warring groups. It, to a much greater extent than the rest of us, must claim its giant's share of responsibility for creating and maintaining vicious conflict around what could be dynamic and energizing differences. The dominating power must create the situation in which all citizens (natives and planters) can work out their own destiny with promise of support rather than in fear of the consequences.' He calls for EC and UN support to be sought for underpinning and developing new structures of government for Ireland.

MR JOSEPH McCULLOUGH of Dublin makes the point that the people and government of the UK, the people and government of the Republic of Ireland, the majority of Northern nationalists and the majority of moderate 'Alliance-type' unionists would accept that a special constitutional framework for Northern Ireland ('not so much a 'failed political entity' as a special political entity') is necessary if significant progress towards a peaceful and stable society is to be made. He believes that some Sinn Féin supporters would almost certainly accept such a framework too. It is mainly the unionists who are against it, because they fear it would too easily become the first step towards absorption into a united Ireland, which they believe would be inimical to their interests. 'However, in maintaining that position, they condemn themselves and their descendants to a continuation of the very insecurity which disturbs them, since they cannot avoid the fact that they live in an Ireland from which, by and large, it does seem that the British would prefer to extricate themselves.' He proposes that to overcome unionist fears of absorption, 'it is most important that any such constitutional solution should be a permanent one, in so far as that is practicable. Bearing in mind the (perhaps remote) possibility of a future anti-unionist majority, unionist strategists perhaps should be attracted to any permanent solution which seemed to protect the interests, as they see them, not only on their immediate supporters, but also of their descendants.'

MR TONY CARLIN, an independent member of Derry City Council, is concerned about the low calibre of candidates often put forward by the traditional parties in Northern Ireland. He suggests the system adopted in Nevada to allow voters to add NOTA ('none of the above') to the ballot paper if they do not want to be represented by any of the candidates named on it. 'If a majority of voters plumped for NOTA, then the election would have to be re-run with the previous candidates barred. The parties would then have an incentive to nominate new, more appealing candidates.'

The American writer SALLY BELFRAGE, who lived for a year in Belfast while writing her book *The Crack*, believes the solutions to the Northern Ireland deadlock are always sought from the same group of pundits — politicians and academics who are constantly selecting and reselecting themselves to be the arbiters of the region's future and the architects of more useless experiments. It is time to abolish the experts and ask the people who 'make the struggle' how it can be ended. She suggests a 'people's referendum'. Among the questions she wants put (to those people 'in the thick of it') are whether or not they envisage the Northern Ireland struggle continuing into their grandchildren's time, and what their view is of 'ethnic cleansing' in the Northern Ireland context. She thinks that the fate of Yugoslavia as a possible 'logical extension' of the Northern Ireland situation should be put to the people. She also suggests large people's conferences (with no one, except the politicians and the self-styled experts, excluded) and schoolchildren's competitions, with as much of them as possible televised. She urges travel bursaries for prizewinners in the latter, and a province-wide lottery with tickets abroad for prizes, on the principle that 'away from it all, Protestants realize they are less 'British' and Catholics less simply 'Irish' than they had thought, and end up, if not enlightened, often huddling together for warmth against the more formidable 'other' of the hostile world.'

SIR OLIVER WRIGHT, the first UK government representative in Northern Ireland in 1969-70 and later ambassador to the US, puts forward 'nine theses for a prosperous future for Northern Ireland':

(1) There has to be an end to terrorism, for investors will not invest sufficiently to enable living standards to rise so long as law and order do not prevail. (2) For terrorism to be brought to an end, there needs to be an agreement on the future of the province between the constitutional parties, for only then will support in the two communities, whether active or passive, for the terrorists wither away. (3) For there to be an agreement between the constitutional parties, the parties must want to come to an agreement. The desire must precede the act, and the desire must include a readiness to compromise. Once there is a readiness to compromise, clever people can draw up the documents registering the agreement. This is no different from any agreement — national or international, private or governmental — anywhere, any time. (4) While there is so far little sign of a desire for an agreement and the Brooke-Mayhew talks seem to have dribbled into the sand, life has moved on outside and within Northern Ireland in ways which ought to make the constitutional parties wish to come to an agreement if only they

could be brought to see the writing on the wall. (5) The Republic has 'gone cold' on the North. The South now has a different agenda: the modernization and Europeanization of the Republic, which is now on the upturn. Obviously there is still a residual and largely romantic wish for the unity of Ireland, but it is on a downturn. The two trendlines crossed at about the time of the election of Mary Robinson as President of the Republic. She symbolizes the new Ireland. (6) Inside the North, the latest census suggests that, while the Protestant community is still the most numerous, the balance is shifting in favour of the Catholic community. (7) A combination of (5) and (6), with (5) acting as a carrot and (6) a stick to the unionists, and with (6) acting as a carrot and (5) as a stick to the nationalists, is there to provide a catalyst to both communities if they wish to take advantage of it. (8) If the opportunity of that catalyst is not taken, the future of Northern Ireland will be that of a forgotten land, bypassed by history. If the opportunity is taken, the talents of this gifted people, well-educated and hard-working, will ensure a prosperous future. (9) The crossroads are approaching. The rewards for coming together will be great; the penalties for not coming together will be equally great. If not now, when?

Other submissions which dealt with political or constitutional issues (among other things) included: Ms Eileen Brown, Mr Garvin Crawford, Pax Christi (London), Very Rev. H. Cassidy, Brother Eoin de Bhaldraithe, Mrs Joyce Agard Evans, Mr John Frost, Mr Michael Gillespie, Sir Alan Goodison, Institute for Social Inventions, Irish Parliament Trust, Mr Seán Martin, Dean Gilbert Mayes, Councillor Randall McDonnell, Dr Samuel McGuffin, Miss Helen McPherson, Miss M. Maguire, Mr John Morrison, Mr Edward Napier, National Peace Council, Northern Ireland Gay Rights Association (NIGRA), Mr John O'Connell, Mr Gearóid Ó Dubhthaigh, Mr Justin O'Hagan, Protestant and Catholic Encounter (PACE), Mr Gerry Rice, and Mr James Stover.

Professor Torkel Opsahl (*L. Doyle*)

Mr Padraig O'Malley (*L. Doyle*)

Lady Faulkner (*The Irish Times*)

Professor Ruth Lister

Professor Marianne Elliott

Mr Eamonn Gallagher (*Lensmen*)

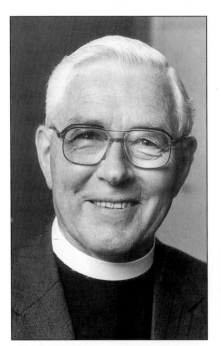

Reverend Dr Eric Gallagher

Mr Andy Pollak (*The Irish Times*)

Sir Kenneth Bloomfield, former head of the Northern Ireland Civil Service, awaits the first hearing at the Old Museum Arts Centre, Belfast, 19 January 1993 (*News Letter*)

General view of a hearing in the Gallery of
the Old Museum Arts Centre, Belfast

Archbishop Robin Eames, Church of Ireland Primate, speaking to
the Opsahl Commissioners, 17 February 1993 (*L. Doyle*)

The Sinn Féin delegation with (left to right) Mitchel McLaughlin, Máiréad
Keane, Bairbre de Brún, Pat McGeown in front of the Opsahl Commission,
20 January 1993 (*Pacemaker*)

(Left to right) Andy Pollak, Maggie Beirne, Siobháin Rainey and Paul Burgess at the Initiative '92 office in Lisburn Road, Belfast (*Pacemaker*)

(Left to right) Eric Gallagher, Lady Faulkner, Torkel Opsahl, Padraig O'Malley and Eamonn Gallagher in the Guildhall, Derry, 25 January 1993 (*Derry Journal*)

Barry Cowan, Chair, and Torkel Opsahl (top) with some participants at
the Belfast Schools Assembly (above), 25 February 1993 (*L. Doyle*)

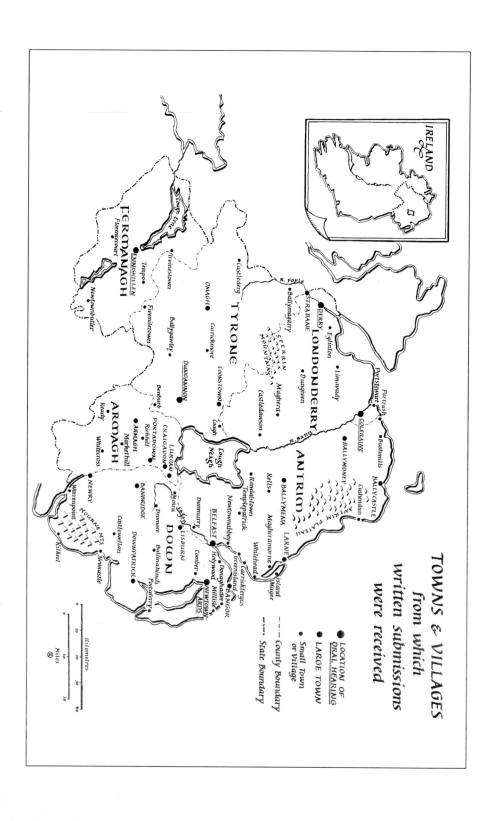

TOWNS & VILLAGES
from which
written submissions
were received

● LOCATION OF
  ORAL HEARING
● LARGE TOWN
• Small Town
  or Village
-·-·- County Boundary
---- State Boundary

IRELAND

FERMANAGH
Florencecourt
ENNISKILLEN
Tempo
Irvinstown
Newtownbutler
Fivemiletown

TYRONE
Castlederg
Ballymagorry
STRABANE
OMAGH
Garrickmore
Ballygawley
DUNGANNON
Benburb
COOKSTOWN
Castledawson
SPERRIN
MOUNTAINS
Maghera
Dungiven

R. FOYLE
DERRY
Eglinton
Limavady
Portstewart
Portrush
COLERAINE
Bushmills
R. BANN
BALLYMONEY
BALLYCASTLE
Ballintoy
Island
Magee
LARNE

LONDONDERRY

ANTRIM
BALLYMENA
Kells
Magherafelt
Randalstown
Templepatrick
Newtownabbey
Whitehead
Carrickfergus
Greenisland
Holywood
BANGOR
Donaghadee
Millisle
NEWTOWNARDS
Comber

ARDAGH
Keady
Whitecross
Markethill
ARMAGH
Richhill
PORTADOWN
CRAIGAVON
LURGAN
Lough Neagh

Dunmurry
BELFAST
LISBURN
Moira
Dromore
BANBRIDGE
DROMORE

NEWRY
Warrenpoint
MOURNE MTS
Kilkeel
Newcastle
Castlewellan
DOWNPATRICK
Ballynahinch
Saintfield

DOWN

ANTRIM PLATEAU

Kilometres
0 10 20 30 40
Miles
0 10 20 30

CHAPTER 12

Submissions' Summary:
Law, Justice and Security II

This chapter begins with summaries of two particularly interesting submissions on the differing attitudes towards law, justice and security which underpin the gulf between people of the two Northern Irish traditions, and on the need for justice issues to be taken up within the region's mainstream organizations and institutions.

PAX CHRISTI IRELAND warn that Protestants and Catholics can have very different approaches to both politics and justice issues. It quotes from a 1986 paper from the Inter-Church Group on Faith and Politics:

Protestant and Catholic theological understandings and traditions have influenced our different cultures and therefore our politics in all sorts of different ways. It is one of the causes of our two communities failing to understand each other and their consequent inability to find agreement. The 'framework' approach of many nationalist politicians and the step by step testing of propositions approach of many unionists is one example of a theological difference brought into politics. We need a much greater understanding of this whole subject, and it is only by honestly talking to each other that we can get it.

Similarly on justice:

In the different religious/national traditions there have developed radically different versions of justice. In a significant part of the Ulster Protestant tradition justice tends to emphasize honest dealing, getting one's just deserts, acting rightly, fair procedures and the punishment of the guilty. Communal justice is not so central. In the Irish Catholic tradition there has developed a victim theology whereby the community sees itself as the victim and identifies with the victims. Justice for the innocent victim and making sure the oppressor gets his deserts are quite central. Peace comes after justice and justice is the right framework. Reconciliation in this perspective is seen merely as giving the other a place in our framework, not trying to create something new.

This radical difference in perspective between the two communities is one of the reasons why they have extreme difficulties in understanding each other in law and order and administration of justice issues. It is, therefore, important that we talk together about our perceptions of injustice in the situation and see if we can reach some understanding, if not agreement.

MS MAGGIE BEIRNE from London, but presently based in Belfast, writes on why she believes that questions of justice and law and order are central in Northern Ireland. However, she begins by noting how she has been struck in Northern Ireland by 'the apparent dichotomy between the many dynamic and innovative grass-roots groups which seems to exist alongside the rather backward stance of many mainstream organizations.' This is exemplified — in the religious sphere — by her impression when she arrived in Belfast that there was nothing as 'progressive, advanced and thought-provoking' as ecumenical groups like Corrymeela and Cornerstone, yet mainstream church services were 'particularly dull and traditional' when compared with their counterparts in England.

A similar truth seemed to emerge whether I looked at women's groups, the trade union movement, the business sector or education generally: on the one hand one could find extremely creative individuals and small groups, and on the other a rather entrenched and conservative 'establishment'.

If this split is a reality, it means that 'the energies of potentially the brightest and the best are being channelled into matters which, however important, are 'subsidiary' in that informal groups rarely have access to the levers of change.' She agrees too with the observation that many activists in the voluntary sector are people of the highest calibre who elsewhere would potentially be involved in mainstream politics — here, on the other hand, they are at risk of being 'siphoned off', or siphoning themselves off, instead of acting as ginger-groups within the established churches, political parties, trade unions and in the public service.

Returning to the question of law and justice, she points out that extremely good work is being done by groups like the Committee for the Administration of Justice (CAJ), but somehow it has not come onto the agenda of mainstream institutions like the above. She believes ways must be found of mobilizing different groups in Northern Ireland around the labels 'security' or 'justice'.

Whatever the constitutional or political arrangements in the future, everyone needs to feel a commitment to law and order *to ensure* justice for all. Unfortunately, at the present time many in the unionist community emphasize law and order first and foremost, and many in the nationalist community emphasize justice — sometimes it seems as though the two principles are contradictory rather than closely related and indeed interdependent. 'Law and order' must rest upon legitimacy, which implies impartiality — it arises from principles of justice; is only feasible when it genuinely promotes the interests of justice, and serious injustices lead inevitably to the breakdown of law and order, since respect for the latter must be earned, not coerced, in democratic states. Similarly 'justice' cannot come into being, or exist, in a vacuum — its principles must be translated into legislative principles of law and order, and then must be abided by, policed and promoted in society.

Ms Beirne believes that the Churches, the political parties and the trade unions should all be seeking to promote dialogue around these questions among their respective followings.

Without such a lead, it is hardly surprising if 'security/justice' remain easy catchwords for 'gesture' politics, or the marginalized concern of a few committed activists.... It is not sufficient that an unresponsive and largely unaccountable security and political apparatus on the one side, and small activist groups like the CAJ on the other, have the field to themselves.

She asks Initiative '92 and the Opsahl Commission to challenge the key organizations and institutions in Northern Irish society to each create an internal working group to look at how their particular organization could 'contribute to an improvement of law and order *with a view to* ensuring justice'. She also urges the Commission to make specific proposals as to HOW its recommendations should be followed up and *who by*: 'only in this way will the important process begun by Initiative '92 have a long-term impact on the key institutions which must become involved in the process of change'.

Changing the Law

THE COMMITTEE ON THE ADMINISTRATION OF JUSTICE (CAJ) argues that protection of human rights must be an essential element of whatever political progress takes place in Northern Ireland. It states: 'Significant violations of human rights in Northern Ireland have not produced peace. Far from it.' Rather than placing human rights concerns in opposition to better law enforcement, human rights should be seen as an aspect of it.

Without effective enforcement of the law against those who break it, society can descend into vigilantism where the rights of none are safe. Without respect for human rights, law enforcement becomes an engine of oppression and itself, the cause of further conflict and deprivation of rights.

Principles such as the need for impartiality, openness, accountability and the use of minimum force, underlie basic international human rights commitments. A Bill of Rights for Northern Ireland would give concrete effect to those principles, according to the CAJ. The European Convention on Human Rights is a ready model.

A Bill of Rights would provide a way of measuring the state's commitment to the protection of human rights and a way of making the state accountable when they were breached. It would provide a public forum for debate on what respecting human rights means in Northern Ireland and a way of checking legislation which is currently rushed through with little parliamentary debate. It would offer a great opportunity to educate all in Northern Ireland on what human rights we have and should protect.

A Bill of Rights should have an equality clause which would tackle an existing major equality deficit in legislation affecting Northern Ireland, where there is prohibition of religious and sex discrimination but no equality law related to race, disability or sexual orientation. The CAJ also endorses a recommendation by the Standing Advisory Commission on Human Rights (see below) for legislation to prevent discrimination in the provision of goods and services on grounds of religion or political belief. An equality clause in a Bill of Rights would provide a means of challenging allocations of public resources believed to have resulted from discrimination or prejudice.

Recommending a code of prisoners' rights, the CAJ says that domestic law does not recognize prisoners as having enforceable legal rights. Without such a code, it is not surprising that disputes escalate and that also, in its absence, abuses and mistreatment can occur much more easily, through neglect as well as malice. The proposed redrafting of prison rules should give prisoners minimum rights to adequate conditions, visits, correspondence, medical care, education, and protection against arbitrary searches. There should be an adequate complaints mechanism, with a strong independent element and 'issues of safe conditions in the jail for both staff and prisoners should take priority over abstract notions of segregation or integration'. The Committee says it also remains concerned about the practice of strip searching.

To lessen the impact of imprisonment on prisoners' families, it has urged changes in relation to release procedures for life sentence and SOSP (held at 'Secretary of State's pleasure') prisoners, as well as to the transfer of prisoners from British to Northern Ireland jails so that they can serve the sentences closer to their families. It welcomes some lessening of restrictions which have taken place, but continues to argue for a more independent element in release decisions.

Lack of accountability for security force use of excessive and lethal force is a serious problem for the legal system and public confidence in it, the CAJ says. It makes a number of criticisms of inquest procedures, including long delays, and contends that 'the inadequacy of the inquest process is simply one example of a marked lack of accountability in the investigative process as a whole'.

The Committee advocates a total ban on the use of plastic bullets. It also urges that the law governing the use of force be brought into line with internationally recognized norms. It states that, unlike the Republic, the jurisdiction in Northern Ireland does not recognize a charge of manslaughter where the force used was permissible but excessive in the circumstances. 'The failure to secure convictions adds to the sense of a lack of accountability for the use of force by members of the security forces.' It says the European Convention standard of 'no more than absolutely necessary' should replace the existing standard of 'reasonable in the circumstances'.

The CAJ believes that there is an urgent need for a public enquiry into evidence of collusion between elements of the security forces and loyalist paramilitaries, citing in particular the case of the double-agent Brian Nelson. It urges that such an enquiry should also recommend 'appropriate' disciplinary action.

It calls for the early repeal of the Emergency Provisions Act 1991 and the Prevention of Terrorism Act 1989, believing that the ordinary law of the land is adequate. It contends that the necessity for many of the powers in the two acts has never been demonstrated and that in several respects 'this body of law fails to meet international standards'.

Although the legislation had been subjected to reviews and official reports, the terms of reference had been designed to narrow the terms of debate, according to the Committee.

By being barred from considering whether emergency legislation *per se* was actually necessary, these reviews have simply contributed to the cosy official consensus, which has ensured that Northern Ireland has never been free of emergency laws. The primary assumption has always been that emergency laws are necessary. Rights are therefore seen as contingent, as something the necessity for which must be proven.

Most people arrested under the Prevention of Terrorism Act are released without charge, the CAJ says, and claims of ill treatment are common, followed by the issuing of many civil proceedings against the authorities. Despite out of court settlements and, in several instances, the inadmissibility of confessions because of police impropriety, it says that not one allegation of assault during interrogation at Castlereagh RUC holding centre has been upheld by the Independent Commission for Police Complaints. (See also Policing.)

THE STANDING ADVISORY COMMISSION ON HUMAN RIGHTS (SACHR) says that, although significant progress has been made, deep divisions remain within the region which need to be resolved. Despite a range of government initiatives over the past 20 years, employment differentials persist between Protestants and Catholics.

Continuing steps should be taken to ensure economic and social advancement in the region. Improving the quality of life will help to redress grievances which may have helped nurture terrorism.

The Commission, reiterating a view expressed in its report on Religious and Political Discrimination and Equality of Opportunity in Northern Ireland, asserts that 'a constitutional framework which provides protection against discriminatory laws and practices is essential if there is to be full recognition in Northern Ireland of basic human rights and fundamental freedoms'.

The recognition throughout Europe of the individual's right to full expression of his/her identity and way of life should encourage the people of Northern Ireland to respect their differences and focus instead upon their many similarities. 'There are in fact a greater number of similarities between Catholics and Protestants than differences, as the Social Attitudes Surveys have shown.'

SACHR cautions that understandable preoccupation with relationships between the 'two main sections of the community' must not blind government to the need to protect the human rights of all sections, including the travelling people and the growing Chinese and Muslim communities in Northern Ireland. It welcomes the concern which, it says, is currently being shown in that regard.

The Commission recommends enactment of an enforceable Bill of Rights for Northern Ireland based on the European Convention on Human Rights. It first expressed that view in 1977. Incorporation of the European Convention would constitute a minimum standard, and the Commission recognizes that there are strong arguments for such a Bill to have considerably wider scope.

A Bill of Rights is necessary in a genuinely democratic society to ensure that governments respect the rights and freedoms of minorities, and to provide an effective legal safeguard against the misuse of power by public authorities.

It envisages enforcement to be within the jurisdiction of the ordinary courts in the region. The question of whether a special court would be required would be a matter for debate between the political parties. SACHR offers its own services.

The Commission ought to have an enlarged role, or a new Commission ought to be created with powers to enforce, promote or intervene in human rights issues. This role ought to be comparable to the role played by the Fair Employment Commission and the Equal Opportunities Commission. The Commission should concern itself also in the education of the public in matters of human rights.

THE COMMITTEE FOR A NEW IRELAND (CNI), in Boston, Massachusetts, says the demand for a Bill of Rights is one of the few matters where there is agreement between the polarized communities in Northern Ireland, and it urges the British government to take steps to introduce one. The Committee's chairman, Mr Michael F. Donlan, who prepared the submission, declares that 'the process of conflict resolution will experience a sea-change if the British authorities should proceed at once to create a constitutional conclave for the political leaders of the two separate traditions in the North to jointly fashion' such a Bill. Its adoption and the process leading to it would constitute some movement out of the dangerous stalemate in the region, he feels.

In part, a Bill of Rights would fill a serious void in the political and social condition of the peoples of Northern Ireland, Mr Donlan maintains, namely 'their lack of empowerment, particularly in the face of an absentee government which is overempowered'.

The absence of accountable government in the North for the past 70 years has been 'one of the great failures of Western democracy', according to Mr Donlan. This led to systematic and institutional discrimination, and decade after decade Britain 'pulled the knot tighter and tighter on themselves' by resorting to emergency legislation in response to republican paramilitaries. Yet in recent years the authorities have begun to realize that they must rectify conditions in the North, hence the 'truly progressive Fair Employment Act'.

There is a much better prospect of a pluralistic society if the constitutional framework for the region is designed to protect the respective diversity of the constituent groups, Mr Donlan states. 'A Bill of Rights helps to fit that bill,' he says. One of its principal benefits is the protection of the interests of minorities from central government excesses.

Mr Donlan argues that the lack of rights in Northern Ireland contributes substantially to the serious alienation between the communities and between them and the government. He states: 'If the people in Northern Ireland could petition to a court, whenever their rights were being compromised by the government, then the government would have to respond in court and show the court that the government was acting within the rule of law and following due process of law. If the government, at the very least, was under an obligation to explain its derogating activities, and in general was seen to be a government which was accountable to courts of law if not to the people, then the government would start to be seen as an institution which was subject to the rule of law.'

More critically, the process of fashioning a Bill of Rights will create a grass-root process whereby the leaders of the two divided communities can come together in an institutional dynamic, for the first time in living memory, and act in common cause. The fashioning of a Bill of Rights for Northern Ireland by these long-divided communities of Northern Ireland is an ideal vehicle by which these communities can find such common cause and broaden the base thereof over time.

A Bill of Rights assures that individuals and groups of individuals are entitled to respect from their government and provides a remedy and recourse in court when the government violates their basic rights. A Bill of Rights is the best means to guarantee that diverse views will be respected and accorded rights of expression. As each community makes common cause with the other to promote a society where diversity is respected, each community will of necessity be in a position to observe and appreciate that their long-opposite rival community is working shoulder to shoulder with them to find means to better the existence of all communities.

DR BRICE DICKSON, professor of law at the University of Ulster, begins with the law on discrimination. He says that, despite progress on several fronts, particularly regarding the enforcement procedures created by legislation like the Fair Employment Acts (1976-1989), 'it is clear that discriminatory attitudes still prevail amidst both the 'establishment' and amongst ordinary people in Northern Ireland'. However, in a separate paper he argues that the 1989 Fair Employment Act is 'one of the few pieces of legislation with the potential to heal wounds in Northern Ireland. If it were extended to protect not just people's employment rights but also their rights when they are receiving goods and services, it would be better still. Of course legislation will never by itself stop people from unfairly discriminating; but it can assist in creating the right climate of openness and tolerance.'

In that paper Dr Dickson is strongly critical of elements in Northern Ireland's legal system for their lack of accountability. He points out that in numerous court cases, including inquests into deaths caused by members of the security forces, the government representatives have issued what are called 'Public Interest Immunity Certificates' in order to 'keep from the court the details of army and police movements or other supposedly sensitive information'. Such unnecessary secrecy serves only to further disillusion the people affected.

Dr Dickson also criticizes the office of the Director of Public Prosecutions for being 'shrouded in mystery' and issuing no reports of any kind, annual or periodic. Another example of an equally alarming lack of accountability is that the powers of the Police Authority for Northern Ireland 'relate only to the inadequacy and efficiency of the force, not to the policing powers it decides to adopt'. The RUC Chief Constable has also refused to allow the scheme by which 'lay' visitors are allowed to inspect cells in police stations to be extended to the three holding centres where terrorist suspects are detained, 'despite the fact that it is from those centres that the vast majority of allegations of serious misconduct by police officers emanates.' He points out that from the creation of the so-called Independent Commission for Police Complaints in 1988 until the end of 1991, there had been no fewer than 1019 allegations of assault laid against police officers by people arrested under the anti-terrorism laws. 'The stark truth is that not one of those allegations has been substantiated after a police investigation. Now even allowing for the inevitable proportion of completely bogus cases, this nil rate of substantiation frankly beggars belief.' He suggests that the best way to increase public confidence in the complaints system would be to appoint independent investigators, at least of serious complaints. The Ombudsman's office could assume this function, as is done in New Zealand and some Australian states. The Chief Constable has said that he would not object to independent investigators if there was a groundswell of public opinion in favour of them. Emphasizing his strong support for the RUC in its terribly difficult and dangerous role, Dr Dickson believes such reforms would be in the force's own interests, in that they would make it more 'acceptable *throughout* our community and in turn make the legal system as a whole more worthy of support'. (See also Reducing the Violence, and Politics and the Constitution: Joint Authority/Sovereignty.)

MR IAN PAISLEY JNR, a researcher for the Democratic Unionist Party, says that the case of the 'UDR Four' is of enormous importance to the criminal justice system in Northern Ireland. The four, he says, 'were members of the 'system' which imposed a miscarriage upon them'. The decision of the Court of Appeal to release three of the men but refuse the appeal of the fourth man 'demonstrates the need for reform and, as such, I propose an agenda for justice'.

All the constitutional parties in Northern Ireland support the introduction of a Bill of Rights, he stresses. He also calls for the inclusion of

Northern Ireland within the remit of the current Royal Commission inquiry into the criminal justice system in the United Kingdom. He supports the Diplock court system 'in view of Northern Ireland's special circumstances — although ideally I would like to see a return to full jury trials.' His main concern is how 'prejudicial' evidence is brought before a Diplock court.

In the current 'trial within a trial' situation, where the judge hears evidence which he/she must rule is prejudicial or not, the evidence is usually uncorroborated statements by the accused. This results in 'a police versus accused' situation being presented to the judge who is trying to determine the truth. In that system, he contends, the evidence of the police can present inherent dangers, since a police officer's credibility is at stake. 'I therefore support and call for the introduction of a safety clause for the presentation of such contested evidence.'

Supporting audio and visual recording of police interviews, Mr Paisley believes that it would protect the rights of both the suspect and the interviewing officer and provide the judge with incontrovertible independent evidence. Calling for the presence of solicitors, on request, during police interviews, Mr Paisley comments: 'Terrorist suspects are so well versed in resisting interrogations, those who suffer from not having access to a solicitor are usually innocent, or at least not 'hardened criminals'. It is the hard men at the coal face of terrorism who should be behind bars.' He urges a system of public access to police holding centres, favouring independent lay visitors 'drawn from sensible sections of the community'.

For the public to feel assured that justice is being seen to be done, the mechanisms of justice must be independent and accessible. 'Forensic laboratories in Northern Ireland should set the pace by becoming independent,' Mr Paisley states.

He also proposes an independent appeals tribunal to deal with the cases of prisoners who claim they have been convicted unfairly. Their cases would be investigated by an appeal commissioner, whose report/recommendations would be considered by the Home Secretary in deciding whether to refer the cases to a second appeal. Once a case was referred, the tribunal would bow out, permitting a normal appeal to proceed. Concerns voiced about the supposed independence of the current police complaints procedure ought to be investigated, says Mr Paisley, while remarking that he has used the procedure himself in the past 'and found it creditable and helpful'.

THE COMMUNITY OF THE PEACE PEOPLE says that the acceptance of violence in its direct and structural forms, is the overriding cause of the problems affecting the people of Northern Ireland. Advocating the repeal of emergency legislation, the Community says that its effect has been to exacerbate mistrust in the security forces, and to create bitterness, frustration and violence.

It calls for a Bill of Rights; restoration of the right to silence; an end to current broadcasting restrictions; abolition of Diplock courts and replacement by a jury system (a three-judge system as an interim measure would be an improvement on the present system); removal of internment from the statute books; and the ending of seven- and three-day detention provisions and exclusion orders.

It also proposes video and audio taping of interviews at police holding centres; immediate access to solicitors for a detained person; legal representation for prisoners before the Life Sentence Review Board and that Board to give reasons in respect of unsuccessful applications for release; abolition of the category 'Secretary of State's Pleasure'; confession evidence admitted in 'terrorist' trials only when corroborated by other non-confessional evidence; a thorough overhaul of the inquest procedure; and abolition of strip searching. (See also Reducing the Violence.)

YOUTH FOR PEACE says that emergency legislation is counterproductive. Rather than dealing with "the terrorist threat', 'it undermines public confidence in the apparatus of the state, thereby creating the dissent in which violence can take root ... we advocate the abolition of emergency legislation in favour of a system of justice in which the entire community can have confidence and where the state forces are publicly answerable for their actions. In short, a system where justice is not only done, but is seen to be done.'

As a group of young people, Youth for Peace is very concerned about the effect on their generation of emergency legislation and the 'extensive powers' of the security forces. It states: 'The detention and sentencing of juveniles is a particular concern of ours. Under no circumstances should juveniles be detained or sentenced to an adult prison...'. It calls for arrested juveniles to be dealt with by specially trained staff, given full access to representation and dealt with in a humane and understanding fashion.

It argues for the creation of an independent commission fully to investigate allegations of security force ill-treatment and for publication of its findings. Prisoners should be granted transfers from jail in England 'and in the meantime there should be better allowances given to families who have to travel to England'.

It suggests that independent judiciary members should replace lay civil servants on the Life Sentence Review Board. The situation in Crumlin Road Prison is 'unacceptable' and the only practical way to reduce tension and violence is to allow segregation. Steps should be taken to reduce the period that prisoners in the jail spend on remand. (See also Policing; and Politics and the Constitution: Autonomy.)

DR STEVEN GREER and MR ANTHONY WHITE, respectively a law lecturer and a barrister, point out that research by another legal academic, Dermot Walsh, had shown that some 40 per cent of the cases in Diplock courts concern alleged offenders with no paramilitary connections. The Government has expressly stated that care must be taken in order to prevent, as far as possible, 'ordinary criminals' being denied the right to jury trial. 'However, it is difficult to maintain with any credibility that those for whom the Diplock courts were designed get a fair hearing, yet non-political offenders who end up there due to the quirks of the scheduling system do not.' They argue strongly for the restoration of jury trials in scheduled, terrorist-type cases. They maintain that the commission which recommended the establishment of the Diplock courts produced no concrete evidence of the twin problems of perverse acquittals and intimidation of juries in such cases in Northern Ireland, with evidence for the latter having never progressed beyond 'sketchy hearsay'. While not denying that such intimidation by paramilitary organizations did exist in the early 1970s, they say that their research shows that 'it has never been proved that this was and is likely to remain such a serious problem that the suspension of jury trial, rather than some other less radical alternative, was and is required'. They then propose a number of safeguards which would allow a return to jury trials in all Northern Irish cases and thus a significant step towards a more democratic legal system there.

Reducing the Violence

THE PEACE AND RECONCILIATION GROUP (PRG), based in Derry, proposes that both the IRA and the security forces initially should make small but important reciprocal de-escalatory military moves aimed at building up trust and achieving an eventual end to violence. Reducing violence is a crucial step towards a solution, it says. 'It offers an opportunity for political leaders to grasp. If they do not, no doubt violence will increase again.'

The group stresses that it does not underestimate the potential for loyalist violence, but points out that loyalist paramilitaries claim that their violence is reactive to the IRA. A de-escalation process is the only way to give loyalists a chance to prove whether their claim is genuine. 'Despite the very serious nature of loyalist violence, we do believe that the effort to remove violence from the political process here has to begin with the 'two sides' of government and the IRA.'

In discussions with the Group, both security forces and paramilitaries had told them that there are peace-building moves they would like to make, but they do not trust the other side. The Group comments:

The British authorities cannot begin to talk to the IRA unless it gives up violence; the IRA cannot give up its campaign unless it knows there will be clear, immediate and specific political benefits for its cause in return; the loyalist organizations say they can make no deals with the IRA, but they could respond in kind to an IRA ceasefire. In every case the demands are too large to be met at once. Each side has told us it would like to make progress towards a more normal society, but no one will make the first move because no one trusts the others.

The Group suggests that the IRA and security forces take specific unilateral steps, clearly signalled to each other so that there is the implicit message — 'we expect a response'. The steps would be such as could be halted and even reversed if the other side 'takes advantage' of them. 'If the other side welcomes them and responds in an appropriate way, gradually they will both discover that some trust is possible. So long as the process is not sabotaged, it will eventually grow to the point where the IRA can risk a ceasefire, and the British can risk talking to them.'

Each side needs help from the other, the Group asserts.

The IRA needs some help in the form of political recognition from the government to reduce its own violence; the security establishment needs help from the IRA if it is to take its pressure off the Catholic side of the community.

The IRA could decide on a small step, such as the elimination of 'coffee jar bombs', or a large one, such as the ending of commercial bombings. Stressing the importance of signalling, privately or publicly, the move, the group explains:

There have been periods of inactivity which the IRA hoped the British Government would read as signals of intent; but we have discovered that the message was not understood. The Government and security forces thought they might be signs of weakness and exhaustion or preparation periods before a new offensive. There must be a clear message.

The Group adds: 'Army officers have told us that a long list has been prepared of possible 'de-escalatory measures'. It is encouraging that the security establishment has worked out some changes which it would be willing to make step by step to answer IRA moves.' Some, such as the introduction of identification cards which army patrols must give to people whom they stop, are already being tried out.

It suggests that steps the security forces might take could include reduced patrolling, the removal of some security barricades and extending lay visiting to police cells to include terrorist suspects. But it would be more effective to signal a major move to the IRA, such as resolving contentious issues in Crumlin Road Prison; an end to repeated searches of the same houses, which it says is interpreted as harassment, or the end of attempts to recruit teenagers as informers.

As the two sides build up trust, a role might develop for international observers, with 'demilitarized zones' being declared, for example, in Belfast city centre or the walled city of Derry and then gradually extending to housing estates, small towns, villages and rural areas.

DR RONNY SWAIN, a psychology lecturer at University College Cork, explains some of the conceptual thinking behind such step-by-step moves. He recalls the GRIT strategy (Graduated and Reciprocated Initiatives in Tension Reduction), devised in 1962 as a means of reducing tension between the United States and the Soviet Union. This was employed by President Kennedy 16 times and on each occasion President Khrushchev reciprocated within 24 hours, Dr Swain explains.

It allows one part in a conflict to take initiatives, rather than reacting to the acts of others and it can be introduced without the prior agreement of the other parties, thus enabling the strategy to operate in the absence of formal talks. Dr Swain points out that because GRIT was originally devised for use in a two-party situation and, since there are many separate parties to the Northern Ireland conflict, it might be more difficult to apply in those circumstances.

He explains its essence:

Suppose that you and I are negotiating about some issue fundamental to our interests. Instead of demanding that you change your position as a precondition to progress, I announce my intention to make a small concession; I then do so in such a way that the action is publicly verifiable. Taking the action involves a small risk for me, but does not entail a major erosion of my position.

I then invite you to reciprocate, but do not demand that you do so. If you engage in behaviour which escalates tension, I retaliate but only sufficiently to restore the status quo before continuing with my conciliatory strategy. As I persevere with my initiatives, it becomes more and more likely that you will make similar concessions. With each exchange of concessions, trust grows and tension is reduced.

MR MICHAEL FARRELL says that the panoply of repressive laws, structures and practices developed in Northern Ireland over the past 25 years 'has become a major factor in perpetuating republican violence, so that those involved in violence today are at least as likely to be motivated by some aspect of the post-1972 repressive apparatus as by the original factors which provoked the growth of the Provisional IRA'.

He does not believe that a cessation of violence should be a precondition to any discussions with paramilitary groups or their political supporters.

Indeed, I think a cessation of violence is most likely to come about through some kind of dialogue with those involved or their political allies. However, an end to the campaigns of violence or even a lessening in their intensity would certainly help the process of discussion about the ultimate future of the area. Perhaps the most practical scenario would be a graduated but steady de-escalation of the violence, and the security measures which mirror and/or provoke it, resulting in a building up of confidence on all sides.

Mr Farrell asks how that could be achieved.

Sinn Féin statements and assessments by informed commentators suggest that there are elements in the republican movement who would like to see an end to violence and to be able to pursue their objectives by regular political means. These elements, however, represent people who are deeply embittered and cynical about the efficacy of political action. Many of these people feel that political action will get them nowhere and that violence is the only thing that produces a response from the powers that be. They point to Irish history and the history of anti-colonial struggles generally as teaching this lesson and reinforce this by citing the treatment of the non-violent civil rights movement in the 1960s and early 1970s, and the way in which loyalist paramilitary groups were allowed to destroy the power-sharing Executive in 1974.

This scepticism about political action has been sharply reinforced in more recent times by the British government's broadcasting ban, which has led to widespread cynicism about calls for republicans to involve themselves in politics. Sinn Féin supporters argue that they were harangued and lectured for years about how they should put themselves before the electorate. When they did so and received a certain mandate, they feel that the goal posts were promptly moved to prevent them getting access to the broadcasting media. They also feel that their treatment on many district councils indicates that there is no will to allow them to participate fully in the political process.

The political vetting of community groups has reinforced this cynicism. Once again republicans were urged to involve themselves with the problems of their local communities. They feel that when they did so, or even when people in their communities who had no links with the republican movement did so, the authorities quickly stepped in to deprive them of funds and undermine them. It seems to many in the republican community that democracy is alright so long as it produces the results the authorities want.

A speedy end to the broadcasting ban and the vetting of community groups, together with equal treatment for Sinn Féin councillors on district councils and in dealings with government departments, would be an earnest of the authorities' good faith in urging republicans to 'go political'. Ending the broadcasting ban and political vetting would not necessarily lead to a cessation of violence, however. There is too much bitterness and anger over other repressive measures — aggressive patrolling and harassment; a police force distrusted by most of the nationalist population, and a highly partisan part-time militia; seven-day detention accompanied by frequent allegations of brutality towards detainees; curtailment of the right to silence; trial by non-jury courts; forced integration of prisoners; refusal to repatriate prisoners from British jails; use of plastic bullets; allegations of a 'shoot to kill' policy, and allegations of collusion between the security forces and loyalist paramilitary groups.'

Mr Farrell points out that this 'panoply of repressive laws, structures and practices' has been repeatedly condemned by a wide range of international human rights agencies, and has contributed substantially to the UK's recently topping the list of states that have been found to have breached the European Convention on Human Rights.

A policy of dismantling these emergency powers and repressive practices so as to conform to international human rights standards, monitored by outside human rights experts, would do a lot to convince the republican community that there was a real desire by the authorities to de-escalate and demilitarize the situation.

Many of the reforms required to secure a return to the rule of law — for example, early release of those who have served long sentences, return to jury trials, and an end to the use of plastic bullets — would be welcomed by loyalists as well as nationalists, Mr Farrell says. A level of consensus has developed among cross-community groups, including trade unionists, on the need to do away with emergency measures, Mr Farrell says. If a return to the rule of law and the development of mechanisms to remedy injustices resulted in an end to republican violence, that in itself would do a lot to reduce tension in the unionist community.

These measures, or some combination of them, might achieve a cessation or suspension of republican and loyalist violence, though I would argue that exceptional measures should be ended anyway, even if there was no immediate prospect of an end to violence, and that we should strive even, or perhaps especially, in times of conflict to conform to the standards of human rights protection to which both the UK and the Republic have committed themselves.

Mr Farrell says that, even if violence ceases for a time, the nationalist population would still be significantly disadvantaged within an already deprived community. 'Unless effective and public measures were taken to redress that disadvantage, nationalist frustration would only build up again.' (See also Politics and the Constitution: Joint Authority Sovereignty.)

MR MICHAEL McKEOWN warns that in many Northern Ireland communities the culture of violence has been endemic for so long that it has become the norm: the availability of arms, the existence of paramilitary castes, the targeting and killing of people have ceased to be an element in a political strategy and have become an end in itself. This, plus the undoubted political successes of the IRA over the past two decades, means that there are many within the Provisional republican movement

who cannot tolerate the idea of abandoning the armed struggle and who are convinced that ultimately Britain will submit to their demands rather than continuing to sustain the drain upon British resources and the affront to British prestige. Since for these activists violence has become a totally acceptable way of life, it is unlikely that they will be responsive to the argument that their campaign can extract no further concession from the UK government. That government has already indicated that it has no continued interest in retaining Northern Ireland as part of the United Kingdom. It cannot and will not go any further because to do so would be to betray not only the unionist community but constitutional nationalism and the government of the Republic.

Mr McKeown believes it likely that 'there are within the republican movement those who accept this reality but are unable to make their views prevail within the councils of the movement'. He suggests that the British government could support this element by some initiatives to enhance their moderating influence. 'A statement by the British government offering a troop withdrawal from the streets, an amnesty for prisoners and a place proportionate to its electoral strength for Sinn Féin at the negotiating table might be the mechanism the republican 'moderates' need to persuade their associates that there are no further political gains to be secured from a physical force campaign.' He concedes that

the British authorities would be very unwilling to take such a step unless they had previously had some assurance that the measure would have its desired effects. To achieve this, secret negotiations would be necessary and possibly at arm's length through an intermediary. The good offices of the new US administration could be availed of for this purpose.... All this indicates a high risk strategy, but it seems to this observer that it is the only one that offers any prospect of securing the essential period of calm to allow all the protagonists to address the longer term task of finding a solution which will hold.

(See also Politics and the Constitution: Other Political Submissions.)

DR BRICE DICKSON, professor of law at the University of Ulster, believes that 'only one initiative is likely to lead to a significant reduction in the level of anti-security force and sectarian violence in Northern Ireland. This is the holding of talks between representatives of the British Government — probably civil servants in the first instance — and representatives of both Sinn Féin and the UDA. Unpalatable as it may be, such talking simply has to occur. It should not, of course, be construed as in any way a concession to political violence — violence cannot be seen to pay, even if in practice (both nationally and internationally) it often does. But talking, by itself, can do little harm.' He would also like to see members of the IRA and UVF participating, perhaps by means of a temporary government amnesty for such people. He would like to see the talks held as much as possible in public, and even be televised; he recalls how much the talks in Poland following the rise of Solidarity gained by being open to public scrutiny in this way.

Dr Dickson believes that new draconian security laws, as with internment and the alleged 'shoot to kill' incidents, would only encourage more young people to join paramilitary groups. 'More would be gained from permitting some emergency laws to lapse as a *quid pro quo* for 'concessions' on the part of the men of violence. Sir Patrick Mayhew admitted as much in his speech at Coleraine in December 1992.' (See also Changing the Law; and Politics and the Constitution: Joint Authority/Sovereignty.)

DR PAULINE CONROY of Dublin, a social policy analyst and EC advisor, examines some issues which may arise in a process of demilitarization during a period of non-war, where peace does not yet exist in Northern Ireland. She lists steps that she feels might have to be taken as a contribution to future discussions between parties which are currently shooting each other. The experience of other conflicts elsewhere may provide guidelines for discussions on the form of an essential demilitarization process which will accompany the cessation of hostilities by the principal protagonists and precede a period of peace, she believes.

Demilitarization might be conceived of as an agreed process, undertaken with respect for the honour and humanity of all parties for the preliminary and orderly and humane demobilization of protagonists in war. The process may be more complicated and full of risk for all sides than the popular view of declaring peace or negotiating a public political solution, on which the mass media has been focused for so many years in relation to Northern Ireland.

Among the steps which may have to be considered are 'the eventual establishment of demilitarization committees which discuss with each other, involving the British army, republican and loyalist organizations. Alternatively, peace monitoring can be undertaken by outside forces such as United Nations Peacekeeping Missions or bodies such as the International League of Jurists. Matters for discussion could include the release of prisoners, the prevention of re-arrest and detention of former prisoners, the identification of arms stockpiles, the re-registration of all legally held arms, the removal of observation posts and other matters in this category.'

Dr Conroy points out that, although unpopular in many quarters, the concept of an amnesty for prisoners has been a central ingredient of the peace process in conflicts elsewhere. It could complement a variety of preceding approaches within the penal system, such as a preliminary amnesty of people convicted as juveniles, accelerated remission already available in Northern Ireland, accelerated parole and day or week release, and prison transfer from and to other jurisdictions.

Demilitarization would also involve providing a small number of people in all communities with a means to leave Northern Ireland, perhaps with the assistance of the United States immigration authorities. The French, when leaving Algeria, recognized such a need when they allowed many people, who feared reprisals, to leave with them, she says.

Members of the British army, RUC and paramilitary groups, 'fatigued' by trauma and crisis, would be able to avail of a specialized form of psychiatric service which is used on occasion of war and conflict. There would have to be discussions with trade union representatives of prison officers and other security forces threatened with immediate job loss, to see their collaboration or neutrality in the demilitarization process. The promotion of confidence in the process and the preparation for an increased supply of job seekers would be helped by the removal of political vetting of community groups, thus facilitating the reintegration of prisoners into their own communities, and the facilitation of economic co-operatives managed by former prisoners.

A SENIOR BRITISH MILITARY OFFICER, in an unattributable oral submission made in a personal capacity, says that no purely political or constitutional way forward will work until the vast majority of the people of Northern Ireland support the system of law and order. He would like to see security co-operation under the Anglo-Irish Agreement developed into a common framework for the whole island, 'so that the same legal and security processes apply in Tipperary as in Tandragee: we are coping with an all-Ireland terrorist problem which requires a mixture of all-Irish procedures to deal with it'. He would like to see the harmonization and equalization of the laws and court systems North and South, and sees the Diplock court system as an abnormal temporary expedient. He says that if the two jurisdictions' security forces — and particularly the Garda Síochána and the RUC — were working under a common system like this, more mutual respect and general public acceptability would result. He believes that if unionists saw such a system significantly reducing IRA violence, they would feel less threatened by it; they would see that the aim of such all-Ireland structures would be 'to put an end to terrorism, to ensure that the terrorists have no hiding place'. He stresses that the police, North and South, would have to be the principal law enforcers, but during the continuing 'temporary insurrection' caused by the IRA, the armies in both jurisdictions would act as 'an aid to the civil power but always under its control'. Both the British and Irish armies should be working under the same rules and instructions in this situation. He believes that the replacement of the Ulster Defence Regiment by the Royal Irish Regiment, with its quota of soldiers from the Republic, is a positive development, and looks forward to the day when soldiers from the Irish Defence Forces and Irish soldiers in the British army are able to train 'in a common European situation'.

A number of submissions suggested that European Community or United Nations forces should replace the British army in Northern Ireland, although no one examined the likelihood or feasibility of such an intervention. MR STEPHEN PLOWDEN from London believes that, because of ancient antagonisms, the British army does not and cannot keep the peace in Northern Ireland.

Would the Europeans be willing to take on this thankless role? If the Community is to be more than a consumers' association, it must involve some willingness to face risk and danger. But the risk is likely to be small. With the British army withdrawn, the IRA would lose its raison d'être and its appeal to the romantic young. The deflation of the IRA would deprive the Protestant paramilitaries of their raison d'être as well. Fighting and revenge killings between the two groups might continue for a long time, but they would increasingly take on the character of gang warfare, unrelated to any political or moral cause.

(See also Politics and the Constitution: Joint Authority/Sovereignty.)

INNATE (Irish Network for Nonviolent Action, Training and Education) outlines its work of mediation and observing in situations of potential conflict. Its members have acted as mediator-observers in potential confrontations during controversial marches in Portadown and Belfast. The group believes there is a twofold purpose in having trained civilians as observers in such situations: (1) it helps all sides to be on their best behaviour because of the presence of such an interested 'neutral' team; (2) to act as mediators if required, attempting to avoid the worsening of any conflict that might develop between those involved. Such observers need to be present in significant numbers so as to be *seen* to be there; they have to be 'mixed' — Catholic, Protestant, women, men, locals, non-locals, young and old; and they have to be specially trained.

QUAKER PEACE AND SERVICE (Northern Ireland Committee) outlines, the work it has done — as a neutral, trustworthy, unthreatening third party — in attempting to build dialogue and keeping channels of communication open between influential people in government, political parties and para-military groups who might otherwise not be able to talk to each other.

'It ought to be self-evident that those who only ever talk to their 'own kind' are not going to have their perceptions challenged by anyone 'other', and if armed conflicts are ever to be resolved, *someone* must establish con-tacts between those dismissed as politically untouchable and those who do the dismissing. This is a role that meditators with accepted good faith can perform.' It cites the work of Quaker mediators in helping to straighten out perceptions distorted by fear and anger as one reason for the remark-ably peaceful end to hostilities and unparalleled magnanimity shown by the victors in the Nigerian civil war.

Quarker Peace and Service points to the long-standing Quaker belief in and experience of the deep structural links between social and economic justice and peace.

Both the state, whichever form it takes, and the community at large, need to accept their full responsibility for avoiding the further marginalization of already isolated groups, and for their being brought back with tact and understanding within the fold of the community. There will be a continuing need for deep listening, healing and conciliatory work on the part of many for-mal and informal groups. And formal structures at all levels both within and outside govern-ment will need to be developed for the promotion of dialogue, allowing Ireland to talk to itself.

Quaker Peace and Service finishes with the words of the American Quaker, Rufus Jones, that Quakers place their trust in, and have been try-ing to create, the "small circles and quiet processes' in which vital transfor-mations can take place'.

PAX CHRISTI IRELAND generally supports the various recommendations on the safeguarding of individuals' rights in Northern Ireland made by Helsinki Watch, Amnesty International, SACHR and CAJ. *Inter alia*, it urges the repeal of current emergency legislation, stringent supervision of interrogations and the introduction of measures to improve the adminis-trations of justice.

It says the British government should be gravely concerned that Hel-sinki Watch, in its 1991 report on Northern Ireland, concluded that:

Human rights abuses are persistent and ongoing, that they affect Protestants and Catholics alike and that they are committed by both security forces and paramilitary groups in violation of international human rights and humanitarian law and standards. It was saddening to find such extensive human rights violations in a democracy such as the United Kingdom and puzzling as to why they had persisted for so long.'

Pax Christi Ireland says that both the RUC and British army operate under current emergency laws and it notes that 'continuous allegations' have been made that the security forces have frequently abused the special powers; that they have been guilty of large-scale abuses of human rights; that the government has tacitly approved or even covered up human rights violations by security forces for political or security reasons and has influenced the administration of justice for security and political reasons. 'It is felt by many that lower standards of justice exist in Northern Ireland than in the rest of the United Kingdom.'

Pax Christi Ireland also states:

However, it must be remembered that, since the present 'troubles' began in 1969, loyalist and republican paramilitary organizations have engaged in a campaign of violence directed against each other, the organs of government, the security forces, members of the legal system, including the judiciary and the civilian population in general. Indeed, their list of 'legitimate targets' seems endless, as do their violations of human rights.

Of the 2900 violent deaths that occurred in Northern Ireland between 1969 and 1989, 2313 were caused by paramilitary groups and 329 by the security forces. Thus, this level of political violence presents extremely serious problems for law enforcement officials'.

The most constructive action which paramilitary organizations could take would be to end their campaigns of violence, it states. 'Pax Christi fully supports the efforts of all those who have engaged in or are still engaged in dialogue with paramilitaries and we earnestly hope that their efforts will be rewarded with success.' (See also Culture, Religion, Identity and Education: Religion; Politics and the Constitution: Devolution.)

MR EUGENE O'SHEA, of Killarney, Co. Kerry, asserts that the sequence of previous initiatives is the wrong way round — the idea of dialogue first, leading to a decision which it is hoped will produce demilitarization in the fullness of time. He advocates demilitarization as the first step in the sequence.

The first requirement of any peace initiative should be the brokerage of a ceasefire, he says. Against a background of violence, talks have little chance of success. Since 'none of the three points of the violent triangle' is likely to be defeated, or surrendered, in the short term, the opposing forces should be involved in a process of 'unilateral, parallel disengagement'.

Mr O'Shea contends that 'such unilateral action (let us say on the IRA's behalf) is considerably more likely to happen in the context of similar parallel movement on the UK government side. Hence the need for brokers.' Non-government agencies should act as brokers since no change seems likely in government policy about not 'talking with terrorists'.

In parallel, unilateral disengagement, 'there would not be a white flag in sight,' he explains. 'Once a formula had been agreed for involving the republican movement in the talks process, both they and the UK government could militarily disengage for ostensibly quite different reasons.'

Mr O'Shea envisages a dialogue stage in two parts: the first, a bilateral, in which the Northern Ireland Secretary of State would seek consensus for the parameters of the next, multilateral stage, would be transformed from those of the past by the existence of a ceasefire and the involvement of Sinn Féin and perhaps the UDA. The first stage could last about three months and, in the event of a threatened walkout or possible breakdown, the Northern Ireland Secretary would hold a referendum on whether he/she had a mandate to move on to the second stage. That stage, which would include a forum-type involvement for the ordinary citizen as well as for political parties and organizations, could last for two years. Its purpose would be to find consensus on a new constitutional status for Northern Ireland. (See also Politics and the Constitution: Other Political Submissions.)

DR JOYCE NEILL of south Belfast emphasizes the need for policing and the maintenance of law and order to be seen as legitimate and fair by everyone. She believes that heavy-handed street patrols and personal and house searches by the British army often lead to the alienation of whole communities and recruitment to paramilitary organizations. She would like to see a carefully monitored pilot scheme, perhaps of limited duration, to find out what would happen in a community if the army's street and search activities ceased. She also emphasizes the need for some sort of panel of 'neutral' monitors of police interrogations in holding centres like Castlereagh.

THE COMMUNITY OF THE PEACE PEOPLE says that, 'when the climate allows', the first step in demilitarizing Northern Ireland should be open dialogue between all the parties to the conflict, including politicians, Churches and paramilitaries. This would be followed by a withdrawal of troops to barracks, a general amnesty, a handing in of all illegally held weapons, further talks on political arrangements and for the creation of a non-violent civil defence system. 'The process should be done in such a way that would entail an equal risk and benefit to all parties. In the meantime there should be attempts to demilitarize Northern Ireland, for instance by declaring Northern Ireland a nuclear-free zone.' (See also Changing the Law.)

SENATOR GORDON WILSON of Enniskillen argues that the Northern Ireland problem is fundamentally a religious one — though 'with little to do with real Christianity' — which needs a political solution based on the Christian virtue of loving one's neighbour.

He sees the cessation of violence as the vital key to a solution, which he projects in two stages. The IRA must by now realize that it is not achieving its goal, he believes. Abandonment of violence would lead to a place for the IRA at peace talks and a reciprocal ending of violence by loyalist terrorists. Without an end to violence, no constitutional settlement will attract the community-wide acceptance needed to make it work. If the people who use the bomb and the bullet do not stop voluntarily, there should be a form of internment on both sides of the border 'which would put all the known 'hard men' behind bars'.

Senator Wilson believes that the removal of the threat of violence would accelerate progress on the second stage, the agreement of a constitution for Northern Ireland, with involvement of the British and Irish governments and the representatives of all parties in the region, leading to a form of government that would include power-sharing. 'The emphasis would be on a shared primary loyalty to a form of government in Northern Ireland, as opposed to a divided one to either London or Dublin, which would be secondary.' He wants a system which allows the two communities to work with, and learn from, each other for the common good.

MS JENNIFER CORNELL, originally from Belfast but now living in New York, outlines a programme of mutual concessions by both communities which were developed with youth club members at Shankill Community House in 1990/91. On the Protestant side, these were: the withdrawal of troops to barracks, the suspension of the UDR (now the Royal Irish Regiment), a reduced level of armed police, and the unconditional involvement of Sinn Féin in subsequent talks. On the Catholic side, they were: the suspension of the Anglo-Irish Agreement, a ceasefire by all paramilitaries, official recognition of the status quo for the present, and all-party involvement in talks. This list of mutual concessions, she suggests, could be presented to people across Northern Ireland via an extensive, door-to-door canvass designed to assess public opinion. She says that she was heartened that young people in the Shankill Road area were receptive to the idea of mutual concessions, not as an ultimate solution, but as a precursor to serious talks.

LITTLE SISTERS OF THE ASSUMPTION in Belfast questions 'the extreme and intimidating use of military technology' in deprived areas, complete with surveillance by cameras, computers and helicopters, and the continual circulation of jeeps and Saracen armoured cars.

The intimidating pointing of guns at ordinary citizens by the army and the frisking of young men, coupled with abusive comments and snide remarks, creates a fertile recruiting ground for paramilitaries. In future, the security forces would need to rid themselves of this unsavoury behaviour and intrusion into individuals' privacy.

(See also The Economy and Society: Social Policy and Community.)

Other submissions on justice, security, legal change and how to reduce violence — among other subjects — came from Amnesty International, Bloody Sunday Justice Campaign, Campaign to Free the Beechmount Five, Centre for Research and Documentation (West Belfast), Committee for the Transfer of Irish Prisoners, Dublin Anti-Extradition Committee, Mr Patrick Dunne, Mr James Eager, Jody Egan, Inter-Church Group on Faith and Politics, Mr Paul Nolan, Lord Jocelyn — a unified all-Ireland or European command for anti-terrorist operations; Rev. G.B. McConnell, Mr James McGeever, Mr Austin McGrogan, United Campaign against Plastic Bullets, and Relatives for Justice — unjust delays and procedures in inquests into disputed killings by the security forces.

A number of other submissions recommended the introduction of a United Nations, European Community or other international peacekeeping force. These included Mr William Connery, Mr Steve Dawe, Mr Patrick Devlin, Mr H.W. Gallagher, Mr Dave Little, Mr M.B. McGovern, Mr J.G. Peile, and Mrs Olive Scott.

Policing

REV. RAYMOND MURRAY, a Catholic priest from Armagh, calls for radical changes in the structure of the RUC, arguing that its present composition, its history and its associations with 'the shoot to kill policy' and other matters, such as 'doubtful court cases', ill-treatment and complaints of harassment of Catholics, have produced a force which does not attract Catholic membership.

Proposing that the Anglo-Irish Intergovernmental Conference should spearhead the change, Father Murray urges consideration of regional divisions or a 'second line police force', in which the paramilitary division would be separate from an unarmed civilian, cross-community, police force which would concentrate on routine, non-military policing.

It is unacceptable, he says, that fewer than 8per cent of the 13,450 complement of the RUC are Catholic, a lower rate than at the start of the conflict in 1968.

There are probably between 200 and 300 RUC officers in Armagh city. I could not name one, and I doubt if a dozen Catholics would know a single member of the force in the Armagh district... The last thing a nationalist in difficulty in Armagh city wants to do is to seek the help of the RUC.... There are no invitations from any of the Catholic schools in the Armagh area to the local RUC to address them, even on such vital matters for children as road safety.... What is wrong?

Father Murray contends that it is wrong to suggest that fear of intimidation is the only reason for Catholics not joining. 'The most important point is that Northern Ireland is made up of two strong cultural traditions, a British one and an Irish one. The RUC caters only for the British tradition. Persons cannot join the RUC and express their Irishness.'

There is the weight of Protestant numbers, often from a very loyalist background, he asserts, and the RUC also has 'elements of the masonic and Orange orders ... and these are anti-Catholic'.

Above all, however, the RUC has traditionally been the defence force of a statelet which practized discrimination against Catholics for 50 years. 'Persons with an Irish identity joining a police force in the North should ideally be able fully to express their religion, their nationalism and their cultural traditions, proudly and without offence or constraint.'

With Catholics comprising half of all young people in the North and a majority in most of its physical area, 'in justice, the sheer weight of the nationalist tradition demands a change in the structures of the RUC'.

REV. BRIAN LENNON S.J. of Portadown, Co. Armagh, stresses the need for an executive role for nationalists in the North, giving them a responsibility for policing matters, and suggests that if the present political division continues, the question of separate community, unarmed police forces for politically divided areas should be investigated.

It is contradictory, he contends, to ask nationalists to take responsibility for an issue such as policing without making the structures available to them to do so. For nationalists, policing is the most important issue to be faced, according to Father Lennon. As with political structures, the key questions are accountability and responsibility. In policing, power effectively rests with the government, although some is devolved to the Chief Constable. 'Unless and until both nationalists and unionists are given an executive role in relation to policy, it is simply not possible for them to take responsibility for it.'

He suggests that if communities cannot act together, there is an argument for separate, unarmed community police forces, together with a 'federal' armed force. Initiative '92 should commission a serious assessment of such a community policing proposal, he feels. The community police forces would have no responsibility in the field of paramilitary crimes; they would be recruited from their divided communities; local community groups and international human rights agencies could monitor their activities.

At present in many areas, it should be possible for the police to make short patrols unarmed, Father Lennon states. This would be public relations, not intelligence gathering. They could also do much more to encourage police-community liaison committees, especially with deprived communities. Rev. Lennon also feels there is an urgent need to investigate whether or not more can be done to protect members of the security forces, perhaps by wider use of technological equipment and better home protection. (See also Politics and the Constitution: Devolution.)

MR DOUGLAS HEGNEY from Belfast outlines how a change in the approach to policing in his area, the Lower Ormeau Road, has achieved positive results for both police and the community. Praising the local RUC subdivisional commander, Mr Victor Shaw, he said that considerable changes have occurred as a result of his 'humane and enlightened' strategy, which Mr Hegney likens to one of 'policing with consent'.

The district has suffered much over the past 20 years, Mr Hegney reports: high unemployment, petty crime. Unfairly branded 'a republican area', it has suffered repeated attacks and killings from loyalist paramilitaries.

He contrasts today's climate of security activity in the area to that of the past. Until recently the police, army and UDR treated the entire population with suspicion and hostility, he says, often launching unjustified searches, accompanied by harassment and intimidation.

But now Mr Shaw readily meets residents and community leaders to discuss their difficulties or advise them of his, and he explains the circumstances of arrests. 'Petty and unjust arrests are few and far between.' Considerable trust has been created and community leaders are able to defuse potential disturbances. Army backup for the police is kept to a minimum and military patrols are always accompanied by at least two uniformed police officers, 'who are clearly in charge of the soldiers rather than the reverse'.

Mr Hegney said that, in fatal incidents, Mr Shaw takes a direct and personal role in dealing with bereaved families, helping to reduce grief and distress. The families greatly appreciate follow-up police visits, offers of help and being kept up to date with progress in the investigations. Mr Hegney points out that all is not perfect on the Lower Ormeau Road, but the residents feel that great strides have been made in spite of continuing horrors, including the betting shop killings when five Catholics were shot dead by loyalist paramilitaries. They are in no doubt that Mr Shaw's fair policing policy has reduced tension and has encouraged the continuing work of local people to reduce social unrest. Mr Hegney says that 'much of the unnecessary hassle and hostility to the police would disappear' if Mr Shaw's policy was extended to the rest of Belfast.

MRS ELIZABETH GROVES, from Andersonstown, Belfast (chairperson of the Falls Community Council, but not speaking in that capacity), made an oral submission on behalf of the tenants, women, youth and pensioners groups she works with as a community development officer in the Greater Andersonstown and Lenadoon areas. She says that local communities in west Belfast have a problem with criminals.

The IRA do go out and take action against so-called anti-social elements — hoods, criminals, whatever label you wish — but they do so simply at the request of the people within the community, simply because policing has been seen to fall down. Policing for normal everyday criminal activity in Andersonstown and greater west Belfast has been seen to be non-existent. People will argue with us that the police cannot go into these areas, but that is a joke. In plain, everyday terms it is a joke because there is not one day in Andersonstown or Lenadoon that you will not see at least 20 to 30 jeeps, Saracens and foot patrols touring around. They can go in when it suits them for other kinds of activity, but very little action is taken against hoods or criminals, with the result that the police have given, in a roundabout way, a mandate for the IRA to go out and take action against the hoods and criminals.

She says that over the past 18 months, at the request of the community, there had been a scaling down of kneecappings and so-called punishment shootings. However, when that happened, the army and the police started to shoot and kill joyriders, and had recently shot dead an IRA volunteer in a stolen car. Now people were saying the kneecappings had increased in the past few weeks.

Many community workers were very fearful of going to the police. Working with young people and senior citizens Mrs Groves said that she had to go into police stations, and had met a few individual policemen who were extremely helpful. She felt they were handicapped in a similar way to her — if they were seen to be 'too giving' to community workers in west Belfast they were 'branded' in the same way that she would be if she was seen associating with the RUC. Some of them genuinely believed in community policing, but were handicapped because they were 'used totally for the military or harassment type of policing'. (See also Politics and the Constitution: Talking to Sinn Féin and the Paramilitarites; The Economy and Society: Social and Community.)

MS PATRICIA MALLON of Belfast says that privately everyone knows that there are still 'no go' areas in Northern Ireland — for example in west Belfast — yet political leaders from John Hume to Margaret Thatcher, as well as the RUC, deny that this is the case.

These denials are at odds with the reality experienced at the grass roots, where an informal justice system has become firmly established and subscribed to not only by those who are generally opposed to the RUC but also by law-abiding citizens who are frustrated by the non-delivery of a policing service. This affects confidence in the police's effectiveness in dealing with crime in those areas. Stories continue to circulate about property recovered by 'whispering in the right ear' of someone in the community, rather than relying on results from the police. At the very least the acceptance of this state of affairs must create an apathetic attitude to policing in these areas by the police themselves. Most people are aware that the police are required to carry out their duty in difficult and dangerous circumstances, but this sympathy does not mean they are excused from that duty.

Every apparent 'shoot-to-kill' incident which is not fully investigated results in countless people giving up the struggle to remain fair to the police and army. When the security forces appear to operate above the law, they do a disservice to those working for a peace process and leave behind deep wounds which do not easily, if ever, go away. Mechanisms should be in place which offer those who are aggrieved an opportunity to see justice done, and I would like to see more openness on the side of the security forces when a 'bad apple' surfaces. This can only strengthen the work of the 'good guys'.

THE COMMITTEE ON THE ADMINISTRATION OF JUSTICE (CAJ) calls for changes leading to openness, impartiality and accountability in the policing system. A new Police Authority, with full-time members, should have statutory duties to establish policing policies and priorities and to ensure they are carried out. It should publish pamphlets to inform the public about its policies. CAJ advocates that the office of the Commissioner for Complaints (Ombudsman) be given the task of investigating complaints against police officers. Incidents of death or injury caused by RUC weapons should be investigated immediately by a senior officer from an outside force. (See also Changing the Law.)

DRUMCREE FAITH AND JUSTICE GROUP, formed by a group of local people in Portadown in response to Orange parades going through nationalist areas, say they would not describe the RUC as a police force, but as a security force. 'For some of us, our only experience of them is one of harassment; coming to the house at 5.00 am and turning it upside down.'

The group, which has also challenged IRA 'oppression', sees merit in the idea of a new Police Authority which would have immediate access to the cases of people detained under emergency powers and which would have a complaints procedure role independent of the RUC Chief Constable. 'It would also have to be able to decide what are policy and what are operation matters because it is within this grey area that many abuses occur.' Members should be appointed by the Northern Ireland Secretary. The membership would have to include community leaders, and nationalists should have membership proportionate to the population.

MR DECLAN O'LOAN, from Ballymena, Co. Antrim, a member of the SDLP, speaks of his party's attitude towards the police and says also that 'old ways' with the RUC have to be changed.

The relationship between a police force and the public is two-way. 'The police must behave properly towards the public, but in turn the public must support the police.' Of course, no one gives unqualified support, but the public supports proper conduct.

Mr O'Loan adds:

In the Northern Ireland situation it is not enough to give the strong impression that our party will only support the police when, at some future time, it can be shown to be perfect in its conduct. We have long complained about a second-class citizenship forced upon us; in our attitude to the police, we abdicate, to some extent, our responsibilities and create a non-citizenship for ourselves. We need to be much more involved in the policing process, criticizing where criticism is due, praising where praise is due, putting forward proposals and accepting some of the stick when things go wrong.'

He warns that, despite reforms that have taken place in the RUC, even one major incident of misconduct does untold damage, and cover-ups even more so. Such incidents remain much too frequent, he says. There is still serious genuine disquiet about interrogations in Castlereagh RUC holding centre, he states, and there is no adequate mechanism to ensure that arrested people are not abused. Mr O'Loan believes that police do not give sufficient recognition to the damage caused by ill-manners or petty harassment, especially of young people.

'The police code of ethics is an unexceptionable document, but the words, Catholic and Protestant, never occur in it. I think that a more direct challenge to certain old ways needs to be exerted within the RUC.' (See also Politics and the Constitution: United Ireland.)

YOUTH FOR PEACE, the youth wing of the Peace People, says that in the absence of normal policing in certain areas, the paramilitaries have inflicted their own brutal 'justice' upon the communities there. The organization believes it unlikely that the RUC in its present form could ever gain the full confidence of certain sections of the community and says that the impetus for local policing, which would deal with non-paramilitary crime, must come from the community where it is needed. (See also Changing the Law/Reducing the Violence.)

DEMOCRATIC LEFT welcomes the growth of police liaison committees, bringing the police more into contact with local community leaders, and calls on all sections of the community to participate fully in the committees. It wants a continuation of the conscious efforts by the police to be even-handed and says that 'the ultimate aim must be the development of a totally accepted community police service.' (See also Politics and the Constitution: Devolution.)

THE GREEN PARTY advocates the presence of a small number of peace-keeping observers from continental Europe alongside British soldiers in Northern Ireland 'for the mutual benefit of all concerned'. The party says 'there is a requirement for a police force which has the respect and support of the entire community and these observers could play a major role in rebuilding public confidence.' (See also Politics and the Constitution: Other Political Submissions.)

MR DAVE LITTLE of Kilkeel, Co. Down, proposes a new community policing strategy as an alternative to the current paramilitary model, in order to gain the maximum level of popular support for the maintenance of law and order and the eradication of terrorism. He refers to the comments last year of the left-wing black commentator, Darcus Howe, on the successful implementation of such a policy in the mixed-race Brixton area of south London.

NORTHERN IRELAND RELIGIOUS FOR JUSTICE AND PEACE (NIRJP), composed of members of Roman Catholic religious orders, urges investigation of the practicality of separate community police forces, dealing with non-paramilitary crime, for nationalist and unionist areas, as well as a mixed force for areas where there is no demand for a separate force. The governing body of the police should be independent of the police and be representative of the communities it serves. In groups with an executive role in regard to policing, residents of deprived areas should have 'a disproportionate influence because it is such areas that suffer most from crime and from bad policing'.

The group says that, the Roman Catholic community in nationalist areas frequently experiences harassment from the security forces. 'Fears are part and parcel of everyday living. These fears are generated through interactions with the security forces, the paramilitaries, the practice of one's religion, the threat to life from loyalist paramilitaries and political pressures from one's co-religionists.' This experience creates anger and powerlessness.

The group asserts that, especially in areas of high unemployment, to put trust in the security forces is seen to be 'putting trust in a dubious authority'. The group state: 'There is a level of faith in the police authorities to handle what might be described as non-paramilitary crime but any collaboration with the police outside of this is fraught with mistrust, more fear and little hope of a just solution.'

It argues that the failure of the Catholic community, through its political and Church leaders, to examine seriously the issue of policing undermines their criticism of the police. 'If Catholic criticism of the police is to be helpful, there is a need for positive proposals that in a different context would enable nationalists to play a prominent role in future policing structures.'

ROSALINE HILLOCK and SISTER ANNA propose, in order to strengthen what they see as an increasing momentum in cross-community contact, that individuals, either singly or in cross-community pairs, should be invited to sign a bond committing themselves not to engage in or to further violence and to respect everyone of a different culture and religion. They suggest that a small button-badge could be worn by those who have made this pledge to live and work against sectarianism. They believe that policing and security — and the need to make them acceptable and trustworthy in minority areas — is 'perhaps *the* most difficult, divisive, sensitive question in Northern Ireland — a running sore'.

Other submissions which dealt with policing, among other things, were the Hilltop ACE Workers Group (east Belfast), the Inter-Church Group on Faith and Politics, and Religious Together (Down and Connor).

Prisons

MR PADRAIC WILSON, a republican remand prisoner in Crumlin Road Prison, Belfast, blames the authorities' prison integration policy for tension and violence in the jail. He asserts that the only feasible solution to the problem is the segregation of republican and loyalist prisoners.

There are three remand wings, he explains: A and B house a mixture of republicans and loyalists and C holds 'non-political' prisoners.

To house republican and loyalist prisoners in separate wings would be the ideal solution but even separation on a landing basis within A and B wings would remove the reasons and opportunities for conflict. It would allow for the implementation of the type of regime already enjoyed by other prisoners. It would also ensure that the control and security of the prison remains in the hands of the prison administration.

Mr Wilson says much of the unrest and disruption springs from limited access to canteen recreation and education facilities. Separate segregated wings would mean prisoners eating all meals in the canteens and having full access to recreational facilities, including the exercise yards. General hygiene and cleanliness within the wings would be greatly improved. Even though access to yards might be slightly curtailed, separate landings would ease tension because prisoners would still be out of their cells more.

Prisoners and staff would gain from segregation, Mr Wilson states. It would remove the threat of violence and risk of injury without requiring major expenditure or physical changes. Under a new or improved system, co-operation could be developed on the basis that any guarantees given and later broken could result in a re-examination of what was on offer.

Mr Wilson says that Lord Colville, in his prisons report, expressed a reservation about separate landings, that exchanges of verbal abuse or throwing of liquids would still be possible. He states: 'This practice has already been stopped by republicans anyway, and could be completely eradicated under a new regime.'

THE REPUBLICAN PRISONERS at the Maze call for a series of changes which they say are aimed at introducing openness into the system for reviewing life sentences. Only when there is openness, can there be proper scrutiny, they state. They call for the scrapping of indeterminate sentences, which they describe as 'inhumane'. Prisoners should be legally represented at Life Sentence Review Board hearings. A prisoner should be told the reasons for refusing to release him or her and should also be given the date of his/her next review. All internal reports on a prisoner considered by the review board should be open to challenge by the prisoner, instead of being secret. Criteria for release should be made known to the prisoner, who should also have the right to know the identities of the people reviewing his sentence and the right to challenge the participation of at least two of them if he/she fears that a fair hearing may be prejudiced.

They say that, although there is considerable uniformity in life sentence cases, no clear pattern of releases has emerged. 'This lack of pattern leaves the prisoner wondering exactly what are the criteria for release. There is no clear definition of what he should do to enhance this release.' (See also Politics and the Constitution: United Ireland.)

THE REPUBLICAN WOMEN PRISONERS at Maghaberry Prison, Co. Antrim, accuse Britain of inflicting human rights abuses on them.

The British do not forcibly strip search women POWs because they fear a threat to security, they do so because the existence of those POWs threatens the very state and social order that they have tried unsuccessfully to impose.

The prisoners contend that in the regime at Maghaberry, which has male and female prisoners, the Northern Ireland Office operates a policy of discrimination against women. They say they are worse off in relation to visits, education, association, exercise and other relaxation activities. They allege they are discriminated against because of their sex and their political beliefs.

The fact that the majority of the women in Maghaberry are Republican POWs makes the NIO even more reluctant to treat them equally to the men. Unlike the male prisoners, the republican women did not change their political beliefs on being imprisoned, so they do not receive the rewards given to the non-political male prisoners.

THE NORTHERN IRELAND ASSOCIATION FOR THE CARE AND RESETTLEMENT OF OFFENDERS (NIACRO) argues that conditions of low income, poor housing and unemployment are closely associated with high levels of crime. In Northern Ireland 'the confrontation between political violence and governmental special powers is manifest in the police stations, courts and prisons no less than in the streets'. On the other hand, 'the criminal justice system is a way of processing the products of social deprivation and division — the alienated, violent, dishonest and despairing people who have taken to anti-social crime. How the system is organized is therefore of major import to the future of our society.'

NIACRO says that in its experience 'people have a highly developed, if often selective, sense of justice. If that sense is offended, then people lose faith in the system and deny [it] that legitimacy which is a precondition of the proper, democratic functioning of what must be, in the end, a mechanism for the enforcement of obedience to the law.' In the particular historical circumstances of Northern Ireland, that will lead to violence. The Association urges that the criminal justice system must be open, equal, fair and accountable, especially in a society where it is mainly staffed by one section of the community. It says that currently there are several elements of the system which fail the test of accountability, three of which it mentions: the operation of the Life Sentence Review System, the detention powers of the Prevention of Terrorism Act, and adjudications on prison disciplinary charges.

THE COMMITTEE FOR THE TRANSFER OF IRISH PRISONERS (CTIP) says there are currently 28 Irish republican prisoners serving long sentences in British jails, many of them serving recommended sentences of 35 years before they can be considered for parole.

The families of every one of these prisoners effectively serves the sentence along with the prisoner. We are sentenced to years of debt, fear, infrequent visits, harassment from the Prevention of Terrorism Act. Our children are sentenced to hardly ever seeing their imprisoned parent and, when they do see them, it will be intolerably stressful. There are elderly relatives who are unable to travel to Britain because of ill-health and who are effectively sentenced never to see their imprisoned child again unless they are transferred to a jail in the North of Ireland.

The Committee says a report from Lord Ferrers of the Home Office gave the clear impression that transfers to Northern Ireland prisons would be granted to Irish prisoners who wanted them. This has not happened: 'The only concession the British government has made is that temporary extended transfers for a period of up to 12 months at a time can be granted to Irish prisoners with families living in the North of Ireland subject to "security consideration".'

Other submissions which dealt with prisons, among other things, came from Mr Stephen Berry, Mr Bernard Conlon, Mr Victor Graham, and Mr John Wills.

CHAPTER 13

Submissions' Summary:
The Economy and Society II

The Economy

MR PAUL TEAGUE, an economist at the University of Ulster, says new policy initiatives are needed to stimulate the region's economy, but warns that success depends on political stability. In a wide-ranging assessment, he lists many of the factors which reflect Northern Ireland's position as the poorest region within the United Kingdom: 8000 entrants to the labour force each year, yet only about 4000 new jobs being created; the UK's highest regional rate of long-term unemployed; one of its highest youth unemployment rates; the highest rate of jobless people with no qualifications; the highest level of regional inequality outside south-east England. The evidence suggests, he says, that the labour market is highly divided, with those at the lower end experiencing low income, few job opportunities and long periods on the dole, while those at the upper end enjoy a relatively comfortable and secure standard of living.

Catholics are 2.5 times more likely to be unemployed than Protestants, but beyond that statistic there is much disagreement about the scale of Catholic disadvantage. Recent evidence suggests that in many sectors the proportion of employed Catholics reflects their share of the labour force. However, research also highlights that many enterprises employ only Protestants or Catholics, indicating that the labour market 'has a strong sectarian tinge. Complaints that Catholics continue to be excluded from higher managerial positions also appear to have some validity'.

In the past 20 years there has been a 'huge contraction' in the region's industrial base, Mr Teague reports. Among the factors in 'this sharp de-industrialization' have been declines in dominant sectors, such as textiles, shipbuilding, tobacco and aircraft manufacture, as well as the withdrawal of multinational companies and the reluctance of others to invest in the region. Between 1973 and 1990 there was a 40 per cent reduction in the number of externally owned plants in Northern Ireland, resulting in a similar drop in employment in that sector. In approximately the same period, employment in small local manufacturing firms dropped from 19,000 to 12,000. Less than 20 per cent of the Northern Ireland workforce is now employed in manufacturing, mostly in low technology and low value-added sectors. In addition, research has shown that the level of technical innovation is well below the UK average; there is a lack of managerial and white-collar staff; management systems are unsophisticated, and many small firms have neither the resources nor the incentive to increase either their workforce's skills or their production technology. As a result, they fall even further behind their competitors.

Against that background, the public sector has come to dominate the local economy, with 44 per cent of the workforce employed directly in it and many more jobs dependent on public spending. The British exchequer operates as the region's economic lifeline, says Mr Teague. Public expenditure outstrips locally raised taxes by nearly two-and-a-half billion pounds. The UK subvention, which makes up the shortfall, excluding spending on security, amounts to about £1300 per annum for each Northern Ireland resident; the cost to the British taxpayer is the equivalent of one penny on income tax. Thus, even with its economic problems, 'Northern Ireland enjoys a standard of living not warranted by the performance of the underlying economy'.

Mr Teague is concerned that the sheer size of the British subvention may have 'negative spillover effects in the local economy'. Northern Ireland has a public sector twice as big as any other UK region, and Mr Teague asks whether the subvention may serve to smother key private sector dynamics, like entrepreneurship, while at the same time being the province's financial saviour. Estimates suggest that local industry is five times more subsidized than its counterparts elsewhere in the UK. Equally, 'in the labour market high unemployment coexists alongside high income inequality, while the industrial sector suffers from low productivity and from poor product quality, despite receiving huge subsidies. It is unlikely that such distortions can be counteracted by piecemeal and selective reform.'

Suggesting a range of economic institutional and policy changes, Mr Teague says, *inter alia*, that 'since it is the source of many of the problems, the half-in, half-out relationship which Northern Ireland has with the UK economy must be resolved. This relationship is highly paradoxical; while the UK is Northern Ireland's financial saviour, it also blocks the emergence of more dynamic and self-reliant economic structures in the province.' Developing more all-Ireland economic strategies may allow a new economic policy regime to emerge in Northern Ireland, he says.

North-South economic co-operation or all-Ireland economic strategies would not involve taking the province out of an economic union with Britain and establishing a similar arrangement in Ireland. The economic and political conditions do not exist for such a strategy. Rather, the project is about forging more intimate and symbiotic relationships between companies, institutions and social partners on both sides of the border so that a new commercial environment may be established.

He also proposes a number of institutional changes, particularly to challenge the 'mendicant commercial behaviour that has become pervasive in the local economy'. One innovation he suggests is the creation of a regional system of industrial relations. This should be aimed at redistributing income more fairly within Northern Ireland: 'Estimates suggest that if people earning over £20,000 were to accept a wage freeze or small pay rises, then thousands of new jobs could be created in the province.' Additional policy changes could include a more co-ordinated attempt to build commercial links between large and small firms; the elimination of 'soft subsidies' from grant provision; and more careful planning of public expenditure.

Mr Teague concludes, however, that these changes would be unlikely to reach their full potential so long as the present political conflict continues.

Traditionally it has been assumed that successful economic development policies can be pursued in spite of the political violence. But this idea is fanciful and unrealistic: political turbulence, be it in Northern Ireland or wherever, produces an uncertain and unstable climate for business. Thus if sustainable good economic performance is going to be secured for the province, a priority must be reaching a political settlement to the present conflict.

THE NORTHERN IRELAND VOLUNTARY TRUST (NIVT) urges the Opsahl Commission to support the calls of economists and business leaders for the compilation of a strategic regional plan with maximum community participation.

The notion of a mini Marshall Plan of recovery for Northern Ireland could captivate the imagination and build upon the ad hoc approaches to date. Northern Ireland currently operates in a planning vacuum totally dependent upon the exigencies of the British economy. Without an indigenous economic and social strategy, we restrict ourselves to a peripheral dependent status with little impetus for change and development. A broad-based regional strategy with challenging goals and targets set within a realistic timescale could transform our political economy. The process of compiling a recovery plan, symbolic of a collective response to adversity and opportunity, could intrinsically be an important part of the healing process that urgently needs to take place in Northern Ireland.

The primary object of the plan would be 'to overcome the horrendous levels of marginalization in our society'. With a strong public sector interventionist role, it would pursue an aggressive industrial development programme and attack poverty in a co-ordinated way, putting in place innovative structures 'to guarantee those socially excluded a quality of life and level of self-esteem that gives meaning to their citizenship'. (See also Social and Community.)

DR GEORGE QUIGLEY, the chairman of the Ulster Bank and former Secretary of the Department of Economic Development (submitting a speech he made first in February 1992), says that as head of a bank which does half its business in the South and half in the North, he has no difficulty with the proposition that Ireland is, or should be, an 'island economy'. 'Both North and South would have singularly failed to give substance to the 1992 concept if, occupying a small island on the periphery of the EC, they neglected or were unable to function as a single market.' He advocates that, for funding purposes, the EC should treat the island as one economic area and proposes the creation of a growth-led Belfast-Dublin 'economic corridor'.

The making of a single market out of the island must be 'an exercise in synergy', he says, 'not a zero sum game where a wholly insufficient quantity of existing island wealth is simply redistributed'. It is important that both parts of the island should perceive such a movement towards greater economic cohesion as beneficial. He stresses the consensus among business people, North and South, that 'making a reality of the island economy is dependent on there being no political agendas, overt or hidden. The island contains too many dealers in ultimates, most of them so far spectacularly unsuccessful.'

Dr Quigley is critical of obstacles to North-South trade and communications, although he acknowledges forthcoming improvements in both road and rail links. However, he is disappointed at a recent survey which showed that 'over two-thirds of companies that sell from Northern Ireland into the South had not undertaken any market research, had no agent or representative there and no branch plant or office'. He points out that Denmark, with a similar population, 'achieves sales levels per capita on its home market *twice* as high as those achieved by the combined efforts of Northern and Southern manufacturers. We desperately need throughout this island the boost to economic growth which greater home sales would provide, bearing in mind that, even if the island economy could grow consistently by 5 per cent per annum, the inroads into unemployment would still be woefully inadequate.' The same survey showed that Northern Ireland firms expected to increase sales to the South by only 20 per cent over the next three years; if the ambitions of firms in the South are equally modest, special steps will be needed to accelerate progress'.

Dr Quigley also singles out for praise the regular meetings between the councils of the main business bodies, North and South: the joint Economic and Social Research Institute/Northern Ireland Economic Research Centre project on the island economy; the EC-backed Co-operation North study on the potential for financial services synergy within the island, which has recommended a permanent island forum to take concerted or complementary action on this question and which has identified the need for a more active primary Irish capital market; the agreement of the Northern Ireland Industrial Development Board and the Irish Export Board to work together to increase the number and range of products supplied within the island; and planned initiatives to open up the field of public procurement on an island-wide basis in order to bid successfully for public sector procurement contracts in the rest of the EC.

He also stresses that an island economy would be in a better position to bring together what has been called an 'interactive industrial network' of firms which cluster in one area to take advantage of ready access to linked suppliers, specialist facilities and services, experienced labour and discriminating customers. On the question of EC support, he applauds the economic progress stemming from EC encouragement of cross-border initiatives, but believes that, instead of simply relating to border counties, 'cross-border' should be redefined 'to embrace the totality of economic relationships within the island, with the EC regarding the island economy as a whole as the relevant entity and directing its attention to the needs of that economic area'. A block of resources should be allocated to the island, for allocation by agreement between the two Governments on a basis agreed with the EC, he proposes. 'The broad terms of reference would be the promotion of a vigorous island economy and the progressive narrowing of the gap between the island and the more prosperous EC countries.'

Dr Quigley concludes by proposing the creation of a Belfast-Dublin 'economic corridor', to serve as the initial focus for a growth strategy which would subsequently expand to encompass other areas on the island. He points to the experience of successful corridor developments in the United States and Europe, with urban and manufacturing centres expanding along a connecting corridor and resulting in a 'regional growth pole'. For obvious reasons, the natural economic tendency of the two largest urban areas in Ireland to develop along a connecting corridor has been constrained in the past. He points to statistics which show the very low rate of telephone calls between Dublin and Belfast (compared to Dublin and Munster); the much lower propensity for passenger traffic by rail; and the high loss of manufacturing jobs on the eastern seaboard, in both jurisdictions, compared with the west.

He believes that the time for such a corridor between Belfast and Dublin is ripe. He urges the co-ordination of government investment policies to create a linked infrastructure to include science and technology parks, university-linked technology incubators, medical and veterinary research facilities and technology transfer processes, as well as the more traditional roads, transportation systems and other public facilities. He believes that the concept of an economic corridor would be an important strategic step to begin to redirect capital flows, which currently leave the country to places where the return is greater, to benefit the island economy. It also 'offers a unique opportunity for partnership between the public sector, through strategically targeted capital projects, and the private sector', with the investment of public sector funds creating a 'platform' for further growth and fostering the climate for the attraction of new business.

In a separate paper (from a speech made in February 1993), Dr Quigley says that he is not at all despondent about Northern Ireland's prospects in the difficult new world of the EC single market. However, he stresses that one of the conditions for realizing the region's 'enormous potential' is 'to get our political act together'. Underlining the need for the whole community, including business, to make a contribution to the regional democratic process, he expresses the wish to see 'Ulstermen controlling the levers of power in Northern Ireland'. He points out that 27 per cent of Northern Irish children live in families dependent on income support; 39 per cent of children live in the 'poverty trap', in families earning less than £122 a week.

My dream would be to see these issues — and a host of others — challenging the political talents of the best and brightest in Northern Ireland, with all men and women of goodwill mobilized to achieve success. To borrow and adapt a phrase from President Clinton's inaugural address, there is nothing *wrong* with Northern Ireland that cannot be cured by what is *right* with Northern Ireland.

MR JAMES ANDERSON, senior lecturer in geography at the Open University, writes that recent interviews with local business leaders (which he carried out in the course of research into the likely effects of European integration on the Northern Ireland conflict) revealed a new enthusiasm for the economic integration of the island of Ireland as an end in itself, and explicitly not as any part of a nationalist agenda. He quotes the director of the CBI in Northern Ireland, Mr Nigel Smyth, who said that partition had been detrimental to industry in both parts of Ireland, and that business people were building cross-border links for sound economic, not ideological, reasons. Many interviewees felt that enthusiasm was stronger in the North than in the South, something that would have been unimaginable in the past.

This enthusiasm starts from the 'economic imperative' to develop the present poor North-South links, Mr Anderson says.

The main stimulus is fear of increased competition from stronger economies in the neo-liberal single market, and the threat of further peripheralization, given the paucity of offsetting interventionist measures by the EC. This fear has concentrated minds on the shared problems and vulnerabilities of the two economies. In the European context both suffer from comparatively low competitiveness, low incomes, poor economies of scale, high unemployment and heavy reliance on agriculture and multinational branch plants with limited domestic linkages. There are real fears that if the two parts of Ireland do not swim together, they may sink separately.

There was broad support among those interviewed for Dr Quigley's ideas, he reports. The dominant view was that the North had benefited from EC membership less than the South, and that, although the Republic and Britain were often on opposite sides in EC debates, the North's economic interests were more usually in line with the Republic's. 'Hence integration with the South was widely seen as offering additional or better international representation, a means of overcoming the North's political peripherality.'

Mr Anderson stresses, however, that, although the case for 'an island economy' may be compelling, integration faces formidable economic, political and institutional obstacles, North and South. He points to the different currencies and tax systems and the unevenness of existing economic links, maintaining that in the Northern Ireland government departments there is no coherent 'state view' on North-South co-operation. Several business leaders, including Dr Quigley, spoke of the lack of informal contacts and mutual distrust in business circles.

Other problems foreseen were increased competition for shared facilities (which is already happening between Donegal and Derry over an airport for the north-west); political obstacles to a single agency to attract inward investment; and Southern tourism interests, which are wary of closer identification with the North. There are also fears that the search for scale economies in the private sector will result in takeovers by Southern companies, with the possibility of asset-stripping and closures. There are fears about competition from the Republic's restructured dairy industry and its larger food-processing conglomerates. Some interviewees felt that the South had legitimate priorities besides North-South integration — not least the inadequacies of its other transport routes — and that there were 'more votes in upgrading Dublin's commuter services than in improving its links with Belfast'. Others thought that North-South transport improvements were stalled because of fears that trade would be diverted from Southern ports to Belfast or Larne.

'Perhaps the biggest obstacle to economic integration is the lack of an adequate institutional framework and political programme', Mr Anderson goes on. 'The experience of cases of successful integration, such as Benelux, suggests it requires concerted political management, democratic involvement and joint institutions with North-South representation to ensure political accountability.' In Ireland, the problems of inter-state economic integration — and because of the importance of the state sectors, integration could not be left to private business — are compounded by the 'troubles' and unionist hostility. 'Rather than economic convergence being the panacea to solve the political conflict, the latter hampers integration.'

He concludes, however, that circumstances are now more favourable for political initiatives on integration, arguing that, contrary to Dr Quigley's position, making a reality of the island economy 'is precisely dependent on there being "political agendas"'. He concludes:

Economic integration is likely to be a central concern in any future talks, and agreeing to effective joint institutions for North-South co-operation may well be part of the price unionists have to pay for a devolved assembly. But, whatever the particular bargaining equation, it is likely that economic and political changes will nudge each other towards greater integration, though at what speed remains to be seen.

THE NORTHERN IRELAND CHAMBER OF COMMERCE AND INDUSTRY (NICCI), the region's largest business organization (and umbrella body for nearly 30 local chambers), says that there is widespread agreement in the region for the view that strengthening the economy to expand employment is a priority. 'Indeed, it is one matter on which agreement exists throughout this community. It provides an opportunity for people to gain a measure of responsibility over the future development of their localities.' The government should build on this agreement by promoting involvement and partnership. Describing the existing structure of central administration in Northern Ireland as 'remote, ponderous and largely unresponsive', the Chamber says it does not facilitate the dialogue required to promote worthwhile community involvement.

The Chamber believes a streamlining of the existing system is necessary to facilitate speedier decision-making and to improve the interface between the administration and relevant interest groups at local level. However, it is important that, where public funds are involved, the accountability and responsibility for which the Northern Ireland Civil Service has an impressive reputation, should be safeguarded.

The Chamber believes that the government decision to enable local councils 'to introduce a levy on ratepayers for economic development (The Miscellaneous Provisions Order 1992) is an important development which, if properly implemented, could promote partnership at local level'. The Chamber is clear that, while an agreed political structure would be a distinct advantage, the absence of consensus on a future central framework must not be allowed to divert attention from economic development. 'It makes sense to focus greater attention on local government, where there are already a number of successful partnership initiatives.'

The Chamber recommends the creation of a central strategic planning committee of private and public sector bodies to produce a programme of initiatives to promote economic development and reduce unemployment. This committee would devise a strategic economic development plan for the province and would establish priorities for spending government and EC funds. A similar approach should be adopted at local government level, with committees establishing development strategies and priorities for local, central and EC funding, and co-ordinating with the central planning committee.

The Chamber concludes by noting that it had been holding a series of meetings with leaders of the main constitutional parties to help produce an agreed approach to local economic development. In addition, it has been instrumental in forming an economic think-tank involving the region's main business bodies and the government, and inviting political leaders to participate. It is encouraging local chambers to consider similar initiatives.

THE CONFEDERATION OF BRITISH INDUSTRY (NORTHERN IRELAND) says that a growth rate of 5 per cent per annum is required if unemployment is to be reduced to average European Community levels. Major policy changes are required to achieve that acceleration. The CBI asserts that a widespread acceptance of the need to achieve exceptional performance is required.

It says that the business community 'remains somewhat remote' from EC support measures, due to lack of consultation and because EC funding is absorbed within the Northern Ireland block grant. Current programmes are largely geared to the public sector, rather than being strategically shaped to the needs of the private sector. Greater business community involvement in the preparation and development of EC support measures could help make them more effective, it suggests.

The CBI estimates that EC structural funding of £1.48 billion is required for 1994-8 to facilitate the necessary growth leading to high self-sufficiency, international standards of competitiveness and dynamic industrial activity. Education and skill levels need to be increased substantially to international levels, with a stronger emphasis on vocational and technical education. Other priority development questions are strategic management skills and international marketing expertise, language skills and stronger business-education partnerships.

EC funds should be used to support the integration of the Northern Ireland electricity network with those of the Republic of Ireland and Britain and to facilitate the introduction of natural gas to the region before 1997. Telecommunications and road network investment is also necessary. The CBI points out that a key element of the EC structural funding sought for 1994-8 relates to proposals with a North-South dimension, developed jointly with the Confederation of Irish Industry. The recent CBI document on the next round of structural funding emphasizes joint ventures with the South in education and training, marketing and trade, industrial investment, and transport and energy infrastructure.

The CBI says manufacturing remains of vital importance to the Northern Ireland economy, employing directly and indirectly more than 50 per cent of those in private sector employment. Over 100,000 are employed in manufacturing and each additional 1000 new jobs in manufacturing results in more than 300 service jobs.

Emphasizing the need for companies to pursue 'world-class standards', the CBI says that the pace of improvement and change within business must accelerate and will require the commitment of business and the focused support of government. The limited success in attracting inward investment to Northern Ireland 'reinforces the need to focus our future on the long-term success and faster growth of indigenous enterprises'.

THE NORTHERN IRELAND COMMITTEE OF THE IRISH CONGRESS OF TRADE UNIONS (ICTU) insists that the need for a major economic recovery programme for the region is 'paramount in tackling disadvantage and poverty'. It is sceptical of the view which it says government expresses, that Northern Ireland has suffered less in the current recession than the rest of Britain because of its heavy dependence on the public sector. According to the Northern Ireland Committee, 'the real weakness in the Northern Ireland economy is the weakness of the private sector, especially in manufacturing, rather than an overdependence on the public sector'.

Calling for economic policies to tackle the acute unemployment problem, the Northern Ireland Committee says that, despite having been 'massaged' downward, on about 20 occasions by government, the official figure in Northern Ireland is more than 100,000. Unemployment in the region has traditionally been double the British average. In some areas — Strabane for example — the officially recorded rate has been over 50 per cent, and in areas like west Belfast it is estimated by community workers at 80 per cent.

The Northern Ireland Committee argues for a new industrial strategy with a different political orientation: a strategy which includes effective manufacturing diversification, involves the social partners more in economic decision-making and efficiently allocates industrial development resources. How to maximise EC support for cross-border co-operation is a key issue. On fair employment, the Northern Ireland Committee says that the current government approach is a significant advance, but it believes that there are 'crucial weaknesses in the general field of human rights and on discrimination with respect to gender'. It stresses that 'progress cannot be achieved while current levels of violence prevail. Within the framework of what is politically acceptable, no security policy is capable of ending violence.'

The Northern Ireland Committee, which has consistently advocated a Bill of Rights for Northern Ireland, calls for the highest standards of human rights and civil liberties to be applied in the region. 'Any departure from these standards is ruthlessly and cynically exploited by paramilitary organizations — which have no respect even for the most fundamental human right, the right to live.' It reiterates its opposition to plastic bullets, strip searching and the use of uncorroborated evidence.

Expressing particular concern about a lack of equality for women in the region, the Northern Ireland Committee calls for training, educational and other initiatives to combat the problem of low pay, low status and poor prospects for working women.

COUNTERACT, the ICTU's anti-discrimination unit, believes that public sector bodies must give greater attention to how they cope with intimidation in the workplace. Following discussions with trade unions, the ICTU equality committee is considering draft guidelines for union procedures to deal with intimidation. Counteract says that it surveyed 26 district councils and eight health education boards on whether their equal opportunities policies contained provisions for dealing with sectarian harassment at work. 'Of all the respondents, only one district council indicated that it was intending to treat this issue as a matter of priority.' An important aspect of intimidation is the issue of hijacking, which affects both workers and local communities, according to Counteract. Promising to focus on the problem, the unit says that the strain placed on victims, some of whom have been forced to transport bombs, has never been investigated.

BELFAST ROTARY CLUB put in four separate submissions, from five individual members, on the Constitution, economics, social concerns and politics. The economic submission, written by Professor Desmond Rea of the University of Ulster, showed that if UK government expenditure was taken as 100, the regional figure for Northern Ireland was 143, compared with 119 for Scotland, 110 for Wales and 96 for England. The submission quotes the *Daily Telegraph*: 'The Union should not depend on handouts and perks.... Quite apart from the fiscal argument for a change of policy, the Celts have travelled far enough down what Hayek called 'the road to serfdom'. A return to the traditional frugality is long overdue.'

However, in considering whether Northern Ireland is treated too generously, the economist John Simpson has argued that one also has to examine the factors which might justify different expenditure levels:

A higher proportion of school-age children affects the education ratio; higher levels of morbidity affect health care, and low income levels affect the call on social services; agriculture is proportionately about four times as large in local employment as in the whole of the United Kingdom; industry and employment is the budget which is directed to narrowing economic disadvantage.

Professor Rea argues strongly that to lower the unemployment level to 'a sensible figure', Northern Ireland requires inward investment, which it will not attract as long as the violence continues. A political settlement is therefore needed 'as a prior step to bringing violence to an end'. Similarly, 'if we are to resist the challenges on the public expenditure front, we need a political settlement involving devolution. With the latter, we can argue more successfully with the British Government and seek more direct lines to Brussels and, incidentally, not be hidebound by ideological Tory policies.'

MANUFACTURING SCIENCE FINANCE (MSF) proposes a ten-year economic development plan for Northern Ireland, funded largely from public investment and designed to re-equip the economy to compete with other

EC regions. In the absence of a devolved political assembly, it proposes a regional Economic and Social Development Authority to draw up this plan, with membership drawn from the trade unions, employers, farmers, Churches and political parties. It also recommends joint cross-border development authorities, estimating that 30,000 new jobs would be created by exploiting the full potential of cross-border trade.

REV. CANON KENYON E. WRIGHT, the chair of the Scottish Constitutional Convention and of the Scottish Environmental Forum, asks whether it might be possible in Northern Ireland to initiate a project similar to the 'national sustainable development plan' which is being formulated in Scotland. Canon Wright says that the widespread participation of decision-makers and the community at large in such an attempt to forge a long-term, ecologically and environmentally sustainable economic plan is as important as the product itself. He notes that the Scottish plan, including a key educational element, 'is not in the immediate sense party political or divisive of the community', and might provide a possible way forward for Northern Ireland.

Other submissions which dealt, among other things, with the Northern Ireland economy, came from Mr Brian Brannigan, Ms Rebecca Johnston — 'tele-cottages' in rural villages; Mr Gabriel O'Keefe — targeting EC funds for small farmers; Northern Ireland Graphical Society, Scrabo Presbyterian Church, Mr Norman Shannon, and Mr Paul Smith.

Social and Community Groups

THE NORTH BELFAST WOMEN, a group of community activists from Catholic and Protestant districts who came together to make a submission, say that north Belfast is 'a microcosm of the Northern Ireland situation, an area deeply fragmented in terms of religious and political divisions'. They point out that there are numerous 'peace lines' which serve to separate communities of different religions. The years of sectarian strife have restricted people's movements and there are continuing sporadic sectarian clashes and killings. Over 580 people have been killed in this relatively small area during the 'troubles'.

They point out that women have played both a pivotal role in drawing attention to the area's social and economic deprivation, and in attempting to resolve its overt sectarian conflicts.

For example, in 1985 it was women who took to the streets in an attempt to stop paramilitaries intimidating Catholic families out of the Manor Street area. The latter situation was so serious that the Northern Ireland Housing Executive eventually decided that the only course of action open to them was to demolish 17 newly built Housing Executive homes.

However, as women community activists with a strong commitment to north Belfast, they are convinced that there is a tremendous amount of goodwill in the area, with people wanting to see an end to the violence and to live in safety and friendship with their neighbours. They list a number of negative influences which have to be overcome to move towards this. First is people's concern about security — from sectarian attack and crime in general. 'It is generally felt that the army's role must be kept to a minimum in order to reintroduce a degree of normality in local areas. In particular, the army should not engage directly in stop-search procedures. This practice causes grave discontent, particularly among the young, fuelling resentment and bitterness.' They urge that community relations training should inform all security force training; greater opportunities for contact with the police, with people knowing how to contact those police personnel involved in community relations and a more effective role for police liaison committees; and the women say that the policy of heavy policing at paramilitary funerals should be reviewed.

It was also felt that 'some areas are being left without any form of protection against crime. This enables the paramilitaries to assume the role of 'protectionists'. While realizing the difficulties involved, it was felt that we need to find an effective mechanism for 'community policing'. There is a need to explore methods used in other countries, particularly the United States.'

While accepting that there is a public demand for security, they are concerned that the authorities' use of environmental walls ('peace walls'), road closures, barriers and buffer zones 'institutionalize and increase residential segregation'. They worry about the long-term consequences of this and want local communities to be consulted about alternatives more geared to long-term planning for integration among the communities. They urge the Government to stimulate a debate about integrated housing for the future. They also say that government criteria on housing needs have made it almost impossible for dereliction and decline in Protestant areas to be tackled, while not significantly increased housing construction and modernization in Catholic areas. 'The continued assertion that in Protestant areas of north Belfast there is 'no housing need' belies the experience of physical and population decline of those communities, and fuels conspiracy theories and actual fears that the Protestant community is being pushed out.'

The group stresses that 'poverty is a central element in the lives of many families in North Belfast and most would say that the standards of individuals and families on benefits have fallen dramatically in the last few years. Most would identify the introduction of the Social Fund as the cause of this deterioration.'

MRS ELIZABETH GROVES makes an oral submission as an individual and a community development officer in the Andersonstown and Lenadoon areas of west Belfast (not as chairperson of the Falls Community Council). She works with groups ranging from tenants' organizations and women's groups to young people and pensioners. She believes that, given the political and military situation and the high levels of unemployment in these areas, the local people have done extremely well in organizing themselves to work for the community.

She says it is hard to motivate young people to go into higher level education because there is so little prospect of a good well-paid job locally after it. 'They are also very much hampered by the high level of army and police harassment on a day-to-day basis on their own streets and in their own community.' The people generally believe the media give a false picture of their areas, particularly at the time of the killing of the two British army corporals in 1988, when the image of Andersonstown portrayed internationally was one of 'morons and gangsters'. In fact, it is 'a very loving, caring community' in which people help each other and have done a lot to help themselves. The people also feel that any initiative in Northern Ireland is always geared towards a 'six-county context' and fails to take into account their community's aspiration towards a united Ireland. (See also Politics and the Constitution: Talking to Sinn Féin and the Paramilitaries.)

Mrs Groves also mentions the fear among west Belfast community groups of 'political vetting', which had inhibited them from coming forward and giving their views to Initiative '92. Community groups had found in the past that if Sinn Féin people became active in their management structures, their funding had stopped.

It is very hard for people from the outside to realize the deep suspicion that has been caused by the history of political vetting of community groups and they certainly find it very, very hard to come out and speak truthfully and honestly. Until people do speak openly, the situation in Northern Ireland is not going to get any better.

She says that people in west Belfast are constantly being made accountable for what they are as a community by the media and the government, but 'nobody seems to be accountable for what they do to us'. She refers to her own mother-in-law, who was blinded by a British army rubber bullet when she was standing at the window of her home while the street outside was under army curfew. 'No one was ever taken to task for blinding her.... She was given some form of compensation which never really repaid her for not seeing any of her grandchildren.' (See also Law and Justice: Policing.)

THE NORTHERN IRELAND VOLUNTARY TRUST (NIVT) calls for the development of 'a strategic vision for Northern Ireland', a regional plan which would encourage dynamic leadership at all levels and be underpinned by action to eradicate social and cultural exclusion. Advocating the incorporation of a community development process into all social and economic planning, the NIVT says that many people are locked into cycles of deprivation in urban ghettos and rural townlands, and feel politically and culturally excluded from the mainstream of society. 'A society which remains indifferent to the levels and degrees of poverty in Northern Ireland also remains indifferent to the existence of peace.'

There is enormous talent within local communities in Northern Ireland, and the spirit engendered by local groups represents 'tremendous hope and aspiration'. Many of these groups 'virtually ignore direct involvement in conventional politics, seeking instead to engage in positive pre-political initiatives aimed at addressing their immediate social, educational, cultural and economic needs'. However, their work is under-recognized and underfunded, and much more could be done to encourage them, says the NIVT. In particular, it refers to the 'phenomenal contribution of local women's groups in keeping hope alive within and between the divided communities'.

The NIVT argues that there has been a failure to incorporate a community development process into our responses to de-industrialization, community divisions, educational inequalities, and health and social services needs. Deprived communities must be involved in the formulation of programmes targeted at their many areas of disadvantage.

People in need will remain so if they have to be the passive recipients of others' philosophies and agendas. Community development enables local people to set their own agenda and begin to meet their own needs. Community development challenges all existing agencies, both statutory and voluntary, to rethink their approaches, and to build participation and redistribution into the overall goals of any programme.

The NIVT also stresses that the plight of young people, often unemployed, alienated and with low self-esteem, has not been tackled with the urgency it deserves. It criticizes Northern Ireland's selective education system for failing to tackle the 'horrendous imbalances' in the vast numbers of young people who leave school at 16 with no formal qualifications. 'Society is often motivated to respond only when young people are perceived to be a threat. This type of intervention can be classified as a deviancy model of youth work.' It calls for a particular recognition of the plight of young people in the most disadvantaged communities and for programmes and resources which, 'as a matter of policy, guarantee a purposeful role in our society for every young person at least until the age of 25'.

Dynamic leadership is a fundamental prerequisite to renewal, regeneration and reconciliation — hence the need to encourage leadership throughout Northern Ireland society, the NIVT states. It points to the benefits of studying models of civic, cultural and commercial leadership in other countries, including some major US cities, and suggests that adult education and community development techniques have much to offer in developing leadership, particularly in marginalized communities. Direct Rule has brought obvious advantages to the more affluent sections of Northern Irish society.

At its worst, however, it bestows resources without any challenge of responsibility. This will never provide the foundations of a balanced society. At every opportunity, the creeping sense of indifference throughout Northern Ireland has to be challenged.

Given the dominance of its role, minimal local political input and the vagaries of Direct Rule, the NIVT believes that the public sector is potentially the single most important catalyst for change in Northern Ireland. The peculiarities of the region necessitate it assuming a leadership role not normally associated with public administration.

It is imperative that the public sector in Northern Ireland accepts that development, encouragement and risk-taking are equal, if not superior, in importance to the traditional roles of regulation, control and accountability. A relatively small number of senior civil servants collectively influence social and economic planning in Northern Ireland. It is incumbent upon those with the responsibility of office to demonstrate vision, statesmanship and purpose.

The NIVT recognizes that, in recent years, the public sector has been willing to experiment with new approaches and structures, with the setting up of the Central Community Relations Unit and of programmes like Making Belfast Work, Belfast Action Teams and the Londonderry Initiative.

The NIVT asks the Opsahl Commissioners to recognize the considerable acts of leadership on the part of the Northern Ireland civil service and encourage more endeavour in this regard. In particular, recognition should be given to the progressive extension of government into the areas of greatest need; yet there is some ground to be made in conversely extending the view of local communities into government. The harmonization of this vital communicative process is vital to achieving a model of government based upon consent rather than imposition. This aspiration is particularly important in all facets of the administration of justice.

(See also The Economy.)

MR KEN HUMPHRIES, a youth and community worker in the Lower Ormeau area of Belfast, says that the sense of powerlessness among people in deprived areas comes from being disenfranchised, not because of anything to do with the vote, but in the wider sense of being 'distanced' by inadequate education, language and contacts from the centres of decision-making. This disenfranchisement grows through people's upbringing, as they 'learn the habit of not having any control over their own direction'. The feeling is shared with their communities, who — apart from a few activists — have 'learned the habit of not having a say in their own development or changes in their own environment or social and economic conditions.'

This is accentuated in a patriarchal society in that women take whatever good or bad men want to give them.... I think that men who learned disenfranchisement in the bigger society impose it on women. I think it is a learned interpretation of how life is and how you can inflict it on others.

Even accents can underline a sense of powerlessness. Middle-class Belfast accents can alienate working-class people of both communities. This is intensified in the nationalist community, 'which is so anti-English inherently perhaps, and those accents symbolize the lack of access that people have to Westminster and for most people in this community decisions could be made in Kuala Lumpur because they have so little possibility to affect them'.

Mr Humphries says the sense of powerlessness among the young people he works with is 'so acute that they are not aware of it'. Most young people are very unpoliticized and do not equate unemployment and economic conditions with powerlessness. 'I think they have a resentment about not being able to have certain goods and lifestyles, but I think it is only those who are highly politicized on an Irish-Ulster front who are very conscious of their situation in terms of political powerlessness.'

Mr Humphries expresses his concern about social and economic issues always taking second place to constitutional issues in local politics. Politicians who espouse them do not have the charisma of fiery loyalist or republican leaders. It would need a Jim Larkin-type leader to rally people to fight against the common problems of economic and social disadvantage.

The people of the Lower Ormeau or Ravenhill cannot identify with someone like John Alderdice — they need someone who has really felt the energy of aggressive republicanism or loyalism, someone who is prepared to stand up and say there are other issues which are more important.

He says women have a greater facility for meeting on common issues:

Men have so much more to lose because of the militaristic conditioning which happens in working-class communities where there is very little kudos or respect to be gained for asking your community to love the enemy. There is much more money to be made and esteem to be engendered for a militaristic stance. I think the middle classes can risk it, and they are the people who have the ability to step above the parapet because their communities do not alienate them to the same extent.

However, Mr Humphries says he has seen young men who have had cross-community experiences and time to ponder the issues of mutual identity between Protestants and Catholics — many of them with very little reason to forgive — demonstrating 'great wisdom and great energy for understanding and forgiving'. He goes on: 'I do not have a very sophisticated view of where that could go but, in that there are young men who have suffered at the hands of 'the enemy' and who are prepared to stand up and say 'I am still a nationalist/unionist, but we have common ground and I am going to put our common ground before any conditions that I have about the Constitution, and if the Constitution changes, so be it'... that is a tremendous laying down of preference and energy.'

He said that the night of the Lower Ormeau bookie's shop massacre in 1992, his group opened a room for people to come to and discuss the issues.

Some of the young bereaved came in, and the fact that some of our volunteers in youth work are Protestants added a new dimension to the discussion. Protestants were among those who were able to express the most care and sorrow, and instances like that had considerable impact. A lot of Protestants attended the vigil and expressed their solidarity with the local people, and some young men who had vengeance on their minds were made to think about the fact that ordinary Protestants had come forward to show that they just wanted to relate to the bereavement. A series of instances like that can eventually accumulate to a wider vision.

The approach of his small youth scheme is to calculate how many years an educated, professional person has spent being educated and prepared for his/her position in society, and then try to replace some of those 10 years that a young person leaving school at 14 is missing because of disadvantage and lack of qualifications. Most young people Mr Humphries knows come out of Youth Training Programmes and ACE (Action for Community Employment) schemes which spend a year trying inadequately to redress the lack of family and school support and the huge advantages in encouragement and expectation enjoyed by their middle-class contemporaries. They come out of these schemes, 'having fulfilled their obligation to the dole, and are now settling down to unemployment as comfortably as they can make it'. He urges a realignment of government resources to allow society to look at ways of 'rehabilitating the whole young person in terms of esteem', and giving them a feeling of being embraced by a group, even if it is not their family which is concerned about their development and their needs.

MR NICK ACHESON of Disability Action contributes a personal submission on the increasingly important role of the voluntary sector in Northern Ireland. He points out that twentieth century voluntary action has its roots in nineteenth century philanthropy, a middle-class response, led by the Churches, to the poverty of the mass of people brought into Belfast by the city's rapid industrialization. The setting up of separate secular voluntary organizations was almost entirely a Protestant phenomenon, with Catholic philanthropy then, as now, tending to be much more parish-based. He gives as an extreme example of the consequences of this, the fact that today the deaf community in Northern Ireland is by and large split on sectarian lines: Catholics use a sign language they learn from Dublin, and Protestants a different sign language learned in the North, 'further isolating an already isolated and marginalized group of people'. This absurd division had its roots in the founding of a school for deaf pupils in Belfast in 1845 which required parents to register their children as Presbyterians or Episcopalians.

Until the 1960s Northern Ireland's major social service bodies had little Catholic participation and were remarkably apolitical. However, during the last 20 years, voluntary organizations have shared in 'the general collapse in the self-confidence of the Protestant community and its loss of hegemony.' This is not only due to the huge new involvement of Catholics, but also to the wider transformation of voluntary activity from philanthropic 'service' to 'action' for social change, and in particular enlarging the social and political rights of marginalized and relatively powerless groups.

The community development surge of the 1970s played a part in this, although efforts to create cross-community resistance to the devastation being wrought on Belfast's inner city working-class areas by redevelopment and the relocation of industry failed for a number of reasons. 'Community development in Catholic areas was based in different systems of community solidarity and a long-standing resistance to the state itself.' Community organizations and associated cultural activities continue to be more lively in working-class Catholic than in equivalent Protestant areas, with the latter having none of the same sense of cultural resistance and community solidarity against the Northern Ireland state.

Mr Acheson points out that if this reads as though the voluntary sector is 'irrevocably a hostage to sectarian divisions', it has to be set against some of the real achievements of the past 20 years 'through which new ideas of social solidarity, citizen action and enlargement of social citizenship have been imported and taken root'. He says a new value system has offered a powerful challenge to the sectarian structures which have historically underpinned so much voluntary action in Northern Ireland. He gives as an example of this the challenge to a 'profoundly misogynist society' posed by the women's movement, which has opened to public view the reality of domestic violence, provided a practical response through Women's Aid, and made 'great inroads into opening up new opportunities for women and in extending legal rights against discrimination'.

He goes on:

In particular the claim that sexual politics is the power relationship which actually shapes women's experiences challenges sectarianism directly. The extent to which it can do this is, of course, the key issue. Can voluntary action of the kind the women's movement epitomizes subvert existing social structures sufficiently to force political change from a changed social agenda? It has never happened in Northern Ireland before — will it now?

Mr Acheson notes that government support for the voluntary sector in Northern Ireland is enormous, around £140 million in 1992/93, with particularly large sums going to housing association grant aid, Training and Employment Agency schemes like ACE, and initiatives like the Belfast Action Teams and Making Belfast Work, which target areas of social need. This reflects the extent to which the social and economic fabric of the region is dependent on public expenditure for survival. The funding, which has increased dramatically since the early 1980s, reflects current British Government ideology which demands that social need be tackled not by government alone but by a partnership of government, voluntary activity and, where appropriate, private companies.

However, the government is anxious that funding going to deprived local communities should not be channelled into the hands of paramilitary organizations, or help to increase the status of those associated with them. This has led to 'political vetting', so that the government reserves the power to remove funding from organizations involving people it does not like. More and more it has avoided the need to do this by channelling the money through the Churches. 'This has been particularly evident in the ACE scheme, where the money has served all too often to reinforce the sectarian divisions of welfare and has given an enormous fillip to the Churches, which are consequently as firmly entrenched as almost any-where else in Western Europe.' It is likely that the Churches will also have access to increasing sums of money for community care through Department of Health and Social Services funding, he believes.

On the face of it, it looks as if the situation is moving back towards the nineteenth-century model of welfare, where the more voluntary organizations are involved in the direct provision of welfare services, the more likely is welfare to be divided along sectarian lines. The irony is that government is also looking to the voluntary sector to improve community relations and new sources of funding are becoming available to projects which may help this.

Emphasizing the extremely powerful role of government, Mr Acheson warns that the 'unintended consequences' of its policy towards voluntary organizations 'may serve to reinforce sectarian divisions where otherwise they might weaken them'. While the evidence suggests that voluntary action brings people from both main communities together in a common cause, the more voluntary organizations are drawn into delivering services in a deeply divided society, the stronger will become the pressures for par-allel welfare systems operating separately in each community. He con-cedes, by implication, that this might not necessarily be totally negative, by using the parallel of the Netherlands. There, almost all welfare pro-grammes, while funded through general taxation, are delivered through separate church-based voluntary organizations, a system which appears to have helped create the conditions for political *rapprochement* by taking off the political agenda potentially divisive education and social welfare issues.

Mr Acheson stresses the importance of the voluntary sector keeping its dis-tance from government, so as to be able to straddle divisions through what he calls 'a studied ambiguity' on the nature of the Northern Ireland conflict.

The task is to create opportunities for dialogue and joint action which will build people's trust and self-confidence in ways which may enable new political formulae to be tried and adopted. Voluntary action is not a substitute for political *rapprochement*, but can contribute to the process whereby it can more easily be achieved.

However, he warns that, given the way in which voluntary action has been embedded historically in sectarian structures,

this kind of agenda will not be easy to put into practice and will create a need for some perhaps painful re-examination of old attitudes within the voluntary sector itself. The first step must be for voluntary organizations to become more self-aware about their values, which in almost all cases are inclusive, participative, respectful of the rights of all individuals, respectful of difference, pluralistic and concerned for the well-being of all citizens whatever their personal beliefs. These are profoundly democratic values and carry a clear message about the kinds of political structures that will both reflect and nurture them. The second step will be to create structures in which this self-reflection can be applied to the sectarian world in which these organizations all must operate. Some way needs to be found to enable people to act on their beliefs in all aspects of life, so that the values developed within the voluntary sector can be applied politically.

Mr Acheson believes the sector, while reflecting society's divisions, can, because of its commitment to deeply human values of social betterment, 'open up a space where these values can come to matter in a political sense'.

He urges, in particular, more reflection on how the voluntary sector can achieve change beyond the immediate concerns of each individual voluntary organization. He sees the task of the next 10 years and beyond as one of working to articulate a 'more mature vision' of what kind of society the voluntary sector wishes for Northern Ireland. He cites, as an example of common values worth striving for, the widespread support in the region for the concept of 'social citizenship' as institutionalized in the National Health Service.

More concretely, he suggests the setting up of a university-based Centre for Voluntary Sector Study and Research, to provide a counterweight to the influence of the Northern Ireland Office, a point of contact with the international debate on the developing role of the voluntary sector, and a set of analytical tools geared to local circumstances. He also calls for funding to support a programme of training and the development of expertise in what he loosely calls 'applied social thought'; and a programme of work within existing voluntary sector networks to explore the links between their aims and local political structures, so that a more common understanding of social issues can be turned into a move towards greater political consensus.

THE 'SPRINGFIELD GROUP' — Ms May Blood, Ms Kathleen Kelly and Mrs Geraldine O'Reagan, all active in deprived Catholic and Protestant working-class communities in west Belfast — call for the creation of Community Development Trusts in local neighbourhoods. They believe that these would help to eliminate the great sense of powerlessness currently felt by local people; improve the economic viability of the district;

offer a focus for new and emerging local leadership, which ultimately could bring new energy to Northern Ireland's political structures.

Such trusts would bring together the public, private and voluntary sectors and would encourage substantial involvement by local people. There should be an equal relationship between the leaders of the trust. The group believes that the potential in the ability and talent of local people has not been fully realized by government or those who finance and support west Belfast.

In our experience many local people in west Belfast work long hours, all day, every day, to provide the basic care that supports the needs of their neighbourhood. This activity is often in support of young people, unemployed, disabled, women and children. In all these areas of activity, local leadership and expertise has developed. Those of us who have experienced this growth of confidence, feel buoyant and confident about the future of our communities.

However, despite government acknowledgment that local people should be involved in the discussions which affect their communities,

in practice people feel that their involvement is often of peripheral interest to those who control these consultations. They have little opportunity to effect change and there is no local accountability concerning the aspects of government policy and resources which are directed towards their communities. Too often those who are in control of the consultative process have access to information and resources which are not within the range of local participants, and this 'not knowing' then leads to a great sense of insecurity and alienation. Frustration on the part of government and statutory agencies at the perceived apathy of local communities misses the point when there is no recognition that consultation too often fails to provide for the possibility of making *real* changes at both policy and operational levels.

Community Development Trusts would have a membership drawn from local people, statutory bodies and local business people, and membership would be on an individual basis, with no one representing a specific interest group. Funding would come from existing statutory funds targeted for an area and the revenue-generating activities of the trust itself, as well as from the International Fund for Ireland, other charitable trusts and business sponsorship.

MRS KATHLEEN FEENAN and MRS MARY LEONARD, from Twinbrook on the outskirts of Belfast, contend that social issues of importance to women, such as housing, child care and training benefits, are not on the political agenda.

In our experience, Catholic and Protestant women find it easy to co-operate when the deliberations and activity are directed towards the issues which matter to their lives. It is our belief that if our party political masters attended to these issues, then talks, and talks about talks, would be more productive.

They say that contempt for the political process is heightened in Catholic areas, especially among youth, by the exclusion of Sinn Féin. The creation of 'real jobs' and wages is central to the well-being of the community, enabling people to clear the benefits system and rent trap. They call for more parental involvement in schools in working-class areas to help overcome problems arising when middle-class teachers do not understand the needs of pupils and to improve parent-teacher communications.

MRS SALLY McERLEAN and MRS EILISH McCASHIN of the West Belfast Parent Youth Support Group say that 'real jobs' could be created by a comprehensive and co-ordinated policy initiated by government. They call for a concentrated effort by statutory agencies to employ local people at local level. The group is experienced in dealing with young unemployed people who 'are sometimes outside the law' and 'disillusioned with life'. The young people come from Catholic areas where unemployment is as high as 80 per cent in some neighbourhoods, resources are few and 'their lives are governed by military and paramilitary forces'. The young people feel that the political process is demeaned by the exclusion from it of Sinn Féin. Unemployment should not be taken for granted, the group stresses. 'There is a need for government to acknowledge that joblessness creates dependency, and that the young people of the local neighbourhoods have ability and talent and that they want to work.'

MS RÓISÍN McDONOUGH says that the Brownlow Community Trust, of which she is director, was set up four years ago to tackle poverty among four priority groups — women, children, the long-term unemployed and the young unemployed — in the deprived Brownlow area of the unfinished 'new town' of Craigavon in Co. Armagh. It was established against a 'crisis' background common to most disaffected working-class communities in which people have been marginalized, the authority of the 'state' is continuously challenged and statutory bodies are often seen 'as remote deliverer of top-down services'. It was set up by community activists helped by senior statutory officials, and operates under the European Commission's Poverty 3 programme, one of 27 'model' action projects throughout the EC 'from which transferable methods and models of good practice in combating exclusion are being learnt to inform social policy at local and European level'.

Ms McDonough says that among its achievements so far have been setting up a creche and a users group in the local health centre; employing six lay health workers; opening a women's centre and a women's training programme; jointly sponsoring an open learning centre; starting a young mothers group, a young girls group and a children's policy forum; drawing cultural resources into the area; co-operating on a debt project; establishing an older people's planning group, and bringing in leading local businessmen to advise groups on starting small businesses.

The Trust is based on the three concepts which are central to the EC Third Poverty Programme: (1) A partnership between statutory bodies and local people to plan for the long-term economic and social regeneration of the Brownlow area. (2) Local people must be involved in decisions about how government bodies and others formulate and carry through their policies in Brownlow. (3) Poverty should be tackled by an integrated approach, bringing together measures in training, housing, education, health, the environment, employment, leisure, culture and income.

Ms McDonough believes that this experiment in partnership between government and people has particular relevance in Northern Ireland, which has limited local democracy and where, in the absence of operational regional or national democratic institutions, constitutional issues have been inappropriately displaced into emasculated local councils, which are ill-equipped to deal with them. Because of the transfer upwards to largely unelected area boards of previously devolved powers like housing, education, health and social services, the relationship between policy-makers, service providers and those on the receiving end in Northern Ireland has been particularly problematic and lacking in accountability. Ms McDonough says that, in this context, 'the concept of active citizenship with 'rights' needs to be further developed'. The question as to whether the Brownlow Community Trust is 'a sustainable alternative model of local democracy' remains to be seen. 'The 'partnership' is in its infancy.'

DR SAMUEL POYNTZ, the Church of Ireland Bishop of Connor, focuses on poverty, unemployment, deprivation and alienation and quotes Cardinal Daly, who called unemployment 'one of the greatest wrongs done to human beings in our society at this time'. He particularly mentions the unemployment and poverty in many Protestant areas, which government initiatives have often virtually ignored. There are many other kinds of poverty, too, he says. Poverty of spirit — a lack of belief in oneself; poverty of education; poverty of possibility; poverty due to poor living conditions; a sense of poverty due to a lack of role models.

Despite praiseworthy improvements in the infrastructure of Belfast, the city still has abnormally high levels of unemployment and a low level of investment; areas such as the Shankill, Falls, Tiger Bay, New Lodge, Tynedale and Rathcoole, have seen the decline in traditional Belfast industries and the drift of inward investment and industrial growth towards more peaceful and environmentally attractive parts of Northern Ireland.

Indeed, if there had been no 'troubles' over the past 20 years, the economic and social reconstruction of many areas in this city would still present a formidable task. Almost any measure one might care to name (children in poverty, unemployment, changes to the benefit system) show that the situation of the poorest has worsened over the past decade.

Despite welcome government and IDB initiatives, the good work done by voluntary and community enterprise groups and the availability of financial incentives, there has been a significant lack of inward investment in north, mid- and west Belfast. 'The numbers of unemployed in west Belfast alone are in excess of 20,000, with many more available for work if jobs were to come on the market.'

Dr Poyntz blames paramilitary violence — republican and loyalist — for deterring inward investment to Northern Ireland and says that 'the evil of violence' is not being adequately faced by all sections of the community. The debate on an economic strategy for Belfast is welcome, he says, and he urges dialogue and partnership between agencies and voluntary groups concerned with economic development in measures to improve Belfast's investment potential.

However, Dr Poyntz adds:

Some of those who vote for Sinn Féin appear to support the continuation of violence or at least have their vote appropriated by that party as support for a continuation of violence. It is important that those who exercise their vote should be aware of the economic realities of the evil scorched-earth policies which, if pursued to the end, will leave Belfast, Northern Ireland and the whole island of Ireland a poor, insignificant place on the periphery of the EC.

West Belfast is frequently portrayed as the great economic blackspot of Northern Ireland. Without denying the needs of this overwhelming 'green' area, I would point out that there are other areas in Northern Ireland which suffer from severe deprivation. Many large estates, predominantly 'Protestant', surrounding Belfast have all but been ignored by government initiatives. Some of these estates are camouflaged by their proximity to areas of considerable affluence, and it is from these deprived districts that evil psychopathic loyalist killers emerge.... I call on the IDB and government bodies to intensify their efforts to attract inward investment to Belfast and I plead for all to work together for the good of all in the community by supporting such efforts.

BALLYBEEN WOMEN'S CENTRE, in a large Protestant housing estate in east Belfast, says there is no real benefit in job training schemes. With no guarantee of employment at the end of training, 'our kids bide their time at the training schemes and then they join the army, whereas the Catholic kids would not do that'. Two years ago half the members of a local youth club joined the British army, which gives them a bit of self-respect and money. Training for the Centre's four part-time ACE creche workers would be of some value if at the end of 12 months their jobs were made permanent, the centre feels. 'Anyone who has left an ACE job here has not got a permanent job, regardless of the training. Yet we are still going through four ACE workers every year.'

THE BLACKMOUNTAIN ACTION GROUP in west Belfast says the skills and ability which exist in communities must be acknowledged by the authorities. It operates in the high unemployment Springmartin estate, a Protestant area on the edge of the greater Shankill, and says its success in establishing good links with the Housing Executive, as well as in developing its administrative office, advice centre and facilities for residents of all ages, has led to higher morale in the estate. The group says that it should be recognized that people want to work in their own areas because of fears for their security if they work in other districts, and there should be more government action to stimulate local employment creation through encouraging small businesses.

THE WOMEN'S INFORMATION DROP-IN CENTRE (WIDC) on the Ormeau Road in Belfast emphasizes the need to find employment for 16-19-year olds. They point to the shortage of places on the 12-24-month Youth Training Programmes, with the result that many young people with no qualifications or incentives to continue in education drop out and are at risk from drugs, alcohol, petty crime and, most seriously, the influence of the paramilitaries. It plans to provide a three-year, on-the-job, skills-related scheme, which eventually will be financially self-sustaining. Trainees will be given training in sculpting, painting, upholstery, internal landscaping and many other artistic skills. The Centre also includes its proposals for the 25-acre Gasworks development area, proposing that it should become an extension of the city centre in the form of an urban village, incorporating a shopping centre, a city farm, sports facilities, restaurants, shops and a whole range of craft workshops, covering such occupations as hand-knitting, pottery, wood-carving, leather-working, silversmithing, weaving and painting.

THE DUNGANNON COMMUNITY RELATIONS WORKSHOP has brought together people from a wide range of backgrounds, from Presbyterian to Sinn Féin, to listen to and discuss with each other their various experiences. In its submission the group says: 'the unique benefit of this educational process is that it derives from listening to the experiences of others which must be considered as valid as one's own. Often stereotypes built and sustained through lack of knowledge are challenged in this way.' It also causes people to become aware of and question their own attitudes.

The Dungannon CRW wants community relations training of this kind incorporated into training programmes for both the unemployed and those in work, small business schemes and graduate training schemes. Because of the polarization of Northern Irish society, such schemes may be the first opportunity for many youngsters to meet people from 'the other tradition'. A community relations element in their training would help them discuss — preferably in mixed groups — the issues of prejudice, stereotyping and sectarianism, as well as equipping them to deal with sensitive situations in the workplace and with their own feelings on political and social matters.

The group also proposes community relations workshops as part of ACE schemes, and suggests that the awarding of government grants to public and private sector employers could be made conditional on them taking up community relations training for their staff. This could start with the civil service. Other groups which could benefit from such training include the security forces, the fire and emergency services, local elected representatives, community, voluntary and special needs groups and teachers. It recommends that schools should be given a budget for the community relations training of *all* teachers — not just those involved with the Education for Mutual Understanding programme. It also suggests that, after taking part in community relations workshops, people might welcome the opportunity to debate the issues raised with their MPs and local elected representatives, a debate that could be co-ordinated by district councils' community relations officers.

THE COMMUNITY RELATIONS COUNCIL (CRC), stressing that it holds no position on a political or constitutional solution for Northern Ireland, says its main strategic aim is 'to increase understanding and co-operation between the political, cultural and religious communities in Northern Ireland'. It recommends that Initiative '92 and the Opsahl Commission should endorse the following objectives in the search for a sustainable political solution: adequate and accurate information by communities about each other's beliefs, customs, culture and attitudes; open and honest communication between people about the differences that divide them, and the fears they have about such differences; a willingness to explore persistent prejudice and stereotyping, replacing it with knowledge based on reality; the development of empathy and respect between people and communities about each other's beliefs, fears and aspirations; the capacity to make principled as opposed to loyalty-based judgments about contentious issues of discrimination and rights, and collectively agreeing on principles of justice; agreement about appropriate ways forward in the development of policing, security and legal systems in which all sections of the community can feel trust and confidence; confidence in handling divisive issues constructively, and a collective acceptance that the use of physical violence to solve conflicts is ultimately destructive to the development of relationships which are tolerant enough to bring about agreed solutions.

In the field of cultural traditions, the Council would like to see: communities feeling confident in the non-triumphalist expressions of their heritage — for example, commemorations, museums, marches and local traditions; a willingness between communities to share information about such expressions of culture and the feelings and intentions behind them — this should be allied to an agreement by the organizers of such activities that they will be sensitive to the perceptions and fears of other communities about such expressions; a capacity to reflect critically upon simplistic analyses of history which prevent communities from moving from fixed positions; an acceptance that the existence of different cultures should be accommodated within any relevant organizational, legal and constitutional structures.

MR PAUL BURGESS of Belfast (who worked as an Initiative '92 outreach worker) is concerned about the rapid development of a government-funded 'reconciliation industry' and warns that the belief that community relations is an end in itself avoids the real issue of constructing a necessary political settlement in Northern Ireland. Pointing out that the government is a major participant, he wonders whether it prefers such an imposed exercise in social engineering to a political settlement not of its choosing. He maintains that pronounced antagonism has been engendered between the Community Relations Council — which is financially 'in favour' with government — and individuals and voluntary agencies dealing with vulnerable groups like the disabled, the elderly, children, and the mentally handicapped, who do not have any cross-community remit.

He also points to a number of impediments to the full implementation of the Department of Education's Education for Mutual Understanding (EMU) programme. First, it is in the hands of teachers, who are themselves the products of segregated schooling and are already overworked because of recent large-scale educational reforms. Secondly, there is no requirement that EMU has to be compulsorily accompanied by actual contact between pupils at Protestant and Roman Catholic schools: schools can satisfactorily meet the guidelines laid down 'without ever having to meet a member of the other community'.

MS PIPPA COOKSON from west Belfast sees women being key people in that area — 'more flexible and open-minded and not so strongly locked into the 'old order''. She is particularly positive about the role of Women's Information Days in providing both facts and future options. She also recommends the use of weekend-long 'future workshops' to discuss such options for Northern Ireland and its local and divided communities. These take the form of three phases: (1) a 'critique' phase, in which everyone in the group says what is wrong with the status quo, allowing people to offload frustrations and identify matters where change is needed; (2) a 'fantasy' phase, in which people are encouraged to let their imaginations run free and outline utopian ideas about the future; (3) an 'implementation' phase, in which people go into subject groups, with the aim of producing specific and detailed plans of action. A future workshop produces projects, designed to specifications based on four basic questions: What is to be done? Who is to do it? When is it to be done? Where are the resources?

MR NICHOLAS SANDERS of Dungannon, Co. Tyrone, suggests a number of Scandinavian models for bringing 'ordinary' people into consultative and planning processes which could be used to help fill the democratic deficit in Northern Ireland. One is the 'search conference', a preliminary stage to the 'future workshops' described above. In Norway this process — involving 30-50 key local people in a 'search' for a better life for their area through studying recent local history and examining the potential of the locality and the strengths and weaknesses of its inhabitants — has played an important part in regenerating economic life in less-favoured regions.

He also recommends the 'workbook method', which is like a written 'future workshop', except that it is not necessary for the participants to meet. The biggest workbook project to date involved 22,000 Swedish members of local Red Cross organizations in planning, discussion and decision-making. A first workbook, prepared by an editorial group of key people, contains basic information and visual material on possible projects (across double-paged spreads), together with sets of questions allowing positive and negative responses, suggestions about who should implement ideas, and room for open-ended comment. It is distributed to everyone with an interest in the subject under consideration or anyone who needs to be informed about it. A second workbook details the initial findings, describes revised and/or new themes and projects and is distributed to the same people, to get them to focus on identified priority issues. A third workbook lists the ideas from the first two books in order of preference and a blank space is provided for respondents to answer questions similar to those posed in future workshops. In this way, a large number of people, many of whom might be inhibited by large, formal meetings, become involved in planning and decision-making.

MRS SHEILA O'HARA of the Gortnamona Parent Youth Support Group in Turf Lodge, a Catholic area of high unemployment in west Belfast, says that 'government has largely ignored the energy and commitment of local people to the development of social and economic resources in their own neighbourhoods'.

A series of government-sponsored training and other initiatives, such as Making Belfast Work, Belfast Action Teams, ACE, YTP, JTP and LEDU, had raised expectations about consultation and better co-ordination between statutory and voluntary sectors, she asserts.

In reality, local groups now believe that these schemes are mainly cosmetic and have a peripheral impact on the lives of those most in need. Most of the schemes are devised out of research sponsored by government and so are influenced by an agenda which is not set by the community. There is a need for a positive recognition by government that these projects at a local level, managed by local people, have the capacity to respond to the very basic needs of the local community.

Mrs O'Hara also calls for a co-ordinated programme of support and rehabilitation to help former prisoners overcome the problems of returning to the community.

PASTOR JACK MCKEE and MR ROY MONTGOMERY are deeply concerned that the dominant 'herd mentality' among young people in areas such as the loyalist Shankill Road in Belfast 'has led to the imprisonment of their own individual character'. Both men run 'the higher force challenge', a programme of personal development, covering Protestant areas of north and west Belfast, aimed at helping young people to break away from crime, drug addiction and anti-social activities. Young people in Northern Ireland, particularly those in sectarian working-class areas, face many problems, they say. 'Paramilitaries, unemployment, alcohol and drugs are a way of life for an ever-expanding number of young people in our community.' The statutory agencies should not be expected to provide all the answers; the local community has a major role to play.

Young people accept that their chances of getting a decent job are slight and they feel that nobody seems to care about their plight.

Paramilitaries are as much a way of life in working-class communities in north and west Belfast as the Boys Brigade and the Boy Scouts would be in other cities throughout the United Kingdom, and for many young people they can aspire to nothing higher in life than to be accepted into their ranks. To be 'one of the boys' is to be regarded as being someone of importance in your particular corner of society. Paramilitary leaders, past and present, are, generally speaking, revered by the young and considered to be working-class heroes. The fear of being rejected by the paramilitaries, and therefore being outside the organizations, is very real for many young people. They feel that they must join if they are not to be considered an outsider. This would cause them to 'lose face' and identity, and worse still, they would be considered 'chicken'. They are encouraged to fight for 'the cause' and are made promises of grandeur, but the reality is detention centres, prison cells, kneecapping or death for an ever-growing number of our young people.

DR KEN LOGUE, a Belfast-based consultant in community development and anti-sectarian work, says that community education, development and relations, while offering no 'solutions' in themselves, are 'important building blocks towards a situation where some kind of accommodation can be possible between the two communities and some progress made towards a more consensual society'. Community development, with its emphasis on the disadvantaged, impoverished and powerless and its values of participation, empowerment and self-help, helps to realize the potential of both individuals and groups. 'In the interests of developing this, potential community development challenges prejudice, sectarianism and the unequal distribution of resources.' It underpins collectivist approaches to education, economic development and the delivery of services in a Northern Ireland society where there have been few opportunities for communities to participate in the democratic process. He recalls that in 1991 the Community Development Review Group, of which he is a member, made a number of recommendations. These included the need for a stated Government policy on community development in Northern Ireland; that government, statutory bodies, local authorities, voluntary organizations and community groups should work together to promote community development to meet social and economic needs; that a small Independent Centre for Community Development be set up to provide a strategic overview of community development in the region; and that a £2 million Community Development Fund be established.

Dr Logue also looks at the complex phenomenon of sectarianism and ways to combat it. He sees a continuum between sectarianism and anti-sectarianism and identifies three levels at which it works and must be tackled: in personal beliefs and ideas, individual and group behaviour, and social structures. Thus he sees sectarianism at the level of ideas in terms of myths about the other community, demonizing its practices and ideology; at the level of behaviour, harassment, intimidation and discrimination against people from the other side; and at the level of social structures, institutional discrimination and social and economic advantage experienced by one community at the expense of the other.

In what he calls 'non-sectarianism', there is, at the level of ideas, an acceptance of cultural diversity and the need for equal treatment; in behaviour — a rejection of harassment and intimidation, and a commitment to equal opportunity and treatment; and in social structures — support for equal resources for both communities and not discriminating because of culture. In 'anti-sectarianism', the following would result: in ideas — a depoliticizing of cultural beliefs, multiculturalism, and having the right to hold contrary beliefs and to accord the same to others; in behaviour — non-acceptance and non-consciousness of sectarian difference in personal relationships and demanding the same from others, not using derogatory terms and not stigmatizing; in social structures — challenging discriminatory practices and structures and implementing programmes to counter them; outlawing intentional and non-intentional discriminatory practices, and overcoming patterns of disadvantage.

PLAYBOARD director Ms Bríd Ruddy says Northern Ireland likes to see itself as a child-centred society, but in fact there is no focus on children at all, with government policies being unco-ordinated. This is particularly serious given the 'no hope' attitude created in many children and young people by generations of poverty and unemployment, so that many children grow up not knowing anyone among their parents or parents' friends who has a job. The sectarian nature of society also impinges upon the play process: play broadens the child's mind, whereas sectarianism narrows it. The physical sectarian divide means that children are afraid to go into different areas and this limits their play space. Working as she does in 'community relations through play', Ms Ruddy believes that 'we need to create questioning stances in children because a lot of research shows the conservative nature of our society and this is reproduced over generations because of a narrowing vision. Since children are not able to express themselves, there is a re-run of the old attitudes, the sectarian voting patterns. It is to be hoped that these can be redressed through early intervention in the play process.' She hopes that provision of play facilities — for example, 'the development of school playgrounds as a way of enriching childrens' culture' — could supplement the Department of Education's Education for Mutual Understanding programme. She warns that if EMU is seen to be an exam-oriented school subject, its effect will be diminished.

THE WORKERS EDUCATIONAL ASSOCIATION (WEA) makes the point that its own work in adult education shows that people in Northern Ireland are capable of coming together in an open and democratic way on issues of common interest.

Voluntary bodies like ours can succeed only if people from diverse backgrounds and beliefs are prepared to work together for the good of the whole society. There is in existence a whole range of voluntary and community bodies which provide the invisible stitching which helps to keep intact the fabric of this society. The individuals and communities who participate in this voluntary movement have learned — both consciously and unconsciously — political skills which are often in advance of those practised by party political leaders. They give the lie to the idea that people in Northern Ireland are hopeless political primitives, and their courage and intelligence must be taken as an indicator of hope that we can come together to overcome our divisions.

The WEA notes that, despite the central political problem of two competing identities, it is wrong to stereotype Northern Irish people as being simply Catholic or Protestant, nationalist or unionist.

In our work in People's History, for example, we find that local identities and local traditions criss-cross sectarian boundaries, and that there are many subterranean cultures and traditions which escape — or avoid — becoming part of any distinct political territory. These are to be fostered and encouraged.

Similarly, the organization stresses its experience that it is in the darkest, most violent times that 'we are most likely to find people prepared to make sacrifices to work for a better and more peaceful society. An anti-sectarian education programme which we launched in 1991, for example, has been showing an astonishingly high take-up from communities all across Northern Ireland'.

THE ULSTER PEOPLE'S COLLEGE (UPC) suggests a 'Charter for Reconstruction' for Northern Ireland, based on the African National Congress's Freedom Charter in South Africa. This would be put together by people like those in community groups, trade unions, women's groups, civil liberties bodies, community employment and co-operative initatives, reconciliation groups, campaigns against health and welfare cuts, progressive intellectuals and Church people — 'all those, in fact, involved in the search for alternative, collective solutions to the crisis in its various forms'. Such a charter would outline general aims and objectives in the matters of concern to these 'activists': unemployment, redevelopment, the subordination of women, social policy, and so on. 'What would mark its novelty and potential popularity would be that it would synthesize these particular aspirations with the popular desire for political accommmodation — in the process both offering a new avenue for the activists to power *and* giving accommodation of 'the two traditions' a new, democratic, inflexion.' The College proposes a process leading to a 'People's Convention' to debate and ratify the charter and set up a new movement to campaign for its implementation.

DR GABRIEL SCALLY, director of public health for the Eastern Health and Social Services Board (writing in a personal capacity), maintains that the domination of public life in Northern Ireland by the 'troubles' and constitutional politics has 'created a deficit in a wide range of social policy spheres'. This deficit is visible not only in terms of public understanding of the major strands of the social policy debate, but also in the poorly developed social policies of the major Northern Ireland parties. He believes that this poverty of social policy debate and understanding 'debilitates Northern Ireland society in grappling with the many substantial problems that affect people, in addition to the problems of violence'. He singles out environment, education and transport as matters where standards in the region have fallen short.

Dr Scally warns that the development of potential democratic government structures will be handicapped by the low level of social policy debate over the past two decades. It has meant that the 'constitutional' parties have been unattractive to those who have a primary interest in social issues. 'Many people who under different circumstances would be contributing to the political life of the province have chosen to encourage the progress they wish to see through their contributions to the civil and public service, voluntary and community organizations.'

He stresses both the importance of increasing the level of social policy debate and involving a wide range of people in it — not just a civil service whose influence has been so substantially increased because of the lack of a democratic structure to which it should be accountable. He therefore proposes the establishment of a series of policy fora to cover the main social policy questions, and to bring in the talents of a wide range of Northern Irish people. The objective of each individual forum should be to explore and develop policy issues through the analysis of problems, and through public debate and the proposing of new measures. The forum would be able to commission research and reports, to invite submissions, and to publish and publicize its proceedings and conclusions. The weight to be given to those conclusions and recommendations would depend on the governmental structures in place at the time. At the very least, a government or executive should be required to consider a forum's recommendations and provide a full response if they are not to be acted upon.

In the health sector, Dr Scally calls for much broader co-ordinated action between the statutory, voluntary and private sectors beyond the traditional ambit of the health service, in order to improve the health of the Northern Irish population. He gives as an example the need for widespread co-operation between local communities, the Department of the Environment, the police, transport bodies and local councils to bring down the high death toll from road accidents. 'The level of death and injury of the roads is far in excess of deaths arising from violence connected with the 'troubles', yet attracts minimal attention.'

LITTLE SISTERS OF THE ASSUMPTION in Belfast long to see 'the state of cynicism and apathy among the general public (which they are often not even aware of) disappear'. They believe that the division between the rich and the poor is at the heart of the Northern Ireland problem, and quote a 1989 report by Dr Paul Doherty of the University of Ulster on the links between poverty and terrorism. They urge strongly that the Social Fund system — they quote the SDLP politician Eddie McGrady calling it 'inequitable and iniquitous' — should be replaced. They say voluntary organizations are becoming the 'safety net for the Welfare State, where applicants are reduced to the status of supplicants, rather than persons with rights to assistance and access to an independent appeals process.' (See also Law and Justice: Reducing the Violence.)

THE BRIDGE centre in Belfast's Lower Ravenhill Road is concerned about statutory agencies' lack of accessibility to the communities they serve. 'There is a sense that professionals and civil servants make decisions from outside which show ignorance of real situations. Access to information or resources is often hindered by cumbersome bureaucratic practices, and yet information means power. Resources are often allocated for use in 'top down' imposed programmes, whereas similar amounts may be more efficiently and effectively used for 'bottom up' schemes with greater success.' The centre stresses that 'there is a need for accessibility, responsibility, accountability, flexibility and insight on the part of government departments and statutory agencies if there is to be a lessening of the powerlessness and hopelessness experienced by communities such as Lower Ravenhill'.

It singles out the Belfast Action Team as a good model, in that it is 'staffed by civil servants who have chosen to work with the community'. They encourage creative initiatives, provide contacts with other agencies, are willing to listen and learn, operate with flexibility and personalize the bureaucracy. On the other hand, 'ACE scheme managers are accountable to civil servants, who often appear to know little about either working with communities or of the difficulties associated with the employment of long-term unemployed people'. Quality control is based on 'book-keeping accuracy and adherence to procedures'.

The centre points to exercises in local consultation by Laganside Development and the Social Security Agency. It welcomes the co-ordination of government departments on the issues of community development and advice services, and also the joint protocol on domestic violence and child abuse, which has brought closer co-operation between the police and the social services.

The Bridge concludes with a detailed list of recommendations. These include: greater accessibility by civil servants to local people and organizations — ultimately they should be accountable to local elected politicians, but only if these are making decisions free from narrow sectarian politics; the establishment of 'cottage' industries in Belfast, given that self-employment is not an option for many people; more real long-term employment rather than short-term training schemes, with their disillusioning and alienating effects on young people; the placement of community development staff to work alongside career civil servants, who in turn should be given experience of inner city communities through placements with voluntary organizations; the co-ordination of government departments to facilitate funding for projects where children, young people and parents are involved *together*, with special encouragement to work with adjoining communities; given that unemployment will continue, the development of cultural facilities to encourage individual and community self-expression and growth.

Other submissions covered problems of employment, poverty, health, and transport at community level. Among those dealing with work in and the problems of local communities — whether in a single community or cross-community context — were: the Belfast Ecology Group, Mrs Pat Campbell, Mr John Cassidy, Mr Don Cheyne, Coleraine Corrymeela Cell Group, the Cornerstone Community, Ms Sharron Darroux, Mr Francis Drake, Healthy Cities Project, Learn and Grow (Belfast), Mrs Kit McClarey, Ms Clare McKenna, Ms Louise McQuillan, Lower Ravenhill Community Association, Royal Victoria Hospital Faculty of Public Health Medicine, and Ms Margaret Walker.

Women's Issues

GRACE BENNETT from north Belfast says that, although women make up 47 per cent of Northern Ireland's population, their voice is unheard, their policies and recommendations are not represented and, in general, they are ignored and marginalized. Over the past 20 years the push for peaceful solutions has come very strongly from movements initiated by women, like the Peace People and Women Together, yet although women do sterling work at the level of community politics, they are not represented in regional or national politics. She believes this is because, first, no Northern Irish party appeals to women and, secondly, 'women do not wish to waste time listening to rubbish, when there is so much to be done in the housing estates'. She proposes that a forum or think-tank should be set up — even on a pilot basis — drawn from women from all backgrounds, from business to the community, to make recommendations about policies that affect women's lives: 'a few hundred Mary Robinsons spread across England and Ireland would do no end of good'. She says that a recent researcher at the University of Ulster found that, of all the Northern Irish parties, Alliance had the best women's agenda and the best women's involvement, yet Alliance would not appeal to 'the large number of women working at the coalface'.

MRS MILDRED SHAW, of Portstewart, Co. Londonderry, maintains that women will not be able to make their full contribution to public life until there are practical improvements in home-child care facilities and changes in working hours which allow upgraded part-time work to be regarded as normal as full-time employment. To remedy underrepresentation in the political talks process involving local political parties and the two governments, she suggests that a panel of woman across Northern Ireland be compiled and, on rotation, a number of them sit-in at the sessions and be given the opportunity to comment. 'They would only have the power of their own personal integrity and their persuasiveness; they would have no vote.'

THE EQUAL OPPORTUNITIES COMMISSION FOR NORTHERN IRELAND (EOC) says that 'the first step in working towards fair and greater participation in public and political life in Northern Ireland is the establishment of targets or goals for female representation by all institutions, political parties and public bodies'. Women comprise only 12.4 per cent of local government councillors in the region and none of the MPs or MEPs is a woman. In 1992 the proportion of women on public bodies was only 25.6 per cent and, of a total of 148 bodies, 24 had no female representation.

The EOC also urges that to ensure a co-ordinated statutory sector policy and adequate recognition for the work of women's groups, there should be a review of statutory policy about the funding of women's voluntary organizations. It is at the level of grass-roots activities that women are pre-eminent, in community support and self-help groups, anti-poverty campaigns, and so on. They are also active through women's groups. These are an important means of empowering women and facilitating their participation in society but, despite the value of their range of work, the groups in which women participate are marginalized, having little economic or political power or influence, the EOC reports.

The Commission urges policy changes towards pro-active responsibility to ensure sex equality in a number of economic and social fields. Present legislation on sex discrimination and equal pay is too limited in scope and cumbersome in procedure. It asserts that 'the failure of sex discrimination legislation to tackle the problems which it was designed to tackle is evidenced by the fact that sex discrimination still exists'. Urgent reform of the present laws should include a unified Equal Treatment Act, covering EC equality law obligations, removing inconsistencies with other legislation, and extending the scope of protection.

The EOC points out that a rise in the number of women in employment has not been matched by an increase in women's economic power. They now represent 49 per cent of the workforce, but the increase over the past decade stems from the rise in part-time service sector jobs. 'Over three-quarters of part-time workers are women, holding jobs which are in the main characterized by poorer working conditions and contracts, low wages, low status and limited prospects.'

Among the matters of concern to the EOC is the provision of equality in education, with a need to develop awareness of gender equality issues and at the higher level to target the needs of women and 'the reality of their circumstances'. The EOC says that government should 'lead the way' in introducing non-discriminatory practices and equal opportunities programmes in the workplace. 'While some changes have been made in the public sector in recent years, much remains to be done to turn broad policy objectives into practical reality.'

THE NORTHERN IRELAND WOMEN'S AID FEDERATION (NIWAF) believes that the traditional political structures in the North could learn much from the principles that women's groups employ, such as consultation, democracy, discussion and 'empowerment'. The activities of women's groups have helped bring about change for very many women and have been 'one of the most positive areas of growth within the wider political arena in Northern Ireland' in the past 20 years, although often unacknowledged by the more established political mechanism, the Federation says.

Overcoming the discrimination against women at every level of society is not simply about equalling up percentages, although that is important — for example, in politics. 'However, what is also important is that the experiences and concerns of women are represented not exclusively by women but by all public representatives.'

The Federation, dealing with the legal processes arising out of domestic violence, says that the legal system needs to be 'more accessible to its users' and must be given due consideration to the apprehension of people whose experience of extreme powerlessness is often reinforced by court procedures. Domestic violence should be a priority on the public and political agenda and requires a multidisciplinary approach, involving statutory agencies, in dealing with victims and treating the abuser.

THE AMALGAMATED TRANSPORT AND GENERAL WORKERS' UNION (ATGWU) REGIONAL WOMEN'S COMMITTEE, voicing its concern about the low pay of women workers, wants government to implement a statutory minimum wage. Since women form the majority of low-paid workers, they would be likely to benefit from the move, the committee feels. Despite equal pay and sex discrimination legislation, there are still major problems about job equality, it says. One of those is a difficulty in ensuring equal access to paid training opportunities for women already in employment. The committee says that training opportunities tend to be directed at management grades, thus effectively excluding most of the female workforce. The committee is concerned about poor working conditions for women and says that short-term contracts, which are on the increase, exclude many women from the already limited range of employment rights.

Accessible and affordable child care and other home facilities are basic to the position of women in the workforce, the committee states, and should be developed on a community basis, rather than being related to individual workplaces. Among its long-term proposals are allocation of EC equality monies on an all-Ireland basis and the establishment of a specialist child care agency, funded by both governments, on the same basis.

PROFESSOR ELIZABETH MEEHAN of Queen's University, Belfast, points out that one recent exciting Northern Irish research project (Wilford and Miller) was inspired by, among other things, 'the frequency with which women everywhere say they are uninterested in or inactive in politics, yet *are* concerned about defence, transport, health policies and so on, and *are* active in trade unions and voluntary associations'. Another (under the auspices of various groups and the Women's Education Project) will build a picture of a citizenship which 'takes account of how women *do* participate to maintain the social fabric'. She goes on:

In the absence even of 'normal' politics, perhaps it would be more surprising than elsewhere if Northern Irish women said they were interested and active in politics, as opposed to specific policy fields. Moreover, the perils of dissent — when protest labelled 'political' can be made to seem associated with paramilitary versions of partisan attitudes — might lead one to expect Northern Irish women to insist, more than others, that their activism is not 'political' but 'community' action aimed at jobs, housing, education and so on. But part of the interest of these projects is that many women's community groups and women party members are saying that the 'troubles' and preoccupation with the single constitutional issue have hidden the more complex range of women's interests and voices for long enough. Though standing up for women's rights anywhere draws on personal reserves, theirs is a badge of courage that feminists, thankfully, do not always have to wear.

(See also Politics and the Constitution: The European dimension.)

THE NORTH DOWN AND ARDS WOMEN'S INFORMATION GROUP (NDAWIG) says that the sense of isolation and powerlessness felt by many women in their areas is only exacerbated by the lack of interest shown in their affairs by local political representatives. They believe that the present party political system at local level does not facilitate women's interests nor their involvement in local politics. They propose that: (1) national political parties should not be represented at local council level; (2) candidates for local elections should be nominated on the basis of their interest and involvement in specific issues of local importance; for example, employment, women's interests, or the environment; (3) women should begin a political learning process by lobbying candidates in Northern Ireland's local elections to impress on them that the issues women consider important should become a priority of incoming councils. These would be state-subsidized child care, an increase in child benefit, equal pay, support for the financial burden of providing school uniforms and dinners, integrated education, and funding for women's groups.

THE METHODIST WOMEN'S ASSOCIATION (MWA) claims that 'the people of our land are now more isolated from each other, more confused, fearful, insecure, and live in a country where there is more homelessness, abuse, poverty, unemployment and insecurity than ever before'. Among other proposals, they advocate the integration of schools and youth clubs, where possible, and a common history curriculum in all schools in Ireland. They also regret that 'the statistics showing the number of women in politics are abysmal'.

Other submissions which dealt with women's issues, among other things (other women's group submissions are in the Social and Community sub-section), were: Baha'i Women's Committee, Ballymagroarty Family Centre (Derry), Derry Well Women, Downtown Women's Centre (Belfast), Mrs Hazel Holmlund, Kilcooley Women's Group (Bangor), Lisburn Women's Group, Lower Ravenhill Womens' Project, Jane Waterson, Women in Media and Entertainment (Galway) and Women's Planning Network.

Discrimination

Surprisingly, despite its seminal influence on the psyche of Catholics and nationalists in Northern Ireland, particularly at the birth of the civil rights Movement in the late 1960s, there were few submission on the subject of discrimination. Professor Brice Dickson deals with anti-discrimination legislation in passing (see Law, Justice and Security: Changing the Law), as do contributors in other sections.

DR GERARD QUINN of University College, Dublin, supports the argument, advanced originally by the government watchdog body, the Standing Advisory Commission on Human Rights, that the British Government should adopt an equality performance indicator in the form of a five-year target for reducing the Catholic/Protestant jobless differential from 2.5 to 1.5.

He argues that the dismantling of the 'barrier' of discrimination, where one community enjoys a position of economic privilege, is a prerequisite if both communities are to engage in purposeful discussions about their future.

Injustice has played a part in alienating Catholics to the point where some of them decided that the state is irreformable, a failed entity. Their decision must not stop us reforming the society, giving it a chance to be a successful entity, solving the inequality problem.

Dealing with the politicians' response to the Catholic-Protestant unemployment disparity, Dr Quinn says that the 'general silence' on the issue plays into the hands of Sinn Féin, which he argues, would lose much of its support to a party that tackled discrimination. 'Unlike the SDLP, Sinn Féin speaks about discrimination regularly, but never presses for a solution. The complaints are geared to keeping their voters indignant, a cynical exercise for propaganda purposes.'

Dr Quinn wants to see more US factories established throughout Northern Ireland and says that they should be staffed 'with the appropriate quotas in accordance with British, or MacBride, or other effective principles'. He says that 'John Hume's outright rejection of the MacBride principles is disheartening' and contends that the subject is so important that the SDLP leader and all sides involved in the issue should come to agreement on principles which could be grafted on to MacBride, a move which he believes would in turn put pressure on Sinn Féin to sever links with violence and work constitutionally.

Dr Quinn points out that the February 1992 statistics showed male unemployment in largely Protestant Ballymena at 15.3 per cent, while Catholic areas were much higher: Derry 33.3 per cent, Newry and Mourne 33.2 per cent, and Strabane 40.5 per cent. Progress towards equal status should have a definite timescale, Dr Quinn says.

The Anglo-Irish Agreement is there to implement reform. Is it not reasonable that the SDLP, and the Government of the Republic, should ask the Northern Ireland Secretary of State to release all possible figures concerning the comparative employment of the two communities, so that analysts can measure progress towards equal status?

He adds: 'If a constitutional party were to obtain and release figures for Catholic unemployment every month, and if those figures showed even slight but steady progress towards equality, the entire nationalist community would soon put faith in the political process, and refuse support for violence.'

Dr Quinn contends that the process of Britain creating economic fair play could have an effect on some traditional Catholic attitudes on nationalism and Protestant attitudes on 'loyalty' to Britain. 'Having shared the unemployment problem, Protestants and Catholics could begin to collaborate as equals in creating new political structures.'

MR FIONNBARRA Ó DOCHARTAIGH, from Derry, sharply criticizes the fair employment record of the Northern Ireland Civil Service and its influence, as he perceives it, on equality legislation. He suggests that a new agency, under the aegis of the Anglo–Irish inter-governmental conference, should oversee reforms within the NICS. Mr Ó Dochartaigh says that many nationalists regarded the Fair Employment Agency as a 'paper tiger' and maintains that its successor, the Fair Employment Commission, which he says is 'still tightly controlled by the NICS', is not a marked improvement. He calls for 'serious changes' in the relationship between the two organizations.

Mr Ó Dochartaigh says that, in spite of inter-governmental agencies, the Anglo-Irish Agreement and greater nationalist representation based on hard-won electoral reforms, the one unresolved item of the original civil rights is religious discrimination in jobs. 'Catholics are still two and a half times more likely to be unemployed than other sections of the workforce. As a result, for countless thousands, and youth in particular, this glaring statistic alone creates a sense of social alienation, firmly rooted in associated poverty and acute feelings of personal and community unfulfilment.'

He accuses the British government of simply 'tinkering with the problem' in setting a target for Catholics in policy-making jobs in the NICS. The current religious makeup of the NICS, Mr Ó Dochartaigh reports, is: 63.2 per cent Protestant; 36.8 per cent Catholic: with senior posts 85.5 per cent Protestant and 14.5 per cent Catholic. He says that civil liberties groups have argued that if Britain was serious about tackling religious discrimination in the workplace, it need only 'turn the economic screw' by linking it to governmental tendering and contract policies.

Provision for taking such affirmative action was actually built into fair employment legislation as recently as 1989, in response to the MacBride principles campaign in America, but has never been used. Only the mildest means of enforcement have been implemented. In the period 1989-91, the only punitive action by the Fair Employment Commission was to fine fourteen companies, who failed to comply with the statutory regulations, an average of £100; hardly more than a slight slap on the wrist.

MS POLLY DEVLIN, the writer, who originally comes from Co. Tyrone, tells of the discrimination felt by a Catholic rural community deprived of something as basic as a decent road.

The shocking fact is that you can tell when you are entering a Catholic rural area by the sudden deterioration of the roads. Whatever the underlying causes of this, and the interlocking circles, it is a remarkable indictment of the system. Driving throughout County Down, say, and into the heartland of Tyrone is to drive from modern well-tarred carriageways into pot-holed, often dangerously narrow, roads. This single feature is, for many residents of the poorer areas, a jolting symptom of their own powerlessness.

In Ardboe, Co. Tyrone, money and goodwill could make a contribution to improvment of everyday life in an area which suffers scars bequeathed by World War II. The parish is severed in two by the derelict, overgrown rem-nants of a wartime aerodrome. No real road connects the two halves and

the traffic of cars, tractors, bicycles and pedestrians has to bump over the remains of the old roads. It really is a perpetual reminder of old sores, as well as being a hindrance to the organic life of the parish (God knows, there's enough division in Northern Ireland anyway, without one small community being divided by something as easily repairable as a road).

Government ministries and the local councils cannot or will not take responsibility for the roads, and so the area lies mouldering.

It is a sad, ugly situation that would, I believe, be unacceptable anywhere else in these islands. It seems perhaps a small matter, where such big matters happen, but Ardboe is a world for the people who live there. The parish suffers through discrimination and political neglect. I really believe that if this aerodrome lay in any other more prosperous, better represented area, the roads would have been rebuilt long, long ago. The population, which is nearly 100 per cent Catholic, feel that asking for help is a fruitless exercise.

Housing

THE SISTERS OF THE CROSS AND PASSION of Larne, Co. Antrim say: 'In order to begin to rid ourselves of ghettos and peace lines, let a big effort be made to create one or more model integrated housing areas, where substantial financial incentives are offered by low rentals to tenants, and preliminary written agreements are entered into by people willing to take on the responsibility of making a go of 'living with difference'.' There should be training of local residents' groups to deal with problems like vandalism, joyriding and sectarian attacks so that 'residents would have a stake in preserving a non-violent environment in which to pursue their everyday lives.' Such experiments would also involve the provision of integrated schools. 'From the creche stage upwards, children would learn together, and divisive labels like "prod" and "taig" would lose their emotive power over time. Apart from the 'model areas', integrated coeducational schools should be options for parents in Northern Ireland provincewide.' They invite proponents of integrated education to educate the Churches and the public about their value, pointing out that there are 'several untried formulae for 'teaching' religious values'.

The Sisters say that 'the idea of people empowerment' should be at the centre of such self-help initiatives. These could also include creating two young peoples' cross-community craft manufacturing co-operatives, in an urban and a rural area, as pilot projects; job-sharing; strict application of equal opportunities legislation; and further funding for women's groups to expand their role in matters such as advising about welfare payments. The churches should be asked to make their buildings available to cross-community groups involved in creches, playgroups and youth clubs. This would enable existing funding to be spread further.

The Sisters applaud the efforts of some clergy to open a dialogue with paramilitary groups and say that as a legitimate party, Sinn Féin, as well as the Workers' Party, have to be included in political discussions: 'preconditions are counterproductive'.

MR D. GORDON KELLY, of Ballynafeigh, Belfast, says that since government recognizes the importance of integration in the workplace and integrated schooling, it should introduce legislation to encourage integrated housing. While peacelines and barriers in Belfast serve a purpose in attempting to prevent inter-communal atrocities, 'I also feel that they represent the concrete expression of a society's reluctance to attempt to reconcile and heal wounds.'

Something must be done to break the cycle of segregation and to facilitate the creation of fully integrated housing layouts, Mr Kelly asserts. An initative would be easier to implement in a new housing estate, where potential tenants were in favour of an allocation policy reflecting the numerical strengths of the two communities, e.g. 60 per cent non-Catholic; 40 per cent Catholic. Thereafter, as a house became vacant, the new tenant would have to be of the same religious persuasion as the outgoing tenant. In the case of existing housing estates, particularly where there were many owner-occupiers, the process would be more complicated. He suggests that there would have to be positive discrimination to achieve the required mix and that topping-up finance from public sources would be necessary to compensate owners who got a lower price for their property by selling into a restricted market.

Mr Kelly, a Quaker, says he feels fortunate to live in a street of 42 houses which represents approximately a 60 per cent non-Catholic, 40 per cent Catholic occupancy. In 1969 less than 20 per cent of the houses were occupied by Catholics and he would not feel threatened if the balance continued to shift towards a reversal of the 1969 position, although he acknowledges that other non-Catholic denominations 'would feel threatened' by that.

Other submissions which covered housing, among other subjects, came from Rev. David Brown and Rev. Joan Scott, Dr Leland Chou, Churches Central Committee for Community Work, Community of the Peace People, Council for the Homeless, Good Shepherd Sisters (Belfast), North Belfast Women — on housing in Protestant areas contracting while the Catholic population expands (see also Social and Community), and Religious Together (Down and Connor).

CHAPTER 14

Submissions' Summary: Culture, Religion, Identity and Education II

Culture

MR MICHAEL LONGLEY, the poet, writes about the importance of the Cultural Traditions Group, set up in 1988 'to encourage in Northern Ireland the acceptance and understanding of cultural diversity; to replace political belligerence with cultural pride'. He says the members of the Group expect 'no quick returns', and compares its long-term work to the energy, optimism and experimentation of the first post-war British Labour government. He lists some of its projects: steering grants to local publishers for good, but not otherwise commercially publishable, books on history, politics, topography, folklore, local history; funding independent producers for radio and television programmes of similar concern; the setting up of the Ultach Trust to fund Irish-language activities; funding local history studies, of which Northern Ireland is probably the most vibrant practitioner in Europe; a survey of local place-names, and the compilation of an Ulster-English dialect dictionary; supporting the John Hewitt Summer School with its 'spirit of interdisciplinary cross-pollination under an ecumenical 'regionalist' umbrella'.

Mr Longley notes that the Ulster tragedy which brought the Group into existence still shapes its deliberations. 'At a recent meeting I suggested that our aim should be to lift the community into consciousness and self-consciousness — the forming of a new intelligentsia, if you like — since it is the intellectual (and, indeed, the emotional) vacuum that makes room for the violence. We are involved in cultural preparation, a constellation of conversions, gradual processes which short-term thinking by Government could easily abort.' He then recounts how, as an Arts Council officer, he was ordered, allegedly on security grounds, to discontinue funding to the Conway Education Project in west Belfast, which offers academic and recreational courses and a wide-ranging cultural programme, and which because of its location inevitably involves Sinn Féin supporters. He had argued that 'espousal of plurality could not be selective in this way; that withholding funds on the stated grounds strengthened the hand of the paramilitaries against moderating influences inside and outside the community; and that the ban not only damaged the trust which the Council's officers had built up on the Falls Road, but also tarnished their reputation for neutrality and thereby made it less safe for them to work in the area.' He believes there was similar short-sightedness when funds were cut to the Glór na nGael language group (since restored).

Patrick Kavanagh's famous distinction between the provincial cast of mind — abstract, imitative, sterile — and the parochial — close, familiar, teeming with life — applies to Northern Ireland in a particular and urgent sense. Terrified of Irishness — the cultural ideology of the Free State and then of the Republic — unionists have clung to what after 1968 has increasingly become known as The Mainland, and to cultural importation. Those who depend on imports run the risk of themselves becoming exports. In his essay 'Crossing the Border', Hubert Butler describes 'the more formidable of Ulster's enemies' as 'those who keep quiet'. '"Time is on our side"', they are saying. ... The province has the artificial vitality of the garrison town and no organic life. ... if ever the pipelines were cut, it would perish.'" Butler ends his essay by suggesting that 'Ulster would no longer be of value to Ireland if she were robbed of her rich history, her traditions.'

Butler thought that reconciliation would not be complete in the South until it had happened in the North; and that it might develop out of regional loyalties. Meanwhile, John Hewitt had begun his work of focusing our attention on Ulster's indigenous cultural resources. 'Ulster', he wrote in 1947, 'considered as a region and not as the symbol of any particular creed, can, I believe, command the loyalty of every one of its inhabitants. For regional identity does not preclude, rather it requires, membership of a larger association.' Hewitt did not seem too bothered as to whether that association might be a federated British Isles or a federal Ireland.

In Ulster, cultural apartheid is sustained to their mutual impoverishment by both communities. W. R. Rodgers referred to the 'creative wave of self-consciousness' which can result from a confluence of cultures. In Ulster this confluence pools historical contributions from the Irish, the Scots, the English and the Anglo-Irish. Reconciliation does not mean all the colours of the spectrum running so wetly together that they blur into muddy conformity. Nor does it mean denying political differences. As William Faulkner said: 'The past isn't dead and gone. It isn't even past yet.' But reconstructing the past or constructing identities has too frequently been a purely propagandist activity in Northern Ireland. The Cultural Traditions approach involves a mixture of affirmation, self-interrogation and mutual curiosity. To bring to light all that has been repressed can be a painful process; but, to quote the American theologian, Don Shriver: 'The cure and the remembrance are co-terminous.'

We are beginning to find in our own parishes the painful, liberating truths.

THE TEMPO HISTORICAL SOCIETY in Co. Fermanagh, a group of rural people, none of them well-off, with different views on the political situation, has become one of the most active historical societies in the country. The Society does not accept the simplistic viewpoint that regards history as a source of division.

Commemorations and celebrations are divisive, but serious analysis and scholarly debate is a different matter. Certainly historians argue, but they always take into account the full picture. Theories are revised and reworked, but the aim is to get as near to the truth as possible, not to strengthen an already held viewpoint.

The Society has learned that history has been taught selectively; found the most inspiring talks given to them by historians were those that revealed unknown facts. They cite Professor John Barkley's revelation that in the nineteenth century the Presbyterian Church was the only Irish Church in which it was compulsory for ministers to learn Irish before ordination.

The United Irishmen are very attractive from a cross-community viewpoint because that was a time when Presbyterians and Catholics united against the establishment. It proved that our divisions are not of immemorial origin and the idealism of that time is inspiring. These are also the roots of republicanism. Can someone not discover common ground here and produce an ideological breakthrough? Our day of lectures, drama and music, called 'A Brotherhood of Affection', was attended by around 100 people from all walks of life and shades of opinion. We are doing our bit in a small way to bring the academics into contact with ordinary people.

The Society says that local history has led its members to an interest in the Irish language. It points out that a positive feeling towards the language has in the past been shared by all sections of the people: for example, Charlotte Brooke, an ancestor of the well-known Fermanagh unionist family, was an important collector of Gaelic literature. They praise the Belfast-based, Irish language body, the Ultach Trust, for 'fostering goodwill towards Irish in a gentle, non-aggressive way'.

The Society also puts on a wide range of women's studies classes. It points out that Northern Ireland does not have one woman politician of high stature and asks why.

Would a woman's solution be significantly different? To move into a military mode of thinking is to deny all feminine values. The values which women try to teach their families, which are also the core values of Christianity, are set aside as irrelevant — we have all been bearing the cost of this.

Another key and popular element in its programme is traditional music: 'our philosophy on music is that it is a common heritage'. The Society points out that musicians from a Protestant background like Len Graham are in the forefront of promoting this musical culture, which is one that belongs to everybody.

Local historical societies are not generally affiliated to any Church or political grouping. This gives them great potential for cross-community mixing.

Unfortunately, our Churches are so efficient at organizing events and clubs for their people that this is one of the chief causes of segregation. There are very few non-aligned societies one can join in Northern Ireland. Adult education is one of the honourable exceptions.... Social meeting and ensuing friendship and trust has got to be one of the ways of improving this society from grass-roots level.

The Tempo Historical Society then lists some of the problems it has encountered:

(1) There must be a neutral venue. Pages could be written about what constitutes a neutral venue. (2) People's attitudes are so ingrained that it is difficult to convince them that you are a genuinely cross-community organization. (3) They are so used to mixing socially in single-religion groupings that they do not consider anything else. (4) They will make judgments about your group by looking at the religion and politics of the majority of its members, rather than

by seriously examining what you are doing. (5) People will pick and choose which history talk they go to, perhaps favouring speakers and topics dealing with their 'side'. This is a very great pity. Anyone who has attended all our events will have had the opportunity to gain a better understanding of all the elements of our society.

The submission concludes by saying that Northern Ireland's problems 'need the application of the very best minds to suggest a way forward. We do not think that these are our politicians.'

PROFESSOR SIMON LEE's submission, entitled 'Lost for Words', argues for the need to think seriously about the language with which we communicate, as part of the process of 'broadening and deepening dialogue which is the hallmark of Initiative '92.' Quoting Vaclav Havel's claim that 'important events in the real world...are always spearheaded in the realm of words', he argues, for example, that

clear thinking about the 'security forces' begins with abandoning that phrase and distinguishing the police and the army whose functions, lawful authority, strengths and weaknesses should not be confused.

The linguistic-starting point for much dialogue, and virtually all policy, concerning Northern Ireland is the assumption that there are two communities, cultures or traditions, one team being Protestant, unionist, loyalist or British, the other being Catholic, nationalist, republican or Irish. Yet a community is not the same as a culture or a tradition. Nor are there only two teams in Northern Ireland. The point is not just that the present rhetoric rules out of existence certain groups, such as Northern Ireland's Chinese, Muslims and travelling people, worrying though that is. The argument is rather that we need the vocabulary to change so as to reflect our present multiple identities.

Within any single aspect of our identities, such as the political one, a community will encompass a spectrum of views from dry to wet, soft-line to hard-line, or diehard, radical through progressive to liberal to moderate to conservative to traditional to reactionary. Adjectival poverty in Northern Ireland, however, conceals the varieties within any group.

The only word much used to criticize developments, or the lack of them, here is 'undemocratic'. This is often a misnomer for 'unelected', part but by no means the whole of the story of rights-based democracy which would insulate various decisions and interests from simple, or even super, majorities. Democracy rests upon a tension between respect for the wishes of majorities and for the rights of minorities. The majoritarian (mis)understanding of democracy can lead to a polarization in which democracy is seen as a zero-sum game. Yet we are all diminished when anyone's rights are violated or left unprotected. The two teams' rhetoric has obscured this truth. The Irish language, for instance, is mistakenly attributed to one team, and any attempts to promote it are then seen in terms of victories and defeats for the two teams. Our vocabulary should instead enable us all to see that we all grow if linguistic or other rights are safeguarded.

In his submission, Professor Lee calls for 'a linguistic world in which we acknowledge the subtle differences between identities based on perceived religious community backgrounds; those based on citizenship, and those based on aspirations for political structures, let alone those based on other facets of our identities, such as gender, class, linguistic fluency, locality'. In such a world, one would be able to distinguish within each of those identities 'those who will identify more strongly or weakly (e.g. believing, lapsed); those who have a more or less urgent agenda (e.g. short-term imperatives, long-term aspirations); those who conform to a tradition and those who seek to change the culture within the community (e.g. moderate, conservative, radical)'. It would be a world 'in which we talk about accommodating the rights of all these diverse people and groups through such democratic notions as proportionality'.

MR SAM McAUGHTRY, the writer, says that 'as a Protestant who has never had a problem with embracing my Irishness, and indeed rejoicing in it, I have been aware for many years that this single gesture brings with it more warmth and goodwill from Catholics than any other Protestant response within the context of our divisions'. Given this, 'Catholics are prepared to accept that, my Irishness notwithstanding, I prefer to live under the United Kingdom system of government'.

There is a fear of things Irish in the Protestant community. In the North the IRA has all but appropriated the Irish language, and the other Catholic Irish speakers are silent on the issue; Fianna Fáil politicians at their conferences have made the language elitist; the Gaelic Athletic Association's ban on the army and the RUC is seen as sectarian; the task of persuading Protestants to encourage the growth of Irish culture, never mind embracing it themselves, is a huge one. But Catholics can help. Already there is support within the GAA for the removal of the Ban, including senior clergy in Thurles, where the GAA began. Northern Catholics who support this stance should be encouraged to speak out. Irish-speaking Catholics should ease the concerns of Protestants by condemning politicians who use the language for political ends. Protestants could be advised that, other considerations apart, it would be a tremendous political gain for them to encourage the spread of Irish culture within their own community. At one stroke it would earn them a new respect from constitutional nationalists, making for a more tolerant climate in future negotiations on the government of Northern Ireland; and it would remove from those who support republican violence one of their most potent weapons — the allegation that unionists are outsiders, aliens, Brits.

Mr McAughtry believes that

by denying their cultural birthright to the degree that they do, Protestants lose credibility in the eyes of the rest of the world. It is sad for someone whose family has been in Ireland for a couple of hundred years to deny being Irish. It is sad to claim Britishness as one's culture; there is no such thing as a British culture — the people in Britain are either English, Welsh or Scottish. It is equally sad to claim that one is an Ulsterman, yet not Irish, since Ulster is a province of Ireland. Protestants should be helped. Everyone else but themselves sees them as Irish. They go into any serious negotiations for good government a goal down because of this.

There were a number of submissions which criticized the role of the media in Northern Ireland. Mr Sam Butler, a former editor of the Ulster *News Letter*, says 20 years of violence and political upheaval have conditioned people, at home and abroad, to judge everything Northern Irish against the background of 'the troubles', to define everything that happens in terms of conflict. This negative attitude has been 'heavily influenced, indeed reinforced, by a media which is driven by violence and political confrontation'. He goes on:

The media cannot be expected to ignore or downgrade deliberately security incidents or some political comments. But the positioning of certain types of stories deserves to be questioned. For example, does a shooting incident in which no one has been killed or injured merit top of the news bulletin or front-page treatment? The violence and political controversy have provided journalists with 'easy' stories. The quality of newspaper and broadcast coverage has been influenced adversely by financial considerations over the past 20 years. Northern Ireland newspapers, in particular, have not had access to the personnel and financial resources to cover the issues thoroughly. Reporting and feature staffs have been reduced. This has left newsdesk personnel facing a dilemma. Security incidents tend to be given an exaggerated priority because newsdesk staff endeavour to cover every such incident to avoid being caught out by an atrocity evolving from what originally appeared to be a minor event. Press releases and statements have gained in importance because they can be processed quickly and easily and help to compensate for the shortage of reporting staff.

(See also Politics and the Constitution: Local Government Reform.)

THE CENTRE FOR RESEARCH AND DOCUMENTATION (CRD), as an organization concerned with the parallels between Irish and Third World experience, 'wants to draw attention to the importance of the colonial legacy for understanding contemporary Ireland, its relationship with Britain and with the wider world'. The Centre argues that there are at least four colonial dimensions to the Northern Ireland situation.

First, along with the South, the North may be a beneficiary of its neo-colonial role as part of the EC. Secondly, to some (albeit a decreasing) extent, the North may be a victim of the economic colonialism of multinationals, with their headquarters elsewhere. Thirdly, it may be argued, as many unionists do, that Direct Rule is a form of administrative colonialism, where Northern Ireland is ruled by British Ministers and a civil service with little local political accountability. And finally, there is the sense in which many of the leading protagonists of the violent conflict still see themselves as 'settlers' and 'natives' after over 300 years of coexistence. Nowadays the terminology itself may be used infrequently, but the mentalities associated with 'settler' and 'native' elsewhere are still rooted in many ways of articulating division and conflict.

The Centre says that one does not have to argue that Northern Ireland is directly comparable to 'settler-native' conflicts in countries like South Africa, Israel and Algeria, to appreciate the extent to which 'settler' and 'native' mentalities can contribute to the intensity of the conflict and hatred which ensues.

Writers on colonialism in the Third World have noted the relentless and mutually destructive reciprocity of settler-native relationships. 'Settlers' need 'natives' and vice-versa. One group defines the other. In Northern Ireland it might be argued that loyalists need republicans or nationalists to demonstrate their own loyalty. Nationalists for their part are often proud to proclaim their disloyalty, making it part of their own communal identity. One of the key aspects of the 'settler' myth is its highly ambiguous relationship with the motherland. The fear of being sold out, the sense of being the carriers of metropolitan civilization in a hostile environment, and the sense of continuous threat from the 'natives' all combine in an ideology of conditional loyalty. A strong sense of self-reliance is threatened by a sense that survival depends on help from the metropolis.

The 'settler' myth denies the accusation of usurpation made by 'natives' by stressing the improving mission of the 'settlers' — their scientific and technical superiority, their more rational forms of religion, their greater entrepreneurial capacity and sense of social discipline, their superior roads, welfare systems and hospitals. The 'native' response is to stress the degree to which such superiority is based on expropriation and privilege while counterposing their own myth of cultural or spiritual superiority.

Even more important than these surviving myths is 'the commitment to coercion which lies at the centre of 'settler-native' mentalities. Basic to the myth of beleaguerment and self-reliance is the 'settler' myth of the right to 'lawfully' coerce the 'native'. Militant 'natives', on the other hand, mirror the 'settler' commitment to coercion and indulge in what Albert Memmi has called the 'nostalgia for arms'. This commitment to coercion has many resonances in Northern Ireland. The primacy accorded to coercion can be seen in demands for ever more soldiers, guns and tougher security policies — in the rhetoric of 'elimination' and 'extermination' of one's opponents and where primacy is accorded to armed struggle.' (See also Politics and the Constitution: Talking to Sinn Féin and the Paramilitaries.)

THE CELTIC LEAGUE (LONDON BRANCH) challenges the 'pernicious myth' that there is an intrinsic link between the Irish-language and Catholicism. They want to establish the principle that 'the indigenous language is and should be of interest to all our people', pointing out that Irish-language movements have provided scope for co-operation and friendship among people of varied backgrounds. They recall the work of the 17th-century Church of Ireland Bishop of Kilmore, William Bedell, in translating the Old Testament into Irish; Protestant Conradh na Gaeilge activists like Rev. Frederick O'Connell, Robert Lynd (a Belfast Presbyterian), Earnán de Blaghd and Douglas Hyde; and, in the present day, the Methodist and Presbyterian Irish-speakers, Risteard Ó Glaisne and Terence McCaughey.

THE HOLYWELL TRUST in Derry — formed in 1989 to 'focus on developing personal and communal empowerment processes in the North-West' — welcomes Initiative '92 as the beginning of a process of opening up to different styles of approach.

Everyone is aware of the complexities of the situation in Northern Ireland and how simplistic 'solutions' may be viewed with a wary eye. We are not putting forward any such solutions. We are much more concerned with setting in train processes which will help to bring about outcomes which are respectful and celebratory of differences (individual and communal) and will thus lead to more appropriate structures and institutions.

The Trust believes that the old attitudes are changing. The traumatic events of the past two decades have shown how 'demeaning and nonsensical' is the old attitude which saw Derry as a peripheral area, peripheral to a world-view which is 'centralist and which measures 'success' only in such quantifiable terms as economic development, levels of unemployment, investment and expenditure and rates of income'.

Developments in technology and communications have underlined the redundancy of such concepts, replacing them with more liberating ideas, such as interdependence, global awareness, individual responsibility, innovation and creativity, and the lifestyles and methods of organization appropriate to those ideas. In this new context, they believe it is the destiny of the people of Derry and the North-West that

> they should play a significant role in facilitating the growth in understanding how individual differences may be celebrated; how prejudice may be reduced; how the environment may be cared for; how neighbourhoods may best be managed; in short, how we may find creative expression and meaning in our lives. With this determination, the city and its communities becomes a place of encouragement, excitement, exploration and enablement, and a significant reference point for people from any part of the planet.

The Trust goes on to identify the elements in its vision for Derry, first under the title 'the North-West as an area of communal celebration'. In recent years these have included the City Council's 'enormously successful pageant' and specially commissioned symphony to commemorate the Siege (or Relief) of Derry, the series of events under the Impact '92 banner, and the 1992 Beyond Hate conference. This latter event followed high-level international conferences held in previous years in the USA, Israel and Norway to study hatred, the 'cancer at the root of human relationships — among individuals and entire nations'. It was opened by President Mary Robinson, and among the many internationally renowned participants were the former Beirut hostages Terry Anderson, Father Lawrence Jenco, Brian Keenan and Terry Waite.

Under the aegis of the Centre for Creative Communications, five prominent people were asked to give a lecture or a workshop and accept an honorary 'city chair', respectively of the environment, liberation, theatrical innovation, compassion and celebration. In May 1992 participants throughout Ireland came together with a panel of international speakers for a Forum on the Changing World of Work. The Different Drums project, initiated in 1991, has brought together young people on a cross-community basis, first in an exchange with young people in New Brunswick, Canada, and then to create a drum troupe based on the different indigenous Irish drums.

Under the title 'the North West as an Experimental Area', the Trust proposes a number of innovative projects. These include exploring the possibility of negotiating agreements with the security forces and the paramilitaries to make Derry a demilitarized zone; making the Foyle basin an experimental centre for harnessing wind, wave and even solar power, and Derry the experimental site for a free, environmentally friendly public transport system; making the city an interpretative centre as an extension of the work done by the Inner City Trust on revitalizing it through building museums, craft centres and heritage centres; building on the work of the Orchard Gallery to make Derry a visually exciting city; a voucher system for voluntary work, by which local government can reward work for the community with 'perks' like tickets to the theatre or to Derry City Football Club; the work that is already going on to create Ireland's first hands-on science centre; a single, accountable, cross-border, decision-making body to manage the ecosystem of the River Foyle; the development of Derry as a cultural centre through building first-class theatre spaces, rock concert venues, hotel accommodation and related infrastructure.

If plans were developed and implemented on the basis of such a vision, then Derry's relationship to the rest of Ireland and the world would change. Derry would be an example. And rather than our city leaders going elsewhere to see how things might be done, others would come to Derry to see how it must be done; to see what must be done to change from dependency and depression to collective creativity and celebration; if a city is to be a place where citizens can find some meaning, some noble meaning, in their lives.

PROFESSOR EDNA LONGLEY says that

the Republic is deeply implicated in the problems of Northern Ireland, in that Ulster Protestants see themselves as making a last stand for the stake of Protestantism in the island as a whole. Conversely, Ulster Catholics are not entirely in the victim-position since they draw strength from the pan-Irish Catholic constituency. Protestant attitudes in the North cannot be divorced from the exclusionary behaviour of the Free State and the Catholic Church towards Southern Protestants (not to mention the burnings and killings of the 1920s). Articles 2 and 3 are a symptom, not a cause. Here I do not urge surrender to unionist positions, but serious recognition, of their cultural basis. Among other things, this means bringing the religious basis of Irish nationalism frankly to the surface. I stress the role of the Republic, because it is the only counter on the board with any freedom to move — a freedom it has been too cautious, immature or indifferent to use.

She believes that 'the vocabulary of Irish — and British — political discourse is misshapen by obsolete and tendentious cultural ideologies. The talks failed for lack of language. Unionism appeals to the lost codes of Imperial Britain, while letting the Republic appropriate 'Ireland' or 'Irish' to itself. This appropriation, internalized at home and exported abroad, has obscured cultural differences throughout Ireland, and driven Ulster Protestants to identify themselves as 'British' rather than 'Irish'. Both these terms are constructs — not God-given truths. The Free State's founding ideology was the least generous and most distorted version of Irishness on offer at the start of the century.'

On cultural grounds, she wants the problem of Northern Ireland to be widened on an 'archipelagic' as well as a European front.

Archipelago can be code for unionism, just as 'this island' (see John Hume) can be code for nationalism. But as a border-zone, a Bosnia, an Alsace-Lorraine, Northern Ireland does not lend itself to domination by any single 'national' ethos. In practice, its citizens pick 'n mix from a range of cultural choices. Thus acknowledgment of *de facto* affiliation to two islands must inform any new institutional framework. A spirit (at least) of condominium would serve to undermine both absolute claims.

Who owns Irish nationalism? Professor Longley asks rhetorically.

There is an asymmetry in the propaganda war because, as a secessionist political creed, Irish nationalism has been getting its act together for 150 years. However, today its case is fragmenting in that ownership of its core values is disputed between Sinn Féin, the SDLP, and the political class in the Republic. Not only 'revisionist' history, but social evolution, places the mentality of most people and politicians in the Republic at a considerable remove from the ghetto tunnel-vision of Sinn Féin — and increasingly from the SDLP. Growing pluralism in the Republic must be explicitly linked to a more sophisticated understanding of the North. I am not so much concerned about the *ethics* of talking to Sinn Féin, as about whether they have anything to say — given that their cultural vocabulary can be seen as either quaintly old-fashioned, or (more malignly) as a sinister throwback to the virulent, Volkish element in late nineteenth century nationalism.

She also believes that 'much trouble is caused by the perception that Dublin and the SDLP share a common agenda, whereas London is distancing itself from the unionists. Also by Dublin's acceptance of SDLP-speak, rather than developing its own vocabulary. London and Dublin should, mutatis mutandis, maintain a similar distance from their Northern clients, and Hume's insistence that 'going to the heart of the problem is the relation between the unionist people and the rest of the people of the island' should be linked to a sense that 'the relationship between the nationalist people of Ireland and the rest of the archipelago' also matters. The massive social and cultural traffic across the Irish Sea seems below the level of government consciousness in both jurisdictions. It is high time that the UK and the Republic sorted out their own relationship within the archipelago and the EC. This would enable them to deal more effectively with the North. Finally, John Hume's view of Ulster Protestants is ignorant, stereotypical and full of post-1921 ideological assumptions.'

On religion and cultural defence she is similarly blunt.

The Churches — especially the Catholic Church — are primarily responsible for 'ghettoizing' this community, and are doing nothing *structural* about it. Increasing apartheid allows totalitarian, fascist and murderous demonization of the Other. The Northern Catholic Church, still locked into a nineteenth-century relationship with nationalism, is also pursuing its own interests, in that Northern Catholics can be kept 30 years less liberal than their Southern counterparts. The perceived necessities of religion-based cultural defence in a frontier-zone has produced the partly irrational victim-psychologies of both communities — witness the Protestant paramilitary escalation.

She finds 'two traditions' to be an inaccurate and unhelpful concept. The work done by the Cultural Traditions Group in Northern Ireland, and begun by the Cultures of Ireland Group in the Republic, is an example of progress at the micro-level which should be attended to and expanded. 'There will be no lasting solution until the simplistic ideologies put in place in the 1920s have been dismantled.'

Professor Longley ends with a number of conclusions:

(1) The Republic, if it were to reflect more deeply on its responsibility for the Northern crisis, has the power to change the situation. (2) The UK and the Republic must work harder on the kind of relationship that befits EC neighbours with exceptionally close cultural connections. (3) 'Archipelago' may be an awkward word, but it is an important idea. (4) The Republic needs a cultural policy, perhaps under Michael D. Higgins's department, which would take the North — and all its cultural ramifications — into account, and spill over into the education reforms now under way. (5) Northern nationalist and unionist politicians must never be allowed to think that they have gained an advantage over their opponents. This may mean treating them equally badly. (6) Dublin and London must speak and act together at all times.

DR BOB CURRAN, of Portrush, Co. Antrim, begins by telling stories about his staunch Ballymena Presbyterian grandmother taking him to an old Catholic woman for a 'cure' for ringworm. Yet she would dismiss the folk tales told by her husband, Dr Curran's Irish-speaking south Armagh Protestant grandfather, as 'nonsense' and 'very Catholic'.

'There were many good Catholics, she insisted, but 'they had a very different culture to us' and it was best not to have too much to do with that.' That was over 35 years ago. Dr Curran was shocked, however, to hear exactly the same views less than five years ago from a 14-year-old boy he was teaching in an almost exclusively Protestant school in Coleraine.

Both he and the rest of his class told me about the superstition of Catholics, of their utter gullibility and of how easily their priests controlled them. They believed, I was told, in banshees, fairies, witches and ancient heroes — not like the Protestants, of course. There were two 'traditions' in Ireland, the boy went on, two different cultures which were both mutually exclusive and distinct. Both traditions were fundamentally opposite to each other and could never, in his opinion, be reconciled. This, he said (though not in these exact words) was the barrier to any political or widespread social progress in Northern Ireland.

Catholics looked towards the culture of the 'priest-ridden and deeply superstitious' Irish Republic, which was anathema to the Protestants, who looked towards England and Britain (which in turn was anathema to the Catholics). The Protestant perspective had to remain on top in Northern Ireland; if the Catholics wanted Irish traditions, let them go to the Republic. This perception was widespread in the community from which the boy had come.

On the other hand, he recalls that young Catholics he grew up with also perceived themselves as having a different 'culture' from their Protestant counterparts, one based to a great extent on the myths and legends of ancient Ireland. Protestants demonstrably lacked such traditions. They also had 'no rich tapestry of traditional music and folk tale' and were the poorer for it. Protestant traditions were often viewed as inferior to their own, a view that frequently translated itself into their perceptions of the Protestants themselves.

Dr Curran believes that the Northern Ireland problem lies not with politics but with something more fundamental — 'our *perception* of ourselves as having two distinct cultures and traditions'. However, he argues that 'there may be more to unite both cultures than to separate them', and much of it can be discovered in a common folklore and folk tradition. 'Rather than there being two cultures to be accommodated, there is a single tradition — that of Northern Irishness — from which certain sections of the community, either by accident or design, exclude themselves.' In his own studies he has found stories, tunes and traditions in Northern Ireland Protestant communities having counterparts in Catholic communities in the Republic. However, among Northern Protestants there is a perception that these traditions are 'nonsense', not worth sharing or passing on, which means they tend to die out because people, and particularly younger people, are encouraged to pursue other interests.

He believes this can be overcome through educating children to value their culture and traditions. He does not see this as a cultural process of 'Irishization' in a narrow religious/sectarian sense, or a move towards a Catholic perspective, but as 'a celebration of our common heritage — both as Catholics and Protestants — within our respective communities and upon the island of Ireland.' He recalls the 18-month long schools-based folklore collection project in the Republic of Ireland during the 1950s, which 'not only established a valuable cultural archive but also created a shared sense of cultural, communal history and identity among the pupils who collected the material'. Pupils were encouraged, for example, to collect from their parents, grandparents and relatives. Such a project could 'provide the basis for a shared community experience and could open the eyes of those who are going to form the next generation in Northern Ireland to the wide and rich spread of tradition which exists in Ireland'. He says that the current provision for teaching 'Irish folklore' in the National Curriculum is totally inadequate and needs far more thought, planning and backup, and suggests courses beginning at primary level which would emphasize the exploration of a shared culture as a 'consciousness-raising' exercise, allowing children to discover how much heritage they had in common.

Protestants have constantly struggled with (or have been hostile to) any concept of an 'Irish identity' because they perceive it as being different and alien to their own. It was almost as if Ulster was not a province of Ireland, but rather one of the English shires. All talk of ancient Irish heroes and study of localized folk tales has been heretofore viewed (by Protestants and Catholics alike) as exclusively Catholic in its tone. Such a view must first be effectively challenged within the classroom. Such a perspective must also be challenged within the Catholic population — folklore, Irish myths and legends must not simply be seen by Catholics as their exclusive province, but rather as having roots within Protestant tradition as well.

The Lower Sixth-Form Group at COOKSTOWN HIGH SCHOOL, Co. Tyrone, a mainly Protestant school, believes it is essential that pupils be given more opportunity to know something about their own tradition. They say that a recent questionnaire in their general studies group revealed some 'disturbing gaps' in their knowledge of Ulster and Irish history, and about Northern Ireland's institutions and prominent people. Pointing out that Education for Mutual Understanding (EMU) and Cultural Heritage courses are not taught to sixth-formers, they ask how they can be expected to learn about the Irish Catholic tradition when they have such limited opportunities to learn about the Northern Irish Protestant tradition, with which they are supposed to identify. They urge that the study of history, from which so much misunderstanding and bias derive, should be made compulsory for all pupils, or some form of Irish/Ulster Studies course be provided. They urge that the writings of the poet John Hewitt should be studied so that young people can learn both about Northern Ireland and about his 'humane and liberal attitudes'.

They stress that many people see integrated education as the most effective way for young people to learn about each other's traditions and religious beliefs. 'Where there is opposition to integrated education, young people should be enabled to understand the reasons for the objections. Would Protestant children, for example, know what is meant by a 'Catholic education', which the Catholic Church tends to regard more highly than integrated education?' They believe many young people have very little understanding of the terms 'Protestant' and 'Catholic'; they accept myths they have picked up; many have prejudiced views — for example, some young Protestants refuse to enter a Catholic Church but are not sure why; there are few if any opportunities in school to learn about Protestantism and Catholicism. Finally they warn Church leaders 'not to lose the respect of young people through over-identification with one tradition'. They question whether a clergyman should be an active member of a political party, much less an MP, party leader or member of a sectarian organization like the Orange Order. 'If young people are to respect the work of religious leaders, it is most likely that they will do so where these leaders are involved in helping the underprivileged and speaking out against injustice.'

MR PADDY FLEMING and SISTER GENEVIEVE, respectively a teacher and a former principal at St Louise's Comprehensive School on the Falls Road, Belfast, propose a number of innovative cross-community cultural projects. Mr Fleming suggests a Media, Arts and Communication Centre to explore culture, tradition and community life in Northern Ireland and to be situated on the Belfast 'peace line'. It would use video, television and the arts to allow both communities to explore issues and challenge commonly held perceptions, and a central element would be the training of young people in media, theatre and other techniques. A preliminary project involving making a series of radio programmes on urban and rural community life is already under way.

Sister Genevieve says concentrating on Catholic and Protestant West Belfast ('where the 'troubles' started and where they will end') should be a priority.

Young parents on both sides of the 'peace line' have to meet in a natural 'setting'. They are totally ignorant about how much they, as pawns in the political game, have in common. What about nursery schools on the peace line? Parents can take their children to these schools in the morning and call for them in the afternoon; there would also be occasions when the schools would have meetings and functions during the year. In this climate the parents will get to know one another. Friendships will be formed gradually. Playgroups might be an idea if nursery schools are impossible.

She also suggests having some Catholic and Protestant teachers in all schools in west Belfast. On another issue, she points out that

there are young men from both traditions in west Belfast who have done time in prison for involvement with paramilitaries a number of years ago. Quite a few have studied with the Open University and all have renounced violence. Both traditions mix naturally and have formed friendships. They want to repay society by doing something positive with the youth. What they need is experienced sensitive leadership which can use these men on projects in their areas.

MR WILBERT GARVIN, an educationalist and musician from Kells, Co. Antrim, says that there is not enough emphasis on the 'creative environment' in Northern Ireland — 'we depend too much on ideas coming in from outside'. He believes Northern Ireland is a small enough unit to tap productively into the creativity of the entire population. 'The addition of high added value depends mainly on the generation of successful ideas, and the bringing of these ideas to fruition.' He suggests the formation of local 'creativity' groups throughout the region to come up with ideas for new products and services. Ideas thought up and agreed by particular local groups should be produced in those areas, thus providing local employment. Royalties should be paid to the groups originating the ideas; ownership of the ideas and the products developed from them would belong to those areas, and both increased local co-operation and inter-area competition would ensue.

Mr Garvin hopes that, in such a system,

less attention would be paid to energy-sapping confrontation and more to co-operative ventures where energy is directed and focused. Inevitably power would be more and more in people's hands since they are the ones generating the wealth. We would thus move towards a more democratic society. People, independent of their background or religious persuasion, would have the opportunity to work together for the good of all. A synergy between different backgrounds — a sort of hybrid vigour — could develop. After working for some time on coming up with ideas for generating wealth, such groups would become more capable of suggesting solutions for all sorts of problems. The collective consciousness of the country moves from one of confrontation to one of creativity.

THE BELFAST ECOLOGY GROUP (BEG) included in a lengthy list of proposals one that Churches should send observers to the services of other denominations as an aid to open-mindedness and tolerance, and stressed the importance of community theatres, culture centres and even radio stations to encourage participation by local people who do not identify with the powerful mainstream institutions of society. It also proposes a Belfast Community Council, with representation from community, voluntary, environmental and peace groups, to run the city instead of the party politicians.

MR PAUL DORAN from Belfast was one of several contributors who emphasized the role of sport in overcoming barriers in Northern Ireland. He believes that the Gaelic Athletic Association is an example of how people having strong nationalist views and identity can assert them without threatening unionists or resorting to violence. He regrets that unionist friends were not able to share in Down's 1991 triumph in the all-Ireland Gaelic football final because they were 'turned off' by the GAA's republican associations. 'It is the task of the GAA to reassure these people, and I was happy to see that they invited representatives of the Shankill Road community to Dublin to discuss the organization.' He believes recent threats to the GAA from the loyalist paramilitaries were a direct consequence of Down's all-Ireland win and the flag-waving victory parades throughout the county — not unlike some other parades that take place every summer in Northern Ireland — which followed it. He asks Initiative '92 to offer 'constructive criticism' of the role of the GAA in Northern Ireland, 'but also to credit it for allowing nationalists to feel comfortable about themselves while not threatening unionists'.

MR ROY ARBUCKLE from Derry proposes an international competition for a 'Third Anthem' — not to support a monarchy, or to fight for an ideal — but in praise of Northern Ireland as a homeland; an anthem that would allow the people of its two different traditions — who are usually unable to sing anything together — to sing together. He wants a song that would be 'equally inspiring to both traditions, a song that our children could begin the day with, a song that all the supporters at a Derry City-Linfield match could sing together, a song that could be used at all occasions when our present anthems are a cause of dissent'. He is not suggesting scrapping the British or Irish national anthems; only that there should be another choice. 'I would see this new song being to us what "God Bless America" is to the USA.'

Religion

The main Churches — and particularly the Protestant Churches — were very receptive to Initiative '92's appeal for submissions. The leaderships of all three main Protestant Churches — the Church of Ireland, the Presbyterians and the Methodists — responded, as did the Quakers, the Reformed Presbyterians and a wide range of ecumenical and reconciliation groups. No member of the Catholic hierarchy responded, although individual priests and groups of religious did submit replies. Outside the Christian Churches, no fewer than nine Baha'i groups sent in submissions.

JOHN and PAULINE COLL of Bangor, Co. Down, contend that 'apartheid' between Protestants and Catholics in Northern Ireland is 'endemic, deep-rooted and pervasive within this society. It is our greatest stumbling block and we can have no progress, no solution, neither peace nor justice until it is faced and eradicated. It exists at all levels of society: in education, in housing, in the workplace and in recreation, but, most significantly, it exists in our minds.' They quote the sociologist Frank Wright that in Northern Ireland 'a pre-condition of friendly relationships is the systematic avoidance of any topic of conversation that might touch on politics or religion and the concealment of everything that, in fact, divides them'. Mr and Mrs Coll continue:

Although we mingle with one another on a daily basis, there is no dialogue, no sharing, no understanding, no contact at any meaningful level. There is no empathy. Our contact seldom rises above a fearful civility.

Apartheid is nowhere more manifested than in our denominational Churches. It appears that no more than lip service has ever been paid, by the leadership within the Churches, to a genuine meeting of minds in this community. There has been, and is, an abundance of window-dressing, but no substance. All the statements and appeals to date have been unbelievably ineffective. The Churches cushion their members against addressing this problem of 'separateness'. It is true that small, committed groups of individuals have endeavoured to make a difference. But if the Churches are to be relevant to the real needs of the community, a major commitment to breaking down this wall of separation must be the urgent priority. At present, fear, suspicion and mistrust are the norm.

We have the highest percentage population of Church attendance in Europe and so our Church leaders have the platform from which to launch a new, concerted movement. We need a major effort, a dialogue to pool new thinking, a fresh approach — an affirmation and celebration of our common faith. We need a vigorous awareness campaign. All levels of Church membership must be motivated, enthused and mobilized and, most important, led from the front. Equally important, the Churches should begin to work on behalf of one another, no Church doing alone what it could do with another. As we see it, this is the primary mission of the Church in Northern Ireland today.

THE CORRYMEELA COMMUNITY points out that the Churches 'have not given priority to the proclamation of a wider Christian solidarity with all victims', transcending the divided cultures which they have had a major part in shaping. 'They have largely remained captive to their particular experiences and cultural forms and they have often reinforced their estrangement from one another.' The Churches, while clearly not the sole cause of sectarianism, may nevertheless

keep people apart with a sense of superiority, whether this is explicit or implicit. We therefore feel it appropriate, as members of an ecumenical Christian community, to make a number of suggestions. We wish to see Churches proclaim the universal love of God in Christ who stands with all the victims. In doing this we do not believe that it is sufficient simply to teach doctrinal concepts or to verbally condemn murder and terror. The witness of the Church must begin to reflect the universal message of Christ through its Christian life and structures. This could be done through the encouragement of ecumenical dialogue, the development of social programmes across community boundaries between Church congregations and parishes, and attempts by the Church leaderships to act together when making comment on political, security and legal matters. Otherwise, the sociological and psychological forces of division will automatically proclaim another message — namely solidarity with our own cultural/religious group.

The Churches need to make provision for regular contact between clergy and laity of different denominations as an integral part of their structures. Inter-denominational relations should not be a matter of 'exceptions'. One of the most common complaints of clergy is that they have 'no time' to do anything about community relations. This could be relieved by raising the priority of inter-community witness within the Churches and by encouraging the laity to undertake much of this activity. Furthermore, the Churches need to be explicitly and openly committed to inclusive programmes where they have influence: in schools, youth work, women's groups, sport's clubs, prayer groups and so on.

(See also Politics and the Constitution: Joint Authority/Sovereignty.)

THE INTER-CHURCH GROUP ON FAITH AND POLITICS stresses that 'the fundamental state of Protestant-Catholic relations in Northern Ireland has been one of enmity and hostility, whether latent or manifest'. To rid themselves of this enmity, people have to acknowledge the fears that exist. Small steps, risks and confidence-building measures have to be taken so that both sides are ready for the new relationships out of which peace can develop.

Nor can politicians do this alone. It is the responsibility of everyone and it will require a profound change of heart and mind. Both communities taking small steps will build mutual confidence and perhaps then the situation will start to spiral upwards.

The Group suggests a number of confidence-building steps, some of who could be taken by the Churches.

It would help if the Catholic Church took more seriously the deep-seated distrust among Protestants of Catholic ecclesiastical power. Changes such as offering communion to inter-Church couples when requested, or not putting obstacles in the way of those who wish to give experiments in integrated education a fair trial, or altering some of the rules for mixed marriages, would be helpful. There is a need for the Protestant Churches to examine honestly their anti-Catholic bias and to show some understanding of the sense of grievance and injustice of many Catholics. Support for the security forces should be balanced by concern for those occasions when there are abuses by them.

The Inter-Church Group concludes its submission thus:

The politics of reconciliation is the only realistic and responsible politics in Northern Ireland. It is either that or our eventual destruction as a community. For a politics of reconciliation to be possible, there needs to be a social and spiritual breakthrough which will change people's views of one another. This breakthrough or change of heart will involve a recognition, in the words of the late John McMichael of the UDA, 'that there is no section of the divided Ulster community which is totally innocent or totally guilty, totally right or totally wrong. We all share the responsibility for creating the situation either by deed or by acquiescence. Therefore we must share the responsibility for finding a settlement and then share the responsibility of maintaining good government.' All of us have met people who have had a change of heart, who have moved from destructive to positive activity and are involved in grass-roots community activities, employment projects, cross-community work and so on. Much more is needed and it may be that the most profound conversion will be required in the apparently more 'respectable' parts of our community.

(See also Politics and the Constitution: Local Government Reform/Role of the Republic.)

In a submission which urges the reawakening of public debate and dialogue in a more socially conscious 'civil society', JAMES NELSON and CLAIRE JOHNSTON from Belfast express the opinion that the Churches are in a strong position to 'take the lead in prompting and enabling active citizenship' in Northern Ireland. This is not something they have taken any great part in to date.

For, although Church leaders are consistent in restating condemnations of violence, the Churches' challenge to the practice of violence has been limited and inadequate. We suggest that, on the whole, the Christian Church has tended in its past to be too privatized, too involved with the things of the heart and the soul, and too concerned with personal sin and individual salvation. For it is the opinion of the majority of Christians that Christ came to declare the kingdom of God, and that kingdom is, above all, a heavenly realm. We believe that when Christ spoke about the Kingdom of God, he talked about it as primarily present, not future, and through his actions he inaugurated it on earth. As Gustavo Gutierrez says: 'The growth of the Kingdom is a process which occurs historically in liberation'.

Mr Nelson and Ms Johnston believe the process of opening up 'public spaces' for debate and dialogue, in the style of Initiative '92, to be fundamental to building a just and reconciled society in Northern Ireland. They urge the Churches to develop strategies, informal and formal, to promote this kind of 'process of talk'. Due to the nature of Church life as a place where people congregate and talk, the Churches can provide an excellent context for the kind of dialogue about fundamental issues Mr Nelson and Ms Johnston want to encourage. The Churches can provide a relaxed, positive, congenial setting for people to express their ideas, to challenge themselves and others, to listen and become informed.

In a more formal way the Churches can significantly contribute to raising the profile of talk. It is the Churches' business to challenge and confront, and all its communication channels — the pulpit, the Sunday school class, badminton matches, luncheon clubs — can hijack this cause.

The Churches must take hold of their role as question-raiser, stimulator and catalyst. Therefore, we suggest that within the existing structures and public arena of the Churches, debate can be formally organized: discussions arranged in youth meetings on poverty, unemployment and the role of terrorist organizations; opportunities created for the elderly to talk about social conditions; meetings set up for business people to debate discriminatory practices and prejudice in the workplace; exchange visits organized between women's groups corporately to talk over issues of child care or adult education.

They emphasize that, because of the influential position of the institutional Churches in Northern Irish society, this debate could attract the participation of many ordinary people.

PAX CHRISTI IRELAND appeals to all professing the Christian faith to make the promotion of respect, tolerance and dialogue with other denominations and faiths 'a priority for prayer, study and action'. They should then begin, 'in a spirit of deep respect for the 'other'', to engage inter-Church or intra-Church groups in discussion on such traditionally sensitive questions as sectarianism, bigotry, prejudice, ignorance and hatred; history, traditions and commemorations; security and policing; and education. Speakers should be invited from the Fair Employment and Equal Opportunities Commissions. Perceptions that, in the Republic, the Catholic Church has undue influence on the state should be carefully studied and, if found to be accurate to any degree, 'an appropriate distance should be defined'. There should be further development of links between Church groups North and South. (See also Politics and the Constitution: Devolution; Law, Justice and Security: Introduction.)

DEIRDRE and ADRIAN RICE, from Islandmagee, Co. Antrim, put forward a proposal for an 'issue-based' adult education programme for members of evangelical Churches in Northern Ireland. They say that the recent decline in Church membership and attendance in the region has also affected the evangelical Churches.

Even within the fundamentalist Churches — normally impervious to frequent allegations of being narrow-minded, ineffective, unrealistic and of no earthly use outside their own Church buildings — many adherents have become disillusioned with the belief that spiritual salvation is of the utmost and only importance. The latter part of the twentieth century has brought with it innumerable demands and challenges for Churchgoers wishing to live useful and effectual lives within their — often divided — communities. Such a situation has persuaded many fundamentalist adherents to consider a symbiotic relationship between body and spirit. This reflection markedly widens the 'mission field' and, consequently, an understanding of secular issues has been identified as an urgent need.

Deirdre and Adrian Rice propose an adult education programme for members of Baptist Churches, Brethren halls, Christian Fellowships and other Church-based groups which are small, evangelical or fundamentalist. The programme, based on the theories of the radical educationalists Paulo

Freire and Ivan Illich, would centre on dialogue, discussion and experiential learning. 'The subject matter would not be analysed exclusively within a biblical context, although reference and analysis naturally would lean towards a biblical framework.' However, they stress that it would be issue-based, not biblically based and therefore it would have a secular focus. Subjects would include abortion, homosexuality, the media, literature, world religions, environmental awareness, feminism, sexuality, sectarianism, tolerance, materialism, evolution/creation, nationalism and racism. The aims would be to bring these Churches' members in touch with issues affecting society and the world at large from which they are often isolated; to increase understanding of such issues within and beyond a biblical framework; to reduce conflict relationships within and beyond Church settings, and to assist personal development.

THE CHRISTIAN RESPONSE TO THE IRISH SITUATION (CRIS) group echoes some of Pax Christi's points. It points to six examples of people's failure to love God and to love their neighbours as themselves in Ireland. Among these are 'ecclesiastical idolatry', putting one's Church before one's Christianity, with the result that many Protestants consider Catholics as sub-Christians (or even anti-Christian), and many Catholics think of Protestants as heretics. Similarly, they are able to condone discrimination, injustice and violence committed in the name of their religious and political cause. 'Most Protestants are willing to accept and justify *all* actions by police and security forces because they are done to combat terrorism and preserve law and order. Many Catholics, on the other hand, regard *all* acts of the police and army as acts of repression against the Catholic community and will find some justification for the vilest atrocities committed by the IRA and other republican paramilitaries.' Both Protestants and Catholics prefer to blame the 'other side' and the British for all their ills. The former 'seem to believe that the terrorist acts of the IRA happen due to the weakness of the Dublin and London governments in not containing them'. The latter blame 'the British colonial past and the current British refusal to leave Northern Ireland, for all the violence plaguing Irish society. Neither side seems to have the moral courage to face the fact that it needs to accept at least part of the blame'.

The groups emphasize that Irish Christians need to learn to put into practice Christ's two commandments to love their neighbours as themselves.

By doing so, they will avoid political and ecclesiastical idolatries, recognize and repent of their sins and failures, have a forgiving heart towards those who have wronged them (as brave individuals like Gordon Wilson have set an example); will be respectful of others' legitimate rights, and will strive to bring about a just and righteous political and social order with full awareness of the fact that they are mere sojourners in this world and that their ultimate loyalty is to God rather than to any political ideology or to any particular country.

In a follow-up submission, one member of the CRIS group, MR ALAN FRENCH, from Dublin, emphasizes the power of 'collective repentance' in the Northern Irish situation. He recounts the liberating experience of another member, an Englishwoman now living in the North, when she repented for what the English had done to the Irish in the past. He is currently preparing a similar confession, as a Southerner addressing unionists, and including what he believes is 'a state of grievance' felt by many Southerners about partition.

It can be compared to two people after a dispute where one side (the unionist) says 'The matter is settled', while the other (the nationalist) says 'No, wait, there is still unfinished business'.

As a Southern Protestant, Mr French also stresses that 'we are *not* living in a state of oppression by the Catholic Church'.

MR BRIAN LAMBKIN of Belfast says that, to date, a consensus about the nature of the Northern Ireland conflict has eluded people there, and this is particularly true on the question of whether it is a religious conflict. He believes that 'consensus on this question is crucial to the achievement of consensus on the nature of the conflict as a whole'. He wonders whether that consensus can be achieved without a large-scale educational programme leading to a clearer understanding of both the historical development of the various religious traditions and their role in the conflict. Mr Lambkin urges support for projects like that proposed by Armagh District Council for a Centre for Religion in Ireland. This, he says, would develop cross-community reconciliation; contribute to understanding by facilitating religious research and study and the dissemination and explanation of its results to Churches, schools and the public; and contribute to the economic development of the area by exploiting such a centre's tourist potential.

MRS MYRTLE SMYTH of Bangor, Co. Down, proposes the building of a 'Thanksgiving Square' in the centre of Belfast, modelled on a similar square in Dallas, Texas. This would be 'a place where people can go simply to give thanks to whatever God they believe in'. It would be 'something beautiful and concrete' — more permanent than ephemeral peace rallies — with space for theatre, music and talks, where people from all denominations and nationalities could meet to learn about each other's cultures and celebrate what they had in common.

The Baha'i Information Office, on behalf of the BAHA'I COMMUNITY of Northern Ireland, says that the worldwide Baha'i community — over five million people from many nations, cultures and classes — is an example of 'a single social organism, representative of the diversity of the human family, conducting its affairs through a system of commonly accepted consultative principles, and cherishing equally all the great outpourings of divine guidance in human history'. The Baha'is encourage such difference — 'we are certain of the value of our experience of unity in diversity as a maxim... Far from being evidence of societal weakness, we maintain that the diversity found within the small compass of Northern Ireland is the most effective foundation for that unity which must be the precursor of real peace.' The Baha'is also urge the acceleration — through education to change the attitudes of policy-makers and people alike — of the process of including women as an active and fully equal force at all levels of society. They emphasize that 'the fostering of spiritual qualities — mercy, tolerance, honesty, trustworthiness, unselfishness, compassion and love — should be at the core of structured educational programmes and not confined to their specifically religious elements'. They also urge a process of re-education, emphasizing world citizenship as 'a prerequisite for the elimination of prejudice in all its forms, dependent as it is on an emotional commitment to ignorance'.

The Baha'is also point to the interesting, perhaps unique, electoral process for the assemblies which are the governing bodies of local Baha'i communities.

All voting is carried out by secret ballot, and electioneering, including the nomination of candidates, is expressly forbidden. Each voter lists nine names, corresponding to his or her preferred assembly membership, and the nine individuals who receive the greatest number of votes are declared to be elected. By this method, maximum freedom of choice is accorded to each elector, and the power-seeking behaviour prevalent in many other systems is avoided. Most importantly, it forms the foundation of a special relationship between the institution and the body of believers. The voter elects with the understanding that he is free to choose, without any interference, whomever his conscience prompts him to select, and he freely accepts the authority of the outcome. In the act of voting, the individual subscribes to a covenant by which the orderliness of society is upheld.

Other submissions came from the Baha'i women's committee, the Baha'i Youth, a group of Baha'i children at Hazelwood Integrated College in north Belfast, the Baha'i Religious Education Committee — criticizing the new core syllabus for religious education for excluding world religions other than Christianity; Baha'i Communities in Ballymena, Carrickfergus, Cookstown, Omagh and Londonderry, and Mrs Vida Blackwell.

Others submissions dealing with religious issues (apart from those coming from mainstream Churches and their religious communities, whose numerous submissions are spread throughout the summary) include Mr Kevin Brennan, Mrs Rita Canning, Mr Ian Carter Long, Ms Dympna Clarke, the Columba Community, the Cornerstone Community, Rev. Denis Faul, Mrs Margaret Forbes (for Dungannon Presbyterian Women's Association), Mr Tony Gasson, Ms Diana Gilpin-Brown, Rt Rev. Brian Hannon (Church of Ireland Bishop of Clogher), Mr T. Hill, Mr Martin Jones, Mr Martin Moorcroft, Mr Joseph O'Donnell, the Long Island

Inter-Church Northern Ireland Discussion Group (New York), Rev. Patrick McCafferty, Ms Thelma Shiel, Rev. Andrew Orr and Rev. Susan Green — as far as possible, clubs, youth and prayer groups, as well as buildings, should be shared between Churches.

Identity

Two of the more interesting submissions in this section, which has an obvious overlap with the previous section, came from a prominent community leader in a Belfast Protestant working-class community and a moderate nationalist academic from a Catholic background.

MR JACKIE REDPATH, the director of the Greater Shankill Development Agency, argues that the social deprivation the Shankill area of west Belfast shares with neighbouring Catholic communities reinforces its sense of siege, and targeting that deprivation is 'a key to liberating the Protestant mentality from negativism, to embracing change and the future as a friend rather than an enemy'. He points out that it is no coincidence that over the past 25 years the areas of greatest disadvantage have been the same as the areas of greatest violence: north and west Belfast, which both the Shankill and Falls Roads run through, has around 45 per cent of Northern Ireland's unemployed and has seen almost 65 per cent of its violent incidents. He stresses that, despite the media image, deprivation is shared by both Protestants and Catholics in such areas, with the Greater Shankill having a 30 per cent unemployment rate (compared to a Northern Ireland average of 19 per cent), rising to 60 per cent in the large housing estates of Glencairn and the lower Shankill, where 95 per cent of residents are dependent on state benefits for part of their income and 50 per cent of households are below the official poverty line.

This Protestant deprivation is now reinforcing the sense of siege and psychology of retreat felt by that community (just as it is widely believed that poverty in the Catholic community reinforced its sense of alienation from the state of Northern Ireland). The sense of siege has been at the core of the Protestant mentality in the province for centuries; the retreat has been sharply felt over the past 25 years. This retreat has been psychological, cultural, intellectual, political, physical and economic. All these factors are felt by the Protestant working class, particularly in Belfast, Derry and the border areas. Some of them are shared with the Protestant middle class. Physically, this retreat is most evident in Belfast, which the Protestant middle class is forsaking for north Down and south Antrim and where the Protestant working class is being driven by redevelopment and the promise of a better life. The Protestant (middle-class and working-class) population of north Belfast has fallen from 112,000 to 56,000 people since 1976. Since 1982 the population of the Greater Shankill area has fallen from 76,000 to 27,000.

While the physical and political retreat — the fall of Stormont, the reduction of powers of local councils, the Anglo-Irish Agreement — is obvious, the intellectual and cultural retreat is 'more insidious'. Mr Redpath recalls the sense of displacement revealed in the words of a community worker — who had changed her name to make it unambiguously Protestant-sounding — at a 1991 conference on community development in Protestant areas: 'My background is Protestant working-class. For a while I was uncomfortable when I realized that I was perceived as a Catholic on the grounds that I was 'alright' — if I was alright, I couldn't be a Prod. I came out of the closet finally when I agreed to facilitate a workshop on women and Protestantism.'

Mr Redpath continues:

The middle class and the educated Protestant community have found little space in their own society for expression in the past 25 years, other than a retreat into business activities. The silence has been loud. This Protestant retreat is all the sharper against the backdrop of a perceived Catholic community in the ascendant, with its growing middle class, and — from its working-class ghettos — a 'successful' guerilla campaign operating for over two decades.

Recognizing and then understanding the Protestant community in retreat is the key to unlocking the door to the future.

To accept its decline as inevitable or to refuse to recognize the need for it to change, Mr Redpath says, will result only in more 'siege violence'. He wants his community to work to shape its own future, rather than have it shaped by outside forces.

To encourage such a renaissance of thinking, society and culture, it is essential that we engage the issue at all levels. It cannot be left to a desperate fight against violence and deprivation in hard-core Protestant areas. The clergy, the business community, civil servants, politicians, poets, academics and the media all have their part to play in building a renewed and confident Protestant community, which will play the lead role in building a new society.... To paraphrase Brian Friel's wisdom about Irish writers and their work — 'We are talking to ourselves, as we must, and if we are overheard by others [in Ireland], England and America, so much the better.'

Mr Redpath says that he understands the constraint on unionist politicians who feel that they always have to look over their shoulders to see if their constituency is following them. But he has 'a notion that for the first time the Protestant community is ahead of its politicians by and large'. He recalls that at the time of the first round of political talks in 1991, the local *Shankill People* newspaper did a survey (not scientific) in which it questioned 202 local people on a number of issues, including whether they supported such talks. 'This was in the knowledge that the talks were about compromise, about accommodating all the traditions here — and 78 per cent of the sample said they supported the talks. There was almost a similar percentage who said 'no' to the next question, about whether they thought the talks would work.' He interpreted this as showing a desire on the part of people for the talks to work, but not a demand that they should work — which allowed the politicians to walk away from them. Mr Redpath believes there has been considerable movement and changes in attitudes among Northern Ireland Protestants over the past 20 years, with more willingness to compromise now. In the same survey 98 per cent of people supported the ceasefire called by the loyalist paramilitaries at that time in order to give the talks a chance to work. 'There was a small number of people, almost entirely young men, who were not for that, and since then we have   seen their answer, and that is the frightening aspect.'

DR BERNARD CULLEN, professor of philosophy at Queen's University, Belfast, believes that within the 'Catholic nationalist' community there is a wide spectrum of opinion on how to make progress towards a widely acceptable form of government for Northern Ireland: from diehard IRA supporters to the many Catholics who consider themselves British to the extent of supporting the consciously unionist Alliance Party. He is concerned to persuade the Opsahl Commission that 'there is a sizeable group of nationalists in Northern Ireland (apart from the Catholics who are quite happy to be *de facto* British subjects) whose political views (in so far as they have any) are not represented by the SDLP's current and recent position'. He writes about his own experience growing up as a Catholic in a strongly loyalist working-class area and learning from his grandfather to revere the heroes of past Irish republican struggles and to abhor the historical injustices perpetrated by the British. Dr Cullen also recalls the kindness and closeness of elderly Protestant neighbours. He says that after rejecting the 'whole nationalist package' as an older teenager, he has come back now to his earlier love of the Irish language, traditional music and Gaelic games.

It is not easy, in our present climate, to be a lover and a defender of the best aspects of a distinctively Irish heritage, including inevitably the vivid collective memories of the Mass-rock and the Penal Laws (but not forgetting 1641), while at the same time insisting that this in no way implies a pathological hatred towards all things English and British, towards all things unionist, and by extension (despite the frequently voiced hypocritical rhetoric about Tone and so on) towards all things Protestant.

He understands (although it also frustrates him) why the Irish language is banned in Belfast City Hall when Sinn Féin councillors brandish it as 'an anti-unionist weapon'. He finds it no surprise that the Gaelic Athletic Association, with its ban on members of 'the Crown forces', should continue to be viewed with suspicion by most Northern unionists. The same goes for Conradh na Gaeilge, the Irish-language organization, whose leadership has, over the past 20 years, been 'distressingly ambivalent' towards the IRA's campaign of violence. So where does that leave people like him, he asks rhetorically. He is referring to   people who have 'a deep-seated but perhaps ill-articulated sense of their Irish identity', who have no sense of allegiance to   British royalty or flags or anthems or feeling for Poppy Day. 'I could go on reciting a long list of 'chill factors' — ways in which manifestations of Britishness in the public and private life of Northern

Ireland either leave many of its citizens cold or excite more or less irrita-
tion. I put it this way because I am referring to nationalists, either for
whom the aspiration to a united Ireland is pushed so far into the future as
to be almost meaningless ('maybe some day, not in my lifetime'); or who
are reconciled to partition, to paying their taxes to a government based in
Westminster and reaping the social and economic benefits of continuing
membership of the United Kingdom; or who would actively resist incorporation into a united Ireland that would look anything like the present
Irish Republic in terms of its economic performance, its social welfare and
educational benefits, and its social and legal illiberality.' The SDLP's
stance does not represent this group, he strongly believes.

Dr Cullen says it was 'profoundly depressing' to hear the Opsahl
Commission testimony of Sir Kenneth Bloomfield, 'a transparently decent
man', who still seemed (from the press reports) to see Northern Ireland's
problems, after all these years, as a purely internal UK affair. It was equally
depressing

to hear the SDLP insist that they will have nothing to do with any administration which does
not involve the Irish Republic in the actual government of Northern Ireland. This is simply
their own updated version of 'Ireland unfree shall never be at peace'. I had really hoped that
we had all come further than this in our appreciation of reasonable unionist resistance to the
involvement of the Irish government in actually governing Northern Ireland — as distinct
from having a legitimate interest in how Northern Ireland is governed.

There is surely middle ground here. We, the people of Northern Ireland ourselves, must
devise means of governing ourselves, in ways which guarantee political, religious, and civil liberties for all our citizens — with the two sovereign governments that have a legitimate interest
in our well-being co-operating *at a distance* in guaranteeing fair play for all. Only so is there
any chance of the present Anglo-Irish Agreement being superseded by a more mutually agree-
able arrangement. I am convinced (and many opinion polls support my contention) that this
fair play and equal treatment within Northern Ireland is the essential demand of many, if not
most, Catholics who live here; and that they are much less concerned with changing Northern
Ireland's position within the United Kingdom. Behind the honeyed words about accommodating both traditions, the SDLP simply does not seem to be prepared to settle for this, which it
derides as an internal settlement. Sensing no urgency as it waits for the Taigs to outbreed the
Prods, the SDLP seems instead to be prepared to go along with that other well-known Provo
slogan: *Tiocfaidh ár lá* — Our day will come.

He stresses too that the SDLP does not represent his view on Articles 2
and 3 of the Republic's Constitution. 'Let me say it loud and clear: I am a
Northern nationalist, and I do not believe that Articles 2 and 3 protect my
'historic birthright' or my minority position in Northern Ireland one iota.
To deal with one frequently floated red herring: in the absence of those
ridiculously imperialistic articles, a simple act of the Republic's parliament
would guarantee that anyone on the island could apply for and obtain an
Irish passport. Indeed, I am convinced that Articles 2 and 3 serve only to
give succour to those who would seek to remove the border by shooting,
bombing and general intimidation; they serve to perpetuate an utterly

fairytale attitude to the divisions on this island, completely out of touch with its social, economic and political realities.' He concludes that they should be 'scrapped forthwith' as being wrong in themselves, rather than being 'part of a *quid pro quo* in a negotiating game'.

Dr Cullen believes that our kind of conflict does not lend itself to resolution: 'the best we can do is learn to cope with the conflict, devise structures which will contain it, while striving to guarantee the best possible life opportunities for all our citizens'. He believes too that the 'nothing is agreed until everything is agreed' approach of the recent political talks is fundamentally flawed, inclining to the view that 'everything' will never be agreed, 'the situation is just not bad enough yet'.

In the Northern Ireland context, the treatment required of all the interested parties to enable the establishment of a lasting settlement would demand painful concessions all round. This, apparently, we are not yet prepared to do.

Sure, there has been a frightening stream of funerals on our television screens; but most of us get on with our lives; we earn enough or get enough from the social security system to pay the bills, buy a few pints and a few vodkas, rent a few videos, and maybe even have a fortnight in Bundoran or Majorca. For most of us, Catholic and Protestant, middle class, working class, and unemployed, the system of direct rule from Westminster via Stormont Castle has been ticking over reasonably well for the past 20 years. My hunch is that matters such as 'the democratic deficit' mean little or nothing to most people. When they see pictures from Sarajevo, I think most people here think we're not so badly off after all — it could be a lot worse! Whatever the reason, the professional politicians simply did not sense in the community at large a sufficient degree of urgency to force them to overcome their many resistances to political accommodation in Northern Ireland.

MR PAUL SWEENEY, the director of the Northern Ireland Voluntary Trust, in a personal submission, begins by stating:

I am a 37-year-old father of four children, deeply rooted in a Catholic working-class background, inextricably scarred by the sectarianism of Northern Ireland, motivated primarily by the pursuit of social and economic justice, rather than nationalist fervour, and desperately committed to contributing to the resolution of the conflict in Northern Ireland in the hope that Catholics and Protestants will develop mechanisms for addressing our deepest divisions without resorting to the act or threat of violence.' He says that, although he abhors violence, many of his peers in Derry did become involved in paramilitarism, and thus, 'with a deep understanding of where political violence emanates from', he avoids 'ritualistic condemnations' of individual acts of violence. 'To eradicate violence, we have to develop structures which redress the underlying causes of violence. Likewise, those actively engaged in violence (by deed or process) must be included in the resolution of conflict.

Mr Sweeney says that his intuitive Irishness

has little to do with Ireland being a Catholic, Gaelic and Free State. I don't have to try to be Irish. I don't particularly pursue Irish ways and customs; indeed, I am so Irish that I don't necessarily feel less Irish by holding a British passport. Culturally and spiritually I am Irish. In terms of citizenship and practicalities, I live under British jurisdiction. I live in two places at the one time. I live in a place where two worlds overlap. For the most part this overlap has been destructive; however, this does not necessarily have to be so. With vision, imagination, leadership and the deliberate management of diversity, a new relationship is possible. This process of 'realignment' has been significantly advanced over the past several year.

He urges recognition of

the significant changes in the management of the Northern Ireland problem in recent times. Rather than feel pressurized to favour one particular solution (there is none), I see merit in the Opsahl Commission outlining a framework for progress and enunciating a plethora of incremental initiatives that can be sponsored to ease the realignment process.

(See also Politics and the Constitution Improving the Anglo-Irish Agreement.)

The submission of the PRESBYTERIAN CHURCH'S CHURCH AND GOVERNMENT COMMITTEE lays great stress on northern Presbyterians' keen awareness of the 'double minority' nature of the conflict between communities in Ireland: a British Protestant minority in Ireland living beside an Irish Catholic minority in Northern Ireland.

The majority in Ireland is positively Roman Catholic and Irish, but *not* British. The majority is thus more hostile to the British than it is to the Protestant churches; hence Roman Catholics have no real problems with ecumenical activity, but have problems with unionism and loyalism. The minority in Ireland is Protestant and British, but *not* Roman Catholic. The minority has as many problems with ecumenical activity as the majority has with unionism and loyalism. On the Protestant side, the main sensitivity seems to be in relationships with the Roman Catholic Church, while on the Roman Catholic side the main problem seems to be political (for example, the British Royal Family, support for the security forces, and so on).

The answer is that both minorities have to be cherished. 'Within the whole island, the significance of the culture, religion and identity of the Protestant minority must be recognized, honoured and protected. Within Northern Ireland, the significance of the culture, religion and identity of the Roman Catholic minority must be recognized, honoured and protected.' (See also Politics and the Constitution: Devolution.)

MR PAUL NOLAN from Belfast talks from his own experience, as an adult education organizer in working-class areas, of the 'essentially binary nature' of the Protestant-Catholic quarrel which seemed to render impotent much of the cross-community exchanges in which he had participated.

It is, of course, more complex than that. The fault line that divides us into Catholic and Protestant, unionist and nationalist, also runs through us as individuals, so that we are all to some extent British and to some extent Irish. Certainly I personally am always aware of living in and between two cultures. Born and raised a Catholic and fed by the dreams of nationalism, I was also at the same time fostered by the British welfare state and able to enjoy the opportunities of the British educational system.

Today I still hope to see a united Ireland, but in my working life I operate inside the framework of a UK structure, visit England, Scotland and Wales frequently, and find that my closest political sympathies are with sections of the British labour movement. I enjoy the traditional music of England and the traditional music of Ireland, the modern English novel and the modern Irish novel, and channel-hop at night between Irish and English broadcasting stations. Not everyone, of course, finds their cultural identity divided so symmetrically, but all of us live in what Edna Longley has called a 'cultural corridor', regardless of which end of that corridor feels most like home.

The point I wish to draw from this is that to inhabit two cultures, two minds, need not be pathologized or seen as schizophrenic; rather, the possibility exists that this diversity can be experienced as a form of enrichment. For that to happen, cultural identity has to be detached from statehood; in other words, people must be reassured that whatever political framework is eventually agreed, their culture and heritage (provided these are not triumphalist or oppressive) will be safeguarded, legitimized and respected.

(See also Politics and the Constitution: Joint Authority/ Sovereignty.)

MR PADDY DOHERTY, director of the Inner City Trust in Derry,   points to the dramatic demographic change that has taken place in Northern Ireland since the last census, and believes that it will continue.

We have a young, vibrant Catholic community, and their energy is channelled into positive things. But if they are faced with a negative approach from those who lead the Protestant population, then they will say to Protestants: we would like you to join us in a united Ireland or a better Ireland, but if you do not want to join us, it is going to happen anyway. I believe it will come; it could come easy or hard, but it will come.

He says that in Derry he is part of an attempt to facilitate the Protestant tradition through, for example, Derry City Council's celebration of the tercentenary of the Siege of Derry, although '95 per cent of those who celebrated it were Catholics'. He had offered to build a museum for the Apprentice Boys, but they were not prepared to accept it: 'there is always suspicion in any move that we would make and it seems to us that any effort is regarded as an attempt to undermine their position. They have a major identity problem having to deal with people like myself — and there are many of us in the community — who are articulate, hard-bargaining and with no great respect for institutions. On the other hand, they are people who have been bred into and have accepted institutions and are stuck in institutional ways.' He thinks that the 'pulling back of Protestants is because there is now a wave of young, educated Catholics who are quite capable of taking power away from them at national level, as well as locally'.

Mr Doherty warns that the intransigent unionist majority on Belfast City Council should be looking at their own stewardship and anticipating what will happen sometime in the next ten years, when they are faced with losing control of the city. In Derry, after being pushed out of power and retreating into a corner, they are now beginning to see that there is a role for them in the city after all. Similarly, in Northern Ireland as a whole, 'it is incumbent upon the Protestant leadership to examine where they will be 50 years from now. I am trying to work for a country which will look after my grandchildren.' He accepts that the Protestant community has suffered terribly from the IRA campaign, 'but it is time that we planned for the future and to do it knowing that Britain will pull out'. He says he is prepared to 'lean over backwards to help them to be part of this community, but I will not accept that Britain has a right of ownership of this country. This is fundamental.' Both sides have to learn to be graceful in a changed situation: Catholics have to ask themselves how they will react in a position of power and Protestants how they will react in a position of powerlessness — or is there a halfway house where no one has to be powerless?'

Mr Doherty admits that before they took over the administration of Derry, Catholics had little or no feeling for the old walled city. But that has all changed 'because Catholics now have a feeling of ownership and the feeling that not only can they make a contribution but they are making a magnificent contribution'. There is 'incredible energy' now. Derry's Catholics, through their community development trust structures, have taken responsibility for their city.

The whole concept of the Trusts — the Inner City Trust, the Northlands Centre, the Creggan Initiative, the Diamond (Protestant) Trust — is about taking from the Government the money needed to create jobs and improve the quality of life, and if the Government withdraws its help, we want to have set up a viable operation which will go on — not one that can close down because the funding is withdrawn. And I think we are getting a good response. There are some very creative civil servants who are beginning to see that if you create a system where local people are involved in economic development, they can succeed. This often results in the barriers coming down as well.

He believes that the real task, in Derry and elsewhere, is to 'create space for people with different and sincerely held opinions to come together to achieve a common goal'. (See also Politics and the Constitution: United Ireland.)

DR BRIAN GAFFNEY of Downpatrick writes as 'a middle-class Catholic now, from a working-class Catholic background, part of a section in our community which is increasing in size. I received my education to third level and beyond free of monetary charge, courtesy of the state system, but, as a member of a large, relatively poor family, at some personal cost to my parents and brothers and sisters ... I have a lot to be thankful for both to my family and to the society in which we live.'

His submission starts with two statements:

(1) I feel, as a Catholic, no sense of belonging to the fabric of society that makes up the official state of Northern Ireland. (2) I have, as a person of liberal values and left-wing political leanings, no means of expressing my views and feelings in a public forum.' Before he elaborates, he states that he abhors violence and does not wish 'to have any association with the furtherance of political or other ends by violent means.

(He feels he has to say this as a Catholic from a 'nationalist' background, if only to 'reassure those people who automatically think the opposite is more likely'.)

Every British government and opposition, and some Northern Ireland political and public figures, have insisted that in Northern Ireland it is possible for Catholics and Protestants to live together and hold widely different political views. They insist that it is perfectly legitimate to hold an aspiration for a united Ireland, even a socialist republic, as long as this is deferred to the far distant future and not pursued by violent means. They also declare that such unity could come about if a majority in Northern Ireland so wished. This indeed makes this issue a respectable political aim for anyone to hold.

However, many of the important structures of Northern Ireland society discriminate against this viewpoint by emphasizing the relative 'superiority' of holding the similarly legitimate wish to maintain the link to Britain. They do this in names; for instance, the Royal Ulster Constabulary. They do it in actions; for example the job discrimination revealed in the district councils, in the main university. They do it by attitude — for example, assuming that finishing the day's television with the British national anthem is not offensive.

Perhaps I am too sensitive and, after all, the only really important issue is that of action, and while there are no jobs to give out there cannot be discrimination and if there are jobs the Fair Employment Commission will ensure equal opportunity. But I do not think this is oversensitivity. I would like to play a role in our society. I would like to feel at home in the city hall of my home city. I would like to assume that my local police constable had my safety and security as high on his or her agenda as my Protestant neighbour's. Indeed, why should I not feel these things are so? I am a respectable member of the community, I wish no one ill, I pay my taxes and so on. But I would like to do all these things and still hold my 'legitimate' aspiration, still feel my Irish identity. Yet if I express these feelings, am I not assumed to be a closet 'Provo'? Am I not forbidden open access to officialdom? These are feelings which I believe prevent a sizeable proportion of the Catholic community from playing a proper role in Northern Irish life. It is my belief also that both sides lose in this situation: we are frustrated in our wish to take part; Northern Ireland is denied the benefit of using our talents and diverse abilities.

Dr Gaffney suggests a number of ways in which this could be changed. First, he says 'the powers that be should initiate a process, either by direction from above or preferably by choice, of disestablishing the unionist ethos from public life. I am not recommending the relegation of the unionist tradition to a secondary role, but the equalization of the two major traditions by having *neither* associated with authority. This should apply at every level, in terms of names (e.g. the Northern Ireland Police Force), actions and eventually attitudes.' Secondly, he supports the setting up of a new political party in Northern Ireland, not linked with historical attitudes the way the traditional parties are.

I feel that the middle classes, who have benefited much even from our troubled society, are prevented from paying anything back in the way of ideas and leadership by the lack of a left of centre, secular, truly non-traditional political party. I look with envy at the success of such a movement in the South, which has a society with many similar traditional divides.

MR ALAN SHEERAN, a community activist in Belfast's working-class Protestant areas, says in an oral submission that action to help young people in the present economic climate is an absolute necessity. It is a cross-community problem. 'Until we give these young people hope, we will keep recycling the problems.' The main thing is to get back some form of democracy and accountability, for people to have some control over their lives and over the 'middle-class' civil service and government-appointed 'quangos'.

The Protestant community needs new ideas, but Mr Sheeran is concerned that the ideas are not liberal or left-wing enough. The Protestant Shankill area of Belfast was always a very strong labour area, full of independent unionists, people who were not happy with the status quo, he says. Rather than being a Labour Party, the SDLP 'restricted the potential for growth from the left'. Mr Sheeran says: 'I think we need to have our own Labour Party, but part of the problem for the Northern Ireland Labour Party was that it was too closely associated with the unionists. It was the wrong time for it.'

Mr Sheeran is worried that terms such as 'the Ulster race' represent the development of 'a racial agenda among suspicious groupings which is being ignored'. Having conducted research work for the Community Development in Protestant Areas group, he says there is 'a search by Protestants for identity and also a desire to cherish what we have'. It has also given him a new view of the value of being a Protestant. He says with reference to the idea of Ulster independence: 'One of my grandparents was Catholic and the other a very staunch Protestant — the two come together within me and I am very proud of this. They both related to being northern. This is why I have some sympathy with the northern-centred aspects of a separatist idea, but a real fear of any argument based on race. I feel angry about being kept apart from the nationalist side of my heritage.'

KAREN SLOAN, a sixth-former at Methodist College, Belfast, says that she hates to be stereotyped.

From various discussions with people both within Northern Ireland and in other countries, I have discovered who I am supposed to be, purely because I am Protestant. Being Protestant means that I am British, most probably leaning towards unionist ideals, totally against any form of Dublin rule, and I probably do not get on with many Catholics. It is precisely this attitude which irritates me most about the classification in Northern Ireland.

In fact, she says, she considers herself Irish (probably because she spent six years in Dublin) and finds unionists and their attitudes (excluding attitudes towards violence) more bigoted than Sinn Féin. 'There are times when I am ashamed to be a Protestant (in the Northern Ireland sense of the word), and I don't think a Stormont government would ever give me reason to be particularly proud.'

She says she is not unique in having 'a relatively negative attitude' towards Northern Ireland, believing that there is no solution to its troubles. However, she concedes that living in Stranmillis and going to Methodist College, attended by both Protestants and Catholics, the 'troubles' do not directly affect her. However, 'I cannot say that they don't worry me. The fact that people are being killed for simply and supposedly being in one of the classifications which I detest so much deeply worries me and maybe explains some of my cynicism concerning Northern

Ireland. Everything is pointless surrounding the killings. I find it difficult even to attempt to be positive in such a situation.'

Next year Karen Sloan is leaving Northern Ireland to go to university and does not know if she will come back. She says that, with three other pupils from Methodist College, she spent a morning at the end of last year with four pupils from St Louise's College in the Falls Road discussing the subjects to be debated at the Initiative '92 schools' assembly. This, she goes on, proved to be one of 'the more worthwhile mornings of my life'.

I learned so much about the Northern Ireland situation which I always rather cockily felt that I was so well informed about.... But 18 is too old to start to learn — why not start in primary school before we learn which category we are classified as? Being fortunate enough to go to Methody, I never gave any other schools much thought, but now I realize how important it is to be given the chance to meet people from all corners of the community. It is only when we realize how much we actually share (in our case that we frequented the same places on Saturday nights!) that we discover there is definitely something concrete to build on. Reconciliation is all about recognizing our differences and realizing that differences which we are supposed to have are not so important after all. The younger we realize this, the better.

She might consider coming back after graduating: 'My greatest dream would be to see Ireland free from problems. I do very much like my country and hate to see it being torn apart.'

MR TONY CROWE, making a submission on behalf of THE APPREN-TICE BOYS OF DERRY, says that Ulster Protestants,

when accused by the world at large of having a siege mentality, often react to the accusation with pride rather than the anticipated guilt. There is, after all, nothing wrong with a siege mentality when you are actually under siege. The historian Alaistair Cook noted in a recent work on the Siege of Derry: 'The lack of magnanimity displayed by many Ulster Protestants emerges naturally and inevitably from their history, and in particular from the siege of 1688-89. The strongest emotions of Ulster Protestants spring not from a sordid triumphalism, but from a deep sense of vulnerability'.

Mr Crowe makes three points:

(1) Research all over the world where there are culturally divided communities shows that peace and stability are attainable only when all doubt about territorial integrity is removed. (2) The historical self-vision of Protestants is one of endless repetition of repelled assaults, without hope of absolute finality or fundamental change in their relationship with their surroundings and neighbours. (3) The revoking of the Anglo-Irish Agreement and the removal from the Eire Constitution of Articles 2 and 3 could help resolve some of the difficulties suggested by (1) and (2).

The PEACE AND RECONCILIATION GROUP SCHOOL STUDENTS in Derry discovered that in their discussions they were not able to settle the question 'United Kingdom or united Ireland?' so it was unlikely that the whole Northern Ireland community would.

We realize too that many nationalists have doubts about Dublin governments, and many unionists have reservations about Westminster rule. Our own hope is that British or Irish identity will become less important as two things develop: first a sense of European citizenship, and secondly a new Northern Irish identity, based on awareness of how much we have in common, and fair and equal treatment for everybody.

MR NIALL FITZDUFF of the Rural Community Network, writing in a personal capacity, believes that the nation-state has less to offer Northern Ireland in the future than 'a much greater focus on local regional identities, not in a unitary sense but also allowing for some fluidity of identity. He emphasizes that the recognition of the importance of local and regional identity will have to 'involve significant investment in processes of community development and political education to evolve new structures to build a much more participative and open society from the bottom up'. However, real progress on this agenda can happen only in the context of an agreed political framework which gives equal acknowledgment to the rights to British and Irish identity within Northern Ireland.

THE RURAL COMMUNITY NETWORK (RCN), which brings together 170 community, farming, environmental, voluntary and statutory bodies, district councils, and individuals in rural areas, focuses on issues of poverty and disadvantage and seeks support for community development and decentralized policies to improve the quality of life for rural communities. It says that community and voluntary organizations often feel limited through self-censorship from facing many of the realities of political life in Northern Ireland. 'This avoidance may be for the best of reasons, but begs the question of how this has diminished the possibilities for dialogue and debate. The question must be faced of whether open and frank discussions within community groups could contribute to solutions to the conflict?'

MR JOSEPH PEAKE, a Catholic who has been involved in the cross-community group Enniskillen Together, says there is very little communication across Northern Ireland's two significant divisions — of religion and class — *about* those divisions (it is where these two divisions reinforce each other that bigotry and paramilitary involvement occur most frequently).

People in Fermanagh tend to make social contact within their own community rather than across the divide. When cross-community contact is made, it tends to be for a particular discrete purpose, such as canoeing, and communication tends not to extend to the nature, causes of, or possible solutions, to the division. Such lack of communication between the communities *about* the communities leads to a grave lack of understanding. Thus the Catholics' perceptions of themselves, of the Protestant community, of the 'facts' about Northern Ireland, and of the issues that need to be dealt with are very different from the Protestants' perceptions of the same items, and often startlingly so. The reverse is also true.

People seem powerless, or at least they think they are. 'People generally ask when will it all end or how is it going to turn out, rather as though 'it' were a thunderstorm or some other event over which we have no control, as opposed to a set of human actions that we can influence and for which we have some responsibility (or for which we must take some responsibility).'

There is alienation in both communities, and the Catholics distrust the state and the security forces. However, it seems to Mr Peake that the Protestants have

a feeling that goes deeper than mere distrust. It is as though the very fabric of society had changed its nature. Democracy in Northern Ireland has been turned on its head. Stormont has been abolished, the 'B Specials' have gone and the UDR is going; local councils are without any real power; an openly revolutionary party that advocates the use of violence gets one-third of the Catholic vote; and the British government, without consulting the elected representatives of the majority, have given a foreign government the right to interfere in Northern Ireland affairs. Just about every 'reform' since 1968 has been made to suit the Catholics and they are still not satisfied — but it is they who get all the world's sympathy. And all this while a campaign of genocide not only goes virtually unpunished, but is openly supported by the votes of at times the vast majority of Catholics in Fermanagh. I think the feelings of puzzlement, resentment and unease (almost as though society had lost its way) are more pronounced in blue-collar than in middle-class areas.

Mr Peake says several facts connected with the above have emerged from his experience of cross-community involvement: (1) It is very difficult to attract Protestants to and keep them in such groups, with organizations that start 50-50 tending to become mainly Catholic, with a scattering of Protestants. (2) The same is true for blue-collar workers. (3) An open meeting to discuss religious differences will attract mainly Catholic middle-class women. (4) 'Members of cross-community committees are generally atypical of our society, having had a life experience which has removed them in some way from their community, such as having lived abroad, given up their religion, or having made a "mixed" marriage.'

Mr Peake then outlines various steps towards improving the situation. There should be more contact between amenable organizations which are not in themselves religious, but are at present nevertheless almost totally Protestant, like the Women's Institutes, and similar almost totally Catholic organizations, like the Credit Unions. Community development (and involvement) schemes are absolutely vital, particularly in working-class areas, not only for developing leadership skills, but also for showing people that by starting a play-group or stopping a new road from going through, they actually have the power to change things. Equally vital is for local Protestant communities to take the lead in inviting Catholics to hear Protestant perceptions and fears (he believes that it is Protestant perceptions and fears which most urgently need to be expressed and understood by Catholics). He concedes that this cannot be done on any large scale, but is sure that there are Protestant clergy in County Fermanagh who, realizing the need for dialogue, would consider approaching a small number of people in their congregations to put such a proposal to them. He emphasizes that some groundwork, using counselling techniques to help reduce fear and alienation among those expressing themselves, would have to be done with each group before such a meeting.

> While there are numerous administrative steps that can be taken to ameliorate our situation, I firmly believe that we are very much like a married couple who have built up a bad relationship over the years. Whatever the faults on both sides, the only possibility of removing bitterness and building a constructive future is to communicate and understand each other, to learn to see with the other's eyes and hear with the other's ears.

He urges the setting up of problem-solving and communication courses — the kind used by marriage guidance counsellors, encounter group leaders and management trainers — for interested people involved in community and cross-community development to find out more about their own prejudices and how other people see things across Northern Ireland's religious, class and sexual divides.

Mr Peake also suggests some administrative steps, emphasizing that it would be better if these were taken as a result of dialogue between the two communities, rather than imposed by government. These include the suggestion that members of the police force should take an oath to uphold the law and not of loyalty to the monarch, and that complaints against the security forces should be investigated by an outside police force, and in serious situations there should be a non-UK observer.

OCTOPUS, the Northern Ireland chapter of the US-based National Coalition Building Institute, leads 'experiential workshops' to develop five specific skills: identifying the information and misinformation which groups learn about other groups; identifying and expressing pride in one's own group; learning how other groups experience mistreatment; learning the personal impact of discrimination; learning how to interrupt prejudicial jokes, remarks and slurs. The Derry-based group says it is vital in Northern Ireland to 'create as many safe spaces as possible for people to learn about the effects of others mistreatment'. Octopus works particularly to develop leadership skills in undervalued groups like young and working class people and women, but also wants to help decision-makers to have 'the skills to enter into dialogue and work towards the non-violent resolution of conflict at a personal and political level'.

MR JAMES CLARK, an east Belfast businessman, believes that imposed solutions will not work in Northern Ireland and that any solutions must come from the ground up. He wants these to be built on what the people of the region already have in common, which he thinks is much more than is generally recognized. He cites the examples of the common needs of mentally handicapped children and of young mothers of children who attend the same playgroup; businesses which depend on each other; and church groups that are working quietly together on joint projects.

Mr Clark would like to see a group of knowledgeable and respected people consulting the citizens and putting together a consensual 'mission statement' pointing the way towards a better life for everyone in Northern Ireland, irrespective of an eventual political solution. This would include such aims as a good education for everyone to reach their maximum potential, a decent place to live, a secure and safe environment, and the development of the arts. To monitor how Northern Irish society measured up to these aims, he suggests the establishment of a special tripartite department — made up of representatives of government, business and community groups — to co-ordinate the activities of existing monitoring agencies like the Consumer Council and the Ombudsman and keep a check on how government and other bodies are falling short of the ideals contained in the mission statement.

DR LEO SMYTH of University College, Galway says that the structure of decision-making facing Northern Ireland's politicians resembles one which has been found, under laboratory conditions, to have predisposing tendencies to conflict.

A willingness to co-operate is blocked by fear of exploitation; mutual accommodation is less desirable than outright winning (which increases fears in the other party of exploitation); a common result is a state of affairs that pleases nobody but has the virtue of being better than exploitation by the other party.

Both nationalists and unionists face the same challenge: to be a majority under one constitutional arrangement is to be a minority under another, with the result that the aspirations of one side are always a threat to the other. The risk in making substantial concessions is the risk of ending up exploited as a permanent minority.

The SOCIAL DEMOCRATIC AND LABOUR PARTY submitted a 1991 analysis paper on the nature of the Northern Ireland problem. The SDLP believes that this problem is 'in essence a conflict between two identities'. After outlining the Irish identity of Northern nationalists, it identifies the 'Irish dimension', acknowledged as valid and legitimate by the British Government in the Anglo-Irish Agreement, as a 'fundamental element of whatever new arrangements might emerge from the current process'.

It then goes on to describe the unionist community's perception of itself as British. This means that, from the unionist perspective, whatever emerges from the current process would 'have to be such as to guarantee their sense of identity and to assuage their fears in terms of the perceived threat posed by Irish nationalism to their ethos and way of life'.

An accompanying speech by party leader Mr John Hume at the opening of last year's inter-party talks quotes from the New Ireland Forum report to encapsulate the SDLP's standpoint. In that report we, along with the other nationalist parties on this island, defined ourselves as those who identify themselves as part of a nation which extends throughout this island, and who seek the unity and independence of that nation. For historical reasons we may in the past have defined ourselves in terms of separation from Britain, and opposition to British domination of Ireland. The more positive vision of Irish nationalism in recent times has been to create a society that transcends all differences and that can accommodate all traditions in a sovereign independent Ireland united by agreement.

It is the SDLP's belief, Mr Hume goes on, that the two communities in Northern Ireland, however they are defined, have certain inalienable rights.

If our strategy for dealing with this problem were to be reduced to its most essential core, it would be the need to create new arrangements in this island to accommodate those two sets of legitimate rights: the right of nationalists to effective political, symbolic and administrative expression of their identity; the right of unionists to effective political, symbolic and administrative expression of their identity, their ethos and their way of life.

No solution is available to us through victory for either of these identities. So long as the legitimate rights of both unionists and nationalists are not accommodated together in new arrangements acceptable to both, that situation will continue to give rise to conflict and instability.

Other submissions covering the cultural, religious, psychological and media aspects of the Northern Ireland situation — among other things — came from Ms Janet Brennan, Cathal and Catherine Brugha, Ms Yvonne Burgess, Mr Noel Conway, Mr M.J. Curran, Mr Robert Greacen, Mr Simon Hall-Raleigh, Mr Paddy Houlahan, Mr Maurice McCartney — a redefinition of the population to include the distinct, liberal community, Mr Joe McCool — the damaging effect of the standardization of postal addresses on rural tradition; Mr Michael McCaughan, Mr Roy McClenaghan (Ekklesia Christian Fellowship), Mr Peter McLachlan, Mr Patrick McVeigh, Ms Anthea McWilliams, Mr David Mason, Mr Edward Orme, Strabane and Omagh Community Relations Forum, Upper Ards Historical Society, Mr Noel Weatherhead.

Education

Thirty-six submissions were received advocating integrated education as a vital link in breaking down religious-community barriers and stereotypes, and helping the process of reconciliation. Few, if any, of them dealt with practical solutions to the problems of extending integrated education in an increasingly segregated society. However, together with the need for a Bill of Rights, this was one of the few subjects that found a wide consensus among people making submissions.

ALL CHILDREN TOGETHER (ACT), the original integrated education pressure group, calls integrated schooling 'a very radical form of reconciliation'. It goes on:

Recent research has shown the positive attitudinal changes which occur when Catholic and Protestant pupils are educated together, particularly at secondary level. This reconciliation does not merely touch the pupil population. There is a cascade of positive influence which touches parents, grandparents, siblings, relations, friends, administrative and ancillary staff. Such influences and contacts, often on a daily basis, are powerful instruments for opening minds to the 'other' community.

The group points out that the Education Reform (NI) Order 1989 states that integrated schools should have a positive religious dimension. It believes that to allow 'a vaguely Christian or wholly secular integrated education system' to develop in Northern Ireland would not be true to the letter or spirit of this law, or truly represent the wishes of most parents or properly benefit community relations. It urges the churches to champion this form of reconciliation 'in a very tangible way' by providing pastoral care for pupils, staff and parents in integrated schools. It also believes that 'shared religious education' is the linchpin of integrated education. All Children Together says that the lack of church support for integrated education demonstrates 'a lack of vision' and is interpreted as 'a desire to hold onto power'.

DR COLIN IRWIN, a lecturer in the Department of Social Anthropology at Queen's University, Belfast, says: 'The tolerant and just societies that we desire must first be created in our schools, and those who oppose such institutional changes must take much of the responsibility for the social failings of their communities.' He insists that segregated education helps perpetuate prejudice and social conflict in Northern Ireland, while integrated education increases cross-community understanding and friendship. Faced with opposition from local community leaders, the Churches and school boards, he argues, the Northern Ireland Office and the Department of Education have failed to provide every child in the region with a real option of attending an integrated school. This should not be tolerated.

Dr Irwin states:

Generations of adults have failed to bring peace to Northern Ireland. Perhaps it is time we gave the young a chance to show us what they can do. They can not do worse. Peacemaking and integrated education is their right.

Experience suggests that integrated education is most successful when it is founded on the principles of freedom of choice, equality and openness in curriculum development. Unfortunately, those who wish to maintain the status quo of social division will continue to deny the social worth of integrated education. But no one is fooled. The children know the truth.

Dr Irwin says that most Church leaders encourage their members to send their children to segregated schools and local politicians frequently try to frustrate the establishment of new integrated schools. He emphasizes that most of the integrated schools are not secular but Christian, offering religious education and guidance in the Roman Catholic and Protestant traditions.

Unfortunately, the Roman Catholic Church in Ireland refuses to make provision for its priests to provide denominational care to the Catholic students at these integrated schools, and at Brownlow College, where a free vote of the parents changed the status of their Protestant state school to 'integrated', the Protestant-dominated regional education authority appointed two governors to the school's board who were opposed to integrated education.

Dr Irwin asserts that availability of integrated education is a human right and says that too many children are turned away because of a lack of schools and places.

Every parent and child in Northern Ireland must be given a real option of choosing integration, starting with their school application and transfer forms. If 10 per cent of the parents and children choose integration, then human rights and the international community must require that 10 per cent of the schools in Northern Ireland are integrated. In this enterprise, government institutions, community leaders, representatives of all the Churches and the various school boards must provide leadership in a spirit of co-operation.

MR TERRY FLANAGAN, principal of Lagan College, Northern Ireland's first integrated school, shares the conviction that segregating children when they reach school age contributes to perpetuating religious divisions. He calls on the Churches actively to support integrated schooling.

Despite considerable goodwill by parents and children for integrated education, what is lacking for the majority of people is the opportunity for their children to experience it. Mr Flanagan says he finds hard to understand

the lack of sustained visible and audible support for integrated education from the Churches. It seems to me that, alongside their high level of visible and audible ecumenism, they should be giving their full support for the children of Northern Ireland to be educated together in schools which will respect and make provision for the children's differing home/community relations.

They should be using their influence with the government to support such schools. That they do not do so seems to me to suggest that their interests are at least vested and are not in the community as a whole. At worst, in theological terms, their lack of visible and audible support may in their own terms be a sin against the God whom they believe did not create the existing distinctive divisiveness.

If the Churches were to openly support the education of children together, it would make it easier for the government of Northern Ireland to be proactive in its support for integrated education. If they cannot/will not do so, then the government, which is charged with seeking the best interests of the whole of society and not any particular group or groups, should seriously consider actively promoting the education together in schools of children of compulsory school age. Perhaps it is time for a symbolic action on the part of both government and Churches.

URSULA and NIALL BIRTHISTLE, who are Catholic parents in Derry, say that, in relation to integrated education, the Catholic Church is not respecting the freedom of conscience of many of its members. They say that pressure should be put on the Catholic hierarchy to refrain from being against integrated schools and to appoint chaplains to them.

In some cases a lot of obstacles have been placed in the way of Catholic parents who send their children to integrated schools. Apart from refusing to appoint chaplains, in some cases there has also been non-co-operation when it comes to these children making their first communion/confirmation and using the local Catholic church.

They also propose integration of the teacher training colleges, peace education in schools during teacher training; Irish language should be offered on the curriculum on state schools where there is a reasonable intake from the Catholic/nationalist community or where a reasonable demand is expressed.

THE FOYLE TRUST FOR INTEGRATED EDUCATION (FTIE), which opened the Oakgrove Integrated Primary School in 1991 and Oakgrove Integrated College in 1992, says that the process of people coming together to plan and set up these integrated schools in Derry has been 'a highly positive, hopeful and heart-warming process of reconciliation'. It also says that it has been an empowering experience in that actual structural change is accomplished by ordinary citizens. Another positive element is that the all-ability nature of integrated schools helps to obviate the social divisiveness of the educational system.

THE IRISH NATIONAL TEACHERS' ORGANIZATION (INTO) believes there is much to be gained through the harmonization of the education systems in Northern Ireland and the Republic. The underlying principles of each have much in common, INTO says, and it is 'through the integration of the best features of both systems that a new base can be created which would ensure genuine equality of opportunity and treatment'. The primary and secondary levels' curricula, with one major exception, are strikingly similar and little difficulty would be encountered in harmonizing them, INTO believes. The exception relates to the Irish language and the significance which it has in the curricula in the Republic. INTO says that the role of Irish within a school curriculum should be related to the educational needs of the child, parental expectations and choice, and the requirements of public policy.

INTO says that 'one of the greatest social evils persisting in Northern Ireland is the continuation of a selective system of education at secondary level'. It has had an adverse impact on the primary school curriculum and categorizes at least two-thirds of our young people as 'failures'. Northern Ireland's higher percentages of A-level passes than England and Wales has been achieved at a disproportionate cost to the rest of the education system, INTO asserts, 'with the result that more children leave secondary education without any form of qualification than anywhere else in the United Kingdom'.

INTO says that in Northern Ireland and the Republic there should be a common age of transfer from primary to post-primary education; second-level schools should have parity of staffing and resources and pursue a widely based common syllabus.

The development of Education for Mutual Understanding as a cross-curricular theme in Northern Ireland is a welcome step, the INTO says. It also proposes further development of a current pilot North-South teacher exchange scheme and says that there should be exchanges within Northern Ireland between maintained and controlled schools.

NETWORK CRAIGAVON, a community relations initiative, supporting integrated education, proposes that it should be mandatory for schools to include information on other cultures and religions, including non-Christian ones, in their curriculum. It suggests that an independent group should be funded to compile a programme of study and perhaps facilitate it within the schools, in a number of pilot schemes. It also suggests that the idea could be developed further, through Parent Teacher Associations and community groups, to give similar information to parents and other adults.

SISTER ANN MARIE McQUADE, principal of the Convent of Mercy in Enniskillen, Co. Fermanagh, advocates a comprehensive system to replace the present selective system of grammar and secondary schooling. Children of all abilities would transfer at 11 plus to a common school where their individual educational needs would be met through the school's internal organization.

The present selective system unjustly labels up to 70 per cent of children as 'failures' at 11, damaging their sense of self-worth and stunting their development educationally and as members of society, she says. It creates two types of schools which are required to deliver the same curriculum and have their success-failure measured by the same yardstick of GCSE results, yet grammar and secondary schools do not enjoy parity of esteem, nor do they start from the same baseline, she asserts. The grammar school has a privileged position in our society, is better resourced and its pupils include the ablest academically, the socially advantaged and those with more positive attitudes to education generally.

The time is right, Sister McQuade believes, to retain what is best in the present system and move on to a better one which takes account of the needs of all pupils.

MRS SHEILA CHILLINGWORTH of Newtownabbey, Co. Antrim, speaks of the intense frustration caused by the educational system and suggests a link between allocation of resources and the high rate of unqualified school-leavers.

The educational authorities must support those who are trying to cope with young people who grow up resenting school, playing truant, joyriding, and leaving school barely literate, to face all the other inner-city social problems as well.

I helped to run a community school in Divis for children like this, so difficult they had been expelled from school. The educational authorities succeeded in closing it. I now run a scheme for poor readers in Ballymurphy and have to beg all my finance from charitable trusts and business firms. The educational authorities refused a grant in an area with a 40 per cent–50 per cent reading retardation rate.

(See also Politics and the Constitution: Talking to Sinn Féin and the paramilitaries.)

MR NICHOLAS SANDERS contributes a detailed paper on the Danish folk high school system and its possible adaptation to Northern Ireland. He recalls that the system's nineteenth-century originator, the Lutheran bishop Grundtvig, wanted the schools to be based not on book learning but on the 'living word', to be imparted by 'the discourses of emotionally engaged teachers, discussion carried far beyond the walls of the classroom, and such relaxations as community singing'. Grundtvig's ideas brought together a belief in the enlightenment of ordinary rural people with the cultivation of social equality and national identity, pride in the latter being firmly placed within a sense of national humility in international relations. Grundtvig's disciples' schools placed the emphasis on teaching citizenship and personal maturity, rather than the tools of a future profession, and to this end avoided formal tests. In the late 1960s and 1970s a new generation of idealistic young people from the cities adapted the schools to bring in urban people looking for adult education courses. However, the schools' continuing emphasis on personal and community development continues to act as an important counterweight to the vocational emphasis in the rest of the Danish educational system. It is this aspect of the folk high schools that should interest Northern Irish politicians, government officials and educationalists, says Mr Sanders, as well as Grundtvig's belief that all people share a need for what he called 'the heartfelt interaction between human beings'. (See also The Economy and Society: Social Policy and Community.)

MR ANDY POLLAK, the *Irish Times* journalist and Initiative '92 co-ordinator, proposes 'a new education and intellectual vision for the future of this island', embodied in the establishment of a new 'Friendship University' located on the Irish border. On a practical level, it would help meet the dramatically increasing demand in the Republic for third-level education places, and provide an alternative for Northern students facing the continuing 'brain drain' from Northern Ireland to universities in Britain. The visionary purpose of the university would be to provide 'a centre of excellence and enlightenment, a place where a new generation of young people — the first for 80 years — can begin to share an all-Ireland perspective in the non-threatening, indeed liberating atmosphere, of learning, debate and research'.

He proposes that the new institution would be set up, not by governments, but by a group of independent people concerned only with education and reconciliation. A precedent for a university being set up in a border region in this way exists in the establishment of the University of Saarbrücken after World War II, as part of the reconciliation process between Germany and France.

Mr Pollak acknowledges that the necessary funding would be huge, and sees such an institution coming about not by government action, but as a partnership between the private and public sectors, with the former playing the major role (as happens in the USA). He believes that such a visionary, yet practical, project would be of interest to EC programmes like INTERREG, the International Fund for Ireland, and wealthy Irish-Americans and US charitable trusts. He believes that, after discussing the project with several university heads, he has identified a number of disciplines which would meet unsatisfied needs in Irish higher education: language studies, rural studies, peace studies, religious studies, business and legal studies, and health studies. One way of avoiding the costs of a 'green field' project might be to form links between existing colleges on both sides of the border, e.g. Sligo Regional Technical College and Enniskillen Technical College, or Monaghan Vocational College and Armagh Technical College. Another less expensive option would be to base the concept on that of a US-style liberal arts college, which could support part of its costs through Irish study courses for visiting US and foreign students. Urging their participation, Mr Pollak says it is high time the so-called 'intellectual class' in Ireland started doing something 'to counter the huge gulf in attitudes, perceptions and interests that exists between the people of the two jurisdictions on this island'.

MR JOHN W. McDONALD, a retired US ambassador who is co-founder of the Institute for Multi-Track Diplomacy in Washington, suggests, among other things, developing programmes for teaching conflict resolution in schools. He refers to the Iowa Peace Institute's courses to train teachers in conflict resolution skills so they can pass them on to their students. This programme, which is now state-wide in Iowa, is also called 'peer mediation' because the young people are trained to resolve their own problems without the involvement of adults.

THE INTERFRIENDSHIP GROUP in Lurgan, Co. Armagh, puts forward a list of suggestions covering a wide range of subjects. Among them are an integrated teacher training college and a training programme, with a strong emphasis on the elimination of prejudice, conflict resolution, community policing, history and culture for all members of the security forces and all candidates for public office.

Other submissions which covered educational issues, among other things, came from All Children Together, Community Relations in Schools, Cookstown High School, Ms Ellen Doyle, the Educational Guidance Service for Adults, Lady Goodison, Ms Rebecca Johnston, Kilcooley Women's Group, Mr and Mrs Morgan, F. John Herriott — Northern Ireland Peace Corps (also Mr Malachy Mahon), Windmill Integrated Primary School (Dungannon), St Patrick's Youth Fellowship (Coleraine), Mr Paddy McEvoy — Steiner schools; Mrs Ann McCay, Ms Nan Magennis, Mothers for Peace (Ilkley), Ormeau Woodcraft Folk — urgent need for young children to mix outside segregated school system, Quaker Peace Education Project (Londonderry), Ulster Humanist Association, Jean and Caroline Whyte, and the Workers Educational Association.

The Environment

There were a small number of submissions on ecological and environmental issues. The GREEN PARTY argued that all decisions should be taken at the lowest possible level, with each sub-district local community in Northern Ireland managing its own education, health, job creation, child care and environmental protection. However, such matters as transport policy, energy distribution and water services, as well as the promotion of intermediate technology and heavy industry should also be pursued at district council and regional administration level. Each community should aim for greater economic self-sufficiency, for example, in the provision of foods from horticultural units, vegetable gardens, orchards and associated food-processing units. Each community should be able to run much of its own industrial production, not only in traditional crafts but also in more modern sectors — for example, computer-related trades like word-processing and desktop publishing, which are both ecologically sound and amenable to decentralization. Some communities would be able to create much of their own energy, by solar panels, windmills, water turbines, biomass units or wave generators. 'It is worth mentioning in this regard that Ireland has the best potential wind power in all Europe.' All communities should be able to recycle and reuse paper, glass, aluminium cans, wood, cloths and vegetable waste. Such traditional thrift-inducing habits as the daily milk deliveries should be encouraged by a tax on the use of non-renewable resources, like plastic milk cartons. All communities should take on the disposal of their own wastes. (See also Politics and the Constitution: Other Political Submissions; Law, Justice and Security: Reducing the Violence.)

THE WOMEN'S PLANNING NETWORK of the Royal Town Planning Institute (Northern Ireland), a group of 12 women planners with an interest in planning and environmental issues, posed a number of questions that people in their profession needed to be asking in Northern Ireland.

Do the recreation facilities provided in our towns and cities cater for the desires and aspirations of women as well as men? Does the layout and location of housing meet the needs of women? How effective is public transport? What is the provision of creches, toilets, play and other facilities in our town centres? Are multi-storey car parks user-friendly? Is our city dominated by road and car users? How isolated are women in peripheral estates? How can women be directly consulted in determining the needs of an area? Are cities safe places for women to live?

Other submissions on environmental issues came from Mr Phillip Allen, Belfast Ecology Group, International Tree Foundation (Omagh), Mr John Leacock, Mr R. Finlay McCance — no democratic control over the Department of the Environment in Northern Ireland, Mr Andrew McLean, Northern Ireland Environment Link, Triangle Recycling Group (Coleraine), and Ulster Society for the Preservation of the Countryside.

CHAPTER 15

The Views of the School Students

James Nelson

As part of the Opsahl Commission's oral hearings, two 'parliamentary' schools' assemblies were held at the Guildhall, Derry and Queen's University, Belfast on 24 and 25 February 1993. Both assemblies were chaired by the broadcaster and film-maker Barry Cowan, and they gave young people from across Northern Ireland the opportunity to voice their concerns and ideas about the region's future.

All secondary and grammar schools in Northern Ireland — Catholic-maintained, state-controlled and integrated — were invited to send two representatives, aged between 16 and 18, to contribute to the debate. In the event, 163 pupils, representing 75 schools, participated. Since all schools were invited but not all responded, it was beyond the control of the organizers to ensure a strict balance of participants across the religious divide. In the end, however, the balance reasonably reflected the religious make-up of the population in the two areas; that is, in Derry the balance was tilted in favour of Catholic maintained schools and in Belfast there were more (mainly Protestant) state-controlled schools represented.

On each day the format was the same. In the morning the students were split into five working groups, each consisting of between 15 and 20 students and led by a member of the Opsahl Commission. Each group had a different topic to discuss and individuals were free to raise whatever issues they wished in relation to that topic. The five groups discussed the following five topics:

> Group 1 — Youth Culture
> Group 2 — Cultural Identity
> Group 3 — Politics
> Group 4 — Law and Justice
> Group 5 — Jobs and Emigration

The informal, intimate atmosphere of the working groups was clearly conducive to open and honest discussion, allowing students to work out points upon which a majority of them could agree. By the end of the morning, each group formulated a motion which reflected their main concerns and this was forwarded, together with a short report, for debate in the afternoon plenary session. While the more heated debate of the afternoon session was to highlight the extent to which these young people displayed entrenched, and at times sectarian views, the commissioners were impressed that, given the right environment, they could establish conciliatory relationships and reach significant levels of consensus.

Not surprisingly, the topics that provoked most debate and aroused most passion in the plenary sessions were Politics, and Law and Justice, followed by Cultural Identity. Youth Culture and Jobs and Emigration produced less discussion, and students expressed little interest, in particular, on the latter topic.

This report will give an outline of students' opinions on the five topics and the motions they passed at each assembly.

Youth Culture

As might be expected, students initially were hesitant about speaking out in this opening debate, particularly in the Derry assembly, but gradually they gained confidence enough to take the floor. The two predominant issues in the discussion of Youth Culture were drugs and sexuality, and there was general dissatisfaction expressed about the way in which these issues are dealt with at present. In terms of the new drug culture, one girl at the Belfast assembly commented:

I do not think adults realize how quickly we grow up because we are subjected to a more open environment than they were and we have to grow up quicker than they did.

On the issue of sexuality, a girl from St Louise's College, Belfast, reporting the findings of her working group, stated:

We decided we needed more education on the emotional side of sexual relationships and we were sick to the back teeth of receiving biological facts and figures.

This claim that young people are forced to deal with issues which their parents are unaware of was certainly highlighted over the two days by the revelation of the extent to which young people had access to drugs. When asked how many people had had contact with drugs (maybe not taken them, but had had access to them), the working group in Derry said that all 17 of them had, and in Belfast 12 out of 17 indicated that they had. The same question was asked in the plenary session in Belfast, where a rough hand-count indicated approximately 70 per cent of the students had had some contact with drugs. The suggestion, therefore, from a boy from Omagh Christian Brothers' School, that, 'adults need to be educated about drugs just as much as the youth', had particular weight.

To help them deal with the problems and difficulties of present-day youth culture, the students had several suggestions. One idea was that, as people with specific needs but no voice, they should have a vehicle for expressing their opinions, either through youth councils, which would advise the political establishment of their needs, or through the voting system, if the voting age was lowered to sixteen. A second suggestion was that advice and information on drugs and sexual issues should be more readily available. A few individuals at the Derry assembly objected to the availability of information on abortion, arguing that such information was a back door route for its eventual introduction. In general, though, there was support for this request. The students, however, did wish to stress that, while they were eager to receive advice and information, it should not come in the form of instruction about what they should or should not do. In the words of one female speaker at the Belfast assembly:

We need alternatives for young people in Northern Ireland, and it is just not enough for adults, teachers and the clergy to say 'Do this or that, and do not touch that!', but we need people who will guide us more.

Exactly where this guidance would come from, however, was a dilemma. Some speakers proposed the best way to get advice would be through 'expert strangers' — for example, guidance counsellors at the Brook Clinic. The fact that such counsellors would not be speaking from any religious or moral bias and were not familiar with an individual's background was, for some students, essential:

I think the 'independent' bit is very important because if you feel you cannot talk to your parents and you could not talk to someone in authority, like a teacher, then it is important that they [the counsellors] would be independent and confidential.

Others, however, felt that having independent counsellors who were unsympathetic to school, Church or parental wishes would create a situation of conflict. One student, speaking from a Catholic background, commented:

If you had an independent counsellor who did not liaise with the school, then there are two philosophies at odds ... independent counsellors would be a good idea but only in conjunction with parents, schools and so on.

When it came to a specific discussion of the Brook Clinic, there was general support for it, but even those who were in favour of Brook believed that it would not be viable in some places because, 'in a small town situation, if you are seen to be going to the Brook Clinic then everyone would know about it in half an hour'. The suggestion, therefore, was that discreet ways of spreading information and offering guidance were more welcome than very public ones.

Motions

In Derry, the assembly passed two youth culture motions: that information on sensitive issues such as sex, drugs and alcohol should be made freely available through specialist organizations, like the Brook Clinic, as well as through schools and churches; this was passed overwhelmingly. The students also passed a motion (by 36 votes to 20) that the voting age should be lowered to sixteen and that youth councils be set up to advise public representatives on issues of concern to young people.

In Belfast, the assembly passed a youth culture motion (by 72 to 2) that the Department of Education should appoint full-time independent counsellors in all schools to advise on all aspects of drugs and sexuality.

Cultural Identity

On the basic question, 'What is our culture?', the students at both assemblies initially attempted to sidestep the Irish/British dichotomy by considering the notions of a distinct Northern Irish identity, or a unifying youth culture. In this vein, some speakers encouraged their peers to 'dwell on the similarities rather than the individualities', but this provoked a frank response from one student in Derry: 'The main political conflict in cultural identity cannot be ignored.' And, as if to testify to this, the majority of the discussion focused on the issue of 'Britishness or Irishness?'

At both assemblies there was, perhaps surprisingly, a clear majority of support for an Irish culture. A Catholic student from Methodist College reported that in her working group in Belfast, 'we felt unanimously that we were all Irish. Even though some of us had British citizenship we felt that our culture was Irish.' There was some opposition to this sentiment. One girl there protested: 'The Protestants of Ulster will never accept the Irish culture.' This particular statement triggered a stream of responses from students attempting to encourage the Protestant tradition to identify with the Irish culture. One typical comment was:

Our culture is there to be enjoyed — it is rich, good and strong and is there to be enjoyed by everybody. It is not for one side to say 'I am a Protestant, so that is not for me'.... It is everybody's culture!

Interestingly, a Catholic student commented that it was not only Protestants who needed to gain greater access to Irish culture. Speaking about his own school, he revealed:

Irish is not promoted at all (about eight people in my year did Irish and it is not offered as an A level option); Gaelic football, hurling and camogie are not promoted and they are very much minority games.

In practical terms, then, there was a request that all schools should give pupils the option to study Irish history and the Irish language ('opportunity' and 'choice' were frequently repeated words in relation to this issue).

History, in particular, was felt to be an essential element of the culture to which to have access. As one student pointed out:

We are the politicians of the future and we should be allowed to learn where we come from, because if we do not know where we come from, we will not know where we are going.

The single greatest factor causing Protestants to dissociate themselves from the Irish culture was considered, by some, to be religion: 'They are afraid that others will think ... they are being swallowed up by the Catholic faith and that they will be ruled from Rome', suggested one Catholic boy at the Belfast assembly. Perhaps it was the manner in which this speaker talked about Protestants as if there were none present which dissuaded them from speaking up, but no Protestant endorsed or disputed this comment. The same speaker concluded that if culture is to be 'for everybody', it should, therefore, have 'nothing to do with religion'. In the Derry assembly, however, the religious element to culture was not so easily dismissed. As one speaker reflected:

We could not talk about cultural identity without discussing religion, and the two are so closely linked in the present situation, you cannot avoid them.

A student from Omagh Christian Brothers' School argued against this linking of religion and culture, saying that cultural differences in Northern Ireland were actually 'a political clash of cultures, rather than a religious clash of cultures; a question of the Union and the border rather than a question of Communion and the Bible.' However, the majority believed that religion was the dominant influence in creating a cultural divide and, by implication, a divide would remain as long as the two traditions existed.

The need to develop a society which accommodated diversity and difference was proposed by one student, who commented, 'I think the problem is less that we have two traditions; more that we have two traditions which cannot respect each other'.

There was considerable support for integrated education. A typical opinion was that 'if people can learn together, they can live together'. A number of speakers, however, attempted to stress the practical difficulties involved in integration. A male student from Lagan College confessed proudly, 'I go to an integrated school, and evidently I think it is the best way,' but he wanted to know, 'how are you going to integrate across the board?' More negatively, another speaker enjoined: 'to have Protestants going over to west Belfast and going to a solely integrated school ... is not going to work'.

Motions

In Derry, the assembly passed a cultural identity motion (by 46 votes to 11) that religion influenced culture and identity in Northern Ireland more than any other factor.

In Belfast, the assembly passed three cultural identity motions: that people should recognize a common Irish culture and a love of Northern Ireland (78 to 10); that education should be integrated throughout the system, not just at secondary level (68 to 16); and that religion should not be married to politics (79 to 1).

Politics

It was the debate on politics, in both assemblies, which created the first friction among the participants. Whereas people could agree to disagree about personal issues such as drugs and sex, and on the vague notions of culture and identity, compromise was possible, politics was something that mattered. But coupled with this sense of immediacy about political matters was a disillusionment and dissatisfaction with the present political climate. The Belfast working group reported: 'Political parties...do not really represent the true views of people', and 'are basically sectarian'. (However, it was soon to become clear in the debates on politics and justice that sectarian attitudes were not confined to political parties.) The Belfast Working Group also revealed that, because of this, no one expressed any wish to vote for any present political party. Feelings on these issues were powerfully illuminated by the extra questions asked by the chairman following the politics debate at the Belfast assembly. Of the 57 young people (out of 93 present) who said they would be inclined to take part in the democratic process, only 18 knew what party they would vote for.

During the plenary sessions, the majority of time was given over to two main issues: the constitutional question of how Ireland could be united, and the debate over whether Sinn Féin and/or the paramilitaries should be involved in any future political talks.

With regard to the question of a united Ireland, a student from Omagh Christian Brothers' School was keen to point out that what his working group had proposed was:

New and radical — not just the old Southern takeover of the North ... what we are proposing is a merger of everything in Ireland, so that everyone can participate.

This would be a united Ireland in which the unionists would play an integral role, the Catholic Church would have less influence, and economic problems would be tackled. The only problem was how to persuade unionists that they had nothing to fear.

One speaker, however, objected to the flow of this argument, pointing out that, 'It is not that they [the unionists] do *not* want to be nationalist; they just want to be British.' In response , the student from Omagh perceptively noted that, for some unionists, their murals, their philosophy, is about the separateness of Ulster, rather than any pro-British theme — they all go on about Cuchulainn, the defender of Ulster, from the Irish enemy, rather than any link with Britain.

Although the motion in support of Irish unity was passed at the Derry assembly, it was clear that several Protestant students still felt that their case was not being fairly represented. A student from Portora Royal School, Enniskillen articulated this dissatisfaction when, after the vote, he interrupted proceedings to say:

We do not have a fair representation of the community here. There are considerably more Catholics than Protestants, and although the motion might be carried here, you cannot really say it is representative unless there are more Protestants.

Interestingly, the response to this comment came from two Protestant girls. One declared:

I am a Protestant and I heard that all schools were invited, and if they did not come, that was their own choice.

The other said she was also a Protestant and had voted for a united Ireland.

Both assemblies spent the majority of their time in the politics debate discussing the question of who should be included in talks about a political solution. For several speakers, there seemed to be no distinction between Sinn Féin and the IRA, and the question of talking to their representatives was, in both cases, dismissed: 'Why should we sit down and be dictated to by people who want to destroy the state?' Others, however, saw two distinct issues: Should we talk to Sinn Féin's elected representatives? And should we talk to the republican and loyalist paramilitaries?

Some spoke out against talking to Sinn Féin because it had 'abused and blackened the name of democracy'. The majority of speakers, though, recognized the fact that 'Sinn Féin is a registered political party' which legitimately represented the republican vote. On this point, one speaker commented: 'If you continue to block off the political avenue, I am afraid we are just going to see another twenty-five years of what is going on.'

It was also suggested that the inclusion of Sinn Féin made that organization more accountable:

Should they not have to answer for the killing, murdering and the hate? The only way we are going to get answers from the IRA is to have them sitting here, and if that is in the form of Sinn Féin, then so be it.

A spin-off of this discussion concerned the credibility of other parties to be at the talks table, particularly the DUP. For Sinn Féin to be barred from talks for supporting violence, and the DUP not, seemed to one girl from Limavady Grammar School to be hypocritical: 'Surely Ian Paisley supports violence', she said. This point was challenged, but it received a fiery reply:

Did the Unionist parties not make up the Third Force? Did Peter Robinson not march through Clontibret and was fined ten thousand punts? Does he not support violence?

On the issue of talking to paramilitaries, opinions were again polarized. 'Paramilitaries have waived their right to be involved in talks', said one speaker. 'You cannot have a peaceful solution when you do not talk to people who are fighting', another retorted.

It was the latter view which gained most support among students at both assemblies. Even one girl, who felt 'perhaps it is not right to give them [the paramilitaries] a political entity' admitted:

these are the people who are making the difference on the streets ... the murderers *are* ruling Northern Ireland, and until people start talking to them, Northern Ireland is going to stay in the quagmire it is in now.

It seemed, therefore, that the vast majority of students (some with preconditions, most without) gave wholehearted assent to the statement that: 'the only way to look forward is to get *everybody* sitting around that table'.

Motions

In Derry, the assembly passed a politics motion (by 39 to 21) that the only viable solution for the Northern Ireland problem is a united Ireland by agreement, and that in the interim there should be an extended period of negotiation involving all parties, including paramilitary organizations, with a view to appointing a constitutional convention whose duty shall be to arrive at a new and balanced constitution for a new Ireland. Students in Derry were also asked to vote separately on the part of the motion which proposed that all paramilitary organizations be involved in political dialogue. This was passed by 51 votes to 12.

In Belfast, the assembly passed a politics motion (by 72 to 3) that, with a view to radical change which would fully recognize the nationality, culture and religion of all sides, there should be a resumption of the talks process involving all parties, including Sinn Féin, providing that the party condemns/denounces violence. Fifty-one also voted that Sinn Féin should be included in party talks now; 27 voted against this.

Law and Justice

Issues of justice and discrimination were stormily debated by both assemblies in the most emotive topic of each afternoon. The working groups on both mornings had been able to establish general agreement on several points, including a need for a review of the Prevention of Terrorism Act; a review of censorship laws; improved justice in the workplace through further integration and an eradication of intimidation; and increased accountability of the security forces.

Yet any sense of consensus was soon lost when the debate in the plenary sessions got under way. In both cases the discussion had barely commenced when the issue arose: 'Justice on whose terms?' In the words of a student at the Belfast assembly:

I think if you are going to get people to go against the paramilitaries, you are going to have to have a system whereby justice is in place.

The clear implication was that if the 'system' is unjust, who can blame someone for turning to the paramilitaries for 'justice'?

In this accusation of injustice against 'the system', the main perpetrators were seen to be the security forces. This issue, in Belfast particularly, seemed to touch a raw nerve on both sides: Catholic students were aggressive in their accusations, and the Protestant students, in turn, were extremely defensive.

On the one side of the argument it was stated in absolute terms: 'Catholics are discriminated against by the security forces'; 'people will take the security forces seriously only when they start doing their job properly and stop intimidating and harassing the minority'. While, from the other side, the retort came: 'If the Catholics showed respect for the security forces then the security forces would show the same back.'

One remark outraged a student from Methodist College: 'I am insulted', she exclaimed, 'by what the previous speaker has just said. I am standing here as a Catholic, not as a terrorist. How dare he link the Catholic community in general to terrorism.'

The polemics continued. 'I think the security forces do a great job: they risk their lives every day and we should be thankful to them', said a boy from a state school. This received the response from a student of St MacNissis College, Carnlough: 'In my community, about 100 per cent of the population find *no* confidence in the security forces.'

At times the speakers displayed stereotypical attitudes towards the other community. 'Protestants never get hassled by the security forces; it is always the Catholics', said one. 'The trouble in Northern Ireland is the IRA', said another.

Even when it came to discussing reform of the security forces, there was little agreement. For example, when at the Derry assembly the suggestion was made that more Catholics should be recruited to the RUC, a student from Omagh Christian Brothers' School responded:

We believe that, of course, every society needs a balanced police force which reflects the community it serves, but how can Catholics join at present? There are several insurmountable reasons — enormous difficulties with regard to their own personal security.... They are not perceived as a community police force ... in very many areas they are perceived as being an agent of British rule. Even the name, the 'Royal' Ulster Constabulary, giving allegiance to the crown, automatically alienates 40 per cent of the community. How in those circumstances are Catholics supposed to join the RUC?

On both days there was general agreement on only two points. First, students felt that there should be measures employed to ensure against corruption and misconduct in the security forces. Secondly, they agreed that a police force is a necessary part of society. But the nature of it ('civil' or 'military'?) and its make-up (Catholic/Protestant) remained unresolved questions.

The strength of feeling on this issue brought the debate to boiling point on several occasions. Only two speakers at the Belfast assembly attempted to step back from the heat of the debate to urge the participants to generate fresh ideas and to adopt a more conciliatory attitude.

The first speaker from Friends' School, Lisburn, expressed his dismay that:

Nothing that anyone has said so far has been truly original.... And as long as such solutions are bandied about as an independent Ulster, which is a cultural absurdity, and an economic and social impossibility; the continuation of the status quo, which only means the continuation of the troubles; and Irish union, which is of course a backward step to an eighteenth and nineteenth-century nationalism that is out of place in today's world; while such solutions are still bandied about, we will not make genuine progress.

When challenged from the floor to offer his own original idea, the speaker responded:

It is perhaps in closer economic, cultural and, above all, closer political integration in Europe as a whole that the long-term solution to Northern Ireland's problems may be found.

The second speaker, from St Louise's College, Belfast, remonstrated:

I am thoroughly disgusted the way we are behaving here. We are allowing some people's bias to influence us and to allow our blood to boil. How are we ever going to get a solution if we continue like this? What are you people doing? You are just letting arguments flow and it is just like the way it goes with the older generation, and if we continue to allow this to happen, we are never going to get a solution, so listen to what people are saying and take it in. Maybe you do not agree, but you have to compromise, and I think the whole thing is that we have to learn to compromise and we are certainly not doing that here.

Motions

In Derry, the assembly passed a law and justice motion (by 22 to 11, with 24 abstentions) in favour of tighter security, more severe sentences and reforms of the police and army to prevent corruption and misbehaviour.

In Belfast, the assembly passed a law and justice motion (by 82 to 3), urging communities to speak out against the paramilitaries. An extra motion, urging more Catholics to join the RUC, was passed by 43 to 18, with 29 abstentions.

Jobs and Emigration

The topic of jobs and emigration created much less discussion in the plenary sessions than the previous topics, and because feelings were still running high after the law and justice debate, some speakers lapsed into making points on political and security issues.

Although the working groups had worked hard in the mornings, only a couple of ideas were discussed in the plenary sessions. On the subject of jobs and employment, the problems were perceived to be the lack of work and intimidation and discrimination in the workplace. To tackle the latter problem, it was suggested that increased cultural integration would be helpful, as would the removal of political symbols from the workplace; for example, 'Shorts Factory, where you have Catholics working under Protestant, unionist, loyalist symbols'.

With regard to tackling unemployment and improving the general economic situation, the idea of an all-party forum on economics gained the consent of the majority of students in Derry. It was their opinion that economics should have a higher priority on the political agenda:

We should be voting on issues of economics and the quality of our lives, rather than an abstract concept of who rules what.

However, it was pointed out that: 'when politicians in Northern Ireland come together, they just get caught up arguing amongst themselves.... I do not think they would end up talking about economics.'

Emigration proved to be a fairly uncontentious topic. Some thought 'it is sad to see people emigrate...for the very fact that they are leaving the country is making it worse', but, in general, there was agreement that 'by going away, we could come back and make Northern Ireland a better place'.

The 'troubles' featured very low in the reasons for leaving. The students considered the major attractions that drew people away to be: university, employment prospects and quality of life. In contrast to this it was pointed out that:

Northern Ireland has the lowest crime rate in the United Kingdom and is probably one of the cheapest places to live.

Indeed, most students felt proud of their country and were annoyed at the manner in which the media chose to represent it:

It has got its troubles, which is undeniable, but it also has good points. The media choose to portray this as a Beirut zone of dodging bullets, but it's not true.

At the end of the Belfast assembly, the chairman asked the participants to vote on two further questions. The responses were revealing and — to some observers — depressing.

Mr Cowan asked how many of those present believed that the troubles in Northern Ireland would be resolved in their lifetime. Twenty believed they would, 54 believed they would not and 16 did not know. He then asked in what direction the students thought the political tide was turning.

Thirty-five believed that it was turning in favour of the nationalist perspective and only two believed it was turning in favour of unionism. There were eight who thought it was turning in an entirely different direction. The others did not raise their hands.

Motions

In Derry, the assembly passed a jobs and emigration motion (by 36 to 21) in favour of the establishment of a type of local assembly that would concentrate on the economic situation of Northern Ireland.

In Belfast, the assembly passed a motion (by 81 to 9), urging a greater attempt to be made to promote trust and understanding between the two sides of the community through more active, though not compulsory, support for integrated education.

James Nelson is a Co. Antrim-born graduate of Stranmillis College and Lancaster University, who worked on the organization of the Initiative '92 schools' assemblies.

Two Commentaries

The Work of Initiative '92:
An Insider's View

Andy Pollak

The idea for Initiative '92 was born out of a conversation in August 1991 in the Cincinnati Cooler Company café in Belfast's Botanic Avenue between the editor of *Fortnight*, Robin Wilson, and the professor of jurisprudence at Queen's University, Simon Lee. They were concerned that, following the collapse of the first round of inter-party talks earlier that summer, the people of Northern Ireland were being reduced to mere spectators at their fate, and they believed there was a widespread desire among all kinds of people for a new means of expressing their views and hopes about the future.

Their idea was for an independent commission of inquiry to which the people of Northern Ireland — and those beyond who were concerned about it — would be invited to submit ideas on possible ways forward for the region. Apart from that, there would be no limitation on what the ideas could be about; they realized it was vital that the terms of reference of such a commission should be kept as open as possible, so that no view would be excluded.

The two men spent the following autumn sounding out opinion about their idea, and bringing together a group of people — most of them active in Northern Ireland's vibrant community and voluntary sectors — to act as a 'steering group'. The project began to get off the ground towards the end of 1991, when three major charitable trusts offered support: the Joseph Rowntree Charitable Trust, a charity known for its readiness to back both innovative ideas and projects aimed at broadening and deepening the concept and practice of citizenship and democracy, came in first with £100,000; it was followed by the Barrow Cadbury Trust with £50,000 and the Northern Ireland Voluntary Trust with £25,000 (see below for details of further funding).

In the meantime the 'steering group' had gathered 150 people from Northern Ireland and beyond to act as the ultimate owners or 'patrons' of the project, to whom a management committee would report on a regular basis. These people came from a wide variety of social, political and religious backgrounds. They included writers like Seamus Heaney, Michael Longley, Jennifer Johnston and Brian Friel; businessmen and trade unionists like Billy Hastings, Seán O'Dwyer and Lord Blease; clergymen like Bishop Samuel Poyntz, the Rev. John Dunlop and Father Denis Faul; and people like the former hostage Brian Keenan, the then chairperson of the Equal Opportunities Commission, Mary Clark-Glass, the student leader Maxine Brady, the former SDLP politician Paddy Devlin, and the peace activist Máiréad Corrigan-Maguire. Others who joined later — we ended up with over 220 patrons — included the trade unionists John Freeman and Joe Bowers, the lawyers Peter Smith, David Hewitt and Paddy O'Hanlon, the singer Paul Brady, and the Sports Council chairperson Don Allen. However, the 40 or 50 most active and committed members of the patrons body came largely from the voluntary sector, community groups and church and recon-ciliation groups.

A number of meetings of patrons in the early months of 1992 approved the setting up of a management committee and charged it with finding a seven-member commission of inquiry of eminent, knowledgeable, fair-minded people and appointing a small secretariat to publicize the project and canvass people to contribute their ideas to it.

Initiative '92's work programme was launched, and the seven members of the Commission were presented to the public, at a press conference in Belfast's Linen Hall Library on 26 May 1992. Their role was then effec-tively put on hold for eight months to allow the small secretariat to canvass the public for submissions.

Through the summer and autumn, speakers criss-crossed Northern Ireland addressing public meetings, womens', Church, business, trade union, rural, student, schools, youth and community groups and confer-ences. Twenty-nine public meetings were organized — all but a couple of them by Initiative '92's workers — in places as far apart (in every sense) as the strongly nationalist border areas of south Fermanagh and south Armagh and unionist north Antrim and Coleraine, from Bangor and Newtownards in the east to Derry and Limavady in the west. Outside Northern Ireland, speakers went to London, Dublin and Cork.

There were many private meetings too. Leading members of the four main constitutional parties were briefed about the project, as were Sinn Féin, Democratic Left and the small loyalist Ulster Democratic Party. There were meetings with senior police and military officers, senior civil servants from both the British and Irish governments, and church, business and trade union leaders.

This period was also spent in the arduous task of raising the necessary extra funding to make up the shortfall in the project's total budget of £228,000. The Nuffield Foundation put in £23,500, and the remainder came from the Tudor Trust (£15,000); the Howard Charitable Trust in

Dublin (£4200); the First Trust Bank (£4000), which co-sponsored the schools' assemblies (with Nuffield); the Baring Foundation (£2500), the Ulster Telethon Trust (£2000), the Community Relations Council (£1400 for focus groups), the Arthur McDougall Fund (£250), and a number of individual donors.

In many ways, this was the most difficult period of the project. It was clear that certain large sections of Northern Irish society could not or would not put their ideas down on paper and send them to an unknown group of people calling themselves Initiative '92. There was great suspicion of us in three particular groups. Among republican-minded community activists in west Belfast, the 'ghetto' mentality, which is suspicious of anything that originates from outside its precincts, was reinforced by our appeal for their ideas on Northern Ireland's *political* future. It became clear that we were being shunned by such people because of the Government's dubious policy of 'political vetting', i.e. removing official funding from community groups on suspicion of being unduly influenced by Sinn Féin and/or paramilitary groups. Understandably in these circumstances, it proved difficult to persuade them freely to express their republican views through Initiative '92's very public process.

In nationalist Derry, where we did get a good response, one patron pointed out that, for many people, the very act of signing their name to a document containing their ideas and sending it to an unknown and unproven commmission — albeit one that kept stressing its independence from governments and political parties — was extremely difficult in a society where trust had broken down and signing statements was identified with false confession evidence extracted under police interrogation.

The same lack of trust, in a different form, was a block to persuading traditional Protestants — although not urban working-class loyalists — to contribute their ideas. Strenuous efforts were made to get the views of border Protestants, described in the Presbyterian Church's submission as 'one of the most vulnerable and terrorized communities in western Europe'. But perhaps for that very reason, we failed: the groups we approached did not have sufficient confidence in our Commission, believing it did not adequately represent the unionist point of view. In vain did we point out that it did not represent the nationalist viewpoint either, and was not meant to, being rather a group of fair-minded 'good listeners' who were prepared to consider all sides' positions.

This demand for the Opsahl Commission to be seen to have a strong unionist representation was also the response when members and supporters of the Democratic Unionist Party were approached. It was as if they did not trust themselves to be able to put their strong unionist arguments convincingly in public, believing that any group of 'outsiders' must by definition be prejudiced against their viewpoint. This extreme lack of confidence — bordering sometimes on paranoia — even led to DUP officials refusing to allow Initiative '92 to have their published policy statements; the ostensible reason being that our Commission had invited Sinn Féin to one of its oral hearings.

As one contributor pointed out, even the word 'process', which we liked to use about the Initiative '92 project — calling it a process of inquiry, debate and dialogue — was suspect to many strong unionists. For them the very idea of 'process' implies movement, and in their present insecurity, any movement can be only in one direction: towards the thing they most fear — the weakening of Northern Ireland's links with Britain, and a shift towards a united Ireland.

In Northern Ireland trust between people is a rare commodity. Many people, especially in the areas most affected by violence, will do something for a person or an organization only if they personally know and trust that person or organization. The work of Initiative '92's outreach workers, therefore, became crucial to our success. To gather the ideas required to initiate a popular debate, we had to win the trust of significant groups across a wide spectrum of civil society.

To the extent that we succeeded in this, credit is due particularly to three outreach workers, Kate Kelly, Paul Burgess, and Helena Schlindwein, the last of whom we could afford to keep on only for a very short time in Derry. These were people who were known and trusted respectively among women and women's groups in greater Belfast, in the Protestant working-class areas of north and west Belfast, and in Derry. The result was that some of the most thoughtful written submissions — and provocative oral hearings — came from individuals and groups in these areas.

Another mechanism we used to gauge opinion among those sectors of society that normally would not participate in an exercise like Initiative '92 was 'focus groups', a method used widely by political parties and social researchers in the United States. We organized six of these confidential discussion groups, assisted by a research consultant familiar with the method, with people from the Shankill Road area of Belfast, south Armagh, south Tyrone, rural mid-Ulster (two) and the Waterside area of Londonderry. According to this method, the participants are chosen as typical 'ordinary' residents of an area and are invited to take part by a number of trusted local intermediaries — ministers of religion, priests, councillors, community leaders and so on. Their discussions about the future of Northern Ireland, led by a trained facilitator, were recorded, transcribed and studied in confidence by members of the Opsahl Commission.

One of the most marginalized groups in Northern Ireland are the prisoners. However, the fact that so many prisoners are paramilitaries or former paramilitaries often means that they are highly intelligent, motivated and articulate. We managed to persuade the prison authorities to allow us to mail an invitation to every prisoner in Northern Ireland, inviting them to contribute their ideas to Initiative '92. As a result, a small number of significant submissions came, particularly from republican prisoners in the Maze and Crumlin Road Prison in Belfast.

At the other end of society, we met some predictable middle-class apathy (see chapter 3), and even hostility. We received reports of dinner conversations that accused us of being 'a middle-class masturbatory exercise'; a commission of foreigners who knew nothing about Northern Ireland; a waste of time and money because only the politicians and the government could change anything; and the authors of one more report on the most researched piece of divided territory on this earth. Our response to such criticism is to ask the critics to study this report. Is a process which involves hundreds, even thousands, of people, in a debate about the future of this little region — one of the least successfully governed in western Europe — a waste of time and money in a society which claims to be a democracy?

On the other hand, some of our strongest supporters were also from the middle classes: Church people, business people, academics, and the group from which the project took much of its energy — young, politically conscious professionals who, whether unionist or nationalist, want to see the return of active, participatory politics to Northern Ireland (however they perceive it) and have strong and often idealistic views on how those politics should be exercised. Many of the most impressive submissions came from this group. The one big disappointment here was the lack of interest in what we were doing from the Northern Catholic bishops, although Father Denis Faul and the Jesuits were enthusiastic in our cause. (The former said that addressing the Opsahl Commission at a Dungannon oral hearing made him feel like a citizen of classical Athens!)

November 1992 brought to an end — for the present, at least — the political talks between parties and governments. Perhaps not surprisingly, this latest withdrawal of the politicians from the negotiating table provoked renewed media and public interest in Initiative '92's efforts to provide an alternative 'citizens' forum'. Submissions started to arrive in their scores at our office in Belfast's Lisburn Road.

As the 11 January 1993 deadline approached, the number of written submissions had reached 500 and they were still coming. In the end there were 554, representing, when those involved in group and organizational submissions are taken into account, the work of around 3000 people. Of these, 414 came from Northern Ireland (193 from Belfast, 45 from Derry city and county, and 176 from the rest of Northern Ireland), 69 came from the Republic of Ireland, 59 came from Britain and 12 came from farther afield. One member of the Commission sensitive to such things calculated

— on the basis of the slightly smaller total of submissions he had then received — that of the submissions originating in Northern Ireland, 45 per cent came from Protestants, 22 per cent came from Catholics, 10 per cent were done jointly, and 23 per cent were from groups or individuals who were neutral or non-identifiable.

The six weeks of oral (largely public) hearings took the Commission from Belfast to Derry (to the Guildhall, the Bogside and the Waterside), to Newtownards, Coleraine, Enniskillen and Dungannon, and back to the Falls and Shankill Roads in Belfast. They were widely reported in the Northern Irish, Irish and — to a lesser extent — the British media, and were generally welcomed as an unusual and imaginative way of giving the voiceless people of Northern Ireland a platform, at a time when their political representatives' voices were stilled (see 'An American at the Hearings'). The media, a conservative body at the best of times — fascinated by 'important' people and generally uninterested in the 'ordinary' citizen — had blown somewhere between cool and cold for the first eight months of our 'citizens' inquiry'. Now, however, even the largely reactive local press (see Sam Butler's strictures in chapter 14), spurred on by some excellent coverage in *The Irish Times*, *The Guardian* and the *Financial Times*, began to see the potential of this unprecedented exercise in Northern Irish society looking at itself. In fact, the unionist *Belfast News Letter* covered the oral hearings on a daily basis — like *The Irish Times* — and went so far as to defend Initiative '92 against criticism from that normally most reasonable of unionist politicians, Ken Maginnis.

The politicians were, perhaps understandably, suspicious of this non-elected group dabbling in what they consider to be their business. One party leader politely asked me to refrain from writing, after the third such letter, to request him to make a submission. However, it was notable, in the event, that senior politicians from three of the four main constitutional parties — the exception being the DUP — put forward their parties' views at the Opsahl Commission's hearings.

Many people who were initially sceptical of Initiative '92's scheme were won over by the high level of debate and interchange of ideas at the Commission's hearings. A visitor from the Republic wrote afterwards about the Commission's

formidable array of intellectual talent, compassion and wisdom. Equally impressive, though, is the willingness of so many ordinary people — submission writers, audience, staff — to set aside the feeling of hopelessness that rises insidiously after twenty years of failed initiatives; to devote effort and patience to reflection and analysis without fear of failure; to try to hold in one conceptual arena painstakingly worked-out proposals for political progress, and a simple but arrestingly eloquent account of life in a disadvantaged area of Belfast. Many gifts, many perspectives, building into the kind of widespread participation without which no progress can be made in Northern Ireland. Already, it's an achievement.

There were, of course, many weaknesses in the Initiative '92 approach.

Paul Burgess, one of our outreach workers, was not the only person who felt that the 13-month timespan meant that many key tasks were done at sometimes self-defeating breakneck speed. First among these was the job of gradually and gently winning the trust of less confident, more marginal, more disenfranchised sectors of society, like women, working-class and rural people. Ideally this would have needed much more time than we had, in between the rest of our multifarious tasks, over the year.

Even members of the 'chattering classes', well-used to articulating their ideas and having them represented on television and in newspapers, confided that they found the prospect of sitting down and writing something on ways forward for Northern Ireland a daunting one. How much more so was this the case among the so-called 'ordinary' people whom Initiative '92 was trying to persuade to contribute? Having become conscious of this, we borrowed tape recorders from the BBC and in the last three months of 1992 outreach workers made a point of seeking out and interviewing articulate working-class community representatives and spokespeople for marginal groups, in particular. Time, however, was not on our side. Ironically, it was in the few weeks immediately before the January 1993 submissions' deadline — fixed because of the need to move on to the second stage of our process, the oral hearings — that we were, for the first time, gaining public profile.

I am confident, had we been given another six or nine months to do more careful work with groups who still needed persuading that they too could and should engage in this unprecedented act of public, political dialogue, we could have doubled or even trebled the number of submissions. As it is, we began to break through the wall of apathy and alienation from politics that nearly a quarter of a century of violence and deadlock had erected. As the Northern Ireland Voluntary Trust said in its submission:

Initiative '92 took upon itself a formidable task. Launched at a time of particular fatalism and despair throughout Northern Ireland, it has contributed significantly to dialogues, discussions and horizon setting.... Our hope is that Initiative '92 will act as a catalyst and signposter of future directions.

The patrons of Initiative '92 have decided to continue the process for another year. Starting in the autumn of 1993, there will be a series of conferences, youth, school and community debates, focus groups, opinion polls and other events to build on the results of the citizens' inquiry detailed in this report. Impressed by the enthusiasm and articulacy of the participants in the two schools' assemblies, and the level of frank, open-minded discussion in those assemblies' working groups (see chapter 15), the patrons hope to lay particular stress on school and youth activities. As we said in the leaflet launching the oral hearings:

The ideas raised and the debate provoked by Initiative '92 and the Opsahl Commission will not be allowed to gather dust on a shelf or die away into apathy and helplessness. Initiative '92 isn't going to go away in 1993; just as Charter 77 in Czechoslovakia didn't go away in 1978. We are going to start a debate about the future of Northern Ireland, a citizens' debate, a people's debate. We're only just beginning... .

Michael Longley, in his poem at the beginning of this report, speaks of a space, a safe space, a clearing in Northern Ireland's jungle, in which people can share their thoughts and words. If such a shared space — in which ordinary people can begin to discuss the difficult issues of politics, justice, and ways forward for Northern Ireland — can be maintained and even expanded, then Initiative '92's work will not have been in vain.

I have a final, personal point. One of the great pleasures and privileges of this job over the past year has been to meet some of the remarkable — even inspirational — people who have been working away quietly for much of the last two decades all over Northern Ireland. The following are just some of those to whom I want to pay tribute for their work in providing the cement that keeps a functioning, and in places a vibrant, Northern Irish 'civil society' ticking over, while others are trapped in apathy, intransigence and violence: Vivienne Anderson and her colleagues in north Belfast; Jackie Redpath of the Greater Shankill Development Agency; Duncan Morrow and his colleagues in the Corrymeela Community; Dougie Hegney, the Belfast Catholic taxi-driver who had lost his son in a sectarian assassination and talked to us about the differences between bad and good policing; the County Antrim Protestant businessman who spends much of his spare time advising community groups in west Belfast; Eamonn Deane and his visionary colleagues in the Holywell Trust in Derry; Paul Sweeney of the Northern Ireland Voluntary Trust; Sheila O'Hara and Geraldine O'Regan in west Belfast; Colm Cavanagh, Anne Murray and their colleagues in the Foyle Trust for Integrated Education; Karen McMinn of the Northern Ireland Women's Aid Foundation. These are the unsung heroes of Northern Ireland. When a society has such citizens, there is real hope for its future.

An American at the Hearings:
An Outsider's View

Lionel Shriver

For Northern Ireland it was a unique experience. Here were people engaging in an intellectual debate about the future of the region, relishing the stimulation of the argument, anxious to propose, anxious to listen, anxious to respond. For the most part, here were no well-rehearsed, iterative, adversarial positions, up for 'negotiation' (as if that was how ideas could, or should, be handled).

Here were sophisticated witnesses: the two most prominent civil servants in the respective histories of the two states, North and South, Sir Kenneth Bloomfield and Dr T.K. Whitaker, brought vast experience and rigorous minds to the table. The Presbyterian moderator, Dr John Dunlop, brought a deep reservoir of knowledge of one of the largest of Northern Ireland's cultural communities.

Here, too, were voices previously unheard — of working-class women community activists in west Belfast, for whom the dominant political agenda appeared largely irrelevant; as irrelevant as the various 'schemes' to deal with the issue that pressed upon them most: unemployment.

In late January 1993, a senior official of the Department of Foreign Affairs in Dublin was already declaring that the Opsahl Commission of inquiry into ways forward for Northern Ireland was a success, for the 'educational exercise' it had already provided.

A radio comment on the first day of hearings in Belfast by Initiative '92's co-ordinator, Andy Pollak, that the politicians had 'failed' and it was now time for 'the people' to come forward, led to a stinging attack from the Ulster Unionist MP Ken Maginnis, who variously accused the initiative of being 'middle-class', 'naive' and 'simplistic'.

Mr Maginnis's attempt to denigrate the commission's work failed. The *News Letter* accused him of acting 'more than a trifle precipitately', said the Commission had given 'a clear indication that it is prepared to seriously address the real issues which have been plaguing the people of Northern Ireland for generations', and asserted that it deserved 'a fair hearing'. Significantly, no other politician rowed in behind Mr Maginnis's attack, and his 'strand two' talks colleagues, Christopher and Michael Mc-Gimpsey, meanwhile made their own submission at a hearing in Newtownards.

But perhaps the most illuminating political response to the initiative came from one of the parties which did make a collective submission to it — Sinn Féin. Here was another unique situation. For the first time, Sinn Féin faced a level playing pitch: no broadcasting ban to restrict it in putting forward its views; no differentiation between other parties and itself in access to the table. How would it shape up? The answer — an answer which may have considerable significance for the debate on how and whether Sinn Féin can be brought into talks — was clear. It just did not perform. One British journalist said it was like listening to the Militant Tendency.

While other cross-examinations provoked a fascinating exploration of ideas, Sinn Féin would neither engage with the questions on the terms in which they were put, nor articulate any possible compromises it might accept on the way to its ultimate goal. Its ideological rigidity precluded either intellectual flexibility or political pragmatism.

The starting-point for the first submission (heard by the Commission in Belfast's Old Museum Arts Centre), by the former head of the Northern Ireland civil service, Sir Kenneth Bloomfield, was perhaps appropriate. With mandarin understatement, Sir Kenneth argued: 'Whatever the ideal future state (and status) of Northern Ireland may prove to be, its present state of limbo is in many respects unsatisfactory.'

Since it was likely that there could be neither broad consent for unification nor for complete integration with Britain, the 'democratic deficit' should be filled by a power-sharing administration with substantial powers, including 'some involvement' in security. (Sir Kenneth is known to have felt keenly the impotence of the 1974 Executive, of which he was secretary, in this regard.) If this could not be agreed, he said, then a Royal Commission-type inquiry should investigate a new tier of administration between the councils and central government, comprising three or four elected authorities.

Addressing the seven-member Opsahl Commission, Sir Kenneth said that the political process in Northern Ireland urgently needed to be 'reanimated'. The Anglo-Irish Agreement, he said, however lofty its motives, had a very serious defect: it made the Republic the 'specific sponsor or guarantor of one section only of our unhappily divided community'. The 'visible alignment' of the Republic's government with one community would and had driven unionists into a 'defensive position'.

The core of the problem was the lack of confidence between the two communities, although external relationships could not be ignored, and 'responsibility-sharing' was the key to developing confidence, as the players in 1974 had shown. The 'top table' of any new administration had to be 'widely based'; minority safeguards like weighted majority requirements were not enough.

The Presbyterian moderator, Dr John Dunlop, told the Commission that Northern Ireland should be seen as a double-minority problem — including the minority unionists perceived themselves to be in an overall Irish context. Dr Dunlop said he hoped the Commission could encourage a move from 'I win, you lose' politics to 'I win, you win'; co-operation rather than confrontation. Often identity had been negatively defined — *not* British or *not* Catholic — rather than positively affirmed. If one was heavily dependent on a negative perception of the 'other' community for one's own self-definition, one was unlikely to be able to enter into relationships with it. He echoed Sir Kenneth's theme of the need for confidence-building measures to encourage agreement.

Dr Dunlop stressed the importance of 'recognizing and honouring' minorities, and suggested a senate for Northern Ireland as one means of protecting minority rights. He did not demur when the former senior European Commission official, Eamonn Gallagher, defined this as an 'equal share in government and power'.

It was important that, in any constitutional arrangements, 'local people' had access to power and that this was not removed from them. Dr Dunlop, too, suggested that the Anglo-Irish Agreement had led to an asymmetrical arrangement, because of Dublin's perception of its minority guarantor role. There was a need to alleviate the unionists' sense of siege, he said, pointing to the flight of Derry Protestants from Cityside to Waterside.

Commissioners effused gratitude for the testimony of Sally McErlean, a burly, plain-speaking representative of the West Belfast Parent-Youth Support Group. Her testimony struck a lively and good-humoured counterpoint to the sedate Presbyterians. McErlean, who did not consider herself to be political, identified the primary ailment of her area as unemployment, which runs to 85 per cent. 'Everyone's talking about recession,' she said. 'We've had a recession for fifty years. We can't lose our jobs. We've never had jobs. Boys' fathers never worked, their mothers. You ask why our kids joyride? They don't have a car.' Yet she expressed disdain for government schemes like the Youth Training Programmes. 'Twenty-seven pound a week! You buy a pair of shoes, you'll pay that. So you have to steal. Would *you* work for twenty-seven pound? I wouldn't!'

Mrs McErlean is the mother of six, one of whom was murdered by the loyalist Michael Stone at Milltown cemetery. None of her children has ever worked — with a single piquant exception. For a year, one child worked for YTP to gather figures on unemployment.

Motivating students to complete their education is difficult when they have nothing to do with their skills once they leave school. 'I had a son was beakin' school,' Mrs McErlean explained. 'When I rang, they said, "Oh, he hasn't been to school in three years!"' Subsequently, she and other Divis residents organized a community school, 'Crazy Joe's', for such truant children. Although the project was later closed down, other home-grown initiatives, like Conway Mill and Springhill, continue to serve students that mainstream schools had written off as hopeless. However, 'parents are so busy struggling', they cannot think about integrated education. 'That's a middle-class thing.'

She considers cross-community summer camp projects equally irrelevant: 'We want something for our kids in our area. Not taking kids away and bringing them back: "I'll take ye to America!" with big sums of money. Because when they come back, they never meet again.'

Mrs McErlean expressed indignation that legally elected Sinn Féin representatives were excluded from the negotiation process. Yet when pressed to say if she had any faith in the talks, her response suggested that Sinn Féin participation might make a negligible difference: 'Politicians can just walk off. They can call talks on and call them off. I got up this morning very narky. They could get up narky and decide, "I don't feel like talking this morning". Everyone has to work together, and it will never happen.'

As with many later testimonies, however, Mrs McErlean was long on woes and short on answers. Government employment schemes were palliative, schools failing, joyriding endemic... . In its search for positive visions for the future, the Opsahl Commission often found a Northerner's eloquence saved for problems of the present, discussion from the floor rapidly degenerating into scrapping with Families against Intimidation and Terror over that organization's fabled list of IRA expulsion orders.

Mrs McErlean did demonstrate confidence in the people of west Belfast: 'We're going to fight for things to get better', she concluded. 'I would die fighting.'

With the members of the Cadogan Group that afternoon, the Commission was unusually hard-hitting. Eamonn Gallagher began by accusing Cadogan's lengthy, bound submission of not according unionism and nationalism equal legitimacy. The Group drew the admittedly difficult distinction that it was all very well for nationalists to express their aspirations, but it was not their right to act on those desires by eliminating Northern Ireland as a state.

'In all your discussion of discrimination,' observed Mr Gallagher, discrimination that the Cadogan Group believes to have been overestimated, 'you don't mention the Special Powers Act at all.'

'We admit that unionists have often been bigoted', Paul Bew said. 'We're not whitewashing the unionist state. But look at the figures: Catholics are improving economically more quickly than Protestants.'

'Could I just come back to my question?' Mr Gallagher asked sharply. 'There is no reference to the Special Powers Act in your discussion of discrimination.'

'I think the answer is probably that we did not regard it as discrimination,' Dennis Kennedy asserted. 'A lot of people are highly critical of the Special Powers Act, *per se*, not as to whether it was used against one community or the other.'

'It was only used against one community, isn't that correct?'

'No, I don't think so,' Dr Kennedy replied.

'No, that is not correct,' Dr. Bew said in support of his colleague.

'Give me examples, if you can, of when it was used against the loyalist community.'

'We could produce them...,' Dr Kennedy faltered, but we can't produce them out of a hat. It is not a subject that is dealt with in the booklet, and therefore we are not equipped to answer questions like that.'

'That's my point. The Special Powers Act is not dealt with in your booklet, though you do discuss discrimination in great detail.'

The Commissioner then asked Dr Kennedy whether the Group excluded from its definition of a civil right the expression of national identity.

Dr Kennedy said he assumed that what was meant by the right to political expression of an Irish identity for a citizen of Northern Ireland was 'the right of a person living inside Northern Ireland who deems himself politically Irish to be able to live within a political unit which is Irish. Now I do not think that is a civil right, or human right. I think it is a nationalist claim.'

'And how', rejoined Mr Gallagher, 'would you expect to attain the consent of the nationalist community to that?'

'By seeking to confront them with reality.'

'I'm sure that would be very helpful to them.' Gallagher's sarcasmwas palpable.

The Cadogan Group urged unionists to understand that they do not own Northern Ireland, and if they are serious about allegiance to the principles of the United Kingdom, they must put fair democratic structures in place. Nationalists must accept in return that Irish unity or even joint authority can be arranged only by consent of the majority. 'That consent is not forthcoming' rang loudly through the Old Museum. The talks were scuppered from the outset because they put proposals for constitutional change on the table which cannot come about. In the Cadogan Group's view, it was time nationalists became practical.

In his presentation the next morning, the Alliance leader, John Alderdice said the price of political agreement for unionists was sharing at every level. But he said it was 'a matter of deep concern' that the SDLP appeared no longer happy with a 1973/74-type arrangement. He also complained of the asymmetry of the two governments' stances. Indeed, a few days earlier he had told BBC that he believed that the British government was now minded to disengage, claiming that Sir Patrick Mayhew saw his role as similar to that of the Hong Kong governor, Chris Patten — a view which Sir Kenneth Bloomfield had said his experience in government did not bear out.

Just as he had warned unionists in the 1970s that they were driving nationalists towards extreme positions, Dr Alderdice said he was now warning constitutional nationalists that they were doing the opposite. 'If people close their eyes to it, then we will gradually slide into a very violent situation.' There was a 'huge responsibility' on the Republic's government to show the generosity that had been promised.

Dr T.K. Whitaker, the former secretary of the Republic's Department of Finance and governor of the Central Bank, said all Dáil parties and the SDLP now accepted the principle enshrined in the Anglo-Irish Agreement that there could be no change in the status of Northern Ireland without majority consent. Logically, this should mean rewriting the territorial claim in Articles 2 and 3 of the Constitution 'in aspirational terms', but a referendum to that effect might be clouded in 'emotional rhetoric'. Therefore, it was best to accept that the commitment in the Agreement already qualified the claim by the consent precondition.

There was a need to secure 'grudging acquiescence' of a devolved arrangement, he said, since this would deliver peace, and peace was more important than any political arrangement. It should be 'evolutionary', however, in allowing either community in Northern Ireland to change its mind about the preferred constitutional status of the region. It was wrong to describe Northern Ireland as a 'failed' entity, but nationalists could never accept abandonment of their ideal, Dr Whitaker said. The new arrangement should be confirmed by a referendum North and South — in which Articles 2 and 3 *could* be reformulated — and there should be a border poll every 20 years or so in the North.

Northern Ireland was an 'abnormal' constituency, however, because the majority built into its foundation meant that a change of government was not possible. Yet 1974-style power-sharing was not appropriate in the long term, because it confirmed matters of argument to the cabinet room and reduced an associated assembly to a 'cipher'.

Dr Whitaker favoured a 70 per cent weighted majority being required for major decisions — for instance, those affecting 'parity of esteem' between the two communities — and a requirement that every Minister be accountable to a committee on which all parties were represented proportionately. There should also be a Bill of Rights.

Under questioning, Dr Whitaker also suggested that the Republic's role was 'excessively focused' on one side in Northern Ireland, which contradicted the principle of seeking majority consent for unity. It was very important not to exclude for very much longer a big section of Northern Ireland from any influence over its own affairs, he said.

Choosing his words carefully, he proposed an 'Ireland Co-operation

Committee' between institutions in the two jurisdictions, with equal representation, and dealing with matters of common interest, such as EC questions. The Council of Ireland had been misrepresented, particularly by the
SDLP, he said. It had not been intended as a 'vehicle for trundling unionists into a united Ireland', but as the apex of institutions with no executive
functions, unless agreed both North and South. Even a 'semblance' of
Irish unity, Dr Whitaker suggested, would go a long way to satisfying the
nationalist aspiration.

The Northern Ireland Religious for Justice and Peace, a committee
from twelve orders of the Catholic Church which works in nationalist
areas on anything from travellers and employment to prisoners and conflict mediation, concentrated its submission on problems of policing.
Middle class themselves, the committee acknowledged that it personally
found the police supportive. In working-class — or rather 'unworking'
class — neighbourhoods, 'asking Catholics to support the RUC is impossible. They believe they have no control, that the police act as judge and
jury. The RUC inspires nothing but suspicion and fear.' Somehow,
nationalists must be given representation in the police force, with an
authority that is real and not just public relations. The committee admitted, 'We don't have a solution. But some whole new structure must be created.'

'I have real sympathy for the police,' acknowledged one woman. 'They
have to combat crime *and* terrorism. But in west Belfast, the police are
simply not acceptable. For example, my car was hijacked and the RUC
wouldn't come up half a mile away. I called twice. Finally I had a friend
drive me to the station. I got out of that car in *terror*. I was shaking. If anyone had seen me or my friend, in our veils outside a police station, we were
in terrible danger — from our own people.'

One of the Commissioners, Dr Marianne Elliott, observed that Protestants often view the Catholic faith as authoritarian and hierarchical,
with a low emphasis on individual responsibility, which aggravates
Protestant mistrust. The committee believed the misconception could
stand clarification. Since Vatican II, Catholicism has focused more on the
individual conscience. In areas like west Belfast, however ironically, 'if
Catholics turn to Sinn Féin, they are in conflict with the teachings of the
Church. They cling to their faith, but politically can't go along with the
demands of its leaders.' This cognitive dissonance has actually encouraged
Catholic intellectual and spiritual independence.

On the subject of integrated education, the committee was less than
optimistic: 'In principle, we see its value. In practice, we were gerrymandered we live in different areas. We would need US-style busing, which
didn't succeed in America, and no one here would support. Integrated
schools aren't realistic when populations are segregated.' The media, the

committee claimed, promotes the idea that only Catholics are opposed to mixed schooling. 'But Protestants are just as fearful of Catholics teaching their children. They're superstitious.'

Dr Elliott observed how nationalists resented the assumption that they all support the IRA, when there is no parallel assumption about unionist support for loyalist terrorism. Was there, she asked, any ambivalence about violence in the nationalist community that could help explain this? In another example of the shifty relationship to language that Presbyterians had observed of Catholics the day before, the Northern Ireland Religious for Justice and Peace failed to answer the question.

In sum, the Religious put forward yet another moving evocation of the problems in west Belfast, and solutions were spoken of largely in terms of why they would not work.

And so to Sinn Féin, whose four-member delegation was led by its northern chairman, Mitchel McLaughlin. He said the goal should be for the two governments to agree on the objective of ending partition. They should aim to conclude this in the shortest possible time, but with maximum consent. To that end, there should be consultation with Northern unionists and nationalists. The European Community should not fund the status quo, but should support moves to unification, and the United Nations should treat the issue as one of decolonization. Rev. Eric Gallagher, the former Methodist president who was involved in the Feakle talks with the IRA in the mid-1970s, made a warm rejoinder: 'I am as concerned as you are for a settlement. Not just a settlement — a just settlement.' He had not changed his position since the Feakle episode and he had read the party's document several times, he stressed. Against that olive branch, he asked what Sinn Féin felt it could do to build trust in the Protestant community in the inclusive 'peace process' it sought.

It was an opportunity for Sinn Féin to propose conciliatory initiatives. But after recognizing that 'only a fool would ignore the very real divisions in our society', Mr McLaughlin quickly shifted the argument back to Sinn Féin's analysis of the problem: Northern Ireland could not be made 'a stable democratic entity', partition had to be debated 'in a forthright way', and the solution was in an 'all-inclusive, national democratic framework'.

It was a pattern to be repeated. The commissioners' countenances grew glummer and glummer as the Sinn Féin team essentially refused to accept the validity of the questions they were being asked and grew increasingly tetchy and defensive.

When the chairman, Professor Opsahl, asked if Sinn Féin could conceive 'a midway point' on the argument about the renunciation of violence and talks, Bairbre de Brún was adamant: negotiations would bring peace, not peace bring negotiations.

When Marianne Elliott asked how Sinn Féin could encourage unionists into dialogue, Mr McLaughlin said unionists would 'sit on their hands' until the British government changed its position as demanded. 'Let the British break the log-jam', he said.

Asked about possible interim stages short of unification, Pat McGeown, a former Maze hunger striker, said, 'Our analysis is that an end to partition is primary in ending this conflict.' Far from amending Articles 2 and 3 of its Constitution, he said, the Irish government should strengthen its position on unity.

Asked by Professor Opsahl what Sinn Féin's stated commitment to pursuing its policy 'democratically and non-violently' meant in the context of IRA violence, Mr McLaughlin said: 'Sinn Féin's attitude to the right of Irish people to use the option to use violence hasn't changed.' It appeared, Eamonn Gallagher reflected, 'to be all or nothing.'

'The headline about Initiative '92 in the *Irish News* says here, STAND UP IF YOU HAVE THE ANSWERS', began Mary Leonard. 'Well, we're sitting here, and we don't have the answers.' She and Kathleen Feenan, both from Twinbrook, were members of the Women's Information Group (WIG) testifying in a purely personal capacity.

'If women were given a greater role politically, would that improve matters?' Dr Elliott asked.

The WIG was more concerned with women's daily lives and with their children. Few women were likely to come forward as councillors or MPs.

'Are schools not fulfilling their roles?'

Hardly. Whole areas fail the Eleven plus. When schools have low rates of passing, 'something should be looked at. It's impossible that all these children are stupid.'

Asked about ACE (Action for Community Employment) schemes, both women were as scathing as Sally McErlean had been about Youth Training Programmes. 'It's only for a year, and the wages are low. To qualify a second time, you have to be unemployed for a year again; now the project is oversubscribed, they've changed it to *two* years. ACE promotes a vicious cycle of unemployment. They take sixteen-year-olds: three months, painting; three months, paint-peeling; three months, brick-laying; three months, street cleaning. Where's the pride in the job — no money, no security? At the end, they hate it.'

One Commissioner, Lady Faulkner, inquired if the women had any positive ideas for the future.

Some groups, like WIG, had proved fruitful; all were grass roots in origin. But each such project was fighting for funds. With some graciousness, Mrs Leonard and Mrs Feenan did not take any evident offence when, after the break between their testimony and Sinn Féin's, three-quarters of the audience and all the television cameras cleared off. When a minor political party that openly supports the use of violence draws a crowd of over eighty and a peaceful cross-community women's group promptly reduces that number to less than twenty, the Opsahl Commission as an event on 20 January testified all too clearly to what attracts public attention.

After two days in Belfast, the Commission moved to Newtownards, where the Ulster Unionist brothers Chris and Michael McGimpsey said they would not be prepared to sit down with Sinn Féin, since it was 'part and parcel' of the IRA campaign. They said that the problem was not insoluble and could be best resolved through 'a benevolent, liberal and pluralist democracy, in which both communities share', a North-South mechanism to facilitate co-operation on economic and social matters, an end to the Republic's territorial claim, and a new treaty, replacing the Anglo-Irish Agreement, taking account of the 'totality of relationships'.

'If Britain should join the ranks of the persuaders, she should persuade unionists to do *what*?'

It was already dark outside the leaded panes of Derry's Guildhall, where the Commission proceeded the following week. As the rest of the city, already off work, was scurrying home, the windows continued to glow on the second floor.

'She should persuade unionists of the value and safety for them in agreeing to new relationships with the rest of the island', replied Mark Durkan, chairman of the SDLP.

Padraig O'Malley of the Commission leaned into the microphone. His voice was soft: 'Should Britain be persuading unionists to accept some form of Irish unity?'

'We would have no objection to Britain performing such a role', Mr Durkan said with a laugh.

The audience chuckled as well, with relief — the atmosphere in the Guildhall had grown tense. Spectators returned to pin-drop silence. It was already 6 p.m.; the hearing was running overtime, but the hall was full, and the rows of spectators on the edge of their chairs did not betray that it had been a terribly long day.

Mr O'Malley pressed: 'You would persuade them to join some kind of all-Ireland state?'

'Mmm — that is .... ' Mr Durkan twisted in his seat. 'Mmm-nnn ... to address their relationship to the rest of the island.'

'Mark', chided Mr O'Malley with an indulgent smile. 'I don't know what that means.'

'If we could get an agreement on how we share the island ——'

'You would be persuading unionists to share the island ——'

'On a basis that respects the rights and requirements of both traditions.'

'Might that exclude a united Ireland of some kind?'

'If that was the agreement that was reached.'

'Or a federal state?'

'Yes.'

'So the phrase "an agreement on how we share the island" doesn't necessarily mean you're talking about any form of all-Ireland state?'

Mr Durkan retreated to 'value and safety', and Mr O'Malley doggedly repeated the question. 'I'm still, I'm sorry, not clear', the Commissioner apologized. 'Could there be an arrangement where the two traditions would "share the island" in which you would not have a unified Ireland, a federal Ireland, or even a confederal Ireland?'

'Uh .... ' There was a protracted pause. 'Yes, obviously at a rational level, yes, that's possible, yes.'

The three yes's recalled Molly Bloom. The audience released a collective breath, and leaned back in their seats. There was a sense that something had happened.

Whether indeed something did happen — whether on 25 January 1993 the SDLP went on record as being willing to accept an internal solution for Northern Ireland — is open to question. Mr Durkan did not necessarily speak for the SDLP. The party leader, under similar duress, might have been more successfully elusive. Moreover, Mr Durkan was under pressure, and with retrospective qualifications, his concession might break no ground, but fit comfortably back into party ideology.

For whether the Opsahl Commission hearings have turned up anything truly new is also open to question. Still, for an initiative that first elicited widespread derision — as more chatter from airy-fairy academics — the hearings have produced some interesting moments. Mr Durkan's testimony was one of them.

Paddy Doherty, director of the Inner City Trust, had begun the Commission's first day in Derry. 'Plantation was a monstrous crime against the Irish people!' he exhorted, with little need of a microphone. 'Northern Ireland as a political entity is an attempt to perpetuate the crimes of the 17th century.'

Commissioners congratulated Mr Doherty on his rejuvenation of the inner city, then confronted him with their impression culled from Initiative '92's 'focus groups' in December 1992: Protestants in the Waterside felt 'marginalized', 'alienated' and 'powerless', a trio of adjectives relentlessly reiterated in subsequent inquiries. Mr Doherty was sympathetic, to a point.

'Unionists are experiencing what we did for 60, 70 years. I'm sorry, I appreciate the feeling.... The ruling junta is leaning over backwards to be fair in Derry. But it's difficult to deal with *perceptions* of inequality', he said.

Asked whether nationalists should be encouraged to join the Royal Ulster Constabulary, Mr Doherty was unequivocal. 'If my son asked me tomorrow, I'd say, you're no son of mine if you join the police.'

Lady Faulkner, widow of the former Northern Ireland prime minister, asserted — not for the first time — that she 'considered herself Irish', perhaps bravely compensating for the disquieting memory that her husband had introduced internment in 1971. Yet it was difficult for her Protestant friends to lay any eager claim to an Irish identity when their people were being killed, 'in the name of Ireland'.

'Congratulations on your own clear statement that you're Irish', Mr Doherty declared.

'I don't need congratulations', said Lady Faulkner, drawing upright. 'It's just a fact.'

Unionist demands for the removal of Articles 2 and 3 of the Republic's Constitution were, according to Mr Doherty, 'unadulterated blackmail'. Protestants were motivated by a desire for raw power: they wanted Stormont back. Yet, like many nationalists, he was cautious about a united Ireland right away. First the South had to 'clean up its act. Were the two communities to reach an agreement in the North, he would allow the South to 'stand outside my door knocking'.

Marlene Jefferson, who, though a former unionist mayor, described herself as 'a housewife', struck a conciliatory tone. Though Protestant, she routinely referred to 'the six counties' and 'the 26 counties', and called the city 'Derry — save for one fluster of 'Derry ... or Londonderry ...' when she sounded suddenly unsure to whom she was speaking.

Mrs Jefferson began by apologizing to the Commissioners that their arrival had been preceded two days earlier by the murder of Constable Michael Ferguson in the city centre. Her submission urged Catholics and Protestants to 'work together', and advocated integrated schooling and a return of power to regional government. She was optimistic that a political settlement was on its way: 'There's a general gut feeling that something is happening out there.' Perpetuation of Direct Rule was 'the easy option', but 'a disgrace'. Through concurring that Waterside Protestants were 'marginalized' and 'alienated', she urged her neighbours to take an active part in all Derry, and to cross the river rather than stock up on rashers in Coleraine. She confessed that, even in Derry, 'if you rub a little under the skin, it's orange or green'.

She herself could not accept a united Ireland, fearing that her fellow Church of Ireland parishioners would dwindle as they had in the South after partition. 'Their population plummeted,' she said dolefully. 'My feeling is personal.' And Mrs Jefferson is one of those unionists that the SDLP is confident it will 'persuade'.

'How would they ever persuade me?' she asked Padraig O'Malley, with a trace of exasperation. 'Is a united Ireland a good idea when neither of our houses is in order? Neither the South's nor the North's? .... Nationalists should accept this is their country. It's hard enough to organize six counties; who needs to try 32?'

Mr O'Malley asked, as he had many citizens placed in the Opsahl dock, whether Mrs Jefferson could see Northern Ireland developing into 'another Bosnia'.

'I don't want that', Ms Jefferson said hastily. 'I don't want to say that.'

'In the event of British withdrawal,' Mr O'Malley pursued, 'do you think Protestants would fight, or sit around the table and hammer out an agreement?'

The woman looked at her hands, silent. Finally she whispered so quietly only the front row could hear: 'They'd fight.'

Frank Curran, former editor of the *Derry Journal*, asserted that partition had been based on a 'myth of homogeneity'. West of the Bann was Catholic, he said, and would never be ruled effectively by Protestants, who even in the whole of the North maintained an increasingly tentative majority. The Protestant population was older, accounting for seven out of ten deaths in the region.

Protestants were retreating to Antrim and Down, already home to 70 per cent of their community, for, 'in a situation of Catholic majority, Protestants move away'. As a people they felt 'happier and safer where they are in the majority'. Watersiders, for example, would never return to the Cityside, which was 'a shame', Mr Curran said. 'They have surrendered the historically Protestant part of Derry.' Not a single policeman lived on his side of the river.

Mr Curran recommended separate, autonomous governments east and west of the Bann, with separate police forces. As Protestant consolidation continued, he saw a 30-county Ireland as plausible — not 32. Unionists would 'never give up Antrim and Down. And the cost of subjecting them would be horrific'. The two counties going it alone, however, would last at most 'several years', depending on the degree of British subsidy.

Mr Curran believed that the nationalist intention to persuade unionists was 'specious'. He said: 'They know perfectly well that unionists won't give in to a united Ireland.' In Protestant minds, their existence was at stake, and a united Ireland was 'equivalent to extinction'.

In counterpoint to a string of community-relations submissions about 'working together', Mr Curran's message was segregationist. Conciliators might find his proposal cynical, others realistic.

Mari Fitzduff, director of the Community Relations Council, argued for mandatory, government-financed education in democracy and conflict resolution for local politicians.

She would not be tempted by one of Mr O'Malley's favourite questions — always asked with palpable relish — about a fairy-tale future: 'The key players have been on the scene for more than 20 years. Do you think it would be useful if all the party leaders called a press conference and announced, "We've given it our best shot, and now we're stepping down. Let the younger generation have a go'?"

Ms Fitzduff replied smoothly that she was not interested in decrying the quality of Northern Ireland politicians. 'We have to work with our current representatives, and get beyond the 'if onlys,' she said, impatiently. 'If *only* Sinn Féin would join the talks, if *only* Articles 2 and 3 were eliminated. Get on with it.'

Should Sinn Féin be in the talks?

'That depends on the level.' Inclusion at the national level was problematic; locally, many Sinn Féin councillors had proved 'quite reasonable'. Should their inclusion continue to be impractical at constitutional talks, perhaps the party could be involved in a round of discussion papers.

Paul Sweeney, director of the Northern Ireland Voluntary Trust, appeared frustrated by queries about Sinn Féin's inclusion and the like: his submission emphasized not politics but poverty. His impatience at questions about whether Britain was truly 'neutral' — when his proposals concerned school-leavers and ghetto development — highlighted the perhaps too broad design of Initiative '92, which solicited suggestions on all aspects of Northern Irish society.

In the hearings, testimonies have been divided as much between economic and political agenda as between unionist and nationalist ones. Mr Sweeney resisted discussing troop withdrawal, keener to confront third-generation unemployment.

From the Guildhall, the Commission moved to Pilot's Row Community Centre in the Bogside — beginning with the Holywell Trust, whose presentation was curiously infiltrated by American therapy-speak. Both republican and loyalist doctrines were 'disabling mythologies'; young men of both creeds needed to 'get in touch with the feminine side of their nature'; no one was dealing with 'bereavement'.

Asked why Protestants in the Waterside might still feel 'alienated' when Catholics had gone out of their way to be inclusive, the Trust explained: 'Twenty years ago, we were bitter.. ... We had to change our thinking to become whole and contented. If we were bitter, our contacts would be unhealthy.' In the 'Beyond Hate' conference in the city in 1992, Protestants had 'shared their pain'.

Like the Holywell Trust, the Bloody Sunday Initiative (BSI) was infected with 'empowerment', a word that seems to have run like a computer virus through nationalist Derry. Its proposal: British withdrawal was the key to peace. Sinn Féin had to be included in negotiations, since constitutional parties also had links with violence — hadn't the DUP been linked to those involved in arms trading with the South African Defence Force? Encouraging Northerners to be 'creative', the BSI hoped that such an inclusive round-table would arrive at the imaginative solution of a united Ireland.

If the outcome of such negotiation be instead an internal solution, would the group accept it?

The BSI replied: 'We are more concerned with *process*,' an obscure noun that pops up frequently. It allowed for the dissonance of both campaigning for an all-Ireland state and conceding that such an outcome was 'unlikely'. The BSI, too, aspired to 'persuade' unionists to join the rest of Ireland, since loyalists might behave differently if they were 'empowered' to make their own decisions.

Surely unionists would prefer to move from being 2 per cent of the United Kingdom's population to 20 per cent of Ireland's? The South, in this vision, transforms into a secular, socialist state, pumpkin to carriage. If there was a transitional arrangement — and in this part of the world, Rev. Eric Gallagher observed, the temporary tended to last a long time — Britain might subsidize the North. Dr Gallagher wondered why, having finally got rid of the place, Britain would have an overweening desire still to pay for it.

Parallels with South Africa were several, including the assertion made in more than one nationalist testimony that unionists had no more right to veto a united Ireland than whites had to veto political progress in South Africa — putting a united Ireland and the black franchise on a dubious moral par. Whatever Protestant 'right' there might be, the Bloody Sunday Initiative allowed, the reality was that unionists could veto an all-Ireland solution, unless the new arrangement was imposed militarily — 'which we won't do'.

On the third day, the commission moved to the Waterside ('marginalized', 'alienated' and 'powerless'). The new Ebrington Business Centre is a converted mill, magnificently renovated under the supervision of Glen Barr, a former leading figure in the Ulster Defence Association. According to the centre's workers, Mr Barr picked out all the paints and fabrics himself, and even dabbed his own share of windowsills. He prefers soft greys and muted purples. The purples of Northern Ireland's future that flashed before Barr's eyes were not so muted.

'We face a holocaust in three to four years unless politicians solve the constitutional crisis.' Young Protestants were flocking to join the paramilitaries, believing that no one listened to talk and the only answer was to imitate the IRA. Waterside youths told him, 'We seem to be losing all the time; we don't seem to be winning anything.'

'At least young people now have a piece of paper', Mr Barr said. 'What I'm warning the government is pretty soon those kids are going to shove that piece of paper into a milk bottle half-filled with petrol.'

Loyalist paramilitaries had become more sophisticated, he cautioned.

Having adopted a cell system, fewer were being caught, and they were shooting 'the right people'. As to whether the North might degenerate into 'another Bosnia', his reply was unhesitating: 'Exactly the same.'

Once former UDA leader Andy Tyrie's right-hand man, Mr Barr pushed the UDA in a political direction in the late 1970s, when he secured its support for negotiated independence. Failure to win any attention from government with its document *Beyond the Religious Divide* had driven the leadership back to military tactics. Impatient loyalists had argued, 'If they want proof we're still here, we'll give them proof.'

'I regret this turn', Mr Barr said. 'We've paid a price for it.'

Mr Barr was making his first public statement for twelve years. He was still advocating independence: 'I'm a first-class Ulsterman, not a second-class Englishman, and I don't want to be a third-class Irishman, either.' Independence might lead to a proper non-sectarian politics: 'It's an indictment of all of us that union jacks and tricolours get people elected.... We've got to convince both communities that to both sovereign powers we're Paddies.... The utopian relationship with our respective guarantors is a lie.'

The UDA man turned community activist suggested that more generous investment in Protestant areas might ameliorate the loyalist sense of being hard-done by, claiming that government funds went almost exclusively to Catholic areas. Until Protestants were treated more equitably, they would not cross the bridge. Not because they felt unsafe, he concluded: 'They just don't want to be part of that city.'

While Mr Barr was a fine advocate for the 'alienated', the occasion was, for the Waterside, a little surreal. After a long session with the Foyle Trust for Integrated Education, devoted to mutual understanding through mixed schools, John Robb and Jim Wilson testified for the New Ireland Group, proposing a federal, albeit secular, all-Ireland state. The Very Rev. Victor Griffin, former dean of St Patrick's Cathedral in Dublin, spoke for tolerance and an end to sectarianism. Topping off an afternoon of staggering goodwill from a community that would ostensibly initiate 'another Bosnia', Tony Crowe took the stand for the Apprentice Boys.

'People perceive the organization as preserving a unique identity', Mr Crowe said — though the version of this identity he put forward was not the one most nationalists in Northern Ireland remember. Chairman of the Diamond Project Trust, pledged to the regeneration of the Waterside, Mr Crowe said he would 'emphasize cultural identity without exclusivity'. The Trust encouraged Protestants to return to the Cityside, to get involved in the whole of Derry. Like the Holywell Trust, he, too, spoke of 'confidence and self-esteem' — a language yards from 'No Surrender'.

'Didn't the Apprentice Boys', asked the Commission chairman, Torkel Opsahl, in his lilting Norwegian accent, 'use to be more divisive?'

'We are *perceived* to be more divisive,' Mr Crowe tried to assure him, 'but the celebration of the past doesn't necessarily open old wounds.' He recited John Hewitt, adding ruefully that the poet would be 'bemused to hear an Apprentice Boy quoting his work'.

Without a doubt, submissions to Initiative '92 do not constitute a reliable social attitudes survey, and to reach firm conclusions by pot luck would be foolhardy. But this brief foray across the Foyle suggested that some unionists in the city have come a long way.

Often held up as an example of 'working together' that might be applied to the whole of the North, Derry frames different photos, depending on whose shutter one is looking through. On the one hand, Mr Durkan said, the city was such a paragon of power-sharing that at one stage some unionist councillors had walked out of the chamber because the city was being used to 'beat other unionists like a stick. Derry is embarrassing to unionists elsewhere on the island.' The mayoralty and council committee chairs were rotated. Nationalists had not, Mr Durkan assured the Commission, been 'triumphalist'.

However, the theme of 'alienation' was recurrent. According to many testimonies during those three days — those of Mr Durkan, Mr Curran, the Holywell Trust, the Bloody Sunday Initiative, and even, to some extent, Mrs Jefferson — Waterside Protestants have alienated themselves, walking out on the city if they can no longer control it. In some of these analyses was an implicit accusation of petulance, babyishness: losing the game, the Prods had scooped up their marbles in a huff and had crossed the bridge.

Mr Durkan claimed that, though Derry had 'bent over backwards' — another recurrent phrase — to pay tribute to *their* heritage with the 1989 tercentenary celebration of the city's siege, most Protestants had boycotted the festivities. And the 1992 campaign in the Waterside to revise local boundaries to create a separate, unionist-dominated council had 'hurt us deeply'. Even in Derry, where nationalists had been so generous, Protestants wanted 'partition' to control their own area — an impulse Mr Durkan found 'telling'.

A rejuvenated town, a model of reconciliation, where power has shifted into the hands of the once oppressed, who magnanimously refuse to take vengeance? Or a segregated, polarized city which harbours an ominously resentful, disinherited underclass, victims of reverse discrimination, and capable of unspeakable horrors in 'three to four years'? Both black-and-whites must contain shades of truth, but the snaps seemed to be shots of opposite shores.

'It concerns me that politicians seem under such pressure to deliver', Kevin Boyle worried when the Commission returned to the Old Museum Arts Centre in Belfast. His joint submission with Tom Hadden warned that

Northern Ireland should not 'rush into any new arrangements' or 'force the pace'. Any progress would have to be 'tentative'.

Several mouths in the audience hung open. Twenty-five years on, with Father Raymond Murray still carping about plastic bullets and Gary McMichael still intoning about 'Protestant fears' only the week before, the winds of change were hardly rushing in anyone's ears that afternoon.

'Politicians are under no pressure', objected Padraig O'Malley from the Commission. 'There is no punishment for failure; indeed, they're expected to fail. And more lives are lost in traffic in Northern Ireland than through violence. In our focus groups, people described the 'troubles' as an inconvenience. Where is this pressure? Professor Boyle asserted that the 'troubles' did affect people's daily lives; that visitors in Ulster for only a few hours were conscious of 'how this conflict drains people'.

By the fourth week of Opsahl hearings, the conflict was certainly starting to drain the Commissioners. The chairman, Torkel Opsahl, a kindly, deferential Norwegian lawyer, had stopped apologizing to local witnesses that he was not from here and needed everything explained to him — if he did not know a great deal more to begin with than he let on, he was inevitably well-informed by week four.

The gentle professor was actually beginning to interrupt from time to time, cutting Father Murray short in Dungannon: 'Our role is to initiate debate — not to sit through it all.' His ritual presentation at the end of each submission of his wedge of wood, 'from the oldest oak forest in Ireland, not to act as a wedge to divide you but as a doorstop to keep the door open', was now delivered with an exaggerated Scandinavian sing-song bordering on parody.

The Boyle and Hadden submission was one of several resorting to Europe as a way out of the local conundrum, an approach that had been developed in more detail by Robin Wilson and Richard Kearney in the Linen Hall Library the week before. Mr Wilson, one of the originators of Initiative '92, was quick to caution the Commissioners to accord their submission no privilege.

Northern Ireland, they claimed, had traditionally been subject to conflicting national sovereignty claims, but in the context of the European Community, national sovereignty had become anachronistic. Instead, the two advocated 'disseminated sovereignty', increased regional autonomy within the larger European scheme, thereby rendering both unionism and nationalism obsolete. In its antiquated absorption with national sovereignty, Northern Ireland was still squabbling about a concept that Brussels found 'laughable', they said.

Mr Wilson and Professor Kearney would design a highly autonomous North with removal of all barriers between North and South, though not trying for a united Ireland — 'we're trying to get beyond that', Mr Wilson said. He would neither support nor modify the consent formula — he would 'get beyond it'.

With the recent rise of militant nationalism in Eastern Europe and Western Europe's baulking at Maastricht, that the nation-state is dissolving into regions within a federation becomes a little hard to credit. Moreover, one gets the curious sense that 'getting beyond' the Irish Question through Europe is *cheating*.

Ray Smallwoods, convicted of involvement in the attempted murder of Bernadette McAliskey in 1981, and Gary McMichael, whose father and leading Ulster Defence Association figure, John, was murdered by the IRA in 1987, advanced the Ulster Democratic Party's document, *Common Sense*.

At its release by the UDA in 1987, *Common Sense* was considered to be an adventurous and unusually tolerant proposal for hard-core unionism, advocating a devolved administration with proportional representation, a Council of the British Isles, and a Bill of Rights. Nowadays, with a wider recognition of the need for an 'Irish dimension' and less vituperation about the Anglo-Irish Agreement, it seems not so radical. To the Commissioners, Mr Smallwoods and Mr McMichael appeared recalcitrant.

At the end of that day, Terry Carlin, Northern Ireland officer of the Irish Congress of Trade Unions, told a discouraging story. Responding to one of the many Opsahl inquiries about policing and how the Royal Ulster Constabulary might be made more acceptable and accountable, he said that the Police Authority had approached him about serving as a member last year. When he had met the chief constable, Mr Carlin and many of his fellow trade unionists were hopeful that he could rejoin the Authority, from which he had been forced to resign once before because the position was too politically sensitive. The meeting, however, was 'a disaster'. Sir Hugh Annesley had made clear straight away that he did not believe the Police Authority should have any control over the RUC; only an Act of Parliament could make the police accountable to the body. Were such legislation passed, he would resign. The chief constable had said that he would pay as much attention to a letter in the *Irish News* as he would to the Police Authority.

So the ICTU's non-participation stood. 'We don't have an anti-police attitude', Mr Carlin told the commissioners. 'We respect their sacrifices. That was a difficult decision. Every society needs a police force.'

Testimonies in Dungannon were even more disheartening. The Dungannon Community Relations Workshop and Cookstown High School were both eager that the 'two traditions' should talk out their differences, but any mention of the murders in the district in the preceding weeks — about which, perhaps, people did need to talk — was noticeably absent. Nor did any amount of 'Education for Mutual Understanding' seem to have taught the Omagh Christian Brothers' School's senior prefects why on earth unionists would find their federated Ireland proposal the least bit objectionable.

Father Murray's hour-and-a-half monologue on the evils of the British state, shoot-to-kill, police harassment and colonial domination might have been recited 20 years ago and not a word would have been out of place. Father Denis Faul admitted that the Catholic Church was 'fearful' of integrated education, which was unworkable because of the importance of 'statues and symbols'. Would such a school put a crucifix on the wall, or not? Rather than face such daunting questions, it was better to stay apart.

Back at the Old Museum in Belfast the next week, Douglas Hegney was a welcome breath of fresh air. A Catholic taxi-driver from the Lower Ormeau making a personal submission, he nervously took the mike to commend, not Sinn Féin advice centres, but the police. Mr Hegney's earlier experience with the Ulster Defence Regiment and the RUC had been predictably unpleasant: searches, demands for identification, all looking up a barrel of an SLR rifle. But when Victor Shaw took over as commander in the area, Catholics were 'treated with respect .... Shaw talks to people.'

Though conceding that nationalists were unlikely to 'tip their hats' to the police, Mr Hegney claimed that the mood in the Lower Ormeau had been transformed since policing had become less aggressive and officers more civil. He was familiar with local policemen, and though 'we don't wave, we don't give each other dirty looks, either.' He cheerfully admitted that when he saw anything wrong, he reported it to the RUC, and his complaints were acted on promptly. The credit went to Mr Shaw.

Rev. Eric Gallagher asked: 'Supposing your man [Victor Shaw] was transferred to the Markets?'

Mr Hegney panicked: 'I wouldn't want him transferred!' Defying stereotypes in truth rather than decrying them in rhetoric, commending concrete progress rather than exhorting to abstract 'ways forward', Mr Hegney's testimony may have been the high point of the Opsahl exercise.

Setting the tone for the Shankill testimonies to follow, Dr Samuel Poyntz, the Church of Ireland Bishop of Connor, called attention to Protestant poverty, often hidden in ward statistics which included wealthier areas. Working-class Protestants, he asserted, were suffering low morale; educational results were appalling, and why? Rev. Walter Lewis explained that in areas like the Shankill, people felt at sea. 'Stormont has been taken away; they feel a lack of dignity.'

The churchmen noted Protestants' increasing territorial paranoia. Loyalists were convinced that whenever demolition took place, 'it's always on their side of the peace wall', even strongholds like Tiger's Bay were going Catholic, and Protestants were slipping in Suffolk. 'Protestants perceive they are being squeezed left and right', Dr Poyntz said.

The Shankill's population had plummeted through migrations, and old houses — torn down for redevelopment — had been replaced by only a third of the housing stock, Mr Lewis said, 'like a deliberate government policy of social engineering'. Dr Poyntz claimed that loyalists felt the government would 'only listen to Twinbrook'. This kind of talk was the province of republicans not so long ago.

Dr Poyntz's description of the beleaguered state of some of his parishioners helped lend credence to Desmond Rea's warning on its heels, that 'republicans could be seen as succeeding'. Professor Rea found this 'dangerous'.

The Commission moved to the Argyle Business Centre in the Shankill the next day, beginning with Mark Langhammer, who demanded that both major British parties contest elections in Northern Ireland. It was 'the only place on earth you can't join the Labour Party', he said. 'You can join in Cork, in Australia — but not in Strabane.'

The British parties, he insisted, would dilute the sectarian nature of Ulster voting patterns, and introduce, for once, 'real politics' beyond flag-waving. Asked whether Protestants would accept a united Ireland if 51 per cent voted in favour of it, Mr Langhammer volunteered: 'I'd join the Irish Labour Party.' The prospect did not seem to distress him too much.

Jackie Redpath took up where Dr Poyntz had left off, despairing of deprivation in the area, poor educational achievement and devastating migration. Protestants, he claimed, were ashamed of their heritage, afflicted with a lack of confidence, and in physical and cultural retreat. He told of one community worker who finally 'came out of the closet' as a Protestant by changing her name; all her friends had assumed she was Catholic because she was 'all right'. Poets and writers 'rubbished' the culture, and many refused to admit they were Prods. Catholics, on the other hand, seemed 'ascendant, going somewhere, on the move'.

Mr Redpath emphasized that there was a strong desire for a political settlement among his community, that Protestants now wanted 'a normal life'. He described unionists as having gone through a 'process of grief'. Until 1969, working-class Protestants felt that they were 'looked after' by the government. However, watching broadcasts of the early civil rights marches in Derry and on the Falls, Shankill residents had pointed at Catholic slums and had puzzled: 'But those houses look just like ours!'

With the fall of Stormont had come 'a sense of loss — real or not', which resembled the process of bereavement. First, anger; next, denial — acting as if nothing had changed; denial turned to apathy, then depression. Mr Redpath urged his community to move on to the final stage of 'acceptance', to learn to cherish their culture and engage in mature self-examination.

Pastor Jack McKee and Roy Montgomery continued this exchange of roles with the 'downtrodden Catholic'. Mr McKee referred to a recent survey in the area that had asked young people, 'Are you depressed?' Eighty per cent had said yes.

'There's a perception among Protestants that Catholic grievances have been dealt with', Padraig O'Malley said, 'and Catholics are playing a clever card and reverse discrimination is taking place.' Yes, Mr Montgomery agreed, that was a clever card. There was still such a thing as the 'down-trodden Catholic', but they had much better housing. A Catholic from Ligoniel had told him recently that he could 'tell the Protestant areas because the houses have concrete windows'. Protestants felt they were being punished because of how Catholics were treated in the past; most government money went into Catholic areas. The Fair Employment Commission was 'as popular with Protestants as the bubonic plague'; it was seen as merely a route to Catholic jobs.

Mr Montgomery reiterated the physical retreat his community was experiencing. 'Show me one street in north Belfast that was Catholic and is now Protestant.' When Divis and Unity Flats came down, the residents would be housed in Protestant north Belfast. 'This reinforces extremists', he warned. 'You have to protect your house.'

The recent rise in loyalist violence was therefore a product of the perception that 'violence seems to pay', Mr McKee said. 'From this side of the fence, it looks as if they've bombed their way through twenty years and got everything they wanted.' He cautioned that young people were taking over the violence in north and west Belfast, and 'the older fellows are afraid of them'. They had once been assured that Northern Ireland would always stay in the UK, and that Dublin would never be part of their future. Disillusioned with the British government, young loyalists were resorting to methods they had learned from the other side of the peace line.

The two were sure that unionists would accept power-sharing now. 'You've no objections', asked Marianne Elliott, 'to unionists going to Dublin?'

Mr McKee retorted: 'I've no objection if they go to *Rome*'. A united Ireland, however, was unlikely, because the South did not want the North. In their submission, they had written: 'If you picked up the phone today and offered it to Albert Reynolds, he would emigrate.'

The North was not an issue in the Republic, Mr Montgomery said. 'They've given up on a united Ireland. We have the idea up here that they walk around dreaming up how to get the six counties back. I had a barman tell me the other day in Dublin, 'You can do whatever you like with the six counties, as long as you do it on your side of the border.'

The tone of the entire day was hard-done-by but conciliatory, and notably cleansed of no-surrender bluster. Shankill witnesses argued for proper politics and the commonality of working-class grievances.

Are the republicans winning? Although Professor Boyle had remarked,

'It's not productive to measure how each side is doing', that's what happens. At any rate, nationalists are in the better mood.

At the Twin Spires building on the Falls Road, the Commission resumed the next day with Sister Genevieve and Paddy Fleming. No amount of depressing questions about what proportion of graduates of St Louise's Comprehensive School, of which Sister Genevieve was formerly principal, actually got jobs or went on to higher education would deter her from trumpeting the achievements of the school. Students there felt 'as good as students from Methody' and 'had something special about them'. The ring of this submission was clarion, with high hopes for the future, confidence in the young — perhaps there was something to the 'ascendant Catholic' after all.

Liz Groves from Andersonstown was concerned with political vetting. Fear of saying the wrong thing and having their funding cut had put many community workers off talking to the Commission, she claimed. Sinn Féin should be included in talks. The IRA knee-capped joyriders because the police, with a military agenda, did not bother with 'hoods'. Asked whether it was true, as the Shankill complained, that most government money went to Catholics, Ms Groves conceded: 'They're probably right.' But she was quick to qualify that: there was not nearly so much money in Catholic west Belfast as loyalists imagined, and locals had little say on how it was spent, the majority of funds going into 'safe, middle-class, middle-of-the-road initiatives'.

The one-time People's Democracy activist, now Dublin solicitor, Michael Farrell, argued that an all-Ireland state was the ideal ultimate solution, but that an interim arrangement of joint authority should precede it. Since he readily admitted that Britain did not want the North, and (less readily) that the South did not either, just yet, dumping the statelet on both governments sounded positively malicious.

The Centre for Research and Documentation draws its leadership from returned development workers, determined to take on the 'third world of Europe' at home. Since they are convinced that Ireland's legacy of colonialism has been left untackled, one does sense they have been away. Further, the organization's claims to being 'apolitical' began to look dubious in a barrage of indignation at abuse of power by the state. Parallels between Northern Ireland and the oppressed of South Africa, the Philippines and El Salvador were copious in their presentation.

In the ensuing public discussion, a Catholic who had followed the hearings from early on, took the floor. 'All the new thinking is among the Prods', he proclaimed. 'All the old thinking is among the Taigs. We're stuck.'

Although there seems to be no danger in either part of town of 'forcing the pace', most spectators of the Opsahl Commission who travelled from the Argyle Business Centre to Twin Spires would have to agree. Though not always taking the form of tangible political compromise, the tone of many unionist submissions through the hearings was surprisingly conciliatory. Protestants may not have moved a full inch, but they have certainly shifted a millimetre or two. In comparison, the nationalist perspective appears to have remained more constant — challenging which fraction, really, is 'intransigent'.

However, the Opsahl Commission may have been given a sanitized version of both communities. For example, Clifford Smyth, formerly of the DUP, appeared to argue a unionist case that he described as 'fair, rational and moderate'. He even said that Protestants 'might accept a united Ireland some day'. Yet a month later, Dr Smyth organized a conference at Orange House w.here his first speaker, Michael de Semlyn, railed that not only was the Pope the anti-Christ and that all Catholics were 'lost on a road paved with idolatry and superstition', but that after the fall of communism the Vatican was poised to take over the world through the evil machinations of the Maastricht treaty. Asked how he felt about the speech, Dr Smyth said he was well pleased.

There is a danger, therefore, in taking the pervading solicitude and reasonableness of some of these testimonies too seriously. Students who perform nicely for teacher will often get up to mischief when they are allowed out to play.

Lionel Shiver is an American writer who covered the oral hearings for Fortnight. *Her latest novel is* Ordinary Decent Criminals (*Flamingo*).

Appendices

Appendix A

Written Submissions

Of the 554 groups or persons who made written submissions, the following indicated that their names could be published:

Mr Nick Acheson, Belfast; Mr Annett Agnew, Kilkeel, Co. Down; All Children Together; Mr W.M. Allen, Belfast; Mr Philip Allen, Belfast; Alliance Party; Amalgamated Transport and General Workers' Union, Region Two Women's Committee; Amnesty International; Anarchists' Animals' Liberation, Yorkshire; Mr James Anderson, Belfast; Mr P. Anderson and Mr P. Burns, Belfast; Mr Roy Arbuckle, Derry; Sir Edward Archdale, Comber, Co. Down; Mr W.J. Armstrong, Tempo, Co. Fermanagh; Mrs Vida Blackwell, Carrickfergus, Co. Antrim; Baha'i Community of Cookstown; Baha'i Community Religious Education Committee, Newtownabbey; Baha'i Information Office Northern Ireland; Baha'i Women's Committee of Northern Ireland; Baha'i Youth Northern Ireland; Baha'i children, Ballymena; Baha'i Community, Ballymena; Baha'i of Londonderry; Ballybeen Women's Centre; Ballymagroarty Family Centre, Derry; Mr Peter Barry TD, Cork; Mr Glen Barr, Londonderry; Mr Harry Barton, Limavady, Co. Derry; Mr Joe Beattie, Belfast; Ms Maggie Beirne, Belfast; Belfast Ecology Group; members of Belfast Rotary Club; Ms Sally Belfrage, London; Mr Stephen Berry, Maghaberry Prison, Co. Antrim; Mr and Mrs Birthistle, Derry; Blackmountain Action Group, Belfast; Rt Hon. David Bleakley, Bangor, Co. Down; Ms Grace Bennett, Belfast; Lord 'Billy' Blease; Bloody Sunday Initiative, Derry; Bloody Sunday Justice Campaign, Derry; Sir Kenneth Bloomfield, Belfast; Mr Patrick Clavell Blount, Surrey; Professor Frederick Boal, Queen's University, Belfast; Mr Samuel Boyd, Gwent, Wales; Rev. John Brady S.J., Dublin; Mrs Evelyn Berman and Mrs Catherine Lyle, Belfast; Mr Kevin Brennan, Downpatrick, Co. Down; Ms Janet Brennan, Dungannon, Co. Tyrone; Dr Michael Brennan, Newry, Co. Down; the Bridge Centre, Belfast; Mr W.J. Britton, Donaghadee, Co. Down; Mr James Brogan, Rosslare, Co. Wexford; Mr Barrie Brooks, Belfast; Mr Garrett Brophy, Ardee, Co. Louth; Mr William Browne, Crossbeg, Co. Wexford; Ms Eileen Brown, Wallasey, Merseyside; Rev. David Brown and Rev. Joan Scott, Belfast; Cathal and Catherine Brugha, Dublin; Mr Ruairí Brugha, Dublin; Mr Sam Butler, Belfast; Mr Aidan Bunting, Omagh, Co. Tyrone; Mr Paul Burgess, Templepatrick, Co. Antrim; Ms Yvonne Burgess, Fife, Scotland; Mr William Burns, West Lothian, Scotland; Mr G.T. Burton, London; Cadogan Group, Belfast; Rev. W. Sydney Callaghan, Belfast; Campaign to Free the Beechmount Five, Belfast; Campaign for Equal Citizenship; Mrs Pat Campbell, Belfast; Councillor James Canning, Dungannon, Co. Tyrone; Councillor T. Carlin, Derry; Carrickfergus Baha'i Community; Dr Michael Carr, Londonderry; Mr Ian Carter Long, Belfast; Sir Charles Carter, Cumbria; Mr John Cassidy, Waterside, Derry; Very Rev. H. Cassidy, Armagh; Mr Colm Cavanagh, Londonderry; Confederation of British Industry (Northern Ireland); Celtic League, London Branch; Centre for Research and Documentation, West Belfast; Dr David Chapman, Stowmarket, Suffolk; Mr Don Cheyne, Lisburn, Co. Antrim; Mrs Sheila Chillingworth, Newtownabbey, Co. Antrim; Dr Leland Chou, North Carolina, USA; Christian

Response to the Irish Situation, Belfast and Dublin; Mr John Christoffersen, New York; Churches' Central Committee for Community Work; Mr Ciarán Clancy, Blackrock, Co. Dublin; Mr Joseph Clancy, Blackrock, Co. Dublin; Ms Dympna Clarke, Belfast; Mr James Clark, Belfast; Mr R.J. Clements, Newcastle, Co. Down; Coleraine Corrymeela Cell Group; John and Pauline Coll, Bangor, Co. Down; Columba Community of Prayer and Reconcilation, Belfast; Committee for National Democracy and Peace, Dublin; Committee for a New Ireland, Boston, Mass.; Committee on the Administration of Justice; Committee for the Transfer of Irish Prisoners, Belfast; Community of the Peace People; Community Relations Council; Mr Bernard Conlon, Brussels; Mr William Connery, London; Dr Pauline Conroy, Dublin; Conservative Integration Group; Mr Noel Conway, London; Mr David Cook, Belfast; Ms Pippa Cookson, Belfast; Cookstown High School, Lower Sixth-form Group; Co-operation North; Ms Jennifer Cornell, New York; Cornerstone Community; Corrymeela Community; Council for the Homeless (Northern Ireland); Counteract; Mr Barry Cowan, Holywood, Co. Down; Mr Jim Creighton, Belfast; Community Relations in Schools; Mr Garvin Crawford, Belfast; Mr Tony Crowe, Londonderry; Professor Bernard Cullen, Belfast; Mr John Cummins, London; Mr Michael Cunningham, Co. Galway; Dr Bob Curran, Portrush, Co. Antrim; Mr Frank Curran, Derry; Mr M.J. Curran, London; Professor John Darby, University of Ulster, Coleraine; Ms Sharon Darroux, Belfast; Mr Steve Dawe, Canterbury, Kent; Sir Robin Day, London; Eoin de Bhaldraithe, Moone, Co. Kildare; Democracy Now, London; Democratic Left; Derry Well Woman; Mr Patrick Devlin, Castlederg, Co. Tyrone; Ms Polly Devlin, London; Rev. Robert Dickinson, Ballymena, Co. Antrim; Professor Brice Dickson, University of Ulster, Jordanstown; Mr Paddy Doherty, Derry; Mr Terence Donaghy, Belfast; Mr Paul Doran, Belfast; Downtown Women's Centre, Belfast; Mrs Ellen Doyle, Belfast; Mr Francis Drake, Lisburn, Co. Antrim; Drumcree Faith and Justice Group, Portadown, Co. Armagh; Dublin Anti-Extradition Committee; Mr Jeffery Dudgeon, Belfast; Dungannon Community Relations Workshop; Dungannon Presbyterian Women's Association; Mr Patrick Dunne, Dublin; Rev. Gregory Dunstan, Ballymena, Co. Antrim; Mr J. Eager, Belfast; Most Rev. Dr Robin Eames, Armagh; East Belfast Community Development Association; East Belfast Protestant and Catholic Encounter Group; Educational Guidance Service for Adults; Ms Jody Egan, Greystones, Co. Wicklow; Dr Brian Eggins, Belfast; Mr Peter Emerson, Belfast; Equal Opportunities Commission for Northern Ireland; Mr Alan Evans, Portadown, Co. Armagh; Ms Joyce Evans, Switzerland; Faculty of Public Health Medicine, Royal Victoria Hospital, Belfast; Mr Michael Farrell, Blackrock, Co. Dublin; Mr Seán Farren, University of Ulster, Coleraine; REv. Denis Faul, Dungannon; Mrs Kathleen Feenan and Mrs Mary Leonard, Dunmurry; Councillor Raymond Ferguson, Enniskillen, Co. Fermanagh; Mr James Finnegan, Letterkenny, Co. Donegal; Dr Mari Fitzduff, Cookstown, Co. Tyrone; Mr Niall Fitzduff, Cookstown, Co. Tyrone; Mr Terry Flanagan, Belfast; Sister Genevieve and Mr Paddy Fleming, Belfast; Foyle Labour Party; Foyle Trust for Integrated Education; Mr Andrew Frew, Belfast; Mr John Frost, Holywood, Co. Down; Dr Brian Gaffney, Downpatrick, Co. Down; Mr H. W. Gallagher, Newtownards, Co. Down; Mr Seán Gallagher, Co. Limerick; Gandhi Foundation, London; Mr Wilbert J. Garvin, Kells, Co. Antrim; Mr A. Gasson, Swindon, Wiltshire; Mr Michael Gillespie, Londonderry; Ms Diana Gilpin-Brown, Whitecross, Co. Armagh; Mr Will Glendinning, Markethill, Co. Armagh; Good Shepherd Sisters, Belfast; Lady Goodison, London; Sir Alan Goodison, London; Mr B. Gordon, Belfast; Mr Bob Gourley, Belfast; Mrs Elizabeth Gourley, Belfast; Mr Victor Graham, Maghaberry Prison, Co. Antrim; Mr John Gray, Belfast; Mr Robert Greacen, Dublin; Green Party, Belfast; Mr Arthur Green, Downpatrick, Co. Down; Mr Steven Greer, Bristol; Very Rev. V.G. Griffin, Limavady, Co. Londonderry; Mrs Elizabeth Groves, Belfast; Mr Wilfred Grundle,

Ballymena, Co. Antrim; Professor Tom Hadden and Professor Kevin Boyle; Mr Simon Hall-Raleigh, Peterborough, Cambridgeshire; Mr Trevor Halliday, Ballymena, Co. Antrim; Mr Jim Hanna, Belfast; Rt. Rev. Brian Hannon, Fivemiletown, Co. Tyrone; Mr John Hayes, Bangor, Co. Down; Healthy Cities Project, Belfast; Mr Joseph Healy Jnr., Belfast; Mr Douglas Hegney, Belfast; Mr Fergal Henchy, Portrane, Co. Dublin; Mr F. John Herriott, Blackrock, Co. Dublin; Mr Jackie Hewitt, Belfast; Hill Top (ACE Workers) Group, Belfast; Mr T. Hill, Newtownabbey, Co. Antrim; Rosaline Hillock and Sister Anna, Belfast; Lord Holme, London; Mrs Hazel Holmlund, Ballymena, Co. Antrim; Holywell Trust, Derry; Mr Ron Horgan, Cork; Mr Paddy Houlahan, Armagh; Mr Alan Houston, Belfast; Mr C.D. Hudson, Irvinestown, Co. Fermanagh; Mr Chris Hudson, Blackrock, Co. Dublin; Mr Ken Humphries, Belfast; Mr Barry Hurley, Dublin; Lord Hylton, Bath, Somerset; Mr Brian Inglis, London; Institute for Social Inventions; Interaid Ulster; Interfriendship, Lurgan, Co. Armagh; Inter-Church Group on Faith and Politics; International Tree Foundation, Omagh; Irish in Britain Representation Group; Irish Congress of Trade Unions, Northern Ireland Committee; INNATE, Belfast; Irish National Teachers' Organization; Irish Council of Churches; Irish National Congress; Irish Parliament Trust; Irish Studies Workshop, Soar Valley College, Leicester; Dr Colin Irwin, Belfast; Mr Gordon Jackson, Banbridge, Co. Down; Mrs Joan Harriet Jackson, Portstewart, Co. Londonderry; Mr Kenneth James, Belfast; Mrs Helena Jamison, Belfast; Mr Stanley Jamison, Belfast; Mrs Marlene Jefferson, Londonderry; Lord Jocelyn, London; Ms Roberta Johnston, Florencecourt, Co. Fermanagh; Dr Roy Johnston, Dublin; Mr Martin Jones, Dungannon, Co. Tyrone; Mr A. Kaluarachchi, Belfast; Mr D. Gordon Kelly, Belfast; Mr Emmet Kelly, Dublin; Mr James Kelly, Bailieboro, Co. Cavan; Mr Michael Kelly, Letterkenny, Co. Donegal; Kilcooley Women's Group, Bangor, Co. Down; Labour '87; Laganside Group; Mr Brian Lambkin, Belfast; Mr Mark Langhammer, Whiteabbey, Co. Antrim; Mr John Leacock, Ballymoney, Co. Antrim; Mr R.B. Leahy, Liverpool; Learn and Grow, Belfast; Professor Simon Lee, Queen's University, Belfast; Rev. Brian Lennon S.J., Portadown, Co. Armagh; Mr Allen Leonard, Cambridge, Mass.; Mr W.A. Leonard, Co. Armagh; Liberal Democrats (Northern Ireland Party); Lisburn Women's Group; Mr Dave Little, Kilkeel, Co. Down; Little Sisters of the Assumption, Belfast; Mr Hugh Logue, Brussels; Dr Ken Logue, Bangor, Co. Down; Long Island Inter-Church Northern Ireland Discussion Group, USA; Belfast; Professor Edna Longley, Belfast; Mr Michael Longley, Mr Dominic Loughran, Newry, Co. Down; Lower Ravenhill Community Association, Belfast; Lower Ravenhill Women's Project, Belfast; Loyalist Ex-Prisoners Group, Belfast; Mr Thomas Lyttle, Maghaberry Prison, Co. Antrim; Mr Alastair MacLurg, Lisburn, Co. Antrim; Mrs Máire Brugha MacSwiney, Dublin; Ms Nan Magennis, Newry, Co. Down; Mr Tom Magner, Coagh, Co. Tyrone; Mr Trevor Magowan, Ballymoney, Co. Antrim; Ms M. Maguire, Belfast; Mr Malachy Mahon, Irvinestown, Co. Fermanagh; Ms Patricia Mallon, Belfast; Manufacturing, Science, Finance, Belfast; Marriage Encounter (Ireland); Mr Seán Martin, Belfast; Mr David Mason, Portaferry, Co. Down; Dean Gilbert Mayes, Co. Dublin; Mr Cormac McAleer, Carrickmore, Co. Tyrone; Mr Sam McAughtry, Comber, Co. Down; Rev. Patrick McCafferty, Belfast; Mr R. Finlay McCance, Belfast; Mr Jack McCann, Ballymena, Co. Antrim; Mr Maurice McCartney, Bangor, Co. Down; Mr Michael McCaughan, Newtownards, Co. Down; Mr Kevin McCaul, Derry; Mrs Ann McCay, Londonderry; Mrs Kit McClarey, Portstewart, Co. Derry; Mr Roy McClenaghan (Ekklesia Christian Fellowship), Belfast; Rev. G.B. McConnell, Warrenpoint, Co. Down; Mr Joe McCool, Dungannon, Co. Tyrone; Ms Jeanette McCormack, Bangor, Co. Down; Mr and Mrs T. McCormick, Bangor, Co. Down; Ms Elizabeth McCullough, Comber, Co. Down; Mr Joseph McCullough, Dublin; Mr John W. McDonald, Washington, USA; Councillor Randal McDonnell, Cushendun, Co. Antrim; Ms Róisín McDonough, Craigavon, Co.

Armagh; Mrs Sally McErlean and Mrs Eilish McCashin, Belfast; Mr Paddy McEvoy, Holywood, Co. Down; Mr James McGeever, Kingscourt, Co. Cavan; Dr Christopher McGimpsey and Mr Michael McGimpsey, Newtownards, Co. Down; Ms Marie-Therese McGivern, Belfast; Mr M.B. McGovern, London; Mr Austin McGrogan, Belfast; Dr Samuel J. McGuffin, Belfast; Pastor Jack McKee and Mr Roy Montgomery, Belfast; Ms Clare McKenna, Belfast; Mr Michael McKeown, Blackrock, Co. Dublin; Mr Peter McLachlan, Belfast; Mr Andrew McLean, Ballygawley, Co. Tyrone; Mr P.A. McNamee, Swanage, Dorset; Professor Paul McNulty, Dublin; Ms Helen McPherson, Carrickfergus, Co. Antrim; Sister Ann Marie McQuade, Enniskillen, Co. Fermanagh; Mrs Anne McQuillan, Newtownbutler, Co. Fermanagh; Ms Louise McQuillan, Belfast; Mr Patrick McVeigh, East Lothian, Scotland; Ms Anthea McWilliams, Belfast; Professor Elizabeth Meehan, Queen's Univesity, Belfast; Methodist Church in Ireland Council on Social Welfare; Methodist College, Belfast (Karen Sloan, Darren Dunn, Reuben Moore); Methodist Women's Association; Mr Brian Minchin, Sussex; Mr Robert Mooney, Bangor, Co. Down; Mr Martin Moorcroft, Richhill, Co. Armagh; Mr Austen Morgan, London; Mr John Morison, Belfast; Mothers for Peace, Ilkley, Yorkshire; Ms Maire Mullarney, Dublin; Mr Charles Murphy, Maghera, Co. Derry; Mr Seán Murphy, Bray, Co. Wicklow; Rev. Raymond Murray, Armagh; Mr Edward Napier, Dromore, Co. Down; National Peace Council, Northern Ireland Working Group; National Platform, Dublin; Dr Joyce Neill, Belfast; Mr James Nelson and Ms Claire Johnston, Belfast; Network Craigavon; New Consensus, England; New Consensus International; New Ireland Group; Newry Plan Group; Ms Clara Ní Ghiolla, Árann, Co. na Gaillimhe; Mr Paul Nolan, Belfast; North Belfast Women; North Down and Ards Womens' Information Group; North Down Labour Representation Group; Northern Consensus Group; Northern Ireland Association for the Care and Resettlement of Offenders (NIACRO); Northern Ireland Community Study Group; Northern Ireland Chamber of Commerce and Industry; Northern Ireland Environment Link; Northern Ireland Gay Rights Association; Northern Ireland Graphical Society; Northern Ireland Office; Northern Ireland Religious for Justice and Peace; Northern Ireland Voluntary Trust; Northern Ireland Women's Aid Federation; Northern Ireland Youth Forum (three groups); Northlands Centre, Derry; Mr Michael Nugent, Dublin; Mr Eoin Ó Cofaigh, Dublin; Mr Fionnbarra Ó Dochartaigh, Derry; Dr Seán Ó Mearthaile, Dublin; Mr Dermot O'Brien, Rathmolyon, Co. Meath; Mr John O'Connell, Dublin; Mr J. O'Connell, Dublin; Mr Joseph O'Donnell, Kincasslagh, Co. Donegal; Mr Matt O'Dowd, Dublin; Mr Gearóid Ó Dubhthaigh, Cork; Councillor James O'Fee, Bangor, Co.Down; Mr Justin O'Hagan, Newcastle, Co. Down; Mr Joseph O'Hanlon, Bangor, Co. Down; Mrs Sheila O'Hara, Belfast; Mr W.J. O'Kane, Maghera, Co. Derry; Mr Gabriel O'Keefe, Newtownbutler, Co. Fermanagh; Mr Philip O'Keefe, Newtownards, Co. Down; Dr Brendan O'Leary, London and Dr John McGarry, Ontario; Mr Declan O'Loan, Ballymena, Co. Antrim; Mr John O'Neill, Belfast; Mr William O'Neill, Belfast; Mr John O'Riordan, Dalkey, Co. Dublin; Dr Máire O'Rourke, Cambridge; Mr Eugene O'Shea, Killarney, Co. Kerry; Mr Ted O'Sullivan, Dublin; Dr Donal O'Tierney, Newry, Co. Down; Oakgrove Integrated Primary School, Londonderry; OCTOPUS, Londonderry; Omagh Baha'i Community; Omagh Christian Brothers' School, Senior Prefects Committee; Mr Edward Orme, Millisle, Co. Down; Ormeau Woodcraft Folk, Belfast; Rev. Andrew Orr and Rev. Susan Green, Lisburn, Co. Antrim; Very Rev. Cecil Orr, Londonderry; Protestant and Catholic Encounter (PACE); Mr Ian Paisley Jnr, Belfast; Mr Andrew Patterson, Wigtownshire, Scotland; Mr H. Patton, Donaghadee, Co. Down; Pax Christi, London; Pax Christi Ireland; Peace and Reconciliation Group, Londonderry; Peace and Reconciliation Group School Students, Londonderry; Mr Joseph Peake, Enniskillen, Co. Fermanagh; Mr J.G. Peile, Craigavon, Co. Armagh; Mr Philip Perry, Oxfordshire; Mrs Ursula

Perry, Oxfordshire; Playboard, Belfast; Mr Stephen Plowden, London; Mr Andy Pollak, Belfast; Portaferry Playgroup, Co. Down; Mr William Potter, Monkstown, Co. Dublin; Rt Rev. Samuel G. Poyntz, Belfast; Presbyterian Church in Ireland, Church and Government Committee; Quaker Peace Education Project, Derry; Quakers Peace and Service, Northern Ireland Committee; Dr George Quigley, Belfast; Dr Gerard Quinn, Dublin; Mr Jackie Redpath, Belfast; Reformed Presbyterian Church, Witness Bearing Committee; Ms Eva-Maria Reidinger, Austria; Relatives for Justice; Religious Together (Down and Connor); Republican women prisoners, Maghaberry; Republican Prisoners, Maze; Belfast; Republican Sinn Féin; Adrian and Deirdre Rice, Islandmagee, Co. Antrim; Mr Gerry Rice, Ballynahinch, Co. Down; Mr Glyn Roberts, Belfast; Mr Hubert Rooney, Newtownabbey, Co. Antrim; Rev. Hugh Ross, Dungannon, Co. Tyrone; Rev. R.S. Ross, Ballymena, Co. Antrim; Mr Gordon Rudlin, Oxfordshire; Rural Community Network, Cookstown; Mr Mark Russell, Richhill, Co. Armagh; Mr Mark J. Russell, Dublin; Mr E. Ruttledge, Derry; Mr Brendan Ryan, Cork; Ms Moya Frenz St Leger, London; Mr Nicholas Sanders, Dungannon, Co. Tyrone; Dr Gabriel Scally, Belfast; Ms Olive Scott, Greystones, Co. Wicklow; Scrabo Presbyterian Church, Co. Down; Mr Norman Shannon, Belfast; Mr Iain Sharpe, Herts; Rev. Desmond Shaw, Portstewart, Co. Londonderry; Mrs Mildred Shaw, Portstewart, Londonderry; Ms Thelma Sheil, Bangor, Co. Down; Mr Stephen Shellard, Dumfries; Mr Alan Sheeran; Ballymena, Co. Antrim; Mr C. Shillington, Randalstown, Co. Antrim; Councillor Jim Simpson, Ballymoney, Co. Antrim; Mr Michael Sing, Londonderry; Sinn Féin; Sisters of the Cross and Passion, Larne, Co. Antrim; Rev. I.R. Sloane, Co. Armagh; Mr Desmond Smith, Dublin; Ms Margot Smith, Portstewart, Co. Londonderry; Mr Paul Smith, Londonderry; Dr Clifford Smyth, Belfast; Dr Leo Smyth, University College, Galway; Mrs Myrtle Smyth, Bangor, Co. Down; Social Democratic and Labour Party (SDLP); South Belfast Constituency Labour Party; The Springfield Group (Ms May Blood, Ms Kate Kelly, Mrs Geraldine O'Regan); St Patrick's Youth Fellowship, Coleraine, Co. Londonderry; Standing Advisory Commission on Human Rights (SACHR); Mr Jonathan Stephenson, Belfast; Stormont Presbyterian Church; Mr James Stover, Saudi Arabia; Strabane/Omagh Community Relations Forum; Stranmillis College Debating Society; Stranmillis College Drama Group; Dr Ronny Swain, University College, Cork; Mr Paul Sweeney, Belfast; Sydenham Methodist Church, Belfast; Mr Nevin Taggart, Bushmills, Co. Antrim; Mr Paul Teague, University of Ulster, Jordanstown; Tempo Historical Society, Co. Fermanagh; Mr M. G. Thompson, Ballymena, Co. Antrim; Mr Gerald Tottin, Belfast; Triangle Recycling Group, Coleraine, Co. Londonderry; Ulster Democratic Party; Ulster Humanist Association; Ulster Motherland Movement, Portadown; Ulster People's College; Ulster Political Research Group; Ulster Society for the Preservation of the Countryside; Ulster Unionist Charter Group; United Campaign against Plastic Bullets, Belfast; Upper Ards Historical Society; Vegetarian Society of Ulster; Ms Margaret Walker, Dunmurry, Co. Antrim; Mr R.L. Walshe, Belfast; Ms Jane Waterson, Saintfield, Co. Down; Mr Noel Weatherhead, Larne, Co. Antrim; Dr T.K. Whitaker, Dublin; Jean and Caroline Whyte, Dublin; Mr John Wills, West Midlands; Senator Gordon Wilson, Enniskillen, Co. Fermanagh; Mr Pádraic Wilson, Crumlin Road Prison, Belfast; Mr Robin Wilson and Professor Richard Kearney, Belfast and Dublin; Windmill Integrated Primary School, Dungannon, Co. Tyrone; Women Together for Peace; Women's Information Drop-In Centre, Belfast; Women's Planning Network; Women-in-Media-and-Entertainment, Galway; Workers Educational Assocation; Mr Gavin Wright, Bangor, Co. Down; Rev. Canon Kenyon Wright, Glasgow; Sir Oliver Wright, Surrey; Youth for Peace.

Appendix B

The Oral Hearings

The following people made presentations at the Opsahl Commissions' oral hearings:

19 January **Belfast**	Sir Kenneth Bloomfield; Church and Government Committee of the Presbyterian Church (Dr John Dunlop, Dr Sam Hutchinson, Dr Godfrey Brown); Mrs Sally McErlean; Cadogan Group (Mr Arthur Aughey, Dr Paul Bew, Mr Arthur Green, Mr Graham Gudgin, Dr Dennis Kennedy, Mr Paddy Roche); Rev. Brian Lennon S.J.
20 January **Belfast**	Alliance Party (Dr John Alderdice, Mr Addie Morrow, Mr David Ford); Dr T.K. Whitaker; Northern Ireland Religious for Justice and Peace (Sister Marie Duddy, Brother Gerard Kearney, Sister Noreen Christian, Father Diarmuid Ryan); Sinn Féin (Mr Mitchel McLaughlin, Ms Máiréad Keane, Ms Bairbre de Brún, Mr Pat McGeown); Mrs Kathleen Feenan and Mrs Mary Leonard.
21 January **Newtownards**	Sydenham Methodist Church (Mr Louis Fisher, Rev. Brian Fletcher); Mr Glyn Roberts; Mr Michael McGimpsey and Dr Christopher McGimpsey; Conservative Integration Group (Mr Alan Love, Mr Leonard Jarvis, Councillor Billy Bleakes); Mr Barry Cowan.
25 January **Derry**	Mr Paddy Doherty; Mrs Marlene Jefferson; Mr Frank Curran; Dr Mari Fitzduff; Mr Paul Sweeney; SDLP (Mr Mark Durkan, party chairman); Councillor John Kerr.
26 January **Derry (Bogside)**	Holywell Trust (Mr Éamonn Deane, Mr Terry Doherty); Bloody Sunday Initiative (Mr Tony Doherty, Mr Robin Percival, Mr Martin Finucane, Mr Paul O'Connor); Derry Well Woman (Ms Karen Meehan, Ms Mary Gill, Ms Anne Monro, Ms Ann McCafferty); Mr Charles Murphy; Peace and Reconciliation Group (Mr John Lampen, Mr Jimmy Duffy, Ms Tanya Gallagher, Mr Colin Miller).

27 January
Londonderry (Waterside)

Mr Glen Barr; Oakgrove Integrated Primary School (Ms Anne Murray, Mr Colm Cavanagh, Mr James Simpson, Mr Geoffery Starrett); the New Ireland Group (Mr John Robb, Mr James Wilson); Very Rev. Victor Griffin; Mr Tony Crowe.

28 January
Coleraine

Professor John Darby; Councillor Jim Simpson; Mr Seán Farren; Mr Declan O'Loan; Corrymeela Community (Mr Duncan Morrow, Mr Colin Craig, Rev. John Morrow).

2 February

Mr Hugh Logue; Professor Richard Kearney and Mr Robin Wilson; Unionist Charter Group (Mr David McNarry, Mr Harry West, Captain Austin Ardill); Mrs Sheila Chillingworth; Northern Consensus Group (Professor Robert W. Stout, Mr Terence Donaghy, Mr John G. Neill).

3 February
Belfast

Ulster Democratic Party (Mr Gary McMichael, Mr Ray Smallwoods); Northern Ireland Chamber of Commerce and Industry (Mr Noel Stewart, Mr Sam Butler); North Belfast women; Dr Clifford Smyth; Northern Ireland Committee, Irish Congress of Trade Unions (Mr Terry Carlin, Mr Jack Nash, Mr Alastair Keery).

4 February
Enniskillen

Councillor Raymond Ferguson; Mr Joseph Peake, Mrs Meeta Sharp, Mr Neville McElderry, Mr Gordon Brand; Mr Gabriel O'Keefe; Senator Gordon Wilson.

5 February

Dungannon Community Relations Workshop (Ms Norma McKeown, Mr Ernie Carroll, Ms Mary Finnerty, Mr Aiden Dolan); Omagh Christian Brothers School Senior Prefects (Mr Ciarán Martin, Mr Gerry Gallen, Mr Mark Rasdale, Mr Tom Conway, Mr Michael McQuaid, Mr Joe Hackett); Rev. Raymond Murray/Relatives for Justice (Ms Eilish McCabe); Cookstown High School, lower sixth, (Ms Leah Barrett, Ms Jayne Cameron, Ms Rachel Finch, Mr Nicholas Laird); Rev. Denis Faul.

16 February
Belfast

Mr Terry Flanagan and Dr Colin Irwin; Dr Brian Gaffney; Mr Douglas Hegney; the Church of Ireland Bishop of Connor, Dr Samuel Poyntz, Mr J.T. McGaffin and Rev. Walter Lewis; Equal Opportunities Commission (Ms Evelyn Collins, Mrs Joan Smyth).

17 February
Belfast

Professor Desmond Rea; Youth for Peace (Mr Paul Smyth and Mr Patrick Corrigan); the Springfield Group (Ms May Blood, Mrs Geraldine O'Regan, Ms Kate Kelly); Professor Tom Hadden and Professor Kevin Boyle; the Church of Ireland Primate, Archbishop Robin Eames.

18 February
Belfast (Shankill Road)

A group of loyalist ex-prisoners; Mr Mark Langhammer; Mr Jackie Redpath; Dr Ken Logue; Pastor Jack McKee and Mr Roy Montgomery; Reformed Presbyterian Church, Witness Bearing Committee (Rev. Andrew Stewart, Rev. George Ball, Rev. Knox Hyndman).

19 February
Belfast (Falls Road)

Sister Genevieve and Mr Paddy Fleming; Mrs Elizabeth Groves; Mr Michael Farrell; Centre for Research and Documentation (Ms Caitríona Ruane, Mr Jimmy Martin; Dr Liam O'Dowd).

22 February
Belfast

Mr David Cook; Mrs Sheila O'Hara; Mr Nick Acheson; Mr Michael McKeown; Committee on the Administration of Justice (Dr Colm Campbell, Mr Stephen Livingstone, Ms Fionnuala Ní Aoláin).

23 February
Belfast

Confederation of British Industry (Mr Roy Bailie, Mr Nigel Smyth); Mr Kenneth James; Mr Desmond Smith; Sisters of the Cross and Passion (Sister Margaret Rose McSparran and Sr. Rosaleen Murray); Irish National Teachers' Organization (Mr Edward Burton, Mr Frank Bunting, Mr Bernard Magill, Senator Joe O'Toole, Mr Des Rainey).

24 February

Schools' Assembly, Guildhall, Derry.

25 February

Schools' Assembly, Queen's University, Belfast.

Appendix C

The Patrons of Initiative '92

Nick Acheson, Samuel Adair, Hazel Aicken, Derek Alcorn, Les Allamby, Don Allen, Ingrid Allen, Vivienne Anderson, Jimmy Armstrong, Jan Ashdown, John Banville, Anthony Barnett, Harry Barnes, Andy Barr, Denis Barritt, George Bell, Craig Birrell, Betty Black, David Bleakley, Billy Blease, John Bowman, Beatrice Boyd, Samuel Boyd, Joe Bowers, Kevin Boyle, Trevor Boyle, Conleth Bradley, Denis Bradley, Maxine Brady, Paul Brady, Terence Brown, Noel Browne, Ruairí Brugha, Patrick Buckland, Pat Buckley, Aidan Bunting, Frank Bunting, Sam Burch, Paul Burgess, John Bush, Peter Cadogan, Eric Cairns, Sydney Callaghan, Colm Campbell, Pat Campbell, June Campion, Jim Canning, Anne Carr, Ernie Carroll, Colm Cavanagh, John Chambers, Ross Chapman, Mary Clark-Glass, Iris Colvin, Chris Conliffe, David Cook, Bob Cooper, Doreen Corcoran, Robert Cormack, Máiréad Corrigan-Maguire, Angela Courtney, Martin Cowley, Tom Craig, Bernard Crick, Maurna Crozier, Bernard Cullen, Gerry Dawe, Dorothy Day, Éamonn Deane, Anne Devlin, Paddy Devlin, Polly Devlin, Aidan Dolan, Geraldine Donaghy, Terence Donaghy, Andrew Dougal, Brendan Duddy, John Dunlop, Séamus Dunn, Éamonn Dwyer, Ruth Dudley-Edwards, Eileen Evason, John Fairleigh, Rob Fairmichael, John Fanagan, Denis Faul, Kathleen Feenan, Brian Ferran, Barney Filor, Mari Fitzduff, Barbara Fitzgerald, Roy Foster, Hugh Frazer, John Freeman, Brian Friel, David Gallagher, Tom Gasson, Norman Gibson, Pip Glendinning, Will Glendinning, Maurice Goldring, Harold Good, Gordon Gray, Graham Gudgin, Adrian Guelke, Tom Hadden, David Hammond, Desmond Hanna, Margo Harkin, David Harkness, William Hastings, James Hawthorne, Séamus Heaney, Fergal Henchy, Brendan Henry, John Herron, David Hewitt, Bronagh Hinds, Erskine Holmes, Helen Honeyman, Deane Houston, Chris Hudson, John Hunt, Michael Hurley, Raymond Hylton, George Johnston, Jennifer Johnston, Ezzat Jalili, Roberta Johnston, Robert Johnstone, Beverley Jones, Philip Kealey, Richard Kearney, Brian Keenan, Alastair Keery, Kate Kelly, Stanislaus Kennedy, Mary Kenny, Tony Kenny, Kevin Lambe, John Lampen, David Latimer, Simon Lee, Brian Lennon, William Leonard, Ken Logue, Barbara Lomas, Edna Longley, Michael Longley, Mary Lyons, Risteard Mac Gabhann, Máire MacSwiney, Alasdair MacLaughlin, Bernard MacLaverty, Brendan McAllister, Sam McAughtry, Tom McBride, Nell McCafferty, Ann McCann, Eamonn McCartan, Felicity McCartney, Michael McCaughan, Minah McCullough, Enda McDonagh, Róisín McDonough, Donal McFerran, Marie-Therese McGivern, Dympna McGlade, Brian McGleenon, Adrienne McGrath, Jim McGrath, Medbh McGuckian, Nancy MacIntyre, Paddy McLaughlin, Paul McMenamin, Karen McMinn, Brendan Mackin, Francie Maguinness, Paddy Maguinness, Benny Marley, Lawrence Mee, Austen Morgan, Seán Morrissey, Duncan Morrow, John Morrow, Robin Mullan, Wilfred Mulryne, John A. Murphy, Pauline Murphy, Tom Nairn, James Nelson, Paul Nolan, Howard Noyes, Eithne O'Connor, Sharon O'Connor, Seán O'Dwyer, Paddy O'Hanlon, Quintin Oliver, John O'Neill, Tony O'Reilly, Cecil Orr, Henry Patterson, Tom Paulin, Joseph Peake, William Pegg, Steve Platt, Andy Pollak, Samuel Poyntz, Deirdre Rice, Foster

Richardson, John Robb, Bob Rowthorn, Tommy Sands, Nicholas Sanders, Gabriel Scally, Helena Schlindwein, J.M. Simms, Audrey Simpson, Desmond Smith, Peter Smith, Fiona Stelfox, Fiona Stephen, David Stevens, Paul Sweeney, Colm Tóibín, Gerry Tyrrell, Charlotte Vij, Brian Walker, Lynda Walker, Dave Wall, T.K. Whitaker, Barry White, Joy Williams, Robin Wilson, Kenyon Wright.

Notes on the Commissioners
and Co-Ordinator

PROFESSOR TORKEL OPSAHL (chair): Professor of Law at the University of Oslo and chair of the Norwegian Institute of Human Rights; 1970-84, Member of the European Commission of Human Rights (Council of Europe); 1973-88, Member of the International Commission of Jurists; 1977-86, Member of the United Nations Human Rights Committee (also Vice-Chair and Rapporteur); adviser on Nobel Peace Prize; has carried out missions for the UN Secretary General in Iran and Iraq and for the Norwegian Foreign Minister in the Baltic countries; currently a member of the UN commission investigating war crimes in the former Yugoslavia.

LADY FAULKNER OF DOWNPATRICK: Former BBC governor for Northern Ireland (1978-85); widow of the late Brian Faulkner, last Stormont prime minister and head of the 1974 power-sharing Executive; formerly a *Belfast Telegraph* journalist and later private secretary to Ulster Unionist Prime Minister Viscount Brookeborough.

MR PADRAIG O'MALLEY: Dublin-born political scientist and Senior Fellow at the John W. McCormack Institute of Public Affairs at the University of Massachusetts in Boston; author of one of the most powerful analyses of the Northern Irish conflict, *The Uncivil Wars: Ireland Today*, (and a 1990 update, *Questions of Nuance*) based on interviews with a wide range of protagonists; also author of *Biting at the Grave*, a study of the 1981 hunger strike; currently working on a three-volume study of political and social change in South Africa.

PROFESSOR RUTH LISTER: Professor of Applied Social Studies at the University of Bradford; formerly Director of the Child Poverty Action Group, in which capacity she had strong links with Northern Ireland; vice-chair, National Council of Voluntary Organizations; author of *The Exclusive Society*.

MR EAMONN GALLAGHER: Former EC Director-General of Fisheries (1977-89) and Deputy Director General of External Relations (1976-77), then the highest position reached by an EC civil servant from the Republic of Ireland; also special advisor to EC President Jacques Delors and EC Observer at the UN (1989-91); formerly Deputy Secretary of the Irish Department of Foreign Affairs; born in Scotland; now retired and living in Brussels.

PROFESSOR MARIANNE ELLIOTT: Lecturer in history at Birkbeck College, London, and professor-elect at the University of Liverpool. Originally from outside Belfast; one of the most respected younger Irish historians and author of the highly acclaimed biography of Wolfe Tone, the father of Irish republicanism; co-founder of the Conference of Irish Historians in Britain; currently working on a history of the Catholics in Ulster.

REVEREND DR ERIC GALLAGHER: Former president of the Methodist Church in Ireland; outstanding ecumenist and worker for peace and reconciliation; one of the Protestant churchmen who had talks with the Provisional IRA in December 1974 which led to a temporary ceasefire; co-author of *Christians in Ulster: 1968-1980.*

MR ANDY POLLAK: Initiative '92 co-ordinator; religious affairs correspondent and assistant news editor with *The Irish Times*; born in Co. Antrim and brought up in London, son of a Czech Jewish father and an Ulster Presbyterian mother; former BBC journalist and editor of *Fortnight*; co-author, with Ed Moloney, of *Paisley* (1986), a political biography.

Index of Contributors